New Applications in
IT Standards:
Developments and Progress

Kai Jakobs
Aachen University, Germany

INFORMATION SCIENCE REFERENCE

Hershey · New York

Director of Editorial Content:	Kristin Klinger
Director of Book Publications:	Julia Mosemann
Development Editor:	Julia Mosemann
Typesetter:	Devvin Earnest, Sean Woznicki
Quality Control:	Jamie Snavely
Cover Design:	Lisa Tosheff
Printed at:	Yurchak Printing Inc.

Published in the United States of America by
Information Science Reference (an imprint of IGI Global)
701 E. Chocolate Avenue
Hershey PA 17033
Tel: 717-533-8845
Fax: 717-533-8661
E-mail: cust@igi-global.com
Web site: http://www.igi-global.com/reference

Library of Congress Cataloging-in-Publication Data

Library of Congress Cataloging-in-Publication Data

New applications in IT standards : developments and progress / Kai Jakobs,
editor.
     p. cm.
  Includes bibliographical references and index.
  ISBN 978-1-60566-946-5 (hardcover) -- ISBN 978-1-60566-947-2 (ebook) 1.
Information technology--Standards. I. Jakobs, Kai, 1957-
  T58.5.N485 2010
  621.39'810218--dc22
                          2009052654

British Cataloguing in Publication Data
A Cataloguing in Publication record for this book is available from the British Library.

All work contributed to this book is new, previously-unpublished material. The views expressed in this book are those of the authors, but not necessarily of the publisher.

Advances in IT Standards and Standardization Research Series (AISSR)

ISBN: 1935-3391

Editor-in-Chief: Kai Jakobs, RWTH Aachen, Germany

Standardization Research in Information Technology New Perspectives

Information Science Reference • copyright 2007 • 300pp • H/C (ISBN: 978-1-59904-561-0)

Standardization has the potential to shape, expand, and create markets. Information technology has undergone a rapid transformation in the application of standards in practice, and recent developments have augmented the need for the divulgence of supplementary research. Standardization Research in Information Technology: New Perspectives amasses cutting-edge research on the application of standards in the market, covering topics such as corporate standardization, linguistic qualities of international standards, the role of individuals in standardization, and the development, use, application, and influence of information technology in standardization techniques.

Also included in this series:

Advanced Topics in Information Technology Standards and Standardization Research

IGI Publishing • copyright 2006 • 348 pp • H/C (ISBN: 1-59140-938-1) • E-Book (ISBN: 1-59140-940-3)

Advanced Topics in Information Technology Standards and Standardization Research is a series of books which features the most current research findings in all aspects of IT standardization research, from a diversity of angles, traversing the traditional boundaries between individual disciplines. Advanced Topics in Information Technology Standards and Standardization Research, Volume 1 is a part of this series. Advanced Topics in Information Technology Standards and Standardization Research, Volume 1 presents a collection of chapters addressing a variety of aspects related to IT standards and the setting of standards. This book covers a variety of topics, such as economic aspects of standards, alliances in standardization and the relation between 'formal' standards bodies and industry consortia. It also offers a glimpse inside a standards working group, as well as a look at applications of standards in different sectors.

The Advances in IT Standards and Standardization Research (AISSR) publishes research findings with the goal of advancing knowledge and research in all aspects of IT standards and standardization. The publications included in this series are authoritative sources and information outlets for the diverse community of IT standards researchers. Information and communication technology (ICT) is the major enabler of the move from an industrial society to the information society to the knowledge society. Yet, this transition will only take place reasonably smoothly if adequate standards are in place, which take into account not only the technical aspects, but also the characteristics of the specific environment within which they will have to function. The Advances in IT Standards and Standardization Research (AISSR) seeks to address the needs of the knowledge society through the betterment and expansion of available research. In covering emerging areas, such as, technological innovation, open source applications, intellectual property, and the standardization of technological applications, the series will create a platform for the continued development of these areas and the information technology

Hershey • New York

Order online at www.igi-global.com or call 717-533-8845 x10 –
Mon-Fri 8:30 am - 5:00 pm (est) or fax 24 hours a day 717-533-8661

Editorial Advisory Board

Table of Contents

Chapter 15

Detailed Table of Contents

Chapter 1

    Shiro Kurihara, Hitotsubashi University, Japan

The standards world has radically changed over the past two decades especially in international standardization, with an increased impact on business and society, although the essential characteristic of standardization in general, namely, to achieve the optimal order in a given context, remains unchanged. In this chapter, such evolution of international standardization, caused by its structural adaptation to changes in its environment as well as the origin and history of standardization and standards are reviewed initially. Subsequently, 'standard studies' is advocated as a new academic discipline to comprehensively analyze the problems of standardization and standards from a broader perspective, transcending predominantly technological concerns. Finally, the need to invest in standards research and education is highlighted.

Chapter 2

    Lynn Crawford, University of Technology - Sydney, Australia
    Julien Pollack, University of Technology - Sydney, Australia

Professional standards are a significant issue for professions such as IT and Project Management, where certification and licensure are either necessary to practice or to demonstrate individual competence and capability. In many professions there is no basis for international reciprocity of professional standards. This chapter documents the development of a standard for global reciprocity between already existing professional standards in the field of Project Management. Data are based on personal involvement by the authors and interviews with participants.

Chapter 3

    Jane K. Winn, University of Washington School of Law, USA

This chapter examines the role of law reform in promoting the development of technical standards for the authentication of parties engaged in Internet commerce. Law reforms intended to improve the security of Internet commerce can only succeed if they address business, technical and legal issues simultaneously. The EU has used commercial law reform and formal standard development to coordinate work on authentication standards, while the US has allowed the market to determine what type of authentication technology is appropriate and has left the development of standards to private consortia. While the EU approach may solve collective action problems more effectively, the US approach may discover end user requirements and may allow business judgments about risk to inform the law more effectively. Neither approach has yet resolved the authentication problems facing businesses engaged in online commerce.

Chapter 4

Josephine W. Thomas, Loughborough University, UK
Steve Probets, Loughborough University, UK
Ray Dawson, Loughborough University, UK
Tim King, LSC Group Limited, UK

This chapter seeks to identify the factors that have impacted the adoption of ISO 10303, the Standard for the Exchange of Product Data (STEP), within the UK Ministry of Defence. The analysis presented in this chapter is based on Diffusion of Innovation (DOI) Theory and the theory surrounding the Economics of Standards. Using a case study approach, the results indicate that several DOI and economic factors have impacted the adoption of STEP. These findings offer insights into some of the technological, organizational, and environmental influences on standards adoption. It is envisioned that these results will make a contribution towards the body of knowledge surrounding the factors and barriers critical to the adoption of standards like STEP, and enable more effective development and adoption of these standards.

Chapter 5

Krzysztof M. Brzeziński, Warsaw University of Technology, Poland

Network Operators (NOs) are the important stakeholders in standardization. For the ongoing development of their infrastructure and service portfolio, they directly use "external" telecommunications standards developed by the SDOs, and both produce and use the company standards, customarily referred to as Operator's Technical Requirements (ORs). It is shown that the specific needs of NOs are not properly reflected in the current structure and contents of the external standards. As a consequence, the process of developing and using the ORs is costly and inefficient. This chapter presents an alternative, formalized methodology for ORs, called OpTeR. A part of this methodology is a lightweight semi-formal notation, which is amenable to handling by a computer support tool. The methodology makes explicit the nature of the current inadequacy of external standards, and allows for a "detour." However, to achieve the optimum performance of the method, the authors propose that the external standards be extended with a new part, called Embedded Capability Relations, that would serve as a common base for ORs.

Chapter 6

Marc Rysman, Boston University, USA
Tim Simcoe, University of Toronto, Canada

This chapter uses citations to patents disclosed in the standard setting process to measure the technological significance of voluntary standard setting organizations (SSOs). The authors find that SSO patents are outliers in several dimensions and importantly, are cited far more frequently than a set of control patents. More surprisingly, the authors find that SSO patents receive citations for a much longer period of time. Furthermore, a significant correlation between citation and the disclosure of a patent to an SSO is found, which may imply a marginal impact of disclosure. These results provide the first empirical look at patents disclosed to SSO's, and show that these organizations both select important technologies and play a role in establishing their significance.

Chapter 7

Aura Soininen, Lappeenranta University of Technology and Attorneys-at-Law Borenius
& Kemppinen, Ltd, Finland

Multiple cases have been reported in which patents have posed dilemmas in the context of cooperative standard setting. Problems have come to the fore with regard to GSM, WCDMA, and CDMA standards, for example. Furthermore, JPEG and HTML standards, as well as VL-bus and SDRAM technologies, have faced patent-related difficulties. Nevertheless, it could be argued that complications have arisen in only a small fraction of standardization efforts, and that patents do not therefore constitute a real quandary. This chapter assesses the extent and the causes of the patent dilemma in the ICT sector through a brief analysis of how ICT companies' patent strategies and technology-licensing practices relate to standard setting and by exemplifying and quantifying the problem on the basis of relevant articles, academic research papers, court cases and on-line discussions. Particular attention is paid to so-called submarine patents, which bear most significance with respect to the prevailing policy concern regarding the efficacy of the patent system.

Chapter 8

Kalle Lyytinen, Case Western Reserve University, USA
Thomas Keil, Helsinki University of Technology, Finland
Vladislav Fomin, Delft University of Technology, The Netherlands

Standards have become critical to information and communication technologies (ICTs) as they become complex and pervasive. This chapter proposes a process theory framework to explain anticipatory standardizing outcomes post hoc when the standardizing process is viewed as networks of events. Anticipatory standards define future capabilities for ICT ex ante in contrast to ex post standardizing existing practices or capabilities through de facto standardization in the market. The theoretical framework offers the following: a) a lexicon in the form of the ontology and typology of standardizing events; b) a grammar, or a set of combination rules, for standardizing events to build process representations; c) an analysis and appreciation of contexts in which standardizing unfolds; and d) logic yielding theoretical explanations of standardizing outcomes based on the analysis of process representations. The authors show how the framework can help analyze standardization data as networks of events as well as explain standardizing outcomes. They illustrate the plausibility of the approach by applying it to wireless standardization to explain standardizing outcomes.

Chapter 9

Firms often acquire other firms to source technology but it is unclear why they might assume such risk by buying before a product standard is established in their industry. This chapter draws upon real options and dynamic capability theories of firm organization to develop an integrated framework that explains why firms might acquire early and which firms are more likely to do so. The authors develop propositions regarding certain firm attributes as predictors of acquisition timing relative to passage of a technology standard. The authors argue that from a real options perspective, the primary reason firms acquire early is related to the firm's knowledge of the technology. However, attributes such as political influence in the standardization process, prior experience making acquisitions, and how the firm resolves uncertainty about the technical expertise of potential acquisition targets are capabilities that also enter the acquisition timing decision. This chapter provides a model based on those propositions and address how it can be empirically tested.

Chapter 10

The purpose of this chapter is to provide insight in recent developments in standardization education. The increasing number of initiatives and activities of the last couple of years indicates that there is a momentum for education on standardization. This chapter provides a structured approach for using this momentum to further develop and implement standardization education. The main topics are: needs for standardization education, audiences and learning objectives, contents of an academic curriculum, and available materials for academic teaching. The authors found an enormous gap between manifest and latent needs for standardization education. The lesson to be learnt from some Asian countries is that this gap can be bridged. First, by a strong national policy which may be part of a regional policy. Secondly, by cooperation between government, industry, national standards body, academia and other educational institutions.

This chapter focuses on the training needed by technical experts and explores the type of academic coursework as well as training that technical experts need in the field of standards and standardization.

Chapter 12

Aileen P. Cater-Steel, School of Information Systems, Australia
Mark A. Toleman, School of Information Systems, Australia

Service management standards such as the IT infrastructure library (ITIL), and now ISO/IEC 20000, provide guidance and tools for effective management and control of IT service delivery. These standards are of increasing importance to organisations around the globe so education about these standards and possibilities for training of IT staff are important. In the main, academics and Universities have not embraced these standards in either research or education about them; however, demand for IT staff qualified to various levels in these standards grows. Universities have a place in this education process and there are significant benefits to them, the graduates and industry in terms of increases in student numbers, enhanced employment opportunities and improvement in service quality, but there are challenges also especially in relating problems in practice to students. Using results from two national surveys and several case studies, this chapter considers the requirements for education about these important standards.

Chapter 13

Knut Blind, Berlin University of Technology, Germany

The dynamic technological changes in information and communication technology (ICT) influence the lifetimes of standards , an important dimension of the dynamics of standards. The need to change or adjust standards according to new trends in ICT has definitely increased in the last decade. Furthermore, some standards became obsolete, because new technologies led to completely new generations of standards. Consequently, standards have a life cycle defined by their publication and withdrawal dates, which represents a core element of the dynamics of standards.

Chapter 14

Carter Eltzroth, DVB Project, Switzerland

The DVB Project is a European-based standards forum which has, for close to 15 years, been developing specifications for digital video broadcasting, many now implemented worldwide. Its IPR policy has several novel elements. These include "negative disclosure": the obligation of each member to license IPRs essential to DVB specifications unless it gives notice of the unavailability of the IPR. This approach contrasts with the more common rule, for example within ANSI accredited bodies, calling for IPR disclosure and confirmation of availability on FR&ND terms. Other notable features of the IPR policy of DVB are arbitration and fostering of patent pooling. This chapter provides a commentary on the DVB's

IPR policy and on its application. It also describes the work of the DVB in resolving IPR "gateway" issues when the perceived dominance of technology contributors, notably through control over IPRs, risked, in the view of some members, distorting new digital markets. In two cases DVB has created a licensing mechanism to dispel these concerns. In addition to the quality of its technical work, DVB's success lies in its novel IPR policy and its ability to achieve consensus to resolve gateway issues.

Chapter 15
Ankur Tarnacha, Pennsylvania State University, USA
Carleen Maitland, Pennsylvania State University, USA

This chapter examines the structural effects of platform certification on the supply of complementary products. Drawing on the exploratory case of mobile application markets, the chapter highlights the broader market effects of competing platforms and their certifications on a platform-based complementary product market. The case suggests that although certification of platforms can increase vertical compatibility, the effects on the complementary product market can be mixed and subtle. The authors present these market effects in a conceptual model that can be applied to understand similar complementary product markets. As such, the article contributes to the literature on compatibility standards by emphasizing some of the complementary product market effects of employing certification in enhancing compatibility.

Preface

THE EUROPEAN UNION'S ICT STANDARDISATION POLICY: CHANGES AHEAD!?

Introduction

During the past three decades, two trends contributed to an increasingly complex ICT standardisation environment:

- the growing importance of ICT[1], and the associated economic importance of standards
- the globalisation of markets.

These were coupled, and further accelerated, by the Internet, which was 'discovered' for commercial use in the mid-nineties. As one result of this discovery, bring own ideas, views, and technologies into the Internet's standards setting process became a major issue for ICT companies.

Further complexity was caused by the liberalisation of the telecommunications markets and the associated emergence of regional bodies, such as ETSI[2] in Europe, and ATIS[3] in the US and TTC[4] in Asia. This was reinforced by the still ongoing merger of the formerly distinct sectors of telecommunications and IT, which caused considerable changes in these markets (David, 1995).

In addition, and as 'external' competitors, standards consortia emerged as a new phenomenon (especially in the IT sector, not so much in telecommunication). This was largely in response to the enormous speed of technical development in ICT and e-business systems. 'Traditional' SDOs – including the European Standardisation Organisations (ESOs) – were widely considered as not being capable of coping with this speed. Well-established consortia include, for instance, the W3C[5], OASIS[6], or OMG[7].

By now, a huge number of consortia and industry fora have entered the ICT (Information and Communication Technology) standards setting arena. Each of these bodies has its own membership, works within its own environment, and has defined its own set of rules. The resulting fragmentation of the standards-setting arena, and considerable overlap of the activities of individual SSBs, means that interoperability between standards from different sources cannot necessarily be assumed. Accordingly, improving co-ordination in ICT standards setting has become a major issue.

At the same time, however, we may observe fierce competition in standards setting. Initially, in the eighties consortia invaded the standardisation territory, which had always been the 'formal' standards bodies' (SDOs[8]) monopoly. This move was also helped by the deregulation of the telecommunication sector. Eventually, the SDOs started fighting back. As a result, these days competition may occur between working groups of different SSBs, and between entire SSBs which cover largely the same ground. In addition, though, WGs of the same SSB may also compete[9].

The SDOs are finding it increasingly difficult to do relevant work in such a competitive environment. Especially human resources are scare, and apparently many companies find it more rewarding to send their staff to consortia's working groups rather than SDOs' committees. And given the inherently global nature of most ICT standards, regional bodies may look like an anachronism to some. This holds particularly for Europe. Here, a well-established standardisation system is in place that is now struggling to keep a high profile in the ICT sector.

The remainder of the paper will first provide some necessary background information. Thus, section 2 will have a look at how the current ICT standardisation environment emerged, and discuss some its characteristics. The various co-operation mechanisms that are in place in standards setting will be described in section 3, for both the international and the European level. This will be followed, in section 4, by a closer look at problems specific to the European Union. Finally, some brief final remarks will be given in section 5.

The Emergence of the Current Standardisation Environment

Over the last three decades, the world of ICT standardisation has changed dramatically, from the fairly simple, straightforward, and static situation that could be found in the seventies.

Back then in the seventies, there was a clear distinction between the then 'monopolist' CCITT[10] on the one hand, and the remainder of the world of ICT standards on the other. CCITT were in charge of standards setting in the telecommunications sector. They was basically run by the national PTTs[11], which still enjoyed a monopoly situation in their respective countries. ISO[12] was in charge of almost all other ICT-related standardisation activities[13]. The various national SDOs developed their own specific standards, but also contributed to the work of ISO.

With the increasing importance of ICT, the economic importance of standards grew as well. A system 'ennobled' by having become a standard held the promise of huge financial gains for its proponents. Likewise, backing a loosing system would imply both severe monetary losses and a severely reduced market share for its supporters. In an attempt to save the day, new consortia could be established to standardise the loosing system. Obviously, this approach increased the number of consortia and led to an even higher complexity of the standards setting environment.

Figure 1. The ICT standardisation universe in the seventies (excerpt)

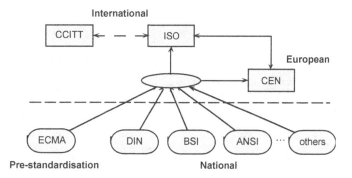

As a result, for a number of years consortia emerged an amazing rate (Cargill, 1995). This was largely in response to the enormous speed of technical development in ICT and e-business systems. 'Traditional' SDOs were widely considered as not being capable of coping with this speed (Besen, 1995), (Cargill, 1995)[14].

To further increase complexity, a proliferation of sector-specific standards may be observed in Europe, especially in the e-business domain. The most prominent representatives here include CEN (The European Committee for Standardization) Workshop Agreements (CWAs), many of which have been tailored towards the needs of a dedicated industry sector.

One effect, which is a direct result of the trends outlined above, is that many companies, especially large manufacturers, vendors, and service providers, are forced to participate in a much higher number of SSBs than they used to, in order to make sure that they do not miss a potentially relevant development (Updegrove, 2003).

The Internet's standards body, the IETF (The Internet Engineering Task Force), plays a somewhat special role thanks to the unprecedented importance of the Internet in today's economy. For many years the IETF had not been accepted as a standards setting body, and its output, the Internet Standards, were not recognised by government procurement regulations (Werle, 2002). This has changed by now, though.

Also, the IETF may be regarded as the role model for many large consortia, such as the W3C and OASIS, which have based their processes on that of the IETF. In fact, many have considered the IETF's process as superior to those of the formal SDOs[15] (Crocker, 1993), (Monteiro, 1995), (Solomon & Rutkowski, 1992).

Eventually, the highly complex web of SSBs we are seeing today emerged, part of which is depicted in Figure 2.

The complex environment outlined above represents a major obstacle for those who are considering active participation in standardisation, as well as for those who are looking for a standard that suits their needs best.

Figure 2. The ICT standardisation universe today (excerpt)

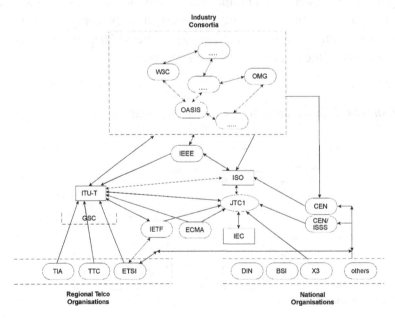

Considering this complexity of the IT standardisation universe, "Where to participate?" is a relevant question for those who wish to actively contribute to standards setting. Functionally equivalent systems may well be standardised in parallel by different SDOs and consortia, and participation in all relevant work groups is well beyond the means of all but the biggest players. The correct decision here is crucial, as backing the wrong horse may leave a company stranded with systems based on the 'wrong' (i.e., non-standard) technology.

In addition to the more practical aspects that need to be considered when selecting the best suited SSB for a particular standards setting activity other, less tangible aspects may play a role in such decision processes, too. In particular, this may include the perceived reputation of an SSB.

Perceptions of the importance and relevance of different types of SSBs differ widely. For instance, Rutkowski offers a rather extreme point of view – *"The Internet standards development process is by far the best in the business."* (Rutkowski, 1995). However, things have changed since the times when the IETF on the one hand and ISO and CCITT on the other were basically the only players in the international ICT arena. These days, the IETF is little else but one of a number of accepted members of the global web of standards setting bodies.

Likewise, the role of the national SDOs has changed. This holds particularly for Europe, where 90% of standards produced are European or international (as opposed to national; this ratio has changed dramatically within a couple of years) (Bilalis & Herbert, 2003). Along similar lines, Ghiladi fears that *"... non-harmonized national standards and rules have the effect of erecting barriers."* (Ghiladi, 2003).

Moreover, in an attempt to improve their position in the competition with consortia many SSBs have introduced 'new deliverables'. These are documents which do not have gone through the full-blown process that leads towards a 'Standard', but are more akin to the specifications issued by consortia (i.e., e.g., they require only a lower level of consensus, and can thus be published quicker). Obviously, this move has introduced further complexity into standardisation.

Many consortia and other SSBs outside the network of formal SDOs have established themselves as recognised sources of standards. Initially, though, their output was considered 'inferior' to that of the formal bodies. This had major repercussions, e.g. in (public) procurement (Heafner, 1988), (Werle, 2002). Here, Europe's commitment to OSI in the 1980-90s was a remarkable example. In addition to its undoubted technical superiority, one of the major reasons why OSI standards were considered preferable to their Internet counterparts was the fact that ISO, where the OSI standards were developed, was a formal SDO, unlike the IETF, which was viewed with considerable suspicion by many.

Similar views could be observed in the private sector. A standards inventory project in the US petrochemical industry, for instance, established rules where *"... preference was given first to international standards, followed by national standards, and then consortium specifications."* (Kowalski & Karcher, 1994).

Yet, by now Europe has recognised that: *"... consortia and fora are playing an increasing role in the development of standards, ... the European Standards Organisations have to recognise these facts and re-design policies, processes and organisational structures, in close collaboration with stakeholders and in particular industry ... "* (EC, 2004b), albeit with some concern: *"It is considered doubtful whether, in the light of the speed of development and the limited participation of experts, the fundamental principles for accountability of standardisation such as openness, consensus and transparency are followed in a robust fashion."* (EC, 2004a). Interestingly, this position has been challenged in (Egyedi, 2003), stating that democracy should not necessarily be required from consortia processes.

These diverse positions already hint at the currently ongoing discussion about the role of consortia in relation to European standardisation.

Coordination at SSB Level: State-of-the-Art

The International Level

The increasingly complex web of SSBs, in conjunction with the equally increasing inter-dependencies between different ICT systems, and between applications and ICT infrastructure, imply an urgent need for co-operation and distribution of labour between the SSBs active in ICT standardisation.

Today, various forms of co-operation between SSBs may be found. In the realm of SDOs, 'horizontal' co-operation between the international SDOs is regulated by a dedicated guide for co-operation between ITU-T and JTC1[16] (ITU, 2001); see also Figure 3. This document specifies different forms of co-operation, including, in order of level of co-ordination, 'liaison', 'collaborative interchange', 'collaborative team'. However, the document also makes it very plain that *"By far, the vast majority of the work program of the ITU-T and the work program of JTC 1 is carried out separately with little, if any, need for cooperation between the organizations"*.

The Global Standards Collaboration (GSC; see Figure 2) covers both vertical (between regional telecommunication standards bodies and the ITU) and horizontal co-ordination (between regional telecommunication standards bodies). It provides for the regular exchange of work programmes and other information between its members. However, it is likely that the progressing merger of the IT and telecommunications sectors will pose additional problems in this respect, such as, for example, the need to include new members (from the IT sector).

In the e-business sector, a specific MoU (ITU, 2000) exists between ISO, IEC (the 'parent' organisations of JTC1), ITU, and UN/ECE (United Nations Economic Commission for Europe). A number of additional organisations have been recognised as participating international user groups, [including, e.g., OASIS, CEN/ISSS, and SWIFT (Society for Worldwide Interbank Financial Telecommunication)]. The objective of the MoU is to encourage interoperability. To this end, it aims to minimise the risk of conflicting approaches to standardisation, to avoid duplication of efforts, to provide a clear roadmap for users, and to ensure inter-sectoral coherence. Most notably, its 'division of responsibilities' identifies a

Figure 3. Co-operation between SDOs at the international level

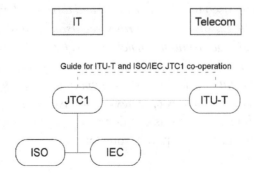

number of key tasks and assigns a lead organisation (one of the four signatories) to each of them. Overall, the co-ordination of the work of the SDOs appears to be reasonably well organised[17].

This does not necessarily hold for the co-ordination between SDOs and standards consortia. Numerous co-operations do exist; however, the current situation can be best described as piecemeal; there is no overarching framework to organise the individual co-operations. The MoU on e-business standards is a good initial step, but its coverage in terms of organisations involved is still rather limited. In this context, the move of UN/CEFACT (United Nations Centre for Trade Facilitation and Electronic Business) to 'outsource' ebXML related activities to OASIS is a notable move, as it represents a unique form of co-operation between an 'official' body and a standards consortium.

'Publicly Available Specifications' (PAS) represent a different, yet highly relevant co-ordination mechanism. The ISO directives state that "... *constitutional characteristics of the* [PAS-submitting] *organisation are supposed to reflect the openness of the organisation and the PAS development process.*" (JTC1, 2004). The PAS procedure is a means for JTC1 to transpose a specification more rapidly into an international standard. The specification starts out as a Draft International Standard (DIS), which, if approved by JTC1 members, immediately acquires the status of an International Standard (IS). This mechanism has primarily been designed to enable JTC1 to transpose specifications that originated from consortia into international standards. In this capacity it also serves as a mechanisms to at least contribute to co-ordination of work done within consortia and the world of formal SDO.

With respect to the co-ordination between individual consortia the situation is even worse. Here as well co-operations occur rather more at the level of technical bodies (if at all) than at SSB level. In most cases, however, the world of standards consortia experiences more competition than co-operation. There is direct competition between consortia covering similar ground, for instance, between RosettaNet and ebXML, and between the Semantic Web Services Initiative (SWSI) and the W3C.

The European Standardisation Landscape

The European Standardisation system comprises three ESOs. Of these, ETSI is in charge of telecommunication standardisation. CENELEC is working in the field of electrotechnical standardisation, and CEN basically covers all other topics. The system is very much based upon the international system, and close links exist between both systems (see Figure 4).

The European Standards Organisations' (ESOs) Joint Presidents' Group (JPG) co-ordinates the standardisation policies of the ESOs based on a basic co-operation agreement (CEN, 2008). Five different modes of co-operation have been defined, including 'Informative relation', 'Contributive relation', 'Sub-contracting relation', 'Collaborative relation', and 'Integrated relation' (CEN, 2008). Moreover, the Directive 98/34/EC (European Commission, 1998) mandates that conflicting standards have to be withdrawn. This is managed internally by each ESO, between the three bodies (through cross-representation at General Assemblies and co-ordination bodies), and 'vertically' with their members, the NSOs.

'Vertical' co-operation between ESOs and their respective international mirror bodies is governed by individual documents. Here, the major need for co-operation and co-ordination is primarily sector-specific.

The 'Vienna Agreement' (ISO, 2001) provides the rules for co-operation between CEN and ISO; analogously, the 'Dresden Agreement'[18] governs relations between IEC (International Electrotechnical Commission) and CENELEC (European Committee for Electrotechnical Standardization). Somewhat surprisingly, only a rather more informal Memorandum of Understanding (MoU) exists for the co-

Figure 4. Co-operation and co-ordination agreements between European and international SDOs (taken from (Jakobs, 2008))

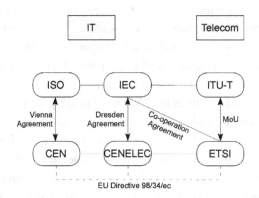

operation between ETSI and ITU[19]. On the other hand, and also a bit unexpected, a dedicated agreement guides the relations between ETSI and IEC[20].

In general, the 'vertical' agreements and MoUs (i.e., those between ESOs and the international bodies) define various levels of co-operation and co-ordination, albeit in comparably vague terms. Nonetheless, co-operation between CEN and ISO, and CENELEC and IEC, has been very successful in many cases, primarily through joint working groups. In contrast, the documents governing the respective 'horizontal' co-operations, are far more rigorous. This holds particularly for the European Directive that regulates the relations between the three ESOs.

ETSI Partnership Projects[21] represent a different, albeit related approach to co-ordination. Covering both SDOs and consortia, such projects co-ordinate a group of regional SDOs and industry consortia working towards a common objective. The '3rd Generation Partnership Project' (3GPP) is the most prominent example.

An initiative jointly taken by the three ESOs is another promising development. The ICT Standards Board (ICTSB) aims to co-ordinate specification activities in the field of Information and Communications Technologies. In addition to the ESOs, ICTSB membership comprises major standards consortia (including, for example, ECBS (the European Committee for Banking Standards), ECMA International[22], OASIS, the Object Management Group, RosettaNet, The Open Group, and the World Wide Web Consortium. The ICTSB's objectives include[23]:

- The analysis and co-ordination of requirements on standardisation.
- The translation of these requirements into standardisation programmes or projects.
- The allocation of work to the most appropriate specifying body (SDO or consortium).

Thus, its approach is quite similar to the one adopted by the MoU on e-business standardisation, albeit broader in scope.

The Global RFID Interoperability Forum for Standards (GRIFS) represents yet another approach to co-ordination. GRIFS a project funded by the European Commission with the aim *"to improve collaboration and thereby to maximise the global interoperability of RFID standards"* (GRIFS, 2008). The GRIFS project is co-ordinated by GS1, ETSI and CEN. It will initiate a forum that will continue to work after the end of the project through a Memorandum of Understanding between key global standard organisations active in RFID.

European ICT Standardisation Problems

A Bit of Background

A number of likely changes in the ICT landscape in the not-too-distant future will (have to) have significant repercussions on the EU's standardisation policy. For example, just like liberalisation of the telecommunication market and the merger of the IT and telecommunication sectors caused significant changes to the standards setting environment, the future merger of broadcast and ICT will contribute to even further changes. These will be all the more important as standardisation will also have a direct impact on the consumer (as signified, for example, by the prevailing uncertainty about future TV standards and their implementation).

The emergence of China as a new powerful player in the ICT arena represents another major development to be taken into account. This holds all the more, given the many unresolved IPR-related issues which still seem to overshadow China's role in (ICT) standards setting. In any case, an EU standardisation policy will need to deal with this emerging potent and robust player.

Nearer to home, the role of standards in support of legislation will have to be re-established. Currently, only standards issued by the ESOs (strangely also including some 'New Deliverables') are referenced in European Directives, policy documents, and in public procurement. Yet, with the increasingly blurred distinction in terms of processes between ESOs and at least some of the major industry consortia [like OASIS or W3C; see, for example, (Jakobs, 2006)], it seems questionable whether this focus on ESO deliverables can, and should, be maintained in the future. The same holds for the role of standards in public procurement processes.

More generally, the relation between ESOs on the one hand and the international bodies and industry consortia, respectively, on the other will have to be re-evaluated. While ESOs are most helpful in dealing with specifically European needs in ICT standardisation, they also represent a somewhat artificial construct, given that most ICT standards are international by their very nature.

Likewise, the overlap of activities going on in both ESOs and in consortia needs to be minimised in order to not waste scarce resources and, more importantly, to ensure interoperability. Here, new ways need to be found to ensure an adequate level of co-ordination and co-operation between ESOs and consortia, but also between the three ESOs.

Another aspect, which may be potentially dangerous in the longer term, refers to the typically unbalanced participation of the different stakeholder groups in ICT standards setting. Different considerations are of importance here. For one, according to recent studies (e.g., Egyedi et al. 2003, Jakobs, 2004, Gerst & Jakobs, 2005, Blind, 2006), SMEs are still dramatically under-represented in both international and European standardisation. Given that SMEs account for 99% of European companies, and provide some 75 million jobs, this is not a sustainable situation. The same holds for consumers, for whom the situation is even worse. Here, adequate measures will have to be implemented to achieve a more balanced participation of all groups of stakeholders where necessary and beneficial.

The same holds for the participation of consumer representatives in ICT/e-business standards setting. In fact, consumers are hardly represented at all in ICT standardisation (with exceptions, thanks largely to ANEC). Yet, many ICT standards directly impact consumers (e.g., those relating to e-inclusion). This will hold all the more with the merger of ICT and broadcasting. Thus, for these standards contributions also from the consumer side would be valuable.

Against this background, and especially with a view at the proliferation and increasing importance of standards consortia, concerns have grown for quite a while now about the (future) relevance of the European ICT standardisation system. Similar earlier concerns – and the wish to get rid of the (perceived) reputation of being slow moving and not really up to the job – had already led to the introduction of 'lightweight' deliverables[24] by the ESO. This time, however, the whole EU ICT standardisation policy is being questioned.

Identified Issues

A report was commissioned in 2006 by the European Commission with the mandate to analyse the state-of-the-art in European ICT standardisation policy, and to provide recommendations on how to adapt it in the future (CEU, 2007). This report observes that various trends, many of them home-grown, are likely to contribute to a reduced importance of SDOs in general, and of the ESOs in particular (compared to standards consortia). According to (CEU, 2007) and (EU-China, 2008), these include, among others:

- **Internal legal issues.** EU legislation (and, to a lesser degree, public procurement) can only reference standards produced by the ESOs. In particular, no standards developed by standards consortia or fora (like, for example, the W3C, OASIS, or OMG), as well as those developed by the IETF, IEEE and the likes the may be referenced. Closely related to that is a
- **Lack of adequate European standards.** EU regulation, legislation and public procurement cannot reference many state-of-the-art standards solely because they have been developed by the 'wrong' standards setting bodies (SSBs; i.e., not by one of the ESOs).
- **Lack of integration of standards consortia.** Here, the prevailing stance remains that "*It is considered doubtful whether, in the light of the speed of development and the limited participation of experts, the fundamental principles for accountability of standardisation such as openness, consensus and transparency are followed in a robust fashion* [by industrial fora and consortia]" (CEU, 2004).
- **Lagging European efforts.** In the ICT standardisation area, EU work is lagging a long way behind market realities. This is not least due to the policies and cumbersome processes deployed by the ESOs (specifically CEN and CENELEC).
- **Lack of adequate links to the R&D community.** The political support is largely limited to indirect support to pre-standardisation. In addition, some dedicated projects looking at the link between R&D and standardisation have been funded.
- **Increasing influence of Asian countries, most notably China**[25] China has recognised the potential of actively pursuing ICT standardisation. This is done on two levels: through the development of national standards, and through strong participation in the international arena (primarily in formal bodies, though, as opposed to consortia).

Envisaged Potential Remedies

To do something about especially the first four issues, the EU needs to re-consider their stance towards non-European SSBs. Specifically, four potential lines of action have been identified (CEU, 2008):

1.   No action at all at EU level.
2.   Modest changes to European ICT standardisation policy, e.g.
     o   create a permanent stakeholders' platform,
     o   encourage deeper integration of the work of consortia / fora into the European standardisation
         system through agreements with the ESOs.
3.   Significant changes to European ICT standardisation policy, e.g.
     o   create the financial and legal possibility to reference non-ESO ICT standards in EU policies
         and legislation,
     o   define ICT standards attributes based on WTO criteria,
     o   use specific standards developed by particular consortia/ fora ('case by case basis'),
     o   clarify the provisions applicable to the use of ICT standards in public procurement.
4.   Comprehensive changes to European ICT standardisation policy, e.g.
     o   recognition / accreditation of fora and consortia as standardisation organisations under Direc-
         tive 98/34,
     o   regulate the treatment of IPR related to ICT standards".

Given the issues listed above (and the numerous others), #1 is hardly an option.

The same holds for option 2. An entity that could easily assume the role of the suggested platform has already been established – the ICT Standards Board[26] (ICTSB). Whether or not consortia actually want to be integrated more deeply into the European standardisation system appears questionable – why should they?

Option 4 would probably bring about a whole host of legal problems that would take considerable time and efforts to be fully resolved. Moreover, given the very diverse policies and bylaws of individual consortia, a 'carte blanche' approach here would not be feasible (see below).

This leaves #3 as the only viable option. The WTO has identified a 'Code of Good Practice for the Preparation, Adoption, and Application of Standards' (WTO, 2000). Compliance with this Code would thus be a minimum requirement for consortia to be accepted as potential sources of officially 'referencable' standards in the EU. It might, however, be advisable to identify additional criteria that should be met by consortia (e.g., about their openness, membership policies, IPR rules, etc). This option should also be implementable with an acceptable degree of legal/administrative overhead.

Some Very Brief Final Remarks

The EU ICT standardisation system is closely connected to the system of international standardisation bodies. Its success within this international context is challenged by various competitors. As far as the 'formal' bodies are concerned, this holds particularly for China. This country is adopting a rather aggressive stance in the attempt to push indigenous technology into international standards. In addition, standards consortia have already marginalised SDOs in many areas of the ICT sector (such as, for example, the Internet, the World Wide Web, and e-business).

Any policy measures to promote the results of the EU's ICT standardisation have to take into account that the most important ICT consortia standards are developed already at a global level. Also, global standards facilitate trade and thus have a strong impact on a country's or region's export performance. Consequently, there is a need for EU actors to be adequately involved in international standardisation processes, in the relevant bodies. The development of strategies to transfer EU ICT standards the international level is crucial in order to gain a competitive advantage.

Since the technological race is becoming faster in the ICT sector, European standards have to be established early and the results should be promoted world-wide. Such international standards based on European input would, however, also enable foreign competitors to imitate European ICT products and systems. This, in turn, will requires a well defined co-ordination of European IPR policies. Furthermore, international standards are a mode of efficient technology transfer in ICT technologies. The European ICT sector can benefit here in those fields in which other regions are in the lead by immediately adapting the respective standards.

Kai Jakobs
Editor

REFERENCES

Besen, F.M. (1995). The standards process in telecommunication and information technology. In R.W. Hawkins, et al. (Eds.), *Standards, Innovation and Competitiveness*. Edward Elgar Publishers.

Bilalis, Z., & Herbert, D. (2001). (IT) Standardisation from a European Point of View. *JITSR, 1*(1).

Blind, K. (2006). Explanatory Factors for Participation in Formal Standardisation Processes: Empirical Evidence at Firm Level. In *Economics of Innovation and New Technology*, 15.

Cargill, C.F. (1995). *Open Systems Standardization – A Business Approach*. Prentice Hall.

CEN (2008). *CEN/CENELEC Internal Regulations - Part 2: Common Rules for Standards Work*. Retrieved from http://www.cen.eu/BOSS/supporting/reference+documents/cen-cenelec+internal+regulations+-+part+2/cen-cenelec+ir+2+-+contents+list.asp

CEU (2004). *Commission Staff Working Document: The challenges for European standardisation*. Retrieved from http://europa.eu.int/comm/enterprise/standards_policy/role_of_standardisation/doc/staff_working_document_en.pdf

CEU (2007). *Final report of the study on the specific policy needs for ICT standardisation*. Retrieved from http://www.ictstandardisation.eu/full_report.pdf

CEU (2008). *Call for Tenders – Future ICT Standardisation Policy: Impact Assessment of Policy Options*.

Crocker, D. (1993). Making Standards the IETF Way. *ACM StandardView, 1*(1).

David, P.A. (1985). Clio and the Economics of QWERTY. *The American Economic Review, 75*(2), 332-337.

Egyedi, T. (2003). Consortium problem redefined: Negotiating 'democracy' in the actor network on standardization. *JITSR, 1*(2).

Egyedi, T., Jakobs, K., Monteiro, E. (2003). Helping SDOs to Reach Users. Report for EC DG ENT, Contract No 20010674.

EU-China (2008). Project Deliverable 3: Review of state of Art – EU & China.

European Commission (2004a). *Commission Staff Working Document: The challenges for European standardisation*. Retrieved from http://europa.eu.int/comm/enterprise/standards_policy/role_of_standardisation/doc/staff_working_document_en.pdf

European Commission (2004b). The role of European standardisation in the framework of European policies and legislation. *Communication from the Commission to the European Parliament and the Council, COM* (2004) 674. Retrieved from http://europa.eu.int/comm/enterprise/standards_policy/role_of_standardisation/doc/communication_en.pdf

Gerst, M., Jakobs, K. (2005). e-Business Standardisation in the Automotive Sector - The Situation of SMEs - Strengthening Competitiveness through Production Networks, Europ. Commission (Ed.), Brussels.

Ghiladi, V. (2003). The Importance of International Standards for Globally Operating Businesses. *JITSR, 1*(1).

GRIFS (2008). GRIFS Brochure. Retrieved from http://www.grifs-project.eu/data/File/GRIFSbrochure-final.pdf

Heafner, J.F. (1988): U.S. Government procurement of open systems products and services. *Computer Standards & Interfaces, 7*(1-2).

ISO (2001). ISO/IEC Directives Supplement – Procedures specific to ISO. http://isotc.iso.org/livelink/livelink/1166946/Supplement_-_Procedures_specific_to_ISO__1st_edition__the__ISO_Supplement____PDF_format___includes_all_forms_.pdf?func=doc.Fetch&nodeid=1166946

ITU (2000). MoU on electronic business between IEC, ISO, ITU, and UN/ECE. http://www.itu.int/ITU-T/e-business/files/mou.pdf

ITU-T (2001). Guide for ITU-T and ISO/IEC JTC 1 Cooperation. http://www.itu.int/rec/recommendation.asp?type=items&lang=e&parent=T-REC-A.23-200111-I!AnnA

Jakobs, K. (2004). The Third Estate - The Role of SMEs in ICT Standards Setting. - Proc. eChallenges Conference, Vienna.

Jakobs, K. (2006). Open Standards and New Deliverables. In P. Cunningham & M. Cunningham (Eds.), *Exploiting the Knowledge Economy; Proc. E-Challenges*. Vienna, Austria: IOS Press.

Jakobs, K. (2008). ICT Standardisation – Co-ordinating the Diversity. In *Proc. 'Innovations in NGN – Future Network and Services. An ITU-T Kaleidoscope Event'*. IEEE Press.

JTC1 (Eds.) (2004). *ISO/IEC Directives, Procedures for the technical work of ISO/IEC JTC 1 on Information Technology* (5th Ed.).

Kowalski, V.J., & Karcher, B. (1994). Industry consortia in open systems. *ACM StandardView, 2*(1).

Monteiro, E. et al. (1995). *Standardisation of information infrastructure: where is the flexibility?* Presented at PICT, London

Rutkowski, A.M. (1995). Today's Cooperative Competitive Standards Environment for Open Information and Telecommunication Networks and the Internet Standards-Making Model. In B. Kahin & J. Abbate (Eds.), *Standards Policy for Information Infrastructure*. MIT Press.

Solomon, R.J., & Rutkowski, A.M. (1992). Standards-making for IT: Old vs. New Models. In *Proc. of the Conference on the Economic Dimension of Standards*.

Updegrove, A. (2003). Major Standards Players Tell How They Evaluate Standard Setting Organizations. Retrieved from http://www.consortiuminfo.org/bulletins/jun03.php

Werle, R. (2002). Lessons learnt from the Internet. Hands off, hands on, or what role of public policy in Europe? *Druzboslovne Razprave (Journal of Social Science Studies), 18*(40).

WTO (2000): Code of Good Practice for the Preparation, Adoption, and Application of Standards. Retrieved from http://www.standardsinfo.net/info/livelink/fetch/2000/148478/6301438/docs_wto/tbt-a3.pdf

ENDNOTES

[1]   Information and Communication Technologies.

[2]   The European Telecommunications Standards Institute.

[3]   The Alliance for Telecommunications Industry Solutions.

[4]   The Telecommunication Technology Committee.

[5]   The World Wide Web Consortium.

[6]   The Organization for the Advancement of Structured Information Standards.

[7]   The Object Management Group.

[8]   Standards Developing Organisations, i.e., the 'formal' bodies like e.g. ISO and ITU at the global level, CEN and ETSI at the European level, and the various national bodies.

[9]   For instance, in the 80s the IEEE groups 802.3/4/5 worked on competing technologies for local area networks. Eventually, Ethernet (802.3) won.

[10]   International Telegraph and Telephone Consultative Committee, the predecessor of the ITU-T.

[11]   Post, Telegraph and Telephone administration (typically the national monopolies).

[12]   The International Organization for Standardization. Please note that ISO is not an acronym, it is derived from the Greek word isos, meaning 'equal'.

[13]   Some related activities were also carried out within IEC, the International Electrotechnical Commission.

[14]   Whether or not this view is justified is a matter of debate. For a slightly different opinion see e.g., (Sherif, 2003) and (Jakobs, 2002).

[15]   See (Jakobs, 2003) for a perhaps more objective discussions of this view.

[16]   Joint Technical Committee One, a committee run jointly by IEC and ISO, covering all IT-related sectors.

[17]   There have been exceptions, though, which need to be avoided in the future. For example, the IEEE 802.11a/b/g activities and ETSI's HIPERLAN/2 covered the same ground and were in direct competition (ETSI 'lost').

[18]   http://www.iec.ch/about/partners/agreements/cenelec-e.htm.

[19]   http://www.itu.int/ITU-T/tsb-director/mou/mou_itu_etsi.html.

[20]   http://www.iec.ch/about/partners/agreements/etsi-e.htm.

[21]   "Where appropriate, ETSI will base its activities on Partnership Projects committed to basic principles such as openness, clear Intellectual Property Rights (IPR) policy and financial co-responsibility, to

be established with partners of any kind (global and regional, Standards Development Organizations (SDOs) and Fora, etc.)" http://www.etsi.org/etsi_galaxy/worldwide/partnership/partnership_a.htm.

[22] Originally the European Computer Manufacturer's Association, now the European association for standardizing information and communication systems.

[23] http://www.ictsb.org/archives_short-cuts.htm.

[24] Like the 'CEN Workshop Agreements' and ETSI's 'Industry Specifications'.

[25] As Chinese officials like to say: third-class companies make products; second-class companies develop technology; first-class companies set standards.

[26] The ICTSB is an initiative from the three ESOs with the participation consortia including, among others, the W3C, ISOC, and RosettaNet to co-ordinate specification activities in the field of ICT.

Chapter 1
Foundations and Future Prospects of Standards Studies:
Multidisciplinary Approach[1]

Shiro Kurihara
Hitotsubashi University, Japan

ABSTRACT

The standards world has radically changed over the past two decades, especially in international standardization, with an increased impact on business and society, although the essential characteristic of standardization in general; namely, to achieve the optimal order in a given context, remains unchanged. In this article, such evolution of international standardization, caused by its structural adaptation to changes in its environment as well as the origin and history of standardization and standards, are reviewed initially. Subsequently, "standard studies" is advocated as a new academic discipline to comprehensively analyze the problems of standardization and standards from a broader perspective, transcending predominantly technological concerns. Finally, the need to invest in standards research and education is highlighted.

EVOLUTION OF INTERNATIONAL STANDARDIZATION

The First Wave Driven by Technology

To date, standards have not been taken up for an academic discipline. Since the development of standards as industrial infrastructure requires the accumulation of considerable data and expert knowledge, it has been entrusted to professional engineers in a business corporation. This is proved by the historical evolution of international standardization. In 1865, an organization concerned with the technology of sending a signal, invented by Samuel F.B. Morse, was launched, a body that has now been succeeded by the International Telecommunication Union (ITU). One of the important tasks today is the allocation of frequencies for mobile phones and the preparation of international agreements published as recommendations. The next international organization was established in 1906 by Lord Kelvin as the International Electrotechnical Commission (IEC) to deal with the electrical technology invented at the time. The third one was set up in 1926, with the focus on mechanical technology, which is the predecessor of the present International Standardization Organization (ISO). Finally in 1987, the Joint Technical Committee 1 (JTC1) was created, together with the IEC and the ISO, in the field of information technology especially related to computer software. The start of these four organizations, each of which corresponds to the then emerging key technologies; namely, communication, electrical, mechanical and information technologies, seems to characterize the technology-led first wave in the history of standards development. As a general rule, the diffusion of a key technology embodied in new products and services calls for such specifications to make them fit for use and acceptable to the times and society. In this sense, the first wave is derived from the adaptation of technological innovation to market or social needs.

The Second Wave Driven by Corporation

The world of standards, however, has been transfigured by a new situation that occurred two decades ago.

In the first place, the rapid progress of the digital revolution brought the importance of consortium or de facto standards to complement de jure standards, the latter of which takes an average of five years to make. This pace is not suitable for shorter-lifecycle products in the infocommunications domain, where many competitors strategically strive to gain a predominant market position. The standards for compact discs, digital audiotapes, or digital video discs were completed in consortium and subsequently absorbed into the IEC. If such procedures become common practice, however, international organizations publicly

recognized as authorities to create standards turn out to be stamping agencies of de jure standards and not involved in the substantial discussion of its contents.

There are significant differences in the standardization methods and procedures used across standards organizations such as the ISO/IEC and the World Wide Web Consortium (W3C) to develop interoperable technologies for leading the Web to its full potential. Some procedures emphasize the need to reach a broad consensus, while others emphasize speed. It is vital to know which procedures are best suited to developing a global standard for a particular product. Digital industries, for example, usually demand faster standardization than the transport sector. Awareness of differences in standardization can be critical for the future of a company or industry.

Second, the managerial angle was introduced as a new perspective for standards. In Europe, harmonization of national standards and regulations was accelerated in the 1980s for the consolidation of markets; and the Quality Management System Standard, which originated in the UK, was adopted as the ISO 9000 series of standards for quality management in 1987. This is concerned with the system and the process of decision-making in organizations that try to respond voluntarily to customer requirements with respect to quality as well as conformity to legal requirements. Such a management system standard has completely changed the old image or fixed idea of the technology standard to specify the product characteristics and testing method. This new type of standard has become the tool of corporate governance linking business and society. A similar ISO 14000 series of management system standard was introduced into the environment in 1996 at the strong urging of the Business Council for Sustainable Development, food safety in 2005, and information security in 2006, respectively, with the social responsibility standard expected to be published in 2008. The ISO has responded on a timely basis to new types of requirements, which has diversified its standards portfolio. It is fulfilling not only strictly technical requirements, but also socioeconomic and ecological ones.

Third, the inauguration of the World Trade Organization (WTO) in 1995 has increased the influence of international standards. The Agreement of Technical Barriers to Trade (TBT) obligates member countries to harmonize national and international standards, while the Sanitary and Phytosanitary Measures (SPS) Agreement comprises the mandatory basic rules for food safety and animal and plant health. Its annex cites the FAO/WHO CODEX Alimentarius Commission (for food), the International Office of Epizootics (for animal health), and the FAO's Secretariat of the International Plant Protection Convention (for plant health) as international standards. These two agreements, which perceive international standards as bridges to trade rather than barriers, have given international standards a predominant position over that in the past General Agreement on Tariffs and Trade (GATT), in which member countries were not obliged to implement international standards as national standards.[2] The German National Standardization Strategy states that "whoever makes the standards controls the market,"[3] and the United Kingdom National Standardization Strategic Framework states that "standards influence everything we do."[4] Even the recently revised United States Standards Strategy states, "The international language of commerce is standards. Adherence to agreed upon product or service specifications underpins international commerce, enabling trillions of dollars of goods to flow across borders, regardless of the spoken language of any business parties."[5] The nations that have abruptly shifted their stance on the strategic value of international standards are not limited to Western countries. China, where virtually all the current leaders are engineers by training, has particularly embraced the need for active involvement in international standards development. Indeed, the program of the May 19, 2005, Beijing Information Technology Standard

International Forum in Beijing clearly articulates China's intentions that "whoever controls the power of standard making and has its technology as the leading standard, commands the initiative of the market. Technology standard has become an important means of global economic competition directly influenc[ing] the competitiveness of an industry, a region or a country" (Purcell, 2005).

Fourth, the network revolution has established the compatibility standard essential for market expansion. The networked economy, which requires interconnection to transcend national borders, has developed globally. Creating a common standard in business circles, followed by the development of a product conforming to the same, is now prevalent in the communication industry. The network externality makes the value of a product of one company, which is compatible with that of another, much higher than it would be otherwise. Such a phenomenon occurs not only in the infocommunications domain, but also the logistics area, targeting global transport through shipping containers.

The changes mentioned previously form the second wave in the world of standards that is driven by a corporation's adaptation to the changes in the business environment; namely, digital innovation, the new requirements of stakeholders, a new international trading order, and network development.

The Third Wave Driven by Market, Government, and Society

In the fifth place of transfiguration, improved awareness of the environment, safety, health, human rights, and social justice from consumers' and citizens' perspectives has highlighted the increased importance of standards. Standards for services such as maintenance, transport, tourism, information technology, and construction have emerged to ensure customer satisfaction and societal security. There is significant demand for conformity to an objective standard based on expert knowledge, or for certification by a disinterested third party. The explanation by a corporation that "you can trust our company to do the work because we pay close attention to environmental conservation and safety" can no longer satisfy the market or customers. However, on the contrary, the market side advances the following claim to a corporation; namely, "show me the objective data related to relevant measures." Stakeholders demand that appropriate measures be taken, not arbitrarily, but based on established rules. The Consumer Policy Committee (COPOLCO) in the ISO has been actively involved in these affairs and contributed much to the publication of international standards of complaints handling, code of conducts, and alternative dispute resolution (ADR) from the viewpoint of customer satisfaction. Its strategy does not involve confronting a business corporation, based on consumers' rights, but getting it to collaborate with consumers to optimally exploit the market mechanism, targeting improved performance beyond compliance with the legal minimums.

Finally, as the sixth, the strategic involvement of national governments in international standardization in high-technology areas from an industrial policy perspective is now critical for countries to succeed in a world dominated by technology and science. The case of high-definition television symbolizes the scramble for the top spot. Japan started to develop it in 1965, but its efforts for international standardization that began in 1974 were postponed without mutual consent. Subsequently, Europe launched the project as one of the European Research Coordination Action (EUREKA) programs in 1985, and the U.S. Federal Communications Commission (FCC) set up a consultative committee for next-generation television in 1987. In 1990, although the standardization was completed in the ITU, multiple formats with varying national origins were standardized in parallel. After innumerable twists and turns, the analog transmission that has been received to date will be completely replaced by the digital alternative by the year 2011 in Japan. International competition in the development of high technology seems too intense for its standardization to be settled normally by a technical committee in the international organization.

These changes seem to form the third wave in the world of standards, which is driven mainly by the market, together with government and society, in having a major influence on standardization.

The Relationship among the Three Waves

These three waves are mapped in Figure 1. The vertical axis shows the subjects or fields of standardization, which are classified into two groups; namely, the technology and management system. Moreover, the horizontal axis represents the main driving forces for standardization; namely, business and society. In case of the first wave, technology itself works as a driving force as well as regarded to be the subject of standardization. The six transfigurations mentioned previously are headed by the corresponding number in each quadrant, while the Roman numerals *I~III* represent the three waves, respectively. Wave *II* is superimposed on wave *I* and wave *III* on top of both. However, this does not mean that the old wave disappears with the advent of the new wave.[6] Standardization of biotechnology, nanotechnology, or renewable-energy technology is an urgent task in wave *I*. The three waves coexist in such a way that each wave occupies a certain space on the same plane. This figure indicates that technology and management system standards have exerted a far-reaching influence on business and society and that these two domains, together with government, increasingly require appropriate standardization to solve the various problems facing them. This conclusion, derived so far from the evolutionary context of mainly ISO, IEC, and ITU, may also be applied to other fields such as international

Figure 1. Subjects and driving forces of international standardization

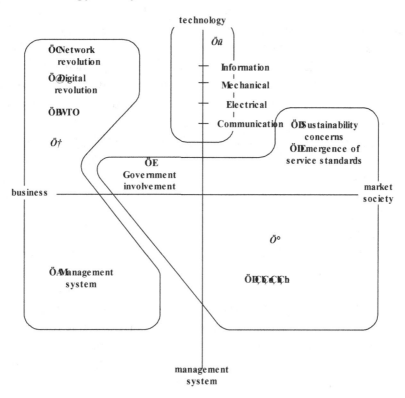

accounting standards. The globalization of the world economy and the establishment of the WTO have vastly increased the social influence of international standards in every field.

The appearance of waves *II* and *III* transformed the world of standards from a mere technological and engineering matter to a more complicated and interconnected phenomenon associated with business and society alongside the environment. The impacts of standards have now expanded ever further to cover virtually all contemporary affairs; namely, corporate governance, international trade, network economy, logistics infrastructure, environment, safety, social responsibility, and deregulation. To understand and analyze such a standard-related development will require the establishment of a new academic discipline entitled "standards studies," which tries to adopt a multidisciplinary approach.

THE ORIGIN AND HISTORY OF STANDARDIZATION AND STANDARDS

To go back in history makes us realize the essence in everything (Anh, 2006). A fundamental idea of standardization is to control or regulate something voluntarily in such a way that conforms to a certain standard aimed at the creation of desirable order. It may safely be said that anything cannot be controlled properly without standards. Its motto is "control by standards."

Standardization of Weights and Measures

A unit of measurement was standardized to facilitate group work, the exchange of goods, taxation of land, and so forth, where common understanding of weights and measures in the physical world between one individual and another—seller and buyer, government and taxpayer—was a prerequisite for improving its accuracy and efficiency. Ancient measures of length called a cubit (approximately equal to the length of a forearm) and feet (corresponding to the length of a foot) were used by ancient Egyptians, Hebrews, and Romans. With this in kind, section 8 of article I of the Constitution of the United States states, "The Congress shall have power to coin money, regulate the value thereof, and of foreign coin, and fix the standard of weights and measures." The origin of the word *norme* in French or *norm* in German, equivalent to *standard* in English, is *norma* in Latin, which means a carpenter's square, an L- or T-shaped instrument used for obtaining or testing right angles. The metrology standard is currently under the control of the International Committee of Weights and Measures (CPIM) and the International Organization of Legal Metrology (OIML). Measurement gives us certain quantitative information that is useful to become more familiar with the object and to facilitate comparison of one item with another, thereby reducing its uncertainty or entropy (Krechmer, 2005). It is quite interesting to know that the origin of the word *rational* in English is *ratio*, meaning the quantitative relation between two amounts. In this sense, the metrology standard lies in the rational foundation of the wider global order.

Standardization of Product Specifications

Shi Huang-ti of the Qin dynasty, the first monarchic government in China, standardized the space between the wheels of a horse-drawn carriage at about 2 meters for tactical reasons. When a carriage moves on an unpaved street, it generates a rut in the form of a wheel track. If the space of the wheels of one carriage differs from that of another, ruts are made here and there, which hamper the progress of the carriage. Standardization of

a wheel space was effective in maintaining the order of the surface of a street and making the traffic faster and more comfortable. Achievement of order in the street brought by standardization consequently yielded military advantage. Following nationwide unification in 221 B.C., he also standardized weights and measures, coins, and languages to rule over a country (Watabiki, 2004). A similar case is found in Europe. The British railway gauge of the distance between the rails is said to be derived from the width of the rear ends of two horses of a Roman centurion, 4 feet, 8.5 inches, or about 143.5 cm.

The need for interconnection of products was widely recognized by the general public about a century ago in the United States when a major fire broke out in Baltimore, Maryland, in 1904. Many fire engines in the surrounding neighborhoods were sent to extinguish the fire, but they had trouble connecting their fire hoses to the fire hydrants in Baltimore because the size differed from that of their neighborhoods. Collaborative work is impossible unless the connection part or interface is standardized to be compatible. A standardized product specification is used as design information by the maker.

The Origin of Standard

The derivation of the word *standard* in English is *estandard* in classical French, used to mean a rallying point; namely, a place where a troop commander stands and a military flag carried on a pole or hoisted on a rope is usually displayed as a mark in order to make each member come together to take concerted action. In this sense, a standard is also considered to be a label, mark, or brand that expresses its distinguishing feature to a group of people who are somehow related to it in some way. In an abstract mode of expression, standard may be termed "prescribed common provisions or rules" indicated by letters, designs, or patterns. In other words, a standard functions as a common language required for communication between the labeled product and its user in order to win the fullest confidence of the market.

A Three-Layer Structure to Classify Standards

A few thoughts concerning the origin and history of standardization and standards suggests a three-layer structure, as shown in Table 1, relating to the functioning of standards. Standardization represents the process or activities consisting of formulating standards; the standard is the product or result obtained from that process. The first column shows the subjects of standardization, the second corresponds to the aims of the standards, and the third illustrates the benefits of standards derived from the corresponding aims in the second column. The bottom layer is related to metrology and cites "comparison" as its main aim of standards. The middle layer concerning "specifications" is characterized by the "achievement of order," while the upper layer is concerned with "labeling," whose derived benefits are the facilitation of communication or commerce. Labeling shows that the labeled object or organization regarding its management system conforms to a certain standard. Comparison, achievement of order or control of variety, and communication in each layer are considered to be the three basic functions of standards. They are also necessary to establish a common understanding of technology or a management system between makers and users or between sellers and buyers. In other words, they decrease various kinds of transaction

Table 1. A three-layer structure to classify standards

Subjects of Standardization	Aims of Standards	Derived Benefits of Standards
Labeling	Common language	Facilitation of communication or commerce
Specifications of	Achievement of order or control of variety	Improvement of performance or efficiency
· Technology		
Product level		
Material		Reduction of cost
Component		
Equipment	Maintenance of interconnection or compatibility	Raising levels of quality
Interface		Safety
		Health
Process level		Protection of the environment
Procedure		
System		
Protocol		
	Voluntary restraints on business process	
Service level		Stakeholders' satisfaction
· Management system		
Testing method	Comparison	
Weights and measures	Common understanding	Objective measure
Terminology	Definition	

costs or risks in a market economy to facilitate the exchange of information and merchandise.

Incidentally, the ISO/IEC *Guide 2: 2004 Standardization and related activities General Vocabulary* defines standardization as "activity of establishing, with regard to actual or potential problems, provisions for common and repeated use, aimed at the achievement of the optimum degree of order in a given context." A standard is defined as "document, established by consensus and approved by a recognized body, that provides, for common and repeated use, rules, guidelines or characteristics for activities or their results, aimed at the achievement of the optimum degree of order in a given context." Generally speaking, standards have various kinds, including legal standards in the form of law, professional standards of medical practice, ethical and moral standards, and standards of sportsmanship. All these have the common aspect of being chosen from among several alternatives or potential variations and determined as mutually agreed rules via the standardization process.[7] In this sense, standardization aims to control, manage, or reduce chaos that may occur spontaneously if left alone. The second law of thermodynamics states that the entropy of a closed system can only increase, and the optimum degree of order can be found somewhere between chaos and cosmos. Standards serve to create the optimum order in a manmade world. Edward H. Chamberlin, an economist famous for the concept of monopolistic competition, referred to the order in the market in a paper published in 1953 (Chamberlin, 1953).

Any producer, by deteriorating his or her product slightly, can reduce cost and increase profits, either by selling at the same price as before, which would give a great profit per unit, or by combining the deterioration with a lower price, which is what happens more commonly, thereby increasing profits by taking business away from rivals. In a succession of such moves, there appears to be no limit until the technological possibilities

of deterioration have been exhausted. In the case at hand, if the producer had put any more gum arabic in the mayonnaise, it would probably have disintegrated. The general tendency described might be termed Gresham's Law of products: bad products drive good products off the market.

The regulation of service and safety in the public utility and transport industries is a familiar example. Standards of safety, for instance, are set and enforced by governments because it is recognized that if they were not, private companies would, in order to maximize their profits, avoid the outlays necessary for this purpose. Similarly, standards of container fill for good products are established because when they were not, some producers had a tendency to maximize profits by converting a given amount of food into more cans of food by putting less food into each can. Similarly, informative labeling as to ingredients is required for some food and drug products as a means of preventing or discouraging certain types of adulteration and as an aid to the consumer in detecting and judging the acceptability of others in light of lower price and other considerations. All that was said earlier about the determination of products by government standards should be recalled at this point. The principle of product deterioration explains such measures of social control in just the same way that the principle of monopoly profits explains the regulation of monopoly.

This indicates a delicate balance in the market. A motive of profit maximization on the side of the seller, if united with imperfect knowledge with respect to certain product aspects on the side of the buyer, may lead to an impermissible degradation of quality, which occurs repeatedly. It is necessary for an appropriate standard to be established as the minimum level of permissible quality in order to solve this kind of problem related to market order. Standards will suppress such activities that cause the market to fall into disorder.

PROPOSAL OF STANDARDS STUDIES AS A NEW ACADEMIC DISCIPLINE

Changes in the world of standards for the past two decades were reviewed in the first chapter, while the essential character, derived from the origin and history of standardization and standards, was illustrated in the second. In this chapter, "standards studies" is advocated as a new academic discipline.

The late Dr. Larry Eicher, ISO Secretary-General from 1986 until passing away in March 2002, remarked in a 1998 speech, "Go to the back of the class if you thought ISO was all about technical requirements, procedures and publication. In fact, ISO is all about communication between people!" The ISO press release Ref. 819, 25 March 2002 states:

During his 16-year tenure, ISO evolved from an institution with a predominantly technological focus to a market-oriented organization whose standards are increasingly recognized as bringing, in addition to solutions to technical problems, wider social and economic benefits. This evolution has been accompanied by the recognition of ISO's leading role in international standardization and the contribution its standards make to facilitating world trade and economic development, and to raising levels of quality, care of the environment, consumer protection, health and safety.

The most fundamental nature of standards developed through the process of standardization seems to me that they are mutually agreed rules based on voluntary consensus and targeting the achievement of the optimum degree of order, primarily in the market economy. The latter, unlike the command economy, is characterized by freedom of competition and choice on the side of many firms and consumers. The variables of equilibrium price, quantity, and quality are determined by the manner or relationship in which the individual firms and consumers are interconnected. The actions of many firms and individuals are constrained by limited information and imperfect knowledge, especially concerning the quality of products for consumers, the recommended solution being the imposition of a quality standard and related informative labeling. Standards will work as guidelines in this way, and the actions of many participants in the market economy are led by the "visible hand" in the right direction. Standards can represent an effective solution strategy to offset the functioning of Gresham's Law of products. Thus, the most important role of standards lies in the creation of order as a whole rather than economic profits for each individual firm, though various benefits can be derived from order.

Figure 2 depicts the complex system of the market economy in which abundant merchandise consisting of goods, services, energy, and information is traded by many heterogeneous participants. This system of transaction is driven by the motive of commerce to mean "with merchandise'" and communication to mean "the sharing or exchange of information." Finance and insurance are required as a supporting infrastructure for the market economy. The arrows show the transactions among business and consumers. The traditional boundary of business is increasingly blurred, and masses of people can participate in a new form of collaborative production like never before, as shown by the arrow from consumer to business (Tapscott & Williams, 2006).

A Global Solution Strategy Utilizing Soft Laws

Since the pace of globalization of the world economy has been accelerating recently, opportunities to optimally exploit international standards as a global solution strategy are increasing. International standards, mainly devised by nongovernmental organizations in a fair, open, and transparent way, have the intrinsic nature of soft laws, the core concept of which is defined as follows (Kirton & Trebilcock, 2004):

Figure 2. The complex system of market economy

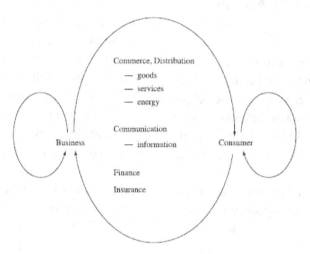

Soft law refers to regimes that rely primarily on the participation and resources of nongovernmental actors in the construction, operation, and implementation of a governance arrangement. Although the parameter of "primarily" permits some ambiguity (as well as flexibility), the key characteristics of a soft law arrangement are clear, in contrast with a hard law arrangement.

First, in a soft law regime, the formal legal, regulatory authority of governments is not relied upon and may not even be contained in the institutional design and operation.

Second, there is voluntary participation in the construction, operation, and continuation. Any participant is free to leave at any time, and to adhere to the regime or not, without invoking the sanctioning power of state authority.

Third, there is a strong reliance on consensus-based decision-making for action and, more broadly, as a source of institutional binding and legitimacy.

Fourth, and flowing from the third, there is an absence of the authoritative, material sanctioning power of the state—police power as a way to induce consent and compliance.

Thus, the essence of soft law seems to be found in informal institutions with voluntary standards or commitments and compliance systems, which are expected to mitigate the deficiencies of formal international law and organizations in several areas, including sustainable development, the global environment, quality of life, the transfer of technology and management systems. Kirton and Trebilcock (2004) point out, "What is new in recent decades is how firms have begun, at the level of the individual firm, business sector, or the whole economy, to design and adopt voluntary codes that extend from their core commercial interests, and closely related issues of public safety, to embrace broader environmental and social concerns, including issues of gender, minority rights, and human rights."[8] They also address several questions about the static coexistence and dynamic interrelationship of hard and soft laws:

- Under what conditions can soft law replace or reinforce the hard law approach of formal legally entrenched commitments and governmentally grounded regulation?
- What are the alternative sequences and mixed resulting forms?
- What are the advantages and disadvantages of each approach and particular blends?

It may safely be said that there is an emerging consensus concerning the proven power and future potential brought by soft law solutions. In my view, the advantage of soft law solutions seems to lie in the fact that they are not imposed from the outside, like hard law solutions, but that they will be generated spontaneously from the inside, based on the consolidated results or justified true information of science, technology, and our experiences, targeting the promotion of optimum community benefits.[9] The European New Approach in 1985 is considered as a good example of combining hard and soft laws. The European directives adopted as hard law by the European Commission set only the essential requirements on safety, health, or environment, and the European standards as soft law are developed by the European standardization bodies in which detailed requirements and/or test methods are laid down to satisfy the European directives. Reflections on the evolutionary change in the subjects of standardization in the ISO, the role of a voluntary standard as a solution strategy within the overall market economy, and the emerging expectations of the future potential of soft law in general may suggest the need for the establishment of "standard studies" as a new academic discipline traversing the fields of engineering, commerce and management, economics, law, ethics, and other social sciences. Standard studies is here defined as follows:

Analysis of the process of development of a voluntary standard and its diffusion or acceptance, their socioeconomic and environmental benefits for business and society, its use as a solution strategy, and the overall impacts on the market economy, including certification and laboratory accreditation.

A Platform for a Next-Generation Innovation

Standardization will bring about the unintended effect of creating a next-generation innovation.

Figure 3 shows the interaction between standardization and innovation. Standardized technology to originate from innovation will diffuse in society after a while and consequently instill a certain degree of order and individual confidence. Subsequently, this situation becomes a platform that will generate radical innovation within the next generation. With this in mind, standardization, which is born of innovation, will in turn give rise to new innovation. Standardization and innovation influence each other accordingly. This unintended effect of standardization on next-generation innovation is often ignored, with only the trade-off between the two being emphasized. Standards are not of eternity or immutability, but of fluidity corresponding with innovations. While innovation is related to the reforming activity, from cosmos to chaos, standardization is concerned with the conservative function, from chaos to cosmos, to achieve a proper balance between uniformity and variety. Cosmos can be defined as a well-ordered whole in a given context, and chaos as complete disorder and confusion.

Figure 3. Interaction between standardization and innovation

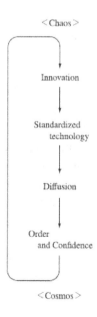

The Core Questions in the Standards Studies[10]

The influence of standards on the market economy and society as a whole is expected to be strengthened and widened. First of all, the general framework of standards studies must be established by asking fundamental questions of standards and standardization, including its aim, process of formation and diffusion, impacts on business and society, conformity assessment, implication for public policy, and appropriate education system.

Standards Studies predominantly focus on the following core questions:

- What subject and what part of it shall or shall not be standardized to target the achievement of the optimum degree of order within a given context?
- What kind of standardization process is best: consensus in a committee, mass collaboration on the Web, or free competition in the market?
- Who will be involved in making standards? Are users recommended to participate in the standardization process in addition to vendors?
- What mechanism of obtaining specialist knowledge and expertise is required for a committee to develop an effective standard?
- What factors influence the speed of diffusion or acceptance of a standard in the market or society and in what way?
- What sort of merits and demerits are yielded to the stakeholders by a standard?
- What variables determine the rate of voluntary adoption of a standard by an individual or firm? Are there any measures to facilitate its adoption?
- By what system and by whom shall the conformity to a certain standard be checked?

- What action shall be taken to eliminate the cause of any detected nonconformity?
- How can the differences in competing standards be reconciled in order not to throw consumers into confusion as to which to choose?
- What conditions are required for a specific single standard to be realized as the de facto market standard through competition among multiple standards?
- How is an old standard replaced by a new standard?
- What kind of relationship between mandatory and voluntary standards is considered appropriate? How is a voluntary standard utilized in the design of regulatory policy, for instance, by making references to standards in laws?
- What kind of system of education in standardization and standards is required at the company, national, regional, or international level?

Specific Subjects to Be Studied Further in Special Fields

The core questions already defined are connected with many existing academic fields. Standards studies are expected to develop by means of asking the following specific questions in each field and accumulating concrete case studies through empirical methods.

Basic themes:
- What is a justification for the existence or role of standards?
- Through what kind of process is an order created in the economy or society?
- What is the relationship between ethics and standards?
- Comparison of standards studies and innovation research
- Creation of a database of global standards development organizations

- Overall taxonomy of standards in a systematic way
- Comparative research on de jure standards, forum standards, de facto standards, and open-software standards, such as Linux, as well as their mutual influences
- System approach to the total system of standardization, certification, and laboratory accreditation, such as mutual recognition agreement

Public Policy:
- How can voluntary standards be applied as a regulatory tool?
- Looking at the standards issues from the perspectives of competition policy
- General inspection of administrative standards and review of the same

Business Administration:
- How can voluntary standards be utilized wisely as a tool for corporate governance?
- The role of standards in overall management, namely in research and development, design, production, purchase, distribution, sales, and accounting
- Next-generation management system standards to integrate quality, the environment, safety, security, and social responsibility
- The development of a sustainable business standard (BSI, 2006)
- What part of a new technology will be protected by the intellectual property right with the other part to be standardized in the form of an open standard, from the viewpoint of profit maximization?
- Why do firms manipulate standards in order to include their patented intellectual property?
- The influence of open standards on the architecture of digital products
- Quantitative analysis of business risk brought by open standards

- Optimal timing for the establishment of a standards forum[11]

Economics:
- Timing of standardization in relation to the progress of research and development
- The relationship between standardization and dominant design
- The role of global standards in international trade
- Compatibility and network externality in network industries
- Quantitative assessment of the economic benefits brought by standardization

Infrastructure or social system:
- Contribution to the global warming problem through the international standardization of energy-saving technologies and renewable energy systems
- Impacts on transport and logistics realized by the international standardization of the intelligent transport system
- A voluntary standard for the optimum distance between two cars going in the same direction on a superhighway to avoid traffic congestion
- Impacts on the economy caused by the international standardization of e-commerce

Jurisprudence:
- What sort of legal order will be brought by voluntary standard, such as a soft law lacking in economic sanctions (e.g., fines)?
- How will an effective compliance and certification mechanism be designed in soft law systems that rely on open, widely participatory, consensus-oriented, multistakeholder dialogue?
- Are hard and soft laws complements or substitutes?
- How can hard and soft laws be optimally combined; for example, with the minimum

requirement set in mandatory standard and the higher level in voluntary standard?

- The role of soft laws in a realm where a formal international treaty remains largely absent

- How are the conflicts coordinated among different voluntary standards?

- The role of voluntary standards in the regime of antitrust competition law or WTO rules; for instance, how to harmonize the promotion of exports with the protection of consumers' interests in the importing countries (Kurihara, 2008)

- How is the precautionary principle handled when setting international voluntary standards?

- How is the code of ethics and responsibilities for professionals designed?

Establishment of an International Institute for Standards Studies

Because the standards problem is too important to be left to standards practitioners, an international institute for standards studies needs to be established. Given the multidisciplinary and global nature of standards studies, the institute should be organized to foster collaborative research among specialists of technology, engineering, science, business, economics, and law, coming from various countries of different cultures and traditions. The mission of the institute is to make policy recommendations and shed new light on the future direction of international standardization for the benefit of international business and the global community, as well as to advance researches into standardization and standards.

THE NEED FOR INVESTMENTS IN STANDARDS EDUCATION

Donald E. Purcell, chairman of the Center for Global Standards Analysis, Catholic University of America, said:[12]

The national economy of every nation depends upon its ability to develop and maintain an effective international standardization system best suited to its needs. Given that standards are the essential building blocks by which every nation develops and maintains a competitive national economy, the challenge is to identify international standards education programs which meet the specific needs of a particular country in their private, public and academic sectors.

For decades, private corporations, government departments and agencies have carried the burden of standards education by preparing their best and brightest employees to work in the complex field of international standardization [in the form of "on the job" training]. There is no question that the international standards education programs offered by private corporations and government departments must be continued and expanded wherever possible. But in today's fast paced and highly competitive world, are these efforts enough? A key question we now must address is whether nations need to make significant investments in creating academic opportunities for their best and brightest students to study the complex field of international standardization.

Standardization courses were already available before 1930, and at the university level, the course of Prof. Kienzle in Berlin, co-founder of the German standardization institute DIN, was offered in the period of World War II. At Helmut-Schmidt-University, Hamburg, Germany, Prof. Hesser provides the course as the world's only full-time professor of standardization at the present time. In the United States, a graduate course in telecommunications standards that used to be offered at the University of Colorado in Boulder started in the early 1980s (Bloomfield, 1999).

A pioneering graduate course on strategic standardization from the multidisciplinary viewpoint was started at the Catholic University of America in 1999 as a joint course between the Schools of Engineering and Law, respectively. The curriculum for this course covered issues such as national standards policies for several countries, regulatory perspectives, technical barriers to trade, electronic commerce, antitrust regulation, intellectual property, professional ethics, health, safety, and the environment. Because Catholic University is located in Washington, D.C., the program was able to attract more than 30 expert guest speakers from corporations, government departments and agencies, law firms, and other universities to add value to the course. Student comments about the course indicate that they became very impressed with the strategic value of global standards to the engineering, business, government, and legal sectors of the United States economy.

South Korea established a university program in 2004 on the significance of international standards that now involves more than 47 universities and 7,000 engineering students. The European Union, meanwhile, created a joint venture that involves two European universities and four universities in Asia and intends to offer a graduate course. In the United States, the national Accreditation Board for Engineering and Technology (ABET) established the study of engineering standards as an education requirement for all engineering schools in the United States beginning in 2000. Further efforts at promoting international standards education have come from the IEC, which in 2005 distributed to its members worldwide a lecture on the "strategic value of international standards."

These recent changes in academic perspectives reflect the changing national perspectives on the value of international standards, part of which were triggered by the inauguration of the WTO in 1995, as well as by the faster pace of innovations.[13] Today's globalization of the national economy and domestic community has triggered an expansion of commerce and communication among people and organizations, which calls for the need to invest in education to teach people the significance of international standards in business and daily life. International standards are needed by business and society as agreed and firmly established rules or guideposts in this ever-changing age of globalization and innovation.

ACKNOWLEDGMENT

The author would like to express deep gratitude to the following people for providing valuable comments and suggestions during my preparation of this article: Masami Tanaka (ISO President), Hiroshi Shima (President of the Japanese Standards Association), Yasukazu Fukuda (Ministry of Economy, Trade and Industry), Donald Purcell (Catholic University of America), Ken Krechmer (Communications Standards Review), John Hill (Sun Microsystems, Inc.), Toshiaki Kurokawa (CSK Holdings Corporation, Affiliated Fellow of the National Institute of Science and Technology Policy), Tineke Egyedi (Delft University of Technology), Henk J. de Vries (Erasmus University), Dan-Bee Kim (Korean Standards Association), Robert Chew (Accenture Pte Ltd.), Dennis Ding (Sun Microsystems [China] Co., Ltd.), Yushi Komachi (Osaka Institute of Technology), Masao Mukaidono (Meiji University), Ruji Shimoda (Tokyo Institute of Technology), Toru Nakakita (Toyo University), Toshiaki Takigawa (Kansai University), Hideo Yamada (Waseda Business School), Takehiko Hashimoto (University of Tokyo), Satoru Tanaka (Kobe City University of Foreign Studies), Bunro Shiozawa (Japanese Standards Association), Kiyoshi Ishizaka (Japan Machinery Federation), Yoshito Hirabayashi (Technofer Ltd.), Toshihiro Fujita (IDEC Corporation); and the following intramural members of the Hitotsubashi Standards Studies Group: Hideo Yamamoto, Toshinori Nemoto (Graduate School of Commerce and Management), Jeffrey Funk (Institute of Innovation Research), Jota Ishikawa (Graduate School of Economics), Tsuneo Matsumoto, Shusei Ono (Graduate School of Law), and Jonathan Lewis (Graduate School of Social Sciences).

REFERENCES

Anh, V.T. (2006). An introduction—The history of standardisation. In W. Hesser, A. Feilzer, & H. de Vries (Eds.), *Standarisation in companies and markets.*

Bloomfield, R.S. (1999). A perspective on advancing standards research and education—Building in the telecommunications scene. *ISO Bulletin, 29*(6).

BSI (Eds). (2006). *BS 8900:2006 guidance for managing sustainable development.* BSI British Standards.

Chamberlin, E.H. (1953). The product as an economic variable. *Quarterly Journal of Economics, Vol. 67*(1).

de Vries, H.J. (2002). Standardization—Mapping a fields of research. In S. Bolin (Ed.), *The standards edge.* Bolin Communications.

Gandal, N., Gantman, N., & Genesove, D. (2007). Intellectual property and standardization committee participation in the US modem industry. In S. Greenstein, & V. Stango (Eds.), *Standards and public policy.* Cambridge University Press.

Higuchi, T. (1996). *Dig shi Huang-ti* (Shikotei wo Horu in Japanese), Gakuseisha.

Kirton, J.J., & Trebilcock, M.J. (2004). *Hard choices, soft law: Voluntary standards in global trade, environment, and social governance.* Ashgate.

Krechmer, K. (2005). *The mathematical basis of standards.* Proceedings of the 4th International Conference on Standardisation and Innovation in Information Technology (SIIT).

Kurihara, S. (2008). Compatibility of free trade with health, safety, and environment. In S. Bolin (Ed.), *The standards edge: Unifer or divider?* Bolin Communications.

Purcell, D.E. (2005). Report to the center for global standards analysis on Beijing information technology standard international forum. Retrieved from http://www.ieee.org/potal/cms_docs/erudation/setf/newsitems/beijingreport.doc

Tapscott, D., & Williams, A.D. (2006). *Wikinomics,* Portfolio.

Watabiki, H. (1994). World history talked by goods (Mono ga Kataru Sekaishi in Japanese), Seibunsha.

ENDNOTES

[1] This is a revised version of the paper entitled *The General Framework and Scope of Standards Studies* published in *Hitotsubashi Journal of Commerce and Management, 40*(2006), 1–18, reprinted in *Polish Journal of Commodity Science, 3*(12) (2007), and reprinted in *Soft Law Discussion Paper Series* COESOFTLAW-2007-6 published by 21st Century Center of Excellence Program "Soft Law" and the State-Market Relationship in Graduate Schools for Law and Politics, the University of Tokyo. The author is very much indebted to anonymous referees for their useful comments to improve the article.

[2] WTO legal texts (http://www.wto.org/english/docs_e/legal_e/legal_e.htm#agreements)

[3] Opening Statement of Wolfgang Clement, Federal Minister of Economy and Labor, *German Standardization Strategy* (2004) (http://www.vde.com/NR/ryonlyres/C06162F7-AB30-426C-AEF7-34C29B21D7E9/0/German-StandardizationStrategy.pdf)

[4] Foreword, *United Kingdom National Standardization Strategic Framework* (2003) (http://nssf.info/resources/documents/Guide_to_NSSF.pdf)

[5] Statement of Donald L. Evans, Secretary of Commerce, from *Standards & Competi-*

tiveness —Coordinating for Results (2004) on the importance of standards (http://www.technology.gov/reports/NIST/2004/trade_barriers.pdf)

6   Alvin Toffler describes the three types of societies based on the concept of "waves" in his book, *The Third Wave*, in 1980; each wave pushes the older societies and cultures aside. First Wave is the society after agrarian revolution and replaced the first hunter-gatherer cultures. Second Wave is the society during the Industrial Revolution, ca. late 1600s through the mid-1900s, featured by standardized mass production. Third Wave is the post-industrial society.

7   "In its simplest terms, a standard is an agreed way of doing something." Quoted from *National Standardization Strategic Framework* (http://www.nssf.info/resources/documents/Standardization.pdf)

8   pp. 9-11, Kirton, J.J., & Trebilcock, M.J. (2004)

9   Note of "3.2 standard" in the *ISO/IEC Guide 2: 2004*

10 As for the transdisciplinary nature of research, Henk J. de Vries made a systematic listing of sciences related to the current and possible standardization research, as shown in the appendix. The author, in cooperation with Osamu Takeuchi, proposed the need to establish "standards studies" as a new academic discipline in *Twenty-first-century Standardology* (in Japanese) published in 2001.

11 Gandal, Gantman, and Genesove (2007) show, by Granger causality test, that while patenting is predicted by participation in earlier standardization meetings, meetings participation is not predicted by earlier patenting.

12 Presentation to the United States National Committee, International Electrotechnical Commission on August 10, 2006. The part in brackets is added by the author.

13 Toshiaki Kurokawa, "Developing Human Resources for International Standards," *Science and Technology Trends – Quarterly Review, 17,* October 2005.

14 This is made by the author based on de Vries, 2002). The parts in brackets are added by the author.

APPENDIX: A SYSTEMATIC LISTING OF SCIENCES RELATED TO STANDARDIZATION RESEARCH[14]

Fundamental sciences:
- Mathematics, Kinematics, Physics, Chemistry, Biology
- [System science]
- [Ecology]
- [Geology]
- Psychology
- Logic
- History
- Linguistics
- Sociology
- [Political science]
- Economics
- Aesthetics
- Law
- Ethics
- Theology

Applied sciences related to the topics of standardization:
- Design, Development, and Construction sciences [Engineering sciences]
- [Commodity science]
- Healthcare sciences
- Management or Business science

Applied sciences related to people and organizations involved in standardization:
- Business science
- Science of Public administration
- [Regulatory science including risk analysis]

Applied sciences related to specific standardization activities:
- Policy science
- Design sciences
- Studies of Technology and society
- Information [and Communication] science

This work was previously published in the International Journal of IT Standards and Standardization Research, Vol. 6, Issue 2, edited by K. Jakobs, pp. 1-20, copyright 2008 by IGI Publishing (an imprint of IGI Global).

Chapter 2
Developing a Basis for Global Reciprocity:
Negotiating Between the Many Standards for Project Management

Lynn Crawford
University of Technology - Sydney, Australia

Julien Pollack
University of Technology - Sydney, Australia

ABSTRACT

Professional standards are a significant issue for professions such as IT and project management, where certification and licensure are either necessary to practice or to demonstrate individual competence and capability. In many professions there is no basis for international reciprocity of professional standards. This paper documents the development of a standard for global reciprocity between already existing professional standards in the field of Project Management. Data are based on personal involvement by the authors and interviews with participants. This discussion addresses different approaches to standardisation, how common issues in the standardisation process have been addressed, and how the hindering influence of the professional associations' proprietorial interest was avoided. Significantly different standards of development processes have been used compared to those typical in Project Management standards development, including: an emphasis on negotiation and joint modification rather than market dominance, and an open access approach, rather than one based on exclusion and gate-keeping.

INTRODUCTION

The role of standards in professional licensure and certification has been an important issue for many years. As early as 1953, Carey wrote that the "… medical profession, the dental profession and the certified public accountants have all used standard examinations for many years and with outstanding success ..." (Carey, 1953, p. 36). In 1962 Milton Friedman commented that occupational licensure was then very widespread (Friedman, 1962, p. 139). Researchers have found continuing agitation to extend standardisation to more professions (Leland, 1980, p. 265), and this does not seem to be reducing, with Blind and Thumm (2004, p. 61) recently finding that the number of standards has "... risen tremendously." In the IT industry, certification has been raised from a hiring tool to a screening tool, with high-level certification being necessary for consideration in many jobs (George, 2002, p. 76).

Standards development should be pursued critically and with care, with some industries needing to revisit the role that standards play within the community. For instance, in the IT industry, certification is often viewed as a vital way to indicate competence. However, studies have found that professional IT certification is not a robust predictor of ability (Cegielski, 2004, p. 105). One study found that "... no statistically significant difference exists between the capabilities of certified network professionals and non-certified network professionals ..." (Cegielski, et al., 2003, p. 97). IT standards of certification and accreditation may even mask a lack of the very qualities that employers are looking for (Schrage, 2004, p. 1).

Over the last decade, the profession of Project Management has moved from one typified by isolated national standards to one struggling with the process of creating global professional standards for knowledge, education, and workplace performance. The profession has developed from clusters of professionals sharing knowledge at a company or industry level, to commonly accepted national frameworks for Project Management, and is now moving towards globally accepted and transferable qualifications in the profession. This paper examines recent efforts to create a framework for global reciprocity between Project Management standards. This is discussed in relation to professional licensure and certification in general, different approaches to standardisation, and recent failures to create globally applicable standards for Project Management.

Project Management Standards: From Community to Profession

Modern Project Management may be considered to have had its genesis in the international arena when, in the 1950s (Stretton, 1994; Morris, 1994), companies such as Bechtel began to use the term "project manager" in their international work, primarily on remote sites. Before long, local communities of Project Management practice developed, becoming formalized in national Project Management professional associations. The development of standards in Project Management began with recognition of shared interests, resulting in fairly informal community gatherings. Through regular meetings and recognition of shared experience, practitioners began to think of themselves as a community and a profession. This led to attempts to define and delineate that profession in order to make it visible and acceptable to those outside the community (Crawford, 2004b, pp. 1389-90).

Dean (1997) identifies seven building blocks of a profession, characteristics that distinguish it from a community. These are: a store or body of knowledge that is more than ordinarily complex; a theoretical understanding of the area of practice; ability to apply theoretical and complex knowledge to a practice; a desire to add to and improve the body of knowledge; a formal process for transferring the body of knowledge and associated practices; established criteria for admission, legitimate practice, and proper conduct (standards and certification); and an altruistic spirit.

Of these building blocks, bodies of knowledge, standards, and certification programs have been of particular significance to Project Management. Before an industry attains a certain maturity, standardisation is of little value. It is less likely to have an interest in standards, or to accept them as valuable. For an immature industry, where new ideas and technologies are in the process of being developed, there is little benefit to investing energy in standardisation, due to the rate of change in the industry (Steele, 2004, p. 42). An interest in standards can then be seen as an indicator of a certain level of maturity within the profession.

A variety of benefits have been identified which accrue from standardisation. General benefits which apply to both technological and professional standardisation include encouragement of technological innovation, guaranteeing marketplace choice, competition, and convenience (JEDEC, 2004, p. 11). Standardisation can also be used as a strategy for fostering economic growth via the broad diffusion of technology and technical rules, and shaping foreign markets according to the specification of local technologies and products (Blind & Thumm, 2004).

At a professional level, standardisation delineates clear professional boundaries, and can be seen as a way of increasing the esteem of a profession. For instance, recent arguments have been made for certification and licensure of HR professionals as a way of increasing respect (Brown, 2005, p. 5). Professional standards are also described as being of benefit to organisations, through acting as "… enablers of more efficient and effective use of resources delivering economic sustainable development" (Bredillet, 2003, p. 464). Furthermore, standardisation can be used as a competitive strategy for new entrants opposing the dominance of existing firms (Baskin, Krechmer, & Sherif, 1998, p. 55).

Project Management Standards: From Local to Global Profession

In the early stages of the development of Project Management as a profession, bodies of knowledge, standards, and certification programs were predominantly developed by independent professional associations, usually taking a proprietary view of the products they developed. This resulted in the proliferation of competing Project Management standards and certification programs, the majority of which were largely local in their origin, and limited in their application to a narrow range of project types within a single culture.

However, by the second half of the 1990s, it was becoming clear that Project Management practitioners and application areas were becoming increasingly global. It is now often the case that projects are shared across multiple international organisations. The application of Project Management had extended beyond international projects, managed offshore by nationally-based companies, to use by global corporations through globally distributed operations and projects (Crawford, 2004b, pp. 1390-1).

Further incentive to develop globally applicable Project Management standards came from outside the profession. The North American Free Trade Agreement, 1993 and the World Trade Organization's General Agreement on Trade in Services, 1994, required the "… development of policies that evaluate professional competence based on fair, objective criteria and transparent (publicly known) procedures" (Lenn, 1997, p. 2). These agreements put pressure on established professions and their professional associations to consider mutually acceptable standards in cooperation with other countries and to actively plan for reciprocal recognition at a minimum.

Unlike the majority of IT standards, Project Management standards are not technical documents. IT standards often describe the characteristics of physical artefacts, algorithms, or processes, that although complex, are unambiguous once understood and can easily transcend cultural and language boundaries. By contrast, professional standards, such as those that apply to certification in the IT industry and Project Management, describe human practice, knowledge, and skills. Such concepts are open to considerable interpretation. This is especially true in the context of an industry that is still defining professional boundaries, and where practitioners from different cultures potentially have inconsistent appreciations of what the profession actually is.

Creating new standards by consensus is a difficult process. Even for technical standards, it "… may not be clear what the best technical solution actually is" (Warner, 2003, p. 7). This ambiguity is exacerbated in the development of Project Management standards, where it is arguable whether there is any such thing as a "best" solution. Rather, standards which reach the marketplace are often the product of lengthy political negotiation and act as accommodated positions between the different professional associations.

Dramatis Personae: Project Management Professional Associations

The Project Management Institute (PMI) is the largest of the Project Management professional associations. PMI originated in North America in 1969, and now has a significant membership. Membership grew at 37.9 percent in 2005, resulting in a total of 212,000 individual members (PMI, 2006). The Institute itself claims that as

…a steward of the project management profession, PMI has the distinction of being one of the fastest growing professional organizations in the world. (PMI, 2005a)

The PMI has developed arguably the most significant Project Management standard, the *PMBOK® Guide* (PMI, 2004), currently in its third edition. The *PMBOK® Guide* is approved as an American National Standard by ANSI and is recognised by the Institute of Electrical and Electronics Engineers as an IEEE standard (PMI, 2005b). However, it has been developed in North America for a predominantly North American audience, and found to describe a form of Project Management that is not culturally suited to some application areas (Muriithi & Crawford, 2003). Nonetheless, the *PMBOK® Guide* has become a

de facto international standard for Project Management knowledge.

The Australian Institute of Project Management (AIPM), is the Australian national project management association, and had over 6,000 members distributed over eight state and territory chapters by 2006. The AIPM remained unopposed as the national Project Management association until 1996, when the first of a number of PMI chapters was chartered in Australia. By 2003, there were PMI chapters in most Australian capital cities (PMI, 2003a), with a total membership of 1,500 (PMI, 2003b). Relationships between the AIPM and the Australian PMI chapters varies from friendly cooperation to active competition (Crawford, 2004b, p. 1395).

By contrast, project managers in South Africa were for many years represented by a PMI Chapter, first formed in 1982. The PMI South Africa Chapter continues to exist, but Project Management South Africa (PMSA), a separate national association, was established in 1997 to satisfy local economic and regulatory requirements. Unlike Australia, because PMSA was essentially formed by members of the PMI South Africa Chapter, there is a far closer and more consistently cooperative relationship between PMSA and PMI. Membership of PMSA increased from 400 at formation in 1997 to over 1,200 in 2003.

In the UK, the Association for Project Management (APM) was formed in 1972, and currently has more than 13,500 individual and 300 corporate members (APM, 2005). APM has developed an independent knowledge standard, the *APM Body of Knowledge* (2006), currently in its fifth edition. This document takes a significantly different perspective on project management than that presented by the *PMBOK® Guide* (PMI, 2004) in terms of both what is considered to be of relevance and how this information is conveyed.

The Japan Project Management Forum (JPMF) is a division of the Engineering Advancement Association (ENAA), which was founded in 1978 as a non-profit organisation based on corporate rather than individual membership. ENAA addresses the needs of industry and corporations, with membership encompassing 250 engineering and project-based companies. JPMF acts as the professional association for individual practitioners. ENAA has published *P2M: A Guidebook of Project & Program Management for Enterprise Innovation* (2002), including an English translation.

Established in 1991 in China, the Project Management Research Council (PMRC) supports over 100 universities and companies and 3,500 active individual members from universities, industries, and government. In 1994 the PMRC initiated, with support from the China Natural Science Fund, the development of a *Chinese Project Management Body of Knowledge* (C-PMBOK), which was published together with the *China-National Competence Baseline* (C-NCB) in 2001.

The International Project Management Association (IPMA), was initiated in 1965 (IPMA 2003; Stretton, 1994). The IPMA has evolved into a network, or federation, comprising 30 national Project Management associations representing approximately 20,000 members, primarily in Europe but also in Africa and Asia (IPMA, 2003). The largest member of the IPMA is the UK APM, which has had considerable influence on the development of the IPMA. An earlier version of the *APM Body of Knowledge* (APM, 2006) was one of the key documents referenced in writing of the *ICB: IPMA Competence Baseline* (IPMA, 1999). So far, the successes of the IPMA has been hampered by its federated structure, by the differing priorities of its national association members, and by lack of funds available for international and global development (Crawford, 2004b, p. 1393).

Blum (2005) divides standards generation processes into public and industrial standardisation. Public standardisation can be managed through national or sector-specific approaches, while industrial standardisation processes can be company based or managed through consortia. In the IT industry "…the competition between public standardization and consortium-based standardization had been won and lost around the turn of the millennium, in favour of the latter …" (Blum, 2005, p. 3).

Nonetheless, in the Project Management community, a variety of public qualifications bodies have ongoing significant influence over the development of Project Management standards. Innovation and Business Skills Australia (IBSA), the South African Qualifications Association (SAQA), and the UK Engineering and Construction Industry Training Board (ECITB) all have their own standards for Project Management qualification, while the New Zealand Qualifications Association has a cooperative agreement with Australia.

Established PM Standards

Project Management standards development has so far relied on a market-based approach. Many of the challenges facing the globalisation of Project Management as a profession and community of practice relate to competition between the various professional associations, which have tended to remain locally focused and exclusionary about the knowledge created by their communities. Qualifications gained under one professional association are not usually recognised for equivalence by other professional associations, although the performance of practitioners qualified by different professional associations may still be equivalent.

There are currently a wide variety of guides and standards, focusing on different aspects of the profession. These have been classified by Duncan (1998) as belonging to one of three categories:

- Projects–focusing on the knowledge and practices for management of individual projects;
- Organisations–focusing on enterprise project management knowledge and practices; and

• People–focusing on the development, assessment, and registration/certification of people.

Existing Project Management standards can be grouped according to these categories (see Table 1). Only some of these standards are discussed here. For a comprehensive review, refer to Crawford (2004b).

Most Project Management standards have been developed through industrial coalitions and consortia, many of which later go on to receive Government endorsement. By far the most popular standards in Project Management are those which focus on projects, the most popular of which have been developed by industry consortia. ISO 10006 and BS 6079 occupy relatively small market shares, compared to the PMBOK® Guide and APM BoK.

Standards focusing on organisations have also been predominantly created by industry consortia, but their emergence is more recent, and are subsequently less prevalent. By contrast, the Project Management standards which focus on people have all been developed publicly, and are generally in the form of performance-based competency standards. The majority of these have been specifically designed for assessment purposes, and provide the basis for the award of qualifications within national qualifications frameworks.

Warner (2003) has distinguished between market-based standards and formal processes for creating standards. "In market-based battles, the standard follows success in the market by definition" (p. 2). The standard is recognised as such because it is the strongest survivor, and success may be based on a pre-existing market or good marketing, rather than inherent value. By contrast, standards created through formal processes are products of negotiation, anticipatory and often pre-competitive. Their development may be the result of a perceived need within the industry, and may have little to do with the existing support, or generation, of a market. This is similar to a distinction made by Baskin, Krechmer, and Sherif (1998, p. 59), who use this approach to categorise standards as either anticipatory, participatory, or responsive (see Figure 1). Project Management standards, whether they focus on projects, people, or organisations, are consistently participatory or responsive standards, describing or helping to define existing practice.

Table 1. Project Management standards focusing on people, projects and organisations

People	Projects	Organisations
Engineering Construction Industry Training Board (ECITB)	A Guide to the Project Management Body of Knowledge (PMBOK ® Guide)	Guidebook for Project and Program Management for Enterprise Innovation (P2M)
South African Qualification Authority (SAQA)	International Project Management Association Competence Baseline (ICB)	Organizational Project Management Maturity Model (OPM3)
National Competency Standards for Project Management (NCSPM)	The Association for Project Management Body of Knowledge (APM BoK)	Office of Government Commerce Managing Successful Programmes (OGC MSP)
	British Standards (BS 6079)	Office of Government Commerce Project Management Maturity Model (OGC PMMM)
	International Standards Organization (ISO 10006)	Projects in Controlled Environments (PRINCE 2)

The current distribution of market share has worked as a hindrance to the process of creating global Project Management standards. "Very often, large companies possessing large market shares will try to establish proprietary *de facto* industry standard ..." (Blind & Thumm, 2004, p. 69). Although the *PMBOK® Guide* only focuses on projects, not people or organisations, it is often considered a de facto standard for the profession as a whole, based on its overall market dominance.

Despite the global presence of the Project Management Institute, over 70 percent of its membership remain located in North America (PMI, 2006). There is considerable reluctance on the part of Project Management professionals in some countries outside the United States to relinquish their independence and genuinely national representation. Furthermore, practitioners in many countries cannot afford the professional membership fees that are acceptable in the United States. In many cases, such as in South Africa, it has been necessary to establish fully national associations in order to meet the needs of local jurisdictions and/or to provide a more affordable alternative.

Previous authors have identified cultural differences between how standards are created in North America and Europe, which may help to explain the reluctance in some countries to adopt the *PMBOK® Guide* as the standard. Bredillet (2003, p. 465-9) identifies that the American standards development favours a market-based approach, where one standard grows to dominance, excluding others from the market. By contrast, a European approach favours negotiation and joint modification of standards. Krechmer (2004) has identified similar differences in the ways that standards have been developed in North America and Europe, providing an example based on the mobile phone industry. He suggests that in North America, a laissez-faire policy was used in the development of mobile phone technologies, where the commercial organisations did as they wished, and it was expected that market forces would result in a clear de facto standard. This policy has resulted in three competing cellular standards. By contrast, a single unified standard was pursued in Europe. "In Europe two equipment developers, Nokia and Ericsson, pulled far ahead of their largest competitor, Motorola, headquartered in North America" (Krechmer, 2004, p. 50).

Minimum Quality Certification

Project Management standards usually take the form of minimum quality certification, instead of licensure. The distinction between these two forms of professional standards is that in situations where licensure is required, the professional may not legally practice without a license, while in situations where professional certification is used the "...governmental agency may certify that an individual has certain skills but may not prevent, in any way, the practice of an occupation using these skills by people who do not have such a certificate" (Friedman, 1962, p. 144). Standards of certification can be considered to be minimum quality standards, used to identify those who

Figure 1. Standards in the product development life cycle (based on Baskin, Krechmer, & Sherif, 1998, p. 59).

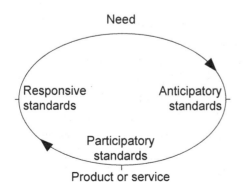

have met the standard, but not to prohibit those who have not.

One of the most common arguments for professional standardisation relates to the protection of public welfare. However, markets using minimum quality standards tend to be typified by information asymmetry, where sellers know the quality of their goods, but buyers do not (Leland, 1979, p. 1329). Over the last few years, certification has proved particularly popular in the IT industry, as a way for personnel to advertise their capabilities. The public is then, in theory, more informed and, as a consequence, buyers have a greater choice, as "... they can buy low-quality goods if they wish" (Leland, 1980, p. 283).

However, just as buyers have to attempt to identify quality, sellers must also communicate this information to buyers. This latter step may be costly or impossible to achieve in some circumstances (Leland, 1980, p. 283). In the case with Project Management certification, where there are multiple levels of certification offered by competing certification organisations, the differences in certifications may be unclear to buyers of services. What follows is that in many cases, if a consumer does not trust their own ability to differentiate between the quality of certified and uncertified products, certification is often treated in much the same ways that licensure is (Leffler, 1980, p. 290).

In such cases, it could be argued that licensure would be more appropriate than certification, as licensure is government imposed over an industry, and so may enforce a level of consistency that may not emerge if an industry is left to its own competing standards for certification. Licensure of professions also allows for government-enforced requirements to be placed on professions, such as the need for continuing professional education, while competing professional associations offering only certification may not be prepared to enforce this requirement on their members.

However, Friedman (1962) found it difficult to see reasons how any argument for licensure

instead of certification could be justified. This is because the usual paternalistic arguments for licensure regarding protecting public welfare are almost entirely satisfied, while certification without licensure provides a good deal of protection against the development of monopolies. The "... elasticity of demand will be fairly large, and the limits within which they can exploit the rest of the public by taking advantage of their special position will be rather narrow" (Friedman, 1962, p. 149). In other words, if certified professionals start charging too much and overly restricting access to certification, then the buying public will simply use uncertified professionals. Certification then seems less open to abuse than does licensure.

Arguments for occupational licensure are often based on issues of public welfare, on the basis of preventing people who are not competent from practicing or on improving the level of competence within the profession. However, many question the assumption of a link between licensure and professional quality (e.g., Clarkson & Muirs, 1980, p. 108). It is not necessarily clear that licensure does raise the standards of professional practice (Friedman, 1962, p. 155), and in many cases "...the considerations taken into account in determining who shall get a license often involve matters that, so far as any layman can see, have no relation whatsoever to professional competence" (Friedman, 1962, p. 141).

It is also not clear whether minimum quality standards maintain the quality within a profession. Sobel (2001) provides an interesting analysis of minimum quality standards for entry into a club, examining the conditions under which standards change over time. He finds that this can be related to variation in judging criteria and the proportion of judges' support necessary to grant entry. Unfortunately, Sobel explicitly makes several assumptions which do not hold for Project Management standards, such as a stable total membership and assessment based on direct comparison between potential and existing members. However, Sobel's general finding that standards have the potential to drop is interesting. Indeed, research has shown that " 'Minimum competency' examinations … fall short of what is needed, as the 'minimum' tends to become the 'maximum,' thus lowering educational standards for all" (National Commission on Excellence in Education, 1983). Sobel (2001, p. 620) relates dropping quality back to the increase in variety of standards, commenting that "[O]ne is tempted to speculate that the proliferation of new qualifications is a reaction to the degradation of existing qualifications."

If the most common argument for professional standards, namely protection of public welfare, is not met, the question remains why standardisation is so popular. The pressure to regulate professions through licensing or certification usually comes from within the profession to be regulated, instead of consumers of their services (Friedman, 1962, p. 140; Wolfson, Trebilcock, & Tuohy, 1980, p. 182). Indeed, such standards are often written more to protect members of the profession from competition, than to protect the public from incompetent practitioners (Leland, 1980, p. 265). Minimum quality standards in general (Leland, 1979, p. 1329) and professional regulation through licensure, certification, and registration (Friedman, 1962, p. 148) have been linked to the efforts of industry representatives or special producer groups to capture monopoly profits.

Research has also shown that professional incomes can be directly related to degrees of regulations. For instance, it has been found that "… television repair prices are higher in areas (Louisiana) with occupational licensure than in those with mere registration systems (California) or no regulation at all (the District of Colombia)" (Clarkson & Muirs, 1980, p. 108). Furthermore, the bodies which administer admission to the profession tend to accrue rents, which can provide an important impetus for licensure (Benham, 1980, p. 14).

In the case of Project Management, the various Project Management professional associations do have commercial interest in that they accrue rents

through the certification of professionals, with maintenance of market share potentially providing a motivator to exclude competitors from the market. However, in many countries, certification is available from more than one professional association, with clear monopolies only occurring in some regions. Certification is also seen by many project managers as a way of overcoming the information asymmetry, by providing a way of advertising their capabilities. Certification clearly provides benefit to those who provide the certifications and to those who gain them, while also providing assurance to employers, who in the face of multiple similar candidates for a position, need some way of making a distinction.

Performance-Based Competency Standards

Glassie (2003, p. 17) argues that conclusions about individual professional competence cannot be reached based on certification status, as certification only measures factors that tend to indicate competence, instead of measuring competence directly. This may be true for some kinds of standards. However, performance-based competency standards are specifically designed for assessment and recognition of current competence. This is assessed independent of how that competence has been achieved. They describe what people can be expected to do in their working roles, as well as the knowledge and understanding of their occupation that is needed to underpin these roles at a specific level of competence. Performance-based inference of competence is concerned with demonstration of the ability to do something at a standard considered acceptable in the workplace, with an emphasis on threshold rather than high performance or differentiating competencies. Threshold competencies are units of behaviour that are essential to do a job but that are not causally related to superior job performance (Boyatzis, 1982).

Models and standards which are based on performance are concerned with outcomes or results in the workplace, as opposed to potential competence, which might be assessed by tests of attributes. In these models, underlying competence in areas which are not easily observed, such as the ability to solve problems, can readily be inferred through performance and results in the workplace. "Performance based models of competence should specify what people have to be able to do, the level of performance required and the circumstances in which that level of performance is to be demonstrated" (Heywood, et al., 1992, p. 23).

Global Standards for Project Management

Work towards the creation of global standards for Project Management first became an issue in 1994, where, at the annual PMI Symposium in Vancouver, Canada, there was a meeting of representatives of PMI, IPMA, APM, and the AIPM, at which "… formal cooperation on several global issues, including standards, certification and formation of a global project management organisation or confederation' were discussed" (Pells, 1996, p. ix). A series of Global Project Management Forums followed.

However, standards-setting organisations must "…remain vigilant to make sure that all its participants are working in the spirit of collaboration" (JEDEC, 2004, p. 11), as "… standard setting is a conflicted, political process" (van Wegberg, 2004, p. 21). Meaningful cooperation between the Project Management professional associations was far from being realised. Informal participation and lip service to cooperation were possible at the Global Project Management Forums. Real progress in the interests of a unified Project Management profession were hampered by political issues and vested proprietary interests. By the thirteenth Global Project Management Forum in June 2003, little real progress had been achieved.

A lack of progress is not surprising, given the open format and range of topics discussed at the Global Project Management Forums. Lack of a tightly defined purpose and scope increases opportunities for those who would subvert the standards-setting process for personal economic gain. The "…standard-setting process is not perfect nor is it foolproof. It can be subverted by participants intent on bolstering their economic advantage over competitors through manipulation, deception and anticompetitive acts" (JEDEC, 2004, p. 11), as JEDEC would well be aware, given their recent complications with Rambus (Stern, 2001).

As an alternative to the Global Project Management Forums, the Global Performance Based Standards for Project Management Personnel (GPBSPMP) Working Group was initiated. The first meeting was in August 2002, set in the UK, hosted by the South African Government. A great deal of lobbying was initially involved to ensure the attendance of qualifications organisations, professional associations, and industry. At that meeting it was decided that a standards framework would be created that would provide a basis for mutual recognition of Project Management standards and certification. The GPBSPMP chose to take a different approach to standards creation than that taken by the Global Project Management Forums, PMI's market-based approach, or the IPMA's federated structure. It was decided that work on the development of global standards for project management practice "…should remain informal, independent of established professional associations" (Crawford, 2004b, p. 1399).

The typical approach to standards development in Project Management has been based on market dominance. However, as "… involvement in standardisation processes is accompanied by the danger that the other participants could use the disclosed and unprotected technological knowledge for their own purposes, R&D intensive companies whose knowledge is either insufficiently protected by IPR or extremely valuable may be reluctant to join standardisation processes" (Blind & Thumm, 2004, p. 62).

Companies which want a market lead ahead of competitors are often reluctant to join standardisation processes (Blind & Thumm, 2004, p. 69). Given that a market dominance approach to standards development was common in Project Management, it was necessary that the professional associations not feel that they were contributing to a standard which may compete with their own products.

The focus of the GPBSPMP was carefully selected. The most widely accepted of the Project Management standards focus on projects or organisations, not people (Crawford, 2004a, p. 1152). In the interests of achieving market dominance, the professional associations have had proprietary interest in restricting reciprocity between their standards and similar standards produced by other associations. By contrast, the standards which focus on people are part of national qualification frameworks, and governments, unlike the professional associations, have shown consistent interest in reciprocity between Project Management qualifications.

Project Management associations have proven to be very willing to share information regarding enabling processes and educational standards, while Project Management knowledge has been consistently regarded as more political. The different Project Management associations also tend to take proprietary positions concerning their bodies of knowledge, which are their primary "products." These observations influenced the approach taken by the GPBSPMP. It was decided that standards development would focus on people, rather than projects or organisations, and would focus on practice rather than knowledge. This provided the opportunity to harness national Governments' interest in reciprocity, while not appearing as a direct competitor to any of the products provided by the various professional associations.

Defining a standard and choosing the words with which it is to be described is a particularly

significant political act. Defining appropriate categories and names in a situation is a process of "… deciding what will be visible or invisible within the system" (Bowker & Star, 1999, p. 44). In this case, effort was taken to define the GPB-SPMP as outside the area of competitive concern of the established professional associations, as not running in the same race. Careful naming can be used as a deliberate tool of forgetting and for delegating attention (Bowker & Star, 1999, p. 280). By focusing on people and practice, the GPBSPMP could be classified as an outsider, and therefore thought of as harmless. As a result, the professional association could participate in the process without it being considered a potential threat.

The GPBSPMP decided to focus on performance-based standards. Standards already existed for the assessment of performance, with the UK, Australian, New Zealand, and South African governments having contributed considerable work to their development since the 1980s. Performance-based competency standards involve more than a test of knowledge. Rather, the Competency standards approach assumes that competence can best be inferred from actual demonstrated performance at a pre-defined acceptable standard (Gonczi, et al., 1993). Such standards are arguably therefore more indicative of practical competence than typical knowledge-based minimum quality standards. Performancebased standards are a way of demonstrating competence gained through practice, such as on-the-job expertise. They provide a way for people who have not had the option to gain qualifications to demonstrate ability and have it formally recognised. As such, this has been a popular approach for governments concerned with equity.

Learning from previous attempts to create global Project Management standards which had been subverted by internal politics, a monetary fee was used as a constraint for entry to the GPBSPMP. Different fees were applicable to organisations and to individuals. Fees were structured to make participation substantially more costly for individuals not representing a subscribing organisation, and subscribing organisations generally were very careful about whom they would allow to represent them. This helped to create a pool of personnel dedicated to, and experienced in, standards development. Participation fees also provided funding, which meant that the process could remain independent of existing associations.

A series of working sessions was initiated, typically involving from 15 to 20 individuals. Organisations who have subscribed and/or sent representatives, excluding those who have specifically requested not to be mentioned, are summarised in Table 2. Table 2 was composed based on internal documentation, after the eighth working session.

All labour on the project was voluntary, excluding secretarial support. It quickly became clear that most progress was achieved while participants were together, so to maximise this, working sessions typically lasted for three days, occurring at least biannually. The process used by the GPBSPMP was as close as possible to ANSI processes and those of the various participating qualifications bodies, in order to facilitate acceptance. This process started with a complete review of existing project management standards.

Primarily the same groups and individuals were involved throughout the development process. Early on the group established a very strong culture focused on cooperation and work. New people were very quickly absorbed into this culture. Political issues were consciously, vocally, and explicitly put aside. Often there was compromise to make the group happy. The focus was on cooperation and producing a good product. The group would be dedicated to the work for three days at a time, with the social aspect of the meeting providing an important focus for creating a strong culture within the group. As many issues were resolved over the dinner table as at a whiteboard.

One of the few areas of political contention related to nomenclature. This can again be related back to the importance of an awareness of classification, and its effect on perceived boundaries,

Table 2. Organisations which subscribed and/or sent representatives

Standards and qualifications organisations	Professional associations	Academic/training institutions	Industry
• Innovation and Business Skills Australia • New Zealand Qualifications Authority • Project Management Standards Generating Body • Services SETA	• American Society for the Advancement of Project Management • Association for Project Management • China Project Management Association • International Project Management Association • Japan Project Management Association • Project Management Institute • Project Management South Africa • Society of Project Managers, Singapore	• Athabasca University • Cambridge International Examinations • Cranfield University • ESC Lille • Middlesex University • University of Southern Queensland • University of Technology, Sydney	• American Express • Living Planit • Motorola • Project Performance Group • Project Services Queensland

as mentioned earlier. In the UK, performance-based standards are referred to as occupational standards, but the use of the term "occupation" was thought by some to be lowering the image of the profession to that of a trade. "Competency" was rejected as a possible descriptor, due to the fears of participants from one country that the standards would imply behaviour and provide grounds for litigation. An interim result was "Global Performance Based Standards for Project Management," but it was thought that this would encompass the organisational and project levels, so "Personnel" was added, resulting in the unwieldy acronym which persisted for the majority of the development process.

Two years, and six working sessions after the work by the GPBSPMP was started, a draft standard was released for public review. At this point, the larger professional associations who already had their own standards and qualifications processes started to withdraw from the development process. Common excuses were that they were "Reviewing their strategy," "Did not have sufficient volunteer labour," and were worried that "Participation sent mixed messages to their membership." At about the same time, one of the professional associations raised concerns regarding the last three letters of the GPBSPMP acronym, which were reminiscent of the name of one of their existing products. This provided the opportunity to adopt a simpler and preferable name—GAPPS (Global Alliance for Project Performance Standards).

Over 100 reviews for the draft standard were received from members of the public. Comments were sorted by the various sections to which they pertained. An adjudication panel was convened to review and decide upon actions in response to comments, on the understanding that unanimous agreement by the panel on actions to be taken was necessary. Reviewers were notified of actions taken in response to their comments. A process to handle appeals to actions was initiated,

with all public reviewers given a right to appeal decisions.

After three years and eight working sessions the GAPPS Global Project Management Framework has been released, and is currently being piloted by a major global corporation. Standards and qualifications bodies involved are addressing their respective local approval processes, with a view towards general adoption as a basis for reciprocity. Similarly, national or other professional associations who don't have their own standards products are currently in the process of examining its suitability and the possibility of adopting it.

CONCLUSION

Two significant differences stand out when comparing the development of the GAPPS standard with more common Project Management standards. First, the standard has been developed as a process of negotiation and joint modification, as opposed to the usual market dominance approach used in Project Management standards development.

Second, minimum quality standards have often been used as a way of ensuring profits for the standards-setting organisation, which then has the opportunity to act as a gatekeeper to those who wish to obtain the professional certification or licensure. Many of the Project Management professional associations could be accused of trying to use such a position to secure a monopoly. A different approach has been adopted in the creation of the GAPPS standard, which, if anything, has been designed to counter any emerging monopoly by focusing on being a basis for reciprocity between existing Project Management standards.

Permission is granted in the standard for distribution, use, modification, publication, and translation of the standard free of charge, although copyright is maintained by GAPPS. GAPPS is making no attempt to act as gatekeepers to the standard. The main benefits to those involved in the production process have been access to developing knowledge and potential increase in reputation through association with the project.

The standard can be seen as an attempt to further the profession, by providing opportunities for countries without existing standards to have a basis for creation of their own and by creating a global basis for professional reciprocity. Open source software has so far had a considerable influence on the software development community. Only time will tell what influence the first open access standard for Project Management will have on its community.

REFERENCES

APM. (2006). *Body of knowledge: Version 5.* High Wycombe, UK: Association of Project Managers.

APM. (2005). Association for project management overview. Retrieved August 24, 2005 from, http://www.apm.org.uk/page.asp?categoryID=3&subCategoryID=21&pageID=0

Baskin, E., Krechmer, K., & Sherif, M. (1998). The six dimensions of standards: Contributions towards a theory of standardization. In L. Lefebvre, R. Mason, , & T. Khalil (Eds.), *Management of technology, sustainable developments and eco-efficiency.* Amsterdam: Elsevier, pp. 53-62.

Benham, L. (1980). The demand for occupational licensure. In S. Rottenberg (Ed.), *Occupational licensure and regulation.* US: American Enterprise Institute for Public and Policy Research, pp. 13-25.

Blind, K., & Thumm, N. (2004). Intellectual property protection and standardization. *International Journal of IT Standards & Standardization Research, 2*(2), 61-75.

Blum, U. (2005). Lessons from the past: Public standardization in the spotlight. *International*

Journal of IT Standards & Standardization Research, 3(1), 1-20.

Bowker, G., & Star, S. (1999). *Sorting things out: Classification and its consequences.* London: MIT Press.

Boyatzis, R.E. (1982). *The competent manager: A model for effective performance.* New York: Wiley.

Bredillet, C. (2003). Genesis and role of standards: Theoretical foundations and socio-economical model for the construction and use of standards. *International journal of Project Management, 21*(6), 463-470.

Brown, D. (2005). Raise HR's stature by raising the bar for qualification. *Canadian HR Reporter, 18*(6), 5-8.

Carey, J. (1953). Uniform standards for professional qualifications. *Journal of Accountancy, 95,* 36-37.

Cegielski, C. (2004). Who values technology certification? *Communications of the ACM, 47*(10), 103-105.

Cegielski, C., Rebman, C., & Reithel, B. (2003). The value of certification: An empirical assessment of the perceptions of end-users of local area networks. *Information Systems Journal, 13,* 97-107.

Clarkson, K., & Muris, T. (1980). The federal trade commission and occupational regulation. In S. Rottenberg (Ed.), *Occupational licensure and regulation.* . US: American Enterprise Institute for Public and Policy Research, pp. 107-141.

Crawford, L. (2004a). Global body of project management knowledge and standards. J. Pinto, & G. Morris (Eds.), *The wiley guide to managing projects.* New York: Wiley, 1150-1196.

Crawford, L. (2004b). Professional associations and global initiatives. J. Pinto, & G. Morris (Eds.),

The wiley guide to managing projects. New York: Wiley, 1389-1402.

Dean, P.J. (1997). Examining the profession and the practice of business ethics. . *Journal of Business Ethics, 16*, 1637-1649.

Duncan, W.R. (1998). Presentation to council of chapter presidents. *PMI Annual Symposium*. October 10, Long Beach, CA, USA.

ECITB. (2002). *National occupational standards for project management: Pre-launch version*. Kings Langley: Engineering Construction Industry Training Board.

ENAA. (2002). *P2M: A guidebook of project & program management for enterprise innovation: Summary translation. Revision 1*. Tokyo, Japan: Project Management Professionals Certification Center (PMCC).

Friedman, M. (1962). Capitalism & freedom. Chicago: University of Chicago Press.

George, T. (2002). Employees raise the bar on certification. *Information Week, 896*, 76-77.

Glassie, J. (2003). Certification programs as a reflection of competency. *Association Management, 55*(6), 17-18.

Gonczi, A., Hager, P., & Athanasou, J. (1993). *The development of competency-based assessment strategies for the professions*. Canberra, Australia: Australian Government Publishing Service.

Heywood, L., Gonczi, A., & Hager, P. (1992). *A guide to development of competency standards for professions*. Canberra, Australia: Australian Government Publishing Service.

IPMA. (1999). G. Caupin, H. Knopfel, P. Morris, E. Motzel, & O. Pannenbacker (Eds.). *ICB: IPMA competence baseline, Version 2*. Germany: International Project Management Association.

IPMA. (2003). *Research and development*. www. ipma.ch/

ISO. (1997). *ISO 10006: 1997: Quality management: Guidelines to quality in project management*. Geneva: International Organization for Standardization.

JEDEC. (2004). White paper: The vital role of standard-setting organizations and the necessity of good faith and fair play among participants. *JEDEC 2004 Symposium: The Future of Standards Setting, Legal, Marketplace and Consumer Implications*. Available at: http://www.standardsconference.org/docs/WhitePaper_1-14-05.pdf

Krechmer, K. (2004). Standardization and innovation policies in the information age. *International Journal of IT Standards & Standardization Research, 2*(2), 49-60.

Leffler, K. (1980). Commentary. In S. Rottenberg (Ed.), *Occupational licensure and regulation*. USA: American Enterprise Institute for Public and Policy Research, 287-295.

Leland, H. (1979). Quacks, lemons, and licensing: A theory of minimum quality standards. *Journal of Political Economy, 87*(6), 1328-1346.

Leland, H. (1980). Minimum-quality standards and licensing in markets with asymetric information. In S. Rottenberg (Ed.), *Occupational licensure and regulation*. USA: American Enterprise Institute for Public and Policy Research, 265-284.

Lenn, M.P. (1997). Introduction. In M.P. Lenn, & L. Campos (Eds.), *Globalization of the professions and the quality imperative: Professional accreditation, certification and licensure*. Madison WI: Magna Publications, Inc.

Morris, P.W.G. (1994). *The management of projects*. London: Thomas Telford.

Muriithi, N., & Crawford, L. (2003). Approaches to project management in Africa: Implications for international development projects. *International Journal of Project Management, 21*, 309-319.

National Commission on Excellence in Education. (1983). A nation at risk: The imperative for educational reform. Washington, US: Government Printing Office (Accessed online at: http://www.ed.gov/pubs/NatAtRisk/findings.html).

Pells, D.L. (1996). Introduction. In J.S. Pennypacker (Ed.), *The global status of the project management profession.* Sylva, NC: PMI Communications, , ix–xii.

PMI. (2003a). *PMI chapters outside the United States.* Retrieved June 26, 2003 from, www.pmi.org/info/GMC ChapterListingOutsideUS.asp#P128 1923

PMI. (2003b). PMI Sydney chapter. Retrieved June 26, 2003 from, http://sydney.pmichapters-australia.org.au/

PMI. (2004). A guide to the project management body of knowledge. PA, US: Project Management Institute.

PMI. (2005a). *PMI chapters.* Retrieved August 24, 2005 from, http://www.pmi.org/prod/groups/public/documents/info/gmc_chaptersoverview.asp

PMI. (2005b). *PMI project management standards program.* Retrieved August 24, 2005 from, http://www.pmi.org/prod/groups/public/documents/info/pp_pmstandardsprogram.asp

PMI. (2006). Project management institute fact sheet. Retrieved March 9, 2006 from, http://www.pmi.org/info/GMC_MemberFACTSheet-Jan06.pdf

Schrage, M. (2004). Hiding behind certification: An over-reliance on IT sheepskins is a recipe for disaster. *CIO, 17*(17), 1.

Sobel, J. (2001). On the dynamics of standards. *RAND Journal of Economics, 32*(4), 606-623.

Steele, R. (2004). Standards as an indicator of maturity? ... and an opportunity for customer and industry advantage? *International Journal of IT Standards & Standardization Research, 2*(1), 42-45.

Stern, R. (2001). More standardization skullduggery. *IEEE Micro, 21*(4), 12-15,69.

Stretton, A. (1994). A short history of project management: Part one: the 1950s and 60s. *Australian Project Manager, 14*(1), 36-7.

van Wegberg, M. (2004). Standardization and competing consortia: The trade-off between speed and compatibility. *International Journal of IT Standards & Standardization Research, 2*(2), 18-33.

Warner, A. (2003). Block alliances in formal standard setting environments. *International Journal of IT Standards & Standardization Research, 1*(1), 1-18.

Wolfson, A., Trebilcock, M., & Tuohy, C. (1980). Regulating the professions: A theoretical framework. In S. Rottenberg (Ed.), *Occupational licensure and regulation. US: American Enterprise Institute for Public and Policy Research,* pp. 180-214.

This work was previously published in the International Journal of IT Standards and Standardization Research, Vol. 6, Issue 1, edited by K. Jakobs, pp. 70-84, copyright 2008 by IGI Publishing (an imprint of IGI Global).

Chapter 3
US and EU Regulatory Competition and Authentication Standards in Electronic Commerce

Jane K. Winn[1]
University of Washington School of Law, USA

ABSTRACT

This chapter examines the role of law reform in promoting the development of technical standards for the authentication of parties engaged in Internet commerce. Law reforms intended to improve the security of Internet commerce can only succeed if they address business, technical and legal issues simultaneously. The EU has used commercial law reform and formal standard development to coordinate work on authentication standards, while the US has allowed the market to determine what type of authentication technology is appropriate and has left the development of standards to private consortia. While the EU approach may solve collective action problems more effectively, the US approach may discover end user requirements and may allow business judgments about risk to inform the law more effectively. Neither approach has yet resolved the authentication problems facing businesses engaged in online commerce.

INTRODUCTION

In 2006, businesses engaged in Internet commerce face a fundamental challenge when trying to implement strong authentication technologies because of the absence of widely accepted standards for the reliable authentication of transacting parties in Internet commerce. For more than a decade, governments have struggled unsuccessfully to create legal frameworks within which businesses can implement strong authentication technologies, and still enjoy the global reach and efficiency of Internet markets. The creation of such frameworks requires the simultaneous resolution of legal, business and technical issues, a result that none of the electronic commerce enabling legislation enacted to date in either the US or EU has managed to achieve. This paper will analyze the strengths and weaknesses of the different approaches taken by the US and EU in recent years, and will suggest what regulatory strategies might succeed in this area in the future.

DOI: 10.4018/978-1-60566-946-5.ch003

The problem of authentication is fundamental to online commerce. Actions taken in online environments can most easily be traced back to particular computer equipment and software, but responsibility for commercial transactions must be attributed to individuals and organizations in the material world, not to computers or software. In order to establish a connection between some action taken online, and individuals and organizations that can be held legally accountable, a system of authenticating computer users must be found. When electronic commerce was based on mainframe computers, and network connections were limited, the scope of the authentication problem was limited. With the commercialization of the Internet in the 1990s and the use of insecure public networks for commercial transactions, the magnitude of the problem of online authentication for commercial transactions increased rapidly. The problem of authentication has so far defied the efforts of developers to produce an effective technological solution that can be widely implemented. Different governments at different times have tried to use "technology-forcing" legislation (Miller 1995) to push technology developers and transacting parties to focus more attention on the problem of authentication, although none have yet succeeded. The question of whether it is possible to develop authentication technologies that can meet the needs of parties using the Internet for commercial transactions is a very real one, but for the purposes of this paper, it will be assumed that such a solution is in theory possible even if it might be prohibitively expensive to implement in the near term.

Assuming that some collective solution to the problem of authentication in Internet commerce is technologically feasible, although it is not yet clear what that solution is, then the question with regard to the regulation of commerce is what form of legal regulation would be most compatible with widespread adoption of such a solution. Standards for authentication technologies are necessary to achieve interoperability and permit transacting

parties to enjoy the positive network effects created by the ubiquitous nature of the Internet. Developing appropriate standards for authentication technology has proven to be a monumental task, and even if appropriate standards can be developed, substantial collective action problems must be resolved in order to achieve their widespread adoption. The US has opted to allow market forces to resolve these problems, while the EU has opted for a more regulatory approach to deal with them.

This paper will analyze different US and EU law reform strategies for promoting the development and implementation of more robust standards for authentication in Internet commerce. National strategies for regulating online commerce have diverged markedly because legal and regulatory cultures vary widely among countries and also because the appropriate relationship between commercial law and technical standards is uncertain. Governments face serious challenges both in trying to identify viable standards and in promoting them effectively with legislation. A decision to refrain from regulating may be equally unacceptable, however, if there is a market failure that leads to underinvest in authentication technologies. Given the magnitude and complexity of the problem regulators face, it should not be surprising that neither the US nor the EU has yet found a way to promote the adoption of standards for effective authentication technologies through law reform. This paper will sketch out the different approaches taken by the US and by the EU in dealing with these issues, and note some of the strengths and weaknesses of each approach. In light of those findings, this paper will suggest that the US and EU have each identified important elements of an effective strategy for identifying and promoting viable standards for authentication in online commerce, and that the differences between those strategies may have a significant impact on the growth of domestic online commerce, and the global competitiveness of domestic online businesses.

AUTHENTICATION AND ELECTRONIC COMMERCE

In order to connect a transacting party to an action taken within an information system, the user must be authenticated. The technical and business challenges to deploying effective online authentication systems within closed information systems may be significant, but they are not insurmountable. Examples of successful, well-established electronic commerce systems that operate in global markets using closed networks of information systems include bank wholesale funds transfer networks, electronic data interchange trading partner relationships that use value-added networks, airline computer reservation systems, credit card systems, automated clearing houses, and automated teller machine electronic funds transfer systems. Participation in each of these systems is either limited by government regulation and licensing systems, or by an individual enrollment process that has significant screening functions, and in some cases, an existing network participant to act as guarantor before a new entrant is accepted. For example, individual consumers could not gain access to these systems in most cases without first establishing an account with a business that would process transactions on the consumer's behalf and that would guarantee the consumer's performance. In such a closed system, the process of formalizing security policies, defining roles, establishing access controls and taking the other steps required to deploy an effective system for authenticating users may be difficult and expensive, but not impossible.

Reliable authentication of transacting parties using open insecure networks such as the Internet is a dramatically more difficult problem to solve. Internet commerce has grown by leaps and bounds, notwithstanding the availability of widely accepted standards for strong authentication, by relying on partial, limited solutions. When Internet commerce first became possible a decade ago, the need for strong authentication technologies and

the possibility of using law reform to engineer a solution to the problem were vigorously debated. Some regulators tried to anticipate how the market should respond to these challenges and passed laws promoting the use of a digital signature/PKI model[2] of authentication. The market did not develop in the manner that these statutes anticipated, however, because this approach was based on misperceptions regarding the nature of the problem on several levels (Ellison and Schneier 2000). While it was always clear to many computer security experts that digital signatures and public key infrastructures could not live up to the hype, these experts were outnumbered by the technology vendors, consultants and misguided amateurs feeding the hype surrounding them in the 1990s (Winn 2001). Regulators in countries that enacted laws promoting the use of digital signatures have found that private parties have continued to resist adopting them for use in commercial transactions (Lamberti 2005).

In the US, the rapid expansion of online commerce in the absence of any mandatory minimum level of information security, including authentication standards, has created a problem of quite a different character. When Internet commerce was still a novelty in the US in the mid-1990s, there was considerable concern about the security of credit card information transmitted over the Internet. When it became apparent that relatively simple technological fixes, such as the Secure Socket Layer communications protocol, could manage at least some of these risks, the perception that the Internet was "open for business" became widespread, and the volume of Internet commerce grew explosively (Willis 2004). By 2006, the consequences of the rapid expansion of Internet commerce in the US without the support of strong authentication technologies were becoming apparent as the volume of Internet fraud involving retail financial accounts also grew explosively. The public debate over the need for strong online authentication systems has been rekindled in the US, but the terms of the debate were quite different than they had been in the 1990s. The focus of the renewed debate is on federated identity systems and harmonizing data protection and electronic commerce objectives, not digital signature certificates and public key infrastructures. The terms of the new debate are defined by a more concrete sense of end user requirements, and a more realistic appraisal of the costs and benefits of establishing and maintaining authentication systems capable of supporting electronic commerce on a large scale in an open environment.

REGULATORY COMPETITION AND ELECTRONIC COMMERCE LAW

"Regulatory competition" describes competition between sovereigns to attract mobile resources such as labor and capital by offering different packages of tax and benefit structures (Tiebout 1956). The notion of regulatory competition has now been applied to a wide range of economic sectors, and the range of regulatory tools used by governments to influence personal and business economic decisions has increased. As a result, the existence of multiple models of regulatory competition must now be recognized (Revesz 2001). For example, competition among different countries with regard to the regulation of labor market conditions may be quite different than competition among different states in a single federal legal system with regard to regulation of financial market conditions. This paper will apply the notion of international competition between the US and EU for control over the technical standards that define global electronic commerce markets, using the problem of authentication in Internet commerce as a case study.

The notion of regulatory competition in the area of standards is well recognized (Egan 2002), as is the idea of international competition to set ICT standards. For example, the European GSM standard for mobile phone communications was clearly more successful than the US alternatives

introduced at the same time (Pelkmans 2001). The notion of regulatory competition between the US and EU with regard to data protection regulations and the technologies used to implement them is well recognized, although not generally labeled regulatory competition (Shaffer 2002, Heisenberg 2005). It has similarly been studied in the area of Java software standards and XML standards for business communications (Egyedi 2001). The problem of defining standards for authentication is part of a larger process of developing standards that facilitate greater automation of business processes, and greater collaboration among trading partners through greater integration of their information systems. The degree of standardization of business processes across firms historically was limited while business processes were largely administered by people, or when computerization was based on internal processes within a single firm. As firms make a greater effort to integrate their internal processes with those of their trading partners, greater standardization among firms is essential (Gibb & Damodaran 2003). Standards for authentication play an essential role in the integration of business processes across firms.

The US is relatively unique among advanced industrialized economies in its enthusiasm for policies designed to "let the market lead" instead of using government to develop a national industrial or economic policy. This has not always been the case—a modern American regulatory state began to take shape in 1887 with the creation of the Interstate Commerce Commission and was expanded dramatically under Roosevelt's New Deal and Johnson's Great Society programs—but since at least 1980, political support for strong regulatory regimes has eroded in the US (McGarity 1996). One aspect of this embrace of market-oriented solutions to social and economic issues is the complex system of diverse and numerous private standard-developing organizations (ANSI 2005b). As ANSI reports, "The U.S. standardization infrastructure...reflects a basic national belief that society will benefit and innovation and creativity will flourish in a system that is free from centralized government control but strengthened through essential government participation." In this context, essential signifies limited to the bare essentials, with government deferring to the market to define standards and, instead of the direct exercise of leadership by the public sector, leveraging the market pull effects of government procurement to promote adoption of specific standards. The National Technology Transfer and Advancement Act of 1995 (NTTAA) directs US government agencies to use standards developed by voluntary consensus bodies whenever available in lieu of government-developed standards to accomplish its regulatory and administrative objectives. These limitations on the role of government in setting standards reflect concerns that if government intervention is not carried out effectively, it will inhibit economic growth by raising costs without any corresponding increase in benefits (Graham 2002).

Member states in the EU, by contrast, are more likely to view standards policy as an integral element of government economic policy and to believe government involvement in the work of a national standards body is an appropriate exercise of regulatory authority (Pelkmans 1987, Hodges 2005, Schepel 2005). Standards are perceived as a legitimate mechanism for coordinating private sector economic activity with national policy goals. Furthermore, EU standards law and policy has played an essential role in the construction of the Internal market through the elimination of technical barriers to trade. The US approach limits government oversight to monitoring for unlawful anti-competitive activities and compliance with minimum procedural requirements, while the European approach includes those functions and adds a framework within which the substance of voluntary, consensus standard-developing efforts can be harmonized with the substance of economic regulation.

The EU system for coordinating law reform efforts with standard-developing efforts is known as the "New Approach" to standardization. Within the New Approach, after legislation has been prepared that requires an associated technical standard in order to be implemented effectively, an associated European standardization effort is initiated by one of the three recognized EU standards bodies. The Commission may send an observer to the standard-developing process, and indeed check that the end result meets the essential requirements of the relevant EU legislation—a directive—but the process of market players coming together to develop the technical standard is otherwise unchanged. The resulting standard establishes a "safe harbor" for regulated entities: compliance with the standard is strictly voluntary, but proof of conformity with that standard creates a presumption of compliance with the corresponding law. If the standard becomes out of date, it can be replaced by withdrawing the first standard and publishing the reference details of a replacement standard in the Official Journal, but no changes need to be made in the text of the Directive or by any member state implementing legislation.

The US market orientation to standard developing has permitted informal standard-developing organizations known as consortia to flourish, while EU regulators have generally regarded the same phenomena with unease (given that many consortia are dominated by US-based companies). In order to promote private sector involvement in standard developing and reduce overlapping research efforts, the US enacted legislation which removed regulatory obstacles to the growth of consortia in 1984 with the National Cooperative Research Act, and in 1993 with the National Cooperative Research and Production Act (Benoliel 2003). While there is concern in some quarters even in the US regarding the transparency and accountability of consortia processes, there is little doubt that consortia are often able to identify demand for specific standards and to complete the process of standard development more quickly and effectively than traditional standard-developing organizations. As a result of the removal by US regulators of legal impediments to their growth, and market acceptance of the standards they produce, consortia have come to play an integral role in the development of global ICT standards generally, although many have reservations about the multiplicity of consortia and solutions, which can be seen as an obstacle to interoperability. EU regulators have responded to the challenges posed by the growth of consortia activities to the *de jure* standard-developing process favored in Europe by looking for ways to increase the effectiveness of European standards bodies.

The US proclivity to let the market lead is also visible in its approach to reforming commercial law to accommodate innovations in the technology of online markets (Bix and Winn 2006). US courts have decided dozens of cases in recent years in which they were asked to decide what legal standards should apply to contracts formed over the Internet. Almost without exception, courts have deferred to emerging business practices even when this requires watering down established legal doctrines regarding formation of contracts. Courts have implicitly accepted the notion that if someone finds unfair the limited disclosures or harsh contract terms imposed by online merchants, they are always free to do business with bricks-and-mortar merchants instead. Courts seem to presume that any attempt by them to mandate "best practices" for online contracting might stifle innovation and reward opportunistic parties who want the benefit of low prices from online merchants but are unwilling to accept the lower level of services they offer which justifies the difference in price. With regard to government regulation of online commerce rather than common law judicial decisions, a presumption that no new regulations should be enacted in the absence of overwhelming, irrefutable evidence of the failure of market mechanisms has limited government efforts. As a former US antitrust official observed, "the essential insight of the 'Chicago School' is not that markets work perfectly, but rather that the market generally works better than government intervention" (Leeds 1997). Even when legislation, such as the CAN-SPAM Act to regulate unsolicited commercial email, is enacted in response to a perceived crisis in online commerce, the legislation tends to be at least as deferential to business interests as it is protective of the larger public interest.

The EU, by contrast, has taken a very proactive approach to regulating the conduct of online merchants, through legislation targeting online business activities, including the Electronic Commerce Directive and the Distance Selling Directive, and through legislation that applies to merchants across the board but has no counterpart in the US, including the Data Protection Directive and the Unfair Contract Terms Directive. These regulations establish high minimum standards that apply either to all merchants, or to all online merchants. Compliance with these consumer protection mandates clearly raises the cost of doing business, but this is accepted as a necessary cost of ensuring the fair treatment of all consumers. One of the justifications for the Electronic signature Directive, discussed in detail below, was a similar desire to make Internet commerce safer for consumers. These regulations are consistent with the regulatory goals announced in 1999, and reiterated on many subsequent occasions, for the eEurope Action plan: ensuring that the information society in Europe is socially inclusive, builds consumer trust and strengthens social cohesion (Commission 1999). This approach to the regulation of online commerce is consistent with greater public anxiety about the social consequences of technological innovation, and a broader consensus in Europe than in the US that government has a duty to manage the risks of technological innovation (Glenny 2001). This regulatory approach requires businesses moving from traditional markets to online markets to internalize more of the costs of managing risks created by the online environment than the corresponding US approach. This divergence between US and EU approaches to market regulation in general and regulation of standard development in particular can be observed in government policies to address the authentication problem.

ONLINE AUTHENTICATION UNDER US LAW

The US, as a common law jurisdiction, benefits from the flexibility of a legal system that can use judicial precedent to adapt existing law to new circumstances. Although the shortcomings of a case law system are numerous, one of the strengths of such a system is the ability to incorporate current business practices into commercial law through judicial precedent, reducing the need for statutory law reform in areas such as contract law. Because US case law had developed to accommodate contracts formed by telegraph, by telex, by telephone, by fax, and by electronic data interchange, many US legal experts felt confident that the common law of contracts would be able to adapt to and accommodate Internet commerce. Other experts, generally with a technical rather than a legal background, argued that while the Internet lowered the costs of discovering and negotiating with new trading partners, it also increased demand for new technologies to authenticate reliably strangers encountered in cyberspace, and that law reform should be used to promote the adoption of such technologies. Some but not all of these experts had an economic interest in promoting specific technologies to solve the authentication problem that were based on a particular model of digital signatures using asymmetric or public key cryptography, combined with a system for issuing identity certificates by trusted third parties.

Some US states took an early lead in regulating online authentication by passing digital signature laws, although these laws were very controversial when they were enacted. Utah was the first to enact such a law in 1995, and several other states soon followed. These laws established licensing requirements to regulate the conduct of trusted

third parties issuing digital signature certificates, and created incentives for the adoption of digital signature technologies by providing enhanced legal enforcement of contracts formed using that technology. Around the same time, some countries in Europe, including Germany and Italy, enacted similar laws. Digital signature laws in the US were roundly criticized as promoting the use of specific technology without regard to whether, as implemented, it was actually a superior authentication technology. In particular, security experts noted that any implementation of digital signature technology that permitted end users to store their private signature keys on the hard drive of a personal computer connected to the Internet was vulnerable to attack. Creating a legal presumption that would make it easier to enforce agreements authenticated by digital signatures produced under such insecure conditions would create an invitation to fraud and expose consumers using digital signatures to unacceptably high levels of risk. The consensus in the US soon turned against such "technology specific" legislation and by 2000 when federal electronic commerce legislation was enacted, it was decidedly "technology neutral." The premise behind such legislation was that market forces, not regulators, should determine what form of authentication is appropriate for online commerce, and that even if the private sector has trouble discerning how business, technical and legal variables should be weighed, legislators and regulators were likely to be even less adept at figuring out what was needed. In 2006, legislation was introduced in Utah to repeal its digital signature law because it was obvious it had become an irrelevant anachronism.

The response of US technology vendors to the invitation offered by technology-neutral legislation to let the market determine the appropriate authentication technology has been to "let a hundred flowers bloom." Neither the federal "Electronic signatures in Global and National Commerce Act" (E-SIGN Act) nor the Uniform Electronic Transactions Act (a model law enacted in nearly all states) provides any mechanism to facilitate the transition from the current *de facto* standard of weak authentication to a stronger standard. In the ensuing unregulated competition among technology vendors, many compelling technical solutions have been brought to market but none has been able to gain decisive market share. As a result, the default for retail Internet transactions in the US remains user ID and password logons even though the security problems associated with such systems are very well known. This appears to be a clear instance of the problem frequently encountered in markets where interoperability is essential to maintain the operation of networks, namely that migration from one standard to another can be very difficult (Shapiro and Varian 1999).

The current lack of reliable, widespread authentication and identity management solutions in the US represents a market failure caused by the inability of markets alone to resolve competing social and economic values including security, convenience and privacy (Blum et al. 2004). The Internet was not designed to support secure transaction processing, and the technical solutions to this problem have been limited in scope and have not been standardized among organizations. Increased use of the Internet in electronic commerce has increased the value of transactions being processed in relatively insecure environments. The vulnerability of Internet electronic commerce has attracted the attention of organized crime, which now operates globally to evade national law enforcement efforts (Cameron 2005).

By 2004, an epidemic of "phishing," "pharming" and "spyware" had forced US regulators and end users to recognize the magnitude of the risks created by the inability to authenticate online merchants reliably. After a "security breach notice" law was enacted in California in 2004, anyone who handles personal information about California citizens and who suffers a breach of security must notify everyone whose personal information might have been compromised that the breach occurred. During 2005, disclosures

by organizations holding personal information revealed that security breaches had exposed the information of more than 50 million individuals in the US. There is even some evidence that American public acceptance of Internet electronic commerce may be declining after years of rapid growth as a result of anxiety about the insecurity of online commerce. In addition to heightened concerns on the part of individual end users, information security issues finally captured the attention of top managers of US companies after the Sarbanes-Oxley Act required them to take personal responsibility for the adequacy of their internal control system.

By the time public outcry had grown over the mounting costs of using weak authentication technologies in online commerce, the process of voluntary, consensus standard developing had been underway in the US for many years. An early attempt to resolve the authentication problem with a proprietary technology was Microsoft Passport, a protocol designed to enable end users to sign onto many different merchants' Web sites after having been authenticated only once to a common server. Launched in 1999, Passport failed to achieve widespread adoption because merchants were concerned about losing control over their customers' information if it was held by Microsoft, end users and regulators were concerned about whether Passport included adequate privacy protections, and security experts noted serious flaws in its security.

The mere threat of Microsoft running an Internet-wide authentication service, however, galvanized its competitors into joining together to look for an alternative solution. In 2001, the Liberty Alliance was founded by technology companies Sun Microsystems and Hewlett-Packard together with industrial companies including General Motors, telecomm companies including France Telecomm, Nokia and NTT DoCoMo, and financial service companies including American Express and Mastercard. Liberty Alliance has developed a model of "federated identity management" to support the model of Internet commerce known as web services. In 2002, another consortium with similar objectives, the Web Service Interoperability Organization (WS-I) was established by Microsoft and IBM together with Hewlett-Packard, Intel, Oracle and SAP AG, among others. In 2005, Microsoft announced that the next version of its operating system would include an authentication product named "Infocard" that will be based on open standards for an "identity metasystem." The intent is to create a visual system allowing users to select among their identities no matter what technology is being used, or who issues them an identity. Among the business problems these products and consortia were established to address was the need for a "single sign-on" (SSO). An SSO permits an end user to access applications and resources from many systems after being authenticated only one time.

By 2006, various US-based private sector efforts to develop standards for strong online authentication systems were beginning to bear fruit. The most visible effort was the Security Assertion Markup Language (SAML), a standard developed by a technical committee of Organization for the Advancement of Structured Information Standards (OASIS). SAML is an XML-based framework for exchanging security information, and is one of the standards incorporated into the Liberty Alliance's "Circles of Trust" model of federated identity management. This security information is expressed in the form of assertions about subjects, where a subject is an entity (either human or computer) that has an identity in some security domain (Cover 2005). The WS-I effort produced a series of WS-Security standards addressing similar issues that are designed to interoperate with other standards such as SAML. Products based on these standards were being marketed, and some had significant numbers of adoptions by 2005. For example, the Shibboleth System, an open source federated identity technology incorporating both SAML and WS standards, is currently being used by many universities worldwide to permit students

and faculty to access online journal subscriptions (Morgan et al. 2004). The US federal government's E-Authentication Initiative, in keeping with the NTTAA, requires participants in federal programs to use strong authentication technologies based on private sector federated identity management standards and products. While it is too soon in 2006 to declare a success of the efforts of US standards consortia, industry experts have expressed guarded optimism that they were likely to have a significant impact within a few years (Blum 2004, LSE 2005).

ONLINE AUTHENTICATION UNDER EU LAW

The EU, as a union of nations with different legal traditions, faces formidable challenges in finding harmonized solutions to problems like the regulation of online authentication technologies. Within the EU, countries responded to the growth of Internet commerce in a wide variety of ways. The United Kingdom, which shares a common law legal culture with the US and which is sometimes nearly as deferential as the US to market forces in its regulatory objectives, refrained from enacting any legislation to regulate the use of electronic signatures. UK regulators, influenced by a strong UK industry reaction against such legislation, generally opposed such legislation on principle, believing that businesses should be allowed to work out what technologies suited their purposes best and confident that UK courts would find a way to sort through whatever evidence the parties might present in the event of litigation concerning electronic contracts. The result was tScheme, an independent self-regulatory scheme set up to review and certify trust services, including electronic signature services. By contrast, Germany was the first country in Europe to enact a Utah-style, technology-specific digital signature law in 1997. The German government and others in Germany, including consumer groups, felt that the stringent writing requirements in German law could only be met by promoting the use of an equally stringent technology such as digital signatures (Kuner 1998A, 1998B). At the time the German Digital Signature Law was enacted, Kuner noted:

The Digital Signature Law is a technical law, since it does not deal with the legal validity of digital signatures; rather, its purpose is to provide the conditions for a secure infrastructure for the use of digital signatures in Germany. While compliance with the Law is "voluntary", the German government is open about its intention to create a de facto standard for the use of digital signatures; for this reason, it is a matter for concern that the Federal Office for Information Security (BSI), [a US National Security Agency]-type government agency, is deeply involved in setting technical standards under the law. (Kuner 1997)

The German law and a similar Italian law enacted soon after also required trusted third parties providing digital signature certification services to be licensed to carry out such services. Other EU countries did not support either the licensing requirement or the technology-specific focus of the legislation, so there was a danger that the internal market for Internet commerce services would be fragmented by inconsistent national laws. The Internal market Directorate of the Commission was given the unenviable task of finding a way to reconcile these apparently irreconcilable positions in order to ensure the free circulation of goods and services in the online version of the European internal market.

The 1999 Electronic signature Directive was the fruit of those labors. It firmly rejects the notion of licensing trusted third parties, but leaves the door open to voluntary accreditation schemes. Trusted third parties that are negligent in providing certification services may be liable to any relying parties that suffer losses as a result of that negligence. Paragraph 16 of the preamble to the Directive provides that the regulatory framework

established by the Directive is not needed for closed systems governed by voluntary agreements among a specified number of participants. Given that closed systems for online commerce are governed by private agreements, this in effect limits the scope of the Directive when applied to online commercial transactions between parties without any prior business relationship.

The Directive established three levels of legal recognition of electronic signatures. At a minimum, it prohibited member states from discriminating against electronic signatures merely on the grounds that they were in electronic form, without regard to the technology used to create the signature. It also provided what was supposed to be a technology-neutral description of an "advanced electronic signature" (AES) but which in fact is merely an abstract, general description of digital signatures used within a public key infrastructure. AES are defined in the Directive as being uniquely linked to the signatory, capable of identifying the signatory, created by a means under the sole control of the signatory, and linked to the signed data in such a manner that any subsequent changes to the signed text is detectable. Four technical annexes to the Directive describe the functional characteristics of AES, and formed the basis of later electronic signature standard-development efforts described below.

The most stringent requirements in the Directive apply to "qualified signatures" which in return receive the greatest legal recognition. Qualified signatures are based on the use of "qualified certificates" (which identify the issuer and the signatory, provide a means of verifying the signature, describe any attributes of the signatory if relevant, give the term during which the certificate is valid, and contain the signature of the issuer), and are created by means of a "secure signature creation device" (e.g., a smart card that holds a private key). Adding a requirement that the private signing key be stored apart from the hard drive of a personal computer greatly reduces the risk of forgery. The Directive creates an incentive for business use of qualified electronic signatures by providing that they shall be treated as equivalent to a handwritten signature under national law. The value of this incentive is limited to the extent that there are few handwritten signature requirements that would apply to electronic commerce. Furthermore, any handwritten signature requirements that existed in 1999 when the Electronic signature Directive was passed should eventually be eliminated by the requirement in the 2002 Electronic commerce Directive that member states eliminate any legal obstacles to electronic commerce (Dumortier 2004).

The Directive was clearly influenced by the structure of New Approach directives, but perhaps should be thought of as a "light" form because it lacks some of the elements of a New Approach directive. In the manner of a New Approach directive, it merely sets forth the general "essential requirements" rather than detailed specifications. The four technical annexes to the Directive spell out functional requirements for "qualified certificates," "certification service providers," "secure signature creation devices," and procedures for signature verification. However, there is no explicit link to one of the European Standards Organizations (the European Committee for Standardization (CEN), European Committee for Electrotechnical Standardization (CENELEC) and the European Telecommunications Standards Institute (ETSI)) to develop standards based on the technical annexes. The Directive provides instead that the Commission may publish in the Official Journal information about "generally recognized standards" for electronic signature products. Although the concept of "generally recognized" standards was left undefined, it appears to bear some relationship to market-based standards.

Notwithstanding the perception of some lawyers that an unambiguously designated electronic equivalent of a legal signature would be essential for electronic commerce, there were in fact no usable market-based standards for the kind of digital signatures that the Directive promotes. As a result,

the Commission issued a mandate to the European Standards Organizations to develop such standards in a collaborative manner with the involvement of market stakeholder interests. CEN and ETSI responded by establishing the European Electronic signature Standardization Initiative (EESSI). This reported to the ICT Standards Board (ICTSB), a strategic group encompassing the three European Standards Organizations and more than a dozen European representatives of consortia. The EESSI provided a work program executed by separate but inter-linked standards groups in CEN and ETSI. The EESSI specifications were published as ETSI Technical Specifications and CEN Workshop Agreements. In theory, they clarify the technical requirements for complying with the functional requirements set forth in the annexes to the Directive, but in practice focused on issues related to qualified certificates rather than to advanced signature issues generally. EESSI standards also addressed a range of issues that were not raised in the annexes but that were felt would be needed by the marketplace when electronic signatures were used in the manner envisaged in the Directive. In July 2003, a Commission decision was published in the Official Journal that referenced three CEN Workshop Agreements (CWAs) as being "generally recognized" as that requirement was set forth in the Directive. As a result of this decision, compliance with the three CWAs published in the Official Journal would indicate that an electronic signature service generally met the requirements of the technical annexes of the Directive. CEN is now upgrading a number of its electronic signature CWAs into formal European Standards (EN).

In 2003, the "Legal and Market Aspects of Electronic signatures" study undertaken on behalf of the commission was published (Dumortier et al. 2003). This study was designed to inform the Commission of the progress made by member states in transposing the Directive into national law, and also to comment on the current state of the market for digital signature products and services in the EU. The study revealed that digital signatures were not being used among private parties with no prior business relationship to authenticate each other as part of a process of forming contracts. To the extent that large numbers of digital signatures and certificates were in use, they were being used in connection with "e-government" programs in those jurisdictions, such as Germany, Austria and Italy, where their use was a mandatory condition for access to certain public sector services. Given that the study was published in 2003, and that the EESSI standards had only been completed in 2002, the absence of private sector adoption of qualified signatures might have been attributable to the normal time lag between the development of a standard and the adoption of technologies based on the standard by end users.

In the years following the publication of the study, there appears to be no new evidence of any growth in private sector adoption of digital signatures in the EU for contracting purposes, although the use of the technology is continuing to grow in response to specific public sector mandates. While the scope of the Directive was not limited to commercial transactions, that was clearly one of the categories of online activities the Directive was intended to facilitate. It has now become apparent that the framework established by the Directive does not provide much value to private parties forming contracts in online environments. Because neither AES nor qualified signatures have gained any significant market acceptance with regard to commercial transactions, the Directive is failing to achieve one of its objectives: reducing the uncertainty associated with migrating traditional business processes into online environments.

A study by the Commission in 2006 conceded that market adoption of electronic signatures had not developed as expected (Commission 2006). The Commission study identifies as possible factors contributing to this failure the complexity of the technology and the reluctance of certification service providers to act as "trusted third parties"

out of liability concerns. As a result, organizations that provide authentication services do so in a manner that prevents those services from being used in transactions with third parties, such as by requiring the use of one-time password devices. Federated identity systems based on single sign-on technologies have been designed with end user convenience in mind, so their complexity is not apparent to individual users. While PKI technologies may be embedded within federated identity management systems, individual users are no longer required to navigate the process of obtaining and validating public key certificates because the PKI functions operate at a lower level of network function than the AES model anticipated.

In 2009, the Commission adopted a proposal to change e-invoicing regulations to remove the obligation to use electronic data interchange or advanced electronic signatures in order for electronic VAT invoices to recognized as equivalent to paper invoices (EU 2009). The 2001/115/EC Directive on Invoicing, as amended by the 2006/112/EC Directive provided that electronic invoices must be recognized as equivalent to paper invoices only if they were authenticated using EDI or AES technologies. The Commission's 2009 proposal to remove the EDI or AES condition to the validity of e-invoices came in response to complaints from the business community received during a public consultation on barriers to the adoption of e-invoicing which targeted burdensome authentication requirements as a fundamental problem. The proposal by the DG Taxation to remove the AES requirement because it had become a barrier to the adoption of new technologies by small and medium sized enterprises in Europe is significant as the first public acknowledgement of the failure of EU electronic signature policies to achieve their stated goals.

The amount of information provided by federated identity systems in order to authenticate an individual or an object (such as a program) is tailored to the situation for which authentication is required, and so much of the information required for an AES may be missing. For example, a user may merely be identified as a faculty member or student covered by an institutional subscription to a journal and not identified by name when authenticated using Shibboleth. The information relevant to the authentication process may not include a public key associated with an individual person as required for an AES because the relevant authentication may be of an organization or an object such as a program. The concept of reliance on authentication information provided by a trusted third party who is not a party to the transaction has been superseded by a more rational, clearer division of responsibility among the party being authenticated, the relying party and the authentication service provider. For example, instead of asking the service provider to manage most of the risk associated with binding an individual person to an online identity, and exposing the service provider to liability for relying party losses that later occur, the relying party may be allocated responsibility for reviewing "assertions" or "claims" made about the party to be authenticated and making a decision about what is an acceptable level of risk associated with those statements. In other words, identity management "best practices" emerging in the 2000s may bear little or no relationship to the 1990s public key infrastructure design incorporated into the Directive.

The Directive has not provided a framework for online commerce as expected in part because the information required for an electronic signature may not be the information businesses needed to enter into online transactions with new trading partners. AES provides information about the legal identity of individuals, yet that information may play a very small role in the calculus transacting parties use in deciding whether to enter into a transaction. In order for the information provided by the certification service provider to be useful to potential trading partners with no prior relationship, it would have to be combined with other information such as creditworthiness, which is outside the scope of the Directive. Another reason

is that there has proved to be no viable business model for certification service providers because their potential liability may be large, yet market conditions did not permit them to charge a high enough price to cover their potential exposure and still be certain to make a profit. The due diligence required to bind an individual person to an online identity is potentially enormous, but the demand for such services has proven to be so minimal that no business model to recapture the true cost of assuring the reliability of certificates has been found (Lamberti 2005). By contrast, the identity management systems emerging as a result of the efforts of the Liberty Alliance and WS-I have grown out of careful analysis of both the business needs of transacting parties and the business objectives of authentication service providers.

At best, the Directive appears to be ineffective at promoting the growth of electronic commerce in Europe. At worst, in member states whose governments continue to promote actively the adoption of digital signature technologies, it may push businesses in those countries to incur significant costs with negligible benefits in return. This is because the PKI model of deploying digital signature models tries to solve too many separate problems at once, and ends up solving none of them particularly well. This shortcoming is demonstrated by the fact that some organizations have been able to make some aspects of the PKI model work in some situations, but attempts to make the overall system work have foundered (Garfinkel 2005). Given that the Directive has some similarities to the highly successful "New Approach" model of legislation, how could the result in this case be such a disappointment? The simplest, most obvious answer is that the Commission put its money on the wrong horse: European and national regulators were aiming to be technology neutral, but in fact fell into the trap of trying to anticipate the "next big thing" in electronic commerce technologies and failed. But this answer just begs the question of why the wrong choice was so attractive to so many people.

The attractiveness of the 1990s model of digital signatures appears to have been due to the appeal of a mistaken analogy for many people steeped in a particular type of legal culture. Some legal cultures place more emphasis on a very formal notion of legal signature than others, just as some political cultures are more supportive of government intervention in markets than others. Some of the most ardent advocates of the most technology-specific aspects of the Directive were from Germany, which has a formalist, regulatory legal culture. Many of the skeptics of the technology-specific approach in the Directive came from the UK, which has a legal system that is relatively flexible and accommodating with regard to what can constitute a legal signature (Wilsher and Hill 2003). In addition, many German legal professionals seem to have a higher degree of confidence than their peers in other legal systems that regulations can determine practical business outcomes. US legal professionals, by contrast, often manifest a high degree of skepticism about the practical impact of regulatory mandates (Tyler 1990).

When belief that an electronic analogue of a very specific notion of legal signature was a necessary precondition to the growth of electronic commerce, and the confidence that law reform designating such an electronic analogue would be adequate to change business behavior intersected with the aggressive marketing efforts of those with rights in a proprietary authentication technology commonly referred to as a "signature," a law reform juggernaut was formed. The resulting *fausse bonne idée*—that the "digital signature" need only be designated by law as equivalent to a legal signature to solve the authentication problem—has proven remarkably resilient. In the context of EU electronic signature laws, it also short-circuited any possible effort to discover what the transacting parties' requirements for authentication technologies actually were, as well as the attendant costs and benefits of different technological models for delivering authentication services were.

HARMONIZING US AND EU APPROACHES?

The recent controversy in the EU surrounding the widespread adoption of radio frequency identifier ("RFID") technology illustrates both the challenges facing the EU system for ICT standard developing, and Commission efforts to overcome those challenges by finding ways to make use of consortia standards to achieve EU policy goals. RFID technology permits automatic identification and data capture by means of radio communications. RFID systems include a tag that can receive radio signals and that can store, and possibly even process, information; a reader that transmits and detects radio waves returned from tags; and a system for collecting data. The earliest predecessor to modern RFID system was used by pilots in World War II to help their ground crews detect whether an incoming plane was a "friend or foe."

Work began on the first RFID standard relevant to current mass-market applications in the ISO/IEC Joint Technical Committee 1/SC 31 in 1997. In 1999, the Uniform Code Council, EAN International, Proctor & Gamble, and Gillette provided funding to the Massachusetts Institute of Technology to establish the Auto-ID Center, which developed the network communications model currently in use in mass-market RFID applications. Since then, many major multinational corporations have worked to develop a wide range of commercial applications for this technology. During the 2000s, RFID tags came into widespread use in certain sectors. GS1, the successor to the Uniform Code Council and EAN International, emerged as the most important international RFID standard-developing organization. GS1 is a standard-developing consortium, and its members include business enterprises from around the world. In 2003, GS1 together with GS1 U.S. formed EPCglobal, a global membership organization that works to promote the adoption of "electronic product codes" and RFID technology. EPCglobal develops standards, provides conformity certification for products, accredits other organizations to provide conformity testing, and provides training, marketing and political advocacy for RFID products and services. Due in part to the promotional efforts of SDOs and trade associations such as EPCglobal, adoption rates for RFID technologies were increasing in the U.S. and in Europe.

Although concern among privacy advocates about potential privacy invasive uses of RFID technology had been expressed since the early 2000s, the controversy surrounding privacy and security issues created by unregulated commercial RFID applications escalated dramatically when Vivian Reding, Commissioner for Information Society, launched a public consultation in 2006. The public consultation was intended to establish global standards for RFID technology and insure their compliance with EU data protection laws. This was followed by a Commission Communication in 2007 articulating the twin EU goals of harnessing RFID as a tool to promote innovation and growth as well as insuring that its use complies with EU law (Commission 2007). In 2008, work began on several projects designed to help coordinate the EU response to RFID developments and contribute to the development of EU-compliant RFID technologies, including Coordination and Support Action for Global RFID-Related Activities and Standardisation ("CASAGRAS"), the Global RFID Interoperability Forum for Standards ("GRIFS"), and the Cluster for European RFID Projects ("CERP"), all of which received major funding through the Seventh Framework Programme, the EU's primary program for funding scientific research.

Although the EU response to regulatory challenges created by rapid adoption of RFID technology has been multifaceted and broad, it has also tended to proceed on bureaucratic time rather than Internet time. In 2009, it is too soon to know what impact EU efforts to change the institutional framework within which RFID prod-

ucts and standards are developed and used will have in global markets. In order to overcome the "privacy invasive" character of RFID standards developed in industry-dominated consortia over the last decade with little input from end users or regulators, significant changes in the design of commercial RFID systems will be needed. In response to the 2007 Commission Communication, Peter Hustinx, the European Data Protection Supervisor ("EDPS"), issued an opinion in 2008 arguing that not enough was being done to insure that RFID applications were deployed in a manner that respected the privacy rights of EU citizens (EDPS 2008). In this Opinion, the EDPS noted the need for clearer guidance on how to apply the current legal framework to the RFID environment and for new EU legislation to regulate RFID use. In addition, the EDPS argued for recognition of the "opt-in" principle for collection of personally identifiable information by means of RFID technology, and the identification of "Best Available Techniques" which would support the privacy-by-design principle. However, a 2008 report issued by GRIFS on the "state of the art" of RFID standards noted, "There have been a number of proposals, particularly from an academic base, to introduce privacy enhancing technologies (PETs) to RFID technologies. Few, almost none, of such PETs are so far present in the devices and air interface protocol standards." (GRIFS 2008 at 110.)

Within the Commission, DG Enterprise has also launched an initiative to reform EU ICT standards policies to reduce the likelihood that ICT technologies such as RFID will be standardized by consortia with little or no reference to EU law or policy. The Commission has suggested that moving from informal coordination among politically based *de jure* and market-based *de facto* international ICT SDOs to formal legal recognition could be based on the criteria developed by the WTO with reference to the Code of Good Practice for the Preparation, Adoption and Application of Standards contained in Annex 3 to the WTO Agreement on Technical Barriers to

Trade (WTO 2000). These principles include openness, consensus, balance, transparency, ongoing support and maintenance of finished standards, public availability, intellectual property licensing on reasonable terms, relevance to market requirements, neutrality and stability, and quality. In 2008, the Commission asked for feedback on the idea that reference might be made to *de facto* standards that comply with these principles in EU legislation (Commission 2008). If the Commission were to adopt such a policy, then it could reference consortia standards in lieu of *de jure* European standards in European legislation or policy documents whenever they appear better suited to the achievement of EU policies. This possibility, in turn, might influence ICT consortia such as GS1 and EPCglobal to focus on EU regulatory and policy issues before standards have been completed and implemented.

CONCLUSION

In 2009, the outcome of regulatory competition between the US and EU with regard to promoting standards for authentication of transacting parties in Internet commerce had not yet been decided because strong, cost-effective authentication technologies were not yet widely in use in either jurisdiction. The EU required member states to enact legislation to promote the use of a particular technology that has not turned out to be effective in meeting the needs of transacting parties. As a result, the legislation has not played much of a role in promoting the growth of online commerce in the internal market by building trust. Although in 2009, DG Taxation announced its intention to abandon efforts promote the use of Advanced Electronic signatures governed by the Electronic signature Directive, DG Information Society and DG Internal market have not made similar announcements, nor have member states such as Germany that have been most committed to promoting the use of this technology.

The US "market-led" approach to promoting the development of standards for strong authentication has similarly failed up to this point to achieve widespread implementation of strong authentication. However, the US approach of regulatory deference to business innovation has succeeded in fueling the growth of online commerce in the US, even in the absence of effective strong authentication technologies. The true costs of having built an architecture for online markets with scant attention to information security problems, including the authentication problem, are only now becoming obvious in the US. It will soon be apparent whether efforts of US-based consortia will succeed in producing standards that can support the adoption of strong authentication technologies. It will take longer to see whether the market-led approach of US regulators will provide adequate incentives for US businesses to implement technologies based on those standards, and so to achieve their widespread adoption once they finally become available. Of course, if the problem of authentication in Internet commerce continues to defy the best efforts of technology developers and transacting parties to find workable solutions, then at some point the assumption that such a solution is technologically feasible will be called into doubt, and no amount of law reform would be able to fix that problem.

REFERENCES

American National Standards Institute (ANSI) (2005a). *United States Standards Strategy.*

ANSI. (2005b). *Overview of the U.S. Standardization System.*

Benoliel, D. (2003). Cyberspace Technological Standardization: An Institutional Theory Retrospective, 18 Berkeley Tech. L.J. 1259 (2003).

Bix, B. H., & Winn, J. K. (2006). Diverging Perspectives on Electronic Contracting in the US and EU. *Cleveland Marshall Law Review*.

Blum, D., Gebel, G., & Moench, D. (2004). *Burton Group Report on the Federal E-Authentication Initiative* (August 30, 2004). Retrieved from http://www.cio.gov/eauthentication/documents/BurtonGroupEAreport.pdf.

Cameron, K. (2005). *The Laws of Identity*. Retrieved from http://www.identityblog.com.

Commission, E. U. (1999). eEurope: An Information Society for All. Communication on a Commission Initiative for the Special European Council of Lisbon, 23 and 24 March 2000. Retrieved from http://europa.eu.int/eur-lex/en/com/cnc/2001/com2001_0428en01.pdf

Commission, E. U. (2006). Report on the operation of Directive 1999/93/EC on a Community framework for electronic signatures. Brussels 15.3.2006 COM(2006) 120 Final.

EU Commission (2007). Communication from the Commission to the European Parliament, the Council, the European Economic and Social Committee and the Committee of the Regions. Radio Frequency Identification (RFID) in Europe: Steps Toward a Policy Framework, COM (2007) 96 final.

EU Commission (2008, February 8). *European ICT Standardisation Policy at a Crossroads: A New Direction for Global Success*.

EU Commission (2009, January 28). VAT: Commission proposes a review of the VAT rules on invoicing with a view to reduce burdens on business and to help Member States tackle fraud. IP/09/132.

Cover, R. (2005). The Cover Pages: Security Assertion Markup Language (SAML). Retrieved from http://xml.coverpages.org/saml.html

Delio, M. (2004). Solving the Identity Crisis. *InfoWorld*, *36*, 34.

Dumortier, J. (2004). Legal Status of Qualified Electronic signatures in Europe. In S. Paulus, N. Pohlmann, & H. Reimer (Eds.), *ISEEE 2004—Securing Electronic Business Processes*. Vieweg.

Dumortier, J., Kelm, S., Nilsson, H., Skouma, G., & Van Eecke, P. (2003). Legal and market aspects of the application of Directive 1999/93/EC and practical applications of electronic signatures in the Member States, the EEA, the Candidate and Accession countries, 20 October 2003.

Egan, M. (2002). Setting Standards: Strategic Advantage in International Trade. *Business Strategy Review*, *13*(1), 51–64. doi:10:1111/1467-8616.00202

Egyedi, T. M. (2001). *Beyond Consortia, Beyond Standardisation? New Case Material and Policy Threads*. Final Report for the European Commission.

Ellison, C. M., & Schneier, B. (2000). Ten Risks of PKI: What You're Not Being Told about Public key infrastructure. *Computer Security Journal*, *16*(1), 1–7.

European Data Protection Supervisor (2008). Opinion of the European Data Protection Supervisor on the Communication from the Commission on RFID in Europe, 2008 O.J. (C 101) 1.

Garfinkel, S. (2005). Design Principles and Patterns for Computer Systems That Are Simultaneously Secure and Usable, MIT Ph.D. dissertation. Retrieved from http://www.simson.net/thesis/

Gibb, B., & Damodaran, S. (2003). *ebXML: Concepts and Application*. Indianapolis: Wiley Publishing.

Glenny, M. (2001, February). How Europe Can Stop Worrying and Learn to Love the Future. *Wired.com*, 9.02. Retrieved from http://www.wired.com/wired/archive/9.02/misha.html

Global RFID Interoperability Forum for Standards (GRIFS) (2008). D1.3 RFID Standardisation State of the Art Report Version 1.

Graham, J. D. (2002). *Office of Management & Budget: An Overview of the U.S. Regulatory System*. Retrieved from http://www.whitehouse.gov/omb/inforeg/pres_mgmt_regulatory_state.html

Heisenberg, D. (2005). *Negotiating privacy: the European Union, the United States, and personal data protection.*

Hodges, C. (2005). European Regulation of Consumer Product Safety. Oxford University Press.

Kuner, C. (1997). *Final Version of the Digital Signature Law with Commentary.* Retrieved from http://www.kuner.com/data/sig/digsig4.htm

Kuner, C. (1998a). *German Consumer Association Denounces EU Draft Digital Signature Directive.* Retrieved from http://www.kuner.com/data/sig/verbrauc.htm

Kuner, C. (1998b). *Remarks of the German Government on the EU Draft Directive concerning Electronic and Digital Signatures.* Retrieved from http://www.kuner.com/data/sig/gov_ger_eu-draft.htm

Lamberti, H.-J. (2005). Securing Electronic Transactions, 9:9 Electronic Banking Law and Commerce Report 5.

Leeds, D. D. (1997). Raising the Standard: Antitrust Scrutiny of Standard-Setting Consortia in High Technology Industries, 7 Fordham Intell. Prop. Media & Ent. L.J. 641 (1997).

London School of Economics (2005). *The Identity Project: An assessment of the UK Identity Cards Bill and its implications.*

McGarity, T. O. (1996). The Expanded Debate over the Future of the Regulatory State, 63 U. Chicago Law Rev. 1463.

Miller, A. S. (1995). Environmental Regulation, Technological Innovation and Technology-Forcing, Natural Resources & Environment, Fall 1995 at 64.

Morgan, R. L., et al. (2004). Federated Security: The Shibboleth Approach. *Educause Quarterly, 27*(4). Retrieved from http://www.educause.edu/apps/eq/eqm04/eqm0442.asp

Pelkmans, J. (1987). The New Approach to Technical Harmonization and Standardization. *Journal of Common Market Studies, 25*(3), 249. doi:10.1111/j.1468-5965.1987.tb00294.x

Pelkmans, J. (2001). The GSM standard: explaining a success story. *Journal of European Public Policy, 8*(3), 432–453. doi:10.1080/13501760110056059

Revesz, R. (2001). Federalism and Regulation: Some Generalizations. In D. C. Esty & D. Géradin (Eds.), *Regulatory competition and Economic Integration: Comparative Perspectives* (pp. 3-29). New York: Oxford University Press.

Schepel, H. (2005). The constitution of private governance: product standards in the regulation of integrating markets.

Shaffer, G. (2002). Reconciling Trade and Regulatory Goals: The Prospects and Limits of New Approaches to Transatlantic Governance Through Mutual Recognition and Safe Harbor Agreements. *Columbia Journal of European Law, 9*, 29–77.

Shapiro, C., & Varian, H. (1999). *Information Rules*. Cambridge: Harvard Business School Press.

Tiebout, C. (1956). A Pure Theory of Local Expenditures. *The Journal of Political Economy, 64*, 416–424. doi:10.1086/257839

Tyler, T. (1990). *Why People Obey the Law.* New Haven: Yale University Press.

Willis, J. L. (2004). What Impact Will E-Commerce Have on the U.S. Economy? *Federal Reserve Bank of Kansas City Economic Review*, 2nd Quarter.

Wilsher, R., & Hill, J. (2003, October 12). A report prepared on behalf of the Department of Trade and Industry into the impact in the United Kingdom of the EC Electronic signatures Framework Directive. DTI TFBJ/C/003/006 IX.

Winn, J. K. (2001). The Emperor's New Clothes: The Shocking Truth about Digital Signatures and Internet commerce. *Idaho Law Review*, *37*, 353.

WTO Committee on Principles for the Development of International Standards. (2000). Decisions and Recommendations adopted by the Committee since 1 January 1995, G/TBT/1/Rev.8, 23 May 2002, Section IX.

ENDNOTES

[1]   I would like to thank Jos Dumortier, Carl Ellison, John Ketchell, Ira Rubinstein, Patrick Van Eecke, Marcus Mueller, Ian Walden, and Richard Wilsher for helpful feedback on earlier drafts. All errors remain my responsibility alone.

[2]   "Digital signature" here refers to a signature formed using asymmetric or public key cryptography and PKI refers to the "public key infrastructure" within which trusted third parties issue certificates binding an identity to a public key. For more information, *see* "What is a PKI?" at the Web site of Public Works and Government Services of Canada, www.solutions.gc.ca/pki-icp/beginners/whatisapki/whatisapki_e.asp.

Chapter 4
A Step Towards the Adoption of Standards Within the UK Ministry of Defence

Josephine W. Thomas
Loughborough University, UK

Steve Probets
Loughborough University, UK

Ray Dawson
Loughborough University, UK

Tim King
LSC Group Limited, UK

ABSTRACT

This article seeks to identify the factors that have impacted the adoption of ISO 10303, the Standard for the Exchange of Product Data (STEP), within the UK Ministry of Defence. The analysis presented in this article is based on Diffusion of Innovation (DOI) Theory and the theory surrounding the Economics of Standards. Using a case study approach, the results indicate that several DOI and economic factors have impacted the adoption of STEP. These findings offer insights into some of the technological, organizational, and environmental influences on standards adoption. It is envisioned that these results will make a contribution towards the body of knowledge surrounding the factors and barriers critical to the adoption of standards like STEP, and enable more effective development and adoption of these standards.

Any comments attributable to UK MoD employees (as part of the interview process) reflect the thoughts of the individuals and not necessarily those of the UK MoD.

INTRODUCTION

Despite a well-documented history relating to the development of ISO 10303, the Standard for the Exchange of Product Data (STEP), a review of the literature shows that there is very limited empirical research into the factors that impact the adoption of STEP. This means that academics and practitioners devoted to the ongoing development and use of STEP still lack a significant body of evidence regarding the factors and barriers critical to the adoption of STEP. In particular, no study has looked specifically at the adoption of STEP in the defence environment. In this article we present findings from a qualitative case study into the adoption of STEP within the UK Ministry of Defence (MoD). We draw upon Diffusion of Innovation (DOI) theory (Rogers, 2003) and the theory relating to the Economics of Standards (Fichman & Kemerer, 1993b) to identify these factors. These two theories were chosen because they are well established and extensively used in information technology and standards adoption research. The first two sections of this article give a brief introduction to the development, current activities, and research surrounding STEP. Following is a review of the adoption-related theories that act as the theoretical foundation of this research. The concluding sections of the article detail the methodology, case background, and findings that have emerged with regards to the factors that influence the adoption of STEP within the UK MoD.

INTRODUCTION TO STEP

Standards have been in existence since the beginning of recorded history (Krechmer, 1996). Some standards were developed as a consequence of man's desire to harmonise his activities, and other standards emerged in response to the needs of an evolving and increasing complex society, and the waves of human progress and technology. This is demonstrated in the development of standards to enable the exchange of product data. As Kemmerer (1999) points out, "the evolution of exchanging product data in an electronic form arose in parallel to the creation and use of computers. As advances in computational and communications technology occurred, emphasis shifted from algorithm/programming to data exchange." The use of these standards to facilitate product data exchange offered a solution to the high backend costs associated with the use of converters for point-to-point customised data exchange, and allowed product data to be shared and utilized without recreating applications or data sets (Albrecht, Dean, & Hansen, 2003).

Over the years, there have been a number of *de jure* and *de facto* data exchange standards in use. However, many of the early standards, for example, the Initial Graphics Exchange Specification (IGES) and Electronic Design Interchange Format (EDIF), were bounded by their restriction to graphical and geometrical information (ProSTEP, 2004). Therefore, in order to override this problem and curb the development of a multitude of standards, work began in the mid 80s on developing a new overarching standard known as ISO 10303—Standard for the Exchange of Product Data (STEP). STEP built upon the lessons learned from the previous standards and had the advantage of not just focusing on basic descriptions of what data are, but on the meanings of data and how data relate to each other (Kemmerer, 1999).

STEP was approved as a full international standard for product data exchange in 1994 under the banner of ISO (International Organization for Standardization), Technical Committee 184 (Industrial-Automation Systems and Integration), and Sub-Committee 4 (Industrial Data) also known as ISO/TC184/SC4. What emerged from the standardisation efforts was a comprehensive series of documents which provided industry with the ability to exchange and share the information used to describe a product throughout the supply chain to the end customer, and throughout the entire life cycle of the product (Mason, 2002). Therefore, the architecture of STEP was built as a series of parts to support the development of standards for product data exchange, sharing, and archiving. Parts 201 to 240 detail the implementable data specifications of STEP known as Application Protocols (AP). Examples of APs are:

- **AP224:** Mechanical parts definition for process planning using machining features
- **AP 210:** Electronic assembly, interconnection, and packaging design
- **AP239:** Product Life Cycle Support

An Application Protocol (ISO 10303-2xx) is in principle first written independently of STEP using the terminology of the application or industry area, resulting in an Application Reference Model (ARM). This model is then mapped to STEP concepts using the EXPRESS data modelling language. The result is an Application Interpreted Model (AIM), which is the actual data model of the application protocol in STEP (Männistö, et al., 1998).

STEP-Related Activities and Research

STEP is extensively used within the CAD community and enables the sharing of the underlying analysis information in industries such as aerospace, automotive, shipbuilding, and construction (Mason, 2002). Indeed, a study commissioned by NIST found that STEP has the potential to save the automotive, aerospace, and shipbuilding industries in the United States approximately $1 billion US per year in interoperability costs (Brunnermeier & Martin, 1999). Other researchers have studied the history of STEP, the implementation technologies surrounding STEP, and the use of

STEP within various industry groups (Loffredo, 1998; Kauhaniemi, 2003; Zhang & Warren, 2003). However, extensive searches of the literature revealed only two specific studies by Dreverman (2005) and Meister (2004) have been carried out to assess the factors that impact the adoption of ISO data exchange standards.

Dreverman carried out a study, sponsored by USPI-NL (The Dutch process and power industry association), on the adoption of three product model data standards in the process industry supply chain. The three standards studied were ISO 10303 (STEP), ISO 15926, and ISO 13584, all of which were developed by the ISO sub-committee ISO/TC184/SC4. The initial problem statement for his research was: The speed of adoption of product model data standards in process industries seems to be lower than in other industry sectors. Consequently, Dreverman (2005) sought to establish the factors that impede or slow the adoption of these standards within the process industry. Dreverman used factor analysis and actor analysis to establish the issues surrounding the three named standards. The factor analysis was based mainly around the factors identified in DOI theory, and the actor analysis described how the motives, power, and actions of the various actors in the process industry affected the adoption of the standards. This study offered insight into the developmental and organizational factors that impact the adoption of these standards.

Meister carried out a longitudinal study of the development and implementation of STEP over 20 years from the perspective of ISO/TC184/SC4 subcommittee members. Meister notes in his study that, "while STEP is in use in companies around the world, its adoption has not been as widespread as initially expected." As a consequence, Meister's research sought to answer two questions:

- Why were organizations not adopting STEP, even if they were participating in its development through the standards writing process?

• Why has STEP adoption been so slow, or at least is it perceived to be?

Meister answered these questions using a single-site interpretive case study approach, based on three theoretical lenses, namely: Economic-based literature, Diffusion of Innovation theory, and Institutional theory. Meister's study offered insight into the developmental and organizational factors that impact the adoption of data exchange standards from the perspective of the ISO/TC184/SC4 community.

Dreverman (2005) and Meister's (2004) research are the only two studies that have been carried out concerning the adoption of standards produced by the subcommittee ISO/TC184/SC4, despite the fact that to date the subcommittee has published 367 standards, including STEP (ISO, 2006). This lack of published studies on the adoption of data exchange standards like STEP validates the need for the research presented in this article, and reinforces Swann's (2000) assertion in his report for the Department of Trade and Industry in the United Kingdom, that "the literature concerning the factors that influence the rate of uptake (diffusion) of standards is limited." This assertion by Swann is further confirmed by authors such as Bryne and Golder (2002), who explicitly state that the literature surrounding IT standards adoption is limited and that there is a need for more empirical studies on IT standards adoption. Therefore, empirical studies into the adoption of IT standards, more specifically data exchange standards such as STEP, are needed to add to the current limited body of knowledge surrounding the adoption of these IT standards.

IT STANDARDS ADOPTION: RESEARCH THEORIES AND APPROACHES

Due to the limited body of work into the adoption of STEP, a broader review of the literature was carried out into the factors that impact the adoption of other IT-related standards. What emerged from the literature was that most diffusion-related research was based on two theories: Diffusion of Innovation (DOI) theory and a theory often termed the Economics of Standards. Most DOI studies build on Rogers' (2003) sociology model for the adoption and diffusion of technology innovations. This model captures the characteristics of the innovation, communication channels, and social system as they interact over time. Rogers (2003) lists five innovation attributes that influence the adoption decision; these include: relative advantage, compatibility, complexity, trialability, and observability. The social system characteristics can be further divided into characteristics of the individual, group, organisation, decision makers, and the roles of opinion leaders and change agents like champions. Communication channels are important to the adopting community for learning about the existence and substance of an innovation. These channels may be internal or external to the organisation and may transmit either formal or informal communications (Prescot & Cogner, 1995). Mustonen-Ollila and Lyytinen (2003) go on to list 28 DOI-related attributes in their meta-analysis of over 200 information system adoption decisions. These DOI studies show that this theory provides a rich explanation of how new innovations are adopted, and how adoption decisions are affected by perceptions of the standard itself as well as the characteristics of the adopters and their environment.

In addition to classical diffusion of innovation theory, the adoption of standards has been studied from an economic perspective (Fichman & Kemerer, 1993b; Katz & Shapiro, 1986). This stream of diffusion research is often labelled the "economics of standards," and focuses on an innovation's inherent economic value for potential adopters. Two main theories have been used within this economic stream. The first related theory is network effects. Network analysis is often based upon the theory of positive network effects, or network externalities, which describes a positive correlation between the number of users of a good and the utility of the good (Katz & Shapiro, 1986). . . A second factor that is often classed under "economics of standards" is switching costs. In this context it refers to a standard specific investment that makes organizations hesitant to change a supported standard.

Other authors have used Game Theory to understand the adoption of IT-related standards (Xia, Zhao, & Shaw, 2003; Belleflamme, 1999). Fichman and Kemerer (1993a) argue that the variety among potential scenarios is so great that no single theory of innovation adoption and diffusion is likely to emerge. However, they do propose that innovations are most likely to be dominant when they score highly on both diffusion of innovation and economics of standards criteria (Fichman & Kemerer, 1993b). West (2003) contends that a more robust and influential framework for understanding technology adoption in an organizational context has been developed by DePietro, et al. (1990, cited in Dedrick & West, 2003). Their model defines a "context for change" consisting of three elements:

- Technology—The model subsumes the five innovation attributes that Rogers (2003) argues influence the likelihood of adoption.
- Organization—Adoption propensity is influenced by formal and informal intra-organizational mechanisms for communication and control. The resources and innovativeness of the organization also play a role.
- Environment—Organizational adoption of new technologies depends on having the prerequisite skills for effective deployment, so as Attewell (1992) found, the availability of external skills (such as through integrators or consultants) is essential for adoption by some organizations.

These three elements, which are often referred to as "TOE," are posited to interact with each other

and to influence technology adoption decisions (West, 2003). However, the "TOE" framework is simply a taxonomy for categorizing variables, and does not represent an integrated conceptual framework or a well-developed theory. Therefore, the "TOE" taxonomy is simply used as a framework to categorise the findings in this article.

RESEARCH METHODOLOGY

Dedrick and West (2003) suggest that a richer framework for understanding adoption decisions can be developed through a qualitative study of a specific standards adoption case. This case study seeks to confirm existing factors surrounding the adoption of IT-related standards like STEP, and explore whether there are any as yet unidentified factors that may influence the adoption of these standards, specifically in the UK MoD. The UK defence community was chosen because the two cited STEP-related studies have not looked at data exchange standards adoption in a defence environment.

Case studies can be used to collect both quantitative and qualitative data; for the purpose of this study, only qualitative data was collected. Different methods were used to collect data, including semi-structured interviews, informal discussions, and the study of archival material and current documentation. The hour-long interviews were carried out with ten implementers and end-users involved in a STEP project called RAMP (Rapid Acquisition of Manufactured Parts). "Implementers" refers to the individuals both within the MoD and in industry, such as consultants and software vendors, who are responsible for the practical implementation of RAMP. The term "end-users" refers to MoD and industry employees who will be working with information systems based on RAMP. Five additional interviews were carried out with MoD employees who had had exposure to STEP.

Case Background

Few commercial organizations or government departments in the UK can compare with the sheer size and sophistication of the MoD, with an annual budget exceeding £30 billion and over 300,000 service and civilian personnel (MoD, 2005). The MoD also works closely with a vast number of prime and sub-contractors or industry partners to achieve its goals.

According to the MoD policy, standardization is key to ensuring the interoperability, quality, safety, reliability, maintainability, effectiveness, and efficiency of the equipment used by the Armed Forces (MoD SSE, 2005a). More specifically, the MoD needs information standards to exchange/share information internally and externally between prime and sub-contractors within the UK, across Europe, and the rest of the world, throughout the lifecycle of a product. For this reason, it has been announced in the Defence Contracts Bulletin that ISO 10303-STEP is the uniform standard of preference for the electronic exchange of product model data. This is further emphasized in the MoD Support Solutions Envelope, which states that: "Current policy is that international and application neutral standards are to be used wherever possible, particularly ISO standards such as ISO 10303" (MoD SSE, 2005b).

To date, the main STEP project running within the MoD is the RAMP project, which is based on the STEP application protocol - AP224 – "Mechanical parts definition for process planning using machining features." The development of STEP-AP 244 emerged from the desire of the US Navy to standardize data exchange to support the RAMP process. The principle of RAMP is that a reduction in the cost of carrying a large spares inventory can be achieved by the storage of electronic definitions of spare parts as opposed to the manufactured items themselves. Components can then be rapidly manufactured on demand from the electronic STEP descriptions.

Therefore RAMP is a form of "just in time (JIT) manufacturing," and the fundamental difference between RAMP and other leading JIT technologies is that the use of STEP-AP224 means that it is a more widely applicable process that is not constrained to any particular computer hardware, software, or vendor-specific implementation (LSC Group, 2002).

In the UK, the navy had a desire to better control its stockholding of spares in order to reduce the size of its inventory, which was very large, and predominately made up of a lot of mechanical parts. In addition to this, the MoD had reasons to move to international standards because they have a vast number of industry partners all dealing with different CAD and proprietary systems. Consequently, the UK Navy saw the use of RAMP, which is based on an international standard and used in the US navy, as an opportunity to deal with these issues. In light of this, in 1998 a pilot project was conducted to prove that the RAMP system worked in the UK operational environment. Following from that, in 2001 a second study was carried out by a large prime contractor to further test the extent of RAMP applicability across a wider range of products. These two projects concluded that RAMP using AP224 could significantly reduce lead times involved in the procurement of mechanical spares and, consequently, cost savings could be realised by an elimination or reduction of stockholding (LSC Group, 2002). In December 2003 a prime contractor involved in the 2001 study embarked on the implementation of the UK's first production pilot application of STEP-based RAMP within an MoD Integrated Project Team.

FINDINGS

This section details the factors and barriers that have been critical to the adoption of the STEP-based RAMP application within the MoD.

Barriers to Adoption

A detailed review of the data collected revealed nine main barriers to the adoption of the standard:

1. **Difficulty understanding the standard (AP224):** This was raised as one of the main barriers to the adoption of the RAMP project. The implementers interviewed felt that the standard was complex. Many of them attributed this complexity to the structure of the STEP standard. As one interviewee noted, *"The concept of the AIM and ARM is preposterous. It's a real impediment to working with the standard."* Many end-users agreed with the idea that they found the standard complex and difficult to understand.

2. **The standards revision process:** According to some implementers, the revisions of the standard had a negative impact on adoption. The implementers found that newer versions lacked backward compatibility with earlier versions of the standard; this caused a certain amount of rework to be done, causing delays in the development of software required to use the standard.

3. **Cost of the standard:** The cost of the standard was an issue that was raised with regards to the fees that had to be paid to access it. Although some interviewees believed that the fees relating to the standard were minimal relative to the project costs, other implementers disagreed with this view. They argued that having to justify the cost of purchasing a copy of the standard was not always easy on a day-to-day basis when dealing with managers who could not necessarily see the need for the extra cost... Eventually, a licence was purchased, which solved the problem.

4. **Legacy technology:** Another issue that emerged was the fact that some of the legacy technologies around RAMP were

a hindrance. As one interviewee pointed out *"The design end was stuck on a UNIX machine; no one is interested in using UNIX machines."* The use of UNIX was a legacy that was inherited from the original implementations of RAMP carried out in the US. Dealing with this problem caused delays and had a negative impact on the time taken to adopt and implement the standard.

5. **Organizational culture:** A commonly cited barrier to adoption was organizational attitudes towards change. The source of this resistance varied among different end-users. Some end-users were resistant to adoption purely because they had traditional ways of approaching work and were not willing to change. Other end-users were resistant to the possible switching costs involved in having to change their current approaches to work. Another source of resistance was based around user attitudes toward standards. Some of the common attitudes were that the use of standards would restrict the way they worked and would cost a lot to implement. In addition to this, some of the end-users indicated that they had a negative view of ISO standards in general, mainly because of their experiences with the ISO standards development community, which they perceived to be a group of academics who were not connected to reality.

6. **Organisational restructuring:** After the 1998 pilot, there was a major reorganisation of the MoD (LSC, 2002). This reorganization may explain the delays that occurred between the first successful pilot in 1998 and the subsequent pilot project in 2001. This reorganisation would have had an impact on the financial and human resources available to work on the RAMP project. In addition to the reviews and restructuring initiatives that take place in the MoD, the other challenge to resource availability is the constant changing of position within

the organization. Most employees change positions every two years, resulting in very little continuity within a project. To further compound the resource availability challenges, the influence and consequences of urgent operational requirements, or wars, requires people to be reassigned to different projects without notice or warning, again making continuity very difficult.

7. **Industries reluctance to adopt AP224:** This has had a significant impact on the adoption of RAMP in the MoD. The industry was reluctant to take on the use of an open neutral standard like AP224 because they believed that this would empower the MoD to take their business to any contractor who was willing to comply with the standard, which could result in a loss of their business with the MoD. However, this resistance by the industry has an interesting impact on the MoD, because even though STEP is the MoD's preferred choice of standard for data exchange, as one MoD employee went on to explain, *"The MoD has large industry contractors that tend to be very traditionally based and [the MoD] is not in a good position to say, if you do not apply this standard then we'll take our business away. We cannot take it to someone else. These large contractors are very powerful. In the United States they have a larger industrial base so they are able to actually apply these technologies and these standards more easily and we tend to be restrained."*

8. **Lack of information regarding the adoption of STEP AP224:** One of the AP224 implementers explained that, *"There are some [AP224] implementations being done... but the companies are keeping [information about the implementations] within their companies, so you are really not sure what is going on. [Different organizations] are not being informative of their work. That makes it very hard."* What this showed was

that information about implementations of the standards in other organization was not being communicated.

9. **Remoteness of the standards community:** Two implementers who were interviewed expressed that they felt the standards community was very remote, resulting in a sense of isolation and a lack of a support network. One of the implementers stated, *"The only real mechanism for engaging with the ISO community is to attend their thrice-yearly meetings."* The implementers went on to state that, *"There is no community out there that people can turn to and have user group meetings and swap ideas around and get suggestions, it can be pretty lonely."* In their view, *"Developers do not do anything for the standard except propagate it and do not support it."* Another implementer who had more input and engagement with developers agreed that, *"There is a complete lack of anybody to support the implementation process, which clearly you would get if you paid for a proprietary system. So the underlying marketing and support that you would expect to receive for starting on any of these processes is transparently absent when you adopt a standard."*

Facilitators of Adoption

A detailed review of the data collected revealed eight main facilitators of the adoption of the standard.

1. **The emergence of RAMP from the US Navy:** There was a positive network effect on the adoption of RAMP in the UK Royal Navy based on the fact that this project was first established in the US Navy. However, due to the general low uptake of STEP across the rest of the MoD and UK industry (LSC Group, 2002), some implementers noted that

there was a lack of a local UK STEP-related support network.

2. **Related implementation technologies:** There was a positive impact from the related implementation technologies, particularly with regards to the use of XML to implement STEP. The use of XML for data exchange into and out of MOD systems is being encouraged wherever appropriate. Hence, the use of XML to implement RAMP encouraged the uptake of RAMP because there was compliance with MoD policy, which states "XML must be used to exchange information between systems within the MOD and between MOD systems and external partners" (MoD CDMA, 2004).

3. **Pilots and demonstrations:** The numerous pilots, demonstrations, and seminars positively impacted the adoption of RAMP and were beneficial in promoting the standard, gaining interest and proving the standard and supporting technologies worked. These pilots were also able to show the benefits that could be achieved from using the standard.

4. **Internal drivers:** The RAMP project leader explained that the main motivation behind the project was that, *"There is a lot of cost [associated with storing parts] and whilst big warehouses full of spare parts can be absorbed in some form of government bureaucracy...you cannot afford to have this asset that is depreciating at six percent per year. And our shareholders are taxpayers!"* Therefore, there were clear economic drivers behind the use of RAMP, which helped facilitate its adoption.

5. **Managerial Influence:** There were key people within the MoD and several consultancies who were vital in championing the benefits of the standard, and were responsible for getting the standard to the current point of implementation that it is in at the moment. As one MoD user noted, *"Once some key*

managers saw the business benefit and were able to see the changes required in light of these benefits, support for the adoption of the standard grew."

6. **Contractual arrangement:** One of the significant factors that encouraged the uptake of the standard by the prime contractor was the gain-share contractual arrangement that was made between the MoD and the contractor. One interviewee explained that the essence of the arrangement was that, *" If MOD says we need 100 spares, the team within this organisation looks at the electronic STEP-based stock holding and would say you do not need 100 you need 10 and they would have saved the MoD 90 spares, so half of the cost that they saved goes back to the contractor."* This contractual arrangement means that both the MoD and contractor share the benefits and risks associated with the project.

7. **Benefits of RAMP:** RAMP was seen as the only standard decision makers believed would bring them the benefit they required. One interviewee who has worked for over 30 years in the MoD explained this point by stating that, *"STEP seemed the logical way to go and the STEP-based approach [RAMP] was the best way. It gave us that degree of neutrality that we did not have to rely on single source supplier and [it] gave us a capability of holding a file neutrally that we could exchange. We did not feel a need to try any other standards."*

8. **MoD position and policy towards standards:** The fact that the MoD has declared that STEP is the standard of preference for the exchange of electronic data is an indication of the fact that the MoD recognises their need for international data exchange standards and was a significant factor in encouraging the uptake of the STEP-based RAMP project. This was best summed by an MoD worker who stated that, *"I have a*

business to run. It is called the Royal Navy. The best way for me to run my business is by applying standards. That is my corporate rule."

DISCUSSION

The factors and barriers identified can be grouped according to the "Technology-Organizations-Environment" categorization. This section discusses the different factors in relation to this categorization.

Technology-Related Factors

The technology-related factors subsume the five innovation attributes that Rogers (2003) argues influence the likelihood of adoption. These factors include: relative advantage, compatibility, complexity, trialability, and observability. All these attributes impacted adoption of the standard. The relative advantage of STEP over other standards made it the only standard considered for the project. Equally, the trialability of the standard through pilot projects had a positive impact on the adoption of the standard. This finding is confirmed by Byrne and Golder (2002), who ascertained that anticipatory standards should have an example installation, which can be used to guide possible implementers and help in the diffusion of a standard. The complexity, compatibility, and observability of the standard had a negative impact on adoption. The complexity of STEP is confirmed by Meister (2004), who postulates that, "STEP is a complex standard because of its scope and requisite details, not because of a fundamental design or development problem." Complexity is one of the main factors that has emerged within other IT standards adoption research (Rogers, 2003; Mustonen-Ollila & Lyytinen, 2003; Dreverman 2005). Inevitably, the main impact of this complexity is in the implementation stages, when

time is lost while implementers deal with the complexity issues.

Compatibility was also described by the interviewees as a very important factor and was discussed in relation to two issues. First, compatibility was discussed in relation to the compatibility of the standard with previous versions. Egyedi and Loeffen (2002) explain that succession in standardization is often a problem, and the advantages of improvements must be weighed against those of compatibility. Clearly, in this study the successive versions caused compatibility challenges for the implementers, and like complexity, compatibility is one of the main issues that has emerged from within IT standards research as impacting the adoption of standards. For example, Dedrick and West (2003) found compatibility a key issue in the adoption of Linux.

Studies done by Rogers (2003) and others (Dreverman, 2005; Meister, 2004) show that observability is a critical factor to support the adoption of an innovation. Many of the interviewees revealed that the main challenge involved in establishing the observability of STEP was a lack of information regarding other success stories, case studies, and implementations of the standard. This challenge points to a key issue relating to communication and information channels, which is another factor that Rogers (2003) and others (West, 1999; Mustonen-Ollila & Lyytinen, 2003) have found to be important in the adoption and diffusion of innovations. The voluntary flow of information between existing and potential adopters is important for creating positive expectations. The general availability of information about the standard has a positive impact on the diffusion of an innovation (Nilakanta & Scamell, 1990).

The final technology-related issue was the pricing of the standards Swann (2000), in his study for the Department of Trade and Industry in the UK, mentions how the rate of diffusion of standards use depends in part on how standards institutions price their standards. Though the pricing of the standard was not a main factor in this case study, there is still further work that can be done to look at how ISO pricing arrangements have impacted the adoption of IT-related standards like STEP.

These findings confirm that the technology-related factors that impact the adoption of STEP within the MoD correspond with the factors that have emerged in other IT standards adoption studies and confirm Rogers (2003) assertion that, "standards that are perceived by organizations as having greater relative advantage, compatibility, trialability, observability and less complexity will be adopted more readily than other standards."

Organizational-Related Factors

Chen (2003) ascertains that "*large government agencies are traditionally said to be strong supporters of standardization efforts.*" This was found to be true in the case of the MoD. As was previously mentioned, the MoD SSE (Support Solutions Envelope) emphasises that standardization is key to ensuring the interoperability, quality, safety, reliability, maintainability, effectiveness, and efficiency of the equipment used by the Armed Forces (MoD SSE 2005a). This strong support for standards is driven by the fact that it is a large organization that is at the top of a supply chain made up of hundreds of contractors and industry partners, and effective exchange and sharing of information and the management of equipment is greatly enhanced by the use of standards. What is interesting to note about the issues surrounding the size and type of organization was that further down the defence community supply chain, the response of prime contractors to the decision to use a standard is not always positive. This was particularly true in the case of the adoption decision process between an Integrated Project Team (IPT) and a prime defence contractor involved in this RAMP project. The contractor was reluctant to take on the use of an open neutral standard like AP224 because the company believed that this would empower the MoD to take business

to any contractor who was willing to comply with the standard, which could result in a loss of their business with the MoD. So in the case of the RAMP project, it was important that a balance was reached, and benefit be seen by both the MoD and prime contactor; this was accomplished through the contractual arrangement. This confirms Meister's finding that adoption of these data exchange standards needs to be thought of in terms of supply chains rather those individual organizations. Indeed, some of SC4 members interviewed by Meister (2004) suggested that customers, like the MoD, should promote STEP "by writing it into contracts," which was the case in this project

The next key issue relates to organizational culture towards change. This problem is commonly cited in the resistance-to-change factors identified by Kotter, et al. (1998) in the *Harvard Business Review*. All the factors in this study point to personal characteristics, which show that some potential adopters are more innovative than others (Fichman, 1992). This was particularly the case in the resistance by some of the older MoD employees who, because of their age, were resistant to the speed at which new technologies were being introduced. Age was also identified as a key moderator of end-user willingness to accept new technologies in a comprehensive study by Venkatesh, et al. (2003) into user acceptance of IT.

The second issue relating to organizational culture was user attitudes towards standards. In other words, the opinions and beliefs of users towards standards. Some of the common attitudes and perceptions were that the use of standards would restrict the way they worked and bring no real benefits, plus some users had a negative view of ISO standards...Meister (2004) had a similar comment from an SC4 member he interviewed; he found that in some countries the term standard meant constriction and a change in current ways of working to match someone else. Coombs, et al. (2001) recognize in their study of the adoption of community information systems that it desirable to attain positive user attitudes towards a system. In their view, this may have a beneficial impact upon user behaviour, ultimately influencing user acceptance of a system. Other authors (Zmud, 1983; Davis, 1993; Al-Gahtani & King, 1999) have provided insight into the impact of user attitudes on system acceptance and adoption. However, these studies focus on attitudes towards information systems and change, and not on specific standards; what emerged from the literature was a lack of studies that dealt specifically with decision makers' attitudes and perceptions towards standards from an adopter-centric point of view. These results have, therefore, given insights into some of the issues surrounding attitudes towards standards, and offered an opportunity for interesting further study to test if these perceptions are valid over a wider population of end-users.

In the end, the contractual agreement and managerial intervention from champions within the MoD were the key drivers behind the adoption of the standard. Indeed, Meister (2004) found that having a strong visionary leader or champion was a common element of every successful STEP adoption story. This confirms work by Rogers (2003) and Prescot and Cogner (1995) who did a longitudinal study into the factors that impact adoption of innovations, and they explain that champion support for an innovation means that someone within the organization becomes a special advocate for the innovation, taking actions to increase the probability of successful adoption and implementation, and this was demonstrated in the study. This is further affirmed by Fichman (1992) who explains that, "the actions of certain kinds of individuals (opinion leaders and change agents) can accelerate adoption."

Environmental-Related Factors

The key factor within the environmental characteristics is the impact of network effects on the adoption decision. There was a positive network effect on the adoption of RAMP in the UK Navy, based on the fact that this project was first established in the US Navy. As one implementer said, *"It was quite a sensible choice to a use an existing standard that did have some support and use."* These findings point to results found in research on network externalities. In network externalities, each buyer of a technology receives greater benefits as the user network increases in size. Examples of this include the telephone service and fax machines (Warner, 2003). These benefits include an increase in support and resources surrounding an innovation. Though this RAMP example is slightly narrow, there was an acknowledgement that by using an international standard there would be an increased benefit as more people work to the standard, and one MoD decision maker noted, *"In the case of an international standard, there is a hope that as more organizations outside the MoD and contractor sector work to the standard, there will be benefit in working with the standard."* This confirms another hypothesized factor in the economics of standards regarding the role of positive network effects that accrue to all adopters of a popular standard (Von Weizsacker, 1984). Therefore, the MoD is positioning itself for greater network benefits as the adoption of AP224 increases.

The other key environmental-related factor is the implementers' concern of a lack of a support infrastructure surrounding the implementation of AP224. The issues surrounding the support infrastructure had to do with implementer relationships with the development community. There appears to be a disconnect between the two communities in this case study and a need for better communication channels, which are a key element for successful diffusion of an innovation (Rogers, 2003; Hovav, et al., 2003). This case study has revealed how poor communication channels among developers, existing adopters, and potential adopters have negatively impacted the adoption of the standard. This finding reinforces the importance of effective and clear communication between the stakeholders involved in the development, use, and implementation of these standards. Steps need to be taken to deal with these communication issues, and it is recommended that an implementer forum be set up to address this issue.

Summary

This case study looked at the factors and barriers critical to the adoption of a STEP project within the UK MoD. The main barriers to adoption were the complexity of the standard, the internal resistance to change, and industry reluctance to adopt the standard. According to the implementers, dealing with the complexity of the standard was an ongoing challenge, and they endeavoured to address this by feeding information surrounding the different issues back to the ISO development community; eventually some of their suggestions lead to changes to the standard. The organizational resistance to change was also a key barrier. However, one interviewee explained that during the early stages of the project they realised that you could never completely eliminate resistance to change so they made a point to address some of the fears of the end-users through a series of training activities, demonstrations, and meetings to discuss and deal with some of the concerns and negative perceptions held by the end-users. In the end the two main factors that inevitably lead to the final adoption of STEP-based RAMP were the MoD's policy towards the use of international standards, more specifically STEP, and to a larger extent the contractual arrangement which was first captured in a business case. This contractual arrangement enabled both the MoD and the prime contractor to see the benefits they could realise from the implementation of RAMP.

These factors are the key issues that impacted the adoption and rate of uptake of the RAMP project within the MoD. All key points fall under DOI theory and the theory surrounding the economics of standards; in spite of some of
the challenges identified, work continues on the RAMP project. The first phase is now complete and tangible benefits have been realised. One report states that to date £60,000 of stock reduction has been realised (Dobson, 2005). With these kinds of results, one of the key stakeholders expressed a belief that if this pilot project is completed and successful, then other IPTs within the MoD could become interested, which would cause the standard to diffuse through the organization. This is in agreement with a secondary adoption strategy described by Gallivan (2001) as the advocacy strategy, where an organization targets specific pilot projects within the firm and the outcomes are observed and used to determine continued adoption of the innovation. . .

CONCLUSION

This case study sought to add to the body of knowledge surrounding the factors and barriers critical to the adoption of data exchange standards like STEP. The results also give insight into the nature of IT-standards adoption in the UK defence community, and these results have been matched to the main theories surrounding adoption-related research, confirming factors that have emerged in previous research. However, the factors surrounding the adoption of data exchange standards like STEP are an area of research that is still in need of empirically-based studies: There is more work that needs to be done in relation to how defence-specific standards are being aligned to international standards, and how adoption of data exchange standards varies in the defence communities of different countries. Additionally, the findings offer opportunities for further research into issues such as the nature of the contractual agreements surrounding standards, the pricing of standards, attitudes towards standards and the ISO body, and the impact of a standards revision process on the final adoption of a standard. Further quantitative research needs to be carried out to test the validity of these issues from a larger population within the defence community. In addition, it would seem likely that these factors may not be able to be generalised and priorities may differ for different STEP Application Protocols and organizations. It is also recognised that this case study has an adopter focus; further work and research has been carried out to establish the factors that relate more specifically to STEP, and interviews have been arranged with members of the ISO subcommittee (SC4) responsible for the development of STEP. Together with these results, a full picture will be built into the factors and barriers critical to the adoption of data exchange-standards like STEP.

REFERENCES

Albrecht, C.C., Dean, L.D., & Hansen, J.V. (2003). Market place and technology standards for B2B ecommerce: Progress and challenges. In J.L. King & K. Lyytinen (Eds.), *Proceedings of MISQ Special Issue Workshop on Standard Making: A Critical Frontier for Information Systems*. Minneapolis: MIS Quarterly (pp. 108-209).

AL-Gahtani, S.S., & King, M. (1999). Attitudes, satisfaction and usage: Factors contributing to each in the acceptance of information technology. *Behaviour & Information Technology, 18*(4), 277-297.

Belleflamme, P. (1999). Assessing the diffusion of EDI standards across business communities. *EURAS Yearbook of Standardization, 2*, 301-324.

Brunnermeier, S.B., & Martin, S.A. (1999). *Interoperability cost analysis of the U.S. automotive supply chain*. Project Number 7007-03, Research Triangle Park. North Carolina: Research Triangle Institute.

Byrne, B.M., & Golder, P.A. (2002). The diffusion of anticipatory standards with particular reference to the ISO/IEC information resource dictionary system framework standard. *Computer Standards & Interfaces, 24*(5), 369-379.

Coombs, C.R., Doherty, N.F., & Loan-Clarke, J. (2001). The importance of user ownership and positive user attitudes in the successful adoption of community information systems. *Journal of End User Computing, 13*(4), 5.

Davis, F.D. (1993). User acceptance of information technology: System sharacteristics, user perceptions and behavioural impacts. *International Journal of Man-Machine Studies, 38*(3), 475-487.

Dedrick, J., & West, J. (2003). Why firms adopt open source platforms: A grounded theory of innovation and standards adoption. In J.L. King & K. Lyytinen (Eds.), *Proceedings of MISQ Special Issue Workshop on Standard Making: A Critical Frontier for Information Systems*. Minneapolis: MIS Quarterly, (pp. 236-257).

Dreverman, M. (2005). *Adoption of product model data standards in the process industry*. Eindhoven University of Technology, Eindhoven, Netherlands.

Dobson, B. (2005). Greater efficiency, reduced cost. *Defence Management Journal, 28*, 25-26.

Egyedi, T.M., & Loeffen, A.G.A.J. (2002). Succession in standardization: Grafting XML onto SGML. *Computer Standards & Interfaces, 24*(4), 279-290.

Fichman, R.G. (1992). Information technology diffusion: A review of empirical research. In J.I. Degross, J.D. Becker & J.J. Elam, (Eds.). *Proceedings of the Thirteenth international Conference on information Systems,* (pp. 195-206).

Fichman, R. G., & Kemerer, C. F. (1993a). Toward a theory of the adoption and diffusion of software process innovations. *IFIP Transactions A-Computer Science and Technology*, A-45, 23-30.

Fichman, R.G., & Kemerer, C.F. (1993b). Adoption of software engineering process innovations: The case of object orientation. *MIT Sloan Management Review, 34*(2), 7-22.

Gallivan, M.J. (2001). Organizational adoption and assimilation of complex technological innovations: Development and application of a new framework. *SIGMIS Database, 32*(3), 51-85.

ISO. (2006). ISO Web site. Retrieved February 22, 2006, from http://www.iso.org/iso/en/isoonline.frontpage

Katz, M.L., & Shapiro, C. (1986). Technology adoption in the presence of network externalities. *Journal of Political Economy, 94*(4), 822-841.

Kauhaniemi, M. (2003). *How STEP and related B2B standards support integrated product data exchange in the Web environment.* T-86.161 Special Topics in Information Technology for Production II. Helsinki: Helsinki University of Technology.

Kemmerer, S. (Ed.). (1999). *STEP: The grand experience.* Gaithersburg, MD: National Institute of Standards and Technology.

Kotter, J.P., Collins, J., Pascale, R., Duck, J.D., Porras, J., & Athos, A. (1998). *Harvard business review on change.* Boston, MA.: Harvard Business School

Krechmer, K. (1996). Technical standards: Foundations of the future. *Standardview, 4*(1), 4-8.

Loffredo, D. (1998). *Efficient database implementation of EXPRESS information models.* Rensselaer Polytechnic Institute.

LSC Group. (2002). RAMP *white paper-Driving down the cost of spares provisioning* (Issue 2). Bath: Warship Support Agency.

Mason, H. (2002). ISO 10303–STEP: A key standard for the global market. *ISO Bulletin,* April (1), 9-13.

Männistö, T., Peltonen, H., Martio, A., & Sulonen, R. (1998). Modelling generic product structures in STEP. *Computer-Aided Design, 30*(14), 1111-1118.

Meister, D. (2004). *STEP through 20 years: Lessons and theoretical implications.* Working paper edn. Faculty of Information Systems, Richard Ivey School of Business, The University of Western Ontario, Canada.

MOD. (2005). *Recent trends in service and civilian personnel numbers, at 1 April each year.* Retrieved November 10, 2005, from http://www.dasa.mod.uk/natstats/ukds/2005/c2/table21.html

MoD CDMA. (2004). *Ministry of defence policy on the use of XML.* Retrieved June 24, 2005, from http://www.cdma.mod.uk/suppinfo/xmlpolicy-v1_0.doc

MoD SSE. (2005a). *Support solutions envelope— Engineering & asset management.* Retrieved March 16, 2005, from http://www.ams.mod.uk/ams/content/docs/sse/v3_3_archive/eam.htm

MoD SSE. (2005b). *Support solutions envelope– Data standards.* Retrieved March 16, 2005, from http://www.ams.mod.uk/ams/content/docs/sse/v3_3_archive/ikm%20&%20c4i/gp_3_ed1.htm

Mustonen-Ollila, E., & Lyytinen, K. (2003). Why organizations adopt information system process innovations: A longitudinal study using diffusion of innovation theory. *Information Systems Journal, 13*(3), 275-297.

Nilakanta, S., & Scamell, R.W. (1990). The effect of information sources and communication channels on the eiffusion of innovation in a data base development environment. *Management Science, 36*(1), 24-40.

Prescott, M.B., & Conger, S.A. (1995). Information technology innovations: A classification by IT locus of impact and research approach. *SIGMIS Database, 26*(2-3), 20-41.

PROSTEP, (2004). *Organization/history (ISO).* Retrieved July 15, 2004, from http://www.prostep.org/en/services/was/orga/

Rogers, E.M. (2003). *Diffusion of innovations* (5th ed). New York: Simon & Schuster International.

Swann, P. (2000). *The economics of standardization.* Retrieved January 24, 2004, from http://www.dti.gov.uk/strd/fundingo.htm#swannrep

Venkatesh, V., Morris, M., Davis, G., & Davis, F. (2003). User acceptance of information technology: Toward a unified view. *MIS Quarterly, 27(3),* 425-478.

Von Weizsacker, C.C. (1984). The costs of substitution. *Econometrica, 52(5),* 1085-1116.

Warner, A.G. (2003). Block alliances in formal standard setting environments. *International Journal of IT Standards and Standardization Research, 1(1),* 1-18.

West, J. (2003). The role of standards in the creation and use of information systems. In J.L. King & K. Lyytinen (Eds.), *Proceedings of MISQ Special Issue Workshop on Standard Making: A Critical Frontier for Information Systems,* (pp. 314-325).

West, J. (1999). Organizational decisions for I.T. standards adoption: Antecedents and consequences. In *Proceedings of the 1st IEEE Conference on Standardisation and Innovation in Information Technology,* (pp. 13-18).

Xia, M., Zhao, K., & Shaw, M.J. (2003). Open E-business standard development and adoption: An integrated perspective. In J.L. King & K. Lyytinen (Eds.), *Proceedings of MISQ Special Issue Workshop on Standard Making: A Critical Frontier for Information Systems,* Minneapolis: MIS Quarterly, (pp. 222-235).

Zhang, J., & Warren, T.L. (2003). *SMEs and STEP.* Contract Number F34601-95-D-00376. Oklahoma State University School of Industrial Engineering and Management: Computer Assisted Technology Transfer (CATT) Research Program.

Zmud, R.W. (1983). The effectiveness of external information channels in facilitating innovation within software development groups. *MIS Quarterly, 7(2),* 43-58.

This work was previously published in the International Journal of IT Standards and Standardization Research, Vol. 6, Issue 1, edited by K. Jakobs, pp. 55-69, copyright 2008 by IGI Publishing (an imprint of IGI Global).

Chapter 5

On Aligning the Properties of Standards with the Needs of Their Direct Users, Network Operators

Krzysztof M. Brzeziński
Warsaw University of Technology, Poland

ABSTRACT

Network Operators (NOs) are the important stakeholders in standardization. For the ongoing development of their infrastructure and service portfolio, they directly use "external" telecommunications standards developed by the SDOs, and both produce and use the company standards, customarily referred to as Operator's Technical Requirements (ORs). It is shown that the specific needs of NOs are not properly reflected in the current structure and contents of the external standards. As a consequence, the process of developing and using the ORs is costly and inefficient. This chapter presents an alternative, formalized methodology for ORs, called OpTeR. A part of this methodology is a lightweight semi-formal notation, which is amenable to handling by a computer support tool. The methodology makes explicit the nature of the current inadequacy of external standards, and allows for a "detour." However, to achieve the optimum performance of the method, the authors propose that the external standards be extended with a new part, called Embedded Capability Relations, that would serve as a common base for ORs.

INTRODUCTION

In this study we focus on the important stakeholder in standardization, and a direct user of telecommunications standards – a Network Operator (NO). The Operator is constrained by the need for interoperability (and thus *conformance* to standards and regulations), his own existing infrastructure /

service capability, and economic aspects. On the other hand, the Operator naturally aims at extending the range and quality of services, increasing the performance of his network, and generally - *differentiating* himself from the competition on a deregulated telecommunications market. The generic task of the Operator is thus the ongoing *development* of his infrastructure and service portfolio. The inherent part of this activity has always been the formulation of *Operator's Requirements* (ORs),

DOI: 10.4018/978-1-60566-946-5.ch005

which are a kind of technical *company standards* (Vries & Slob, 2006). The company ORs are related to the "external" standards issued by the diverse Standards Organizations: SDO (Standards Developing Organizations), SSO (Standards Setting Organizations), consortia, and industry fora (Schoechle, 2003), but are not selfsame.

Technical standards and the development trajectory (or a life-cycle) of technical artefacts are interrelated. The underlying idea of the product development process is to apply consecutive transformations to descriptions, towards a final outcome of the process – a product. Technical standards are used within the development process of the majority of complex technical systems to influence, guide and constrain the transformations, the descriptions being transformed, or both. This understanding is consistent with the well-known definition of a standard, formulated by ISO (ISO/IEC, 2004).

In the domain of ICT (Information and Communications Technology), a *product standard* normally contains a description of a certain aspect of a product. This description is usually referred to as a *specification*. In this context, the terms "standard" and "specification" are often used interchangeably (Robinson, 1999; Dickerson, 2007; Shapiro, Richards, Rinow, & Schoechle, 2001). In this sense, a standard is thus an entity that is being transformed. Its structure, level of detail and formality, completeness, internal consistency, modularity / granularity, notation (means of expression) – all these formal (i.e., concerned with the *form*) aspects are important for the process. A standard may have a form that is suitable, or unsuitable, for a transformation that is about to be applied. The subject who applies transformations, and thus is a *direct user* of a standard, is justified in expecting that his needs will be met.

A standard is also a technical artefact – a product of its own development cycle (Egyedi, 2002; Sherif, 2001; Vries, 2001b). In theory, the needs and expectations of the users of this product, if properly identified and expressed, should provide

feedback to the development process, and eventually – bring a change to the characteristics of a standard, if these prove to be inadequate.

The aim of this study is to identify the deficiencies of the current practice of formulating the ORs, and to propose improvements that concentrate on modifying the *structure* and *notation* of both the ORs and the external standards from which the ORs draw information. The proposed methodology for the development and use of ORs is called OpTeR (Brzeziński et al., 2008). The modifications on the part of a NO are fully realistic – they can be introduced by adopting OpTeR as a company meta-standard (i.e., a standard concerning standards and standardization), and have been tried out successfully in a number of large projects. The change on the part of a Standards Organization is more problematic, but we provide arguments and precedents for a decision to extend the structure of standards with a new part (ECR – *Embedded Capability Relations*), aimed at a particular class of direct users. The modified structures are shown to be closely aligned with the patterns of their intended use (the needs of a NO) and to be "*fit for the purpose*" (ETSI MBS, n.d.) The proposed notation for ORs / ECR is an example of a lightweight formalism (Heitmeyer, 1998) that will greatly benefit from the use of computer support tools, but that can also be sensibly used without such tools.

NEED PATTERNS OF NETWORK OPERATORS

Among the parties (market players, stakeholders) that are to benefit from telecommunications standards, ETSI MBS names "*manufacturers who implement the standards in their products*" and "*telecoms operators who buy the products to install in their networks*". The emphasis is thus on products that are implemented, bought and installed, and the underlying criterion of success is *correctness* of the products w.r.t. the provisions of standards. However, this statement conveys the outdated perception of the role of Network Operators. It seems to originate from the era of close ties between the NOs (the then monopolistic, state Telecoms), their representatives in SDOs, and equipment manufacturers. According to Egyedi (2002), at that time *"tight vertical integration made the technical agreements between* (PTO's and their national equipment providers) *akin to - what in other sectors would be seen as - intra-firm standards"*. In post-monopoly telecommunications, a NO is not bound to a single supplier, and its competitive business strategy and technical needs are unlikely to be directly reflected in the available standards (Dickerson, 2005). What follows, a NO seeks a methodology for precisely stating and documenting their needs and requirements – *precisely*, because these requirements can no longer be implied. The place to do this is a company standard – the OR (Operator's Requirements) document.

The change in the relations of a Network Operator with other stakeholders is accompanied by the technical evolution of system(s) in the domain of a NO, and the corresponding evolution of the external standards that define the elements of such systems. The telecommunications standards have evolved from defining a single product class with a well defined functionality, through a *broad specification* (Artych, 2003) that defines a large class of possible implementations, from which one has to be identified by choosing the *options* to be implemented, to the current situation, in which the entities to be standardized are not self-contained and self-sufficient devices that just have to be correctly implemented – they are *platforms*. Additionally, the technical domain of a NO is *"based on a number of different standards, each covering only a part of the entire product"* (Moseley, Randall, & Wiles, 2004). Some of these standards define closed functionalities, some – broad classes of parameterized, but otherwise fully specified and "non-negotiable" functionalities,

and some – platforms with only partially specified functionality and applicability.

The generic rôle (and a dictionary meaning) of any platform is to carry and support. The properties of a platform constrain what can possibly be carried, and the properties of the "load" put constraints on the required features of a platform. A signalling platform allows higher-level functionalities and services to be conveniently realized. For example, the ISUP protocol has been designed to directly support a set of well-defined functionalities (basic services - the establishment and disconnection of circuit-switched network connections) and a relatively stable set of inbuilt supplementary services. Other services (external w.r.t. the standardized specification of ISUP, such as DCR - Diverted Call Rejection) often need to be supported by signalling capabilities in a manner that, initially, was not presumed or even imagined. Apparently identical services, even the inbuilt ones, can be realized using drastically different sets of signalling capabilities.

In this setting, the Operators do not only *buy* products that implement one of the standardized functionalities – they non-trivially *co-develop* their infrastructure and service portfolio. The essence of Operator-specific development tasks is now deciding *which* capabilities are needed, for *what purpose* and *how* they should be used, and assuring consistency of such decisions. Making such choices requires the handling of relations between available, actually used, and "idle" functions and mechanisms of a network, such as signalling, and services that are readily or potentially implementable (or not implementable at all). These choices are guided by the *usefulness*, *availability* and *cost* (or other suitable measure) of capability groups in a particular technical context and business case, which clearly could not have been envisaged and expressed in a generic, SDO-designed external standard. On the other hand, the capabilities themselves, and their correctness-related mutual relations, are *pre-defined* in an external standard.

It can be concluded that the Operator's task now resembles a multi-criterion optimization problem. Such profound evolution of the needs should have brought about the change in the understanding of the rôle, notation, and use patterns of structures in which these needs are captured and handled – the Operator's Requiremens. But this change has not happened on a global scale yet. The methodology presented in the sequel is one of the potential solutions.

The ORs are formulated in order to serve the needs of a company itself, and are designed to be used both *within* the company (to work out, store, and internally communicate decisions to other divisions, e.g., business and marketing) and *between* the company and its partners (other Operators and Service Providers, equipment manufacturers and vendors, end-users, possibly – the relevant state agencies). Depending on the context, the "requirements" in the OR concept can mean:

- simulations and projections: "let us see what else we *will need* if we decide to provide service *x* by using capability *y*"
- self-commitment: "we *decide* to provide service *x* in our network by using capability *y*";
- external request, as, e.g., in the equipment procurement procedure: "we *need* and *will buy* capability *y*";
- obligation statement, e.g. towards the users or other companies (Operators): "we *will* provide service *x* if requested by means of *z*".

The ORs are usually issued in the context of a particular step of the apparently continuous development process. A *concrete* OR document pertains to a particular (actual, or postulated) version and configuration (down to a single device or functionality) of the technical and service infrastructure of a Network Operator. Traditionally, concrete ORs have been mostly issued within the context of equipment procurement.

As noted by Vries & Slob (2006), company standards may be formulated by reference to, modification, sub-setting (but also, possibly, super-setting), and composition of other, "external" standards. This is typical in telecommunications, where a Network Operator will consider the external standards as *given*, i.e., treated as the existing and momentarily stable outcome of the standardization process, and *binding* (in a *voluntary* way, mainly for reasons of interoperability). Defining and using the relations with external standards is thus one of the most important elements of ORs, which is directly reflected in the notation. However, in order to assess the "traditional" notations for ORs, and to propose improvements, it is necessary to agree on a very general model of a standard. This model will define the important terms that so far have been used informally: "properties", "capabilities", "requirements", and "specification".

DEFINING, SPECIFYING, AND REQUIRING: A MODEL

A *property* is a distinguishing characteristic (an attribute) that is shared by all the members of a certain class of systems. Logic, and model theory in particular, stipulates what it *means* for a system *s* (which in general is not a formula) to have (or satisfy, or be a model of) a property *P* stated as a formula (write: *s* sat *P*). Another, complementary (and the simplest possible) picture would be to treat a property *P* as a one-place predicate over terms that denote individual systems; *Px* is then a formula which is true exactly for those systems *x* that have property *P*. In the domain of telecommunications systems, the properties that are expressed in standards are predominantly *behavioural* properties – those that pertain to the externally perceivable behaviour of identifiable objects: nodes / devices / subsystems (*protocol-related* properties) and whole systems of interconnected objects (*service-related* properties).

A class of systems may be defined by directly giving its *extensional characterization*, e.g., by exhaustively enumerating all the fitting systems (which is usually unrealistic). There may be no system to list or point to, if none has been produced yet. In any case, the alternative, *intensional* definition may be used. The intensional *property-based* definition of a concept (or a class of systems) consists in stating *all* its properties that are considered essential at a chosen abstraction level, e.g., a set $\{P,Q,R\}$. There may be many actual and potential systems (or none at all) that jointly satisfy all these properties, and thus, by fitting the concept being defined, form its extension: $\{sS \mid Ps\,Qs\,Rs\}$. Alternatively, an intensional definition may be given by a *model*: an object that represents the selected aspects of a system, by "encoding", within itself, the relevant properties (this is but one of the many meanings of "model").

A definition should not be confused with a *specification*. According to the Hornby's Oxford Dictionary of English, a specification is "*a definitive statement of properties (design, materials, instructions) of something made (done) or to be made (done)*". We propose that a specification be divided into two logically distinguishable parts: a definition, and a *modal clause* that states the relation of the defined *concept* to real *objects*. Depending on this modal clause, a specification may be:

- a design specification: "the object that is being developed *from* this specification is *required* to obtain (inherit) the defined properties";
- a user requirements' specification: "the defined properties are *needed* / expected" (ITU-T Z.150, 2003);
- a product / system specification: "this system *has* the stated properties" (even it they are not actually required or needed); essentially the same as system description / documentation;

- a normative specification: "the indicated system(s) *must* have the stated properties" (regardless of whether they have been developed taking into account this specification, or not).

It is also usually implied that a specification be *detailed* and stated *formally*, (i.e, at least in an organized way; not *ad-hoc*), although the perception of what is "detailed" and "formal" differs widely. In general, a specification should be sufficiently detailed and formal so as to be conducive to the task at hand.

The modal clause is often implied by the context. A specification that appears in the context of the development process is understood to be a design specification, and the term "design" is then customarily dropped. ITU-T Z.450 (2003) defines such specification as a "*prescription of the design of an aspect of a product or a set of products*". It consists of a definition (property-based and/or model-based) of behaviour, and modal statements – "requirements". There are many misconceptions regarding the notions of specifications and requirements. For example, the well known "key words to indicate *requirements* levels" stated by the IETF and ETSI meta-standards (IETF RFC 2119, 1997; ETSI SR 001 262, 2004), such as "SHALL", "SHOULD", "MAY", etc., when used in textual (narrative) standards, give rise to quite fundamental doubts (e.g., *who* "should"...). One possible way of resolving this terminological and conceptual conundrum is illustrated in Figure 1. This model will be implied throughout the present chapter.

Let us distinguish a *specification document* – a container for entities that will be further described. The physical form of a technical standard is a specification document. An abstract object (the behaviour) that this form expresses (evokes) is the *object of specification*, or simply, in a narrow sense, a *specification* (*Spec* in Figure 1). This object *has* properties – either given directly (a

Figure 1. Relating specifications, requirements, and implementations

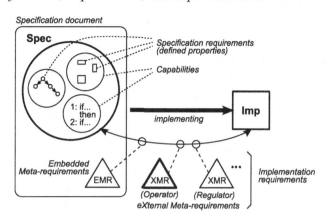

property-based specification), or inferred from a given model (a model-based specification). The relation between a specification and defined (stated) properties can be reversed: a specification *is required* to have every stated property, in order to retain its identity. In other words – the stated properties are *specification requirements*, and pertain exclusively to the specification itself. This view is supported, e.g., by Leduc (1992), who notices that "*the notion of validity of an implementation w.r.t. a specification is not expressed in the specification itself*".

In order to relate abstract specification to its *implementation Imp* (which, when embodied in a real, physical object, is also called a *realization*), it is necessary to state which specification requirements are also required to apply to an implementation. These "requirements imposed upon requirements", or *meta-requirements*, become the *implementation requirements*.

It is often the case that a specification object is *broad* – it represents "too many" behaviours, and only a specific sub-set of these behaviours (and thus a specific functionality) is required to be implemented. For pragmatic reasons, it only makes sense to state a meta-requirement w.r.t. a semantically meaningful group of specification requirements. Such a group is called a *capability*. Meta-requirements state the *implementation status* of capabilities.

Some meta-requirements are placed in a specification document, and define all the combinations of capabilities that are sensible and allowed in an implementation. These *embedded meta-requirements* are exactly the modal clauses, or "requirements", of a design specification. It is postulated that these meta-requirements be kept separate from a specification itself – from those fragments of a specification document that define the specification requirements. Mixing (either conceptually or notationally) these two completely different kinds of requirements is, unfortunately, quite common.

Other implementation requirements (in the form of meta-requirements) may also be formulated. Those *external meta-requirements* (i.e., not contained in a specification document) may be imposed, e.g., by network operators or regulatory bodies. The Network Operator's requirements that are the main subject of this chapter are, predominantly, external meta-requirements.

TELECOMMUNICATIONS STANDARDS

The very general idea of the Operator's Requirements should already transpire from the preceding discussion: the ORs refer to the external standards in order to state the implementation requirements concerning the individual capabilities defined in these standards. The constituent properties of these capabilities are not "touched", as they determine the formal correctness of an implementation of a standard, and it is assumed that a standard is voluntarily accepted to be followed. It is thus important to be able to identify the capabilities defined in a standard, together with their Embedded Meta-Requirements. This is the starting point and a precondition for the development of ORs that refer to standards. Unfortunately, in the current state of meta-standardization, this is a surprisingly difficult task.

The (narrative) text of base standards is the obvious place to look for capabilities, but the major obstacle is that this text is "non-structural". Each chapter/point of a base standard pertains to a certain capability or a set of capabilities. However, the relation between a chapter and a capability is usually not one-to-one, and notational relations between chapters within the whole standards document do not reflect the relations between capabilities.

"Standardized feature lists" are usually meant to provide some sort of a general guide to the text of standards, and they look as if they were an effective source of meaningful capabilities. Indeed, they are being routinely used for documenting the capabilities of individual implementations, comparing different implementations, and stating requirements. Unfortunately, the lists are misleading: we have identified cases in which two dual documents (from ETSI and ITU-T) provide lists with different contents, one being apparently "more thorough" than the other. It is quite easy to imagine an *even more thorough* and detailed list – what will then be the meaning of having more capabilities on a list? It is also interesting to note that the list is very different from the contents of respective ICS documents (see below).

Initially, the inbuilt implementation requirements (the Embedded Meta-Requirements in Figure 1) used to be "hidden" in a standard - literally mixed with the text of a specification. This changed with the adoption of the *conformance testing* methodology (ISO/IEC 9646), introduced to enable the verifiable and repeatable ways of checking conformance of products w.r.t. the provisions of standards. The main actors of this methodology are *equipment suppliers* (manufacturers) and *test laboratories*. To support their needs, the standards have been extended. In addition to a specification itself, a specification document now contains a distinct ICS part (Implementation Conformance Statement proforma; PICS for Protocol ICS), in which the capabilities are explicitly identified, and their respective implementation requirements are stated by giving their *implementation status*. An ICS proforma is handed over to a supplier (manufacturer), who fills in the *support answers* to declare which capabilities have actually been implemented. In the terminology of conformance testing, the embedded meta-requirements, stated in ICS, are called *static conformance requirements*, and the respective specification requirements (defined properties) stipulated by a given capability are called *dynamic conformance requirements*. Jointly, these two kinds of requirements state that any implementation of a given standard should behave as prescribed by the dynamic conformance requirements, within a range of actually implemented capabilities (out of those that were allowed by the static conformance requirements to be jointly implemented).

Note that, *per se*, the notation for ICS documents (Figure 2, after ETSI EG 201 058, 2003, Tab.A.1) does not directly support the task of stating which combination of capabilities (out of a great number of such combinations *allowed* by a standard) is actually *needed*. [ETSI_MBS] remarks that "*an implementer is usually more interested in what has to be done and less concerned about why it has to be done or how the requirement was derived*". An ICS proforma is thus expected to express statements such as: "*(In every implementation of this standard), feature X*

Figure 2. Example of an ICS proforma

Item	<Item description> Call direction	Reference	Status	Support
1	Incoming call	1.1, 5.4.3	m	
2	Outgoing call	1.2, 7.1.2.1	o	

must be implemented. Feature Y may be implemented. If it is, then features K and L must also be implemented".

ICS proforma documents are "*a structured synopsis of a standard*", which "*focuses on different aspects of a protocol*" (ETSI MBS, n.d.). As a reflection of the already existing contents of a base standard, ICS documents should be very easy to develop. This is, however, not the case, as discussed by Brzeziński (2007). Even the relevant meta-standards openly admit that a problem exists ("*Producing an ICS proforma should not be seen as a systematic task ... neither should it result in a systematic search of all "shall" to identify the mandatory capabilities and all "may" to identify the optional capabilities*", ETSI EG 201 058, 2003 ch.8.2). Similar difficulties seem to affect any semantic interpretations of a standard.

A completed ICS document (i.e., with support answers) is used by a testing laboratory to check static conformance (support answer vs. the implementation status of each capability) and to suitably select the tests for checking dynamic conformance.

Further parts of a standard (other than a specification document) that are directly related to *testing* have also been developed. They include the TSS&TP (Test Suite Structure and Test Purposes) part and the ATS (Abstract Test Suite for conformance tests).

A TSS&TP document explicitly reflects the hierarchical relations between the capabilities to be tested, in a more methodical way than the text of a specification. For a given capability, several tests may be provided, and each of these tests has its own explicit *test purpose*, which may be regarded as a re-statement of the essence of a sub-capability being tested. The number of test purposes defined for a single capability gives some indirect indication of the internal complexity and consistency of this capability.

For test purposes, a standardized notation (basically – a structuring imposed upon a narrative text, with distinguished keywords) has been recently adopted: the TPLan language (ETSI ES 202 553, 2008). This lightweight formalism is accessible to users who are not the experts in testing, and greatly aids the understanding of what a given capability is actually about.

A test suite is the "implementation" of test purposes. Being written in a complex programming language (TTCN-3: ETSI ES 201 873, 2008), the tests are much too technical and involved to allow the extractiof of information *from* them. Instead, with a proper technology it is in principle possible to automatically transform a specification and test purposes *into* a valid test suite. Research on the methodology of fully automatic test generation and selection has progressed to a point where it is *almost* possible to apply it to industrial cases of modest size. However, the practice of SDOs (e.g., ETSI) still involves the manual development of test suites, which is extremely costly and time-consuming; a very rough estimate is 100 thousand Euro and two years for a relatively large suite.

Recently, a methodology for interoperability testing has been standardized (ETSI EG 202 237, 2007). This methodology introduces the IFS proforma documents (Interoperable Features Statement) with a notation derived from ICS, and the Interoperability Test Suites (ITS) written in a TD (Test Description) "language" – a structural textual notation. ITS tests are normally not written in TTCN-3 for reasons that seem "ritual" and ill-justified (Brzeziński et al., 2008), but this, at least, makes them accessible for clarifying the understanding of capabilities.

Altogether, a typical telecommunications standard now consists of a suite of individual parts, aimed at particular direct users (formally, these parts are divided into *base standards*: a specification, ICS proforma, and IFS proforma, and *testing standards* that contain the remaining parts). Our experience shows that it is not easy at all to identify the genuine, meaningful capabilities of a standardized specification, and that all these parts *together* are necessary.

THE IDEA OF FORMALIZED OPERATOR'S REQUIREMENTS

The idea of referring to an external standard in order to formulate a company standard is quite clear, but its practical realization is not. The survey of current and past practices (Brzeziński, 2005b) revealed that Network Operators used to create the consecutive versions of concrete OR documents using various *ad-hoc* notations, including:

- the *integral text* of an external standard, with Operator-specific, narrative modifications (additions, deletions, clarifications);
- *delta* or *reduced delta* notation – the headers taken from the text of a standard, with annotations such as "applicable" or "not applicable";
- the *feature list* that enumerates (what is considered as) capabilities of a standardized specification, with informal annotations concerning their implementation status; this device is sometimes ironically referred to as a "laundry list".

The resulting OR documents have been found (*ibid.*) to exhibit a number of serious deficiencies. They are informal, verbose, arbitrary, and prone to conflicting interpretations. They also appear to be a singular effect of some unspecified, expensive, poorly documented process, which involves company "gurus" - consequently, their consecutive generations (issues) bear no verifiable relation to each other. From the methodological point of view, the joint effect of these deficiencies is breaking the formality chain of the development path that has been carefully fostered for many years by the telecommunications research community (Artych & Brzeziński, 1999). From the practical point of view, the ensuing inability to promptly, exhaustively and unambiguously express the needs of a NO, and to verify whether these needs have been met, puts the NOs at a costly disadvantage.

The identified deficiencies of existing ORs (and the actual dissatisfaction of Network Operators with these ORs) have led to a number of projects aimed at developing a formalized methodology for ORs. The ORs that we have assessed and (re-) developed include those concerned with the crucial components and functionalities of "traditional" telecommunications networks: DSS1 (Digital Subscriber Signalling System No.1), INAP (Intelligent Network Application Protocol), ISUP (Integrated Services User Part), packet-mode services for ISDN (Integrated Services Digital Network), PHI (Packet Handler Interface), the AO/DI functionality (Always On / Dynamic ISDN), and remote management mechanisms.

The initial approach to lightweight formalization of ORs (Brzeziński, 1998; Artych & Brzeziński, 1999; Artych, 2003) was loosely based on the idea of *requirement lists* (ETSI ETS 300 406, 1995 ch.8.2.1), which were originally used for conformance testing of profiles. Such a list contains the capabilities taken from an ICS proforma, together with their new, Operator-specific implementation status (which must be consistent with the original status). The assumption was that almost all the interesting properties of a service / protocol must have already been identified and named (at the proper level of detail) in the available ICS parts of relevant standards. This approach worked satisfactorily for DSS1, marginally well for INAP protocols, but failed completely for ISUP - the contents of its ICS proforma proved to be incomplete and, in practice, almost useless for the purposes of ORs.

In virtually every case, the ORs developed according to the "traditional formula" displayed severe deficiencies identified previously, and the burden and costs of the repeated development effort where reported to be surprisingly high. When re-developed according to our original idea, the ORs were also not entirely successful. The common cause of these failures seems to be the external standards, to which the ORs had to refer to. These standards were different for each project, but each of them was "traditional" in form and structure. The conclusion was that *the current structure and notation of telecommunications standards does not properly support the activities of Network Operators. In particular, the ORs have very little to sensibly and unambiguously refer to*. The lack of explicitly identified capabilities (the case of very "sparse" ICS documents) was only part of the story. Even if the capabilities themselves were identified and named, the *relations* between them remained buried in the text of a specification. The resulting ORs were, still, best suited for application in procurement procedures, and the applications of ORs for development proper did not materialize.

This failure led to the reconsideration of the idea of ORs and to the development of our current methodology for Operator's Requirements - OpTeR (Brzeziński, 2005a, 2005b, 2007; Brzeziński et al., 2008). Namely, we propose that the *concrete* ORs be regarded as a parameterized, frozen, and possibly paraphrased instance of *generic* Operator Requirements. These generic ORs reflect a *capability space* – a concept that denotes a collection of inherent, both hierarchical and non-hierarchical relations between the capabilities of the subject matter: the components of a system, a set of services, a protocol, a set of protocols, or a protocol stack.

A capability space can be expressed as a set of statements such as: "*Capability X is composed of X1 and (X2 or X3). X1 makes use of Y1 and Y2. X2 makes use of Y1 and Y3. Implementing Y1 and Y2 allows the capability X to be implemented*". A generic OR document normally refers to a number of different standards. Each one of them has its own capability space, and relations between the capabilities belonging to this space are *embedded* in the standard. When extracted (elicited) and expressed in a suitable notation, these relations form a structure called *Embedded Capability Relations* (ECR). The OR document thus contains a number of "cores" – Embedded Capability Relations for external standards that are referenced. Additionally, it may also contain a "private" ECR, for company standards that, technically, can be handled in the same way as external standards.

When loaded into the OR document, the individual ECRs may then be cross-linked, to reflect the relations between the capabilities of separate standards. These relations are no longer "embedded" – they are imposed by a user of ORs. The generic OR document constructed as described above contains only "static", rarely modified information. However, the OpTeR methodology allows this information to be dynamically used in a number of different scenarios that correspond to the generic tasks of a Network Operator. In particular, the generic ORs can be used as:

- a stable, rarely modified *working document*, which would allow a NO to perform "what if" studies leading to non-arbitrary decisions as to *why* the individual capabilities are needed in a given network, and *how* the required functionality is to be achieved;
- a *placeholder* for particular design decisions;
- a *generator* of concrete, more focused ORs (e.g., issued for a particular type of network equipment, as in a technical annex in an invitation for tenders).

Figure 3. Entities in the OpTeR methodology for ORs

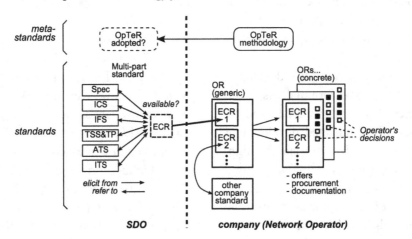

As the ECRs are a part of the OR document, the notation for ECRs is a proper subset of the notation for ORs. This notation should be suitably, but not excessively formalized, so that its contents would be (in principle) machine-processable and automatically verifiable (Artych & Brzezinski, 1999). This postulate is of paramount importance, as the subject matter of ORs in the area of telecommunications is getting extremely complex - the specification part of a single standard may occupy many hundreds or even thousands of pages. Vries & Slob (2006) in their research on the "best practice" model of company standardization also consider a similar postulate ("*IT tools are used in developing and writing the standard*"). However, the ORs should also be usable without a tool.

For the construction of generic ORs it is necessary that the relevant ECRs be present, i.e., they must have been produced *somehow*. The capability space of a standard is a concept that is always there, but, in the current state of standardization, it is not translated into any tangible form – there is currently no part of a standard called "ECR". Consequently, in order to use this structure, the Network Operator must extract it from a standard himself. The one-off task of eliciting the capability space and translating it into the form of Embedded Capability Relations is most delicate, time-consuming, and expensive. However, once the

generic ORs have been developed, the Operator obtains a powerful tool that allows for the *routine* generation of consecutive, concrete ORs. This expensive "detour" may, or may not be acceptable, depending on the priorities of a NO.

In addition to the internal development process and equipment procurement needs, the important use of ORs is *between* the Operators - to assess the prospects for interconnection and/or chances for real, service-level interoperability. For concrete ORs to be directly comparable, their structure should be essentially identical. However, each Operator, while developing his generic ORs, could have taken a slightly different view of the "objective" capability space. The solution is to use a standardized capability space, developed and published by a Standards Organization, as a *common base* for the ORs developed by individual Operators. Apart from technical advantages (consistency), this would bring the reduction of the global effort and expense.

The overall idea of the OpTeR methodology is illustrated in Figure 3.

We envisage that the proposed solution be embodied in a number of standards:

- a company meta-standard, which describes the OpTeR methodology itself; it is postulated that this meta-standard could also

Figure 4. The structure of the OR notation

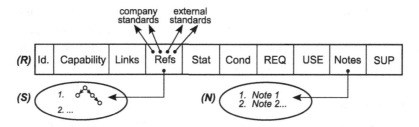

complement the body of external meta-standards used by the SDOs;

- an external standard: the ECR part within a suite of documents that constitute an external standard (the existence of this part is postulated, but cannot be taken for granted);
- a company standard: a generic OR document that *uses* the externally standardized ECR (if available), and *is used* for repeated (in fact – continuous) development work and production of concrete ORs;
- company standards: a number of concrete OR documents produced repeatedly from a generic OR standard.

Expecting the prompt adoption of the elements of OpTeR by the SDOs may be overly optimistic. Jakobs (2003) remarks that some stakeholders *"would rather buy products that more or less meet their immediate needs than get involved in setting standards that may eventually fully meet their requirements"*. This may be travestied into: "Network Operators would rather use external standards that (barely) meet their immediate needs than get involved in setting external meta-standards that may eventually cause the SOs to provide the ECRs". However, the peculiarity of OpTeR is that it does provide for a "detour" and can be implemented even without the cooperation of the SDOs.

THE SEMI-FORMAL OR / ECR NOTATION

The Operator's Requirements are expressed in a structure, shown in Figure 4, which can be used directly as a human-readable document (either printed or displayed on-screen), or handled by a computer support tool. For reasons explained later, the latter is strongly postulated, and a human-readable document can always be produced on-demand by the tool.

The notation is hybrid. It consists of three sub-notations, to be used in three distinguishable parts/areas of an OR document:

- the tabular notation for meta-requirements (R), which is the main component of innovation in our approach; it glues together the other elements of ORs, both stated and referenced;
- the notation for internal specifications (S) of Operator-specific features (capabilities) not defined in the referenced standards. This notation is not prescribed by the OpTeR methodology; it can be chosen according to the task at hand and the availability of methods / tools in the company framework: narrative text, tables, diagrams, particular Formal Description Techniques (e.g., SDL), etc;
- the "free" area for additional notes and explanations; the methodology postulates that the ORs should be fully understandable (semantically complete) without the

need to consult the notes, as these are not intended to be machine-processable.

Each row of the *R* table contains a short identification of a single, distinguishable capability, and a related Operator's meta-requirement, expressed in the form of an implementation status. The columns of the *R* table are described below.

Id (Identifier). Unambiguously identifies a capability within the OR document. To exploit a familiar metaphor, it can also be thought of as providing the number of an OR *chapter* that deals with the identified capability. The static structure of the OR document is thus hierarchical – chapters may have sub-chapters, and may be the subchapters of higher-level chapters.

Capability. States a name of a capability – its "title" or very concise, yet meaningful characteristics.

Links. This novel mechanism allows for defining not only hierarchical (as with chapter inclusion), but *arbitrary* relations between the capabilities listed in the OR document. It contains a list of pointers (notation: "^Id_nr") to (the identifiers of) those capabilities, to which a given capability is related. The relations between capabilities are, in general, asymmetric. For reasons of flexibility, the OpTeR notation does not predefine nor explicitly name a relation induced by a particular use of a Link. According to our experience gained so far, one of the most frequent applications of Links is to point to those capabilities that are *used* or *relied upon*. For example, links in rows (chapters) concerned with signalling procedures may contain the *Ids* of messages/parameters used in these procedures.

Ref (References). Points to definitions (specifications) of a capability, contained in a specific chapter of a standardized specification document, a table/point of an ICS, a group of test purposes in a TSS&TP, or in another company standard. Reference may also be made to a capability defined by the Operator in the *S* area of the OR document. Jointly, the referenced fragments should allow the comprehension of a capability, an in particular – the unambiguous identification of a group of *specification requirements* (required properties, dynamic conformance requirements) that constitute this capability. Additionally, for *traceability*, it is important to refer to, e.g., a group of tests that pertain to a given capability, even if this capability was not actually derived *from* these tests.

Stat (Standard status). Contains an original status value (integral implementation meta-requirement) assigned to a capability by a referenced standard, irrespective of any needs or expectations of an Operator. This value may be inferred from a specification, or obtained from an ICS document. It is likely that many capabilities of a capability space will not appear in ICS tables (due to different purposes of these two documents) and will not be directly identified in the text of a standardized specification. However, if the original status *is* present, then it may be used to automatically check whether the Operator's meta-requirement is consistent with the embedded meta-requirements of a standard.

Cond (Condition). An expression that controls the actual Operator's meta-requirement specified in the *REQ* field, depending on a particular combination of other capabilities being implemented or not (which is reflected by the value of the *SUP* field). Syntactically, the expression is composed of the identifiers of rows that contain these other capabilities, combined by the logical operators (OR, AND, NOT). The value of the expression is computed by substituting the actual values of *SUP* fields of identified rows. If the computed value of the expression is "Y" ("true", i.e., a condition is met), then the Operator's meta-requirement listed first in the *REQ* field is assumed. If the computed value of *Cond* yields "N" ("false"), then the meta-requirement specified in *REQ* after the keyword *else* is assumed, or, if no *else* close is specified, the *n/a* meta-requirement is implied. The absence of any specified condition expression is interpreted as if its value was "Y".

REQ (*Operator's meta-requirement*). An implementation status of a capability, assigned by the Operator and applicable to a given product being developed or described. The set of possible status values is based on implementation status values specified for ICS documents (ETSI EG 201 058, 2003 ch.8.3):

- "M": implementation of a capability is *mandatory*;
- "O": implementation is allowed, *optional*;
- "O.1": implementation of *exactly one* of a set of capabilities annotated with this meta-requirement is required;
- "O.m": implementation of *one or more* capabilities thus denoted is required;
- "X": implementation is *excluded* (prohibited);
- "NR": *not required* (neutral) - the Operator does not care if a capability is implemented (and, presumably, is not willing to pay for it). This meta-requirement does not invalidate a standard status value (if identified): if this embedded meta-requirement was "M", then the capability would still need to be implemented to claim conformance to the original standard;
- "n/a": *not applicable* - the capability is not a part of the current configuration of a product under design, and no specific implementation requirements can or need be stated (may appear, e.g., as a result of the evaluation of a condition);
- "i": *informative* - a capability is out of scope, but it is important to know whether it has been implemented or not, e.g. in order to parameterize the remaining requirements (unlike in ETSI 2003, where "i" means *irrelevant*);
- "H" for "Header": a pseudo-requirement, used for structuring purposes (as will be described further on).

USE. An auxiliary field. Contains an indication whether a capability is (or is intended to be) actually *used* in a given system. For example, the pair (*REQ*="M", *USE*="N") indicates that a capability is not used, but it is / should be available for (future) use.

Notes. Points to a section in the *N* area of the OR document, where an explanatory note concerning a capability may is placed.

SUP (*Support.*) A placeholder for the declaration of the actual implementation of a given capability. The field takes three values: "Y" (equivalent to logical 1), "N" (equivalent to logical 0) and "-" (undetermined). These values are used to evaluate the *Cond* expressions. Depending on the use pattern of the OR document, the *SUP* field is filled by the Supplier (in a scenario similar to the regular use of ICS documents), or by the Operator.

To illustrate the "look and feel" of the notation, a fragment of the Operator's Requirements document (of its R table) developed for the ISUP protocol and related services is shown in Figure 5. In this large project, about 1000 capabilities were identified and cross-linked, and the current state of availability/presence of individual capabilities was recorded. Basing on this form of reusable development information, many Operator-specific services and functionalities were successfully specified in concrete OR documents and communicated to the relevant company departments and vendors/manufacturers.

USING THE NOTATION

We now illustrate the structural properties of the OR notation with some generic patterns of its use. We have assumed that the Operator *needs* and actually *uses* the external standards in his development activities. The initial task is thus to "fill" the empty OR document with its basic contents – the Embedded Capability Relations, i.e.,

Figure 5. A sample of Operator's Requirements

1.4.4	ISUP Availability Control		[A4]2.13 [C31]A.13/24			H
1.4.4.1	Ability to send a User part test message.	^6.1.1.4.8	[C32]IBC_V_8_2_2	O	ANY	O
1.4.4.1.1	Include in UPT a Message compatibility information parameter with compatibility information as specified in *S34.	^2.7.5.2	[A4]ZA *S34	O	^1.4.4.1	M else n/a
1.4.4.1.2	On sending a User part test message, release calls in progress with cause #41"temporary failure".	^6.2.1.18.41	[B4]2.13.2	O	^1.4.4.1	O else n/a
1.4.4.1.2.1	Operator-configurable option of releasing / not releasing calls in progress.				^1.4.4.1.2	M else n/a
1.4.4.1.3	Repeat procedure on failure to receive acknowledgement (any message, including a User part available message and a Confusion message), at interval T4.	^7.1.4	[C32]IBC_V_8_2_3	O	^1.4.4.1	M else n/a
1.4.4.2	On receipt of UPT send a User part available message, if ISUP is available again.	^6.1.1.47	[C32]IBC_V_8_2_1	O	ANY	O
1.4.4.2.1	Include in UPA a Message compatibility information parameter with compatibility information as specified in *S35.	^2.7.5.2	[A4]ZA *S35	O	^1.4.4.2	M

the cross-linked capabilities, with their standard status and proper references. In the current state of meta-standardization, the ECRs are not part of external standards, and need to be extracted by the Operator himself. This is a creative and challenging task. Certain features of the OR notation were meant to help accommodate (or bridge) the structural deficiencies of the current standards. If, as we postulate, the ECRs become a part of an external standard, then the Operator will be relieved of this complex task.

Identifiers introduce the hierarchical numbering of OR *chapters*. In Figure 6a, a capability named "Large capability" is dealt with in chapter 2.1. The capability has two sub-capabilities, each with its own meta-requirement. These meta-requirements become "active" only if the large capability itself is supported (i.e., implemented). Capabilities can be added at the end of the current numbering level, and new sub-capabilities – anywhere, without the need to renumber other chapters. Note that renumbering is trivial for a computer support tool, but is very cumbersome if the ORs are handled as a printed document.

It is often the case that a chapter in an external "narrative" standard contains a definition of multiple, loosely correlated (or not correlated at all) properties. By finding these properties grouped within a single chapter, a user of a standard is misled into giving them joint consideration (joint meta-requirement, joint support answer expected). The "standardized feature lists" share this deficiency – one of their degenerate forms is simply a list of selected chapter headers of a standard, regardless of whether they identify meaningful capabilities, or not. A notational device of ORs that can be used to cope with this phenomenon is a pseudo-requirement "H". A row with a "H" in its *REQ* field is a *header* or a *grouping* chapter (Figure 6b). The capability thus defined has no meta-requirement of its own, and must be interpreted by inspecting all its constituent parts. A header row can also be used to introduce a "new" (i.e., not previously named) chapter containing the related capabilities listed in lower-level chapters. In this way, the OR document may be organized into separate parts (e.g., *Basic services, Supervision, Supplementary services, Charging,*

Figure 6. Intrinsic structural properties of the OR notation

	Id.	Capability	Links	Cond	REQ	SUP
	2.1	Large capability			O	
	2.1.1	Sub-cap. 1		^2.1	O	(N)
a)	2.1.2	Sub-cap. 2		^2.1	M	
	3.1	Group capability		^2.1.1	H	
	3.1.1	Constituent cap. 1			M	
b)	3.1.2	Constituent cap. 2			O	
	5	Service A				
	5.1	Interaction A1	^6			
		•••				
	6	Interactions			H	
		•••				
	7	Service B				
c)	7.1	Interaction B1	^6			
	0.1	NTE (parameter name)			i	(Y)
	0.2	LE (parameter name)			i	(N)
	9.8.2	NTE-specific cap.		NTE	M	
d)	9.8.3	LTE-specific cap.		LE	O(->n/a)	

etc.). If a header row is accompanied by a condition which evaluates to "False", then the whole chapter becomes *omitted*, which means that the meta-requirements of all its sub-capabilities take the value "*n/a*".

A feature of "narrative" standards which is, in a sense, dual to the one identified above is that different manifestations (aspects) of the same capability may be defined in different (often distant) chapters/sections of a standard. This is typical for, e.g., properties concerned with the interaction of supplementary services. Any single capability can only be placed in the OR document *once*: either as a given interaction *with service X* (i.e., in a chapter concerned with service X), or as a given *interaction* with service X (i.e., in a chapter concerned with interactions). Regardless of which option is taken, the capabilities may be additionally *linked* to a header chapter that represents the other perspective, as shown in Figure 6c. An arbitrary number of "viewpoints" on the capabilities can be handled this way.

The preceding discussion was concerned with rephrasing the contents of external standards and expressing them as Embedded Capability Relations. The Operator will also normally have to complement the OR document with the Capability Relations embedded in a "private" part of a specification, defined in the *S* area of ORs. This task may be very similar to what was already described (if this custom specification is taken from the already existing company standards), or qualitatively different, if the Operator designs the custom part of a specification *in parallel* with its ECR representation, and thus can avoid the previously discussed pitfalls.

For flexibility and readability, it is extremely useful to be able to parameterize the ORs with mechanisms like: "IF these ORs pertain to a Network Transit Exchange THEN this chapter becomes applicable". To this end, the names of *informative* capabilities may serve as parameters, as illustrated in Figure 6d. Such a name, used in a condition, evaluates to the support value of its row. In this case it is the Operator who provides this support value. It is convenient to group such parameters (in our case, by convention, in a chapter numbered 0). By providing a vector of parameters, the Operator may easily change a generic OR document into a concrete one, which can be used, e.g., as a technical annex in a contract with a vendor/manufacturer. Parameters may be used to select not only the type of equipment (local exchange, transit exchange...), but also, e.g., a particular phase of the development of Operator's services and infrastructure.

Just two of the design-related functions made possible by the proposed notation, but realized by the support tool (if one is used), are: establishing the *application density* of a particular capability (e.g., in order to find "dead" or superfluous features), and warning against an attempt to delete (or make "excluded" or "not required") a capability, to which there are "live" references throughout the ORs. One of the seemingly trivial, but pragmatically important functions is to sort the contents of ORs in a lexical order of references to a particular source document in the *Ref* field (Brzeziński, 2005b). This operation yields the ORs in a form similar to traditional list of annotations.

Several generations of support tools for ORs have been developed, and the usefulness of the automated support functions has been confirmed. One of the tools provides the company-wide access (via intranet) to particular cuts, fragments, or extracts of the current version of ORs, which demonstrates the feasibility of the *"publishing on demand of the always right version"* concept (Vries & Slob, 2006).

OPTER METHODOLOGY AND STANDARDS RESEARCH

Initially, research that led to the development of the OpTeR methodology was conducted basing on the goal-oriented, real industrial cases, without seeking explicit guidance and justification in the results of research *about* standards and standardization (Jakobs, 2003). The general methodical framework was limited to the theory and practice of formalized specification and verification, and

the available meta-standards. In this section we will relate, *a posteriori*, our work to the wider body of standardization research.

Stability and Flexibility

In *Critical issues in ICT standardization* (2005) it is remarked that *"on the ICT market, the players... have commercial incentives to achieve end-to-end interoperability... while allowing for competitive differentiation of applications and services"*. To rephrase, the general purpose of telecommunications standards is *"almost always to define the minimum set of requirements to enable the product or service to be introduced to a multi-vendor market - to achieve interoperability, leaving room for product differentiation"* (ETSI MBS, n.d.). This is in fact a re-statement of the general question of balancing the role of standards as agents of *stability* and *change* (Schoechle, 2003). The peculiarity of telecommunications is that these two elements are complementary, rather than contradictory. Egyedi (2002) treats differentiation and change as aspects of *flexibility*, and notes that *"there is little literature on the relation between standards and system flexibility"*. In fact, flexibility is central to our discussion. In de-regulated (post-monopoly) telecommunications, the element of stability (understood as a solid platform) can be provided by the external standards developed by SDOs, and the element of change can be handled by the company standards of active market players - product providers (here: Network Operators). These seemingly contradicting aims can be achieved in a harmonized manner, if the external and company standards are conceptually and notationally related to each other. One of the possible ways of defining this relation is through the OpTeR methodology, using the ECRs. Flexibility, achieved by the vastly improved ability to effectively develop consistent Operator's Requirements, directly contributes to the objectives listed by Egyedi (2002): reducing vendor dependence, system extendibility while preserving earlier investments, reduced development and maintenance costs, easier integration, etc. Replacing the one-off, repeated effort spent on developing "pre-ECR" Operator's Requirements by a methodical approach may provide, on a global scale, considerable cost, time and quality advantages.

Specialized Devices: Proliferate or Contain?

One of the options for assuring the required generality of standards is to equip them, in addition to the specification part, with multiple *specialized* devices (parts, notations), provided specifically for the support of particular patterns of use. The IT / telecommunications standards concerning services and protocols seem to evolve towards this "multiple specialized devices" approach, as admitted in ETSI SR 001 262 (2004) ch.5.1.1: "*In particular the aspects of a product which will be of separate interest to different parties (e.g. manufacturers, operators, ...) shall be clearly distinguished, preferably as parts of an ETSI deliverable or as separate ETSI deliverables*". An almost identical statement can be found in ISO/IEC (2004) p.12. For example, the operation of adding the parts concerned with conformance testing has been quite drastic, as it at least tripled the volume of standards, and yet it was considered *important* and *indispensable* for the overall success of standardization in telecommunications. This avenue is currently being taken for interoperability testing (Moseley et al., 2004; ETSI EG 202 237, 2007), which uses the additional Interoperable Features Statement (IFS) documents derived from the idea and structure of ICS.

Our proposal for amending the standards with the ECR part follows the same pattern. It would be hard to justify leaving out the specific needs of Network Operators, while the needs of equipment manufacturers and test houses enjoy full support.

Using the "multiple specialized devices" strategy might impose the danger of proliferation of fine-grained parts of a standard. Superficially, this might be interpreted as *escalation of complexity*. Sherif (2003) warns against the situation in which a standard gets "*hopelessly entangled in attempts to satisfy the requirements of all parties involved*" (p.23). However, this is rather the argument *for* using specialized instruments in standards (the application of the *separation of concerns* principle). Furthermore, in telecommunications, the number of key standards user *types* and their generic roles (activities) appears to be fairly limited. The idea of ORs as company standards allows the diversity of particular, non-generic needs of individual Operator companies not to seep into the external standards, to which Sherif (*ibid.*) clearly refers. Using multiple specialized devices in a standard can also be regarded as a step towards "*simple, small, and lightly modularized*" standards (Egyedi, 2002) - if a given user just looks into those parts that are of direct interest to him.

The "devices" that were referred to above, are mostly understood as deliverables – parts of a standard that are ready to be used by their intended users. Another, quite valid meaning of the term is a "mechanism" or "tool". Some of the specialized parts contain, at least in theory, no new information. It there were a strong, mature, dependable, and *standardized* methodology of transforming information contained in one part of a standard into another, specialized form, then it would be sufficient to provide only basic, common information, and the specialized tools. This is currently possible (in principle) for testing – automatic test generation is gradually reaching the industry-grade level of sophistication. There is essentially no reason why the base specification could not "transform itself", using a proper (so far nonexistent) tool, into the ECRs.

One particular research avenue seems to be relevant to this idea. An *ontology*, or the "specification of conceptualization" (often confused with Ontology as a philosophical study of existing entities), is a formal and explicit representation of a set of concepts and their relationships within a certain domain. Initially researched mainly in the context of knowledge engineering, database systems and Artificial Intelligence, ontology seems an attractive topic also for standards research. In 2006, the first International Workshop on Ontologizing Industrial Standards (OIS) was held. The workshop deals with "mechanized and semi-automatic transformation of existing industrial standards into useful ontologies". A few other publications also deal directly with the application of ontologies in standardization (Gessa, 2007). If the concepts present in a standard are semantically classified and related in an explicit way (i.e., not only in the mind of the reader), then automatic transformations on the semantic level become possible.

Usability and Formality

Preparing a generic OR document is a complex task. Practical experience proves that this *can* be done. However, much more important is to assess if the whole exercise is *worthwhile* – if a user of company standards and external standards built according to the OpTeR methodology will find them *really useful*, in the technical sense. This aspect of standardization is present in standards research, although has been mostly discussed in very general terms. For example, in their "six dimensions" of standards, Baskin, Krechmer, & Sherif (1998) do not distinguish the dimension of the mechanisms of technical usefulness at all. According to Dickerson (2005), one of the postulates for Open Standards (should we say: any good standard?) is that they reflect user requirements. Here we concentrate on a *direct* user – the one that actually reads and manipulates a standard (a Network Operator), not the end-user who consumes the telecommunications products that embody the provisions of a standard (this distinction is identified, e.g., in Vries & Slob, 2006). Dickerson

(2005) notes that Service Providers (whom we also count as Network Operators) have identified their needs and requirements, but their real influence on the Standards Organizations has decreased over time. Here we realistically propose the OpTeR methodology as a *company* meta-standard (which circumvents this lack of influence), and we give arguments for the eventual adoption of this methodology by the Standards Organizations, should favourable conditions emerge.

Vries & Slob (2006) call a standard "*successful if it is used and appears to solve the problem for which it was developed*", and posit that, in order to be really useful, it should be user-friendly. The problem itself, and solutions stipulated by OpTeR, have already been discussed. What is, and what is not user-friendly, ultimately depends on the perception and experiences of a user. While the end-users may only be questioned about their perception and are unlikely to change their habits for the higher good, the direct users of standards are professionals, who could be educated and persuaded to gradually (although with gritted teeth) accept the new and unfamiliar formula. The problem is well known in the domain of formal methods, and the OpTeR methodology does belong, although one may say – only marginally, in this domain. Rushby (2000) provides a comprehensive diagnosis and some solutions. He states that "*formal methods generally require a formal specification or model that is quite different to the other documents and descriptions (...) and whose construction is an additional burden (...)*". (p.95). He repeats the, rarely challenged, opinion that "*benefits of formal specification outweigh the cost of their introduction*", and admits that probably "*the best way forward is to develop a workforce for whom formal specifications are the primary means of documentation and communication*". However, he also immediately notes that the "*path to reach that goal from current practice is difficult, and it is hard to persuade practitioners to undertake it if there are few intermediate rewards along the way*". The pragmatic solution is to let the apparently non-user-friendly aspects of formal methods "disappear" by integrating them with the familiar tools and practices. This is one of the reasons why we strongly postulate using the computer support tools to handle the ORs. Some important tasks of the Operator (such as the production of concrete OR document, given a set of parameters) will then acquire the "press-the-button" functionality (which was also postulated by Dickerson, 2007). That this functionality is real, and not only "academic", has been verified in large and medium-sized projects.

To give a hint of *what* can actually to be hidden from view by the support tools for OpTeR, consider the multi-valued logic of computations on the support values. If a support value is undetermined (has not been given *yet*, or is not expected to be given due to the *n/a* meta-requirement), then for *some* condition expressions it may be impossible to calculate a binary value. The third value '?' is then produced, and its interpretation depends on the mode of use of the OR document. This multi-valued logic is a part of a formal system – the Requirements Calculus (RC), which constitutes the underlying semantic base of the current OpTeR methodology and support tools. We will skip the discussion of this formal system, referring the interested reader to a short exposition of the earlier version of RC by Artych & Brzeziński (1999). The full treatment is provided by Artych (2003).

Tool Support

In the previous section, tool support was considered as the means to hide away the semantic complexity of the "formal side" of the OpTeR concepts. We now look into the wider context of using tools, out of necessity or for convenience, in the preparation (production) and use of standards.

One of the aspects of standardization is fostering the development of tools that would facilitate and automate the handling of their contents. This

issue is emphasized in ETSI EG 201 058 (2003), in the context of PICS documents. For testing purposes, tool support is based on the standardization of the TTCN-3 language and the adoption of this language as the notation for standardized test suites. Apart from full programming environments, there are several TTCN-3 editors available, with specialized functions. For ICS documents, it is envisaged that "*style harmonization will foster the development of ICS editors and interpreters*" (ETSI EG 201 058, 2003). There is still a widespread understanding that a standard consists of text and graphics (drawings), and meta-standards often provide the templates, macros, and conventions (patterns) for "officially recognized" text editors. ISO/IEC (2004) urges to "*derive the maximum benefit available through automated text processing techniques and computer-aided translation*" (p.11).

For ECRs and ORs, tool support seems almost indispensable for purely quantitative reasons, for the effective handling of a very large number of cross-referenced items. Specific, automated functions that cope with this need become then available (searching, filtering, re-numbering, hypertext-like functions, translating, etc.), as previously described. By handling the ECRs by hand (as a text document), the users would deprive themselves of many advantages, such as inherent capabilities for automated validation of the resulting ORs, but such use still remains possible.

A standard "*should be comprehensible to qualified persons who have not participated in its preparation*" (ISO/IEC, 2004 p.10; ETSI SR 001 262, 2004). It is not really expected that the contents of a standard be easy to read and understand, in absolute terms. ORs are highly detailed documents of a technical nature, and a suitable, even very complex notation is appropriate, if it serves its purpose. The contents of a standard written using such notation can be regarded as "*computer code*", to which ETSI guidelines apply (ETSI SR 001 262, 2004 ch. 31 and Annex B.2).

Accordingly, the idea is to present a standardized ECR document as an electronic attachment to a standard.

Antiproducts and the Quality of Standards

We have argued for amending the current structure of (telecommunications) standards with a new part – the Embedded Capability Relations (ECR). This would be yet another extension. The previous waves of extension were motivated by the need to empirically verify the products that claim to embody the provisions of standards, first by conformance testing (ISO/IEC 9646) and recently – by interoperability testing (ETSI EG 202 237, 2007).

The ECRs and the testing-related parts of the standards are targeted at different direct users (the Network Operators and test laboratories, respectively), but both serve the same generic purposes:

- streamlining the activities of their direct users, who are the important stakeholders in standardization;
- improving the overall quality of products developed from standards;
- and, indirectly, improving the quality of standards themselves.

The last point deserves particular attention. Within the ICT companies, e.g., Siemens (Warken, 2006), there is a recent trend towards the *antiproduct* development paradigm. This idea consists in developing, in parallel, two products: a "main" product, and a product that is necessary for assessing (checking, verifying, validating, testing) the main product. These two development processes are, at least in theory, assigned equal status in the "food chain", and each team can consider its product as the "main" one. The current results of one development cycle can (and are expected to) influence the other at any stage, resulting in the synergy of efforts and early resolution of doubts / inconsistencies. If the two products are: a base standard and a testing standard, then the quality of both is improved: "*the development of test materials helps to enhance the quality of specifications by identifying aspects of the specification that are ambiguous, contradictory or unimplementable*" (W3C, 2004 ch.1.3.).

In telecommunications, there may be as many as four products in an antiproduct-like relation under quasi-parallel development (see also ETSI MBS, n.d.):

1. a base specification;
2. an "early implementation" to validate the implementability of a base specification;
3. a test specification – to validate the testability of requirements contained in a base specification, as "*...Only such requirements shall be included as can be verified.*" (ISO/IEC, 2004 A.4), and to validate the adequacy of a test system (as the state-of-the-art test systems based on the standardized TTCN-3 technology are not "universal" and require the additional effort for designing the specialized modules: coders/decoders and adapters, to run even a standardized test suite);
4. a test system to check the implementability of a test specification, and to eventually run the specified tests against an implementation of a base specification.

The antiproduct paradigm is also present in the general idea of standards that are developed in an interactive way, in lock-step with the development of technology that is their subject matter. Such *participatory* (Sherif, 2001), *pro-active* (Jakobs, 2003) or *enabling* (Sherif, 2003) standards are distinguished in opposition to *anticipatory* and *responsive* standards (for more classifications of standards see Vries, 2001a). Sherif (2003) characterizes participatory standards as those that had the chance of being verified / validated against their (first) implementations before their adoption.

This seems to be the current view of ETSI (ETSI MBS, n.d.), and also, by definition, that of the IETF, which expects at least two independently developed, working implementations ("The Evolution of Global Networks", 2001).

We now draw an analogy, and postulate that developing the ECRs, as a particular type of anti-product, in parallel with the development of standards that are the "donors" of capabilities, would bring similar benefits. The preceding discussion of circumventing the structural deficiencies of current standards for the purposes of deriving sensible ECRs can be regarded as a step towards defining the rules for cross-validating these two "antiproducts".

Repositories of Reusable Components

A generic OR document stores, directly and indirectly (as references), a large number of pieces of information (capabilities, test purposes, tests, fragments of specification from various referenced standards) that are available from one place, and can be manipulated (within certain rules) for various purposes. In this sense, these elements of ORs are "reusable", and the OR document is their repository.

This idea, common to all phases of our research, seems to re-appear in different contexts. Some similarity can be found in Krechmer (2002). An idea surprisingly similar to ours is presented by Rycroft & Tully (2007). They strive to provide a single point of reference for related facts from different standards. They break down the standards into constituent parts (in our case – into capabilities), cross-reference them, and provide the means to access (query) this information from one place. Their experience is also very similar to ours. They have found that: extracting meaningful "chunks" of information from standards is intellectually challenging and time-consuming; it is certainly not enough to copy and paste the text from standards; and there is a danger (or rather certainty) of be-

ing subjective in "distilling" standards. This last observation is one of the reasons why we consider so important the development of a single, common, standardized ECR (per standard).

Building and using a repository of reusable information is also the central idea of the IPv6 Testing standardization project (ETSI EG 202 568, 2007). The project is focused on testing, but the concept is quite general. A repository is built, in which the fragments of multiple standards (pieces of specification, requirements, test purposes, and reusable fragments of test programs) are stored. These components are selected and combined to quickly develop the test suites. The components are cross-linked, so that limited semantic checks and queries are possible.

CONCLUSION

Egyedi (2002) realises that "*standards are artifacts like any other artifact*", and notes that little systematic research has been done in the field of their intrinsic characteristics. To address this research niche, we have concentrated on the syntactic, semantic and pragmatic level of a technical standard itself – on how the contents of standards are currently structured and expressed, and how this structure could be improved, given the needs of the direct users of standards.

The proposed OpTeR methodology supports a Network Operator in his development-oriented tasks, in which the company standards – Operator's Requirements – are designed and used. The methodology proposes a lightweight semi-formal notation, which can be handled by a support tool. However, the characteristic feature of OpTeR is the lack of "all-or-nothing" approach: the ORs can also be handled as a printed document, and can be used even if the postulated change in the SDO-developed standards does not materialize.

The ideas presented in this chapter have been gradually developed for over 15 years. OpTeR is the current result of the ongoing research program (Brzeziński, 1998; Artych & Brzeziński, 1999; Artych, 2003; Brzeziński, 2005b, 2005a, 2007). Research was started in 1993 with the first version of Operator's Requirements for the ISDN DSS1 suite of protocols, developed using the traditional approach (so our current criticism has empirical grounds). The methical foundations of our approach allowed it to adapt to the evolving context – the evolution of the rôle of a Network Operator in developing its infrastructure and service portfolio, and the evolution of both the technical contents of telecommunications standards and the state of meta-standardization. It was also shown that the elements of the OpTeR methodology are generally consistent with the current paradigms and identified trends in the evolution of technical standards.

ACKNOWLEDGMENT

The author wishes to thank professor Józef Lubacz for fruitful discussions on the philosophical aspects of the development process and for constant support. The early work was done with dr Rafał Artych. Michał Grzegorzewski developed the more recent computer support tools. The concepts and tools presented herein have been developed over the years partly in the context of consecutive R&D projects carried out on contract from the TP (Telekomunikacja Polska), the leading Polish network operator. The TP has kindly agreed to the publication of selected information on these works. The author was also partly supported by the Research Grant No. N517 008 31/1429.

REFERENCES

Artych, R. (2003). *Methodology for the Design of Useful Implementations of Communications Protocols*. Unpublished doctoral dissertation, Warsaw University of Technology. (In Polish)

Artych, R., & Brzeziński, K. M. (1999). External Conformance Requirements: Concepts, Methods and Tools. In *Proceedings of the 12th International Workshop on Testing of Communicating Systems (IWTCS '99)* (pp. 363–378). Budapest: Kluwer.

Baskin, E., Krechmer, K., & Sherif, M. (1998). The Six Dimensions of Standards: Contribution Towards a Theory of Standardization. In L. Lefebvre, R. Mason, & T. Khalil (Eds.), *Management of Technology, Sustainable Development and Eco-Efficiency* (p. 53). Elsevier.

Brzeziński, K. M. (1998). Towards Formality of Technical Requirements for Protocols. In *Proceedings of the 9th European Workshop on Dependable Computing (EWDC '98)* (pp. 71–74). Gdańsk.

Brzeziński, K. M. (2005a). Embedded Capability Relations to Aid the Industrial Usability of Telecommunications Standards. In *Proceedings of the 4th International Conference on Standardization and Innovation in Information Technology (SIIT 2005)* (pp. 55–63). Geneva.

Brzeziński, K. M. (2005b). Formalizing Operator Requirements for the Development of Telecommunications Networks and Services. In *Proceedings of the 8th International Conference on Telecommunications (ConTEL 2005)* (pp. 611–618). Zagreb.

Brzeziński, K. M. (2007). Network Operators' Requirements and the Structure of Telecommunications Standards. [JITSR]. *International Journal of IT Standards and Standardization Research*, 5(1), 103–117.

Brzeziński, K. M., Gajowniczek, P., Grzegorzewski, M., Karwowski, K., Kukliński, S., Średniawa, M., et al. (2008, December). *Converged services in a heterogeneous NGN / CSN environment. Volume 1–3*. (Research Project no. 501E/1036/4470). Warsaw: Warsaw University of Technology, on contract from CBR TP (Telekomunikacja Polska, R&D Department). (In Polish; not publicly available)

Critical Issues in ICT Standardization. (2005, April). ICT Focus Group report. ICT Standards Board. Available from http://www.ict.etsi.org/publications.htm

de Vries, H. J. (2001a). IT Standards Typology. In K. Jakobs (Ed.), *Advanced Topics in Information Technology Standards and Standardization Research* (Vol. 1, pp. 1–26). IGI Publishing.

de Vries, H. J. (2001b). Standardization - a New Discipline? In *Proceedings of the 2nd IEEE Conference on Standardization and Innovation in Information Technology* (SIIT 2001) (pp. 91–105).

de Vries, H. J., & Slob, F. J. C. (2006). Best Practice in Company Standardization. *International Journal of IT Standards and Standardization Research, 4*(1), 62.

Dickerson, K. (2005). *The Paramount Importance of Standards to Operators, Vendors and Users.* Keynote speech at the 4th International Conference on Standardization and Innovation in Information Technology (SIIT 2005).

Dickerson, K. (2007). *BT's use of Open Standards and Open Source.* Invited speech at the 5th International Conference on Standardization and Innovation in Information Technology (SIIT 2007).

Egyedi, T. M. (2002). Standards Enhance System Flexibility? Mapping Compatibility Strategies onto Flexibility Objectives. In *Proceedings of the EASST 2002 conference.*

ETSI EG 201 058. (2003). *Implementation Conformance Statement (ICS) proforma style guide* (V1.2.4).

ETSI EG 202 237. (2007). *MTS; Internet Protocol Testing (IPT); Generic approach to interoperability testing.* (V1.1.2).

ETSI EG 202 568. (2007). *MTS; Internet Protocol Testing (IOT); Testing: Methodology and Framework* (V1.1.3).

ETSI ES 201 873. (2008). *MTS; The Testing and Test Control Notation version 3.*

ETSI ES 202 553. (2008). *MTS; TPLan: A notation for expressing Test Purposes* (V1.1.1).

ETSI ETS 300 406. (1995). *MTS; Protocol and profile conformance testing specifications; Standardization methodology.*

ETSI MBS. (n.d.). *Making Better Standards.* Electronic publication. Available from http://portal.etsi.org/mbs (accessed 15 Jan. 2009)

ETSI SR 001 262. (2004). *ETSI drafting rules.*

Gessa, N. (2007). *An Ontology-based Approach to Define and Manage B2B Interoperability.* Unpublished doctoral dissertation, University of Bologna.

Heitmeyer, C. L. (1998). On the Need for Practical Formal Methods. In *Proceedings of the 5th International Symposium on Formal Techniques in Real-Time Fault Tolerant Systems (FTRTFT)* (p. 18-26). (Invited paper)

IETF RFC 2119. (1997). *Key words for use in RFCs to indicate requirements levels* (S. Bradner, Ed.).

ISO/IEC. (2004). *ISO/IEC Directives, Part 2. Rules for the structure and drafting of International Standards* (5th ed.).

ISO/IEC 9646. (n.d.). *Conformance testing methodology and framework.*

ITU-T Z.150. (2003). *User Requirements Notation (URN) – Language requirements and framework.*

ITU-T Z.450. (2003). *Quality aspects of protocol-related Recommendations.*

Jakobs, K. (2003). *Information Technology Standards, Standards Setting and Standards Research.* Presented at Stanhope Center's Roundtable.

Krechmer, K. (2002). Cathedrals, Libraries and Bazaars. In *Proceedings of the 2002 ACM symposium on Applied computing* (p. 1053-1057).

Leduc, G. (1992). A Framework Based on Implementation Relations for Implementing LOTOS Specifications. *Computer Networks and ISDN Systems, 25,* 23–41. doi:10.1016/0169-7552(92)90122-7

Moseley, S., Randall, S., & Wiles, A. (2004). In Pursuit of Interoperability. *International Journal (Toronto, Ont.), 2*(2), 34–48.

Robinson, G. (1999). There are no Standards for Making Standards. In *Proceedings of the 1st IEEE Conference on Standardization and Innovation in Information Technology (SIIT 1999).* (Invited paper)

Rushby, J. (2000). Disappearing Formal Methods. In *5th Int. Symposium on High Assurance Systems Engineering (HASE)* (pp. 95–96). Albuquerque. (Invited paper)

Rycroft, S., & Tully, M. (2007). Building an Information Security Meta Standard. *BT Technology Journal, 25*(1), 37–40. doi:10.1007/s10550-007-0006-8

Schoechle, T. (2003). Digital Enclosure: The Privatization of Standards and Standardization. In *Proceedings of the 3rd IEEE Conference on Standardization and Innovation in Information Technology* (SIIT 2003) (pp. 229–240).

Shapiro, S., Richards, B., Rinow, M., & Schoechle, T. (2001). Hybrid Standards Setting Solutions for Today's Convergent Telecommunications Market. In *Proceedings of the 2nd IEEE Conference on Standardization and Innovation in Information Technology (SIIT 2001)* (pp. 348–351).

Sherif, M. H. (2001, April). A Framework for Standardization in Telecommunications and Information Technology. *IEEE Communications Magazine, 39*(4), 94–100. doi:10.1109/35.917510

Sherif, M. H. (2003). When is Standardization Slow? [JITSR]. *International Journal of IT Standards and Standardization Research, 1*(1), 19–32.

The Evolution of Global Networks. (2001). In *Global Networks and Local Values: A Comparative Look at Germany and the United States* (pp. 23–45). National Academy Press.

W3C. (2004). *QA Framework: Test Guidelines (Working Draft, 25 Feb. 2004).*

Warken, M. (2006). *From Testing to Anti-product Development.* Presented at the TTCN-3 User Conference (T3UC), Berlin.

Chapter 6
The Performance of Standard Setting Organizations:
Using Patent Data for Evaluation

Marc Rysman
Boston University, USA

Tim Simcoe
University of Toronto, Canada

ABSTRACT

This article uses citations to patents disclosed in the standard setting process to measure the technological significance of voluntary standard setting organizations (SSOs). We find that SSO patents are outliers in several dimensions and importantly, are cited far more frequently than a set of control patents. More surprisingly, we find that SSO patents receive citations for a much longer period of time. Furthermore, we find a significant correlation between citation and the disclosure of a patent to an SSO, which may imply a marginal impact of disclosure. These results provide the first empirical look at patents disclosed to SSO's, and show that these organizations both select important technologies and play a role in establishing their significance.

INTRODUCTION

Voluntary standard setting organizations (SSOs) provide a venue for market participants to develop compatible standards on which to develop new products. These organizations provide an opportunity for markets to reach compatibility without relying on possibly costly and inefficient government regulation and market-based standards wars. Given their potentially important role in high-technology markets, SSO's have been the subject of substantial amount of research using social science methods, with *JITSR* being an example. However, this research has primarily focused on determining the incentives of market players to participate and implement standard setting, and on the optimal internal organization of SSOs. Our knowledge of the economic and technological impact of these institutions remains quite limited. Evaluating the role of SSOs is difficult because they operate in diverse markets and their effect on outcome variables such as price and quantity are often uncertain.

This article attempts to evaluate the contribution of SSOs to the innovative process. We exploit patents disclosed in the standardization process as a metric for measurement. The treatment of intellectual property is an ubiquitous problem for SSOs and participants regularly must disclose relevant patents to SSOs in the process of negotiating a standard. In this article, we use these patents as a window into the role of SSOs in technological innovation. Patents are easily compared across time and industries, and many properties are well-known as a result of a large amount of research in economics and related fields.

Following the literature on patents, we use patent citations as a measure of economic and technological importance (Jaffe & Trajtenberg, 2002). Citations are well-known to be correlated with economic measures of the importance of a patent, such stock market valuation and the likelihood of renewal. We use patents identified in the intellectual property disclosure records of four SSOs: the European Telecommunications Standards Institute (ETSI), the Institute for Electrical and Electronic Engineers (IEEE), the Internet Engineering Task Force (IETF), and the International Telecommunications Union (ITU). We construct control samples based on technological class and application year of the patents.

We show that patents associated with standard settings differ from control patents in several important dimensions. They are more likely to be part of international families, more likely to be continuation applications, and much more likely to be litigated. Importantly, we find that SSO patents receive far more citations than an average patent, around 3.5 times higher. More surprisingly, SSO patents receive citations over a much longer time period. We show that the average age at which a citation is received is higher for SSO than control patents and that the difference is economically and statistically significant. Interestingly, this difference is greater when we compare SSO patents to a group of highly cited control patents. One explanation for this long-lived citation pattern may be that innovations associated with standards are subject to lock-in and network effects, leading them to be important for a longer period than the average patent.

Two reasons that SSO patents differ from other patents are that the SSO *selects* patents that represent important technologies and that the SSO actually *causes* technologies to have the citation profile we observe. That is, we may wonder whether SSO patents would have had similar citation patterns if they had never been associated with an SSO. The selection effect is natural given that SSOs explicitly attempt to identify the best technology to serve a given need. Finding that the selection effect is important suggests that SSOs are successful in identifying important technologies. The causal effect may arise because an SSO embeds a technology in a standard that then exhibits long-lasting economic importance because of network effects and lock-in. Another source for a causal effect may be that because an SSO disclosure represents a public announcement, it attracts attention to a patent. Finding a causal effect for SSOs suggests that over and above the stated goals of SSOs in facilitating interconnection between complementary markets, SSOs have a further role in determining the path of technological innovation into the future.

In this article, we exploit the timing of disclosures to separate between the selection and causation effects. That is, the extent to which the citation pattern changes after a patent is disclosed to an SSO gives a measure of the causal effect of the SSO. We are cautious in this interpretation as the timing of disclosure depends on the economic environment. In subsequent paragraphs, we discuss why the endogeneity of disclosure could lead us to over or under-estimate the causation effect. However, given the lack of a truly exogenous determination of disclosure, we find this approach a logical starting place.

Our regression approach compares disclosed to undisclosed SSO patents and compares patents before and after disclosure. We find an economically and statistically significant correlation of citations with disclosure. To the extent that we measure the causal effect of an SSO, it appears that the causal effect represents between 25% and 40% of the difference in citations between SSO and non-SSO patents.

This article contributes to a growing empirical literature that examines the impact of particular institutions on the process of technological change. Examples of this research include Furman and Stern's (2004) study of biological resource centers and studies of the university-industry interface, including Mowery et al (1999) and Markiewicz (2004). In the next section, we describe the four SSOs that are examined in this article and how they treat intellectual property. The Data section describes the data set, while the Citation Patterns section takes an initial look at the difference in citation patterns between the SSO and control samples. The Selection vs. Causation section examines the postdisclosure increase in citation rates. The Conclusions section offers some conclusions.

SSOs AND INTELLECTUAL PROPERTY

Before using patent data to study the role of SSO's in the innovation process, it is important to understand the role of patents and intellectual property in the standard setting process. This section describes the four organizations studied and describes how each of them deals with intellectual property.

We use data collected from four major SSOs. These groups are the European Telecommunica-

tion Standards Institute (ETSI), the Institute of Electrical and Electronics Engineers (IEEE), the Internet Engineering Task Force (IETF), and the International Telecommunications Union-Telecommunication Standardization Sector (ITU-T, or often, ITU). Both ETSI and the ITU are international institutions that focus primarily on telecommunications standards. While international in scope, the IEEE and IETF draw the majority of their participants from North America, and are usually associated with the computer hardware and software industries although some of their most significant standards are communications protocols.

Of the four SSOs that we examine, the ITU is the oldest, with origins dating back to around 1865. Its original mission was to promote international coordination among the various rapidly expanding domestic telephone networks. The ITU is based in Switzerland and is associated with the United Nations. Its membership consists of delegates from member nations along with representatives of the larger firms or network operators in each of these countries. The organization's standard setting activities continue to emphasize the protocols used to operate the international telephone network, with work areas that include numbering and addressing, network services, physical interconnection, monitoring and accounting, traffic management, and quality of service.

The IEEE is only slightly younger than the ITU. It was founded in 1884 by several pioneers in the field of electrical engineering. Although the IEEE is a professional society whose members are individual engineers, it is possible to become a corporate member when participating in its standard setting activities. The IEEE's standard setting efforts cover a wide range of subjects, from electrical safety, to cryptography, to standards for semiconductor testing equipment. In recent years, the IEEE's most commercially significant standards work has revolved around the 802.11 specifications for wireless computer networking.

ETSI was formed in 1988 to provide a less formal and more industry-driven forum than the ITU for European telecom standardization. The organization is located in southern France and participants are typically firms—as opposed to the member-state representatives of the ITU. ETSI has played a prominent role in creating several generations of mobile telephony standards that are in use throughout Europe and much of the rest of the world. In particular, it is the forum where a variety of network operators, electronics suppliers, and cellular handset manufacturers reached key agreements on the GSM and 3G wireless protocols.

Finally, the IETF is the least formal of the four SSOs studied in this article. This organization grew out the ARPANET engineering community that emerged during the 1970s, and did not resemble a formal SSO until the late 1980s or early 1990s (Mowery & Simcoe, 2002). The IETF creates a host of protocols used to run the Internet. Prominent examples include the Internet's core transport protocols (TCP/IP and Ethernet), standards used to allocate network addresses (DHCP), and specifications used by popular applications such as e-mail or file transfer. From its inception, membership in the IETF and its various working groups has been open to any interested individual. Much of the IETF's work takes place in online forums sponsored by individual committees and is visible to the general public.

Because all four of the SSO's examined in this article are more or less "open," each of them must deal with the increasing tension between open standards and intellectual property protection. The goal of most SSOs is to promote widespread implementation and adoption of the specifications they produce. However, these goals often conflict with those of individual participants who may hold intellectual property rights in a proposed standard. Patent owners frequently seek royalty payments for the use of their technology—even (or, perhaps, especially) when it is essential to the implementation of an industry standard. Moreover, many firms realize that owning intellectual property rights in an industry standard can result in substantial licensing revenues. This creates strong incentives to push for one's own technology within the SSO, and may lead to long-delays or breakdowns in the standard setting process (Simcoe, 2004).

While most SSOs would like to avoid the distributional conflicts and obstacles to implementa-

Figure 1. Intellectual property disclosures

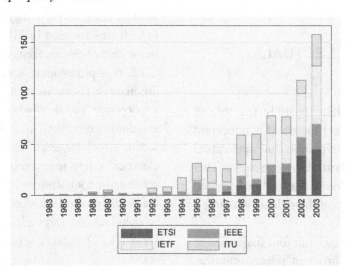

tion that patents can produce, they often have no choice other than to evaluate a variety of proposals that are subject to some type of intellectual property protection. In part, this is because of the well-documented surge in patenting that began in the mid-1980s. This increase reflects a growing awareness of patents' strategic significance, as well as the actions of courts, policy-makers, and patent offices. Awareness of the tension between SSOs and their patent-holding members has also increased because of a number of high-profile legal conflicts.

Given the increasing importance of the intellectual property issue, many SSOs have been debating their own policies for dealing with patents. Lemley (2002) presents a survey of the various policies that SSOs have adopted. All four of the SSOs examined in this article use variations on the relatively common policy of "reasonable and non-discriminatory licensing" (RAND). Under this policy, SSO members agree to disclose any known property rights as soon as they become aware of them. (They are not, however, obliged to carry out a search.) When a patent or other piece of intellectual property is discovered, the SSO seeks assurances from the owner that they will license the technology to any interested standards implementor on reasonable and nondiscriminatory terms. While SSOs and their individual committees are generally inclined to search for technologies that are unprotected or available on a royalty-free basis, their job is to evaluate the potential tradeoff between technical quality and openness.

Table 1 illustrates the growth in intellectual property disclosures at the four SSOs that we study. (We define a disclosure is an announcement by a single firm on a given date that it potentially owns one or more pieces of intellectual property.) While the number of intellectual property disclosures was initially quite small, it began to grow during the early 1990s. By the late 1990s, all four SSOs were experiencing significant growth.

For our purposes, the rise in intellectual property disclosures means that we have access to a publicly available list of patents associated with standard setting. Many features of patents, such as the number of citations they receive, are easily compared across different industries and time periods. We utilize the information contained in intellectual property disclosures to identify standards-related patents whose citation rates may provide a window onto the potential impact of SSOs.

Our study builds on the large literature in economics utilizing patent data. Jaffe and Trajtenberg (2002) describe patents and their citations as a "paper trail" following the innovative process, allowing researchers to track the flow of ideas over time and space. Because citations legally delimit the scope of the citing patent, citations should have an economic implication. A number of papers have established the relationship between the number of citations a patent receives and its economic importance. For instance, Pakes (1986) uses patent renewal decisions and Hall, Jaffe, and Trajtenberg (2005) use stock market valuations of patent holders. In this article, we do not take a strong stand on the meaning of a patent citation, on optimal IPR policies or even on whether patenting encourages innovation or not. Rather, we exploit existing framework for patenting and IPR disclosures to obtain a method for systematically evaluating the role of SSOs in the innovative process. Naturally, this approach does not give us a representative sample of all standards that an SSO generates, and we have a restricted set of SSOs to begin with. However, we hope that even conditioning on the data we have, we are able to provide important insights into the impact of SSOs.

A note of caution: patents may be disclosed for proposals that never become standards, and proposals may become standards but not require licensing of every patent that was disclosed in relation to the proposal. We observe only intellectual property disclosures, not whether they were included in the final standard, whether the proposal became a standard or often even what proposal they were disclosed in relation to. Making these distinctions might be useful for a number of questions but such data are not available to us at this time.

DATA

This section describes the sample of SSO patents that we use to study the standard setting process. All of these data were collected from the publicly available records of ETSI, the IEEE, IETF, and ITU. We begin by describing the complete sample of intellectual property disclosures. We then examine the 1,113 U.S. patents contained in one or more of these disclosures. After discussing some of the issues associated with these patents, we conclude by describing the creation of our initial control sample.

Although the four SSOs in this study have similar intellectual property policies, the scope and specificity of individual disclosures varies dramatically across organizations. These differences reflect variation in the participants, policies, and objectives of the four institutions. In order to provide some intuition for the type of disclosure information provided by these SSOs, we group the data using a particular definition of "disclosure." We define a disclosure as an announcement by a single firm on a given date that it owns (or may own) one or more pieces of intellectual property related to a single standard setting initiative. When a firm claims that a single patent covers two or more standards, each one counts as a separate disclosure. When a single announcement lists more than one patent or patent application, we will refer to each piece of intellectual property in the disclosure as a claim. Since we do not work with the claims data from individual patents, this should not lead to much confusion.

Table 1 illustrates some of the variation in how intellectual property is disclosed across the four SSOs in this study. First, the data for each organization begin at a different point in time. While the ITU disclosures begin in 1983, intellectual property did not become an issue at the IETF until 1995. Second, there are substantial differences in the number of claims per disclosure. While the ITU has the largest number of disclosures, almost all of them contain a single claim. At ETSI, on the other hand, the median disclosure makes four claims, and one contains more than 1500. Finally, individual claims vary in their level of specificity. For example, it was a common practice at the IETF for several years to "disclose" the existence of an unpublished patent application without providing any information that could be used to verify its existence. This variation in claim-specificity can be seen by comparing the number of patents disclosed to the total number of claims at an SSO.

Table 1. Intellectual property disclosures

	Disclosures		Claims per Disclosure			Patents	
	Earliest	Total	Mean	Median	Max	All Patents	US Patents
ETSI	1990	262	36.5	4	1582	847	672
IEEE	1988	125	3.4	1	37	313	252
IETF	1995	314	1.5	1	27	193	97
ITU	1983	821	1.0	1	2	339	188

The final column in Table 1 shows the number of U.S. patents contained in the data set. This figure is smaller than the number of patents claimed at each SSO for two reasons. First, many disclosures list non-U.S. patents. This is particularly true at ETSI, where the large number of claims per disclosure often reflects the disclosure of patent families which cover the same invention in several legal jurisdictions. Second, there are several patents that get disclosed more than once (both within and between SSOs). For example, there are a number of cryptography patents that seem to be disclosed on a regular basis when SSOs deal with issues of computer security.

After removing all of the foreign patents, patent applications, and duplicate observations, the intellectual property disclosures made at ETSI, the IEEE, IETF, and ITU yield a sample of 1,113 unique U.S. patents. We do not claim that these patents are broadly representative of the technology evaluated by these four SSOs. More likely, they are concentrated within several of the most commercially significant standard setting efforts. Nevertheless, these patents provide a unique opportunity to study the role of SSOs in the innovation process.

We obtained citation data for these patents by linking the SSO sample to the NBER US patent data file (Hall, Jaffe, & Trajtenberg, 2002). These data also contain several important patent characteristics, such as application and grant dates, and the name of assignees. Figure 2 shows the distribution of grant dates for the patents in the SSO sample.

It is clear from Figure 2 that the majority of patents listed in SSO disclosures were not granted by the USPTO until the mid-1990s. This is not surprising, given the surge in patenting and the timing of the disclosures in Table 1. However, because these are relatively new patents, it is important to consider the issue of sample truncation. In particular, many of the SSO patents were granted near the end of our sample (our citation data extend to 2004). While we would like to study the long run impacts of SSO affiliation, the data are not sufficient to consider what happens to SSO patents after about 15 years. This issue becomes even more severe when we focus on comparing the pre and post disclosure periods which in many cases may only last one or two years.

Throughout the analysis, we will be comparing the SSO patents to a control sample. The baseline control sample was chosen by selecting all of the patents with the same application year and primary 3-digit technology classification as any patent disclosed to one of the four SSOs.

Figure 2. Grant dates of SSO patents

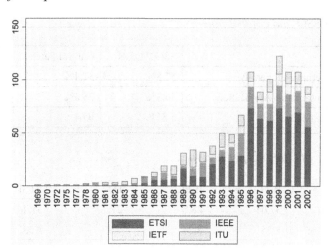

CITATION PATTERNS

In this section, we examine the distribution of forward-citations to patents in the SSO and control samples. We are primarily interested in the age profile of citations—the average citation rate conditional on patent age. Hall, Jaffe, and Trajtenberg (2002) refer to this statistic as the lag distribution. Several papers examine the shape of this distribution for various sets of patents. Much of this work is collected in Jaffe and Trajtenberg (2002). See Hall and Trajtenberg (2002). We begin with a direct comparison of the average citation rates for SSO and control patents. We then turn to an econometric model with application-year and citing-year fixed effects to account for time trends in citing propensity and differences in the "fertility" of inventions across vintage years.

Before presenting data about citations, we begin a few simple measures of the importance of SSO patents. We provide three comparisons of the difference between SSO patents and the control sample. Results appear in Table 2. First, we consider we see that patents that are disclosed to SSOs are more likely to be part of an international family. That is, the patent holder applied for protection in multiple countries at once. Naturally, these would tend to be more valuable patents. Second, SSO patents are more likely to be

continuation patents. A continuation patent is one for which the patent application was altered after the initial application. These patent applications can typically maintain their original priority date that establishes their technological precedence with respect to competing applications. Finally, SSO patents are almost nine times more likely to be litigated than control patents. Obviously, litigation is a sign of the economic importance of a patent.

First, we compare the number of citations that each group of patent receives. Table 3 shows the average number of citations per patent at each SSO and at their associated control group. SSO patents receive substantially more citations than patents from similar technology classes, ranging from 3.5 to more than 4 times greater. This result is not surprising as we know that most patents receive very few citations and we expect that patents that would be important enough to be disclosed would also represent important technologies.

More surprising is that SSO patents receive citations over a longer period of time. Hall, Jaffe, and Trajtenberg (2001) establish that most patents exhibit a peaked citation pattern, with a distinct peak occurring in age 4 or 5. We show that SSO patents exhibit a much smaller peak with substantial number of citations coming relatively late in the patents life. To see this, we compute the

Table 2. Comparison of SSO and control patents

	SSO Patents	Control Patents
International Family	57.8%	31.4%
Continuation Applications	36.3%	25.4%
Litigated	5.51%	0.64%

Table 3. Average number of citations per patent

	IETF	IEEE	ITU	ETSI
SSO	37.03	28.8	27.77	31.44
Control	8.55	8.24	7.97	8.53

average number of citations received at each age for SSO and control patents separately. Figure 3 graphs these results with the lines normalized to integrate to 1. That is, we can interpret these graphs as probability distribution functions over the age at which a patent receives a citation. In each case, control patents exhibit the highly peaked pattern common to groups of patents that have been studied in the past (e.g., Hall, Jaffe, & Trajtenberg, 2001). In contrast, SSO patents have much lower peaks and instead have a much greater probability of receiving citations later in the age process.

One of the most striking facts about Figure 3 is the particularly long citation life exhibited at the IETF. A quick search reveals that there are several notable patents appearing in the tail of the age profile for the IETF, as well as the IEEE. These patents include numbers 4,405,829 and 4,200,770, which cover the basics of public-key cryptography, as well as 4,063,220 which describes the Ethernet networking. These are exceptional patents in many respects—including the fact that they are disclosed on separate occasions in more than

one SSO. So, while these patents are excellent examples of the potential impact of an SSO on the innovation process, it is hard to believe that the *average* patent from among the 400 disclosed at these SSO's in 2003 will turn out to have a similar citation trajectory. Nevertheless, it is interesting to consider whether the importance of the inventions embodied in these early patents could have enhanced the future influence of their respective SSOs.

It is straightforward to use our data to compute the average age at which an SSO receives a citation. Doing so provides simple summary of the graphs in Figure 3 and makes it straightforward to compute whether the differences between SSO and control patents are statistically significant. Table 4 presents the average age (since application) at which a patent receives a citations. Strikingly, SSO patents have a higher age in each case, by 1 to 3 years. The small standard errors associated with these estimates indicate that these differences are statistically significant.

One concern may be that the high average age of a citation in the SSO sample stems from the

Figure 3. Distribution of citations over age for SSO and control patents

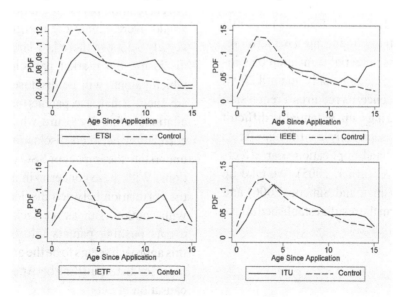

103

Table 4. Average age (since application) of a citation

	IETF	IEEE	ITU	ETSI
SSO	5.38	7.55	6.34	5.47
	(0.063)	(0.073)	(0.055)	(0.023)
Control	3.62	4.20	4.72	4.26
	(0.006)	(0.005)	(0.005)	(0.004)
Highly Cited Control	3.69	4.30	4.87	4.26
	(0.009)	(0.007)	(0.008)	(0.006)

fact that SSO patents represent important technologies. That is, it might be true that all highly cited patents exhibit age profiles like we see for SSO patents. In fact, that is not the case. To show this, we define a set of highly cited patents for each control group. Highly cited patents are in the top decile of citations received for their application year. In this way, highly cited control patents have an average citation rate as least slightly greater than SSO patents for each SSO. Table 4 presents results for highly cited patents in the third row. Strikingly, the average age for highly cited patents may be slightly higher than the entire control sample, but is still well below that of SSO patents.

One should exercise caution in drawing conclusions based on the unconditional age profile. These computations do not make any adjustment for differences in the application-year or citing-year, which Hall, Jaffe, and Trajtenberg (2001) establish as potentially important. Furthermore, they do not address potential truncation bias inherent in observing citations only up until 2004. Addressing these concerns requires a regression framework and brings up potentially difficult questions of how to separately identify age effects from citation-year and application-year effects (Hall, Mairresse, & Turner, 2005). We take up these issues in Rysman and Simcoe (2006) and remarkably, confirm the results established above in the raw data.

SELECTION VS. CAUSATION

The previous section showed that patents disclosed to SSOs are cited at higher rates than the average patent. We interpret this as evidence that these patents embody significant inventions. However, this evidence is insufficient to distinguish whether SSO's select technologies that would have been important regardless or whether SSOs actually influence on the importance of these technologies. In this section, we use the timing of intellectual property disclosures to distinguish these affects. Our goal is to use the disclosure event to estimate the marginal impact of the standard setting organization on patent citation rates.

To be clear, this interpretation depends on the date of disclosure being an exogenous event. This condition is unlikely to be met in practice and the sign of the associated bias is difficult to predict. Suppose the selection effect dominates and patent holders tend to disclose important patents to SSOs, but they do not realize the importance of patents for some number of years. Then, they may choose to disclose patents at the time they can predict that citations will increase. In that case, we will observe an increase in citations around the date of disclosure but presumably, the patent would have experienced the increase without disclosure and the correlation between citations and disclosure would overestimate the marginal impact. Conversely, suppose there is a large causal effect of disclosure but market participants can predict which patents will be disclosed some period in advance. In that case, patents may begin to receive citations before disclosure, which would cause the correlation between disclosure and citations to understate the impact of SSO disclosure on citations. With these concerns in mind, we interpret the correlation between disclosure and citations with caution. But as we lack truly exogenous events pushing patents into SSO negotiations, this approach seems to be the appropriate starting place for distinguishing between the selection and causation effects.

We estimate the impact of disclosure in two ways. In the first approach, we are interested in comparing the size of the SSO effect to the size of the disclosure effect. That is, we want to measure the extra effect on an SSO patent of being disclosed. We use the following regression framework:

$$C_{it} = f(\alpha_y, \alpha_t, \alpha_a, \alpha_c, \alpha_i^{SSO}, \alpha_{it}^{DISC}, \varepsilon_{it})$$

In this equation, the dependent variable is the number of citations to patent i in year t. The variables of primary interest are α_i^{SSO} which is a dummy variable for SSO patents and α_{it}^{DISC}, which is a dummy variable for patent i having been disclosed by period t. That is, the variable is "on" for all periods after disclosure. The control variables are a series of dummy variables for the application year, α_y, the year in which cites are received (the application year of patents that cite patent i), α_t, the age of the patent, α_a, and the 3-digit technology class from the NBER patent database, α_c. Note that age is defined to be $a = t-y$, which implies that the age variables are a linear function of the year and cohort variables and hence, not separately identified. To address this issue, we assume that a single age coefficient applied to all ages greater than 11, by which time most patents receive very few citations. The term ε_i captures unobservable terms. In practice, we estimate with a Poisson regression, which predicts count data like what we observe. We construct robust standard errors that allow for errors that are clustered around each patent.

In this regression, the disclosure dummy coefficient is estimated entirely from within-SSO variation. For instance, if all SSO patents were disclosed in the same year or at the same age, α_{it}^{DISC} would not be identified. Implicit in this approach is the assumption that the age process is the same for SSO and control patents, even though Figure 3 suggests that the age profiles are different for SSO patents. In fact, it we could include a set of age dummy variables for SSOs only and interpret them as the *difference* in the age profile for SSO patents and control patents. However, capturing the SSO effect in a single dummy variable makes the size of the SSO effect easily comparable to the size of the disclosure effect. Results for the disclosure dummy are very similar if we allow for a set of SSO age dummies.

Table 5 presents results. We present only the coefficients of primary interest. Not surprisingly, the SSO dummy is positive and precisely estimated for all four SSOs. In addition, the disclosure dummy is positive and significant as well for all but the IETF. If we interpret the dummy on disclosure as representing the marginal impact of the SSO on the citation count, we can say that between 25% and 40% of the high citations counts for SSO patents are due to being disclosed to an SSO, and the rest is a selection effect. We computed these numbers based on the percentage increase in the number of citations from making a patent an SSO patent and then disclosing it. This result strikes us as very reasonable, although we do not have strong priors over this statistic.

These results suggest an economically significant disclosure effect. In addition, we find similar results if we define disclosure to occur one year after the reported disclosure year in order to account for some sort of lag. However, it would be interesting to do more complex analysis. For instance, we might be interested in how citations vary in the years just before and after disclosure, or how age profiles change when we control for disclosure. We are limited in our ability to answer these questions because of the scarcity of data when using only within-SSO variation. For these purposes, we are currently exploring the use a control sample comparison. While the process of matching patents to a control sample brings up well known problems with unobserved heterogeneity, the larger sample size allows us to pose new and interesting questions.

Table 5. Results for importance of disclosure

	IETF	IEEE	ITU	ETSI
SSO	1.225	0.818	0.868	1.058
	(0.086)	(0.082)	(0.094)	(0.065)
Disclosure	0.114	0.412	0.291	0.285
	(0.198)	(0.169)	(0.112)	(0.063)
% Disclosure	24.8%	40.0%	36.0%	31.6%
observations	197,851	458,734	519,865	301,050
SSO obs.	922	2,482	2,405	6,329

Notes: A Poisson regression of citations on control dummies and dummies for SSO patents and for the periods in or after disclosure to the SSO

CONCLUSION

While the importance of SSOs has been widely remarked by academics and practitioners, there have been few attempts to systematically measure their role in economic performance or technological change. Moreover, since much of the evidence for SSOs' importance is based on specific examples of technologies they have endorsed, there continues to be some debate over whether they actually influence the process of cumulative development or merely choose to select and evaluate important technologies. This is the first article to address these issues using patent citations as a measure of SSO performance.

Using data from the patents disclosed in the standard setting process at ETSI, IEEE, IETF, and the ITU, we showed show that the SSO patents collect many more citations, typically around three times as many. Furthermore, they have a different age profile of citations, receiving them over a longer time span. Finally, we exploited the timing of SSO patent disclosures to show that there is a correlation between citations and the act of disclosure, representing more than 20% of the total difference between SSO and non-SSO patents.

Subject to concerns about the exogeneity of the disclosure event, the large selection effect suggests that SSOs are successful in identifying important technologies. Furthermore, the significant causal effect suggests that current SSO decisions impact the path of future technological innovation. This may occur because SSOs embed technologies in standards that are difficult to switch away from because of network effects. Alternatively, it may be simply the attention attracted to a technology by a disclosure, possibly due to the disclosure's indication that a patent-holder is willing to license its technology.

The treatment of intellectual property at SSOs is a subject of interest to many in the technology policy-making community, and a number of recent events have increased the prominence of this issue. These events include the Rambus case, the surge in intellectual property disclosures at SSOs, the W3C's (an SSO that sets Web-based standards) decision to adopt a royalty-free licensing policy, and the Standards Development Organization Act of 2004, which extended certain antitrust protections originally contained in the National Cooperative R&D Act to American SSOs. While this article emphasizes the positive question of SSOs' role in technological change, the finding that these institutions not only select important technologies but also may influence their future significance suggests that the policy interest in these issues are justified. While we hope to address a number of these questions in future research, we should acknowledge that it is hard to draw any clear welfare implications from the current results. In particular, the impact of having patents in an industry standard will depend on the rules of the SSO, participants' willingness to license any essential intellectual property, and whether they do so on "reasonable and non-discriminatory" terms. Nevertheless, this article provides some of the first large-sample statistical evidence related to the patents disclosed in the standard setting process, and should be an important starting point for future research.

REFERENCES

Blind, K. (2004). *Economics of standards.* Northampton: Elgar.

Chiao, B., Lerner, J., & Tirole, J. (2005). *The rules of standard-setting organizations: An empirical analysis.* Unpublished Manuscript, Harvard Business School.

Furman, J., & Stern, S. (2004). *Climbing atop the shoulders of giants: The impact of institutions on cumulative research.* Unpublished Manuscript, Northwestern University.

Gandal, N., Gantman, N., & Genesove, D. (2005). Intellectual property and standardization committee participation in the U.S. modem industry. In S. Greenstein, & V. Stango (Eds.), *Standards and public policy.* Cambridge: Cambridge University Press.

Greenstein, S., & Stango, V. (Eds.). (2005). *Standards and public policy.* Cambridge: Cambridge Press.

Hall, B., Jaffe, A., & Trajtenberg, M. (2002). The NBER patent citations data file: Lessons,

insights, and methodological tools. In A. Jaffe, & M. Trajtenberg (Eds.), *Patents, citations and innovations: A window on the knowledge economy.* Cambridge: MIT Press.

Hall, B., Jaffe, A., & Trajtenberg, M. (2005) Market value and patent citations. *RAND Journal of Economics, 36*(1), 26-38.

Hall, B., Jaffe, A. & Trajtenberg, M. (2002). The NBER Patent Citations Data File: Lessons, Insights, and Methodological Tools. In A. Jaffe & M. Trajtenberg (Eds.), *Patents, citations and innovations: A window on the knowledge economy.* Cambridge: MIT Press, 2002.

Hall, B., Mairesse, J., & Turner, L. (2005). *Identifying age, cohort and period effects in scientific research productivity.* Unpublished Manuscript, University of California at Berkeley.

Jaffe, A., & Trajtenberg, M. (2002). *Patents, citations and innovations: A window on the knowledge economy.* Cambridge: MIT Press.

Lemley, M. (2002). Intellectual property rights and standard setting organizations. *California Law Review, 90,* 1889-1981.

Markiewicz, K. (2004). *University patenting and the rate of knowledge exploitation.* Unpublished Manuscript, University of California at Berkeley.

Mehta, A., Rysman, M., & Simcoe, T. (2005). *Identifying age profiles of patent citations.* Unpublished Manuscript, Boston University.

Mowery, D.C., & Simcoe, T. (2002). Is the Internet a US invention? An economic and technological history of computer networking. *Research Policy, 31*(8-9), 1369-1387.

Pakes, A. (1986). Patents as option: Some estimates of the value of holding European patent stocks. *Econometrica, 54*(4), 755-784.

Rysman, M., & Simcoe, T. (2006). *Patents and the performance of voluntary standard setting organizations*. Unpublished Manuscript, Boston University.

Simcoe, T. (2004). *Design by committee? The organization of technical standards development*. Dissertation, University of California at Berkeley.

Toivanen, O. (2005). *Choosing standards*. Unpublished Manuscript, University of Helsinki.

This work was previously published in the International Journal of IT Standards and Standardization Research, Vol. 5, Issue 1, edited by K. Jakobs, pp. 25-40, copyright 2007 by IGI Publishing (an imprint of IGI Global).

Chapter 7
Patents and Standards in the ICT Sector:
Are Submarine Patents a Substantive Problem or a Red Herring?

Aura Soininen
Lappeenranta University of Technology and Attorneys-at-Law
Borenius & Kemppinen, Ltd, Finland

ABSTRACT

Multiple cases have been reported in which patents have posed dilemmas in the context of cooperative standard setting. Problems have come to the fore with regard to GSM, WCDMA, and CDMA standards, for example. Furthermore, JPEG and HTML standards, as well as VL-bus and SDRAM technologies, have faced patent-related difficulties. Nevertheless, it could be argued that complications have arisen in only a small fraction of standardization efforts, and that patents do not therefore constitute a real quandary. This article assesses the extent and the causes of the patent dilemma in the ICT sector through a brief analysis of how ICT companies' patent strategies and technology-licensing practices relate to standard setting and by exemplifying and quantifying the problem on the basis of relevant articles, academic research papers, court cases and on-line discussions. Particular attention is paid to so-called submarine patents, which bear most significance with respect to the prevailing policy concern regarding the efficacy of the patent system.

INTRODUCTION

Background

Our society is filled with various types of standards, commonly agreed ways of doing things.

Standards may be sociocultural, political, economic, or technical. Language is a standard, the metric system is a standard, and so is our social etiquette (Cunningham, 2005). Technical standards could be defined as any set of technical specifications that either provide or are intended to provide a common design for a product or a process. They range from a loose set of product characterizations to detailed and exact specifications for technical interfaces. Some of them control product interoperability, some ensure quality or safety, and some are so-called measurement standards (Grindley, 2002).

Particularly interoperability/compatibility standards are paramount in industries such as information and communications technology (ICT) that are dependent on interconnectivity. In fact, the telecommunications industry has relied on them throughout its history. These standards define the format for the interface, allowing different core products, often from different manufacturers, to use the same complementary goods and services, or to be connected together as networks (Grindley, 2002; Teece, 2000). Thus, interoperability standards enable gadgets to work together and thereby they further the goal of increased communicative potential. This follows that their use may also lead to financial benefits due to so-called network externalities (Cunningham, 2005; Shurmer & Lea, 1995). These strong network effects are present when a product or a service becomes more valuable to users as more people use it. Examples of products that benefit from network effects include e-mail, Internet access, fax machines, and modems (Shapiro & Varian, 1999).

A further economic effect of interoperability standards is that they reduce the switching costs from one supplier to another by preventing producers and consumers from being locked into a proprietary system. Standards, however, do not totally eliminate switching costs. When producers and users become committed to a particular system or standard, and the longer they stay with it, the more expensive and difficult it is for them to switch to another that is comparable (Blind, 2004). Consequently, due to these strong economic effects, control of the outcome of standard setting may yield significant economic advantage on the sale of both core and related products (Hjelm,

2000). Patents that provide their holders with a defined right to prevent others from making, using and selling an invention can be used to gain that leverage or to control the adoption of a standard. Therefore, potential conflicts between patent rights and the need for standardization affect the ICT industry and the consumers at large, and these economic effects need to be bared in mind when examining the deficiencies of prevailing standard-setting procedures and the legal framework.

This article studies the patent-related dilemmas that may arise both in the course of standard setting and after the standard has been established. Potential conflicts and their causes are identified and exemplified on specific case studies, and the study of Blind, Bierhals, Thumm, Hossain, Sillwood, Iverser, et al. (2002) is used to quantify the problems further. The aim is to find out whether the problem with patents, particularly with so-called submarine patents, is substantial, or whether it is only a minor concern that has attracted undeserved attention. Term "submarine patent" is used here for patent applications and patents that may yield significant economic power because they "read on" a standard and come to the fore after it has been established.

Standardization and Patents in General

Standards can be established in many ways: the markets determine *de facto* standards, and organized standards bodies agree upon *de jure* standards. These bodies could be said to include government legislators, official standards organizations, various industry committees, and consortia. Unlike de facto standards, de jure standards are usually established in advance and are later implemented by multiple vendors (Grindley, 2002; Messerschmitt & Szyperski, 2003; Mueller 2001).

Standards emerge from all the sources in the ICT sector listed previously. The Internet Society (ISOC), the Organization for the Advancement of

Structured Information Standards (OASIS), the World Wide Web Consortium (W3C), and the Internet Engineering Task Force (IETF) could be mentioned as examples of bodies active in the field of software and the Internet. Then again, the European Telecommunications Standardization Institute (ETSI), the American National Standardization Institute (ANSI), the International Telecommunications Union (ITU), and the International Organization for Standardization (ISO) could be mentioned as organizations operating in the telecommunications industry (Rahnasto, 2003).

A further distinction is that between open and proprietary standards. The purpose of open standards is to provide an industry with well-documented open specifications that could be implemented without prior business and legal arrangements (Caplan, 2003; Messerschmitt & Szyperski, 2003). Furthermore, with open standards, unlike proprietary standards, development of the specification is open to participants without restrictions. The openness may not always be absolute, however, and as a consequence the term "open standards" has various interpretations in practice (Caplan, 2003; Messerchmitt & Szyperski, 2003). In fact, although patent-free standards have traditionally been preferred in the interests of ensuring their success and promoting their use, it has become more difficult to design standards that do not contain any patentable inventions. This holds true particularly when the aim is to choose pre-eminent technology for a standard (Frank, 2002; Soininen, 2005). Therefore, it is not rare to call a standard open even if it includes patented technology providing that licenses are accessible to all. This definition has been adopted in this article as well.

As to the connection between de facto and de jure standards and open and proprietary standards, privately set de facto standards are typically proprietary in nature (Lemley, 2002) meaning that the patent holder controls their utilization. Then again, official standards organizations typically

promote open standards, and those originating from various industry groups and consortia may fall in either category or somewhere in between depending on whether everyone has been able to participate in the selection of the technical specification, or whether the standard has been agreed upon by a handful of companies having the technical knowledge in the area and who then have it adopted throughout the industry (Rahnasto, 2003). The focus of this article is on open, commonly agreed de jure standards.

As said earlier, although open standards are in principle available for anyone to use proprietary technology may be involved in their implementation, and using the specification may require a license (Rahnasto, 2003). Consequently, many official standards organizations and also some consortia have policies that permit their members to contribute proprietary technology under certain conditions: disclosure of the contributor's essential patents may be required, and before the technology is elected, patent holders are asked whether they are willing to offer a license at least on a non-discriminatory basis and on fair and reasonable terms (Frank, 2002). The purpose is to protect the patent holder's interests while fostering standards that incorporate the best technology and have the capacity for worldwide promulgation (Berman, 2005; Soininen, 2005). These organizations are called together as "standards bodies" or "standards organizations" from now on.

From the companies' perspective the dilemma between patents and open standards arises from the need to ensure returns on R&D investments through the exclusion of others while interoperability requires the inclusion of other parties. In fact, patent holders are free to refuse licensing altogether or they may choose the licensees and the licensing terms freely as long as the practice complies with relevant legislation, such as competition regulation/antrust regulation. Thus, companies appear not to be very willing to license their patented technologies to everyone, particularly not to their competitors, on a royalty-free basis or for low returns. It seems, however, that in the context of common standards a limited exception can often be made for business reasons (Interview data U.S., 2004). Indeed, the use of common protocols and interfaces may expand the markets for networks of products that implement them, and producers then compete by innovating on top of the standardized functions (Peterson, 2002a). Nonetheless, even if a company decided to take part in standard setting, the interests of firms, individual contributors and users participating diverge and patents may be utilized strategically to achieve patent holder's objectives. Consequently, the standardization process may turn out to be burdensome as the mere existence of vested interests, for example, intellectual property rights (IPRs), complicates matters (Farrell, 1996; Shurmer & Lea, 1995; Soininen, 2005). Identifying relevant patents and agreeing on their beforehand cause complications and delays to the standardization process.

The relationship between ICT companies' patent strategies and technology licensing practices discussed earlier in general and in respect to open standards is one of the main questions that need to be addressed further in order to find an explanation to why it is that patents may raise such thorny issues in respect to standards. Moreover, attention has to be paid to the standards organizations' practices and bylaws aimed at reducing that tension in practice.

Standardization and Submarine Patents

As mentioned earlier, different types of standards bodies play an important role in establishing standards in the ICT sector, and many of them allow patented or patentable technology to be submitted, but specifically require disclosure of the patents and occasionally even of pending patent applications during the standardization process, as well as their licensing. This is to clarify relevant rights during the process of standard development and reduce the risks of submarine patents so that patent holders cannot claim infringements afterwards, and thereby prevent others from using a standard, or to extract overly high licensing fees. If all essential, relevant rights are clarified during the process, a well-informed decision can be made (Kipnis, 2000). It might also be possible to design around the identified patents and patent applications, or to choose another technology for a standard. In fact, since patent-free standards are often the first choice, disclosure may have a negative effect on what technology is chosen (Soininen, 2005). For instance, when selecting the GSM standard another viable option was apparently rejected because it was considered too proprietary (Bekkers, Verspagen, & Smits, 2002).

Since proprietary technology may easily be discriminated, companies may even have an incentive to manipulate the standardization process and hide the fact that they have relevant patents. Standardization namely gives patents market power they did not have before (Rahnasto, 2003), which in turn improves the holder's negotiation position following the election and adoption of a standard. Furthermore, the disclosure requirement has its shortcomings and therefore companies may not even need to break the rules to capture an industry standard. The disclosure requirement is not necessarily extended beyond the personal knowledge of the individual participant, it may not be practically possible for a company to clarify all the patents and patent applications, and the obligation does not always cover pending patent applications, especially unpublished ones (Lemley, 2002). Consequently, a large share of the rights is not necessarily considered during the standardization process. Moreover, since standard setting may take a long time, many years in some cases, undertakings usually continue their R&D projects and file more and amend their existing patent applications during that period. Therefore, if the obligation to disclose does not hold throughout the standard setting, it is even more likely that patents will surface after it has been established (Soininen, 2005).

The optimal scope of the disclosure requirement, what happens if the guidelines are breached, and what course of action should be taken if there was no contractual duty or even a recommendation to disclose patents or pending applications and a patent surfaces after the adoption of the standard, remain matters for debate both outside and inside the courts. The submarine patent risk stemming partially from non-disclosure also involves third-party patents. Indeed, as Lemelson's submarine patent tactic has demonstrated, it is ideal from the patent holder's perspective to have a patent claiming technology that becomes widely adopted within an industry (Soininen, 2005). In fact, the submarine patent scenario could be said to have become more probable in recent years as numerous cases have been reported in which, despite efforts to identify relevant patents, claims have surfaced after the standard has been agreed upon (Blind et al., 2002). Furthermore, the importance of patents in business has increased in many respects and the legal framework constituting of patent laws and competition/antitrust regulation that may pose limits to the utilization of patents could also be described as pro-patent even though the system has been severely criticized (FTC, 2003; OECD, 2004). This has resulted not only in a higher number of applied-for and granted patents, but also in more aggressive enforcement and increases in technology licensing, bare patent licensing and cross-licensing, which in turn has the potential of generating more conflicts (Peterson, 2002). In fact, it appears that there is an increase in all types of patent claims and charges that relate to standards, and particularly in telecommunications, negotiations over such matters cause delays in the development of standards worldwide (Krechmer, 2005). Therefore it is essential to study the patent landscape in the ICT sector further, take a closer look at realized disputes and examine the loopholes of the system. Only by understanding how it is failing, it is possible to implement better practices.

Standardization and Licensing

There is another quandary involving patents and standards in addition to the submarine patent dilemma described earlier, and that has to do with licensing. This dilemma relates mainly to the mainstream obligation to license one's essential patents on fair, reasonable and non-discriminatory terms (RAND). The problem is that this problem may be limited in firms' patent statements in various ways, resulting in unexpected hold-ups. Companies may, for example, agree to license only patents that are essential for using that portion of the standard they have suggested, or they may impose limits by stating that licenses are available to any qualified applicants (Frank, 2002; Rahnasto, 2003; Soininen, 2005). One typical qualification is that licenses are offered only to companies that offer reciprocal treatment or promise not to threaten patent litigation against the licensing company (Berman, 2005). Moreover, specific licensing terms are not typically agreed upon during the standardization process so that the standards organization would play a role in it (Kipnis, 2000). Each company negotiates terms separately, which allows it to apply its own interpretations of what is considered fair, reasonable and nondiscriminatory (Frank, 2002; Rahnasto, 2003). In fact, it is for this reason that manufacturers participating in standards committees may even be forced to delay the standards development in order to negotiate acceptable terms before the final vote. The worst-case scenario is that the sum of license fees exceeds the total profit available to a product manufacturer, and that the standard never becomes adopted (Krechmer, 2005). Ultimately, consideration of the fairness, reasonableness and nondiscriminatory nature of the terms is left to the courts (Soininen, 2005). So far, however, the courts have not provided proper guidelines on how to determine what is fair, reasonable and nondiscriminatory (Rahnasto, 2003).

Thus, the problems related to the adoption of standardized technology may have to do with disagreement over the content of a company's licensing statement, even in the absence of submarine patents. One might even wonder, considering the large number of patents that are being reported as essential in the course of standardization, whether the disclosure obligation bears any significance in practice. Therefore, it is not enough to concentrate merely on the submarine patent problem and its causes when there is a possibility that limiting that particular risk might have only minimal effect.

Research Objective and Methodology

Standard setting is the cornerstone of today's economy, and it is essential particularly in the ICT sector. The most important feature of open standards is that they have the potential to become widely promulgated and used without undue restriction: this is essential to their success and to the very idea of something being or becoming a standard. Patents may, however, be used exclusively and therefore they may jeopardize the purpose for which standards have been created. Indeed, submarine patents as well as perplexity regarding proper licensing terms may result in increased costs in the form of excessive licensing fees, or they may force the industry to abandon the standard altogether meaning that the societal benefits may be lost. Since patents help companies to gain leverage over the standard-setting procedure and the adoption of the standard, potential dilemmas addressed in this article are also a policy concern. One may ask particularly in the context of so-called submarine patents whether the patent system fulfils its goal. These patents have factually been hidden and thus they have not contributed to technological development of that specific industry, as is the purpose of the patent system.

This article examines the patent-related dilemmas and analyses their causes by exemplifying and quantifying them on the basis of newspaper stories, online articles, research papers, and trial

documents. Further data was collected from interviews with eleven Finnish ICT companies and eight U.S. ICT companies in order to illustrate the relationship between patent strategies and licensing practices in general and in the context of standard setting. The interviews with the Finnish companies focused on patent strategies and were conducted by the author in 2003. Those with U.S. companies based in the Bay Area, CA, were more general and related to their innovation models, appropriability strategies and licensing practices. They were conducted by the author in cooperation with Pia Hurmelinna-Laukkanen and were completed in 2004. The interviewed firms included different types of ICT companies operating in the fields of information technology (software, hardware and related services for different purposes), chip interface technology, audio technologies, and digital entertainment products designed for computers and the Internet, and telecommunications. It should be noted that most of the U.S. case companies were larger than the Finnish companies, their revenues spanning from $60 million to $19,000 million. Furthermore, the size of their patent portfolios was substantially larger and varied mostly between 300 and 2,000 issued patents (one of the companies did not have patents at all). Only one Finnish company had a substantial portfolio of over 5,000 issued patent families, two of them had a medium-sized portfolio of approximately 60 issued patent families and close to 200 pending applications, and the rest had less than 10 issued patents/pending patent applications. The U.S. companies were also more actively involved in standard setting than the Finnish companies.

Obviously, it is difficult to make generalizations on the basis of such limited data. Thus, the data are used to complement other studies and views presented in the literature. In some cases, however, there were common features applicable to all of the firms, or several of them were found to have certain common denominators. Then again, some of the results are presented as examples of corporate operational models. One reason for this is that the interviews were in-depth in nature, meaning that the discussion was sometimes focused more on certain areas, and it would not therefore be possible to say whether the expressed views were common to all of the companies or not. Furthermore, in some situations less than 8 (U.S.) or 11 (Finnish) companies yielded relevant data: only a few companies in the Finnish sample were involved in setting standards. In the following, I refer to the interview data as interview data U.S. (2004) and interview data Finland (2003).

I will start by re-examining the submarine patent concept because the original meaning of submarine patents has largely disappeared as a result of legislative amendments. Nevertheless, certain aspects of the current patent law still contribute to their existence. I will then study ICT companies' patent strategies and technology licensing practices in order to demonstrate the general developments in the area and tensions between proprietary and open operation models and their implications on standardization. After that I will review the disclosure and licensing challenges that have been reported in the context of standardization and patents, and examine the likelihood of such conflicts. I conclude the article by considering the extent of the problems and whether the submarine patent problem really exists and can be limited, or whether it is merely a red herring that needs no further attention. It should however be noted that the sufficiency and flexibility of the prevailing legal framework applicable to solving potential conflicts is not particularly examined in this article even though it is clear that applicable legal tools influence companies' negotiation power, and thereby their behavior during and after standard setting. These legal tools could also prove helpful in minimizing the harmful societal effects of submarine patents. This type of in-depth analysis would be the next phase following the recognition of the prevailing problem, its magnitude and main causes.

THE ORIGINS OF SUBMARINE PATENTS

The term submarine patent has been traditionally used to refer to (U.S.) patents that are issued after a long, intentionally delayed pendency at the patent office. The purpose of prolonging the application period by filing continuation applications, for example, has been to keep the invention secret as long as necessary for the industry to mature on the basis of the technology. When the industry is faced with the challenge of changing the technology, the patent is allowed to be issued, and the patent holder is in a position to prevent others from utilizing the invention and to demand royalties from those who began to use the technology while the application was pending (Heinze, 2002). Indeed, in the U.S. it is possible to file continuation applications and to preserve the priority date of the parent application as long as the parent application and the following continuation application disclose the same invention. There are no limitations on how many times a parent application can be continued (Graham & Mowery, 2002). The application period may thus last over a decade, and all this may happen even if the patent has not made any contribution to the development of the technology it covers: if it has been secretly pending for a long time, no-one has had the opportunity to find out about the invention, design alternative technologies, or develop the patented technology further. Thus, the trade-off between the inventor (the right to exclude others) and society (detailed information about the invention), the keystone of the patent system, is not in balance (Soininen, 2005). Figure 1 illustrates the popularity of continuations in relation to software and other patents in the U.S.

It is clear from the statistics in Figure 1 that continuations are filed frequently. Nevertheless, submarine patents as defined earlier are rare. In many cases it is inefficiency in the patent office that causes long delays rather than intentional postponement on the patentee's part (Ferguson,

Figure 1. Continuation patents as a proportion of issued patents: Software patents compared with all other patents, 1987-1999 (Graham & Mowery, 2002)

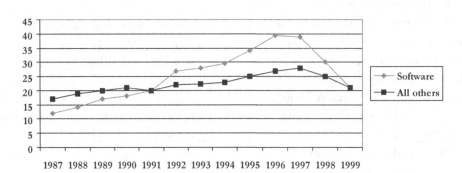

1999). Nonetheless, Jerome Lemelson's patents in particular, issued after decades of pendency at the patent office, have attracted a lot of public attention (Stroyd, 2000; Vanchaver, 2001). Lemelson, who was above all a visionary who anticipated where technology was heading, applied for patents for inventions that he did not himself implement, and amended his applications when necessary to prevent them from being issued. Some of his applications were continued half a dozen times, potentially adding years to the process each time (Varchaver, 2001). He claimed a total of more than 500 patents on basic technologies used nowadays in industrial robots and automated warehouses, as well as in fax machines, VCRs, bar-code scanners, camcorders, and the Sony Walkman. His "machine vision" patent No. 5,283,641 was issued after 42 years of pendency (Stroyd, 2000; Ferguson, 1999; The Lemelson Foundation, n.d.; Soininen, 2005).

Lemelson was active in enforcing his rights. Once someone had developed a product that had some relation to one of his patents, the potential violator was confronted and reasonable compensation was demanded. Aggressive enforcement continues even today, after the death of Lemelson himself. Although quite a few of his patents have been challenged in court, over 750 companies paid royalties for them in 2001 (Soininen, 2005; Stroyd, 2000; Varchaver, 2001). Lemelson is not

the only one to have used submarine patenting tactics, however. Another famous example is Gilbert Hyatt, whose patent for a single-chip microcontroller was issued in 1990 after 20 years of pendency. It was successfully challenged by Texas Instruments, but by that time Hyatt had already been able to collect approximately $70 million in royalties. Submarine patentees also include Olof Soderblom, whose patent for token-ring technology was pending in secrecy in the USPTO for 13 years until it was granted in 1981 (Heinze, 2002). While the application was pending, other companies developed token-ring technologies independently. This development took place in connection with a public-standard-setting process carried out by the Institute of Electrical and Electronic Engineers (IEEE). Since Soderblom's patent surfaced companies have been forced to pay him more than 100 million dollars in royalties (IPO, n.d; Soininen, 2005).

Legal Changes and the Tactics of Submarine Patenting

Since Lemelson's, Hyatt's, and Soderblom's times the U.S. Congress has taken action and amended patent laws in order to discourage submarine patenting. The change from the 17-year patent term counted from the day of issuance to a 20-year term starting from the application date took place in 1995 in accordance with the GATT agreement (Graham & Mowery, 2002). Consequently, a prolonged application period reduces the life of an issued patent. Another amendment made in 1999 was related to the publication of patent applications within 18 months from filing. Although there are exceptions to this rule, the change has reduced the prospect of surprising an industry before 1999 all patent applications filed in the U.S. remained secret until the patent was issued (Graham & Mowery, 2002; Heinze, 2002; Soininen, 2005). A further modification to the Patents Act that would obligate disclosure of all patent applications within 18 months has also been proposed recently before Congress. The introduced bill, H.R. 2795: Patent reform Act of 2005, is currently in the committee hearing phase (GovTrack.us, n.d.).

Furthermore, the U.S. Court of Appeal for the Federal Circuit held some years ago in the Symbol Technologies et al. v. Lemelson case that the equitable doctrine of prosecution laches, which is one of the defenses that can be used in patent infringement cases in order to demonstrate that even though there was a patent infringement, the patent should be held unenforceable, can be applied when the patent is issued following an unreasonable and unexplained delay by the applicant during the patent prosecution. Here, it does not matter whether the patentee's practice of keeping the application pending for many years has been accomplished strictly in accordance with the rules or not (Calderone & Custer, 2005; Soininen, 2005; Symbol Technologies Inc. v. Lemelson Medical, Education & Research Foundation, 277 F.3d 1361, 1363 (Fed. Cir. 2002); *See also* Symbol Technologies, Inc et al. v. Lemelson Medical, Education & Research Foundation, LP et al., 422 F.3d 1378 (Fed. Cir. 2005)).

Thus, it has been confirmed that the doctrine of laches, a defense based on prolonged patent application period, can sometimes be used for protecting an infringer from the harmful effects of submarine patents. Moreover, it is not only after

the patent has been granted that the doctrine of prosecution laches can be applied. The Federal Circuit made it clear in the In re Bogese case that it is possible for the USPTO to address the issue before the patent is granted, and to reject it on this basis (In re Bogese II, 303 F.3d 1362, 1367 (Fed. Cir. 2002)). As far as Europe is concerned, patent applications have traditionally been automatically published within 18 months from filing, and the 20-year patent term has begun from the filing date. Moreover, although it is possible to file divisional applications, continuations are not allowed (Graham & Mowery, 2002; Soininen, 2005).

Submarine Patents Today

If submarine patents are defined narrowly as meaning patents issued after a long, intentionally delayed, secret pendency at the patent office, they do not seem to exist. Nonetheless, despite the legal amendments, circumstances in which patent applications are concealed long enough for the industry to start using a technology without knowing about the lurking patent arise particularly in fields characterized by fast technological development. In some parts of the ICT industry, for example, 18 months of secrecy may already be too long, and prolonging the application phase intentionally is not required for achieving the intended result (Soininen, 2005). Furthermore, patent applicants filing only in the U.S. may currently opt out of the 18-month publication rule and file continuations in order to detect industry developments and to postpone the grant of the patent for five years or so. Since the U.S. is a large and relatively lucrative market, particularly in the computer and software sector (Mueller, 2001), many companies do not even seek international patent protection. Also, provided that the numbers of filed ICT patent applications and granted patents continue their upward trend (OECD, 2005; OECD, 2004), it is getting more and more difficult to be aware of all relevant patents and applications. Especially if inventions are systemic, and innovation is fast and cumulative, multiple patented or patentable inventions may be incorporated into one innovation (Bessen, 2003; FTC, 2003), and therefore infringement is not merely a coincidence that can be avoided but is likely no matter how well the patents and pending patent applications are screened (Interview data U.S., 2004; Watts & Baigent, 2002). For this reason, published patent applications and granted patents may, in reality, be hidden (Soininen, 2005).

Another issue that has to be taken into account is that the scope of a patent typically changes during prosecution. Patent examiners often come up with patentability bars during examination, and require that the scope is limited in some way. Furthermore, as mentioned, the applicant may be able to add and amend patent claims during prosecution so that the scope will better reflect developments in the industry. Here the original application sets the limits for such changes, as its claims must support the new claim and no new matter can be included (EPC, Art 123; Mueller, 2001). As a consequence, although patent application might have been deemed non-essential at the time it was first published, the situation may change before it is granted. Certainly, one element of surprise relates to claim interpretation. Although a patent is a relatively well-defined right, the boundaries are never exact. The scope is not clear until it has been tested in court.

The concept of the submarine patent is understood in this article as broadly referring to patent applications and patents that surface after the standard has been established and take the industry by surprise. Here it does not matter, whether the patent application has been secretly pending or not, even though this possibility certainly contributes to the problem.

Tensions between patents and standards are examined in the following, and the problem of submarine patents and its causes are identified and exemplified further. ICT companies patent strategies and technology-licensing practices are analyzed briefly at first in order to place the

dilemmas between patents and standards into a broader context and to find those practical elements that may contribute to them.

PATENT STRATEGIES AND TECHNOLOGY LICENSING PRACTICES IN THE ICT SECTOR

General Developments

With the shift from an industrial economy toward an information economy, the importance of intellectual property rights (IPRs) has increased. Today, a large proportion of companies' assets constitute intangibles, and IPRs are used to protect and profit from certain of these. Patents, for instance, provide their holders with the right to forbid others from utilizing patented inventions. Holders may thus gain competitive advantage due to their ability to stand out from the competition, or they may use their position to choose their licensees, which is one of their core rights due to the exhaustion doctrine (Kipnis, 2000). Then again, if the patent holder issues a license, as a rule he is entitled to secure any monetary or other compensation he is able to extract from the licensee (Shurmer & Lea, 1995) as long as the licensing terms are coherent with relevant regulation. The objective of licensing is to generate more revenue for the undertaking than it would be able to produce if it manufactured the patented products or utilized patented methods only by itself. Indeed, a well-reasoned licensing program helps a company to position itself favorably in the market place (Megantz, 2002; Soininen, 2005).

Obviously, there are differences between industries with respect to licensing tendencies, but generally speaking, the markets for technology licensing the component of which patents have grown. In fact, in a survey conducted by the OECD/BIAC, 60% of the responding companies reported increased inward and outward licensing, and 40% reported increased cross-licensing. Other types of knowledge sharing have become more common too, and collaboration takes place in the form of sponsored and collaborative research, strategic alliances, as well as in mergers and acquisitions. This has been said to stem from the growing technological complexity, increased technological opportunities, rapid technological change, intense competition, and the higher costs and risks of innovation. As a consequence, companies have namely become more focused on certain areas while they acquire complementary technologies increasingly from other undertakings and universities (OECD, 2004).

The features mentioned previously apply also to the ICT sector, and companies lean heavily on cooperation and networks. Contemporary academic literature refers to this type of innovation as the open innovation model, in contrast to the closed model that used to dominate. Companies applying the closed model seek ultimate control and do everything themselves, while those adopting open innovation realize that valuable ideas do not only originate within their firms, and that it does not have to be the company itself that releases these ideas in the market. Whereas making innovation proprietary and exclusive is a central feature of the closed innovation model, open innovation is characterized by the exploitation of intellectual property in order to create value. The boundary between the company and its environment is said to have become more permeable, enabling ideas and knowledge to flow more freely (Chesbrough, 2003).

One further characteristic of the competitive environment of the ICT sector is so-called coopetition that was pointed out by one of the U.S. interviewees. Coopetition basically means that companies may very well be business partners in some fields and compete aggressively in others (Interview data U.S., 2004). Naturally, all the elements mentioned before signaling the importance of networks, openness in innovation, and coopetition are reflected in ICT firms' patenting practices, the use of patents in their business, enforcement

and infringement avoidance. Furthermore they affect the technology licensing tendencies and licensing terms. Similarly it is possible to detect their implications on standardization and also on settling of disputes as some of the example cases discussed later on demonstrate.

The U.S. Patent Landscape

The patent landscape of the U.S. ICT sector could be described as a thicket to the birth of which strong patent system, technological complexity and fast technological development have contributed. Thus, although a reading of the patent laws gives the impression that there is a correspondence between a product and a patent, this is not necessarily the case: patents may overlap, and the manufacture of one product may require access to hundreds or thousands of patents, or one patent may "read on" many types of products, not just one (FTC, 2003). Therefore, in order to avoid the resulting hold-up problem, many U.S. ICT companies employ defensive patent strategies, and if they have the resources to do so they build large patent portfolios in order to guarantee that others cannot prohibit them from innovating. This in turn increases the number of relevant patents in the industry. Naturally, in addition to the better negotiation position and increased ability to agree on the licensing and cross-licensing they facilitate, patents also provide the means to prevent outright imitation in these cases (FTC, 2003; Interview data U.S., 2004; Soininen, 2005).

In general, the significance of patents as protection mechanisms used to exclude others and thus to generate competitive advantage appears not to be very high in the ICT field, and it is rather competition that spurs innovation in this sector (FTC, 2003). This was reflected in the patent-enforcement activities of the U.S. companies that were interviewed, and which operated on the basis of a defensive patent strategy. Unlike the company that employed an offensive patent strategy and attempted to generate its revenues from technol-

119

ogy and patent licensing, defensively operating firms focused more on their core businesses of making and selling products rather than devoting resources to detecting infringements (Interview data U.S., 2004). Similarly, Messerschmitt and Szyperski (2003) have observed that the exclusionary use of patents is less common in the software industry than in some other industries such as biotechnology and pharmaceuticals. In their opinion this is in part because patents tend to be less fundamental and they can be circumvented easily. Furthermore, according to a quantitative study of U.S. manufacturing firms conducted by Cohen, Nelson, and Walsh (2000), compared to other appropriability mechanisms such as secrecy, other legal tools, lead time, complementary sales, services and manufacturing, patents ranked rather low in effectiveness in fields such as the manufacture of electrical equipment and electronic components, semiconductors and communications equipment, all of which are connected to the ICT sector. Moreover, there were substantial variations between industries: patents appeared to be most important in the chemical industry. This does not mean that they are not acquired for other purposes, such as those indicated earlier, and naturally all of their functions are based on the patent holder's ability to prevent others from utilizing the invention.

Since many ICT companies are dependent on one another as indicated earlier and patents are not vital for protection, they generally have no reason to complicate their business relationships by claiming patent infringement. However, while particularly large U.S. ICT firms seem to be aggressive in building patent portfolios mainly for defensive purposes, offensive patent strategies tend to predominate for individuals and small software companies (Messerschmitt & Szyperski, 2003). Indeed, various sources have reported an increase in companies that derive their revenue purely from patents. These companies, also called patent trolls, do not typically have any R&D of their own, nor do they manufacture any

products themselves: unlike most ICT companies therefore, they are not dependent on other firms. Their business is to force companies involved in manufacturing to license their patents by claiming patent infringement (FTC, 2003; Interview data U.S., 2004; Peterson, 2002b; Surowiecki, 2006). Patent trolls seek for direct licensing revenues and do not usually benefit from a cross-license. Therefore a defensive patent strategy that might otherwise help certain ICT companies to maintain their freedom-to-operate, and that has proven successful also in the context of standards as will be illustrated later has only minimal influence on them.

It is not only patent trolls that seek to make better use of their patent portfolios, however. The prevailing trend in the U.S. has been to found patent-licensing programs, sometimes by forming a separate patent-licensing unit, for the purpose of generating extra revenues mainly from inventions that are not considered core to the company's main operations (Rivette & Kline, 2000). This trend is likely to have an effect also on standardization as standards are becoming more and more vital for the ICT industry and thus they also carry a lot of economic significance. Consequently, having a patent that claims a broadly adopted standard may be a dream come true for a company seeking licensing revenues and not operating in that particular technology area.

Basically, patents are viewed as core elements of corporate business strategies in the U.S. ICT sector. They are employed for multiple purposes in different contexts. They may be used as protection measures and as components in joint ventures, in patent pools, and technology licensing arrangements. A license may also be a pure patent license or a broad cross-license providing a company with not-to-sue coverage. Furthermore, patents may be used to attract other types of resources to the company. They serve as indicators of innovativeness, and can be helpful in attracting financing: they can be used as collateral and are seen as a positive indication in the eyes of venture-capital investors and potential buyers. In fact, one trend that is detectable in the U.S. is the increased tendency of selling and buying patent portfolios and individual patents (FTC, 2003; Interview data U.S., 2004). This may happen in conjunction with the acquisition of an entire company, or patents may be bought from bankrupt firms. This follows that it is not easy to avoid patent infringement as patents may easily find their way to unknown parties meaning that a notification of potential patent infringement may practically come from anyone.

There is one further feature about the U.S. patent landscape that should be noted. It has been claimed that a substantive number of patents are being granted particularly in new areas such as software and the Internet that do not actually fulfill the patentability requirements. These so-called bad patents have contributed to various patent-related difficulties and they have been deemed to be one of the main reasons why the U.S. patent system is not in balance (FTC, 2003).

The European Patent Landscape

So far Europe has not faced patent trolling on a large scale, which could be explained by the fact that the consequences of litigation and infringement are less severe: while the average cost of patent litigation in the U.S. amounts to more than $2 million per side (Vermont, 2002), in Finland the figure for hearing an infringement the case in the district court is closer to EUR 150 000 per side. Of course the total amount of litigation costs may be fundamentally higher if the case involves various phases such as a precautionary measure claim, and both infringement and annulment actions. Moreover, the damages issued are substantial in the U.S. For instance, in 1990 the Federal District Court awarded $910 million in damages to Polaroid in its patent-infringement litigation against Kodak, Alpex Computers was awarded $260 million for patent infringement (litigation against Nintendo) in 1994, and in 2003

Microsoft was forced to pay Eolas $521 million for infringement of an Internet browser patent (PwC Advisory, 2006). By way of comparison, the largest amount of damages ever awarded in Finland was EUR 252,282 (Labsystems Oy v. Biohit Oy, HO S 94/1922, Court of Appeal).

Furthermore, the patent web in the ICT sector appears to be less complex in Europe than in the U.S., although there are certainly variations between different technology areas. For instance, the European mobile-phone industry and the electronics field are areas in which large patent portfolios are common (OECD, 2004; Watts & Baigent, 2002). However, with the exception of the large telecommunications and electronics companies, patents seem to be regarded not so much as strategic assets, but rather as legal tools applied and used for protecting the results of the company's own R&D efforts, and occasionally for licensing (DLA, 2004; Interview data Finland, 2003).

It was evident, for instance, from the interviews with the Finnish companies that were not involved in the mobile-phone area as manufacturers, and had less than 70 issued patent families, that small-scale portfolio building was the preferred strategy for avoiding otherwise weak patent protection. There were no cross-licenses, however, and the companies appeared to be able to operate freely without paying much attention to the patents of others (Interview data Finland, 2003). In general, the patent application part of the patent strategy was well thought out, although it should be noted that the process was technology-oriented and lacked the type of business acumen that was present in the U.S. (Interview data Finland, 2003). In fact, this is a conclusion that has been shared also by others. For instance Kratzman (2005) pointed out in his research:

Finnish patents tend to be academic and not written to generate revenue. They are not commercial nor do they cover multiple applications, an essential element in generating licensing interest. (p. 14)

With respect to the utilization of the patents in the company's business transactions and the infringement surveillance, they could be described as incidental, perhaps because patents were not regarded as important contributors to the company's revenue stream, and most Finnish companies had so few of them. Lead time, constant innovation and, in the area of software, copyright protection, were considered more important (Interview data Finland, 2003). Furthermore, attitudes towards patents appear to be largely negative, even indifferent, in the software industry in particular (Interview data Finland, 2003), which, based on Blind et al. (2001), applies not only to Finland but also to the rest of the Europe as far as independent software developers are concerned. It should be noted, though, that even small and medium-sized companies are beginning to realize the importance of strategic patent management, perhaps partially as a response to the attention paid to patents by investors. Generally speaking, there is a steady increase in the propensity of filing patents in the European ICT sector (OECD, 2005), which in turn will probably increase the likelihood of patent-based conflicts, and make it more difficult to design around the patents when selecting a standard, for instance. Currently, however, European companies appear not to be employing their patents as aggressively as U.S. undertakings and therefore there is a chance that even though European companies had patents that could be characterized as submarines, this would not create substantial hindrances to the industry. On the other hand, markets for technology are international and as the case with GSM standard that will be discussed in the licensing section of this article illustrates, also patent strategies of U.S. companies tend to influence European standardization efforts.

Licensing Practices in the ICT Sector

As regards to companies licensing practices, some companies tend to be more open in their operations than others. Usually it is rather easy to outsource the manufacturing of products, their distribution and marketing, but it is the development that R&D-intensive companies prefer to keep to themselves. This could be detected in the technology-licensing practices of the U.S. ICT companies, which, given the reported increase of 4000% in licensing revenues from 1980 to 1990 (Vermont, 2002) and the recent fascination surrounding the success of open-source software licensing, were surprisingly closed, particularly in terms of licensing in external technologies.

One of the interviewees explained the situation by saying that it was difficult to find useful technologies, and counting on outside technologies was usually considered risky due to potential problems with third-party rights and quality issues, for example. In-house R&D was simply trusted more. When companies did rely on external technologies, they rather acquired the entire company than licensed-in the technology. If they did license-in it was largely limited to non-core elements and design tools. As for licensing-in open-source software, the companies were very careful, and typically had tools in place to make sure that they audited what came in (Interview data U.S., 2004).

When it comes to licensing out their technologies interviewed companies tended to be more open, and there was one company whose business model was based mainly on this. Furthermore, licensing out was used in order to integrate in-house technologies into other companies' products and to make them compatible so that the market for that technology would expand. The licensing models adopted in the interviewed software companies were basically very broad for distribution purposes, and they licensed software to their customers as a package and to other companies to be used as embedded in their products. However, with the exception of commonly established standards, other types of technology licensing that did not involve a complete product were limited (Interview data U.S., 2004).

The licensing terms companies follow naturally vary depending on the subject matter, the business model adopted for the particular product or technology, and the parties involved. Nevertheless, there are certain typical configurations that reflect the extent of control the licensor or the licensee has. The scope of the license is paramount: the licensor retains more control over the technology if he or she grants only non-exclusive rights, which appears to be the most common form in the ICT sector. The possibility to define the degree of exclusivity, for example, in terms of geographic areas or certain uses, and the ability to assign and sublicense the rights are other key elements in determining the scope of a license (Poltorak & Lerner, 2004). Incorporating technical assistance also gives the licensor control over the licensed technology. In the case of trademarks in particular, the licensor has good reason to control the quality of the licensed products, and to put in place certain procedures for testing them and inspecting the licensee's production facilities (Megatz, 2002). It is also advisable to include a termination clause to enable either party to get out of the contractual relationship if necessary. One of the most intriguing termination clauses that reflects the atmosphere in the ICT industry relates to patent peace: such clauses are frequently used in open-source licenses, for instance, and in their broadest form they provide the licensor with the right to terminate the license in the face of claims by the licensee regarding infringement on any of its patents. Representations, warranties, and indemnification clauses related to risk allocation, as well as royalty rates, also affect the balance of the contractual relationship.

Most importantly, however, attention needs to focus on terms relating to modifications, improvements, and therefore also grant-backs. From the licensor's perspective, it is often advantageous to obtain the rights to any improvements developed by the licensee, preferably including the right to sublicense the improvements to other licensees. This would prevent the licensee from using a fundamental improvement or an extensive new development to gain control over the licensor's core technology. Then again, access to improvements developed by the licensor is important for the licensee in ensuring the continued viability of the licensed product or technology (Megantz, 2002).

Some of the companies interviewed had adopted a very restrictive approach to modifications, allowing them only rarely and even then often requiring grant-back terms. Control was maintained through the heavy involvement of the licensor's engineers in the implementation phase, and through quality control. The licensor also typically maintained the right to modify the license terms. Then again, in the context of software licenses, the licensees had very few rights, the source code was seldom provided, and reverse engineering was typically prohibited. Obviously, this depended on whether it was an end-user license, an OEM agreement or a VAP bundle agreement. On the other hand, some companies had adopted a more open approach and operated on a more flexible and market-driven basis. Interfaces were opened up, for instance, and one of the companies even licensed out its software under various open-source agreements (Interview data U.S., 2004).

It could be concluded from previous discussion that R&D intensive ICT companies have rather control-seeking licensing models, but they may be flexible too if it suits the company's business model. Thus, since standards are of crucial importance in this industry, exceptions are often made for the essential purpose of securing product compatibility, interoperability and interconnection (Interview data U.S., 2004). In fact, since many companies may be developing equipment or software for the same systems and platforms, for example, and there are inevitably huge numbers of relevant patents involved (Watts & Baigent, 2002), standardization may prove effective in providing access to essential patents held by various firms. On the other hand, it must be remembered that companies' prevailing licensing practices tend to show also in the standard-setting context, and although the patent policies of standards organizations typically give specified options to the patent holder, different licensing terms can be used to maintain control over the technology as indicated already in the background section of this article. Furthermore, it is only the essential patents need to be licensed when a company participates in setting a standard. As one of the interviewees pointed out, this constitutes a fairly thin layer. Only patents that are technically or commercially necessary to ensure compliance with the standard must be licensed, and only to the extent that it is necessary. Therefore, if the patent holder has waived its rights, for instance, patents cannot be asserted for complying with the standard, but they can be asserted if something extra is being done (Interview data U.S., 2004). Then again those companies that do not benefit from a common standard or are after royalties have generally no interest in taking part in standard setting because doing so could require the licensing of their rights under royalty-free or RAND terms.

The licensing quandaries will be discussed later on, and I will now turn to a more detailed analysis of the submarine patent risk stemming from deficient identification of essential patents to which some of the factors presented in this and the earlier section clearly contribute. Generally speaking the highlighted importance of intellectual property rights and their substantial role as part of companies' business strategies has made it more difficult to avoid conflicts of interests.

STANDARDIZATION AND SUBMARINE PATENTS

Both patents providing their holders with exclusive rights, and open standards expected to be widely promulgated without exclusive control are important to the ICT sector. As they both want different things resolution is not always easy (Cunningham,

2005). From the perspective of this article the core element contributing to the tension between patents and standards, is that it is not always known in advance whether undertakings have patents or pending patent applications that might cover the standards technology. This complicates matters, since patents that surface after the adoption of the standard may, in the worst case, result in no other choice than abandoning it. Although both licensing and patent identification quandaries that were introduced briefly already in the background section may lead to significant economic losses, it is more difficult to anticipate the consequences and to avoid problems in the latter case. Therefore, submarine patents that surface after a standard has been elected and adopted are not only a practical dilemma but also a policy concern. Submarine patents may face the industry with unpredictable predicaments, and ultimately harm consumers. Cases in which unidentified patents of standard setters have caused concern and resulted in legal disputes include Dell and Rambus litigations. Third-party submarines contain the patents of Forgent Networks, Inc and Eolas Technologies, Inc among others.

The most effective way to reduce the possibility of hidden patents that have the potential to cause complications with respect to the adoption of a standard is to conduct a proper patent due diligence periodically and to agree upon the contravening issues beforehand. This is where the patent policies of standards organizations that are aimed at creating shared expectations among standardization participants with respect to licensing and disclosure rules come to the fore (Interview data U.S., 2004; Ohana, 2005). Indeed, if companies participate in setting a standard they usually do their best to follow the standardization organization's patent policies, and consider any deviation unethical (Interview data U.S., 2004; Ohana, 2005). Sometimes the rules are simply not very transparent, and since different standardization organizations have different types of policies it may be burdensome to be aware of and to comply with them all, particularly if the company is involved in many standards organizations. In fact, about 40% of companies in Blind et al. (2002) sample group reported that they had problems due to the unclear IPR structure, resulting, for instance, in the late identification of the patent holders. There is a need for rules that hold as few surprises as possible (Interview data U.S., 2004; Ohana, 2005).

The standards organization's patent policies and their shortcomings with respect to the disclosure obligation are examined in subsequent paragraphs. Since companies adopting the standard ultimately bear the responsibility for patent infringement, there is then a brief glimpse into that part of companies' patent strategies that is aimed at reducing that risk. Combined with what has been said earlier about the patent system and the patent landscape in the ICT sector, these sections constitute the analysis of the causes contributing to the likelihood of infringing others' essential patents in the ICT sector and the challenges companies face in settling these disputes particularly due to the emergence of so-called patent trolls. Case studies illustrate the situation further and give examples of actualized disagreements. The fact that many disputes have been handled in court demonstrates that it has not been possible to settle the issues amicably and that there are significant economic interests involved.

Patent Policies

Many, although not all, standards bodies that are responsible or involved in coordinating the development of standards have implemented explicit IPR or patent policies for handling issues to do with standardization and patents. These policies aim at discouraging the manipulation of the process in order to gain market power, and at easing the tension between the open nature of standards and the proprietary nature of IPRs (Feldman & Rees, 2000; Kipnis, 2000; Soininen, 2005). The policies guide the participant's behavior, and from the legal point of view their nature and content affect the determination of whether a company participating in standard setting and failing to disclose its relevant rights has breached a contract, defrauded, competed unfairly or deceptively or abused its dominant position, for example. Therefore, if the patent policy is deficient, it is difficult to challenge the patent holder's right to prevent all others from using his invention, discriminate among licensees or to condition the license however he wants to as long as this is done in accordance with relevant laws. In the following attention is paid to the nature, extent, scope and timeframe of the prevailing disclosure obligations of different organizations such as ITU, ANSI, ETSI, W3C, OASIS, and IETF and their ability to reduce the risk of submarine patents is assessed.

Nature of the Policy

It has been argued that without legally binding policies standards could easily become the subject of "hold-up" because once a standard has been established, all the patents necessary to comply with it become truly essential. The more widely the standard is adopted, the more power the patent holders gain (Shapiro, 2001). Nonetheless, not all standards organizations aspire to control their participants through imposing on them explicit contractual obligations, and many use their policies more as a "code of practice" (e.g., ITU-T Patent Policy, n.d.). ANSI, for example, has taken the position that it does not mandate disclosure or impose licensing obligations on patent holders because this would overburden the process. It relies more on its participants to voluntarily act in accordance with the policy. Nevertheless, according to Marasco (2003) it has not so far faced abuse of the process. Actually, even though the guideline-nature of the disclosure requirement may narrow down the possibilities to enforce it in court and to claim damages in case of an infringement, non-obligatory rules may also bear significance when it is determined whether a certain participant has operated in good faith under some other principle of law, such as Federal Trade Commission Act, Section 5 that prohibits unfair and deceptive business practices. The case studies of Dell and Rambus examined later will demonstrate this issue further.

The Duty to Disclose

The patent policies of standardization organizations differ in their approach to disclosure in terms of duty to disclose, the scope of the disclosure and its timing. For the most part, they tend to rely on their participants (submitters or members [Perens, n.d.]) to voluntarily disclose all patents that could influence the standard. This is by no means a simple task, and failing to disclose patents that are essential for using the standard may happen by accident. Searching the portfolio is time-consuming and expensive, and therefore companies may not want to make the expense of searching them. Also, it is not always easy to recognize all essential patents and patent applications. This follows that particularly in big companies with large portfolios a company's representative in a standard-setting process may not know whether a proposed standard incorporates a patent within his company's portfolio (Kipnis, 2000; Peterson, 2002b; Soininen, 2005).

It is probably for this reason that standards organizations generally take no responsibility for finding all relevant IPRs, or for verifying the information disclosed by the contributors (e.g., ANSI, 2003b; IETF, 2005; OASIS, 2005), and they are not keen on imposing such obligations on their participants. Thus, many of them do not require disclosure that goes beyond the personal knowledge of the discloser (e.g., IETF, 2005; OASIS, 2005), nor do they require their participants to carry out patent searches (e.g., ANSI, 2005a; ETSI, 2005; ITU-T, 2005; OASIS, 2005; W3C, 2004), which in turn increases the probability that relevant patents remain undisclosed (Soininen, 2005).

Scope of the Disclosure Requirement

Another contributing factor to the submarine patent risk is that it is not necessarily required for companies to disclose their pending, particularly unpublished, patent applications (e.g., ANSI, 2003b; ANSI, 2003a; Kipnis, 2000; Lemley, 2002). The W3C disclosure requirement is an exception, however. It also extends to the unpublished patent claims that were developed based on information from a W3C Working Group or W3C document (W3C, 2004). The OASIS policy also requires the disclosure of all patents and/or patent applications known to the technical committee member (OASIS, 2005). The problem with announcing pending patents is that, although the protection provided by a patent is always unclear until confirmed in court, the scope is even more ambiguous until the patent is issued, and it is therefore not possible to assess whether it will be essential in order to use the technology. It is also possible that it will never be granted. The problem is, however, that if there is no obligation to disclose pending patent applications, waiting until the standard has been agreed upon before allowing the patent to be issued does not constitute a policy breach. In fact, given the need to make informative decisions about standard "characteristics," there has been discussion on whether participants should also be obliged to disclose their potential patenting activity. The U.S. patent system includes a so-called grace period, which allows the inventor to file for a patent up to one year after disclosing it in a printed publication. Thus, it is possible for a company that has submitted a technical proposal to the standards body to then file for a patent covering it after the standard has been elected.

Opinions on the scope of the disclosure obligation are divided. Some people feel that, although companies were required to state their possible interest in patenting their technology, it is never certain that they will apply these patents in reality, or that they will be granted or even essential. On the one hand, if companies had to announce their potential pending patents, other committee members could take them into account when decisions about standardized technology were made (Kipnis, 2000). At the same time, there might be a risk of "sham" announcements in these cases (Soininen, 2005).

Timing of the Disclosure

The timeframe of the disclosure requirement also bears significance in respect to the causes of the submarine patent problem. Since standardization may be valid for years and companies' R&D development is definitely not frozen during that time, it is likely that pending patent applications will be modified and new applications filed during the process. Therefore, although a company may have no pending patent applications or granted patents at the beginning, it might have them when the standard is finally set. For this reason, some standards bodies, such as W3C, have patent policies that incorporate an obligation to disclose essential patents throughout the entire process (W3C, 2004). The ETSI IPR Policy also requires each member to make reasonable efforts to inform the ETSI in good time about any essential patents, both its own and third-party, of which it becomes aware at any stage (ETSI, 2005). Then again, the IETF policy encourages contributors to update their disclosures if the claims are modified, or if a patent is granted or abandoned (IETF, 2005).

Third-Party Patents

Standards organizations patent policies can never bind third parties and even though some patent policies do encourage also other interested parties as well as contributors to bring attention to potential third-party patents (e.g., IETF, 2005; ITU-T, n.d.; ITU-T, 2005; OASIS, 2005), this is not enough to record all of them. One option to increase the awareness of third-party rights would be to conduct a patent search. Standards bodies are not typically involved in such an activity,

however (e.g., IETF, 2005; OASIS, 2005). On the other hand, ETSI is now considering an ex ante approach to declaring relevant patents with respect to the Long-term Evolution (LTE) standard (Informamedia.com, 2006). This would at least diminish the likelihood that new essential patents emerge after the standard has been elected and it remains to be seen whether this approach will be adopted on a broader scale.

It could be concluded that patent policies are helpful in reducing particularly the risk of standard setters' submarine patents and even though they could be strengthened in many ways to narrow down the possibility of manipulating the process in order to gain market power, some of the difficulties are mainly practical. Therefore it might not be possible to avoid them even if companies were posed an obligation to disclose their potential patenting activity, for instance. The only effect of doing so could be that companies are discouraged from participating which in turn would increase the risk that patents remain undisclosed and generate problems at a later stage.

Patent Strategies to Avoid Infringement

There may be a room for improvement in standards bodies patent policies but it is not only loopholes in them but also deficiencies in companies' own patent strategies that contribute to the fact that relevant rights may remain unnoticed and standard adopters may face predicaments due to them. Obviously, it is the company incorporating a standard into its products and services that ultimately bears the risk of infringing others' patents, and therefore identifying relevant rights is not by any means only the responsibility of standards organizations. Indeed, in addition to enhancing a company's own patenting, licensing and enforcement activities, a proficient patent strategy also helps in avoiding patent infringements.

A major goal in managing corporate patent liability is to avoid being sued and paying substantial royalties to other patent holders. What is even more important is to avoid being prevented from using a particular technology, which could force the company out of a lucrative market (Miele, 2000). Furthermore, the costs of patent litigation, particularly in the U.S., could be substantial and a drain on financial and human resources (Knight, 2001). Thus, if it is necessary to prevent significant liability, the company should consider refraining from using technology that infringes others' rights. In some cases this is not possible, and the company has to employ such technology that has been patented by others in order to operate in a particular market. Keeping both situations in mind, there are certain steps that could be taken in order to reduce the liability, the likelihood that patent holders will assert their rights against the company, and the amount of royalties that should be paid in cases in which patent liability cannot be avoided (Miele, 2000). One of these steps includes identifying patent problems early in the product cycles. For instance, a freedom-to-operate search conducted on the basis of patent classification numbers and certain keywords might be useful for identifying close references, which could then be examined in more detail (Knight, 2001) before the product is released onto the market. Another step is to monitor the patent activities of the company's closest and biggest competitors because companies are often particularly sensitive to infringing activities that originate from their competitors (Miele, 2000).

In practice avoiding infringements is not that easy and companies' patent strategies are not flawless. No patent search is or can be 100% thorough (Knight, 2001), and as many Finnish interviewees mentioned, it may be difficult to identify relevant rights and to make sense of the scope of patent rights (Interview data Finland, 2003). Sometimes, a company may not even have any specialized infringement surveillance. Indeed, in Finnish companies infringement checkpoints were rarely incorporated into R&D projects. This does not indicate, however, that there was no knowledge whatsoever about the patent landscape: information regarding other companies' patent position can be obtained as a side product when the company is considering patenting its own inventions and conducts prior art searches for that purpose (Interview data Finland, 2003). As far as the U.S. companies were concerned, the extent of due diligence with regard to others patents varied depending on the situation: some technology areas were more important, and some were known to be more heavily patented than others, thus requiring more thorough clarification. Nevertheless, these companies typically did not have any systematic patent clearance (Interview data U.S., 2004).

A further risk-reducing alternative to freedom-to-operate analysis and other types of patent surveillance is to use the porcupine approach discussed earlier in the section on patent strategy in the ICT sector. This means that a company builds a defensive patent portfolio aimed at reducing potential infringement allocations and making settlement easier. It may also have broad cross-licenses in place, thereby removing a huge block of patents from its surveillance list (Interview data Finland, 2003; Interview data U.S., 2004). This is a strategy that has been favored by large U.S. and multinational Finnish ICT companies, but unfortunately it does not work well against individual patent holders or so-called patent trolling companies. The fact that patents are being assigned more than before, further increases the risk that they find their way to such parties that do not come up in competitor surveillance and remain unnoticed for that reason.

In sum, companies may take certain precautions to prevent patent liability, but even if they do, the risk of patent infringement remains particularly high in areas in which it is simply not possible to keep track of new filed applications and issued patents. As one of the U.S. interviewees stated, there is always a risk that others' patents will read on your product. You can do all the clearance work and look at all the patents that are out there, but the next week a new patent may be granted (Interview data U.S., 2004). Nevertheless, there are many improvements that could be made in order to strengthen the infringement surveillance, and instead of fighting only their own battles during the standard-adoption phase, companies could pool their expertise and resources and help to limit the submarine patent risk already before the standard is established.

Case Studies of Standard-Setters' Submarine Patents

Standards organizations' IPR policies related to disclosure do not cover every situation, which is understandable, since weight must also be given to the flexibility of the process. Also the means ICT companies have currently implemented in order to avoid infringement of other companies' patents do not help much in identifying relevant rights. The unfortunate consequences are that despite the efforts there still is a high risk that patents surface after the establishment of the standard, and these (essential) patents are much more valuable then than they would have been previously: it gets more difficult to change the specification as time passes and the technology becomes adopted. Therefore, particularly if they are not breaching IPR policy, some patent holders may seize the opportunity and seek to hide the fact that they have essential patents, or pending applications—otherwise the standard could be modified so that it no longer covers them.

The problem with standard-setters' submarine patents is not only theoretical, because the risk has actualized also in reality. Cases that have involved undisclosed patenting activities and have resulted in legal disputes include Dell, Rambus and Unocal from which Dell and Rambus cases are discussed in the following. These examples demonstrate further the importance and role of a proficient patent policy since it does not merely help to reduce the submarine patent risk beforehand but it also influences the possibilities to solve

the problem later on. The previously-mentioned example cases indicate, for instance, that competition authorities do not take misbehavior during standard setting lightly and are keen on examining doubtful situations even though the merits of the case may not be sufficient in order to find fault from the defendant's side. In the end the result is dependent on the wording of the policy and proof of misbehavior. In a way legal tools that are available provide the last means to solve actualized conflicts. Luckily, litigation is not always needed. For instance IBM's behavior in relation to ebXML standard implies that consequences of the failure to disclose are not always detrimental. Since many ICT companies are largely dependent on one another it may be possible to reach an amicable solution rather easily in some situations.

Federal Trade Commission v. Dell Computer Corp. (1995)

In the Dell (1995) case the Federal Trade Commission (FTC) accused Dell Computer Corporation, on the basis of Section 5 of the FTC Act which prohibits unfair or deceptive business practices, of intentionally concealing its patent during the Video Electronics Standards Association (VESA) VL-bus technology standardization process. Although VESA's IPR policy required that its members disclose any potentially conflicting patents, Dell certified that it did not have such patents. After the standard had been widely adopted in the marketplace, Dell sought to enforce its patent against VESA members. The Commission found that even if Dell's actions were not strictly speaking intentional, the company had failed to act in good faith. It also stated that had Dell disclosed its patents properly, VESA would have incorporated different technology into the standard. Dell's misrepresentation therefore caused restraints on competition resulting in the hindrance of industry acceptance and increased costs in terms of implementing the bus design (Federal Trade Commission v. Dell Computer

Corp., FTC File No. 931 0097 (2 November 1995)) (Soininen, 2005).

In the end, a consent decree was agreed upon and Dell promised not to assert its patents against computer manufacturers that complied with the standard (Balto & Wolman, 2003; Hemphill, 2005; Lemley, 2002). It should be noted, however, that even though a satisfactory result was reached through a settlement the case was not decided in court leaving the industry with ambivalence about the proper interpretation. In fact, the Rambus litigation discussed later indicates that the conclusion could have been different if the case had been litigated further.

Rambus, Inc v. Infineon Technologies AG (Fed. Cir. 2003) and Federal Trade Commission v. Rambus, Inc.

Rambus has faced two litigations due to its actions in the Joint Electronics Devices Engineering Council (JEDEC). The first one, Rambus, Inc v. Infineon Technologies AG (2003), arose when Rambus sued Infineon for synchronous dynamic random access memory (SDRAM) patent infringement. Infineon counter-claimed that Rambus had defrauded it when it failed to disclose patents and pending patent applications during its membership of JEDEC and while JEDEC was developing the industry standard for SDRAM. More specifically, Rambus had filed for a patent '898 for Rambus DRAM technology in 1990, it cooperated in forming the standard from 1992 until 1996 when it resigned from the standards body just before the final vote, and both during and after its participation it had filed continuation and multiple divisional applications based on the original 898 application, and by doing so it amended its patent protection to cover the SDRAM technology. Later, it allowed these patents to be issued, and began to defend its own patents aggressively, requiring companies to pay royalties. Nonetheless, the Federal Circuit came to the conclusion that Rambus had not fraudulently failed to disclose

its patent applications, but held that its duty to disclose as a JEDEC participant applied only to those containing claims that could reasonably be considered necessary in order to practice the proposed standard, and that this obligation arose only when the work had formally begun. The court held further that the duty to disclose did not cover the participant's future plans or intentions, that is, filing or amending patent applications, and criticized JEDEC's patent policy for its staggering lack of defining details. It thereby left its members with vaguely defined expectations as to what they believed the policy required. (Rambus, Inc v. Infineon Technologies AG, No. 01-1449 [Fed. Cir. 2003]; Soininen, 2005).

The second litigation, FTC v. Rambus, Inc was based on Section 5 of the FTC Act, and it is still pending. The FTC has accused Rambus of a series of anti-competitive acts and practices, claiming that through deliberate and intentional means it has illegally monopolized, attempted to monopolize, or otherwise engaged in unfair methods of competition in certain markets related to the technological features necessary for the design and manufacture of a common form of digital computer memory. It further claims that Rambus's anti-competitive behavior has, among other things, increased the royalties associated with the manufacture, sale, or use of synchronous DRAM technology, and has reduced the incentive to produce memory using it and to participate in JEDEC or other industry standard-setting organizations or activities (Administrative Complaint, 2002; Soininen, 2005).

The difference between FTC v. Rambus and the Dell case is that in the former the FTC is attempting to demonstrate that Rambus gained market power through its misbehavior, and thus that the industry is locked into the JEDEC's SDRAM standard. According to the FTC, "It is not economically feasible for the industry to attempt to alter or work around the JEDEC standards in order to avoid payment of royalties to Rambus"

(Administrative Complaint, 2002). In its initial decision released on 24 February 2004, Judge MacGuire stated that the FTC "failed to sustain their burden of establishing liability for the violations alleged," and dismissed the complaint. In her opinion there was no evidence, for example, that Rambus had violated JEDEC patent policy, or that the challenged conduct had had anti-competitive effects (Initial Decision, 2004; Soininen, 2005). To conclude, even though a standard setter has operated unethically and the other participants disapprove his conduct, it may be difficult to challenge it in court particularly if proper guidelines are lacking.

IBM and the ebXML Standard

Even though Dell and Rambus attempted to enforce their rights against those who had adopted the standard, patent holders do not always seek royalties although a patent emerges after the standard has been established. One reason for a submarine patent holder to comply with the standards organization's policy is the bad publicity, which may result in the loss of credibility as a fair standardization participant (Sarvas & Soininen, 2002). For example, IBM claimed in April 2002 that it had one patent and one patent application that were relevant for implementing the open, royalty-free ebXML standard developed by OASIS in cooperation with the United Nations, and that it was willing to license them on RAND terms. IBM's announcement caused strong reactions in the public and in the industry, particularly because IBM had participated in the design of the standard. Furthermore, IBM had previously announced that it was willing to contribute to the standard without any restrictions, but had nevertheless made comments regarding the licensing terms and conditions of the two patents. However, soon after the news reached the public, IBM agreed to license the patents royalty-free (Berlind, 2002a; Berlind, 200b; Wong, 2002).

Case Studies of Third-Party Submarines

Those companies that do not benefit from a specific standard simply do not participate in setting it and therefore it may happen that third parties who are not covered by patent policies have patents that "read on" the standard, and do not appear before its adoption. If the patent holder then decides to enforce his rights, the benefits of the standard may be lost. In fact, many businesses that received patents during the technology boom were either purchased by other companies or landed in holding companies. Thus, in some cases a standards organization may adopt a standard believing it is royalty-free, and then find out that the new owner, which did not participate in the standard-setting process, is aggressively trying to enforce its IPRs (Clark, 2002). For instance, the director of intellectual property at Jupiter Networks Inc has observed a sudden surge in these types of third-party patent-infringement assertions, some of which are valid and some are not. This surge is understandable in his opinion, because patent holders hope to profit from the wide deployment of products that must implement Internet standards. He described a typical patent-assertion scenario in which a patent holder dusts off issued patents directed to old but related technologies or modifies claims in pending patent applications to read on published standards, and then targets standards-compliant networking-equipment manufacturers (Lo, 2002). The case studies presented in subsequent paragraphs illustrate the type of legal disputes that may arise if a third-party patent holder attempts to enforce his rights. Basically, the accused infringer can defend itself by claiming non-infringement or unenforceability, or by attempting to invalidate the patent. These are the strategies followed also in the case studies presented.

Forgent Networks and the JPEG Standard

A third-party claim arose in 2002 when Forgent Networks Inc searched its portfolio of 40 patents and found that it had a patent (US Patent 4,698,672) related to the implementation of a baseline version of the ISO/IEC 1098-1 standard, that is, the JPEG image standard that is one of the most popular formats for compressing and sharing files on the Internet, and is also used in various industries in products such as digital cameras, personal digital assistants, cellular phones, printers and scanners. In its desperate search for profits, Forgent estimated the solidness of its infringement claim and entered into a multi-million-dollar licensing agreement with the Japanese companies Sony and Sanyo before making a public announcement in July 2002 of potential JPEG patent infringement and starting to pursue licensing fees from a range of companies. Forgent had, in fact, obtained the patent in question through the acquisition of Compression Albs Inc. in 1997. Since the inventors who originally filed for the patent in 1986 had not participated in the JPEG standardization process that was going on around that time, according to Forgent, no abuse of the standardization process had taken place (Clark, 2002; Lemos, 2002; Markoff, 2002; Reingold, 2006).

As a result of Forgent's aggressive patent enforcement, many U.S., European, and Asian companies agreed to license the '672 patent, and by April 2004 it had generated approximately $90 million in licensing fees. Those who did not agree to license willingly were sued for patent infringement. Indeed, on 22 April 2004 Forgent's subsidiary Compression Labs, Inc sued 31 major hardware and software vendors, including Dell and Apple Computers, for patent infringement, and on 6 August 2004 it initiated litigation against 11 companies (Asaravala, 2004; Forgent Networks, 2006).

Professionals in the field of compression technology and representatives of the JPEG committee doubted the validity of the patent and stated that there could be prior art available that would render it invalid. These doubts have been manifested in legal actions, such as those taken by 24 companies that filed a counter-complaint against Forgent and its subsidiary in the Delaware District Court seeking declaratory relief as to non-infringement, invalidity, and unenforceability of the patent. Even Microsoft, which had not been sued by Forgent at that time, filed a complaint against it on 15 April 2005, claiming that the patent had been obtained fraudulently. Furthermore, the non-profit Public Patent Foundation has filed a request for re-examination of the '627 patent in November 2005. In late January 2006 the U.S. Patent and Trademark Office (USPTO) made a decision to review the patent, which will in any case expire in October 2006 (Forgent Networks, 2006; Lemos, 2002; Reingold, 2006; Red Herring, 2006).

EOLAS and HTML Specification

Another third-party submarine example is the EOLAS case. Here, the dispute arose when Eolas Technologies Inc, which had licensed a patent from the University of California, sued Microsoft for the use of the patented invention, that is, the widely used feature of HTML, the format that describes the format of Web pages. After a long stream of litigation the Federal Circuit (2005) also found the patent valid and infringed (Eolas Technologies Incorporated and the Regents of the University of California v. Microsoft Corporation, Case Nr. 04-1234 (Fed.Cir, 2005)), and the Supreme Court refused to hear the case (Malone, 2005). At the request of W3C the Eolas patent was also re-examined by the USPTO, which released two preliminary findings claiming that it was invalid. Ultimately, the patent office kept the patent in force, however (Perens, n.d.).

Although a patent holder has a very strong negotiating position if the patent accidentally "surfaces" after the adoption of the standard and those who are accused of patent infringement can mainly defend themselves by trying to invalidate the patent, third-party patents do not always create problems. In many cases reasonable licensing terms can be agreed upon. As with the cases in which the patent holder had participated in the standard setting, business relationships and bad publicity may also be reasons why third-party patent holders comply with a standardization organization's policy and license the patents royalty-free, for instance, although they may have no obligation to do so.

The Risk of Patent Problems and How to Reduce It?

It could be concluded from previous discussion that it is important to implement proficient patent policies that are clear, concise and transparent and hold as few surprises as possible. These policies should be drafted with an intention of influencing companies' behavior both during and after standard setting so that misconduct could be diminished and potential problems solved. The nature, extent, scope and the timeframe of the disclosure requirements are examples of such disclosure terms that could be clarified in order to reduce the submarine patent problem, which taking into account the recent litigations and the fact that 40% of companies in Blind and Thumm's sample group reported problems regarding unclear IPR structure (Blind et al., 2002) is not only theoretical. Furthermore, one way of reducing the problems that may result when not all patents are known prior to the establishment of a standard could be to require that essential patents granted in the future will be identified and potentially licensed under the same terms as the disclosed patents. In fact, it is a common requirement in patent pools for essential future patents to be subject to grant-back and thus to contribute to the pool. This requirement may occasionally have anticompetitive effects, however, Balto and Wolman (2003) and patent holders would probably consider this type of requirement too restrictive.

As regards to third-party patents that are becoming a more and more relevant concern there is a lot that could be done in order to reduce the risk they may pose to the adoption of a standard. First of all, the standard-setting participants could be encouraged to conduct more thorough patent searches already during the standardization procedure, and to let the standards organizations know about potential third-party claims. Secondly, third parties could be reserved an opportunity to make a patent statement early on, and thirdly, standards organizations could take a more active role in finding relevant patents themselves. Otherwise, if dealing with the increasing number of third-party patents was only left to companies implementing the standard, they would be in different positions and the openness of the standard could be endangered: only those companies that already have cross-licensing agreements in place, have enough leverage in order to negotiate a good deal with the patent holder, or have the resources to fight the patent in court might be able to adopt the standard.

A further way to limit the risk of submarine patent-related troubles arising from both standard-setters and third parties, and to help companies to solve the conflicts better and therefore to reduce the harmful consequences of such patents would be to renovate the legal framework. The possibilities and the need to do so have not been estimated in this article, however. Obviously, when considering the actions needed, the advantages and disadvantages should be estimated and balanced carefully. Therefore, it is in place to examine also the other patent and standard related quandary that has to do with licensing. These problems are similar to those experienced with submarine patents, and in fact, the GSM example presented later is in essence a submarine patent case. What basically differentiates submarine patent cases and those in which a patent has been properly disclosed is, however, the possibility to make informative decisions about the adoption of a standard, and to design around it or agree upon licensing terms in advance, and thus avoid great societal losses that would occur had the standard been already broadly adopted and if the parties were not able to solve the conflicts.

LICENSING OF PATENTS AND STANDARDIZATION

In case a patent holder has disclosed that it may have patents or pending patent applications that are essential for using a standard, standards bodies typically pose certain licensing alternatives for that company. The patent holder's options are usually the following: (1) the patent holder may state that it is willing to license its essential patents on royalty-free terms, (2) the patent holder may refuse from licensing altogether, (3) the patent holder may promise to license, but negotiate the terms separately, or (4) the patent folder may make a statement of licensing on fair, reasonable and nondiscriminatory terms (RAND). These alternatives are discussed further in subsequent paragraphs, and case studies are used to illustrate the licensing perplexities. The necessity and effects of addressing the submarine patent problem are estimated on this basis.

Royalty-Free Licensing

Royalty-free standards often have more chances of being broadly accepted and widely used than standards requiring licensing payments. For instance, the Internet has been said to require freely available standards in order to work effectively. Patent-based standards requiring royalty payments inhibit its development because they slow down or discourage the adoption of new technologies. As a consequence, companies frequently agree to make their patented technology available on a royalty-free basis, and hope to generate more profits by selling products that use their standardized technology (Clark, 2002; Interview data U.S., 2004).

As mentioned, given the benefits, standardization participants are often willing to license their patents on a royalty-free basis for the specific purpose of using the standard. This holds true particularly if they are able to make sure that the patents could nevertheless be utilized for defensive purposes if the need arose (Interview data U.S., 2004). Naturally, participation and agreement to license to everyone require that such conduct is in accordance with the firm's commercial interests: having its superior technology chosen for a standard may provide it with a head start in incorporating that technology into its products, for example. Then again, companies seeking licensing revenues through incorporating their proprietary inventions into a standard do not typically have a business motivation to participate in designing royalty-free standards (Soininen, 2005).

Refusal to License

If a royalty-free licensing scheme cannot be negotiated, and the patented technology cannot be designed around, it may nevertheless be in the interests of the public to get the patent holder to agree to license it at least on RAND terms. If the patent holder refuses to license on these vague terms, the standardization process is halted and other solutions are sought (Hjelm, 2000). Refusing to license at all is rare, however, although it is the most influential form of leveraging one's patent rights (Rahnasto, 2003). As the following case study demonstrates it has nevertheless played a major role in making the ETSI Wideband Code Division Multiple Access (WCDMA) standard backward compatible with the IS-95 standard favored by Qualcomm Inc, for instance (Soininen, 2005).

What happened in the WCDMA dispute was that Qualcomm accused ETSI of intentionally excluding Qualcomm's technology from its standards, thereby creating an unfavorable position for Qualcomm in the European third-generation telecommunications market. In order to make its voice better heard, the company claimed that the key technologies needed for WCDMA infringed its patents, and refused to license this technology unless the WCDMA was made backward compatible with the IS-95 standard. It seems that Qualcomm expected that a harmonized standard would increase its licensing revenues fundamentally (Hjelm, 2000; Westman, 1999; Soininen, 2005).

Ericsson, who was another key patent holder in the technology involved, was of the opinion that Qualcomm's patents were not infringed, and to gain a better negotiation position it also sued Qualcomm for the infringement of Ericsson's CDMA patents (one of the U.S. standards) Qualcomm was employing. Finally, consensus was reached as a result of cooperation between Qualcomm and Ericsson. The companies entered into a series of definitive agreements that resolved all disputes relating to CDMA technology, and as a part of the settlement Ericsson acquired Qualcomm's terrestrial CDMA wireless infrastructure business, including its R&D facilities. Furthermore, the companies gave a promise to license essential WCDMA patents (Hjelm, 2000; Westman, 1999). The standardization process was practically frozen during this period, which lasted roughly a year (Sarvas & Soininen, 2002).

Indeed, as the previous example demonstrates companies operating in the ICT sector are dependent on each other and therefore conflicts in one area may result in complex legal battles in another. Nevertheless refusing to license may be a feasible strategy for a company that opposes a certain standard. A firm may also wish to delay the acceptance of a standard to give it more time to develop products that incorporate it.

Blank Promise to License

Firms typically agree to license their patents royalty-free, or on RAND or other terms, or they may merely agree to license but make no statement of the the terms and conditions. Particularly if the last-mentioned option is available and chosen, there is likely to be a fight over the proper licensing conditions. One example of a disagreement over proper licensing terms was the one that arose during the formation of the European GSM standard in the 1980s, which was first coordinated by CEPT (Conference Europeenne des Administrations des Postes et des Telecommunications) and later by ETSI. In fact, this particular licensing dilemma, which involved Motorola, contributed to the change in patent culture that took place in the European telecommunications sector in which patenting had until that time been regarded as a secondary issue—specifically among the national telecommunications service providers whose markets had previously been monopolized but were now deregulated (Bekkers, Verspagen, & Smits, 2002; Granstrand, 1999).

What basically has been presented in literature to have happened in the context of the GSM standard was that a U.S. company, Motorola, for which patenting was a natural and integral part of doing business, entered the European scene and employed the aggressive patent strategy it was used to. While other standard setters operated in accordance with a "gentleman's agreement", shared their ideas and specifications during the standardization process in an open atmosphere, and refrained from patenting once the basic technical decisions had been made, Motorola pursued patent protection in the course of the process (Granstarand, 1999). Furthermore, Bekkers, Verpagen & Smits (2002) have argued that while most other companies agreed on licensing their essential rights on fair, reasonable and nondiscriminatory terms, Motorola refused to make general declarations. It declined monetary compensation and was only willing to cross-license its patents to certain companies. Although Siemens, Alcatel, Nokia and Ericsson were able to negotiate cross-licenses, Motorola's licensing strategy effectively prevented various other companies from entering the market. When a number of non-European companies finally managed to obtain all the necessary licenses to built GSM terminals in the late 1990s, the cross-licensees had already built up a strong market position. Moreover, since the cumulative licensing fee paid for a GSM handset was very high as confirmed by studies of Bekkers, et al., the price made it difficult to compete if the company was not part of a cross-licensing agreement. In fact it has been argued that the licensing fees have totaled as much as 29% of the costs of the GSM handset (Bekkers et al. 2002)

RAND-Licensing

Even under the RAND system, specific licensing terms are typically not agreed upon during the standard setting. Revealing the terms after adoption can generate conflicts and hamper the parties' ability to compete in the affected market. Peterson (2002b) lists the following situations that could arise in this context: (1) the patent holder seeks a broad grant-back that appears non-discriminatory but has different effects on different parties; (2) the patentee requires a minimum annual royalty based on "administrative costs", which may have the effect of excluding smaller rivals and new entrants; (3) the patentee seeks royalties from downstream providers such as manufacturers of finished goods, and refuses to license to suppliers of upstream inputs such as IC vendors, and thus to increase its income, which however may increase competitors' costs and time to market; (4) the patent holder acquires admissions of infringement and validity, and/or retains the right to immediately terminate a license if the licensor challenges infringement or validity; (5) the patentee requires acceptance of venue, which might constitute a major problem for small companies or foreign competitors; and (6) the patent holder seeks a royalty that it considers "fair" but that exceeds the average profit margin of all the parties who need licenses. For instance, one of the U.S. interviewees mentioned that his company had been approached with a royalty requirement as high as 10% (Interview data U.S., 2004).

Furthermore, even though the company may have made it clear in its licensing statement that the license was only available under certain conditions it considered as fair, reasonable and nondiscriminatory, these terms may come as a surprise to some and cause disputes. For instance, the Townshend v. Rockwell International Corp. and Conexant Systems (N.D.Cal.2000) litigation arose when Townshend, whose patents "read on" the V.90 standard for 56K chipset modems and who had promised to license them on certain terms, filed a patent-infringement suit against Rockwell and its successor Conexant. In response Rockwell and Conexant asserted two antitrust counterclaims based on the Sherman Act Sections 1 (conspiracy) and 2 (monopolization and its attempt) among others, and claimed that Townshend and 3Com had conspired to restrain trade by deceiving the ITU into incorporating Townshend's patent into the industry standard, denying competitors access to the technology, and filing a patent-infringement lawsuit to prevent Conexant from using Townshend's technology. Furthermore, Townshend and 3Com were accused of having attempted to monopolize the market for 56K modem chipset products (Kirsch, 2000; Townshend v. Rockwell International Corp. and Conexant Systems, Inc., 55 U.S.P.Q.2d 1011 (N.D.Cal.2000)).

I am not going to go into the legal specialties of the case here, but the Court found all Rockwell's and Conexant's counterclaims unfounded. With regard to the antitrust-based claims it noted, among other things, that there had been no collusion, and since 3Com—to which Townshend had non-exclusively licensed its essential patent prior to the setting of the ITU V.90 standard—had declared during the standardization procedure that Townshend had relevant patents pending, ITU had not been deceived. Since 3Com had also made a proposition prior to the acceptance of the standard to license those patents for a per-unit royalty fee, or to cross-license them in return for technologies that were specified in the standard, or related to it and were otherwise practically necessary or desirable for technical or economic reasons in order to make a commercially viable product compliant with the standard, and further that it had not been shown that Rockwell and Conexant could not have obtained a license under those terms, Townshend's actions could not be held anticompetitive (Kirsch, 2000; Townshend v. Rockwell International Corp. and Conexant Systems, Inc., 55 U.S.P.Q.2d 1011 (N.D.Cal.2000)).

The previous case illustrates that it is particularly difficult to defend oneself against such patent holders that have disclosed their patents properly and declared their licensing terms during the standard-setting procedure. Indeed, due to the flexibility in the interpretation of RAND, having patents in standardized technology could also become a valuable source of royalties or other resources. For instance, Qualcomm relies on a royalty stream resulting from others utilizing its patented technology incorporated into various standards. In fact, the pricing of Qualcomm's licenses has led to huge disagreement between Qualcomm and six other companies involved in the WCDMA 3G standard. Basically, Broadcom, Ericsson, NEX, Nokia, Panasonic Mobile Communications and Texas Instruments have all claimed that Qualcomm, who promised to license its essential WCDMA patents on RAND terms, is charging excessive and disproportionate royalties for them. Qualcomm has been claimed to charge the same royalty rate on the WCDMA 3G standard as it does for the CDMA2000 standard adopted in the U.S., although it has fewer essential patents in it. Furthermore, it offers lower royalty rates to handset customers who buy chipsets exclusively from Qualcomm than to manufacturers of chipsets for mobile phones, making entry into the market more difficult for chip makers (Nokia, 2005a; Outlaw.com, 2005; Nokia, 2005b).

As a result of this disagreement, all six of the previously-mentioned companies filed complaints to the European Commission in October 2005 requesting it to investigate and to put an end to Qualcomm's anticompetitive conduct (Nokia,

2005a, 2005b; Out-law.com, 2005). Qualcomm has responded to the allocations stating that they are legally without merit, and appear to be nothing more than an attempt by these licensees to renegotiate their license agreements. In a separate move, Qualcomm then filed a patent-infringement action against Nokia claiming that Nokia was infringing 12 of its patents that related to GSM, GPRS, and EDGE standards (Jacobs, 2005; Nokia, 2005c; Wireless Watch, 2005b).

This is not the end of Qualcomm's legal disputes, however. Previously, in July and again in October, the company had filed infringement suits based on the previously-mentioned patents against Broadcom. These actions were a follow-up of Broadcom's claims that included a patent-infringement action filed against Qualcomm in May 2005, a complaint with the U.S. International Trade Commission (ITC) suggesting that Qualcomm was unfairly importing products that infringed Broadcom's patents and requesting that the ITC investigate Qualcomm's imports, and a separate antitrust suit raised in July. This U.S. antitrust claim was based on similar grounds as the complaint made to the European Commission. In its antitrust complaint Broadcom charged Qualcomm with abuse of the wireless technology standards-setting process, failure to meet its commitments to license technology for cellular wireless standards on RAND terms, and various anticompetitive activities in the sales and marketing of chipsets based on CDMA technology (Gohring, 2005a, b; Regan, 2005).

As can be seen from the volume of suits and counter-suits discussed earlier, Qualcomm's strategy of using its essential patents as revenue generators is challenging and particularly litigation-sensitive, and it is not considered viable by all technology/patent-licensing firms even though their business model would support such activity. One of the U.S. interviewees stated, for example, that taking into consideration the current legal situation and the IPR policies adopted by many standards bodies, it was not beneficial for it to take any part in the standardization. Its business was based on technology and patent licensing, not on manufacturing products, and there was simply not enough monetary compensation involved in standards (Interview data U.S., 2004).

Cross-Licensing

As mentioned earlier, agreeing upon exact licensing terms is not part of the standard-setting procedure, and negotiations are held between the companies interested in using the standard. This follows that another reason beyond the technological benefits for promoting the selection of patented technology for a standard is the possibility to cross-license patents with those of other participants that also "read on" the standard. The more patents companies have, the less they have to pay others for using the standard. Cumulative royalties might otherwise reach the point of unprofitable manufacture (Alkio, 2003; Soininen, 2005). For this reason, companies have an incentive to obtain patents that are essential for using the standardized technology. They may therefore amend their pending patent applications and file for new ones during the standardization process in order to make sure that if a certain technology is chosen for a standard, their patents cover some of its elements. For example, with regard to the CDMA2000 standard, Qualcomm held 28%, Nokia 16%, NTT DoCoMo 13%, Ericsson 8%, Motorola 7% and Hitachi 5% of the essential patents involved. Then again, Ericsson has 30%, Nokia 21%, Qualcomm 20% and Motorola 14% of the essential patents included in the WCDMA standard (Alkio, 2003). In fact, it has been estimated that some of these major patent holders will end up with a total royalty of 7% of costs or less, while a nonpatent holder could pay 25% of the wholesale price in GSM and WCDMA royalties (Wireless Watch, 2005a).

In order to diminish the problem with too high royalties, some manufacturing firms and operators have declared that they would prefer to agree upon cumulative royalty caps beforehand (Wireless Watch, 2005a). For instance, Nokia was behind such a proposal in respect of 3G patents (Naraine, 2002a). Nevertheless, there are different views on whether agreeing on licensing terms is the job of the standards organization at all, and Qualcomm, in particular, has opposed the royalty-cap proposition actively (Naraine, 2002b). Also one of the U.S. interviewees pointed out during the interview, that in the end, the markets determined whether a product was feasible at a certain price or not. This was not the licensor's responsibility. He further noted that the game in the industry seems to have turned into a price competition rather than the building up of value to customers and communicating that value to them (Interview data U.S., 2004). However, as far as the next version of the 3GPP-based radio standard, Long Term Evolution (LTE), is concerned, ETSI is considering getting all relevant patent holders to sign up to a pre-agreed cumulative cap of approximately 5% for royalties on the cost of LTE equipment (Informamedia.com, 2006).

Licensing and Submarine Patents

As explained earlier, standardization participants have diverging business interests that, combined with control over certain aspects of technology, complicate the standardization process and the adoption of standards particularly if monetary or other licensing compensation is pending. In fact, quantitative research conducted by Blind et al., (2002) has indicated that the dilemma is not rare at all: over 30% of European companies reported that they had faced dilemmas involving the high licensing fees demanded by the IPR/patent holders, and approximately 25% had had problems with cross-licensing (Blind et al., 2002; Soininen, 2005). However, if there were no compensation, fewer patent holders might be inclined to allow anyone to utilize their patented inventions, and technologically inferior technology might be chosen for the standard. In fact, it has been suggested that incentives offered to patent holders are not sufficient given the positive effects of standardization. Another quantitative study also conducted by Blind and Thumm (2002) demonstrated that the tendency to join standardization processes is lower if an undertaking has intense patent activity than if it does not. It is suggested that this could be an indicator that the use of IPRs, reflecting the success of the company's own R&D activities, and participation in standardization are, to certain extent, alternative innovation strategies (Blind et al., 2002, Soininen, 2005). Unfortunately this finding also indicates that a large chunk of patents may fall into the category of third-party patents that have a high likelihood to remain unnoticed.

What basically differentiates submarine patent cases and those in which a patent has been properly disclosed is the possibility to make informative decisions about the adoption of a standard, design around it or to agree upon licensing terms in advance. However, standards organization's patent policies only require a general promise to license on RF or RAND terms. Exact licensing conditions are negotiated separately between the parties and this is often done after the standard has been elected. Therefore, with an exception of the fact that a licensing statement has been given and therefore there are more changes of challenging the company's licensing terms, these situations bear a lot of similarities to submarine patent cases. Obviously, if licensing terms were specified better and RAND terms were determined in accordance with the situation that has prevailed prior to the establishment of the standard, there would be less room for interpretation, and the patent holder would not be in such a good negotiation position. This follows that, even though it was possible to diminish the dilemma with submarine patents discussed earlier, licensing perplexities would probably continue to prevail. On the other hand early disclosure could at least diminish those significant economic losses that would occur if the submarine patent surfaced after

the standard had been used broadly and various complementary products and services had been based on it. It should be pointed out, however, that the advantages of clearing all relevant patents beforehand also depends on whether the standard is such that it is constantly evolving as new features are incorporated into the system after the original standard has been set, or whether it remains unchanged after its establishment. In the former situations it would be important to be able to gain information also on those rights, which are essential for the purposes of implementing the standard in its amended form, while those rights that were initially essential may no longer be relevant at this phase.

DISCUSSION

In the previous sections I have identified multiple situations in which patents have caused concern during and after cooperative standard setting. These situations could basically be divided into those in which the holder of the disputed patent has participated in setting the standard and those in which the patent holder is a third party. Furthermore, a distinction could be made between patents that have been properly disclosed to the other participants, and the rights that come as a surprise either because the patent policy has not required their disclosure and no attention has been drawn to them, the patent holder has intentionally concealed them despite the patent policy, or the rights holder has accidentally neglected to disclose them.

The number-one reason for the disputes that have arisen in the previously-mentioned situations is that patent holders use their position of being able to prevent others from using an invention that is essential for operating the standard to require licensing fees or other terms that are unacceptable to companies operating in the industry. When talking about properly disclosed patents, the patent holder may have made a declaration prior to the publication of the standard specification to the effect that it was willing to license its essential patents royalty-free, or that it was willing to license them on fair, reasonable and non-discriminatory terms. Here, the patent holder may have posed certain limitations, or the patent holder may have made only a blank promise of RF or RAND licensing, and a dispute may arise afterwards over what the correct interpretation of such a promise is. Sometimes, there may not be any kind of a promise.

The consequences of the patent holder refusing to license at all, or on terms accepted by most companies, depend on when the dilemma comes to light. The longer it takes for the dispute to arise the worse are the consequences from a societal perspective. Before the standard is set it may well be possible to design around the patents or to choose other technologies over heavily patented ones, and even after the standard specifications have been published, the abandoning of the standard altogether, or its modification, may not be detrimental as companies may have alternative standards to choose from. Of course, the time and the money invested in setting a standard would be lost. On the other hand, if the standard has already been broadly adopted it may be difficult and very costly to change the specifications without losing the network benefits. Ultimately, doing so would harm consumers who are already using a system in which various products are interchangeable and interoperable. Obviously, from the patent holder's perspective, the situation is reversed: the later his patent comes to the surface, the more leverage he gains.

I posed the question in the title of this article whether especially the submarine patent problem truly existed or whether it was a red herring. Although the evidence is largely anecdotal and further quantitative research is needed, I have to conclude that problems to do with unidentified patents do come to the surface after the standard has been established. Obviously, even though there is a high likelihood that plenty of relevant patents

remain unnoticed, it is only a minor aspect of the variety of conflicts that patents give rise to during or after standardization, and plenty of standards can be adopted without actually having to face troubles with submarine patents. Particularly those situations in which it can be proven that a standard-setting participant breached the patent policy and purposefully concealed the existence of relevant patents or patent applications and thus misled the industry and manipulated the process in order to gain market power, appear to be rare. Companies typically try to do their best to comply with the patent policy.

Avoiding problems with submarine patents seems to be getting more challenging all the time, however. This is because ICT patents, some of which are valid and some of which are not, are increasing in number making it more difficult to avoid infringement. Furthermore, patents are being assigned more often than before and therefore they may end up in companies that did not participate in setting the standard. Patents are also utilized more aggressively in the field, and the more patent-holding companies are seeking to extract as high royalties as they can get from those implementing a standard the less likely it is that an amicable solution can be reached. As a consequence, particularly the U.S. red herring population seems to be growing quickly in number, even though certain legal provisions such as the U.S. Sherman Act, sections 1 and 2, which prohibit conspiracy and monopolization or its attempt, and the FTC Act, section 5, which prohibits the use of unfair and deceptive business practices, have been and could be used in an attempt to wipe out the most colorful individuals. Other legal tools include fraud, equitable estoppel that prevents a party that has not operated fairly from enforcing his rights, the doctrine of prosecution laches applicable to patents that have been issued following an unreasonable and unexplained delay during patent prosecution phase, and the implied-license and patent-misuse doctrines (Lemley, 2002; Mueller, 2001). Furthermore, non-infringement clarification and patent invalidation either in court or as an opposition (EPO) or re-examination (USPTO) procedure in the patent office could be attempted. In Europe the EC treaty, Art 81 (prohibits agreements and concerted practices that prevent, distort or restrict competition) and 82 (prohibits the abuse of dominant position) could offer limited help as well. Unfortunately, the legal means have not appeared to be very effective so far. The fact that legal disputes have arisen demonstrates that the dilemmas are serious and that they bear significant economic weight, however.

What makes particularly the submarine patent problem interesting from the societal and patent policy perspective is that in this case companies implementing the standard have not, for some reason or other, been able to identify the relevant rights or to plan their operations so as to avoid infringement. Moreover, the consequences of not being able to continue to use a specific standard may have far-reaching effects not only on the competition in a certain field but also on consumers. Therefore, the purpose of the patent system—to promote innovation and facilitate technology transfer through granting the inventor an exclusive right in return for publishing his invention—may not merely restrain trade in the traditional sense, that is, legal monopoly versus free competition, but may also contravene the public interest in a way that is no longer reasonable given the role of patents in enhancing innovation. This, incidentally, has been seriously questioned in areas such as software and semiconductors. In fact, patents and standards are a policy concern linked to a more general concern regarding IPR protection and the possibility of using it in order to control product interoperability.

This article suggests that further attention should be paid to analyze the efficacy of the legal framework and the need for legislative amendments particularly in the context of standards and so-called submarine patents that come to surface after the standard has been established and adopted. As a practical matter for diminish-

ing potential conflicts, clarifying patent policies in respect to disclosure and licensing obligations, conducting more thorough patent due diligence, and developing guidelines on how to determine RAND terms are recommended. It is further noted that limiting only the risk of submarine patents will not get us far in reducing the conflicts between patents and standards.

REFERENCES

Administrative Complaint (2002), Docket No 9302, 18 June 2002.

Alkio, M. (2003, March 9). Kovaa peliä patenteilla. *Helsingin Sanomat*, p. E3.

ANSI. (2003a). *Guidelines for implementation of the ANSI Patent Policy.*

ANSI. (2003b). *Patent policy.*

Asaravala, A. (2004, April 24). Forgent sues over JPEG patent. *Wired News*. Retrieved August 29, 2006, from http://www.wired.com/news/business/0,1367,63200,00.html

Balto, D.A., & Wolman, A.M. (2003). Intellectual property and antitrust: General principles. *IDEA The Journal of Law and Technology, 43*(3), 396-474.

Bekkers, R., Duysters, G., & Verspagen, B. (2002). Intellectual property rights, strategic technology agreements and market structure. The case of GSM. *Research Policy, 31*, 1141-1161.

Bekkers, R., Verspagen, B., & Smits, J. (2002). Intellectual property rights and standardization: The case of GSM. *Telecommunications Policy, 26*(3-4), 171-188.

Berlind, D. (2002a, April 16). IBM drops Internet patent bombshell. *Tech Update.*

Berlind, D. (2002b, April 25). The hidden toll of patents on standards. *Tech News on ZDNet.* Retrieved August 29, 2006, from http://news.zdnet.com/2100-9595_22-891852.html

Berman, V. (2005, January-February). Is it time to reexamine patent policy for standards? *IEEE Design & Test of Computers*, 71-73.

Bessen, J. (2003). *Strategic patenting of complex technologies* (Working Paper). Research on Innovation.

Blind, K. (2004). *The economics of standards.* Edward Elgar.

Blind, K., Bierhals, R., Thumm, N., Hossain, K., Sillwood, J., Iverser, E., et al. (2002). *Study on the interaction between standardisation and intellectual property rights* (EC Contract No G6MA-CT-2000-02001, 2002).

Blind, K., Edler, J., Nack, R., & Strauß, J. (2001). *Micro- and macroeconomic implications of the patentability of software innovations. Intellectual property rights in information technologies between competition and innovation* (Study on Behalf of German Federal Ministry of Economics and Technology).

In re Bogese II, 303 F.3d 1362, 1367, Federal Circuit (2002).

Initial Decision (2004). Docket No 9302, 23 February 2004.

Calderone, L.L., & Custer, T.L. (2005, November). *Prosecution laches as a defense in patent cases.* Flaster Greenberg Attorneys at Law. Retrieved August 29, 2006, from http://www.flastergreenberg.com/pdf/PatentArtic_prf3.pdf

Caplan, P. (2003). *Patents and open standards* (White paper prepared for the National Information Standards Organization).

Chesbrough, H. (2003). *Open innovation.* Harvard Business School Press.

Clark, D. (2002, October). Do Web standards and patents mix? *Computer*, pp. 19-22.

Clark, R. (2002, July 19). *Concerning recent patent claims.* Retrieved August 29, 2006, from http://www.jpeg.org/newsrel1.html

Cohen, W.M., Nelson, R.R., & Walsh, J.P. (2000, February). *Protecting their intellectual assets: Appropriability conditions and why U.S. manufacturing firms patent (or not)* (NBER Working Paper Series).

Cunningham, A. (2005). Telecommunications, intellectual property, and standards. In I. Walden, & J. Angel (Eds.), *Telecommunications law and regulation.* Oxford.

DLA. (2004). *European intellectual property survey.*

Eolas Technologies Incorporated and the Regents of the University of California v. Microsoft Corporation, Case Nr. 04-1234, Federal Circuit, 2 March 2005.

ETSI. (2005). *IPR policy.*

Farrell, J. (1996). *Choosing the rules for formal standardization.* UC Berkeley.

Federal Trade Commission v. Dell Computer Corp., FTC File No. 931 0097, 2 November 1995.

Feldman, R.P., & Rees, M.R. (2000, July). The effect of industry standard setting on patent licensing and enforcement. *IEEE Communications Magazine*, pp. 112-116.

Ferguson, K. (1999). 20/20 foresight. Retrieved August 29, 2006, from http://www.forbes.com/1999/04/19/feat.html

Forgent Networks. (2006). *Intellectual property, '672 patent cases.* Retrieved August 29, 2006, from http://www.forgent.com/ip/672cases.shtml

Frank, S.J. (2002, March). Can you patent an industry standard? *IEEE Spectrum.*

FTC. (2003). *To promote innovation: The proper balance of competition and patent law and policy.*

Graham, S.J.H., & Mowery, D.C. (2002, June 6-8). *Submarines in software? Continuations in U.S. software patenting in the 1980s and 1990s.* Paper presented at the DRUID Summer Conference on Industrial Dynamics of the New and Old Economy—Who is Embracing Whom?, Copenhagen/Elsinore.

Granstrand, O. (1999). *The economics and management of intellectual property.* Edward Elgar Publishing.

Grindley, P. (2002). *Standards, strategy and policy.* Oxford.

Gohring, N. (2005a). Qualcomm files a second suit against Broadcom. *InfoWorld.* Retrieved August 29, 2006, from http://www.infoworld.com/article/05/10/21/HNqualcommsecondsuit_1.html

Gohring, N. (2005b). Qualcomm files patent infringement suit against Nokia. *InfoWorld.* Retrieved August 29, 2006, from http://www.infoworld.com/article/05/11/07/hnqualcommsuit_1.html

GovTrack.us. 109th Congress, H.R. 2795: Patent Act of 2005. Retrieved August 29, 2006, from http://www.govtrack.us/congress/bill.xpd?bill=h109-2795

Hahn, R.W. (2001, March). Competition policy and the new economy. *Milken Institute Review,* 34-41.

Heinze, W.F. (2002, May). Dead patents walking. *IEEE Spectrum,* 52-54.

Hemphill, T.A. (2005, January). Technology standards development, patent ambush, and US antitrust policy. *Technology in Society, 27*(1), 55-67.

Hjelm, B. (2000). Standards and intellectual property rights in the age of global communication: A review of the international standardization of third-generation mobile system.

IETF. (2005). Intellectual property rights in IETF technology.

Informamedia.com. (2006, March 1). ETSI acts on unfair, unreasonable and discriminatory IPRs. *Informamedia.com.*

IPO. (n.d.). *21st Century Patent Coalition: "Submarine patents" ARE a significant problem.* Retrieved August 29, 2006, from http://www.ipo.org/contentmanagement/contentdisplay.cfm?contentid=7334

ITU-T (n.d.). *Patent policy.*

ITU-T (2005). *Patent policy implementation guidelines.*

Jacobs, P. (2005, December). Qualcomm defends patent licensing programme. *wirelessweb.* Retrieved August 29, 2006, from http://wireless.iop.org/articles/news/6/12/6/1

Kipnis, J. (2000, July). Beating the system: Abuses of the standards adoption process. *IEEE Communications Magazine,* pp. 102-105.

Kirsch, E.D. (2000). International standards participation: Lessons from Townshend & Dell. *International Lawyers Network. The bullet"iln", 1*(2). Retrieved August 29, 2006, from http://www.ag-internet.com/push_news_one_two/internationalstandards.htm

Knight, H.J. (2001). *Patent strategy for researchers and research managers.* John Wiley & Sons.

Kratzman, V.A. (2005). *Technology transfer mid-term report next step recommendations.* FINPRO.

Krechmer, K. (2005, January). *Communications standards and patent rights: Conflict or coordination?* Paper presented at the Economics of the

Software and Internet Industries Conference, Tolouse, France.

Labsystems Oy v. Biohit Oy. HO S 94/1922. Finnish Court of Appeal.

The Lemelson Foundation. (n.d.). Jerome H. Lemelson. Retrieved August 29, 2006, from http://www.lemelson.org/about/bio_jerry.php

Lemley, M.A. (2002). *Intellectual property rights and standard setting organizations* (UC Berkeley Public Law and Legal Theory Research Paper Series, Research Paper No. 84).

Lemos, R. (2002, July 23). Finding patent truth in JPEG claims. *CNET News.com*. Retrieved August 29, 2006, from http://news.com.com/Finding+patent+truth+in+JPEG+claim/2100-1001_3-945686.html

Lo, A.M. (Jupiter Networks, Inc). (2002). *A need for intervention: Keeping competition alive in the networking industry in the face of increasing patent assertions against standards*. FTC/DOJ Hearings on Competition and Intellectual Property Law and Policy In the Knowledge-Based Economy—Standard Setting and Intellectual Property, 18 April 2002.

Malone, S. (2005, November 1). *Microsoft loses Eolas Supreme Court appeal*. PC Pro. Retrieved August 29, 2006, from http://www.pcpro.co.uk/news/news/79431

Marasco, A. (ANSI). (2003, October 30). *IPR and standards*. Presentation at AIPLA.

Markoff, J. (2002, July 29). Patent claim strikes an electronics nerve. *The New York Times*.

Megantz, R.C. (2002). *Technology management. Developing and implementing effective licensing programs*. John Wiley & Sons.

Messerschmitt, D.G., & Szyperski, C. (2003). *Software ecosystem*. The MIT Press.

Miele, A.L. (2000). *Patent strategy: The manger's guide to profiting from patent portfolios*. John Wiley & Sons.

Mueller, J.M. (2001). Patenting industry standards. *John Marshall Law Review, 34*(897).

Naraine, R. (2002a, May 8). Nokia calls for 5% cap on 3G patent royalties. *internetnews.com*. Retrieved August 29, 2006, from http://internetnews.com/wireless/article.php/1041561

Naraine, R. (2002b, May 10). Qualcomm rejects Nokia patent cap proposal. *internetnews.com*. Retrieved August 29, 2006, from http://www.interetnews.com/wireless/article.php/1116381

Nokia. (2005a, October 28). *Leading mobile wireless technology companies call on European Commission to investigate Qualcomm's anti-competitive conduct*. Retrieved August 29, 2006, from http://press.nokia.com/PR/200510/1018639_5.html

Nokia. (2005b, October 28). *Leading mobile wireless technology companies call on European Commission to investigate Qualcomm's anti-competitive conduct*. Retrieved August 29, 2006, from http://europe.nokia.com/BaseProject/Sites/NokiaCom_CAMPAIGNS_57710/CDA/Categories/PressEvents/_Content/_Static_Files/transcript.pdf

Nokia. (2005c, November 7). *Nokia responds to reports of Qualcomm GSM patent infringement suit*. Retrieved August 29, 2006, from http://press.nokia.com/PR/200511/1019958_5.html

OASIS. (2005). *IPR policy*.

OECD. (2004). *Patents and innovation: Trends and policy challenges*. Retrieved August 29, 2006, from http://www.oecd.org/dataoecd/48/12/24508541.pdf

OECD. (2005). *Compendium of patent statistics*. Retrieved August 29, 2006, from http://www.oecd.org/dataoecd/60/24/8208325.pdf

Ohana, G. (Cisco Systems, Inc). (2005. October 6). Intellectual property rights: Policies in standard-setting: Areas of debate. In *Proceedings of From A to Veeck: Standardization and the Law, 2005 ANSI Annual Conference*. Retrieved August 29, 2006, from http://public.ansi.org/ansionline/Documents/Meetings%20and%20Events/2005%20Annual%20Conference/Legal%20Conference/Ohana-Panel%20I.pdf

Out-law.com. (2005, November 31). Mobile-makers say 3G patent licensing breaks antitrust laws. Retrieved August 29, 2006, from http://www.out-law.com/page-6280

Peterson, S.K. (Hewlett-Packard Company). (2002a). *Consideration of patents during the setting of standards*. For FTC and DOJ Roundtable, Standard Setting Organizations: Evaluating the Anticompetitive Risks of Negotiating IP Licensing Terms and Conditions Before A Standard Is Set, 6 November 2002.

Peterson, S.K. (Hewlett-Packard Company). (2002b). *Patents and standard-setting processes*. FTC/DOJ Hearings on Competition and Intellectual Property Law and Policy in the Knowledge-Based Economy, 18 April 2002.

Perens, B. (n.d.). *The problem of software patents in standards*. Retrieved August 29, 2006, from http://perens.com/Articles/PatentFarming.html

Poltorak, A.I., & Lerner, P.J. (2004). *Essentials of licensing intellectual property*. John Wiley & Sons.

PwC Advisory. (2006). *2006 patent and trademark damages study*.

Rahnasto, I. (2003). *Intellectual property rights, external effects, and anti-trust law*. Oxford University Press.

Rambus, Inc v. Infineon Technologies AG. No. 01-1449. Federal Circuit, 29 January 2003.

Red Herring. (2006, February 3). JPEG patent reexamined. Retrieved August 29, 2006, from http://www.redherring.com/Article.aspx?a=15582&hed=JPEG+Patent+Reexamined&sector=Industries&subsector=Computing

Regan, K. (2005, July 5). Broadcom suit accuses Qualcomm of antitrust tactics. *E-Commerce Times*. Retrieved August 29, 2006, from http://www.ecommercetimes.com/story/44395.html

Reingold, J. (2006, January). *Patently aggressive*. 102. Retrieved August 29, 2006, from http://www.fastcompany.com/magazine/102/patents.html

Rivette, K., & Kline, D. (2000). *Rembrandts in the attic*. Harvard Business School Press.

Sarvas, R., & Soininen, A. (2002, October). *Differences in European and U.S. patent regulation affecting wireless standardization*. Paper presented at the International Workshop on Wireless Strategy in the Enterprise, Berkeley, California.

Shapiro, C. (2001). *Navigating the patent thicket: Cross licenses, patent pools and standard setting*.

Shapiro, C., & Varian, H.R. (1999). *Information rules*. Harvard Business School Press.

Shurmer, M., & Lea, G. (1995, June). Telecommunications standardization and intellectual property rights: A fundamental dilemma? *Standardview, 3*(2).

Soininen, A. H. (2005).Open Standards and the Problem with Submarine Patents. Proceedings SIIT 2005 pp. 231-244 4th International conference on standardization and innovation in information technology.

Stroyd, A.H. (2000). *Lemelson bar coding patents: Attempting to sink the submariner*. Retrieved August 29, 2006, from http://www.mhia.org/PSC/pdf/Lemelson.PDF

Surowiecki, J. (2006, December 26/January 2). Blackberry picking. *The New Yorker*, Financial Page.

Symbol Technologies Inc. v. Lemelson Medical, Education & Research Foundation. 277 F.3d 1361, 1363. Federal Circuit, 2002.

Symbol Technologies, Inc et al. v. Lemelson Medical, Education & Research Foundation. LP et al., 422 F.3d 1378. Federal Circuit, 2005.

Teece, D.J. (2000). *Managing intellectual capital.* Oxford University Press.

Townshend v. Rockwell International Corp. and Conexant Systems, Inc., 55 U.S.P.Q.2d 1011. Northern District of California, 2000.

Varchaver, N. (2001, May 3). *Jerome Lemelson the patent king.* Retrieved August 29, 2006, from http://www.engin.brown.edu/courses/en90/fall/2003/Lemelson%20Fortune%20may%2014%202001%20article.pdf

Vermont, S. (2002). The economics of patent litigation. In B. Berman (Ed.), *From ideas to assets. Investing wisely in intellectual property.* John Wiley & Sons.

Watts, J.J.S., & Baigent, D.R. (2002). Intellectual property, standards and competition law: Navigating a minefield. *IEEE*, 837-842.

Westman, R. (1999, October). The battle of standards—And the road to peace. *On—The New World of Communication*, pp. 26-30.

Wireless Watch. (2005a, November 29). Mobile patents war shifts to email. *The Register.* Retrieved August 29, 2006, from http://www.theregister.co.uk/2005/11/29/mobile_email_patents_war/

Wireless Watch. (2005b, November 15). *The Register.* Qualcomm IP battle hots up. Retrieved August 29, 2006, from http://www.theregister.co.uk/2005/11/15/qualcomm_ip_battle/

Wong, W. (2002, April 18). IBM ebMXL patent plan royalty-free. *Tech Update.*

W3C (2004). *Patent policy.*

This work was previously published in the International Journal of IT Standards and Standardization Research, Vol. 5, Issue 1, edited by K. Jakobs, pp. 41-83, copyright 2007 by IGI Publishing (an imprint of IGI Global).

Chapter 8
A Framework to Build Process Theories of Anticipatory Information and Communication Technology (ICT) Standardizing

Kalle Lyytinen
Case Western Reserve University, USA

Thomas Keil
Helsinki University of Technology, Finland

Vladislav Fomin
Delft University of Technology, The Netherlands

ABSTRACT

Standards have become critical to information and communication technologies (ICTs) as they become complex and pervasive. We propose a process theory framework to explain anticipatory standardizing outcomes post hoc when the standardizing process is viewed as networks of events. Anticipatory standards define future capabilities for ICT ex ante in contrast to ex post standardizing existing practices or capabilities through de facto standardization in the market. The theoretical framework offers the following: a) a lexicon in the form of the ontology and typology of standardizing events; b) a grammar, or a set of combination rules, for standardizing events to build process representations; c) an analysis and appreciation of contexts in which standardizing unfolds; and d) logic yielding theoretical explanations of standardizing outcomes based on the analysis of process representations. We show how the framework can help analyze standardization data as networks of events as well as explain standardizing outcomes. We illustrate the plausibility of the approach by applying it to wireless standardization to explain standardizing outcomes.

INTRODUCTION

Over the past decade, successful standard-setting has become critical for innovation, while Information and Communication Technologies (ICTs) have become networked, ubiquitous, and complex (David, 1995; Mansell & Silverstone, 1996). ICTs are technologies dedicated to information processing; in particular, they involve the use of computers and software to convert, store, protect, process, transmit, and retrieve information (Wikipedia, 2005). Recently, traditional standard-setting mechanisms have become rife with problems: They do not respond well to the increased scope, pace, and complexity of technological and market change associated with ICTs (Garud, et al., 2002; Schmidt & Werle, 1998; Werle, 2000). This is the case, in particular, with the exponential growth of *anticipatory* ICT standards—standards that embed significant technological or process innovations into the technical specification—and which are "intended to guide the emergence of new technologies and consequently indicate far ahead in advance of the market's ability to signal the features of products that users will demand" (David, 1995, p. 29). Anticipatory standards define future capabilities for ICTs in contrast to recording and stabilizing existing practices, or capabilities *de facto*. Failures with anticipatory ICT standardizing are common (Steinmueller, 2005; Markus, et al., 2006) and our ability to explain their failure with the existing body of knowledge is poor.

In this article we advance process theorizing of ICT standardizing—the mission of describing, revealing, understanding, and explaining processes, features, and outcomes of ICT standardizing (Weick, 1995). To this end we formulate a theoretical framework which helps formulate plausible, generalizable, and valid explanations of *why* and *how* certain ICT standardizing outcomes emerged (Weick, 1989). The framework posits that ICT standardizing can be seen as a network of events that create and coordinate the adop-

tion of institutionally-bound and contextualized technological repertoires (capabilities) among a set of heterogeneous actors. We draw upon Actor Network Theory (ANT) and Social Construction Of Technology (SCOT) studies (Howcroft, et al., 2004) to explicate these necessary theoretical constructs.

ICT standardizing is viewed in this study as collective engineering of technical specifications (David, 1995; Steinmueller, 2005; Baldwin & Clark, 2005). By drawing upon SCOT (Bijker, 1987), we view anticipatory standardizing as technology framing—sense-making—which at the same time builds durable socio-technical networks (Callon & Law, 1989; Latour, 1995). The framework analyses of event networks of such engineering, sense-making, and negotiation activities offers: a) a *lexicon* in the form of ontology and typology of standardizing events; b) a *grammar*, or set of combination rules for events to build *process representations*; c) an analysis of *contexts* in which events unfold; and d) a set of *logical rules* to yield explanations of standardizing outcomes.

The proposed framework is not *a process theory* of anticipating ICT standardizing outcomes. First, it is not a theory of anticipatory *standards* as ready-to-adopt fixed artifacts, but instead it moves towards theorizing about *standardizing as a stream of social, political and design events which connect ideas, artifacts, people, and institutions to yield a specific technical specification.* Like all process theories, it cannot be used to accurately predict standardizing outcomes, but rather to analyze why specific processes took place in the way they did, and why certain outcomes emerged (Mohr, 1982; Markus & Robey, 1988; Langley, 1999) as to anticipate outcomes of future standardization situations. Second, it is not a complete process theory, as it offers at current state theoretical constructs to compose statements to understand and explain concrete standardizing outcomes.

The remainder of the article is organized as follows: In the second section we define anticipatory ICT standardization and critically review past literature on anticipatory ICT standards to identify core concepts for our integrative framework. In the third section, we build on this review by integrating concepts from the review and developing our theoretical framework, which consists of process theories, the lexicon, the grammar, the context analysis, and the logic. We show how these concepts can account for anticipatory ICT standardizing outcomes. In particular, we illustrate the benefits of the framework by analyzing a small standardizing episode. The fourth section summarizes the main findings, compares the proposed theoretical framework with other accounts of standardization, and explores avenues of future research.

RECEIVED STANDARDIZATION THEORY

Anticipatory ICT Standardizing Defined

In general, "a standard defines a uniform set of measures, agreements, conditions, or specifications between parties (buyer-user, manufacturer-user, government-industry, or government-governed, etc.)" (Spivak & Brenner, 2001, p.16). Technology standards offer agreed upon, external points of reference to which the physical and performance characteristics of current or future technologies can be compared (Hawkins, 1995; Spivak & Brenner, 2001). For this article, we limit ourselves to anticipatory ICT standards that integrate and embed significant technological innovations[1]. Such standards are very challenging to formulate and enforce as they do not just record existing practices (e.g., quality standards), or establish some new practices that need just to be coordinated (e.g., measures). Their intent is to

generate new principles to existing solutions, or to create totally new solutions. Because of this they offer significant upside economic yields and embed significant challenges related to intellectual property, scale of economic benefits and costs, and means to enforce standards and their deviations, yet also pose significant risks of failing.

We define *anticipatory ICT standardizing* as a process in which two or more actors come to agree upon and adhere in a contract to a set of publicly available original and novel technical specifications for an ICT system, service, or capability, including its parts, features, or functionality (David & Greenstein, 1990). Typically, anticipatory ICT standards emerge as multi-firm agreements about technologies, e.g., Bluetooth standard (Keil, 2002) and GSM standards (Moully & Patet, 1991), as vertical industry standards, e.g., Markus, et al., 2006; Damsgaard and Lyytinen (2001),; as de facto standards constituting an open standard, e.g., SUN's Java platform (Garud, et al., 2002), or as open specifications which later can become de facto standards, e.g., IETF's RFCs (Tuomi, 2001) or W3C drafts or RFCs (Berners-Lee, 1999).

Due to its *innovative* nature, anticipatory ICT standardizing is akin to cooperative, multi-actor R&D and indicative of *collective engineering*, where standard setters create capabilities to displace existing capabilities (David, 1995), and seek thereby new markets (Gabel, 1991). Because of this, anticipatory ICT standards share four features: 1) they record and coordinate advances in information and communication technology capabilities (Mansell & Silverstone, 1996); 2) they are intended to guide future compatibility or interoperability requirements-related ICTs, including physical products, service platforms (David, 1995), or data exchange or process standards (Markus, et al., 2006); 3) they are often created in international and/or national institutional contexts to promote industry-level coordination (Hawkins, 1995); and 4) they are conveyed in public domain documents to which different parties have *open access* and can thus be influenced through institutions (Gabel, 1991).

FOUR PERSPECTIVES OF ANTICIPATORY ICT STANDARDIZING

An in-depth review of all research in anticipatory ICT standardization is beyond the scope of this article. Rather, we will in the following summarize four broad theoretical perspectives and examine how each stream has approached anticipatory ICT standardizing problems (Table 1 (a/b)). We will discuss what specific theories have been deployed in each perspective and what are the strengths and weaknesses of each perspective

Practitioner Literatures

There is a relatively large body of practitioner-oriented literature that discusses practice-related issues relevant to ICT standardization (see, e.g., Cargill, 1989). While this literature covers the whole process of standard creation and selection, thoroughly documents standardization institutions and associated processes, and offers useful rules of thumb for approaching standardizing situations, it lacks a theoretical underpinning that limits its explanatory power to account for standardization processes and outcomes.

Economic and Management Theories of Standardization

In a second stream of research, standardization has been analyzed as an economic or managerial decision problem (Shapiro & Varian, 1998; Swann, 2000). It is driven by the following research questions: Why do producers or users choose a specific ICT standard, and what is their rational justification for such a choice? In addressing these questions, researchers use economics or management theories to explain the economic benefits of

standards and identify conditions that maximize individual users' or collectives' welfare. Early economics literature focused on market-based selection (Farrell & Saloner, 1985; Farrell & Saloner, 1986). Recent studies have also focused on explaining the dynamics of standard adoption by utilizing asymmetric switching costs (e.g., Brynjolfsson & Kemerer, 1996; Farrell & Saloner, 1988a), network externalities (David & Steinmueller, 1994), or increasing returns (Arthur, 1989). Relatively few studies have analyzed standard selection within standardization institutions, or within hybrid arrangements, such as standardization alliances (Axelrod, et al., 1995).

While the body of economics literature is large and growing, these studies suffer from a number of deficiencies when we try to understand anticipatory ICT standardizing. First, these studies focus completely on standard choice and ignore technological, social, structural, or institutional forces that shape standard creation and selection (Markus, et al., 2006; Weitzel, et al., 2006). Accordingly, a standard-to-be-selected is assumed to be a natural state to which companies and other actors respond passively. Yet, this is not the case with anticipatory standards. While economic models often provide deep insights into counterintuitive outcomes of standard choices, they are limited in analyzing relatively simple choice situations where the choice shifts fast and unpredictably. Accordingly, they are not well suited to account for outcomes of complex anticipatory standardizing that have had a significant strategic impact (Funk, 2002; Markus, et al., 2006). In addition, these studies ignore the influence of social or institutional context and the "shadow" of history that affects standard creation.

Legal and Public Policy Studies

Although most legal and public policy studies do not address the issue of standardization *per se*, many such studies have either analyzed the broader context in which standardizing takes

Table 1a. Theories to analyze anticipatory ICT standarding outcomes

Perspective	Theory	Domain/Focus/ Phase	Research Question	Explanatory mechanisms	Strengths /Deficiencies	References
Practitioner	A-theoretical	**Domain:** ICT standard **Focus:** Any standard **Phase:** Standardization as a process	How are standards created and how do standardization institutions operate?	Rules of thumb, normative principles, descriptive narrative	*Rich descriptions of actual processes and rules of thumb* What should I do or how should I go about in standardizing in this situation. Lack of theoretical underpinnings, difficult to generalize	(Cargill, 1989; Schmidt & Werle 1998)
Economics	Game theory: Standard creation	**Domain:** General **Focus:** Any standard **Phase:** Standard Creation	Selection of a type of standardization strategy	Rational expectations of firms in game setting	*Explains choice of body.* General focus, and domain, ignores nature of standardization, little emphasis on process, no explanation of technology	(Farrell &Saloner, 1988a)
	Game theory: Standard selection	**Domain:** General **Focus:** Any standard **Phase:** Standard Selection	Selection of de facto standard	Rational expectations of firms in game setting	*Explains choice of existing standard.* General focus and domain can take into account innovation by risk/ yield, no emphasis on standardization process, no explanation of technology	(Farrell &Saloner, 1986; Weitzel, et al., 2006)
Management	Increasing returns and network effects	**Domain:** General **Focus:** Any standard **Phase:** Standard Selection	Selection of de facto standard	Network effects, positive externalities	*Explains choice of existing standard.* General focus and domain, with no focus on social context, no emphasis on standardization process, and no explanation of technology	(Arthur, 1989; David, 1985; Katz, 1986; Shapiro & Varian, 1998; Weitzel, et al., 2006)
	Asymmetric switching cost	**Domain:** General **Focus:** Any standard **Phase:** Standard Selection	Selection of de facto standard	Asymmetric switching cost due to installed base	*Explains inertia in switching between standards.* General focus, ignores nature of standard and social forces, no emphasis on standardization process, no explanation of technology	(Brynjolfsson & Kemerer, 1996; Farrell & Saloner, 1988b; Shapiro & Varian, 1998)
Legal and Public Policy	Theories of regulation	**Domain:** General **Focus:** Any standard but recently mainly ICT **Phase:** Standard as a regulation	How do intellectual property rights and antitrust law affect standards and vice versa? How can a standard be viewed as regulation?	Standard as regulation. Regulatory actors. Intellectual property rights and antitrust law	*Provides rich explanation of the context for standardization processes.* Static view of technology, fails to develop a process perspective of regulation	(Lessig, 1999a; Hosein, et al., 2003; Jarvenpaa, et al., 2003; Patterson, 2002)

Table 1b. Theories to analyze anticipatory ICT standarding outcomes

Perspective	Theory	Domain/Focus/Phase	Research Question	Explanatory mechanisms	Strengths/Deficiencies	References
Sociology of Technology	Actor Network Theory (ANT)	**Domain:** General **Focus:** Any standard **Phase:** Standardization as a process	How are standards created? How do standards become selected so that technologies become stable?	Enrolment into actor networks through translation. Paths in networks. Passage points	*Explains how standards are stabilized within socio-technical networks and how they become irreversible.* Descriptive language to explain standardization processes and outcomes as a set of translations. General theory of technology as inscriptions. Focus on structure of the actor network, downplays individual's innovative role in anticipatory standards	(Allen, 2004; Callon & Law, 1989; Faraj, et al., 2004; Hanset, et al., 1996; Howcroft, et al., 2004; Latour, 1997; Law, 1992; Mangematin & Callon, 1995; Mähring, et al., 2004; Ramiller, 2005; Walsham, 1997, Walsham & Sahay, 1999)
	Social Construction of Technology (SCOT)	**Domain:** General **Focus:** Any standard **Phase:** Standardization as a process	How do standards embody specific problem-solving strategies? How do standards reach a closure, i.e., become standard ways of defining technology?	Designer and user communities. Technology frames. Closure	*Explains how technology is interpreted over its lifetime and how such interpretations stabilize.* Descriptive language to identify and analyze design choices and rationale associated with standards. Views design and use of ICT systems as a framing process. Focuses mostly on sense-making after design, little focus on sensemaking during design. No process study methodology	(Bijker, 2001; Davidson, 2002; Orlikowski & Gash, 1994; Pinch & Bijker, 1987; Sahay & Robey, 1996; Swanson & Ramiller, 1997)

place, or subsumed standardization as a form of regulation. This connection is obvious as regulatory environments provide the context in which standardizing takes place and standards are enforced. For instance, legislation about intellectual property rights (Patterson, 2002; Weiser, 2003) and antitrust legislation (Sheremata, 1998; Teece & Sherry, 2003) directly influence anticipatory standardizing. By the same token, new anticipatory technological standards and their proliferation generate forces that shape regulation (Hosein, et al., 2003). This has led some scholars to suggest that standards can be viewed as a form of regulation (Hosein, et al., 2003; Jarvenpaa, et al., 2003; Lessig, 1999a, b). For instance, Jarvenpaa, et al. (2003) draw parallels between standardization and regulation by arguing that any market player that affects the ICT architecture is acting as a regulatory agent.

Although legal and public policy studies of standardization improve our understanding of how standardization processes are embedded in an institutional context, and are shaped by and contribute to enacting this context, these studies are limited in their ability to inform our understanding of anticipatory ICT standardizing. First, the institutional regulatory environment and the standardization contexts differ radically. Regulation is carried out by national or international legislative institutions based on a public mandate and force. By contrast, anticipatory standardizing takes place in a wide variety—ecology—of institutions that range from informal alliances within an industry to formal standard development organizations associated with nation states (SDOs) (Schmidt & Werle, 1998). This difference suggests that a less institution-bound theory might be needed for standardizing.

The literature that focuses on technology standards as a regulatory actor has also been criticized as static (Hosein, et al., 2003). In particular, within anticipatory ICT standardizing, a more dynamic view is needed that covers simultaneously the emergence of new technologies and the social forces–institutions–that are tied with these technologies and shape actors' expectations, channel resources, and mobilize bias (King, et al., 1994). Finally, the regulatory literature, while emphasizing parties' incentives to create regulatory mechanisms, has failed to provide a process theory of how regulatory mechanisms themselves are created (Croley, 1998). This also weakens the suitability of this stream to explain anticipatory ICT standardizing outcomes.

Social Theories of Standardization

A fourth stream of standardization research is rooted in the sociology of technology research (Williams & Edge, 1996). The bulk of this literature draws upon either the Actor Network Theory (ANT) (Latour, 1997, 1999) or the Social Construction of Technology research (SCOT) (Bijker, 1987). For a general overview and discussion of both literatures, we refer to Howcroft, et al. (2004). Both of these literatures share an interest in examining standardization as interactions between socio-technical elements in which the technology-to-be-standardized becomes invented, introduced, invested, and stabilized (Latour, 1999). Though recently these two approaches have converged, as actor-centered analysis has been extended into broader settings of technology assessment (Sørensen & Williams, 2002), these literatures are somewhat distinct in how they account for technology creation and adoption.

In SCOT, the emphasis is on the evolution and mobilization of interpretive schemes and associated engineering skills as the technology becomes invented and stabilized. Its *leitmotif* is to explain why technology obtains a certain shape and how such shaping is socially conditioned and produced. This explanation is organized around a theory of *technology frames*–a set of community-wide, shared mental schemes "composed of... the concepts and techniques employed by a community in its problem solving" (Bijker, 1987, p.168). In particular, SCOT research has suggested the notion of *closure conditions* (Pinch & Bijker, 1987) that determine when and how technology frames stabilize. Accordingly, an investigator of standards should trace backwards from a "closed" technology standard to situations where specific alternatives were excluded while addressing critical challenges during standard design (Hughes, 1987). This unpacking reveals why and how technological choices are made. SCOT complements economic research in that it identifies and narrates interpretive processes associated with design and foregrounds *sense-making* associated with any technical innovation—including anticipatory standards (Pinch & Bijker, 1987).

Actor-Network Theory seeks to understand why and how a technological solution was created as a carrier of a network of *both* technical and social relations. It aspires to reveal how a technology "embodies the innovator's beliefs, social and economic relations, patterns of use, legal limits, and assumptions as to what the artefact is about" (Akrich, 1992a). ANT leads an investigator to ask the following questions: How did actors become aligned? (Callon, 1986) What reasons did they have for entering the network and how did this change their behaviors (inscriptions) (Akrich, 1992a)? To explain anticipatory standardizing, ANT would trace the designed and agreed standard back into set of "translations" (Callon, 1986) where actors became "enroled" in a network. Though ANT theorists do not assume sequential processes in such network constructions, nearly all ANT studies explain network emergence as an orderly sequence of specific types of events (Callon, 1986). This ordering is subordinated to a movement towards an *obligatory passage point* (Callon, 1986): "a situation through which the heterogeneous actors involved… must be made to pass" (Ramiller, 2005, p.57). One such passage point, for example, would be the agreement about the final contract, while another one would be to make the technology to behave as specified in the standard.

ANT shares with SCOT the interest in revealing why standardizing followed one trajectory and thus stabilized, and by doing so excluded other alternatives. Yet, the notion of stabilization in these streams is different. In ANT, stabilization is seen to result from an expanding enrolment that leads the actor-network to grow whereby the content and intensity of the connections in the network changes (Mangematin & Callon, 1995). The ANT literature thus provides insights into how increasingly complex socio-technical networks emerge, and how, due to intricacies of the translation *process,* the standards become *stable,* i.e., *agreed* and *irreversible*. In SCOT, in contrast, standardizing is about closing, typifying, and objectifying frames that "read" technologies-in-making.

Both ANT and SCOT have been adopted in ICT standardizing, or innovation, research. SCOT researchers have studied managers' sense-making during IT innovation (Swanson & Ramiller, 1997), how users and designers interpret requirements (Davidson, 2002), how users make sense of the technology (Orlikowski & Gash, 1994), and how technologies maintain interpretive flexibility (Sahay & Robey, 1996). Past ANT research has studied system implementations as translations through passage points (Mähring, et al., 2004; Ramiller, 2005), and how systems create social orders (Walsham & Sahay, 1999).

Research focused on ICT standardizing has also drawn upon both strands of social theory. First, Hanseth, et al. (1996) examined how standards are inscribed during standardization processes by using ANT. Likewise, Egyedi (2005) analyzed how the institutional context of SDO affects standardization outcomes based on ANT. She investigated negotiations within an actor-network in explaining standardizing outcomes. She analyzed, in particular, the meaning, purpose, or role of the network, actors' positions in the network, and the boundaries of the network. Likewise, Jakobs (2006) examined relationships between standardization and user-side innovation by using SCOT. He observed mutual influence between standardization and innovation sense-making in which technology standards are being developed. Likewise, Stewart and Williams (2005), drawing upon SCOT, discussed user sense-making during innovation and suggested that "in this process, artifacts are often reinvented and further elaborated ("innofusion")" (Stewart & Williams, 2005, p.195).

Despite their merits in explaining technology evolution, ANT and SCOT remain broad theories of technological and social orders. This makes them too general to capture critical aspects of anticipatory ICT standardizing. They suffer among others weaknesses in accounting anticipatory ICT standardizing as collective engineering in specific institutional contexts. From the ANT viewpoint this introduces a challenge in explaining who should be enroled, why, and how, and what is the organization of the network when design is fluid, shifting, and ambiguous. Some ANT assumptions, like actors' interests, remain relatively stable (Allen, 2004); they know within whom/what they need to enrol, and are not plausible in this context (Ramiller, 2005). During anticipatory standardizing, designers do *not* know what networks they must pull together: Designs remain ambiguous, their consequences cannot be predicted, and most relationships between the actors are up for grabs (Van de Ven, et al., 1999). Actors discover their interests dynamically by enroling in different networks in different ways over time, and their interests emerge hand-in-hand with advances in various designs (Ramiller, 2005).

Likewise, SCOT suffers the lack of integrating individual creativity in its concept of technology frame. It is not clear what role breakthrough ideas, novel innovations, and exceptional individual talent play in the evolution of technology if technologies are directed and shaped by community sense-making. In addition, SCOT views "technology framing" primarily as a user-related sense-making around finished designs (Pinch & Bijker, 1987). Yet, as a form of innovation, anticipatory standardizing involves surprises that unexpectedly change the direction of design, and it is driven by shifting individual design-triggered framing. These shifts are produced by individual designer's wits in framing their designs *differently,* which, in turn, will affect how they locate into social and technological networks. When designers weigh in new design options, both the design and its interpretation change, and "they are themselves transformed, 'redesigned' as actors, as they learn about the possibilities of the technology" (Ramiller, 2005, pp.71-72). Thus, due to both SCOT and ANT's focus on established and fixed actor networks, or community wide "technology frames," they are limited to accounting for how an individual designer and later a design team can shape standardizing outcomes. Although some attempts to resolve this problem have been made (Akrich, 1992; Faraj, et al., 2004), how individual cognition is currently brought to bear in understanding standardizing is limited to finished designs.

Motivation for the Proposed Process Theory Framework

ANT and SCOT together offer an excellent starting point for developing a process theory for anticipatory ICT standardizing. They both focus on processes that make technologies stable and irreversible—a goal also shared in anticipatory standardizing. However, both approaches are broad descriptive "sensitizing devices," and do not aspire to produce process explanations that are specific to ICT standardization context. They offer little guidance how accounts of ICT standardization processes can be formulated and systematically analyzed. We believe, however, that more localized theoretical frameworks can be useful in building process theories of standardizing that are accurate and theoretically adequate to identify, analyze, and synthesize standardizing events and their connections into networks. These networks can then be used to build explanations

155

why and how an ICT standardization outcome was produced (Langley, 1999). In what follows, we formulate a process theory framework to build anticipatory ICT standardizing theories (Weick, 1989).

A PROCESS THEORY FRAMEWORK FOR ANTICIPATORY ICT STANDARDIZING

A theoretical framework for standardizing process theories consists of a set of constructs (lexicon) and their relationships (a grammar) that help formulate process theories (a theory logic), and a set of criteria to evaluate such theories (Bacharach, 1989). A general discussion of process theories is beyond the scope of this article (see Langley, 1999; Van de Ven, et al., 1999; Pentland, 1999; van de Ven & Poole, 1995; Mohr, 1982). We just note that process theories differ mainly in types of constructs, their relationships, and the logical way inferences are made from the data (Mohr 1982; Van de Ven, et al., 1999). A problem in available process theory guidelines is that they are about broad social processes and do not take into account differences, e.g., in accounting a small project change, a disruption in a team's behavior, or a strategic change. They are mainly distinguished by the level and nature of constructs used, type of analysis method, or complexity (Langley, 1999). To build process theories of anticipatory standardizing demands, however, it is necessary that we increase the domain level detail (vertical theorizing) among constructs used and the richness in their connections (Weick, 1989). This must be reflected in the consequent choice of constructs and the ways in which we advance explanations with those constructs.

In general, we define a *process* as a set of events that unfold over time in a context (Pettigrew, 1997). We call any set of such events organized over time an *episode*. Standardizing events accordingly range from imagining use

scenarios to designing specifications and testing, to choosing between design options[2]. An ICT standardizing process theory is about the types of events that unfold, how they relate, and how they explain standardizing outcomes (Markus & Robey, 1988; Mohr, 1982; Van de Ven & Huber, 1990). In short, it explains *why* and *how* an ICT standardizing outcome emerged.

We propose the following constructs following Bacharach's (1989) suggestions for theory building to build ICT standardizing process theories:

1. A *context* in which the events take place. This construct is critical for two reasons: a) most process explanations are context-dependent and the notion of context is needed for increasing internal validity, and at the same time b) context is necessary for generalizing across other situations and improving external validity of the proposed theory. Overall, context construct is needed to align with Bacharach's (1989) idea of the utility of the conceptual relationships and their explanatory potential and related assumptions.

2. A *lexicon* of event types and outcomes. The lexicon defines the content and granularity of standardizing events that will be brought to bear in explaining the outcome. This element corresponds with Bacharach's (1989) concept of theory constructs that define theory variables, and the theory's scope.

3. An *event grammar* that characterizes the nature of relationships into which the standardizing events enter. The grammar establishes a focal means of arranging events into relationships and chronicling event networks as defined by their temporal ordering, or by other relationships. This element relates Bacharach's (1989, p. 510) concept of construct relationships and criteria by which one assesses the logical adequacy of those relationships.

4. A set of *logics* to infer from the events, their networks and contextual relationships, statements how and why the process was organized as it was, and why certain outcomes emerged. This element corresponds to Bacharach's (1989) demand for theory-based explanations that are grounded on propositions.

THE CONTEXT

Generally, a process emerges from interactions between events and a context (Van de Ven, et al., 1999). A context is instrumental in process explanations, as it relates events into nested arrangements of associated structures and processes (Pettigrew, 1997). Accordingly, we need to examine how events "of one period lead to changes in the context that affect action in the subsequent periods" (Langley, 1999, p.703). In line with this approach, we assume that standardizing events are constrained by the context, but they also shape that context by preserving or altering technological capabilities, modifying institutional arrangements, or changing the actors (Pettigrew, 1997).

During standardizing, the context can be separated into a nested structure of focal actors, the technological environment, the market environment, and the institutional environment. The technological environment includes existing and emerging ICT technologies, past design choices in deploying these technologies, and emerging technological trends. The technological environment defines what is technologically possible and desirable. Actors include firms, organizations, and individuals who are directly participating in the standardizing process. In anticipatory ICT standardizing, firms from varied industries as telecommunications equipment, telecommunications services, information technology, semiconductor manufacturing, packaged software, or many user industries participate. Organizations such as the ITU, ETSI, or other industry associations might participate actively in standardizing. The market environment includes existing or emerging markets that the standard is targeting or that might be influenced by the emergence of the standard as well as the firms and organizations or individuals operating in these markets. Finally, the institutional context includes institutional arrangements as well as regulatory and legal frameworks within which the standardizing takes place. Institutional arrangements might include standardization fora, alliances, or standardization bodies in which the standardizing takes place. In particular, regulations about the telecommunications or information technology domain and anti-trust laws play an important role in shaping the standardizing.

A LEXICON OF EVENTS

We assume each such standardizing *event* accounts in some way, either directly or indirectly, for the observed outcome. This defines the profile of each event, and covers the type of outcome, its content (what the event is about), and related actors. We assume that standardizing events can be analytically distinguished based on their primary outcomes–the content–and that each event is associated with an output of a specific type (as reflected in resulting documents, ideas, artifacts, or agreements). Such output is later regarded instrumental in explaining the ensuing process and its outcomes. Events that do not have such impact can always be discarded during the process as irrelevant for the current theory building effort. An event can be triggered by other events, or by changes in the context, and such causes of events need to be identified in the event description.

In general, several different types of outputs can be related to any standardizing episode, such as a standards meeting. These episodes have multiple and diverse outputs that need to be carefully separated and associated with specific individual events. In addition, to account for the temporal dimension, each identified event must be tagged with start and end times so that they can be ordered in temporal sequences. Such baseline sequences of events offer a basis for formulating process explanations.

Traditionally, process theories have used a singular concept of an event, which is defined as an observed change in the process state marked by a point in time. In this regard, we find current process theories to be too general, and propose here a richer domain-specific typology which classifies standardizing processes into three types of events. As our primary interest lies in understanding what goes on during standardizing while an ICT standard emerges as an "agreed upon" specification, we need a typology that distinguishes between various aspects of standardizing in the same manner as Simon (1977) distinguished between different aspects of decision making. Simon drew his distinctions based on the idea of cognitive orientations that characterize three recursive phases of decision making that completely describe decision outcomes. His cognitive orientation included a set of cognitive elements and processes that had to be foregrounded in each phase. Completeness was about finding out which types of cognitive orientations were necessary so that a decision-making process could be successfully completed. Accordingly, he proposed three decision phases 1) *intelligence:* defining a problem space; 2) *design:* structuring a problem space; 3) *choice:* searching in that space. He also demonstrated their completeness in exhaustively explaining decision outcomes.

Likewise, we will define ICT standardizing events based on their essential *cognitive orientations.* We distinguish three cognitive orientations whereby ICT standardizing can be broken down into: 1) *design,* 2) *negotiation,* and 3) *sense-making.* Here, 1) *Design* orients itself towards the creation of technical specifications and draws upon engineering principles that lay out design architectures, components, and their specifications; structural, functional and observable behavioral features (e.g., reliability) of the artifacts

dominate the reasoning; 2) *Negotiation* orients itself towards reconciling technical solutions with regard to the interests of the involved actors; strategies and interests of actors and anticipations of their behaviors towards other actors dominate the reasoning, and 3) *Sense-making* orients itself towards "reading" technical specifications in ways that relate them to the life-worlds associated with the use of produced artifacts and/or shaping institutional contexts that surround specified technology. Here, design artifacts' relationships to users' experience, designer' experience and others' life-worlds dominate the reasoning. All these types are necessary to define and produce an anticipatory standard. Design events are necessary to yield specifications that can include novel principles which are shown to work. Negotiations are needed to reach agreements between actors, while sense-making is needed to contextualize the specification and negotiation events into an unfolding business, institutional, and user context (Weick, 1995).

In formulating the typology, we also recognize the notion of a closure and stabilization that is needed in creating the standard. Each event type distinguishes a separate dimension along which standard setters must stabilize the standardizing results. Consequently, a successful anticipatory ICT standardizing includes: 1) *a design closure:* the technical specification has been formulated and fixed completely in light of engineering goals and criteria (Simon, 1977), 2) a *negotiation closure:* actors know what has been agreed upon, and what the implications of such agreement are for their interests. Most actors are also aware that such an agreement has been achieved (Callon, 1986), and 3) a *sense-making closure:* each actor interprets the standard in relation to technological, social, and business contexts in a meaningful and stable way. The meaning of technology has become typified and institutionalized for involved actors, and they enact relatively stable technology frames (Pinch & Bijker, 1987).

Design (D-Events)

Anticipatory standards emerge neither by God's finger nor by recording existing practice. They involve spurts of innovation where technical designs are proposed, implemented, and evaluated. Anticipatory ICT standardizing is fundamentally about *collectively engineering a new tangible (or intangible) technical artifact through a set of design events (D-Events)*. Design events echo the "science of the artificial: finding occasions for making a decision, finding possible courses of action, choosing among courses of action" (Simon, 1977). Design choices are made by selecting from alternatives that have been deemed possible during preceding D-events. Identification of D-events unpacks a standard setter's winding cognitive process and his or her constant struggle to articulate design alternatives and make choices.

A design closure is achieved through a set of D-events which gradually produce a technical specification that is innovative, i.e., defines novel technological capabilities that can be implemented and at the same time submits to good engineering practices. Such principles include general design goals and architectural norms that state that specifications need to be simple, elegant, efficient, and involve acceptable and better trade-offs between performance, cost, and reliability, than existing solutions, etc. When engineers/ designers reach a closure, they will know collectively how the new technology will work, what its basic properties will be, and how it changes engineering, design, manufacturing, or use practices. A failure to reach a design closure involves a failure to produce technical specifications, or to produce specifications that include errors, are ambiguous, too complex, or costly to implement. This is either due to a failure to generate feasible design options or a failure to choose correctly among them.

When explaining how a design closure is reached, investigators need to come to grips with how technical specifications can actually be derived. This resembles the process of trial and error learning (March, et al., 1991). Accordingly, ICT standardizing takes place predominantly in distributed laboratories, but also covers joint work in committees where technical specifications are reviewed, revised, and modified in all minutiae (Schmidt & Werle, 1998). A large proportion of standardizing is about "every day" engineering–arduous elicitation, elaboration, and refinement of the technical details, and arguing about design options. Accordingly, D-events are communicated in genres appropriate to these communities: technical reports, memoranda, prototype solutions, test results, etc.

The scope of design events ranges from simple design tasks, such as specifying a software or hardware interface, to decisions concerning the encompassing design architecture around which the whole standard will be built and which will affect a trajectory of future innovations and standard refinements (Baldwin & Clark, 2005). For example, the design of a wireless phone standard involved myriad design choices: articulating the architecture of the system (and its service model); specifying open and proprietary sub-system interfaces; and validating their non-functional features (reliability). But, it also involved smaller events such as specifying a speech codec or usability constraints for the interface (Manninen, 2002; Fomin & Lyytinen, 2001). The designs are path dependent in that they draw upon existing technological capabilities and factor in installed base compatibility and interoperability. Designs are also path dependent in that they build on previous technological advances and well-known solution spaces.

The collective and heterogeneous nature of standardizing designs adds *complexity* to the process and forms a significant barrier to reaching a stable design. This can be due to a great number of proposed solutions or due to the need to apply multiple conflicting design principles or requirements. This complexity is reflected in massive piles of documents and large committee sizes. For instance, a complete GSM standard already covered thousands of pages of detailed technical documents (Mouly & Pautet, 1992) and the complexity of 3G standards has grown exponentially. Standard setters must master this complexity by setting their ambitions wisely, and by applying modular designs (Simon, 1977). Good architectural control becomes crucial as architectural decisions define critical interfaces and allow separate communities to work in parallel (Simon, 1977). Thereby multiple parallel and iterative design processes are implicated when engineers choose a modular design for standards. Likewise, higher ambitions lead to increased uncertainty and a larger number of iterations. For instance, during Bluetooth standardization, the first version of the standard was delayed since its technological implementation proved significantly more complex than expected due to its high ambition level (Keil, 2002).

Negotiation (N-Events)

In the end, each standard is about excluding alternative technical specifications in light of "positive" political and economic consequences of such exclusions. Designers become negotiators when they ask how their designs will align with other actors' interests[3]. Therefore—metaphorically speaking—during standardizing, a set of technical specifications transforms itself from a "pure" cognitive state–a design idea–into an institutional force to reckon with embedded in the standard. This transformation happens through negotiation between actors. In fact, great or less than great design ideas can travel to the material world only through the gates of negotiation (Suchman, 2000), and an anticipatory standard "can be conceived as a complex (socio-technical) system resulting from a long and laborious process of negotiation" (Gherardi & Nicolini, 2000). Such a negotiation result creates irreversibility as "the displacement, the creation of a link that did not exist before and that to some extent modifies the original" (Latour,

1999, p.197), while actors enter into irreversible networks (Hanseth, et al., 1996).

The standard as a negotiated order contains binding technical repertoires that are institutionally bound, recognized, and legitimate. Accordingly, *we call a standardizing event an N-event if it supports the goal of reaching an agreement about a specification through negotiation.* Each result of N-events defines the nature, content, and form of a part or a whole set of specifications *as agreed* and thereby declares commitments, rights, and duties implicated by the agreement across standard setters, adopters, and other parties (e.g., regulators). Per definition, the final standard is established if and only if the whole specification is closed by an agreement concerning the substance of technical specifications and its implications for each actor. Moreover, all actors must recognize the agreement as legitimate. The final agreement must be preceded by a set of other N-events that gradually transform the status of non-legitimate and dis-agreed upon specifications into legitimate and agreed upon. Thus the set of final specifications create formal contractual relationships between standard setters and can also produce new regulations for standard-setting institutions. A failure to reach negotiation closure leads actors to reject technical specifications or their implications, and in so doing, break down the network.

The negotiations are also *path dependent* in that they draw upon existing contracts, contractual arrangements, and instutional practices that recognize, record, and enforce such contractual arrangements (regulatory statutes by standardization organizations, patent laws, trade secrets, etc.). Negotiations are also *path dependent* during the standardization in that they build on previous negotiation moves as well as known "negotiation spaces" in which actors have entered previously. This intrinsic connection between negotiation and network irreversibility explains also the immense difficulty of creating anticipatory standards. Standard setters can ensure the durability of technical repertoires only if the agreed upon standard will travel well across time and space. This occurs only if subsequent N-events constantly create, solidify and expand *new* actor-networks, which require either connecting to, or demolishing existing networks – both of which are extremely difficult to accomplish.

The form and content of N-events vary depending on the institutional context. Negotiations are not necessarily carried out during a single N-episode. As noted, they often refer to earlier umbrella agreements, rest on prevailing practice, or trigger a series of additional N-events across multiple institutional contexts (Schmidt & Werle, 1998). Negotiations take place often at official meetings, but often the deals are struck in hallways and in unofficial discussions (Haug, 2002). Negotiations are carried out by spokespersons who have a mandate (Latour, 1987). These include prominent engineers, strategy and IPR professionals, technology managers, and even politicians. The mandates are defined and enabled through the intermediation of rule makers and enforcers (other spokespersons, standard-setting organizations, committee chairpersons, etc.). The mandates are about technical choices, licensing, sharing of IPR, market shares and market making, enrolment of new actors, or their disconnection. Each mandate is defined by its characteristics, including the scope of technical specifications, types of contracts, IPR pool documents, etc.

Sense-Making (S-Events)

Anticipatory standardizing exhibits a form of technological imagination that writes technology repertoires for the future world (Latour, 1999). Metaphorically it is "persuasive and constitutive storytelling about the future" (Suchman, 2000, p.319). By telling a different story, standard setters expand their horizons and become aware of prejudices they bring to their interpretations of current technology use (Gadamer, 1975). Such story telling is named in ways from organizing visions, futuristic scenarios, to technology fads

(Swanson & Ramiller, 1997) and documented in policy and market reports, strategy formulations and technology road maps, consumer focus group reports, or memos that record ongoing conversations among standard setters (e.g., minutes).

Overall, standardizing creates and enacts meanings about designs, artifacts, design and use processes, agreements, and actors and their identities which, over time, transform and renounce standard setters' interpretive frames about the technology (Karnoe, et al., 2005; Latour, 1992). Actors at the same time attach meanings (perspective making) to standards and make sense of others' meaning projections (perspective taking) (Boland & Tenkasi, 1995). In so doing, they rationalize what they are doing or have been doing, and shift their cognitive strategies in relation to the technology-to-be-standardized, the actors involved, or the institutional context (Callon, 1986; Latour, 1995; Weick, 1993). This ebb and flow builds and questions technological frames and leads to the attribution of new meanings to standards, actors, and the context (Bijker, 1995).

No anticipatory standard will be agreed upon unless actors *make sense* of it and can imagine the types of repertoires embedded in it operating in a future world. In a narrow sense (no pun meant here), sense-making is about how the design meets set-up engineering criteria, such as simplicity or elegance in design. In a broad sense it embraces a broader set of cognitive tasks that help designers understand how proposed designs relate to the future social, technological, and institutional world, and how they shape and are shaped by these worlds. In the following, we will talk about sense-making in a broad sense.

After Weick (1995), we define sense-making as an actor's interpretive response to observed and imagined changes that result from design or negotiation events, or changes in the standardizing context. *Events that read meanings into anticipatory standardizing events and actors are called sense-making events (S-events).* Sense-making closure means that there is a set of S-events that produces a set of stable interpretive frames among the involved actors, which defines the meaning of the standard for their context. A failure to reach such a closure is common. It signals controversies around what the technology is supposed to do, or how it relates to future use or institutional contexts.

S-events draw upon actors' past experience and inherited technology frames that coordinate sense-making. Therefore, anticipatory standardizing poses significant challenges when such frames diverge or break down. For instance, in the early phases of the Bluetooth standardization, participants from the computer and telecommunications industries had to pour significant efforts into formulating a joint understanding of the scope of the technology-to-be-standardized because their views on what would make the standard successful differed (Keil, 2002). Failures in sense-making generate unstable technical specifications, shifting actor identitites, and a fluid institutional context, all of which can result in disagreements.

Though anticipatory sense-making is proactive, it is simultaneously retroactive. Standardizing starts with a retrospective reading of current technology that erects a context that is *path dependent*. Anticipatory standardizing becomes proactive when it attributes a *different* meaning to a not-yet-invented technology, and thus enacts a new environment (Weick, 1995). It generates mindfull deviations so that the technology becomes re-defined, re-evaluated, and re-contextualized (Garud, et al., 2002).

EVENT GRAMMAR

An event's significance is produced by its place and role in an event sequence. We need therefore to combine identified events into sequences. Such networks of events connect all events to process outcomes (Pentland, 1999). Given that anticipatory ICT standardizing is highly complex, non-linear, and chaotic (Markus, et al., 2006; Nickerson &

Zur Muehlen, 2006), and takes years to unfold, the event grammar–a way to connect events–has to be built on assumptions about the complexity. We therefore assume non-linearity among design, sense-making, and negotiation events: They can be connected by relationships that exhibit circularity, concurrency, and hierarchical organization. We next extend the process analysis to event network analysis. We explore first how events will be organized into sequences and thereafter how we can infer why and how outcomes relate to such sequences.

We devise an *event grammar* that articulates multiple heterogeneous relationships between design, sense-making, and negotiation events. The grammar consists of two levels. The first level–called *binary grammar*–describes how any two events can be positioned into adjacency pairs. Second, a *choreography grammar* offers a set of principles that help string adjacency pairs into larger sequences. Overall, the proposed *grammar*– by organizing events into sequences–integrates three separate perspectives that underlie design, negotiation, and sense-making activities. In so doing, we account for a problem noted by Langley (1999): How can different theoretical perspectives be combined in process explanations? In our analysis, each event type is germane to understanding one critical dimension of anticipatory standardizing. Yet, each dimension alone is insufficient in explaining the final outcome. Utilizing multiple perspectives simultaneously and by integrating them through the event grammar, offers a feasible strategy to carry out a multi-perspective analysis and arrive at plausible process theories.

Binary Grammar

The binary grammar detects *reasons* for moving between the events and expresses their natural temporal order (before, after, and parallel). The first step in the analysis is therefore to relate any event to its preceding and/or succeeding events. Each event can thus be connected to two sets of adjacency pairs: a set of events that lead to this event, and a set of events that follow it.

Building our binary grammar rests on two main principles. First, events of *any type* can be organized into adjacency pairs based on their temporal properties (before and after). These properties arrange events into sequences that maintain chronological (topological) order. Second, any event can trigger and be triggered by any other event type. For instance, a new design can trigger sense-making about potential technology applications in the market, it might trigger negotiation about intellectual property rights regarding the design, or it might trigger additional design to integrate it into a new architecture. Third, we distinguish in each event an actor's *choice* that shifts his or her cognitive orientation from one type of "activity" into another, or from one activity into another activity within the same type. These relationships define the "logic" of standardizing events, and will form the kernel in explaining the outcomes. We do not expect that any preceding event will *causally* determine the type or the content of the succeeding event. Rather, any event type can trigger another type of event, subject to the outcomes of the preceding events, and actors' conscious or unconscious choices, and the impact of contextual conditions. For instance, a technical design can trigger negotiation among actors in the same industry who share a similar understanding of its application, while the same design can trigger sense-making in a broader community that needs to relate the design to its environment as to arrive at a common understanding. Succeeding events can also be multiplied into several sub-events through decomposition. For instance, during negotiation, sense-making events might be triggered to find out how each design alternative relates to the goals of engaged actors. Negotiation can thus only continue after the sense-making in each alternative path is completed.

Table 2 classifies a space of possible event adjacency pairs. Many of the defined patterns were identified in several empirical investigations that we have listed in the table. In the table each row defines a type of the preceding event and each column a type of the following event. Overall, the table lists a set of possible event pairs and reasons why they are connected together. The table was derived based on a content analysis of empirical investigations of standardization processes as shown by the references. Within each reference analyzed we identified a set of two different types of events and then analyzed what triggered the shift from one event to the next. Overall, the table outlines a number of event pair *archetypes* and helps identify typical event pairs. For instance, a design-design event pair consists first of an earlier event that triggers a later decomposition refinement. A typical negotiation-sensemaking pair could consist of first negotiating technical commitments and then engaging actors in sense-making to explore what this compromise entails in the future market. The table is not, however, complete in the sense that the reasons for these relationships were empirically identified and additional reasons to connect events might emerge from future studies. Nor does it replace an in-depth analysis of detailed relationships between events and their context. Overall, the binary analysis demands a careful articulation how events and their contexts interact in order to find specific reasons why such moves took place.

Event Network

An event network identifies the connections among *all* standardizing events organized over time as defined by temporal and adjacency relationships. A network of events thus represents how standardizing reached a closure with respect to design, negotiation, and sense-making, and overall produced a standard, or how it failed to do so, and if so, what events "failed." We need this level of aggregation in our analysis as event pairs alone show how events relate to one another, but not why specific standardizing results emerged. By integrating the events into a network, the

Table 2. Binary Relationships Between D-, N-, S- Events

Preceding/ Following Event	D-event	N-event	S-event
D-event	**DD1:** Decompose and refine technical specifications (Baldwin and Clark 2005) **DD2:** Test, Evaluate (Manninen 2002, Haug 2002)	**DN1:** Compromise between designs; (Haug 2002) **DN2:** Agree on final design; (Manninen 2002) **DN3:** Agree on design parameters/ evaluation criteria (Manninen 2002)	**DS1:** Justify design feature (Fomin and Lyytinen 2001) **DS2:** Evaluate use scenarios (Schmidt and Werle 1998) **DS3:** Imagine new contexts of using technology (Keil 2002)
N-event	**ND1:** Refine and search for a negotiated solution (Haug 2002) **ND2:** Develop a solution to counterattack existing designs (Funk 2002), (Garud et al 2002)	**NN1:** Negotiate rules; (Manninen 2002) **NN2:** Negotiate actor composition; (Garud et al 2002, Keil 2002) **NN3:** Negotiate after disagreement (Haug 2002)	**NS1:** What does a compromise mean? (Haug 2002) **NS2:** Does the negotiated standard make sense? (Garud et al 2002) **NS3:** What does the standard mean for technology evolution? (Haug 2002)
S-event	**SD1:** Develop a new scenario to reconsider design (Manninen 2002)	**SN1:** Change use context to negotiate design options (Faraj et al . 2004)	**SS1:** New use scenario triggers sense making of other technologies (Funk 2002)

result is shown to be generated by a multi-path event sequence that takes place in a set of shifting contexts. It involves both chronological and activity-based relationships between events. By increasing the complexity of the network level analysis, we increase the accuracy in our process accounts (Weick, 1989).

In formulating an event network, we can deploy visual mapping techniques (Langley, 1999) that use graph theory to organize event pairs into networks depicting both time and activity-based dependencies between events. These graphs can be analyzed for their structural properties and at the same time they offer a holistic overview of the event networks. We build an event network in three steps. First, we aggregate events into a *temporal sequence* by sorting events into chronological chains by utilizing their start and end times. Temporal ordering creates a timeline of the standardizing process and allows us to identify both sequential and concurrent events. Second, since each event

can be triggered or trigger other events, we need to aggregate event pairs into *sequences according to their functional outcomes*, i.e.,their activity-based relationships. We further need to identify which events change the context, or are shaped by the context. An *activity-based ordering* creates a functional map of the standardizing processes and observes which events are decomposed into sub-events (Simon, 1977), and which events lead to other events by changing the type of the event, its content hops between types of events, or the content of the event.

In a third step, we *compare and integrate the temporal, functional, and activity-based networks*. The resulting event network describes a) temporal (x ended before y), b) functional (x produced input to y, or x needed type-y input), and c) activity-based dependencies (what types of events x lead to an event y). This network organizes events *sequentially, in parallel, and iteratively*. The outcome is not a pure sequential model that most process theories utilize (Pentland, 1999), as it integrates multiple, including iterative, connections between events.

PROCESS LOGIC

Logical Inference Rules and Deductive Process Explanations

The event networks chronicle event sequences that either lead to a standard (closure) or fail to do so. By being grammatically "correct," the choreography conveys one logical premise to explain the observed outcome. Yet, knowing which design, sense-making, and negotiation events took place, and when and how they were related, does not explain yet what generated the pattern and its outcome (Pentland, 1999). To explain why such outcomes emerged, we need to draw upon logical and theoretical rules that are applied to the "structural characteristics" of the event network and the context (Pentland, 1999). An analogy with stories might help here to illustrate our point: grammatically correct sentences are necessary, but not a sufficient condition of telling a plausible story. To be plausible, a story requires a narrative (a story line) in addition to being composed of grammatically correct sentences. Similarly, the story of a standardizing process requires a narrative (story line) that informs why events were strung together the way they were. To accomplish this, explanations require a logical narrative from the used process representation that creates a plausible scenario of how the standardizing unfolded, and how and why a standard emerged. To create such narratives, we need theoretical and logical rules that conceptually connect events and outcomes (Pentland, 1999). Discovering these connections, however, does not yield a strong causal explanation: event sequences are *not* both necessary and sufficient conditions for producing the outcome. In contrast, we show why Y resulted in process

X though there can also be other situations under which Y can be achieved.

While crafting process explanations we draw upon a set of inference rules. A *rule of inference* is a scheme for constructing valid inference. In logic, such schemes establish syntactic relations between a set of formulas called *premises,* and an assertion called a *conclusion*. These relations are used in inference to arrive at new, true assertions. Rules also apply to semantic and pragmatic arguments, but here their formulation is more difficult and controversial (Toulmin, 1959). Yet, the discovery and use of rules and associated theoretical models that connect events, standardizing contexts and standardizing outcomes in plausible ways equates with the goal of building process theories (Pentland, 1999; Langley, 1999). In our case, this calls for formulating inferences that address the following question: Why and how was a standardization closure reached given the event sequence and the context? Formulating such an explanation poses a significant intellectual challenge since inference rules for process data are not well axiomatized as are rules of inference for variance-based explanations (Shadish, et al., 2003). For example, the validity and reliability of process explanations are difficult to establish (Pentland, 1999).

We are often left with our imagination in formulating such rules and must rely on their intuitive appeal. No wonder that Langley (1999) calls process theorizing a "synthesis" and claims that no matter how carefully we execute the process analysis, this alone does not guarantee a good result. Synthesis requires leaps of imagination to organize events into plausible narratives by inventing new worlds and logics (Weick, 1989). Langley (1999) suggests theoretical triangulation and matching of heterogeneous models as one means of developing such rules. This was already followed above in formulating rules to build up event networks. This construction by itself generates iterations between data and their explanations. Though unavoidable, we think that such iterations can be further reduced by applying some rules to analyze a given event network at any time point during the analysis.

One method of reducing iterations is to match taxonomies of generative mechanisms with produced event networks. Pentland (1999) suggests the following mechanisms: 1) life cycle; 2) teleological (goal seeking); 3) ecological (variation, selection, and retention); and 4) dialectical "motors" (Van de Ven & Poole, 1995). Yet, these taxonomies do not provide good "meta-rules" regarding which type of explanation one should choose for a given data set. In fact, most process descriptions can be cast into multiple explanations (Pentland, 1999). For example, standardizing can be viewed as a teleological process from an actor's viewpoint, as an ecological process from the viewpoint of a technological system, or as a dialectical process from the viewpoint of multi-actor negotiation. Many generative mechanisms can be matched with any observed process "surface structure" leading to what Langley calls the "alternative templates strategy," where an investigator proposes "several alternative interpretations of the events based on different, but internally coherent sets of a priori theoretical premises" (Langley, 1999, p.698). This strategy is followed in our process framework in that each sequence of types of events (closure) imposes alternative explanations about the process. Yet, none of them offers a complete account, and therefore dynamic interactions between design, sense-making and negotiation, and associated local perspectives need to be accounted for in the analysis.

Inductive Inference Rules Based on the Content of Event Networks

We propose next an inductive strategy to craft process explanations. This strategy helps exclude alternative explanations by iteratively applying inference rules that explore and test internal validity threats associated with proposed explanations. These rules can be organized according

to increasing complexity and generality. We differentiate between inference rules that operate on: 1) singular events, 2) binary event pair rules, and 3) event network rules.

Singular Event Rules

These rules operate on each event and seek to confirm that the event description reflects the empirical reality, and that its classification into event types and a related event profile is valid. These rules guarantee that the narrative that will follow is based on validated events and event constructs.

Rule SER1: *The description of each design, sense-making, and negotiation event needs to be complete for a valid narrative to emerge (Pentland, 1999).*

Here, complete means that each event description must fully express critical properties, i.e., input, output, type of event being applied, actors associated with the event, and context and timing of that event. Applying this rule improves the internal validity of explanations. Omitting elements leads to misleading inferences, given the complexity of anticipatory standardizing and the frequency of unforeseen events, such as new technological possibilities, or changes in the context. A more complete description helps clarify the reasoning behind an actor's moves that underpin events. In particular, when we explain *why* actors behaved in a particular way and *why* specific events ensued, completeness is the first criterion for internal validity. In addition, a careful depiction of events in a narrative form helps detect serendipities that shaped the process trajectory (like unexpected technological discoveries).

Rule SER2: *The classification of events into design, sense-making, and negotiation events integrates alternative theoretical perspectives to account for the process and its results and* *helps detect multiple explanations for observed events, and excludes or foregoes proposed explanations.*

By using this rule we improve the internal validity of the explanation by urging the investigator to apply multiple theoretical perspectives to the same set of events, thereby applying and excluding alternative explanations. Multiple perspectives allow the investigator to identify additional events that might be triggered by other events. For instance, when an event is analyzed through the design, sense-making, and negotiation lenses, it might become apparent that while it is a design event, during the event, a sense-making or negotiation event is spawned that was instrumental. Particularly, when events sequences fail to reach closure, such spawned event might be the underlying reason for the failure. For example, an investigator may ask why there was no closure on sense-making. Was it because the design was so novel and incomplete that actors could not imagine the implications of its use, or was it just not designed well?

Binary Event Pair Rules

Binary event pair rules operate on event pairs and seek to validate and infer explanations of changes in actors' cognitive orientations.

Rule BEPR1: *Shifts in event types signal changes in the actors' cognitive orientation.*

When one or more standardizing events produce a standardizing event of a different type (e.g., a design event triggering a sense-making event), we can detect two reasons for this change. First, when one cognitive activity is completed, that is, the event is finalized, standardizing will continue with a new event type. For instance, once the design of a set of components has been completed, the actors might proceed to sense-making or negotiation on how to integrate these

components into the system. Identifying the event pairs in which new types of events were triggered helps the investigator to trace change in cognitive orientation during different time periods.

Rule BEPR2: *Shifts in event types prior to reaching closure help identify critical events that changed standardizing trajectory.*

More important than events that trigger just new event types are events that trigger new event types before the process reaches a closure. For instance, during design the engineers might encounter technical alternatives that would force them to select through sense-making multiple new use scenarios and then to negotiate which of these scenarios help drive design. Events that trigger these different event types before a closure is reached signify situations where main challenges (Hughes, 1987, calls them "reverse salients") that emerge during standardizing were resolved by adopting a fresh approach. By applying this rule, investigators can observe critical moments in the standardizing process and identify what shifted when critical path dependency shaping and breaking events took place.

Event Network Rules

Event network rules operate whole event sequences. Here we seek to use pattern matching rules to increase the internal validity of explanations by generating all possible explanations for the observed outcome, and excluding them iteratively. Such internal validity analysis is applied to event sequences for one standardizing process at a time.

Rule WCAR1: *All event paths in the event network should be consistent with the observed process outcome.*

The first rule at the event network level is that all event paths should be consistent with the observed outcome. For instance, if a standard fails to emerge, the observed process sequence should include a failure to reach closure either in design, negotiation, or sense-making. Similarly, if a successful standard emerges, the narrative should entail a sequence that explains closure in all three types. Event sequences that are inconsistent with the observed process states suggest omission of critical events or the omission of critical interactions with the context.

Rule WCAR2: *Deviations from the process signify important junctions in standardizing.*

Per definition, a complete standardization plan should define activities that lead to closure in design, sense-making, and negotiation. In most cases, such completeness is lacking and difficult to achieve due to a high level of ambiguity in anticipatory standardizing. Comparing the actual event network with the planned process activities provides important insights into episodes that explain the different process outcome. It first shows the level of ambiguity and incompeteness in the original plan. Second, deviations show when the standardizing process became chaotic and therefore moved to an unanticipated trajectory. This happens often when the external environment shapes the process in an unexpected way, or the process generates unexpected outcomes. For instance, a deviation from the plan can suggest that critical events shaped the context that triggered unforeseen sense-making or negotiation events.

DEVELOPMENT OF THE MOBILE SWITCHING SYSTEM (MTX) FOR THE NMT SYSTEM

We will next illustrate how to use the process theory framework by analyzing the standardizing of the Mobile Switching System (MTX) for Nordic Mobile Telephone (NMT) by drawing upon the rich description offered in Manninen (2002).

The NMT 450 standard was published in 1979–3 years before the first NMT service–and it formed the first public standard for mobile telephony. The standardizing of a key component of the standard–its switching platform (MTX) specification–offers a vivid and interesting episode for analyzing anticipatory standardizing processes. Due to its virgin origin NMT standardization, it involved high levels of uncertainty both in terms of service, architecture, and technology choices. Using Manninen's (2002) narrative as a baseline, we identified first all key events in the standardization process (Appendixes 1 and 2). Then applying event rules SER1 and SER2, for each event we identified type, context, timing, actors involved, as well as input and output (preceding and following events—see Appendix B).

Having compiled the complete event list enabled us to draw a visual representation of the events and their relationships (Figure 1) for the subsequent analysis. This MTX choreography needed to be interpreted in the overall context of the NMT's mission: (1) its ambiguous scope and unclear objectives; (2) and the rapid change in digital switching capabilities during the standardization process. The graphical representation forms a matrix, where rows contain event types (context, design, negotiation, and sense-making), and the columns–timing (the start date) of each event. The process presentation shows how the MTX standardizing process was carried out through D-, N-, and S-events, and how these events connected. The final graphical representation can then be used for subsequent process analysis by applying binary and network event rules.

From the graphical representation, we can identify clusters of events that were critical in producing the final standard. To illustrate how some of these clusters can be identified we will focus next on some clusters. We can note first in Figure 1 several critical context events (market and technology change) marked by squares (e.g., MC1, MC2, TC1, TC2,TC4, and TC5). These concentrated in two intervals–at the outset of the project in 1969, and around 1975, when the digital switching technology became available and a decision had to be made about it. As shown, the project initiation context was dominated by the design and sense-making activities (S1 and D2). The MTX design choice (N4) contributed critically to the overall NMT success, since not only was closure reached in design, negotiation, and sense-making about switching, but these closures also critically influenced other standardization activities within the NMT standardization as can be seen by analyzing the outward links from S7 or D9. Overall, multiple closures were reached which correspond to four core design issues faced with MTX development: 1) the type of network (N4), 2) the network architecture (S7), 3) the specifications for the MTX (D9, N16), and 4) the adoption of the MTX (N17).

Several insights emerge from the process analysis. When we investigate Figure 1, we can identify two periods where either D-, S-, or N-activities dominated the process. Between 1975 and 1977, we observe more design (D) and negotiation (N) activities, while after 1977 the design activity diminished and the sense-making (S) intensified.

These centres of activity highlight one feature of event network analysis, i.e., what was the main focus of the process at different time periods. Figure 1 also shows how the context and the process interact, how events trigger and interact with each other, and what types of changes take place as a result (the symbols refer to Table 2 transitions above). Finally, it shows the linearity (e.g., S1, D2, and S2 events), temporal dependencies (S1 comes before S2), functional dependencies (D3 and D5), iteration (D5-D7, or N17 as a repeated attempt of N14) and decomposition in the process structure (D7 should have been followed by N9, but instead S7, N8, and D8 were triggered for the process to proceed, or failure to reach closure in N14 triggers N15 and N16).

Finally, from the methodological standpoint, we can see how the analysis follows the analysis rules outlined above (Table 3), and how the application of these rules increased the reliability and internal validity of the analysis. It allowed building of a systematic explanation of process outcomes that could be described as an emerging process theory of the NMT standardizing. Specifically, graphical representation presents

Figure 1. MTX event choreography

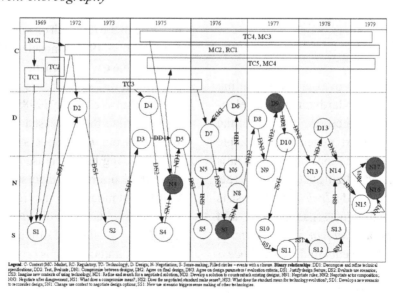

Table 3. Application of inductive inference rules for process analysis

Rule	Application
Rule SER1:	Each event type was derived from a detailed description of events using standardization committee minutes and interview data. Their classification is complete and all events that resulted in outcomes were identified.
Rule SER2	The classification of events to event types allowed us to identify moments where new ideas of mobile telephony emerged and where these were negotiated with other players like telecommunication manufacturers.
Rule BEPR1	We could observe significant shifts in standardization focus as a result of event type changes. One example is the re-thinking of service concepts after the initial design is completed–an example is a realization that the cost MTX exceeds the expectations, which results in rethinking the network structure and the number of suppliers: D6-D7-S7-N8-D8.
Rule BEPR2:	We observe situations where a failure to shift standardization focus leads to a successful closure–an example is the failure to start design again after D9, to which Ericsson did not yield (N16).
Rule WCAR1:	We could detect all observed closures based on the analysis of preceding events.
Rule WCAR2	The shift to design a digital switching platform resulted in a deviation in the original standardization plan (TC1, S1, D2), but at the end defined a different capability and scope for the service (TC5, MC4, S7, D9).

vividly the overall complexity of the process. Besides giving a simple yet comprehensive view of interdependencies between different events, we also gain a more accurate description of the dynamics of the process (changing patterns of the event networks). We also obtain a better grasp of the dominating cognitive orientations based on which event types dominated the process at any given period of time.

DISCUSSION

This article set out to improve our understanding of anticipatory ICT standardizing by developing a process theory framework. The aim of the framework is to support generating plausible and generalizable explanations of *why* and *how* anticipatory ICT standardizing outcomes emerge. To this end, we developed a *lexicon* that consists of a typology of design, sense-making, and negotiation events, a *grammar* in the form of combination rules for events to develop *process representations* of anticipatory ICT standardizing events, *logic* rules that yield theoretical explana-

tions based on the inductive analysis of process representations, and a discussion of the *contexts* in which standardizing unfolds.

CONTRIBUTIONS TO SOCIAL THEORIES OF STANDARDIZING

We expand process theories to explain ICT standardizing. The past years have seen a dramatic increase in the research on anticipatory ICT standards (David, 1995; Mansell & Silverstone, 1996) while we have witnessed increased problems with traditional ICT standards research (Garud, et al., 2002; Schmidt & Werle, 1998; Werle, 2000). While all recognize the increased role of *anticipatory standards,* our *actual* understanding of successful standardizing has decreased. Our article inches toward an improved understanding of anticipatory ICT standards by moving from the study of *standards* to the study of *standardizing*. This is a significant intellectual shift as it suggests that the study of standardizing is pivotal to our ability to understand this complex phenomenon.

The main contribution of this work lies in the expansion and integration of concepts derived from social theories of technology to anticipatory standardization research. Recent research in ANT and SCOT (e.g., Hanseth, 2006; Jakobs, 2006; Stewart & Williams, 2005) has begun to recognize that design, negotiation, and sense-making are all critical for understanding many standardizing processes. However, this work has remained largely fragmented. Our article addresses this weakness by developing an integrated, yet modular, framework that explicates relationships among these key concepts, and defines roles each theoretical perspective can play in explaining anticipatory ICT standardizing. Due to its complexity (Hawkins, 1995), process explanation needs to decompose the phenomenon into smaller building blocks (Hanseth, 2006). Yet, rendering a meaningful explanation of the whole and its outcomes demands an integration of these building blocks. We proposed here that design (D), negotiation (N), and sense-making (S) activities and their analytically controlled interactions offer one set of such building blocks.

The strength of this framework is that it draws on multiple streams of research on standardization in ICT: social process theories, where each is well suited to examine a specific "simpler phenomenon" in isolation. It organizes them into modular and comprehensive process accounts. The novelty of our work is not necessarily in *what* concepts we introduce, but in *how* we position them, and how we conceive them as a family of interrelated theoretical lenses. By bringing the design, sense-making, and negotiation elements together, we outline a basis for formulating rigorous, theory-based process analysis of ICT standardizing. This helps conceive each successful anticipatory ICT standard as, "a specific configuration of knowledge and industrial structure–it involves distributed knowledge, a precise definition of physical interfaces between components in a system, and an industrial struc-

ture with considerable division of labour and specialisation" (Steinmueller, 2005).

Anticipatory standardizing demands that individual designs, collective designs, and shifts in technology framing interact. Our emphasis on individual and distributed sense-making expands SCOT's "technology framing" from a user-related activity about finished designs (Stewart & Williams, 2005) to sense-making about early designs by engineers and standard setters. This expansion is important given that anticipatory ICT standardizing embodies one key engine of ICT innovation and involves technical discoveries. Our study also goes beyond recent accounts of anticipatory ICT standardization offered by SCOT and ANT by highlighting the importance of collective engineering. Anticipatory standardizing rests on inventing genuine designs, as actors constantly generate designs and reconcile them. Focusing on the criticality of design has broader implications for Actor Network Theory studies. Anticipatory ICT standards will entail novel changes in technological capabilities and involve a high level of uncertainty. Accordingly, designers are simultaneously building multiple ambiguous and poorly understood networks, and they cannot predict consequences of their designs (Van de Ven, et al., 1999). This renders construction of actor networks an iterative process that has not been accounted for in ANT's linear view of translation. We argue that such insight should also be reflected in process accounts. Therefore, we have outlined an iterative model of process analysis, which circumvents the limitations of linear process models.

CONTRIBUTIONS TO PROCESS ANALYSIS AND EXPLANATIONS

Our article makes a useful research contribution to process theorizing (Mohr, 1982; Langley, 1999; Pentland, 1999; Van de Ven, et al., 1999).

Past research on processes has not explicitly discussed the refinement of process ontologies that are sensitive to the studied domains. For example, Langley's (1999) excellent review focuses mainly on how process approaches can manipulate one-dimensional event data to yield process accounts. However, she never explores different *types* of events as one critical aspect of formulating explanations. We feel that our amendment offers one useful way to improve the accuracy of process theories while keeping them still relatively simple (Weick, 1995).

Proposing a separate analysis layer of a "grammar" offers a flexible way to organize events into event sequences. The concept or grammar allows us to control how much iteration and parallelism will be allowed in process explanations. Most past process models assume a linear sequence either through successive stages, e.g., ANT's translation model, or through linear sequences associated with a specific narrative (Pentland, 1999). While both templates are useful, the proposed expansion helps control the level of complexity and, if need be, tap into chaotic and random processes involving iteration that are frequent in innovative contexts (van de Ven, 1999). Finally, introducing a separate layer of inductive inference rules augments the narrative-based deductive "grand narratives" of process theorizing (van de Ven & Poole, 1995) with a set of validity-enhancing rules. The more complex process structures generated by our method can draw upon the improved computer-based tools that have been proposed (see, e.g., Ethno at http://www.indiana.edu/%7Esocpsy/ESA/home.html). We expect that such tools will help to better manage inherently complex process traces resulting from our analysis. Such more rigorous modeling of event interactions and sequences will also offer possibilities to simulate process behaviors using system dynamics, and to predict their outcomes under different contingencies[4]. Another alternative is to use emerging computational models of dynamic network analysis (Carley, 2006)

LIMITATIONS AND FUTURE RESEARCH

We emphasize that the proposed framework is not the same as a complete process theory. Rather, it offers an ontology of events and event sequences, a way to organize and represent event sequences and a set of rules geared toward formulating plausible process explanations. As a general theoretical framework, in its current form it is not open to direct empirical validation. *We emphasize that only local theories formulated by using such a framework can be used explain standardizing processes and can thus be subjected to empirical validation.* The intellectual value of the framework lies in its domain-specific, systematic formulation of theoretical concepts that will permit investigators to craft, formulate, advance, and validate new types of empirical claims about anticipatory ICT standardizing. Such a framework hopefully will promote systematic building and validation of process theories that account for complex ICT standardizing phenomena.

Due to its modular structure, the proposed framework is not closed. In fact, any part of the framework–its lexicon, grammar, and inference rules–is open to further expansion and refinement. Such expansions are welcome when the framework is applied in local research settings. In future, we expect that the framework can be used to build process theories that approach anticipatory standardizing as a non-linear, emergent, and path-dependent process. Some recent research drawing upon our ideas suggest that this avenue is fruitful (Virilli, 2003; Mitra, et al., 2005) and they show that different standardization processes allow for design, sense-making, and negotiation events in proportions and they organize them differently over time. They also show that processes are chaotic and non-linear. Beyond these studies, we expect research in the following areas in the future: What designation of non-linearity–random or chaotic–can be detected (Van de Ven, et al., 1999) in ICT standardizing? Do specific sequences exhibit tipping effects towards a closure (Axelrod, 1984)? Can different types of event sequences be related to increasingly innovative outcomes (Autio, 1997)? What context changes create deviations from prevailing standardizing paths, and are there differences in how to respond to such deviations (Karnoe, et al., 2005)?

The framework can also be used to derive empirical accounts of some aspects of anticipatory ICT standardizing. For example, fast cycles between both D- and N-events punctuated by diffusion and experimentation resulted in successful standardization during Internet development in contrast to traditional SDO standardization where a long cycle of D events was followed by a singular N event (Abbate, 1999). Likewise, incentives and governance structures within the actors may radically shape interactions between the events (Benkler, 2001) raising the following question: How do the events shape the organization of standardizing actors? Finally, the framework can help critique and expand normative ICT standardization models that originate from product development and regulation theories (Schmidt & Werle, 1998). These models view ICT standardizing mainly as a linear refinement over one dimension: design or negotiation. Yet, our framework suggests that such models are inadequate as they prioritize design over negotiation or vice versa and ignore sense-making.

ACKNOWLEDGMENT

We are grateful to John King, Ari Manninen, Juha Knuuttila, Ping Gao, and Joel West for inspiring discussions that led to some ideas in the manuscript. Thanks go also to Dick Boland, Michel Callon, Michael Cohen, Sandeep Purao, Timothy Schoechle, Francesco Virili, Karl Weick, Youngjin Yoo, and Lynne Markus for detailed comments on earlier version of the manuscript. Apologies for remaining errors apply.

REFERENCES

Abbate, J. (1999). *Inventing the Internet*. Cambridge, MA: MIT Press.

Akrich, M. (1992). The description of technical objects. In J. Law, & W. E. Bijker (Eds.), *Shaping technology/building society: Studies in socio-technical change*. Cambridge, MA: MIT Press.

Allen, J. P. (2004) Redefining the network: Enrollment strategies in the PDA industry, *Information Technology & People 17*(2), 171-185.

Arthur, W. B. (1989). Competing technologies, increasing returns, and lock-in by historical events, *The Economic Journal, 99*(394), 116-131.

Autio, E. (1997). New, technology-based firms in innovation networks: Symplectic and generative impacts. *Research Policy, 26*(3), 263-281.

Axelrod, R. (1984). *The evolution of cooperation*. New York: Basic Books.

Axelrod, R., et al. (1995). Coalition formation in standard-setting alliances. *Management Science, 41*(9), 1493-1508.

Bacharach, S. (1989). Organizational theories: Some criteria for evaluation. *Academy of Management Review, 14*(4), 496-515

Baldwin, C. Y., & Clark, K.B. (2005). Designs and design architecture: The missing link between "knowledge" and the "economy." Advancing Knowledge and the Knowledge Economy. Washington, DC.

Benkler, Y. (2001). Coase's penguin, or, Linux and the nature of the firm. *Yale Law Journal, 112*(3), 367-445.

Berner-Lee, T. (1999). *Weaving the Web: The original design and ultimate destiny of the World Wide Web*. San Francisco: Harper.

Bijker, W.E. (1987). The social construction of Bakelite: Toward a theory of invention. In W.E.

Bijker, T. P. Hughes, & T. Pinch (Eds.), *The social construction of technological systems.* Cambridge: MIT Press.

Bijker, W. E. (1995). *Of bicycle, bakelites, and bulbs: Toward a theory of sociotechnical change.* Cambridge: The MIT Press.

Boland, R. J. J., & Tenkasi, R. V. (1995). Perspective making and perspective taking in communities of knowing. *Organization Science, 6*(4), 350-372.

Brynjolfsson, E., &Kemerer, C.F. (1996). Network externalities in microcomputer software: An econometric analysis of the spreadsheet market. *Management Science, 42*(12), 1627-1647.

Callon, M. (1986).. Some elements of a sociology of translation: Domestication of the scallops and the fishermen of St Brieuc Bay. In J. Law (Ed.), *Power, action and belief: A new sociology of knowledge?* London: Routledge & Kegan Paul.

Callon, M. (1992).. Techno-economic networks and irreversibility. In J. Law (Ed.), *A sociology of monsters: Essays on power, technology and domination.* London: Routledge.

Callon, M., & Law, J.(1989). On the construction of sociotechnical networks: content and context revisited. *Knowledge and Society, 8,* 57-83.

Cargill, C. F. (1989). *Information technology standardization: Theory, process, and organizations.* Redford, MA: Digital Press.

Carley, K. (2006). Dynamic network anlysis: Summary of the NRC workshop on social network modeling and analysis. In R. Breiger, & K. Carey (Eds.), National Research Council, Washington D.C.

Croley, S. P. (1998). Theories of regulation: Incorporating the administrative process. *Columbia Law Review, 98*(1), 1-168.

Damsgaard, J., & Lyytinen, K. (2001). The role of intermediating institutions in the diffusion of electronic data interchange (EDI): How industry associations intervened in Denmark, Finland, and Hong Kong. *The Information Society, 17*(3), 197-210.

David, P. A. (1985). Clio and the economics of QWERTY. *The American Economic Review, 72*(2), 332-337.

David, P. A. (1995). Standardization policies for network technologies: The flux between freedom and order revisited. In R. W. Hawkins, R. Mansell, & J. Skea (Eds.), *Standards, innovation and competitiveness: The politics and economics of standards in natural and technical environments.* Aldershot, UK: Edward Elgar.

David, P. A., &Greenstein, S.M. (1990). The economics of compatibility standards: An introduction to recent research. *The Economics of Innovations and New Technology, 1*(1/2), 3-41.

David, P. A., &Steinmueller, W.E. (1994). Economics of compatibility standards and competition in telecommunication networks. *Information Economics and Policy, 6*(3,4), 217-241.

Davidson, E. (2002). Technology frames and framing: Socio-cognitive investigation of requirements determination. *MIS Quarterly, 26*(4), 329-358.

Egyedi, T. (2005). *Consortium problem redefined: Negotiating 'democracy' in the actor network standardization.* Unpublished working paper, Department of Information and communication Technology, Faculty of technology, Policy and Management, Delft University of Technology.

Faraj, S., Kwon, D.,& Watts, S.(2004). Contested artifact: Technology sensemaking, actor networks, and the shaping of the Web browser. *Information Technology & People 17*(2), 186-209.

Farrell, J., &Saloner, G. (1985). Standardization, compatibility, and innovation *Rand Journal of Economics, 16*(1), 70-83.

Farrell, J., &Saloner, G. (1986). Installed base and compatibility: Innovation, product preannouncements, and predation. *The American Economic Review, 76*(5), 940-955.

Farrell, J., &Saloner, G. (1988a). Coordination through committees and markets *The RAND Journal of Economics, 19*(2), 235-252.

Farrell, J., Saloner, G. (1988b). Dynamic competition with switching costs. *The Rand Journal of Economics, 19*(1), 123-137.

Funk, J. L. (2002). *Global competition between and within standards: The case of mobile phones.* New York: Palgrave.

Gabel, H. L. (1991). *Competitive strategies for product standards: The strategic use of compatibility standards for competitive advantage.* London: McGraw-Hill Book Company.

Gadamer, H.-G. (1975). *Truth and method* (G. Barden & J. Cumming, Trans.). New York: Seabury Press.

Garud, R., Jain, S., & Kumaraswamy, A. (2002). Institutional entrepreneurship in the sponsoring of common technological standards: The case of Sun Microsystems and Java. *Academy of Management Journal, 45*(1), 196-214.

Gherardi, S., &Nicolini, D. (2000). To transfer is to transform: The circulation of safety knowledge. *Organization, 7*(2), 329-348.

Hanseth, O., Monteiro E., & Halting, M. (1996). Developing information infrastructure: The tension between standardisation and flexibility. *Science, Technologies, and Human Values, 21*(4), 407-426.

Hanseth, O., et al. (2006). Reflexive standardization: Side-effects and complexity in standard-making. *MIS Quarterly,* forthcoming.

Haug, T. (2002). A commentary on standardization practices: Lessons from the NMT and GSM mobile telephone standards histories. *Telecommunications Policy, 26*(3-4), 101-107.

Hawkins, R. W. (1995). Introduction: Addressing the p*roblématique* of standards and standardization. In R. W. Hawkins, R. Mansell, & J. Skea (Eds.), *Standards, innovation and competitiveness: The politics and economics of standards in natural and technical environments.* Aldershot, UK: Edward Elgar.

Howcroft, D., Mitev, N., & Wilson, M. (2004). What we may learn from social shaping of technology approach. In J. Mingers, & L. Willcocks (Eds.), *Social theory and philosophy for information systems.* Chichester: John Wiley, pp. 329-371.

Hosein, I., Tsiavos, P., &Whitley, E.A. (2003). Regulating architecture and architectures of regulation: Contributions from information systems. *International Review of Law Computers & Technology, 17*(1), 85-97.

Hughes, T. (1987). The evolution of large technological systems. In W. Bijker, T. Hughes, & T. Pinch (Eds.), *The sociological construction of technological systems.* Cambridge, MA: The MIT Press.

Jakobs, K. (2006). Shaping user-side innovation through standardisation: The example of ICT. *Technological Forecasting & Social Change, 73*(1), 27-40.

Jarvenpaa, S., Tiller, L.E.H., &Simons, R. (2003). Regulation and the Internet: Public choice insights for business organizations *California Management Review, 46*(1), 72-85.

Jørgensen, U., & Sørensen, O. (1999). Arenas of development: A space polulated by actor-worlds, artefacts, and surprises. *Technology Analysis and Strategic Management, 11*(3), 409-429.

Karnoe, P., &Garud, R. (2005). Path creation and dependence in the Danish wind turbine field. In J. Porac, & M. Ventresca (Eds.), *Constructing industries and markets.* New York: Elsevier.

Katz, M. L., & Shapiro, C. (1986). Technology adoption in the presence of network externalities. *Journal of Political Economy, 94*(4), 822-841.

Keil, T. (2002). De-facto standardization through alliances–Lessons from Bluetooth. *Telecommunications Policy, 26*(3-4), 205-213.

King, J. L., et al. (1994). Institutional factors in information technology innovation. *Information Systems Research, 5*(2),139-169.

King, J. L., &West, J. (2002). Ma bell's orphan: US cellular telephony, 1974-1996. *Telecommunications Policy, 26*(3-4), 189-204.

Langley, A. (1999). Strategies for theorizing from process data. *Academy of Management Review, 24*(4), 691-710.

Latour, B. (1987). *Science in action: How to follow scientists and engineers through society* (1st ed.). Milton Keynes: Open University Press.

Latour, B. (1992). Where are the missing masses? The sociology of a few mundane artifacts. In W. E. Bijker, & J. Law (Eds.), *Shaping technology/ building society: studies in sociotechnical change.* Cambridge, MA: MIT Press.

Latour, B. (1995). *Social theory and the study of computerized work wites.* Paper presented at the IFIP WG8.2, Cambridge, UK.

Latour, B. (1997). *On actor-network theory: A few clarifications.* ANT Resource, Centre for Social Theory and Technology, Keele University.

Latour, B. (1999). *Pandora's hope: Essays on the reality of science studies.* Cambridge, MA: Harvard University Press.

Law, J. (1992). Notes on the theory of the actor-network: Ordering, strategy, and heterogeneity *System Practice, 5*(4), 379-393.

Lessig, L. (1999a). *Code and other laws of cyberspace.* New York: Basic Books.

Lessig, L. (1999b). The law of the horse: What cyberlaw might teach. *Harvard Law Review, 113*(2), 501-549.

Lyytinen, K., &Fomin, V.V. (2002). Achieving high momentum in the evolution of wireless infrastructures: The battle over the 1G solutions. *Telecommunications Policy, 26*(3-4), 149-170.

Manninen, A. T. (2002). *Elaboration of NMT and GSM standards: From idea to market.* Unpublished PhD Thesis, University of Jyvaskyla.

Mähring, M. et al. (2004). Trojan actor-networks and swift translations: Bringing actor-network-theory to IT project escalation studies. *Information Technology & People, 17*(2), 210-238.

Mangematin, V., & M. Callon. (1995). Technological competition, strategies of the firms and the choice of the first users: The case of road guidance technologies. *Research Policy, 24*(3), 441-458.

Mansell, R., & Silverstone, R. (1996). *Communication by design: The politics of information and communication technologies. Oxford:* Oxford University Press.

March, J. G. (1991). Exploration and exploitation in organizational learning. *Organization Science, 2*(1), 71-78.

Markus, L., et al. (2006). Industry-wide IS standardization as collective action: The case of the US residential mortgage industry. *MIS Quarterly,* forthcoming.

Markus, M. L., & Robey, D. (1988). Information technology and organizational change: Casual structure in theory and research. *Management Science, 34*(5), 583-598.

Mitra, P., Purao, S., Bagby, J.W., Umapathy, K., & Sharoda, P. (2005). *An empirical analysis of development processes for anticipatory standards.* NET Institute Working Paper No. 05-18 http://ssrn.com/abstract=850524

Mohr, L. B. (1982). *Explaining organizational behavior.* San Francisco: Jossey-Bass.

Mouly, M., & Pautet, M. –B. (1992). *The GSM system for mobile communications.* Palaiseau, France: Michael Mouly and Marie-Bernadette Pautet.

Nelson, M. L., Shaw, M. J., & Qualls, W. (2005). Interorganizational system standards development in vertical industries. *Electronic Markets, 15*(4), 378-392

Newman, M., & Robey, D. (1992). A social process model of user-analyst relationships. *MIS Quarterly, 16*(2), 249-266.

Nickerson, J. V., & zur Muehlen, M. (2006). The social ecology of standards processes: Insights from Internet standard making. *MIS Quarterly,* forthcoming.

Orlikowski, W., & Gash, D. (1994). Technology frames: Making sense of information technology in organizations. *ACM Transactions on Information Systems, 12*(2), 147-207.

Patterson, M. R. (2002). Inventions, industry standards, and intellectual property. *Berkeley Technology Law Review, 17*(3), 1-42.

Pentland, B. T. (1999). Building process theory with narrative: From description to explanation. *Academy of Management Review, 24*(4), 711-724.

Pettigrew, A. M. (1997). What is a processual analysis? *Scandinavian Journal of Management, 13*(4), 337-348.

Pinch, T. J., & Bijker, W.E. (1987). The social construction of facts and artifacts: Or how the sociology of science and the sociology of technology might benefit each other. In W. E. Bijker, T. P. Hughes, & T. J. Pinch (Eds.), *The social construction of technological systems: New directions in the sociology and history of technology.* Cambridge: MIT Press.

Ramiller, N. C. (2005). Applying the sociology of translation to a system project in a lagging enterprise. *Journal of Information Technology Theory and Application, 7*(1), 51-76.

Robey, D., & Newman, M. (1996). Sequential patterns in information systems development: An application of a social process model. *ACM Transactions on Information Systems, 14*(1), 30-63.

Sahay, S., & Robey, D. (1996). Organizational context, social interpretation and the implementation and consequences of geographical information systems. *Accounting, Management and Information Technologies, 6*(4), 255-282.

Schmidt, S. K., & Werle, R. (1998). *Coordinating technology: Studies in the international standardization of telecommunications.* Cambridge, Massachusetts: The MIT Press.

Shadish, W. R., Cook, T.D., & Campbell, D.T. (2002). *Experimental and quasi-experimental designs for generalized causal inference* (2nd ed.). Houghton Mifflin.

Shapiro, C., & Varian, H. (1998). *Information rules: A strategic guide to the network economy.* Cambridge, MA: Harvard Business School Press.

Sheremata, W. A. (1998). New issues in competition policy raised by information technology industries. *The Antitrust Bulletin, 43*(3/4), 547-582.

Simon, H. A. (1977). *The new science of management decision* (rev. ed.). Englewood Cliffs: Prentice-Hall.

Sørensen, K. H., & Williams, R.(2002). *Shaping technology, guiding policy: Concepts, spaces and tools.* Cheltenham: Edward Elgar.

Spivak, S. M., &Brenner, F.C. (2001). *Standardization essentials: Principles and practice.* New York: Marcel Dekker, Inc.

Steinmueller, E. (2005). *Technical compatibility standards and the co-ordination of the industrial and international division of labor.* Paper presented at NSF Academics conference on Advancing Knowledge and the Knowledge economy.

Stewart, J., &Williams, R. (2005). The wrong trousers? Beyond the design fallacy: Social learning and the user.In H. Rohracher (Ed.), *User involvement in innovation processes: strategies and limitations from a socio-technical perspective.* Munich: Profil-Verlag.

Swann, P. (2000). *The economics of standardization.* Final Report for Standards and Technical Regulations Directorate, Department of Trade and Industry. Manchester Business School, University of Manchester.

Suchman, L. (2000). Organizing alignment: A case of bridge-building. *Organization, 7*(2), 311-327.

Teece, D. J., & Sherry, E. F. (2003). Standards setting and antitrust. *Minnesota Law Review, 87*(6), 1913-1994.

Van de Ven, A. H., et al. (1999). *The innovation journey.* New York: Oxford University Press.

Van de Ven, A. H., & Poole, M.S. (1995). Explaining development and change in organizations. *Academy of Management Review 20*(3), 510-540.

Van de Ven, A. H., &Huber, G. (1990). Longitudinal field research methods for studying processes of organizational change. *Organization Science, 1*(2), 213-219.

Virilli, F. (2003). Design, sense-making and negotiation activities in the Web services standardization process. In J. King, & K. Lyytinen (Eds), Standard making: A critical research frontier for information systems. Proceedings of a Pre-conference Workshop at ICIS, December 12-14, Seattle, 2003, Washington, available at http://www.si.umich.edu/misq-stds/proceedings/index.html

Walsham, G. (1997). Actor-network theory and IS research: Current status and future prospects. In A. Lee, J. Liebenau, & J. DeGross (Eds.), Information systems and qualitative research. London: Chapman and Hall, pp. 466-480

Walsham, G., & Sahay, S. (1999). GIS for district level administration in India: Problems and opportunities. *MIS Quarterly, 23*(1), 39-66

Weick, K. E. (1989). Theory construction as disciplined imagination. *Academy of Management Review, 14*(4), 516-531.

Weick, K. E. (1993). The collapse of sensemaking in organizations: The Mann Gulch disaster. *Administrative Science Quarterly, 38*(4), 628-652.

Weick, K. E. (1995). *Sensemaking in organizations.* London: Sage Publications.

Weiser, P. J. (2003). The Internet, innovation, and intellectual property policy. *Columbia Law Review, 103*(3), 534-613.

Weitzel, T., Beimborn, D., & König, W. (2006). A unified economic model of standard diffusion: The impact of standardization cost, network effects and network topology. *MIS Quarterly,* forthcoming.

Werle, R. (2000). *Institutional aspects of standardization: Jurisdictional conflicts and the choice of standardization organizations.* Koeln: Max-Planck Institute for Social Science Research.

Wikipedia. (2005). Retrieved September 9, 2005 from, http://www.wikipedia.org/

Williams, R., & Edge, D. (1996). The social shaping of technology. *Research Policy, 25,* 865-899.

Woiceshyn, J. (1997). Literary analysis as a metaphor in processual research: A story of technological change. *Scandinavian Journal of Management, 13*(4), 457-471.

ENDNOTES

[1]   The list of such standards is growing but covers, among others, standards on mobile technologies. See http://www.3gpp.org/; Web services–see http://www.w3.org/2002/ws/ (GSM)–see http://www.gsmworld.com/index.shtml; mobile services (OMA)–see http://www.openmobilealliance.org/; Interoperability and loosely coupled computing services around the Semantic Web–see http://www.w3.org/2001/sw/; short range communication standards (Bluetooth)–see http://www.bluetooth.com/; programming platform standards (Java)–see http://java.sun.com/; networking standards (IETF)–see http://www.ietf.org/; web standards (W3C)–see http://www.w3.org/; or vertical information standards (Rosettanet)–see www.rosettanet.org

[2]   We could as well use the term "activity," but because the existing literature on process theories extensively uses the term "event," we will follow this term.

[3]   To engage in such events designers must do one of the following: a) signal their willingness to reach an agreement or accept another's invitation about designs; b) accept the principal concept and scope of the agreement; c) agree on the content and technical form of the agreement; d) agree on "gives" and "takes" (commitments) in relation to the standard and its outcomes (e.g., IPRs); e) agree on how to access the agreement; and f) agree on what conformance to the agreement means.

[4]   We are thankful to one of the reviewers for pointing this out.

[5]   Further in text as PTTs.

[6]   Further in text as PTTs.

APPENDIX A

The Narrative of the MTX Development Process

The idea of a pan-Nordic cellular telephony system was conceived at the Nordic Teleconference in 1969. The decision included a plan to investigate possibilities for creating a common traffic radio system–as it was called at that time–for Nordic countries (Denmark, Finland, Norway, and Sweden). This decision (sense-making) was prompted by the market context–the growth of manual national car-telephone systems beyond expectations. The original design idea established a lasting technology context was about *creating a common and compatible Nordic auto-radio service*, which required novel market and regulatory context. Because of this, the scope of the innovation, during NMT standardizing was open for a long time and involved multiple designs over the next six to seven years while their feasibility and service quality was evaluated. The aforementioned events forming the context for the launching of the NMT project can be presented as follows:

MC1: The growth of manual national car-telephone systems beyond expectations.
Event Type: Sense-making (Market Context–MC); Timing: 1969; Input: none; Output: TC1; Actors: National PTTs[5]; Context: Growth of car-telephone systems.

TC1: Investigate possibilities for creating a common auto-radio service.
Event Type: Design (Technology Context–TC); Timing: 1969; Input: MC1; Output: S1; Actors: National PTTs; Context: Idea to create a pan-Nordic radio telephony system.

MC2: Creating a novel pan-Nordic market for the proposed common auto-radio service.
Event Type: Sense-making (Market Context–MC), Timing: 1969; Input: MC1; Output: S1, D2; Actors: National PTTs; Context: Idea to create a pan-Nordic radio telephony system.

RC1: A need for new regulatory context for the proposed common auto-radio system.
Event Type: Sense-making (Regulatory Context–RC); Timing: 1969; Input: MC1; Output: S1, D2; Actors: National PTTs; Context: Idea to create a pan-Nordic radio telephony system.

The design of the MTX subsystem formed a crucial element in the design of the NMT. Its design would largely determine the future of Nordic mobile telephony service–for example, how closely it would resemble normal telephony and how relationships between actors during mobile telephone use and installation were arranged. The architectural choice centered on the switching strategies, and whether to use digital switching platforms. This choice had not been fixed when the decision to develop the service was originally made (TC1). One reason for this was the lack of expertise among people who advocated the new radio system–radio engineers, and their inadequate knowledge of switching–which constituted a specific technology context (TC2). Because of the lack of expertise, the first system design idea (TC1) of possibly automatic switching gave way to an idea (sense-making) of an intermediary manual system (S1) (Fomin & Lyytinen, 2000).

S1: An understanding that an intermediary manual system would serve the needs.
Event Type: Sense-making; Timing: 1969-1975; Input: TC1, TC2, MC2, and RC1; Output: D2; Actors:

National PTTs; Context: Idea to create a pan-Nordic radio telephony system. Inadequate knowledge of switching of the radio engineers for the development of automatic switching system.

When the idea of developing an intermediary manual system had been accepted, possible design solutions for the manual system were proposed (D2). The NMT group made a summary of the types of exchanges (MTX), which were to be used for connectivity with fixed networks (PSTN) in the 1980s. Each of the proposed solutions was investigated for the suitability for MTX use (S2).

D2: A need to develop an intermediary manual system.
Event Type: Design; Timing: September 1972-September 1973; Input: S1, MC2, and RC1; Output: S2; Actors: National PTTs; Context: Idea to create a pan-Nordic radio telephony system. Initial MTX design scope.

S2: Inquiry about the suitability of the exchanges for MTX use.
Event Type: Sense-making; Timing: September 1973-October 1975; Input: D2; Output: N3; Actors: National PTTS; Context: Idea to create a pan-Nordic radio telephony system. Initial MTX design scope.

These events formed the first stage of the MTX development process. In 1975, the development context had changed–in 1975 automatic switching (D4) was chosen based on economic criteria (N4) (Toivola, 1992) after the NMT work group had analyzed the cost of alternative switching systems (S4). Yet, the design of an automatic switch after the decision was not something that could be easily done. At that time, cellular communication design was dominated by radio system concerns without considering the needs of switching (Lyytinen, et al., 2000) as radio engineers did not have expertise in designing automatic switches (TC3). As one switching engineer who participated in NMT development noted (Lyytinen, et al., 2000):

What the radio people were saying was that the challenge is now here on the radio side.... They didn't talk about analogue or digital switches, because they didn't have a clue about those, or microprocessor-controllers, anything....

To overcome this weakness, MTX design was carried out by expanding the actor network to Nordic telecommunication manufacturers (TC4, MC3). The design evolved between 1975 and 1978 through several cycles of design (architecture, switching capability, and service concepts), negotiation (cost, commitments and feasibility aspects), and sense-making (receiving feedback from manufacturers re-evaluating the service concept) (see Appendix B for the complete list of events).

The MTX design contributed critically to NMTs success (TC5, MC4) as it implicated several closure points for design, negotiation, and sense-making. Overall, five closures were reached which corresponded to four core design issues faced with MTX development–the type of network (N4), the network architecture (S7), the specifications for the MTX (D9, N16), and the actual adoption of the MTX (N17):

- **N4–The type of network and service concept**. The decision on an automatic digital switch was critical for the future sense-making and negotiation. When the issue was closed it affected broadly how the future service was conceived, the composition of the actor network, and added a new set of negotiations.

- **S7–The network architecture**. The Closure in the MTX sensemaking affected the whole image of the network-to-be among system developers. This closure was critically influenced by the technological expertise offered by telecom manufacturers and their market knowledge. As a result, designers re-conceptualized the network architecture. This resulted in a closure in sensemaking, as the new conceptualization–an idea of a regular phone service in cars across all Nordic countries–had to be implemented in the network.

- **D9–The complete MTX specification**. The final specifications from three manufacturers were received in 1977 and the design specifications were frozen,i.e., the standard reached the design closure.

- **N16–The contract negotiation. Intensive negotiations took place around the MTX procurement.** Though specifications were frozen, the NMT group demanded changes as costs and service ideas need to be matched. The vendor–LM Ericsson–refused to make changes, closing negotiation.

- **N17–Sealing the MTX deal.** The negotiation closure was reached when the Finnish PTA finally gave in.

APPENDIX B

The Complete Event List

The Initial Context for the Commencement of the Project

MC1: The growth of manual national car-telephone systems beyond expectations.
Event Type: Sense-making (Market Context–MC); Timing: 1969; Input: none; Output: TC1; Actors: National PTTs[6]; Context: Growth of car-telephone systems.

TC1: Investigate possibilities for creating a common auto-radio service.
Event Type: Design (Technology Context–TC); Timing: 1969; Input: MC1; Output: S1; Actors: National PTTs; Context: Idea to analyze the technical feasibility of a pan-Nordic radio telephony system.

MC2: Creating a novel pan-Nordic market for the proposed common auto-radio service.
Event Type: Sense-making (Market Context– C); Timing: 1969; Input: MC1; Output: S1, D2; Actors: National PTTs; Context: Examine the need for a pan-Nordic radio telephony system.

RC1: A need for new regulatory context for the proposed common auto-radio system.
Event Type: Sense-making (Regulatory Context–RC); Timing: 1969; Input: MC1; Output: S1, D2; Actors: National PTTs; Context: Idea to anticipate the regulatory needs of a pan-Nordic radio telephony system.

Initial MTX Design Scope

S1: A inquiry to develop an intermediary manual system.
Event Type: Sense-making; Timing: 1969 to 1975; Input: TC1, TC2, MC2, and RC1; Output: D2; Actors: National PTTs; Context: Idea to create a pan-Nordic radio telephony system. Inadequate knowledge of switching of the radio engineers for the development of an automatic switching system.

D2: A plan to develop an intermediary manual system. The NMT group made a summary of the types of exchanges (MTX), which were to be used for connectivity with the fixed network (PSTN) in the 1980s.

Event Type: Design; Timing: September 1972 to September 1973; Input: S1, MC2, and RC1; Output: S2; Actors: National PTTs; Context: Idea to create a pan-Nordic radio telephony system. Initial MTX design scope.

Investigating the Suitability of the Exchanges for MTX use

S2: NMT group made preferences for the choice of suitable exchanges: AKE-13 (LM Ericsson) for Denmark, 11B, 11C (STK) for Norway, ARM (LM Ericsson) for Finland, A-205 (Teli) for Sweden.

Event Type: Sense-making; Timing: September 1973; Input: D2; Output: D3; Actors: National PTTS; Context: Idea to create a pan-Nordic radio telephony system. Investigating the suitability of the exchanges for MTX use.

D3: PTTs make their choices for exchanges: Denmark chose AKE-13, "unless there was a cheaper solution." Norway chose AKE-13 for Oslo and Östland, separate MTX for other regions. Sweden chose A-205. Finland voiced no opinion.

Event Type: Design; Timing: September 1973 to January 1975; Input: S2; Output: D5; Actors: National PTTS; Context: Investigating the suitability of the exchanges for MTX use.

Choosing between Manual and Automatic Switching Systems

D4: NMT group considers an automatic switching system as a replacement for the manual one.

Event Type: design; Timing: 1975; Input: TC3; Output: S5; Actors: National PTTs; Context: Choosing between manual and automatic switching systems.

S4: Analyzing the development and maintenance (operational) costs of manual versus automatic switching systems.

Event Type: Sense-making; Timing: 1975; Input: D4; Output: N4; Actors: National PTTs; Context: Choosing between manual and automatic switching systems.

N4: Automatic switching system chosen based on economic considerations.

Event Type: Negotiation; Timing: 1975; Input: S4, TC4, and MC3; Output: D5, TC5, and MC4; Actors: National PTTs; Context: Choosing between manual and automatic switching systems.

Making Rough Draft for MTX Specifications

D5: NMT group started to work on MTX specifications. The specifications scheduled to be completed by May 1976.

Event Type: Design; Timing: September 1975 to June 1976; Input: D3; Output: S5; Actors: National PTTs; Context: Making rough draft for MTX specifications.

S5: In May 1976 potential suppliers were identified.

Event Type: Sense-making; Timing: May 1976; Input: D5; Output: N5; Actors: National PTTs; Context: Making rough draft for MTX specifications.

N5: Completed in June 1976, draft specifications sent to the suppliers.
Event Type: Negotiation; Timing: June 1976; Input: S5; Output: N6; Actors: National PTTs, suppliers; Context: Making rough draft for MTX specifications.

Bi-Lateral Negotiations with the Suppliers on the Technical Specifications of their Proposed MTXs

N6: Negotiations with suppliers were held in August 1976.
Event Type: Negotiation; Timing: August 1976 to October 1976; Input: N5; Output: D6; Actors: National PTTs, suppliers; Context: Bi-lateral negotiations with the suppliers on the technical specifications of MTX.

D6: On October 15, 1976, eight preliminary MTX offers received.
Event Type: Design; Timing: October 1976; Input: N6; Output: D7; Actors: National PTTs, suppliers; Context: Bi-lateral negotiations with the suppliers on the technical specifications of MTX.

D7: Evaluation of the received preliminary MTX offers. Decisions reported in December 1976.
Event Type: Design; Timing: October 1976 to December 1976; Input: D6, TC5, and MC4; Output: S7; Actors: National PTTs, suppliers; Context: Evaluation of the preliminary MTX offers for the economic and technical feasibility.

S7: The cost of MTXs was found to exceed the expectations (the smallest capacity MTX /1000-7000 subscribers/considered unsuitable). As a result, the number of ordered MTX was reduced significantly, which had a direct bearing on the network structure.
Event Type: Sense-making; Timing: December 1976 to December 1977; Input: D7; Output: N8; Actors: National PTTs; Context: Evaluation of the preliminary MTX offers for the economic and technical feasibility.

Limiting the Number of Suppliers

N8: NMT group negotiating on the number of manufacturers, which will be receiving the final MTX orders.
Event Type: Design; Timing: October 1976 to Q1 1977; Input: S7; Output: D8; Actors: National PTTs; Context: Limiting the number of suppliers for the initial MTX specifications.

D8: It was finally decided to limit the number of manufacturers to the following five: LM Ericsson, Motorola, NEC, C. Itoh, and Telefenno.
Event Type: Design; Timing: Q1 1977; Input: N8; Output: N9; Actors: National PTTs, suppliers; Context: Limiting the number of suppliers for the initial MTX specifications.

Sending Out Tender Invitations for MTX bids

N9: A tender for MTX specifications bids sent out to suppliers, requesting the bids to be received by December 1, 1977.

Event Type: Negotiation; Timing: September 1977 to December 1977; Input: D8; Output: 9; Actors: National PTTs, suppliers; Context: Tender for the initial MTX specifications.

D9: LM Ericsson, Motorola, and NEC have submitted their bids.

Event Type: Design (closure); Timing: December 1977; Input: N9; Output: D10; Actors: National PTTs, suppliers; Context: Tender for the initial MTX specifications.

Evaluation of the Bids

D10: Upon receiving bids from the manufacturers, the proposed MTX specifications are evaluated.

Event Type: Design; Timing: December 1977; Input: D9; Output: S10; Actors: National PTTs; Context: Evaluation of bids for the initial MTX specifications.

S10: A rough assessment has shown that there were shortcomings in LM Ericsson's offer, incompleteness in Motorola's offer, and minor weaknesses in NEC's offer.

Event Type: Sense-making; Timing: Q4 1977; Input: D10; Output: S11; Actors: National PTTs; Context: Evaluation of bids for the initial MTX specifications.

Re-Working the Deficiencies of the Initial MTX Specifications (Proposals)

S11: The uncertainties in the manufacturers' bids necessitated the NMT group to send a list of questions to the manufacturers in order to obtain clarifications.

Event Type: Sense-making; Timing: February 1978 to May 1978; Input: S10; Output: S12; Actors: National PTTs, suppliers; Context: Re-working the deficiencies of the initial MTX specifications (proposals).

S12: Reliability assessments were finished.

Event Type: Sense-making; Timing: December 1977 to May 1978; Input: S11; Output: S13; Actors: National PTTs; Context: Re-working the deficiencies of the initial MTX specifications (proposals).

MTX Delivery Negotiations

S13: Estimates of the costs stemming from the delay with NMT system's introduction are made. Sweden projected the loss of SEK 16 million if the NMT was delayed by one year.

Event Type: Sense-making; Timing: Q1 1978; Input: S12; Output: N14, Actors: National PTTs; Context: MTX delivery negotiations.

N13: LM Ericsson promises to ship the MTX to Sweden on May 1, 1981, to Norway on July 1, to Denmark on September 1, and to Finland on November 1.

Event Type: Neogtiation; Timing: August 1978; Input: D9; Output: D13; Actors: National PTTs, LM Ericsson; Context: MTX delivery negotiations.

D13: NMT recommends that the National Authorities to sign the corresponding contracts for the proposed MTX specifications. Denmark, Sweden, and Norway intend to sign the contract with LM Ericsson.

Event Type: Design; Timing: August 1978; Input: N13; Output: N14; Actors: National PTTs; Context: MTX delivery negotiations.

Signing a Contract for MTX

N14: All but Finnish National Authorities sign a contract with LM Ericsson. Finland considers the offer too expensive, seeks supplementary offers from LM Ericsson and NEC.

Event type: Negotiation; Timing: August 1978; Input: D13; Output: N15; Actors: National PTTs, LM Ericsson; Context: Signing a contract for MTX.

NMT Group Proposing Changes to MTX Specifications

N15: The NMT group approached LM Ericsson with the request to make changes to MTX specifications.

Event Type: Negotiation; Timing: 1979; Input: N12; Output: N16; Actors: National PTTs, LM Ericsson; Context: Choosing LM Ericsson's AXE exchange as the MTX for all Nordic countries.

N16: LM Ericsson refuses to implement the changes to MTX specifications, unless the delivery dates are postponed.

Event Type: Negotiation; Timing: 1979; Input: N15; Output: N17; Actors: National PTTs, LM Ericsson; Context: Choosing LM Ericsson's AXE exchange as the MTX for all Nordic countries.

LM Ericsson's AXE Exchange–The MTX of Choice in all Nordic Countries

N17: Reaching closure on negotiation–Finland signs the contract with LM Ericsson.

Event Type: Negotiation; Timing: 1979; Input: N14; Output: none; Actors: Finnins PTT, LM Ericsson; Context: Choosing LM Ericsson's AXE exchange as the MTX for all Nordic countries.

This work was previously published in the International Journal of IT Standards and Standardization Research, Vol. 6, Issue 1, edited by K. Jakobs, pp. 1-38, copyright 2008 by IGI Publishing (an imprint of IGI Global).

Chapter 9
Integrating Real Option and Dynamic Capability Theories of Firm Boundaries:
The Logic of Early Acquisition in the ICT Industry

Alfred G. Warner
Penn State Erie, USA

James F. Fairbank
Penn State Erie, USA

ABSTRACT

Firms often acquire other firms to source technology but it is unclear why they might assume such risk by buying before a product standard is established in their industry. We draw upon real options and dynamic capability theories of firm organization to develop an integrated framework that explains why firms might acquire early and which firms are more likely to do so. We develop propositions regarding certain firm attributes as predictors of acquisition timing relative to passage of a technology standard. We argue that from a real options perspective, the primary reason firms acquire early is related to the firm's knowledge of the technology. However, attributes such as political influence in the standardization process, prior experience making acquisitions, and how the firm resolves uncertainty about the technical expertise of potential acquisition targets are capabilities that also enter the acquisition timing decision. We provide a model based on those propositions and address how it can be empirically tested.

INTRODUCTION

Competition in industries where product standards define winning technologies has been compared to a particularly chancy casino game: Not only are outcomes and risks unknown, but the rules for competition emerge only in the process of playing (Arthur, 1996), defining (or re-defining) which firm skills, abilities, and know-how are valuable. Entering early (i.e., before the successful or standardized technologies are defined) with particular skills or resources is risky because they could be the wrong resources and ultimately have no value. This problem is exacerbated when firms enter via acquisition of another firm, as acquirers notoriously fail to realize value after the purchase. Yet, in the information and communication technologies (ICT) industry, firms have increasingly chosen to enter this way and do so well before standards are established.

As an example, Table 1 shows acquisitions in the ICT industry in three key technologies over the period 1995-2000. Public records show that although almost all acquisitions of firms providing Fast Ethernet technologies occurred after the Institute of Electrical and Electronics Engineers (IEEE) generated the 802.3u standard, about half of the acquisitions in Gigabit Ethernet occurred

Table 1. Acquisitions in three technologies in the ICT industry, 1995-2000 (acquisitions prior to standard in italics)

Acquirer	Target	Date
FORE Systems	*Applied Network Technology*	*Jun-95*
Cisco	Grand Junction	Sep-95
Siemens	ORNET	Sep-95
Cabletron	Enterprise Networks	Nov-95
Compaq	Networth	Nov-95
FORE Systems	ALANTEC Corp	Feb-96
Bay Networks	NetICs	Dec-96
Intel	Case Technology	Jan-97
Intel	Dayna Communications	Sep-97
Cabletron	NetVantage Inc	Jun-98
Lucent Technologies	Lannet, div. of Madge Networks	Jul-98
Lucent Technologies	Enable Semiconductor	Mar-99

Fast Ethernet acquisitions (IEEE 802.3u, effective July 1995)

Acquirer	Target	Date
Cisco	*Granite Systems*	*Sep-96*
FORE Systems	*Scalable Networks*	*Nov-96*
Bay Networks	*Rapid City Communications*	*Jun-97*
Cabletron	*Yago Systems*	*Jan-98*
Lucent Technologies	*Prominet Corporation*	*Jan-98*
ODS	*Essential Communications*	*May-98*
Level One	Acclaim Communications	Jun-98
FORE Systems	Berkeley Networks	Aug-98
Alcatel	Packet Engines	Oct-98
Level One	Jato	Nov-98
Intel	Level One Communications	Mar-99
Intel	XLNT	Mar-99
Vitesse Semiconductor	XaQti	May-99

Gigabit Ethernet acquisitions (IEEE 802.3ab, effective June 1998)

continued on following page

Table 1. continued

Acquirer	Target	Date
Cisco	*Telesend*	Mar-97
Cisco	*Dagaz*	Jul-97
Cisco	*NetSpeed Inc*	Mar-98
Cabletron	*Ariel*	Jun-98
Cabletron	*Flowpoint*	Jun-98
Marconi	*Reltec*	Mar-99
Cisco	*Fibex Systems*	Apr-99
Cisco	MaxComm Technologies	Aug-99
Netopia	StarNet Technologies	Oct-99
Terayon	Radwiz	Oct-99
Efficient Networks	Flowpoint	Nov-99
Westell Technologies	Teltrend Inc.	Dec-99
Nortel Networks	Promatory Communications	Jan-00
Intel	Ambient Technologies	Feb-00
Intel	Basis Communications	Mar-00
Terayon	Raychem Access	Mar-00
Orckit	EDSL Networks	May-00
Virata	Excess Bandwidth	Jun-00
Virata	Agranat Systems	Jul-00
Infineon	Savan Communications	Dec-00

ADSL acquisitions (ITU G.992.2, effective June 1999)

before 802.3ab was accepted. At about the same time, firms like Cisco and Cabletron were acquiring asymmetric digital subscriber line (ADSL) startups well before the ITU G.Lite 992.2 standard was accepted in 1999. Acquisition has become an increasingly common mode of entry and a key element in how firms manage technology (Chaudhuri & Tabrizi, 1999; Karim & Mitchell, 2000) but it is not obvious why firms would choose to spend millions or billions of dollars to enter new technologies in standards-based industries before the standard is defined and uncertainty about outcomes is high. In this article, we integrate recent work in real options and dynamic capabilities

theories as an explanation and framework for further empirical research.

Real options logic (ROL) is a theory of governance or firm boundaries with emphasis on how firms manage uncertainty. It has historically been viewed as the purchase of the right to make staged investments where the value lies in the ability to defer further expenditures (Adner & Levinthal, 2004; Kogut & Kulatilaka, 1994). Currently, however, researchers have developed the idea that value can also derive from growth opportunities if firms can invest to secure technological positions or access to new capabilities (Folta & O'Brien, 2004; McGrath, 1997), particularly if managers can act strategically to influence the standardization outcome (McGrath, 1997). For example, when Cisco Systems acquired AuroraNetics for their resilient packet ring technology in 2001, other members of the IEEE 802.17 working group reportedly feared that Cisco could then dominate the standard-setting process (Matsumoto, 2001). Both internal development projects and acquisitions can be considered the purchase of a real option (Folta & O'Brien, 2004); accordingly, in this article we argue that early acquisition represents the purchase of a growth option.

However, if growth option ROL can explain *why* firms might acquire before a standard is adopted, it is ambiguous with respect to *which* firms might do so and is therefore incomplete as a theoretical explanation. Firms purchasing this sort of real option should be concerned with two issues: Will the technology acquired become part of the standard and, if so, will the acquirer be able to exploit that opportunity? A more complete understanding of the early acquisition decision requires the integration of another theory of firm boundaries where specific capabilities of the acquiring firm play a key role.

Dynamic capability (DC) theory is an extension of the resource-based view (RBV) of the firm. In the resource-based view, competitive advantage derives from the control of valuable, rare, and difficult to imitate resources (Barney,

1991; Peteraf, 1993; Wernerfelt, 1984). These include assets such as specialized equipment, human skills, technical knowledge, and organizational abilities (Eisenhardt & Martin, 2000). Dynamic capabilities are regarded as higher-level resources in that they address how firms manage in turbulent environments through reconfiguration or transformation to achieve greater effectiveness (Teece, Pisano, & Shuen, 1997; Zollo & Winter, 2002). This is an alternative view of why firms make the governance choices they do, but it fails to specifically address what resources are best for future competitiveness. Success depends on the firm having superior knowledge about the future value of a resource or making a fortuitous buy (Barney, 1991; Eisenhardt & Martin, 2000). Some have argued that this lack of clarity on resource identification until after the fact makes the RBV/DC tautological (Priem & Butler, 2001). For these reasons, we believe that early acquisition can be better explained if growth oriented ROL and the RBV/DC are regarded as complementary rather than competing explanations. Firms might manage the rules of competition by entering early enough to influence the shape and structure of the standard (i.e., purchasing an option on growth opportunities to secure what could be extremely valuable resources), but this only makes sense when the decision to buy is supported by a set of key organizational capabilities. ROL and DC theories address different phases or aspects of the same resource acquisition process, and a synthesis of the theories might be useful in explaining acquisition timing.

Using the ICT industry as a frame, we develop a theory of how specific firm-level attributes can explain early acquisition. First, we argue that a significant gap in firm resources is the primary motivation for early acquisition as a real option, but that it is not a sufficient cause. We further describe how capabilities such as alliance experience and political power moderate and reinforce the real option by helping to manage the uncertainty problem. We also posit that other capabilities,

such as acquisition experience, are important in managing integration of acquired firms. If the acquiring firm succeeds with the option play, effective and efficient integration improves the likelihood of a win in the market.

Theories of governance or firm boundaries involve what activities the firm will conduct internally and what activities will be conducted outside through market or alliance. As Leiblein (2003) observes, such theories are often treated as independent explanations, whereas integration of relevant theories would enable the development of a more robust theory of governance. Our article represents a step toward that objective, as we argue that neither real options nor the resource based/dynamic capabilities view is sufficient to explain acquisition patterns in the ICT industry, but that as complements, they can. Though this article is not intended to be an empirical analysis, it does develop a basis for testing the extent to which these governance theories can be integrated.

BACKGROUND AND THEORY

Acquisition as a Real Option Investment

Real options are likened to financial options because the purchase of the option conveys the right, but not the obligation, to make further investment (Adner & Levinthal, 2004; Kogut & Kulatilaka, 1994). To illustrate, a financial option might be the purchase of a call on a stock at some time in the future. If the price of the stock rises high enough, the investor can strike the option by purchasing the shares at the option price and then re-selling them at the higher, actual price. If the price does not rise high enough, the investor can abandon the option. The key attributes of this model are the uncertainty about the future price, the contrast between limited downside risk and unlimited upside potential, and the property rights conveyed by ownership. Similarly, ROL argues that managers can undertake projects that more traditional valuation techniques, such as net present value analysis, might undervalue if they have discretion in the timing of investments, can wait for the resolution of uncertainty (Leiblein, 2003), and then choose to take further action, defer, or even abandon the opportunity (Bowman & Hurry, 1993). Real options have generally been used to assess internal development decisions (such as R&D for new technologies), but have also been applied to investments between firms, such as joint ventures. An emerging line of real option theory recognizes that growth options emerge if particular capabilities (Folta & O'Brien, 2004) or technological positions (McGrath, 1997) can be generated by investment under high uncertainty. Growth options are particularly valuable in high technology environments because they create the opportunity for firms to participate in subsequent generations of products (Leiblein, 2003).

Real options logic has recently been applied to technology development in a standards environment in several important ways. Modularity or task splitting in overall system design (such as computers or local area networks) can lead to the components of the system comprising a "portfolio of options" (Baldwin & Clark, 2000), the value of which is greater than that of a unitary design. More specifically, Gaynor and Bradner (2001) have shown that the competition between modularized technical solutions in an open standardization process creates real options for participants. They also clearly demonstrate how uncertainty about which technologies will be used, and how, permeates the standardization process. For example, they observe that asynchronous transfer mode (ATM) technology was standardized as a potential competitor to other LANs, but became most successful in high-speed IP routers and DSL technologies, which exemplifies the unpredictability of standardization.

This uncertainty is key to the value of a real option. First, because managers cannot accurately foretell the future, the option permits them to secure a position with property rights when uncertainty is high and wait until the uncertainty is resolved to take further action. An incremental approach limits downside risk (the price of the option) while endowing the owner with potential upside gains (Amram & Kulatilaka, 1999; Gaynor & Bradner, 2001). In technological opportunities, the uncertainty can be decomposed into several components. Initially, it is often unclear whether a particular technological approach will work. This has been termed "technical" uncertainty and can be resolved endogenously by investing in development (Dixit & Pindyck, 1994; McGrath, 1997), which is a function of the property right implicit in the option. Later, as technologies compete, the "market" uncertainty about which technology prevails is resolved in terms of a particular solution. In formal standardization, as Gaynor and Bradner's (2001) ATM example shows, resolution may come first as a win in the standards process and subsequently as a win (or loss) in the actual market competition between standardized technologies.

Second, the uncertainty around which technology wins is usually considered exogenous and outside the control of the firm (Amram & Kulatilaka, 1999), but scholars have recently developed the idea of a third form of uncertainty external to the firm but, unlike market uncertainty, subject to strategic intervention (McGrath, 1997; McGrath, Ferrier, & Mendelow, 2004; Miller & Folta, 2002). In these circumstances, managers can invest and act strategically to shape how the uncertainty is resolved.

Firms can secure growth options in several ways. The most often used example is entry into a new technology through internal development, which may clearly be construed as the exercise of the right generated by an investment in R&D as described above. How real options logic applies to inter-firm arrangements is less clear, but a property-rights perspective can be seen as parallel to internal development. Internal projects are the property of the firm that undertakes them, so it is clear they have a right to invest further or abandon the project. In the sense of securing an equivalent position, acquisition of another firm conveys equally strong property rights to the buyer and, if undertaken when the relevant uncertainty is still high, is strategically equivalent to the same stage opportunity created by internal investment. For this reason, Folta and O'Brien (2004) consider entry through internal development and entry through acquisition as theoretically parallel in their analysis of "dueling options." Thus, either internal development or acquisition into a standards-based technology before the uncertainty over which technology will prevail is resolved can reflect a positioning response to innovation or a growth option (Folta & O'Brien, 2004).[1]

The decision to secure a growth option through acquisition should be a function of the firm's relevant knowledge about the emerging technologies. Technological change ranges from incremental to radical (Anderson & Tushman, 1990), but this is relative; heterogeneity in firm investments, history, and resources suggest that within a particular industry, firms will regard the significance of technological innovations differently. Firms with relevant knowledge resources might view imitation of a new technology as relatively straightforward because it is near their existing capabilities and their prior investments have generated absorptive capacity (Cohen & Levinthal, 1990) or the ability to integrate and apply new knowledge. Firms that have made long-term and irreversible commitments to competence in other domains will find they lack the proper resources for imitating new technologies because they lack relevant absorptive capacity. These organizations might try to develop the skills internally but find that the time required to learn cannot be condensed easily or inexpensively. While this can be partially overcome through accelerated investment (Kim, 1997), there are time compression diseconomies involved that restrict the return to investment in learning (Dierickx & Cool, 1989). Even hiring talent away from competi-

tors can be difficult because the resources might not be easily tradable or accessible in the market (Barney, 1991; Teece, et al., 1997).

The effect of timing further complicates the choice of how to develop a response to new technologies. Late entry can adversely affect profitability (Ali, Krapfel, & LaBahn, 1995), market share (Lawless & Anderson, 1996), and even survival (Christensen, Suarez, & Utterback, 1998; Mitchell, 1989). In standards-based industries, entry timing can have another role. Since formal standards are often established in anticipation of market competition, solutions that eliminate particular approaches can put firms at a competitive disadvantage relative to those whose technologies are supported by the standard. This suggests that the critical time for entry and intervention is before the standard has been established, and firms lacking relevant knowledge resources must find a way to acquire them so they can compete or else be compelled to enter late and face the challenges of playing "catch-up." Therefore, firms increasingly turn toward acquisition to acquire the requisite high-technology skills (Chaudhuri & Tabrizi, 1999).

We therefore argue that initial differences in knowledge endowments for firms facing innovation will dictate the sort of real option purchased. We would expect firms that have relevant resources to attempt internal development first and if they acquire, they would be more likely to do so after the standard is complete. If firms that lack the relevant resources cannot learn about the technology quickly enough to attempt internal development, we argue that the real option perspective should lead them to acquire before the standard has passed. For example, Cisco CEO John Chambers once characterized the firm's most likely competition as IBM and Nortel (O'Reilly, 1998). If, as we discuss below, technical knowledge can be proxied by patent portfolios, IBM's wealth of patents in relevant fields and Cisco's lack in the same should imply that Cisco would be more likely to acquire early and IBM acquire late, if at all. This closely reflects the acquisition patterns that actually occurred. Clifford Meltzer, another Cisco executive, explained the strategy: "We don't believe we are smart enough to know all the important technologies over the next few years. You pick some, and then watch the industry" (Rogoski, 1997). We thus propose:

Proposition 1a: *Early acquirers (i.e., firms acquiring before the standard is accepted) will be more likely to lack relevant technical knowledge than will late acquirers.*

We also argue that the extent of overall invention in the industry moderates the value of resident knowledge stocks. If there is relatively little inventive work occurring, then the chances of a firm's stock of knowledge being made obsolete are less likely. If, however, the rate of invention is high, firms might be compelled to look outside for knowledge resources, particularly if there are multiple approaches to solving a technological problem (Steensma & Fairbank, 1999). That is, the intensity of the "trigger" for the investment decision can vary (Zahra & George, 2002). In optical networking, for example, Nortel had established a very strong position in SONET/SDH technologies research and development (Arellano, 1999). However, the emergence of dense wave division multiplexing (DWDM) technologies, evidenced by a surge in US patents, apparently outstripped Nortel's capacity to leverage earlier optical expertise. DWDM systems are complex and includes component such as laser modules, modulators, pump lasers, receivers, multiplexers, among many elements (McEuen, 2000). Although the firm was able to internally develop some components such as tunable lasers, Nortel eventually turned to acquisition to meet the demands of market pace (LaBarba, 1999), buying firms such as Cambrian Systems for metro DWDM capabilities, Qtera for long-range optical signaling, Xros for optical routing, and Core Networks for their tunable lasers. Accordingly, we propose:

Proposition 1b: *When the rate of invention in a technology family is high, firms will be more likely to perceive themselves as lacking relevant technical knowledge and will be more likely to acquire early (i.e., before the standard is accepted).*

How Dynamic Capabilities Moderate the Acquisition Decision

If the uncertainty around the standard is exogenously resolved, this gap in knowledge assets should be sufficient motivation for firms to make the real option acquisition and we should expect no other regularities among earlier acquirers. However, if managers can act strategically to affect outcomes (McGrath, 1997), then characteristics internal to the firm should emerge as commonalities among early acquirers. We argue that firms undertaking early acquisition will seek both the right technology and the right target, that is, a technology that shows promise and a target that can be successfully integrated and exploited by the acquiring organization. Meeting either objective will depend on specific firm attributes that directly support the option investment and/or the process of acquisition, and therefore moderate the acquisition decision. Such attributes are best characterized in a dynamic capabilities framework, since they become routine, learned processes, refined through experience. According to Eisenhardt and Martin (2000), these capabilities are "the antecedent organizational and strategic routines by which managers alter their resource base—acquire and shed resources, integrate them together, and recombine them—to generate new value-creating strategies" (p. 1107), and advantage goes to firms that use these capabilities sooner or more effectively than the competition.

Recent work illustrates three such routines or capabilities which can directly support the option aspect of the acquisition: political, alliance, and integration skills (Eisenhardt & Martin, 2000; Zollo & Singh, 2004). We expect that acquirers will exhibit differences in political or process power and that more powerful firms will find it beneficial to enter when their power can be deployed. As Wernerfelt and Karnani (1987) note, the ability to influence outcomes is itself a sufficient motivation to enter when uncertainty is still high. We also argue that acquirers with alliance experience should be able to asymmetrically resolve some of the technical uncertainty around the option, which also influences timing. Capabilities can also affect how well the acquisition process is managed. Alliance experience serves a second role here in that firms can more effectively determine if partners would be good acquisition targets and integrate well. Finally, firms that are experienced in integrating acquisitions should better understand the time, organizational, and cultural requirements of such purchases. We examine each capability below.

Political Capabilities

The standardization process in the ICT includes the work of several types of bodies ranging from the formal international structure (such as the International Telecommunication Union (ITU) and the International Electrotechnical Commission (IEC)) to the formal regional organizations, such as the European Telecommunications Standards Institute (ETSI). Further, many of the standards in the ICT industry are developed by "gray standards bodies," a classification that includes self-organizing regional entities such as the Institute of Electrical and Electronics Engineers (IEEE) and the European Computer Manufacturers Association (ECMA), as well as industry groups such as the ATM Forum. These groups are open in process and multi-vendor oriented (Egyedi, 2000) and vendor firms can sponsor technologies and participate in the process that accepts or rejects those technologies.

The influence of firms is such that they are increasingly regarded as a dominant force in standard-setting worldwide (Heywood, Jander, Roberts, & Saunders, 1997), but we argue that

firms will differ in their power in this context and those with greater perceived influence will be able to move markets or the processes that lead to markets. We anticipate that the specific standardization process will moderate this ability.

Standardization has been described as a social exercise in the construction of technology in that actors collectively establish processes and routines for the definition and solution of problems (Tushman & Rosenkopf, 1992). To the extent that the social construction also reflects the competitive orientation of the vendor firms involved, differences among the firms should enter the analysis. For instance, standardization processes are increasingly complemented by the work of block alliances that expedite technical testing and coordination. Examples include the Fast Ethernet, Gigabit Ethernet, and 10 Gigabit Ethernet Alliances that coexisted with and complemented the work of the relevant IEEE 802.3 committees as well as the Universal ADSL Working Group and its recommendation to the ITU. These block alliances are explicitly vendor based and, in gray standardization work, usually comprise firms that are concurrently involved in the standards process (Warner, 2003). Even if firms are not directly involved in the formal standardization process, the effect of power can persist if the work of the block alliance is included in the standard. The power of firms to influence how that work is developed at the alliance level is then reflected in the ultimate formal document.

Thus, firms that have more market or financial power (Munir, 2003; Wernerfelt & Karnani, 1987) or are central firms in long-term networks (Soh & Roberts, 2003) might be able to influence outcomes based simply on their choice of technologies. Soh & Roberts (2003) have mapped the networks in the US data communications industry and show that network central firms were early entrants and leaders of coalitions. Central firms may also form cliques that can dominate the technological decision process (Rosenkopf & Tushman, 1998). For example, in the work between the ADSL Forum and the Universal ADSL Working Group, Forum vice-chairman Bill Rodey argued that contention over technologies within the groups was minimized because the major firms had banded together (Oakes, 1998).

In addition, success in leading market entry strengthens or maintains the dominance of central firms for the next technological opportunity (Soh & Roberts, 2003) or for advances within the technology (Chiesa, Manzini, & Toletti, 2002). Finally, firms may seek to employ individuals they feel are influential in the standardization process or influence who staffs key administrative positions in standards committees (van Wegberg, 2004) or simply swamp the process with voting representatives (Heywood, et al., 1997). Therefore, firms with more power or clout should be more likely to enter early (particularly in gray standardizations processes) because they would be better positioned to shape outcomes.[2] While this capability supports the real option for either internal development or acquisition, with respect to acquisition in particular, we propose:

Proposition 2: *Early acquirers will be more likely to have greater influence in the relevant standardization community than will late acquirers.*

Alliance Capabilities

Alliances present opportunities to not only learn what partners know, they also allow firms to learn *about* partners more deeply and thus moderate the option investment decision in two ways. First, alliances allow partners to judge the content and applicability of the knowledge and skills the other brings to the collaboration (Grant & Baden-Fuller, 2004), which can reduce uncertainty about technical merit. Second, the process of establishing and maintaining an alliance provides information about each partner's culture, capabilities, and systems beyond the expressed motive for the venture (Zollo, Reuer, & Singh, 2002) which affects the ease and likelihood of successful integration.

Those with alliance expertise should have better information about (and be better able to judge) partners/targets than firms that do not have such experience. This expertise can vary along dimensions of investment level and scope.

How alliances are structured in terms of ownership can affect the level of information generated. Firms that have equity investments in candidate targets privately reduce information asymmetry relative to other potential acquirers and are in a better position to assess the relevance of the target's technology. Equity alliances are frequently used in R&D ventures because of the problems associated with knowledge expropriation (Gulati, 1995; Oxley, 1999). In order to gain financial backing, managers of private, capital-seeking firms must reduce information asymmetry by disclosing important information about their firm to potential backers including financial records, plans, and assets (Janney & Folta, 2003). This privileged access gives firms the ability to assess candidate technologies and reduce technical uncertainty. Provided the technologies meet the acquirer's relevance test, these firms should be more desirable acquisition targets than firms about which the investor does not have equivalent information.

Furthermore, firms vary in the extent to which they have developed alliance portfolios or strategies. In the late 1990s, some firms in the ICT industry began to operate not only as technology producers but also as managers or coordinators of venture capital funds, taking equity stakes in a wide array of firms with emerging technologies. Intel is a good example in that they have three equity funds (the Digital Home Fund, Communications Fund, and the China Technology Fund) and investments for each fund are publicly available (Intel, 2005). Other ICT firms that have implemented similar approaches in the past include Nokia (Nokia Venture Partners, now known as BlueRun Ventures), Lucent's New Venture Group, Nortel's Business Venture Group, and Cisco's Business Development Group. At the same time, non-equity based consortia or block alliances became popular ways to generate rapid standard development and interoperability testing and to coordinate the contributions of firms to standardization (Warner, 2003). Firms in these blocks should therefore have information not available to those outside. Overall, these alliance structures should allow participating firms to develop a richer acquisition environment and are capabilities that directly support both the real option and the subsequent integration process. We propose:

Proposition 3a: *Early acquirers will be more likely to have had an equity alliance with the target than will late acquirers.*

Proposition 3b: *Early acquirers will have larger alliance portfolios than will late acquirers.*

Integration Capabilities

Extracting value from acquisitions, particularly in the sense of integrating new knowledge, is difficult and firms often fail to achieve desired objectives (Chaudhuri & Tabrizi, 1999). First, learning takes time even under good conditions. Transferring skills within the organization can be difficult and time consuming (Teece, et al., 1997; Zander & Kogut, 1995) and the problem is exacerbated when acquirers and targets have different prior knowledge sets. The two organizations must establish a common ground for discussion and exchange before the new knowledge can be exploited.

Second, even when the new knowledge is "understood" by technicians and managers on an individual level, it must be transformed into routines and processes that the firm can use, which involves changes at many levels in the organization. This process can be blocked if the implementation too strongly challenges existing technical and managerial systems (Leonard-Barton, 1992). Recent research focusing on in-

novation output after acquisition has concluded that firms commonly underestimate the difficulty of integrating new information into the organization (Ahuja & Katila, 2001). Finally, integration is more difficult when there are significant size, structural, cultural, or other differences between the acquirer and target firm (Inkpen, Sundarum, & Rockwood, 2000).

Given these difficulties, prior acquisition experience has been shown to positively affect subsequent performance (Haleblian & Finkelstein, 1999; Hayward, 2002). This is due to several learning related causes. First, experience can lead firms to develop more efficient screening of acquisition candidates (Vermeulen & Barkema, 2001). Second, experience creates a more informed understanding of the time and skills required to integrate an acquisition and extract the value from the knowledge resources. Zollo and Singh (2004) argue that the process of codifying experience for application to subsequent purchases is key to managing the acquisition and assisting in the integration of targets. These assessment and integration routines are learned and practiced and constitute a dynamic capability (Eisenhardt & Martin, 2000). Experienced acquirers should be more conscious of the time investment to make a purchase successful. As a general illustration of these ideas, we note that Cisco is well known as a remarkably successful acquirer. Some of the reasons advanced for this include the due diligence process by which the firm qualifies targets with a strong focus on the social and cultural characteristics of the proposed target, identifying the prospects for a good fit with Cisco (Mayer & Kenney, 2004). For this reason, the firm prefers to target relatively young, small firms it can more easily integrate, particularly with respect to retention of key personnel. This conservative approach, according to CEO John Chambers, means that Cisco "has killed nearly as many acquisitions as we've made" (O'Reilly, 1998, p6). Another reason for Cisco's success is in the integration process itself. Once the deal is closed, Cisco's ten-step systematized integration process took over. Those steps include merging information systems such as conversion to Cisco's MRP, vendor evaluation and rationalization, and implementation of statistical process controls (Wheelwright, Holloway, Kasper, & Tempest, 1999), and were played out in 90- and 180-day programs (Mayer & Kenney, 2004). Because of the importance of experience in forming acquisition integration practices, we propose:

Proposition 4: *Early acquirers will be more likely to have prior acquisition experience than will late acquirers.*

To summarize our propositions, we argue that in the ICT industry, the timing of acquisitions reflects both the need and ability of some firms to invest in real options. Early acquisitions will more likely be undertaken by firms that lack appropriate knowledge resources which still seek to enter the market in a timely fashion and manage the outcome of the standards process *vis-à-vis* that technology purchase. This will be moderated by the rate of invention in the industry: When the level of invention is high, we anticipate that firm knowledge stocks will tend to be less relevant and increase the likelihood of early entry through

acquisition. Certain capabilities will support the likelihood of option purchase. Early acquirers will more likely possess political influence or clout because firms lacking this power would regard the resolution of the uncertainty as exogenous and out of their control, and are thus disincented to enter before the standard is passed. We also argue that acquisition timing reflects asymmetries in knowledge about potential candidates. Alliances eliminate some uncertainty for acquirers in this strategy and partners from prior alliances, especially partners in which the acquirer has had an equity stake, will more likely be acquired early. Finally, acquisition timing will be a function of preference and experience in the process. Firms might historically prefer acquisition as a sourcing mode and thus have developed skills and knowledge stocks regarding acquisition integration. Under these conditions, acquisition is likely to be early. Figure 1 provides a simple illustrative model of the relationship between our propositions and early acquisition.

DISCUSSION

As it stands, our model describes how we expect firms to behave with respect to acquisition and

Figure 1. Factors affecting entry timing

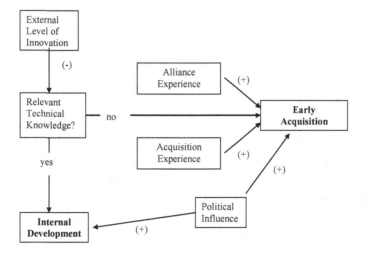

entry timing in the ICT industry. However, there are normative implications to an integrated approach. Earlier work in real options theory was prescriptive in the suggestion that the firm be viewed as a bundle of options (Bowman & Hurry, 1993). That is, when conditions are uncertain, firms should invest in a series of options to preserve flexibility and position. A key assumption is that the uncertainty will be resolved exogenously, which means that all firms are on an equal footing. In other words, the only issue for firms is if they have the wherewithal to purchase the option. Even so, a recent critique of the theory observes that real options promoted as a general means of creating firm-wide flexibility are "oversold" (Barnett, 2003) and that they are better as a project-specific tool. Barnett (2003) also notes that developing effective options is resource intensive, much like creating key organizational capabilities. We believe this is an important argument on several grounds.

First, as we have discussed here, acquisition can be construed as a real option but one that requires investment beyond merely purchasing the target. In order to make the acquisition successful, firms will need to leverage a number of other capabilities in the wake of the purchase. Thus, these growth options are not simply a "buy and wait" proposition, but require active management. Second, particularly in this context, we would argue that these real options are not merely "like" developing capabilities, but are expressly developing them. This occurs on several levels. If the acquisition is successful, the firm has acquired new technical skills that are not only useful in current applications but as a springboard for future development within the same technology. Moreover, the acquiring firm has reinforced the political and integration capabilities that supported the acquisition, improving their position for subsequent option investments. Thus, from a normative position *contra* earlier options reasoning, we argue that not all firms are capable of taking these options and that undertaking acquisitions as an option

can be a highly risky process for firms lacking the supporting capabilities.

Our integrated model is testable. If early acquirers fail to show some, if not all, of the regularities we predict, then the theoretical integration is superfluous. We consider several issues in empirically testing these propositions since operationalizing the variables we propose will require some judgment. The dependent variable–acquisition timing–is a good example. Because agreement on standards evolves, and at some point prior to actual adoption the debate has ended and there is no longer opportunity to influence the outcome, acquisition is "early" only if conveys at least the opportunity to affect the shape of the standard. One way to define this is to track the actual course of discussion within the standard process and to assert that acquisitions made when disagreement was still high should be considered early. However, not all such processes can be easily monitored because they might involve off-line actions (such as vendor groups), they are difficult for researchers to access, or because they are concluded and acquiring the relevant primary information is not possible. We suggest that a first cut approach might simply establish a cutoff time prior to standard passage that distinguishes acquisitions made under greater or lesser uncertainty. For example, the set of acquisitions made at least six or twelve months prior to the first passage of a standard should have been made under conditions of much greater uncertainty than the set of later acquisitions. This time frame reflects how the pace of standardization has increased over the past decade and what once took years might now only require months (Rada & Berg, 1995).

Another issue will be operationalizing technical knowledge. We suggest the use of patent portfolios as a general metric. Patents have served as proxies for the stock of codifiable knowledge–that which firms draw upon to learn (DeCarolis & Deeds, 1999; Dierickx & Cool, 1989) and in the ICT industry, patents have been used to model technological competence (Madden, Rao,

& Galvin, 2002; Rao, Vemuri, & Galvin, 2004). Further, patents will be useful in such a study because they are classified by technology, which provides information on both the rate and direction of inventive change (Archibugi & Pianta, 1996). Though recent work has argued that firms with significant knowledge assets, such as patents, may resist joining standardization movements to avoid knowledge spillovers (Blind, 2006), we note that this analysis addressed ten industries (and did not include the ICT industry) where firms with sufficient market power could take effective unilateral action outside the standards process. However, the modularity of system design in the ICT industry (Baldwin & Clark, 2000) constrains the ability of firms to opt out of standardization and introduce proprietary products. While this suggests that standards may vary across industries in their perceived downstream importance, and opens up research possibilities into the interaction between importance and standardization participation, it does not obviate the use of patents in this industry as one measure of technical knowledge.

Measuring prior acquisition experience should be straightforward because if the acquirer or target is a publicly held firm (and virtually all acquirers in the ICT industry are publicly held), acquisition is a matter of public record. The issue for research is the extent to which the marginal returns to learning through acquisition persist. That is, are more acquisitions always better or do the marginal benefits of learning how to integrate purchases disappear after some (presumably small) number of acquisitions?

Alliance portfolios will be more difficult to measure than acquisition experience as firms do not face the same reporting requirements. There are several potential approaches to this problem using available information. First, non-equity alliances, particularly memberships in industry groups and consortia, are generally announced either by firms party to the alliance or, in the case of industry groups, by the group itself and are a matter of record. Information about equity

alliances is sometimes retained because it can convey strategically important information to competitors, but investments are increasingly announced by investors or the recipients. For example, if firms have corporate venturing portfolios, the information about firms in the portfolio is publicly available. Finally, if a publicly held firm has a stake in an acquisition target, this is always disclosed in the announcement of purchase.

The ability to influence processes is a complex variable that poses a number of measurement challenges. Based on the work cited above, we expect that operationalizing influence will include firm characteristics such as size, and the extent to which the firm is or has been a leader or founder of successful industry consortia. Alternatively, researchers may turn to network analysis tools to assess how central firms are in the industry, particularly over time. The work of Soh and Roberts (2003) may provide a direct measure of centrality as would a cumulative measure of membership in consortia, particularly founding membership.

CONCLUSION

This article has developed a descriptive model showing how early entry through acquisition can be explained by integrating the principles of real options and dynamic capabilities theories of firm boundaries. Real options theory explains why firms may generally invest in a new technology through acquisition but does not specifically inform us as to which firms might be so inclined. The dynamic capability perspective shows us which firms could best incorporate new resources but not how to select those assets, suggesting that acquiring resources that convey competitive advantage is sometimes just a matter of fortune. That is, dynamic capability theory provides a more useful explanation after the resources have been acquired. In combination, however, real options and dynamic capabilities show how firms can identify opportunities and, if they possess the requisite capabilities such as political, integration, and alliance skills, purposefully move to acquire resources and take the actions that make those resources valuable. This integration should help explain why and which firms acquire early in the ICT industry.

REFERENCES

Adner, R., & Levinthal, D. A. (2004). What is not a real option: Considering boundaries for the application of real options to business strategy. *Academy of Management. The Academy of Management Review, 29*(1), 74.

Ahuja, G., & Katila, R. (2001). Technological acquisitions and the innovation performance of acquiring firms: A longitudinal study. *Strategic Management Journal, 22*, 197-220.

Ali, A., Krapfel, R., Jr., & LaBahn, D. (1995). Product innovativeness and entry strategy: Impact on cycle time and break-even time. *Journal of Product Innovation Management, 1995*(12), 54-69.

Amram, M., & Kulatilaka, N. (1999). *Real options.* Boston: Harvard Business Press.

Anderson, P., & Tushman, M. L. (1990). Technological discontinuities and dominant designs: A cyclical model of technological change. *Administrative Science Quarterly, 35*(4 Dec), 604-633.

Archibugi, D., & Pianta, M. (1996). Measuring technological change through patents and innovation surveys. *Technovation, 16*(9), 451-468.

Arellano, M. (1999). Fast company: Nortel's long involvement with OC-192 research is helping it dominate the market. *Tele.com, 4*(17), 42.

Arthur, W. B. (1996). Increasing returns and the new world of business. *Harvard Business Review*(July-August), 100-109.

Baldwin, C. Y., & Clark, K. B. (2000). *Design rules.* Cambridge, MA: The MIT Press.

Barnett, M. L. (2003). Falling off the fence? A realistic appraisal of a real options approach to corporate strategy. *Journal of Management Inquiry, 12*(2), 185.

Barney, J. (1991). Firm resources and sustained competitive advantage. *Journal of Management, 17*(1), 99-120.

Blind, K. (2006). Explanatory factors for participation in formal standardisation processes: Empirical evidence at firm level. *Economics of Innovation and New Technology, 15*(2), 157-170.

Bowman, E. H., & Hurry, D. (1993). Strategy through the options lens: An integrated view of resource investments and the incremental-choice process. *Academy of Management Review, 18*(4), 760-782.

Chaudhuri, S., & Tabrizi, B. (1999). Capturing the real value in high-tech acquisitions. *Harvard Business Review, 77*(5), 123-130.

Chiesa, V., Manzini, R., & Toletti, G. (2002). Standard-setting processes: Evidence from two case studies. *R & D Management, 32*(5), 431.

Christensen, C. M., Suarez, F. F., & Utterback, J. M. (1998). Strategies for survival in fast-changing industries. *Management Science, 44*(12), S207-S220.

Cohen, W. M., & Levinthal, D. A. (1990). Absorptive capacity: A new perspective on learning and innovation. *Administrative Science Quarterly, 35*, 128-152.

DeCarolis, D. M., & Deeds, D. L. (1999). The impact of stocks and flows of organizational knowledge on firm performance: An empirical investigation of the biotechnology industry. *Strategic Management Journal, 20*(10), 953-968.

Dierickx, I., & Cool, K. (1989). Asset stock accumulation and sustainability of competitive advantage. *Management Science, 35*(11), 1504-1513.

Dixit, A. K., & Pindyck, R. S. (1994). *Investment under uncertainty.* Princeton, NJ: Princeton University Press.

Egyedi, T. M. (2000). Institutional dilemma in ICT standardization: Coordinating the diffusion of technology? In K. Jacobs (Ed.), *Information technology standards and standardization: A global perspective,* 48-62. Hershey, London: Idea Group Publishing.

Eisenhardt, K. M., & Martin, J. A. (2000). Dynamic capabilities: What are they? *Strategic Management Journal, 21,* 1105-1121.

Folta, T. B., & O'Brien, J. P. (2004). Entry in the presence of dueling options. *Strategic Management Journal, 25,* 121-138.

Gaynor, M., & Bradner, S. (2001). *The real options approach to standardization.* Paper presented at the Hawaii International Conference on Systems Sciences, Honolulu, HI.

Grant, R. M., & Baden-Fuller, C. (2004). A knowledge accessing theory of strategic alliances. *Journal of Management Studies, 4,* 61-84.

Gulati, R. (1995). Does familiarity breed trust? The implications of repeated ties for contractual choice in alliances. *Academy of Management Journal, 38,* 85-112.

Haleblian, J., & Finkelstein, S. (1999). The influence of organizational acquisition experience on acquisition performance: A behavioral learning perspective. *Administrative Science Quarterly, 44*(1), 29-56.

Hayward, M. L. A. (2002). When do firms learn from their acquisition experience? Evidence from 1990-1995. *Strategic Management Journal,* 23(Jan), 21-39.

Heywood, P., Jander, M., Roberts, E., & Saunders, S. (1997). Standards: The inside story. *Data Communications*(March), 59-72.

Inkpen, A. C., Sundarum, A. K., & Rockwood, K. (2000). Cross-border acquisitions of US technology assets. *California Management Review, 42*(3), 50-71.

Intel. (2005). *Intel Capital Portfolio,* Vol. 2005.

Janney, J. J., & Folta, T. B. (2003). Signaling through private equity placements and its impact on the valuation of biotechnology firms. *Journal of Business Venturing, 18*(3), 361-380.

Karim, S., & Mitchell, W. (2000). Path-dependent and path-breaking change: Reconfiguring business resources following acquisitions in the U.S. medical sector, 1978-95. *Strategic Management Journal, 21,* 1061-1081.

Kim, L. (1997). The dynamics of Samsung's technological learning in semiconductors. *California Management Review, 39*(3), 86-100.

Kogut, B., & Kulatilaka, N. (1994). Operating flexibility, global manufacturing, and the option value of a multinational network. *Management Science, 40*(1), 123.

LaBarba, L. (1999). Nortel tunes into lasers: New units push envelope toward sparing concept. *Telephony, 236*(9), 22.

Lawless, M. W., & Anderson, P. C. (1996). Generational technological change: Effects of innovation and local rivalry on performance. *Academy of Management Journal, 39*(5), 1185-1217.

Leiblein, M. J. (2003). The choice of organizational governance form and performance: Predictions from transaction cost, resource-based and real options theories. *Journal of Management, 29*(6), 937-961.

Leonard-Barton, D. (1992). Core capabilities and core rigidities: A paradox in managing new product development. *Strategic Management Journal, 13,* 111-125.

Madden, G., Rao, P. M., & Galvin, P. (2002). *Technological competency of leading ICT firms: US patent data evidence.* Paper presented at the International Telecommunications Society, Seoul, South Korea.

Matsumoto, C. (2001). Rivals vie to reshape net topology. *Electronic Engineering Times*(1183), 1,16.

Mayer, D., & Kenney, M. (2004). Economic action does not take place in a vacuum: Understanding Cisco's acquisition and development strategy. *Industry and Innovation, 11*(4), 299.

McEuen, D. (2000). DWDM: Increasing the capacity of optical networks. *ElectronicNews, 46*(27), 16.

McGrath, R. G. (1997). A real options logic for initiating technology positioning investments. *Academy of Management: The Academy of Management Review, 22*(4), 974-996.

McGrath, R. G., Ferrier, W. J., & Mendelow, A. L. (2004). Real options as engines of choice and heterogeneity. *Academy of Management: The Academy of Management Review, 29*(1), 86-101.

Miller, K. D., & Folta, T. B. (2002). Option value and entry timing. *Strategic Management Journal, 23*, 655-665.

Mitchell, W. (1989). Whether or when? Probability and timing of incumbent's entrance into emerging industrial subfields. *Administrative Science Quarterly, 34*(2), 208-230.

Munir, K. A. (2003). Competitive dynamics in face of technological discontinuity: A framework for action. *Journal of High Technology Management Research, 14*(1), 93.

O'Reilly, C. (1998). Cisco Systems: The acquisition of technology is the acquisition of people. In S. G. S. o. Business (Ed.). Palo Alto, CA: Stanford University.

Oakes, C. (1998). ADSL Standard: Divided Tech, United Companies: Wired News.

Oxley, J. E. (1999). Institutional environment and the mechanisms of governance: The impact of intellectual property protection on the structure of inter-firm alliances. *Journal of Economic Behavior & Organization, 38*(3), 283-309.

Peteraf, M. A. (1993). The cornerstones of competitive advantage: A resource-based view. *Strategic Management Journal, 14*, 179-191.

Priem, R. L., & Butler, J. E. (2001). Tautology in the resource-based view and the implications of externally determined resource value: Further comments. *Academy of Management Review, 26*(1), 57-66.

Rada, R., & Berg, J. (1995). Standards: Free or sold? *Communications of the ACM, 38*(2), 23-27.

Rao, P. M., Vemuri, V., K. , & Galvin, P. (2004). The changing technological profile of the leading ICT firms: Evidence from U.S. patent data, 1981-2000. *Industry and Innovation, 11*(4), 353-372.

Rogoski, R. (1997). *In the past, the future: Cisco System's RTP chief says partnering key to firm's success.* Bizjournals.com (Feb 10).

Rosenkopf, L., & Tushman, M. L. (1998). The co-evolution of technology and organization. *Industrial and Corporate Change, 7*, 311-346.

Soh, P.-H., & Roberts, E. B. (2003). Networks of innovators: A longitudinal perspective. *Research Policy, 32*(9), 1569.

Steensma, H. K., & Fairbank, J. F. (1999). Internalizing external technology: A model of governance mode choice and an empirical assessment. *The Journal of High Technology Management Research, 10*(1), 1-35.

Teece, D. J., Pisano, G., & Shuen, A. (1997). Dynamic capabilities and strategic management. *Strategic Management Journal, 18*(7), 509-533.

Tushman, M. L., & Rosenkopf, L. (1992). Organizational determinants of technological change: Towards a sociology of technological evolution. *Research in Organizational Behavior, 14,* 311-347.

van Wegberg, M. (2004). Standardization and competing consortia: The trade-off between speed and compatibility. *International Journal of IT Standards & Standardization Research, 2*(2), 18.

Vermeulen, F., & Barkema, H. (2001). Learning through acquisitions. *Academy of Management Journal, 44*(3), 457-476.

Warner, A. (2003). Block alliances in formal standard setting environments. *International Journal of IT Standards and Standardization Research, 1*(1), 1-18.

Wernerfelt, B. (1984). A resource-based view of the firm. *Strategic Management Journal, 5,* 171-180.

Wernerfelt, B., & Karnani, A. 1987. Competitive strategy under uncertainty. *Strategic Management Journal, 8,* 187-194.

Wheelwright, S. C., Holloway, C. A., Kasper, C. G., & Tempest, N. (1999). *Cisco Systems, Inc: Acquisition integration for manufacturing.* Cambridge, MA: Harvard Business School.

Zahra, S. A., & George, G. (2002). Absorptive capacity: A review, reconceptualization, and extension. *Academy of Management Review, 27*(2), 185-203.

Zander, U., & Kogut, B. (1995). Knowledge and the speed of the transfer and imitation of organizational capabilities: An empirical test. *Organization Science, 6*(1), 76-92.

Zollo, M., Reuer, J. J., & Singh, H. (2002). Interorganizational routines and performance in strategic alliances. *Organization Science, 13,* 701-713.

Zollo, M., & Singh, H. (2004). Deliberate learning in corporate acquisitions: Post-acquisition strategies and integration capability in U.S. bank mergers. *Strategic Management Journal, 25,* 1233-1256.

Zollo, M., & Winter, S. G. (2002). Deliberate learning and the evolution of dynamic capabilities. *Organization Science, 13*(3), 339.

ENDNOTES

[1] Internal development and acquisition are clearly not the only ways of entering new markets. Firms can use alliances or product licensing as alternative entry modes. However, these governance modes typically do not convey property rights, such as the ability to modify or customize supplied products. This inability was one reason cited in Cabletron's acquisition of FlowPoint in 1998 (Sweat, 1998). The real option right to decide to abandon or invest further is a specific outcome of how the option purchase conveys property rights.

[2] We are indebted to an anonymous reviewer who points out that the effect of such power may not be linear. In some processes, the efforts of very large firms are stymied by a coalition of other firms or entities, suggesting a liability to perceived power. Therefore, we agree that the effect may be curvilinear and that there may be decreasing returns to these measures of political strength.

This work was previously published in the International Journal of IT Standards and Standardization Research, Vol. 6, Issue 1, edited by K. Jakobs, pp. 39-54, copyright 2008 by IGI Publishing (an imprint of IGI Global).

Chapter 10
Standardization Education:
Developments and Progress

Henk J. de Vries
Erasmus University, The Netherlands

Tineke M. Egyedi
Delft University of Technology, The Netherlands

ABSTRACT

The purpose of this chapter is to provide insight in recent developments in standardization education. The increasing number of initiatives and activities of the last couple of years indicates that there is a momentum for education on standardization. This chapter provides a structured approach for using this momentum to further develop and implement standardization education. The main topics are: needs for standardization education, audiences and learning objectives, contents of an academic curriculum, and available materials for academic teaching. The authors found an enormous gap between manifest and latent needs for standardization education. The lesson to be learnt from some Asian countries is that this gap can be bridged. First, by a strong national policy which may be part of a regional policy. Secondly, by cooperation between government, industry, national standards body, academia and other educational institutions.

A few years ago, universities in Korea hardly spent any time on standards and standardization. Since a few years, however, standardization courses at Korean universities are attended by thousands of students per year. Korea's stance is that standards shape the market for products and services. As it wants to increase its influence in the process of developing these standards and help its companies profit from standardization, it indeed understands the need for education.

This chapter presents developments and progress in standardization education and builds on a previous paper in which we reported about the main results of an international workshop on standardization education we organized in 2007 (de Vries & Egyedi, 2007). In this chapter we use the same structure:

1. Overview of standardization education initiatives
2. Need for standardization education
3. Audiences and learning objectives

DOI: 10.4018/978-1-60566-946-5.ch010

4. Contents of a cross-academic course on standardization
5. Inventory of existing educational material

The first three sections address standardization education in the widest sense, whereas the last two sections focus on academic teaching.

OVERVIEW OF STANDARDIZATION EDUCATION INITIATIVES

Korea's initiatives in standardization education spearheaded a flurry of activity internationally. Since 2003, the number of activities has increased rapidly. A few examples are as follows.

- The first Strategic Standardization Workshop of the Korean Standards Association is held (KSA, 2003).
- Secondary school program on standardization education in Thailand (2003-2006), 2,354 teachers are trained and 444,600 students receive standardization education.
- Asia Link Project on Standardization Education (2004-2006), a cooperation between six universities of two European and four Asian countries (Hesser & Siedersleben, 2008), resulting in a e-learning modules and a book (Hesser, Feilzer & de Vries, 2007).
- An article about the need for standardization education is published in the Japanese Journal for Science and Technology Trends Quarterly Review (Kurokawa, 2005).
- In the framework of the IEC Centennial (International Electrotechnical Commission), two publicly available lecture series are developed: one series for engineers (Purcell, 2005) and one for business schools (Egyedi, 2007).
- The International Cooperation for Education about Standardization (ICES) is founded (2006) and organizes a yearly workshop or conference about standardization education.
- KSA organizes its first International Standards Education Seminar (2006).
- The Hitotsubashi University Project (Japan) on "standardology" starts (2006-2009).
- ITU (International Telecommunication Union) organizes a consultation meeting called Cooperation between ITU-T (ITU Telecommunication Standardization Sector) and Universities in Geneva, January 18 to 19, 2007, followed by conferences for academics and practitioners.
- The International Organization for Standardization (ISO) presents its e-learning modules on international standardization (Gerundino, 2005; 2007).
- Ministers of the member countries of the Asia Pacific Economic Cooperation agree to give priority to education about standards and conformity. They encourage the APEC members to develop reference curricula and materials to address the significance of standards and conformance to trade facilitation in the region (Joint statement issued at the 18th APEC Ministrial Meeting, Ha Noi, Vietnam, 15-16 November 2006) (Choi (ed.), 2008).
- ISO organizes an award to encourage and recognize successful programs for higher education in standardization (ISO Focus, 2007). Winner is China Jiliang University, Hangzhou. Second prizes are won by universities in Egypt, France, Japan, Korea and The Netherlands. The 2009 winner is Rotterdam School of Management, Erasmus University, Rotterdam, The Netherlands. The other finalists were educational institutions from Belarus, Egypt, France, Korea, and Ukraine (ISO Focus, 2010)
- Two European projects, COPRAS (Cooperation Platform for Research and

Standards) and INTEREST (Integrating Research and Standardisation), finalized in 2007, address how to feed the R&D (research and development) results of universities and companies into standardization and include educational issues.

- The International Journal of IT Standards & Standardization Research organizes a special issue on standards education (2007).
- The APEC project on standardization education starts, led by Korea. Indonesia, Japan, Singapore, Thailand, the USA, and Vietnam participate (2007-2010) (Choi (ed.), 2008; Choi, de Vries & Kim, 2009).
- The national standards bodies of Argentina and Brazil report growth in standardization education activities (Amorim, 2008; Marin, 2008).
- The Japanese Ministry of Economy, Trade and Industry (METI) organizes an International Workshop on Standardization Education, December 4-5, 2008.
- The International Journal of IT Standards & Standardization Research and the Journal on Cases in Information Technology organize a common special issue on standards education (2009).

This incomplete listing suggests a surge of interest in standardization education worldwide, and a momentum for discussion and collaboration.

NEEDS FOR STANDARDIZATION EDUCATION

Insight in what needs or demands there are for standardization education may help drive, focus, and structure new initiatives in this area and in a practical sense legitimize them. Four approaches ease identifying needs for standardization education: (1) deducing needs from current course offerings, (2) deducing needs from standardization-related tasks, (3) deducing needs from standardization-related problems, and (4) systematically studying aspects of the standards phenomenon and inferring related needs.

Inventory of Current Courses

In case of supply, demand may usually be presumed. In line, studying the supply of standardization education may well indicate what needs there are. In most countries the number of universities paying attention to standardization education is very limited (Acyl & Borde, 2003; Borde, 2004; Center for Global Standards Analysis, 2004; Choi (ed.), 2008, Krechmer, 2007; Kurokawa, 2005; M&E Consultants, 2001). In the USA, the Accreditation Board for Engineering and Technology (ABET) Criteria for Accreditation of Engineering Programs require that universities pay attention to engineering standards in the curriculum of undergraduate students in all engineering fields (Spivak & Kelly, 2003). However, the extent to which this requirement has been effectuated is unknown. Special courses on standardization tend to attract only a small number of students. The major share of academic education on standardization can be found in Asia, mainly in China, Japan (Kurokawa, 1995), and Korea, but also in Thailand and, thanks to the common European-Asian Asia Link Project on standardization education, in Indonesia, Sri Lanka, and Vietnam as well (Hesser, Feilzer, & de Vries, 2007).

Nonacademic teaching is offered in many countries, mainly in the form of courses for technicians about certain standards. For some of these standards courses, the number of students is huge, for example, in the case of standards for IT service management (Cater-Steel & Toleman, 2007). The national standards bodies of certain countries, for example, Austria (Stern, 2003), Germany, the USA, and Vietnam, also offer some more general courses on standardization, next to the ISO courses (Calzadilla-Sarmiento, 2005). However, compared to the number of people involved in standardization, the supply of education is very restricted (de Vries, 2005; Krechmer, 2007). This indicates a limited manifest need for education.

Courses for Standardization-Related Tasks

Verman (1973) was the first to call standardization a discipline for which professional knowledge is needed. Standardization activities are carried out by people who may need specific knowledge and/or skills to do their job. Their educational needs can be identified by determining what they must do during specific stages of the standards process irrespective of where standardization takes place: at a company, national, regional, or international level in the committees of consortia or formal standards bodies.

For those who develop standards professionally, the education required will usually differ from those who are merely indirectly involved. Currently, the most extensive education for standardization professionals is offered by Professor Song and his colleagues at China Jiliang University in Hangzhou, People's Republic of China (ISO Focus, 2007). Several international, regional, and national standards bodies offer short courses for standards professionals and standards officers in companies (e.g., the German national standards institute DIN). However, most participants in standardization committees have had very little training, if any. As a result standardization activities in companies, consortia, and standards bodies are carried out in a rather primitive way (de Vries, 2005). For example, the quality of standards and the speed of the process are up for improvement (de Vries, 1999).

A similar observation can be made about people for whom standardization activities only constitute part of their job. They are usually not aware that they can profit from training and education. This applies to the management level as well as to the workers on the shop floor.

Whereas those who work in standardization appear to feel little need for education, literature on the matter does identify a need. To give an example, an important argument for increasing the awareness of and education in standardization is that standards increasingly act as soft law (Kurokawa, 2005). In the European Union, for example, a certain group of standards is related to legislation by means of so-called New Approach mandates, but is not mandatory (Hanson, 2005). Many companies are insufficiently aware of this and would benefit from a better understanding of the relation between standardization and regulation. This applies more generally, as Mary Saunders, chief of the Standards Services Division of NIST (National Institute of Standards and Technology) points out in ASTM Standardization News ("Standards Education in the Unites States: A Roundtable," 2003): "The critical need is for training that addresses why standards are important and why an individual should participate in standards development activities."

Education to Solve Problems

According to John Hill, former standards manager of Sun Microsystems and initiator of ICES, "companies as well as standards bodies need well-educated standardization experts. Standardization processes should keep up with the times. Who will progress the theory and practice of standardization? Will universities provide us with such people?" His concern is echoed by Kurokawa (2005), who says Japanese companies, too, experience difficulties in creating standards specialists for the longer term; on-the-job training is costly and insufficient.

Doede Bakker, responsible for standardization issues at the Dutch trade association for the technology-industry sector (FME-CWM), notes that companies that want to achieve a leading market position have to set the relevant standards themselves. Therefore, education on all company levels is needed, in particular at the managerial level. Managers need to be convinced about the importance of standards by clearly demonstrating and quantifying the benefits of standardization.

The national, regional, and international standards bodies are facing the problem that technical experts for standards development are scarce. Moreover, an important part of those who are currently active will be retiring in the coming decade without there being enough successors. This demographic development partly explains the timing of present interest of standards bodies in education.

Academic Approach to Needs

De Vries (2005) describes an academic approach to determine standardization education needs. This approach starts out by asking questions regarding what is done in practice (in this case, by the people involved in standardization), how it is done, why it is done, and why it is done in a certain way. By means of a general model, first, processes in standardization are defined, then the people related to these processes, and, finally, the education they need to carry out their tasks. This model can be applied to different standardization settings, for example, at a company, intercompany, national, or international level in different business sectors, in technical as well as nontechnical areas, and for different kinds of standards. Moreover, these settings can be studied from different scientific angles.

Concluding Remarks

An enormous gap can be observed between latent and manifest needs for standardization education. Countries like Korea, Thailand, and Turkey show that to bridge this gap, a national strategy is needed, as is cooperation between a country's government, industry, national standards body, academia, and educational institutions (Choi, de Vries & Kim, 2008).

AUDIENCES AND LEARNING OBJECTIVES

The question why one should have knowledge of standardization should be the starting point of standardization education. It determines which audience should be targeted and what should be taught (learning objectives). Literature shows different answers to the questions about who should be educated on standardization (what audiences there are) and why (which learning objectives match these audiences). Krechmer (2007) argues that, since the development and implementation of most standards are done by scientists, engineers, and technicians, they should be the main target groups for standardization education. Other authors distinguish different groups. Kurokawa (2005), for example, discerns three target groups: general standards users, those who actually work with standards, and those who strategically address standards. Each group requires a different kind of education. De Vries (2005) uses yet another approach. He analyzes the process of standardization to identify target groups and the competencies they need to have. Most of these people can be found in companies and standards bodies.

Korean education started off by targeting students of engineering. The reason for starting with future engineers was that a main significance of standards stems from the fact that they are embedded in products. The Korean courses focus, for example, on creating awareness about the significance of standards, and on what standards are and how they influence the world market. A main lesson learned by the Koreans is that teachers of standardization education are an important category of people for standardization education ("teach the teachers").

In a brainstorm session, the 2007 workshop came up with a list of audiences who would benefit from standardization education (de Vries & Egyedi, 2007):

- Audiences in the regular educational system, for example, those in primary school, secondary school, vocational training, and universities, including MBA students, PhD students, postdocs, teachers, and university professors. For example, in Thailand, Turkey, and Korea, children of primary and secondary school age receive standards education. In Korea, summer camps are organized. As far as academic teaching is concerned, needs range from general (e.g., cross-academic courses) to specific education (e.g., focused on students in engineering, business, medicine, and law; see also de Vries, 2005; Hesser & Czaya, 1999; Reihlen, 1999).
- Audiences in job training programs, for example, for standards developers, implementers, corporate managers, and managers of functional units (e.g., purchasing department); researchers; policy makers; those in public administration; lobbyists, for instance, in an industry sector; and media people. In addition, there should be education for the wider public. There are those who will make a fulltime career out of standardization, which applies to a group of standardization experts in China, and those who end up in this area at a later stage of their career, as is mostly the case (Simons, 1999).

Choi and de Vries (2010) developed a framework for standardization education for different target groups.

The best example of education for fulltime standards professionals is the set of courses offered at the China Jiliang University (ISO Focus, 2007). The types of students are as follows.

- Postgraduate students from mechanical and electronic engineering disciplines
- Postgraduate students from technology-testing and meter-measuring disciplines

- Undergraduate students from standardization and quality management

The learning objectives for the bachelor level are the following.

- To work in company standardization jobs
- To serve the standardization management sectors of the government at different levels
- To serve the medium servicing organization for standardization.

The objectives for the master level are the following:

- To draft professional, local, or national standards
- To participate in regional or international standardization activities as a representative of the organization
- To engage in standardization management affairs in government and big companies

The curriculum may lead to a qualification in standardization (i.e., a license for ISO 9000 auditor). More than 70% of the students get a standardization-related job after obtaining their bachelor's degree.

People usually come into contact with standards via their profession (e.g., in a specific technical area). They may sometimes already be acquainted with specific standards, such as standards for technical drawing or standards for the safety of low-voltage installations, through regular education at the lower, intermediate, or higher vocational level. However, in the long run this knowledge will not suffice as new standards emerge and existing standards are changed or withdrawn. So, once people really get involved in developing or applying standards in their professional life, they will need continuous education, for example, by means of a course offered by a national standards body.

The regional and national policies on standardization education and the educational settings differ widely, and, as a consequence, so does educational content. The policies and settings range from becoming a strong player on the international market (Korea) to preparing the country for EU membership (e.g., Turkey) and improving student chances for employment abroad (Sri Lanka, exporting people vs. products). That is, each country may have a different focus, and therefore a different view on what students need to prepare them for work.

Three types of interrelated learning objectives can be distinguished: attitude-, skill-, and knowledge-related objectives. According to Françoise Bousquet (ZFIB Conseil, Paris), there is a need both for knowledge (understanding the importance of standardization, knowing and understanding the process and the standards procedures) and know-how (how to behave, and how to lobby, represent, report, and collect information).

Knowledge-related learning objectives range from the strategic value of standards for industry (competitive intelligence), countries, and regions (trade facilitation) to the standardization strategies of countries and standards bodies (e.g., France, Japan, Korea, Sri Lanka). For example, one of the learning objectives of an MBA course in Sri Lanka is "to present the importance of standardization as a strategic tool and provide an understanding of different standardization strategies" (according to Professor Niranjan Gunawardena, University of Moratuwa, Sri lanka).

CONTENTS OF AN ACADEMIC CURRICULUM

Standardization courses differ in the topics they address (Bloomfield, 1999; de Vries, 2005; Hesser & Czaya, 1999; Zachariades, n.d.). Most curricula seem to be composed in a rather pragmatic way, strongly depending on the specific knowledge of the designer.

In one of the bigger projects on standardization education, the Asia Link Project (Hesser, Feilzer & de Vries (eds), 2007), the determination of the curriculum content also started off by using a pragmatic approach. Project participants proposed topics, which were grouped into 20 modules, and then checked with de Vries' (2005) more fundamental approach for omissions. Next, the project group defined which topics were to be addressed per module. The authors of the different modules had quite an amount of freedom in writing them. To fine-tune and extend the set of modules, a second edition of the project book has been prepared (Hesser, Feilzer & de Vries (ed, 2007).

In academic education on standardization, there is a choice between developing a separate course and integrating standardization in another course. The interdisciplinary character of standardization and the amount of relevant topics would seem to make a separate course worthwhile. Table 1 shows possible themes for such a course: themes identified in the ICES workshop 2007 (de Vries & Egyedi, 2007) and the curricula in Korea (KSA, 2007), the Catholic University of Washington (Purcell, 2006), and the Asia Link Project Standardization in Companies and Markets (Hesser, Feilzer & de Vries (eds), 2007) as indicated by chapter headings. This is no more than a tentative comparison for a theme in one course may encompass three themes in another course. So, having fewer themes mentioned does not mean that a course is less complete. Moreover, because circumstances differ per country, the contents need not be the same in each country.

AVAILABLE MATERIAL FOR ACADEMIC TEACHING

In any area of education, the availability of teaching materials is a prerequisite. For standardization, a fair amount of books (e.g., Için, 1994; KSA, 2007; Simons & de Vries, 2002), e-learning environments, digitally available lectures and Internet

Table 1. Elements of standardization curricula

Theme	Curriculum			
	Korea	Asia Link	Washington	ICES Work-shop
Importance and effects of standards	X	X	X	X
Definitions	X	X	X	X
Classification of standards	X	X	X	X
Functions of standards	X	X		X
History of standardization	X	X		X
Importance of international standards	X		X	
Organizations for international standardization	X	X	X	X
Processes of international standardization	X		X	X
Industrial standardization in Korea	X			
Measurement standards	X	X		
Company standardization and quality management	X	X		X
Application of company standards	X	X		X
Conformity assessment	X	X	X	X
Standards & IPR	X	X	X	X
Economic aspects of standardization		X		
Development of standards		X		
Standardization in product development and design		X		
Standardization within a company – a strategic perspective		X		X
External standardization as a company strategy		X	X	X
Standardization and innovation		X		X
Standardization and international law		X		X
The European standardization regulatory framework		X		
Standardization policy of the European Union		X		
Standardization and law in the Federal Republic of Germany		X		
The European Union and its New Approach		X		
Quality management and ISO 9001		X		
Implementation of the ISO 14000 environmental management system		X		
Agricultural standardization		X		
National standards policies			X	X
United States standardization system			X	
Consortia		X	X	
Regulatory perspectives (USA)			X	
International trade and standardization		X	X	X
International competition			X	
Health, safety and the environment			X	

continued on the following page

Table 1. continued

Antitrust, competition and trade regulation		X	
Value of standardization for different actors			X
Lifecycle of standards and technologies			X
Structure of standards documents			X
Standards and cultural diversity			X
Skills in standard setting			X

courses (e.g., Egyedi, 2007; Purcell, 2005), bibliographies (e.g., for Greek small and medium-sized enterprises and for U.S. engineering students), and other educational material exist. However, the vast majority is written in Chinese, Dutch, Japanese, Korean, Turkish, and so forth and is, as such, not easily accessible. Only a small proportion is available in English. One such exception is the Asia Link course book (Hesser, Feilzer & de Vries (eds), 2007) and the corresponding e-learning curriculum. The Internet curriculum, to which one can subscribe, consists of 22 learning modules. Like in the Korean courses, the Internet is not used only to offer course material. It is also a means to do exercises, to exchange information within groups and between teachers and students, and to store and retrieve documents. The e-learning curriculum includes a frequently-asked-questions section, a glossary, and examination questions (Hesser & Siedersleben, 2007).

There are, of course, also teaching materials with a more narrow focus (e.g., an Internet site about two standards in the batch processing industry, www.batchcentre. tudelft.nl), and books and Internet sites that do not specifically target education but may provide useful input for education. Examples are the books from Spivak and Brenner (2001), Blind (2005), and Jakobs (2001, 2006), and the COPRAS Web site www.copras.org (i.e., guidelines to facilitate interfacing between research projects and ICT standards organizations).

In many Western countries, it turns out to be difficult to attract students. This problem may be related to the educational material used. Standardization is not known for being "fun" and "sexy". Although, for example, case studies are very useful and essential to illustrate standardization issues (de Vries, 2006), and invited speakers, in particular, from industry, liven up courses (e.g., Korea and USA), overall teaching cases that involve role playing and helping students experience standardization are lacking. A notable exception is the one developed by the ISO for educating standardizers. The course takes as a starting point the interests of a company from the imaginary country Southistan and facilitates learning by doing. Courses like these, which aim at standardizers, would also seem useful for academic teaching (Gerundino, 2005; 2007), and the material developed for academic teaching may well be applicable in other educational settings.

The manner in which standardization education is offered (pedagogical means) is one thing. The context in which it is presented is another. Françoise Bousquet's positioning of standardization as an industry tool for competitive intelligence is a good example. This makes explicit that standardization is a means and not an end. Moreover, possibly the need for standardization can be more compellingly demonstrated if expressed as a derivative of and tool for a higher, strategic goal such as it being a tool for competitive intelligence, safe working conditions, effective production process, reduced health risks, and so forth.

Even given our bias toward material provided in English, the content of (Internet) courses and books showed much overlap. Only a limited number of subjects was not or not equally covered, such as the following.

- Different national and regional standardization education strategies (e.g., included in a U.S. course)
- The history of standardization (e.g., Vu, 2006)
- The impact of cultural diversity on standardization (addressed by a CEN focus group [Comité Européen de Normalisation, European Committee for Standardization])

Regarding these issues, more research is needed as an input for education. The need for more research also applies to the impact of standards, a subject that, despite recurrent efforts, remains difficult to argue and quantify. Better insight on this matter would very much ease getting standardization education on the political agenda of more countries.

CONCLUSION AND FUTURE DEVELOPMENTS

An enormous gap exists between manifest and latent needs for standardization education. Few policy makers notice the contribution of standards to industry and society. Company managers lack awareness of the strategic importance of standards for their company in terms of market share and the effectiveness of the organization. People who do the standards work, for example, experts who participate in standards committees, mostly do so without any education or training. They are not aware that findings in standardization research and training in professional skills could enhance their effectiveness considerably. The lesson to be learned from some of the Asian countries is that the gap can be bridged: first, by a strong national policy that may be part of a regional policy, and second, by cooperation between government,

industry, national standards bodies, academia, and other educational institutions.

A diversity of target groups can be identified, each with different educational needs. However, catering to the needs of these target groups need not start from scratch, as the experience gained in different countries and the educational material already developed show.

The increasing number of initiatives and activities of the last couple of years indicates that there is a momentum for education on standardization. The above stated lack of awareness suggests itself as a possible theme for ICES and other people and organizations interested in standardization education. That is, how can we make governments, industry, and universities aware of the strategic importance of standards and standards education? Or, focusing on educator problems, we can ask the following.

- How can students be drawn to courses about standardization?
- What pedagogical means can best be used to trigger their interest?
- In what manner can teachers secure institutional support for such courses?

REFERENCES

Acyl, A., & Borde, J. M. (2003). *Training and education for standardization in Europe – Volume 1 – Survey report*. Paris: Akela Business Engineering.

Amorim, C. S. (2008) Global perspectives and Strategies for Education about Standardization. Presentation at 3rd ICES Workshop, Gaithersburg, 2008-02-21—22, http://www.standards-education.org (last accessed 2008-11-09).

ASTM Standardization News. (2003). Standards education in the United States: A Roundtable. *ASTM Standardization News*, *31*(6), 41–47.

Blind, K. (2004). *The Economics of Standards – Theory, Evidence, Policy.* Cheltenham, UK / Northampton, MA, USA: Edward Elgar.

Bloomfield, R. S. (1999). SA perspective on advancing standards research and education – Building on the Telecommunications Scene. *ISO Bulletin, 30*(6), 17–20.

Borde, J.-M. (2004). *Training and education for standardization in Europe – Survey report.* In F., Bousquet et al. (Eds), *EURAS Proceedings 2004* (pp. 157-170). Aachener Beiträge zur Informatik Vol. 36. Aachen, Germany: Wissenschaftsverlag Mainz in Aachen.

Calzadilla-Sarmiento, B. (2005). Training services Supporting International Standards development. *ISO Focus, 2*(3), 16–19.

Cater-Steel, A., & Toleman, M. (2007). Education for IT Service Management Standards. *International Journal of IT Standards and Standardization Research, 5*(2), 27–41.

Center for Global Standards Analysis. (2004). *Report on a Survey of Schools of Engineering in the United States concerning Standards Education.* Washington, DC: The Catholic University of America.

Choi, D. (2008, Ed.). *APEC SCSC Education Guideline 1: Case Studies of How to Plan and Implement Standards Education Programs.* Singapore: APEC.

Choi, D. & de Vries, H.J. (2010). Standardization as Emerging Content in Technology Education at all Levels of Education. *International Journal of Technology and Design Education, 20*(?) (forthcoming).

Choi, D., de Vries, H. J., & Kim, D. (2009). Standards Education Policy Development: Observations based on APEC Research. *International Journal of IT Standards and Standardization Research, 7*(2), 43–63.

de Vries, H. J. (1999). *Standardization – A Business Approach to the Role of National Standardization Organizations.* Boston / Dordrecht / London: Kluwer Academic Publishers.

de Vries, H. J. (2005). *Standardization Education.* In M.J. Holler (Ed.), *EURAS Yearbook of Standardization, Vol. 5, Homo Oecomomicus, XXII* (1) (pp. 78-80). Munich: Accedo Verlagsgesellschaft.

de Vries, H. J. (2006). Competing E-Purse Systems: A Standards Battle. *Journal of Cases on Information Technology, 8*(1), 1–15.

de Vries, H. J., & Egyedi, T. M. (2007). Education about Standardization – Recent Findings. *International Journal of IT Standards and Standardization Research, 5*(2), 1–16.

Egyedi, T. M. (2007). *IEC Lecture Series: The importance of Standards.* Geneva: IEC (CD).

ISO Focus (2007). Education for all. Special issue. *ISO Focus, 4*(11).

ISO Focus (2010). Special issue on education. *ISO Focus, 7*(1).

Gerundino, D. (2005). Learning-by-doing: the ISO e-learning programme. *ISO Focus, 2*(3), 12–14.

Gerundino, D. (2007). ISO e-learning completed! – A convenient, practical and fun way to become a standardization expert. *ISO Focus, 4*(11), 39–43.

Hanson, D. (2005). *CE Marking, Product Standards and World Trade.* Cheltenham, UK / Northampton, MA, USA: Edward Elgar.

Hesser, W., & Czaya, A. (1999). Standardization as a subject of study in higher education – A vision. *ISO Bulletin, 30*(6), 6–12.

Hesser, W., Feilzer, A. J., & de Vries, H. J. (Eds.). (2007). *Standardisation in Companies and Markets* (2nd ed.) Hamburg: Helmut Schmidt University.

Hesser, W., & Siedersleben, W. (2008). Standardization goes East – The European-Asian academic network – International and multimedia-based. *ISO Focus*, *4*(11), 21–24.

Için, O. (1994). *Standardizasyon ve Kalite.* Istanbul: Türk Standardlari Enstitüsü.

Jakobs, K. (2001, Ed.). *IT Standards and Standardization: A Global Perspective.* Hershey, PA: Idea Group Publishing.

Jakobs, K. (2006, Ed.). *Advanced Topics in Information Technology Standards and Standardization Research, Vol. 1.* Hershey, PA: Idea Group Publishing.

Krechmer, K. (2007). Teaching Standards to Engineers. *International Journal of IT Standards and Standardization Research*, *5*(2), 17–26.

KSA. (2003). *International Workshop to develop a Standardization Education Model.* Seoul: KSA.

KSA. (2007). *Future Society and Standards.* Seoul: KSA (in Korean).

Kurokawa, T. (2005). Developing Human Resources for International Standards. *The Quarterly Review*, *5*(17), 34–47.

Marin, L. J. A. (2008) Global perspectives and Strategies for Education in Standardization. Paper presented at 3rd ICES Workshop, Gaithersburg, 2008-02-21—22, http://www.standards-education.org (last accessed 2008-11-09).

M&E Consultants. (2001). *Report on a survey of other NSBs Educational Activities.* East Barnet, Herfordshire, UK: M&E consultants.

Purcell, D. E. (2005). *IEC Lecture Series: International Standardization in Business, Industry, Society and Technology.* Geneva: IEC (CD).

Purcell, D. E. (2006). *Strategic Standardization Syllabus.* Washington, DC: Catholic University of America, School of Engineering.

Purcell D. E. & Kelly, W. E. (2003). Adding value to a standards education: lessons learned from a Strategic Standardization course. *ISO Bulletin*, 34-34. .

Reihlen, H. (1999). Is standardization a standard career? *ISO Bulletin*, *30*(6), 2.

Simons, C. A. J. (1999). Education in standardization – Getting structured common sense into our society – The personal opinion of a standards-educator. *ISO Bulletin*, *30*(6), 13–16.

Spivak, S. M., & Brenner, F. C. (2001). *Standardization Essentials – Principles and Practice.* New York / Basel: Marcel Dekker Inc.

Spivak, S. M., & Kelly, W. E. (2003). Introduce strategic standardization concepts during higher education studies… and reap the benefits! *ISO Bulletin*, *34*(7), 22–24.

Stern, J. (2003). Train the standardizers, or how to become step-by-step an expert in standardization. *ISO Bulletin*, *34*(7), 20–21.

Verman, L. C. (1973). *Standardization – A New Discipline.* Hamden, CT: Archon Books.

Vu, T. A. (2006). *An Introduction – The History of Standardization.* In W. Hesser, et al. *Standardization in Companies and Markets* (pp. 35-60). Hamburg: Helmut Schmidt University Hamburg.

Zachariades, A. (n.d.). *Protypation Digest – Contents' plan.* Thessaloniki, Greece: Union of Hellenic Scientists for Protypation and Standardization.

Chapter 11
How Engineers Learn about Standards

Ken Krechmer
University of Colorado, USA

ABSTRACT

This chapter focuses on the training needed by technical experts and explores the type of academic course-work as well as training that technical experts need in the field of standards and standardization.

INTRODUCTION

Standardization has been practiced for a long time. Until recently, the people who attended standardization meetings were skilled in the technical field associated with the standardization efforts. As the Internet has become more important to all of society, more people recognize the importance of standardization; some Internet standardization activities (e.g., ICANN) now attract significant non-technical participation. While standards impact many fields (e.g., law, economics, business, etc.), creating functional standards in every technical area still requires technical experts. This paper focuses on the training needed by technical experts and explores the type of academic coursework as well

as training that technical experts need in the field of standards and standardization.

Successful technical courses are quite different from successful non-technical courses. Lucky (2006) states that, "We engineers are used to building on the foundation of a relatively small set of rules - Maxwell's Laws are the proto-typical example - where everything can be reduced to the application of a few equations. This kind of ordered world fits very nicely into textbooks and test questions." Some existing standardization courses focus on technical students successfully (see below), but no existing standardization courses describe standardization using a relatively small set of rules where the use of such rules allows inference into future system behavior.

The current focus of standards and standardization education is on standardization, the process of

DOI: 10.4018/978-1-60566-946-5.ch011

creating, implementing or using a standard, usually with examples of different standardization processes. A "standard" describes a concept or realization based on common agreements. While learning about standardization is desirable, as it offers insight into the importance of standards in every technical and commercial field, this short paper argues that academic courses would be better to focus on teaching the relatively small set of rules that underlie standards and standardization and use specific standardization examples for demonstration that the rules function as proposed.

With the view that there are basic rules underlying it, the entire field of standards and standardization is a science and thus can be termed *isology* - the science of standards. The author argues that studying the science of standards is an academic endeavor while creating standards is a practiced skill.

REVIEWING STANDARDIZATION EDUCATION WORLDWIDE

A 2003 European survey on standardization education, Acyl (2003) states, "...the survey shows that very little effort is done in Europe related to standardization training and Education. It also shows that although standardization is above all an issue of business more than a technical issue, Business Schools are not in general involved in any curriculum or session in a curriculum on this matter. More important, it appears a general feeling of lack of understanding about the subject itself [sic]." Courses with some standardization focus identified in this survey include IT Security, Quality Engineering and Software Engineering.

In a report on the Standards Education in Korea - University education program, Kim (2006a) indicates that a common standardization course is given in 35 technical universities and has achieved an enrollment of 2,639 spring semester and 2,323 fall semester students (roughly 100 students per course in 2005) with a good satisfaction rating

from the students. Initially the courses suffered from low enrollment, but recommendations from previous students, some publicity and the course being required by the engineering schools increased enrollment (Kim, 2006b).

A course on strategic standardization was offered jointly by the School of Law and the School of Engineering at Catholic University Washington, DC from 1999 to 2001. In three years, 18 students attended. The course was then discontinued (Purcell, 2003).

In a US engineering school survey in 2004 (Center for Global Standards Analysis, 2004), the major findings were:

1. Standards education is not a priority issue among schools of engineering in the United States;
2. Schools of Engineering in the United States do yet not accept the critical nature of standards in the new 21st century global economy.

A survey of standards-related education in Japan conducted by Kurokawa (2005) of the Science and Technology Foresight Center, identified 28 different universities with current standardization courses. These courses are focused on technical students and include lecturers from local standardization organizations. The survey's author also indicates that the Chinese have a program of standardization education similar to the Koreans.

At two universities in the Netherlands which teach a standardization course, each course attracts between 10 and 30 students per year. The professor teaching the courses notes the difficulty in attracting students to a course in standardization (deVries, 2005, p. 80).

For further standardization course examples see the EU's European Commission (2006) catalogue of academic institutions involved in research and training related to standardization.

Reviewing these surveys in more detail suggests the following:

- The focus of most of these academic courses is on standardization in a specific functional area, industry or market segment.
- Academic standardization courses on specific standardization areas such as: metrology, IT security, safety standards, software engineering or quality have little in common.
- Even considering the academic courses, most standardization training is done by the hundreds of existing individual standardization organizations.
- The Korean courses success appears to be due to its focus on engineering students and inclusion in technical curriculums.

Throughout the course of history, the functions of standards have evolved. As the importance of measurement standards to increase trade became more obvious, measurement standardization became the task of governments. The expanding need for new standards as the industrial revolution developed, gave rise to commercial standardization. Both a governmental interest in standardization and a commercial interest in standardization are realistic. Many countries continue to view standardization as a governmental issue. The United States government tends to consider standardization a commercial issue as standardization is seen as a means to achieve commercial ends (Congress of the United States, 1990). This view is one reason for the limited academic interest in the field in the United States.

THE PROBLEMS WITH TEACHING ISOLOGY TODAY

The effects of standards are very broad and include expanded communications, increased quality and decreased cost (for the manufacturer, service provider and consumer), increased trade (local, regional and international), increased uniformity, new markets (innovation or location), information dispersion, market control and regulation. The widespread use of standards increases compatibility, interchangeability, interoperation and usability. In micro-economics literature, the impacts of standards have been identified as coordination, scaling and learning, network, and gateway effects. All these different effects may have significant ramifications on society. And these effects expand as technology becomes more critical to society. Trying to comprehend such a broad range of effects without an effective model of the causes is not realistic. This is one more reason for the low interest in the West in existing standardization courses.

The models and rules that apply to all standards and every standardization process are still developing. Recognizing that every standardization process can be seen as anticipatory, participatory or responsive relative to the appearance of products and services is recent and just beginning to be supported in the literature (Baskin, 1998). The idea that standards can be seen as a series of successions over recorded history with each succession having a different form of economic impact is new (Krechmer, 2000). Recognizing that the concept of a standard can be defined in mathematical terms is still contentious (Krechmer, 2005). Whether or not these specific theories are valid, the lack of widely accepted models and rules that offer insight into the field seriously diminishes the value of academic training in the discipline.

The lack of agreement on the models and rules underlying standards and standardization has many ramifications:

- Definitions of the terms standard and standardization are not agreed or rigorous.
- Reference standards, metrology standards, manufacturing standards, and Information and Communications Technology (ICT) standards are not linked together as a unified discipline.
- The relationship between economic theory and standards theory is not developed

sufficiently to allow the economic effect of a standard to be quantified.

- The necessity of a priori agreements, which may be standards, for any communications is not widely understood.
- There is no broadly accepted theory explaining the layered nature of standards (Verman, 1973).

The lack of such basic definitions, rules and models is a major reason that:

- There is no text book addressing the entire field, which introduces theory, develops rules and models, offers examples of how the theory applies and includes exercises for the student.
- Standards concepts are often not included in the other disciplines they strongly impact including: business, strategic management, engineering, science, micro-economics, patent law, history of technology, public policy and social sciences.
- There is no succinct understanding of the importance of standards and standardization in the general population.

Academic courses are needed to address the importance of standards, provide theory to allow analysis of the field as well as identify what students should be aware of in their field of interest.

Sometimes young engineers do not consider carefully enough the requirements, specified in public standards, for the functions they are designing. Training to consider applicable standards needs to take place within existing engineering courses, while an elective course, perhaps at a graduate level, would focus on teaching the general concepts that apply to both standards and standardization. Training within existing engineering courses would, as a byproduct, identify standardization as an important activity in each affected field. Then the student who has further

interest may be motivated to take additional courses that focus on isology. This view is supported by other researchers in the field. (deVries, 2005, p. 77-78).

Hayek (1973) notes that standardization may occur by accident, assumption, convention, committee or fiat. In the cases where standardization is a committee effort, the give and take of standardization under the procedures of a specific committee is a practical art learned by reviewing the committee's training materials or attending meetings. Many engineers, the author included, have learned the practice of standardization by going to specific standardization meetings and participating in the work.

Of course, an introduction to a specific process of standardization is desirable for new standardization participants. Many standardization organizations now make available materials to teach new participants how their specific standardization committees function. Considering how little overlap there is in policy and procedures between different standardization organizations, ISO and the ITU as example, it makes little sense to learn about the operation of a specific standardization organization before there is a desire to participate.

Teaching the practice of standardization is valuable only when applied to a specific standardization process. Practical training in specific fields of standardization may not be very useful to technical students as most engineers are well advanced in their careers before they become active in standardization work. All professional people desire to learn the rules that apply to their discipline. Without an understanding of the rules of isology, the student does not acquire the tools to analyze either the impact of different standards or how future standardization actions may impact their field of endeavor. For isology to offer serious training to technical students, rigorous rules and models are necessary.

BASICS OF STANDARDIZATION

Standardization is the selection part of a system which creates variations and makes selections - just like an evolutionary system. Evolutionary systems function to increase the likelihood of survival by minimizing risk, rather than reduce the total energy used. Different standards proposals are often combined into a final standard so that each proposal "survives," which is not always energy or operationally efficient. Currently engineers are trained to create efficient designs, not minimize risk. Minimizing risk requires a very different approach from creating efficient designs. Teaching engineers the need to balance these conflicting goals is an important task of isology education. Important enough that students are likely to recognize the need to learn it.

Balancing the multiple interests represented in a standardization committee requires consensus standardization. Each standardization participant must find their interest acceptably represented before they can agree to a new standard. In this light, the concept of the "best" standard does not really exist. Standardizing two or more ways to achieve the same result, while less energy efficient, may minimize both short and long term risk. Choosing how to balance multi-party interest and single standard efficiency is often the most difficult task in a standardization process.

An example of the need to balance efficiency and interest is a "standards war," when two different technical approaches to a standard vie to be defined in the standard. Standards wars usually occur when the different technical approaches represent value to different organizations or groups of organizations. The public does not care about who wins a standards war. The public only cares about receiving the product or service that a needed standard helps define (Shapiro, 1999).

A standards war pits two or more technical approaches against each other in competition to be included in an eventual standard. Usually a single standard is considered a goal to reduce

inefficiency and cost. However computers (e.g., in cell phones or PCs) are changeable and can therefore allow multiple choices. One example is support for both the Mozilla and Microsoft Internet Explorer browsers in a single personal computer. Where it is economically practical to support multiple implementations of the same function, when a standardization organization deadlocks over the technical approaches, the choice should be to include all the economically acceptable variations. Such a choice can offer a balance between efficiency and commercial interests.

Considering standardization as a tool in the service of society is the basis of the view that only sanctioned standardization bodies produce standards. Sanctioned standardization bodies are considered by some to operate for the good of society. Private or non-sanctioned standardization organizations are assumed to operate for private gain. This is too narrow a view. Even while respecting the public good, standardization often entails choices that favor some and reject others. Such choices are made in sanctioned standardization committees as well as private consortia, the only real difference is the procedures used to make the choices. Standardization, the process of creating, implementing or using a standard, may be a service to society, but it also creates winners and losers.

Successful standardization entails a recognition that the "best" may be what is politically possible rather than what is technically most efficient. In standardization the idea of "the politically possible" is fraught with negative connotations. It is more productive to understand "the politically possible" as the solution that provides the lowest risk to the largest number of participants.

TEACHING STANDARDS

Focusing on the rules and models underlying standards rather than the process of standardization will create more compelling academic courses that are more directly related to the interests of technical students. While isology is a cross-disciplinary science, the creation and implementation of standards is the practice of scientists, engineers and technicians. It is the use of standards that impacts aspects of other fields such as business, economics and law. Other academic fields which may study standardization include social sciences, the history of technology and public policy. Non-technical students should learn how the concepts underlying standards and standardization impact their field. Technical students should be introduced to the practice of standardization as part of their specific technical curriculum. Then academic courses on isology should be available for those who wish to study the field in more depth.

Some standardization courses are fragmented by attempts to address in a single course three real, but separate, needs:

1. Teaching a non-technical audience the importance of standards. Attendance demonstrates that teaching a non-technical audience the importance of standards is often unsuccessful. Non-technical students usually do not see a need to learn about standards. As technical students become increasingly interested in isology other students will recognize the value in understanding the discipline.
2. Teaching technical students what they need to know about standards in their field. This requires a technical course. Such courses currently seem to be the most successful. Serious technical students are often not interested in non-technical courses.
3. Teaching the policy and procedures of individual standardization committees. This is only valuable to people who are planning to attend specific standardization committees in the near future.

Teaching technical students about isology should occur in two phases. First, an introduction to the subject should be a part of existing technical

courses. A big gap in existing isology education is the paucity of discussion of the general field in secondary and undergraduate technical courses. Few physics courses address the importance of standards for mass, time and space to the understanding and use of all physical phenomena. Trade and technical courses often do not address the importance of specific standards in each trade or technology. Standards are perceived much like air, necessary but not noticed, in technical education today. It is in such trade and technical classes that a recognition of standards and their impact on modern society should be first presented. With such introductions to isology it is reasonable to expect an increased interest in higher level, specific courses on isology.

The second phase of isology teaching would be a separate technical course developing and explaining the rules and models that illuminate isology. One successful approach to teaching a technical discipline has been termed the Modeling Method which has the following objectives:

*   To engage students in understanding the physical world by constructing and using scientific models to describe, to explain, to predict and to control physical phenomena.
*   To provide students with basic conceptual tools for modeling physical objects and processes, especially mathematical, graphical and diagrammatic representations.
*   To familiarize students with a small set of basic models as the content core of physics.
*   To develop insight into the structure of scientific knowledge by examining how models fit into theories.
*   To show how scientific knowledge is validated by engaging students in evaluating scientific models through comparison with empirical data.
*   To develop skill in all aspects of modeling as the procedural core of scientific knowledge.[1]

Following the Modeling Method, the curriculum of an academic isology course would develop the basic model of standards (successions) correlated with mathematics, history and economics, the basic concepts (evolutionary processes) behind standardization, as well as examples of the practice of standardization to illuminate the theory. Analysis of the impact of standardization in a specific technical discipline should be included in the appropriate courses in that discipline.

If academic courses in the field are to be successful, they need to attract and provide useful training to scientists, engineers and technicians. This requires acceptance of and instruction in models describing standards concepts and standardization processes, as well as validation by experimental evidence.

VALUE TO THE STUDENTS OF ISOLOGY

The creation of standards worldwide has become a large, rapidly growing field employing more than a half million people at least part time.[2] Many of the most successful companies in the high technology markets control key standards relating to their markets. Controlling patents that apply to a successful standard in the market has become a means to demand very large payments. An example of such very large payments is the Research in Motion (producers of the Blackberry) royalty payment to NTP (a patent holding organization) of over $600 million. College students are often interested in entering a field with financial promise. Standards increasingly impact the market success of every technical product. At the intersection of business, law and every technology, isology is a promising new field.

Technical students who wish to focus on this new field may find direct employment with: research organizations developing new technologies which will require new standards, development organizations bringing new products and services

to market that need to implement existing or create new standards, production organizations which can benefit from their own standardized use of various products and services, government agencies that support the introduction or use of standardized products and services, or standardization organizations themselves.

Students with interest in a specific technical field will find that an involvement in standards and standardization brings opportunities for greater industry visibility and senior level technical positions. In addition, students from business, law, economics, social science, public policy and history of standards will find that studying isology offers new ideas, insights and direction in their field. The study of isology is a multi-disciplinary science. Multi-disciplinary fields provide some of the fastest growing employment opportunities.

THE FUTURE OF STANDARDS AND STANDARDIZATION EDUCATION

Current academic courses on standardization have not been as successful as desired. This may be improved by greater focus on the technical aspects of the discipline and greater integration of standards concepts in specific technical courses. Once accepted models and rules are available and verifiable, then a formal technical education in standards and standardization can develop and academic courses of interest to technical students can emerge.

Training current and future teachers and professors of technical courses to recognize the importance of standards to their students may take time. To accelerate the process, these teachers should be among the first students of each new isology class. Perhaps a web-based course on isology promoted to existing teachers of technical curriculum would be helpful.

Once the rules underlying isology are identified, the scientific nature of the field becomes clear. Now an area that has been seen mostly as an application, rightfully becomes a discipline of its own. This opens the discipline to new and much needed research as well as attracting students who find technical subjects interesting and challenging. The science of isology has much to teach us all.

REFERENCES

Acyl, A. & Border, J.M., (2003). *Training and education for standardization in Europe, Volume I, Survey report*, October 20, 2003.

Arthur, W. B. (1988). Self-Reinforcing Mechanisms in Economics. *The Economy as an Evolving Complex System* (pp. 9-31). SFI Studies in the Sciences of Complexity, Addison-Wesley Publishing Co.

Baskin, E., Krechmer, K., & Sherif, M. (1998). The six dimensions of standards: Contribution towards a theory of standardization. In L. A Lefebvre, R. M. Mason, & T. Khalil (Eds.), *Management of Technology, Sustainable Development and Eco-Efficiency* (pp. 53-62). Amsterdam et al: Elsevier.

Center for Global Standards Analysis. (2004). Report on a Survey of Schools of Engineering in the United States concerning Standards Education, March 2004, The Catholic University of America, Washington, DC.

Congress of the United States. (1990). Office of Technology Assessment, Critical Connections, US Government Printing Office. Darwin, C. (1895). *The Origin of the Species by means of natural selection*. D. Appleton and Co.

de Vries, H. J. (2002) Vries, Standardization – Mapping A Field Of Research. In S. Bolin (Ed.), *The Standards Edge* (pp. 99-121). Ann Arbor, MI: Bollin Communications.

deVries, H. J. (2005). Standardization Education. In M.J. Holler (Ed), *EURAS Yearbook of Standardization, Vol. 5, Homo Oecomomicus, XXII* (1) (pp. 78-80). Munich: Accedo Verlagsgesellschaft.

European Commission. (2006). *Website, Enterprise and Industry, Standardization*. Retrieved from http://ec.europa.eu/enterprise/standards_policy/academic_network/catalogue.htm#Universities #Universities

Hayek, F. A. (1973). *Law, Legislation and Liberty, Volume 1: Rules and Order.* London: Routledge & Kegan Paul.

Hesser, W., & Inklaar, A. (1998). *An Introduction to Standards and Standardization*, DIN Normungskunde Band 36 (p. 35). Berlin: Beuth Verlag GmbH.

Kim, D. (2006a). *Standards Education in Korea– University Education Program*. Presentation at The Future of Global Education in Standards conference in Tokyo, Japan, February 6, 2006.

Kim, D. (2006b). Private email to the author from D. Kim, researcher at KSA (Korean Standards Association) directly responsible for the "university standardization course," November 16, 2006.

Krechmer, K. (2000). *Standards Mark the Course of Economic Progress.* A revised version of a paper presented at the International J.A. Schumpeter Society Economics Conference, Manchester, England.

Krechmer, K. (2005). *The Mathematical Basis of Standards*. Presented at Standards and Innovation in Information Technology (SIIT), Geneva, Switzerland.

Kurokawa, T. (2005). Developing Human Resources for International Standards, Science and Technology Trends . *The Quarterly Review, 17,* 34–47.

Lucky, R.W. (2006, September). Unsystematic Engineering. *IEEE Spectrum.*

Purcell D. E. & Kelly, W. E. (2003, July). Adding value to a standards education: lessons learned from a Strategic Standardization course. *ISO Bulletin*, 34-34.

Shapiro, C., & Varian, H. R. (1999). Waging a Standards War. In *Information Rules* (pp. 261-296). Boston, MA: Harvard Business School Press.

ENDNOTES

[1]   http://modeling.asu.edu. The Modeling Theory of Physics Instruction approach to reforming curriculum design and teaching methodology is the focus of educational research by David Hestenes and collaborators since 1980. Implementation through Modeling Workshops for high school teachers has been supported by grants from the National Science Foundation from 1989 to 2005. The documented success of the workshops and the enthusiastic response of the teachers has stimulated institutionalization and expansion of the program through increased involvement of university physics departments.

[2]   The author makes this estimate based on 30 major standardization organizations worldwide with the largest having 30,000 participants. For example, the IEC has 10,000, the IEEE 20,000, VDE 33,000, and the ASTM 30,000 based on their current web site information. Estimating that an average sized, major standardization organization has 15,000 participants, then 30 x 15,000 ~ 500,000.

Chapter 12
IT Service Management Standards:
Education Challenges

Aileen P. Cater-Steel
School of Information Systems, Australia

Mark A. Toleman
School of Information Systems, Australia

ABSTRACT

Service management standards such as the IT infrastructure library (ITIL), and now ISO/IEC 20000, provide guidance and tools for effective management and control of IT service delivery. These standards are of increasing importance to organisations around the globe so education about these standards and possibilities for training of IT staff are important. In the main, academics and Universities have not embraced these standards in either research or education about them; however, demand for IT staff qualified to various levels in these standards grows. Universities have a place in this education process and there are significant benefits to them, the graduates and industry in terms of increases in student numbers, enhanced employment opportunities and improvement in service quality, but there are challenges also especially in relating problems in practice to students. Using results from two national surveys and several case studies, this chapter considers the requirements for education about these important standards.

INTRODUCTION

In recent years, a quiet revolution has occurred in IT service management. Over the last 20 years, the ITIL phenomenon has spread from the UK government data centres to the IT departments of private and public organisations around the world. With the evolution of ITIL from a 'company' standard

DOI: 10.4018/978-1-60566-946-5.ch012

to its ratification in December 2005 by the International Organisation for Standardization (ISO) as an international standard (ISO/IEC 20000), growth in its adoption has accelerated. As at January 2009, there are 318 organisations spread over almost 40 countries certified to the standard (itSMF, 2008).

IT service managers are responsible for an increasingly diverse and crucial infrastructure. They are under pressure to reduce costs while helping the organisation generate revenue, and to provide fast, cost effective service to their customers. Over the last few years, many organisations have adopted the IT infrastructure library (ITIL) to provide effective management and control of IT service delivery and support. The ITIL best practice framework enables managers to document, audit, and improve their IT service management processes.

An important feature of ITIL which has facilitated its acceptance is the internationally recognised certification of accredited ITIL training courses. Today, many consulting firms offer ITIL training in response to the demand for ITIL certified staff. Despite this sweeping adoption by industry, most academic institutions appear to be reluctant to include ITIL in their IT curriculum. Accompanying this is a general lack of interest by information systems researchers in ITIL adoption, as noted by Venkataraman and Conger: "The best practice processes and principles that are part of ITIL: Service Management, Service Delivery, Applications Management, etc. are very much in-line with the teaching objectives of MIS departments. Despite this, however, the level of understanding and interest of ITIL in academia, both on the research and teaching dimensions, significantly lags industry activity" (2006). There are exceptions, such as the research effort led by Cater-Steel (Cater-Steel, 2009; Cater-Steel & McBride, 2007; Cater-Steel & Pollard, 2008; Cater-Steel, Tan, & Toleman, 2006; Cater-Steel & Toleman, 2007a, 2007b, 2009; Cater-Steel, Toleman, & Tan, 2006; Iden, 2009; Praeg & Spath, 2009; Tan, Cater-Steel, Toleman, & Seaniger, 2007), Hochstein, Tamm and Brenner (2005), Niessink and van Vliet (1998), Potgieter, Botha and Lew (2005), Praeg and Schnabel (2006), Praeg & Spath (2009), and Iden (Iden, 2009), all of whom have undertaken empirical research into the ITIL phenomenon.

There have been recent attempts to raise general awareness of the need for education on standardization (Purcell, 2006). In particular, communities engaged in vocational training and university education are urged to recognise their

important role, alongside business and government, in ensuring that standardization is effective and practical. "Their specialized knowledge can form a vital contribution to standards development, while integrating the principles of standardization into the curricula allows students to carry them forward into the workplace: an investment in the future" (BSI Education, 2006).

Standardization and certification are two separate issues, but are often confused (Kruithof & Ryall, 1994). Many IT service departments adopt standards to improve service, consistency of performance, and productivity. These standards are sometimes developed in-house, or adapted from vendor, national or international standards. Standards adoption may be motivated by a corporate compliance or improvement program, or undertaken as a separate exercise within the IT department.

Depending on the standard, certification by a third party may apply to individuals, as is the case of ITIL qualifications, or apply to an organisational unit, for example subsequent to an ISO/IEC 20000 audit.

A recent survey of Human Resources (HR) managers and IT employees in the United States found strong evidence of the increasing acceptance, prevalence and benefits of certification of IT staff in business and industry (Wonacott, 2003). The US study focussed on certificates awarded by vendor organisations such as Microsoft and Cisco, as well as professional associations such as the Project Management Institute and the American Institute of Certified Public Accountants. The HR executives and IT employees reported that certificates related to IT education were of great benefit in the recruitment and job application process; both felt that an IT certificate was a clear signal of not only specific IT knowledge and skills, but also of desirable motivation and attitude (Wonacott, 2003).

The objective of this paper is to describe the evolution of ITIL from a company standard to international standard, and to consider the growing need for training and the possible role of universities in providing education to assist students gain certification related to IT service management. To meet this objective, two research questions are posed:

RQ1: Is there a demand for education related to IT service management standards?
RQ2: Should universities include IT service management standards such as ITIL in their curricula?

The paper is structured as follows. Firstly, the methodology used to gather evidence is described. Then a detailed explanation is provided of the ITIL framework, its origins, growth and certification. The evolution of ITIL to an international standard is explained. The role of universities in providing education related to IT service management, ITIL, and standardization is then discussed. In the final conclusions section, suggestions are made for further research.

METHODOLOGY

As well as reviewing recent literature on ITIL adoption and training, the authors have conducted four surveys and many case studies of ITIL adoption with IT service managers. The analysis is based on the data gained from these sources. The case studies used structured interviews based on an instrument developed by Hochstein et al. "to identify insights which can be logically followed and transferred to other organisations" (2005). Structured interviews were conducted with the managers of ITIL implementation projects in six large organisations between March and September 2006. The organisations were selected on the basis of their response to a survey which was conducted at the IT Service Management Forum (itSMF) Australian national conferences in 2005 and 2006. These six case studies complement the survey data and enable both a broad view of the

phenomenon as a whole and a richer, more detailed picture of a few organisations (Groves, Nickson, Reeve, Reeves, & Utting, 2000). The interviews were recorded and transcribed, checked by the researchers and confirmed by the interviewees as a valid record of the interviews. The completed survey forms provided background information prior to each interview and supplemented the interview data.

IT INFRASTRUCTURE LIBRARY (ITIL)

Origins of ITIL

In response to the serious economic downtown in the late 1980s, the Central Computer and Telecommunications Agency (CCTA) in the United Kingdom developed the Government Information Technology Infrastructure Management framework to reduce costs and better manage IT service delivery (Sallé, 2004). Since 2000, the ITIL framework has been administrated by the Office of Government Commerce (OGC), an independent office of the UK Treasury.

The core of ITIL version 2 as released in 2001 comprised five service support processes, one service support function and five service delivery processes. Service support processes apply to the operational level of the organisation and include the service desk function, incident management, problem management, configuration management, change management and release management. The service delivery processes are tactical in nature and comprise service level management, financial management, capacity management, IT service continuity management, and availability management (OGC, 2006).

The ITIL Refresh Programme Board released ITIL version 3 in 2007. The project produced five new core texts: Service Strategy; Service Design; Service Transition; Service Operations; and Continual Service Improvement (itSMF, 2007).

Table 1. Summary of key aspects of six case study organisations

Case	Organisation Type	# of screens supported	ITIL start date	Initial process implemented	Subsequent processes
A	Government Dept	600+	Mid 2002	Incident, problem, change mgmt	Service level, configuration, availability mgmt
B	University	5,000	Early 2003	Change mgmt	Service desk, problem, configuration mgmt
C	Government Dept	12,500	2001	Financial, service level, change, configuration mgmt	Incident, problem mgmt
D	Government Dept	35,000	Mid 2001	Change mgmt	Release, incident, problem mgmt
E	University	11,000	2003	Incident mgmt	Problem, change mgmt
F	International Finance Co	70,000	2003	Incident, problem, change mgmt	BS 15000 ISO/IEC 20000

Adoption of ITIL

ITIL has a strong following in Europe, especially in the government sector, and adoption is growing in North America and other countries (Barton, 2004). Recent surveys and case studies have reported an upsurge in awareness and adoption of ITIL (Axios Systems, 2008; Casson, 2005; Hochstein et al., 2005; Nerney, 2003; Niessink & van Vliet, 1998; Schuller & Wheeler, 2006; Thibodeau, 2007; Violino, 2005). A recent survey of 255 IT professionals in the UK, America and Australia revealed that an overwhelming majority of organisations (87%) now follow the ITIL guidelines with one in three organisations intending to adopt ITIL within a year, and another third (36%) considering it (Axios Systems, 2008). Axios believes that this increase in adoption is due to the launch of ITIL V3 and recognition of the value it brings to the business. Australia is at the forefront of ITIL adoption, possibly due to the strong links between Australia and the UK: "ITIL in Australia has seen rapid adoption through consultancy and education programs since the mid 1990's" (ITIL Survival). Although de Vries' research (2006) suggests multinational companies would be more likely to adopt standards from other countries, the surveys conducted at the itSMF Australian conference did not support this suggestion. Strong adoption of the UK-based ITIL framework was reported by Australian-based private and public sector organisations; it did not appear that multinational companies are more likely to adopt the framework (Cater-Steel & Tan, 2005).

In this section, the salient points from the interviews of the six organisations are presented and illustrated with quotations from the managers interviewed. Due to the commercial sensitivity of the information and comments, the actual names of the organisations cannot be disclosed. The six cases are referred to as Case A to F with the interviewees referred to as Manager A to F and the corresponding organisations as Organisation A to F. The key aspects of the six cases are summarised in Table 1.

The cases investigated provide strong evidence that ITIL enables standardization of IT service management processes and terminology across organisations, and that such standardization is vital to ensure a consistent and reliable level of service:

We had built our practices and processes formally on the 9000 series of standards and we could see that the ITIL framework was much more aligned with an IT service management business. So when we started, it was clear to see that there would be an evolving standard around IT service manage-

ment that we would be able to adopt. [We wanted] really to align ourselves with an industry reference framework or an industry reference model that made more sense to us than trying to adopt an esoteric principle within 9001. (Manager A)

[Previously] they didn't define processes. They had little islands of expertise and islands of practice with very little connections, or standardization across them ... ITIL is something that they could use as a framework to standardise some of their processes, and keep in mind, many of these processes did exist already, we just may have used different terms, different names, different labels, and they may be at different levels of maturity. (Manager B)

[Previously] you had maverick and cowboy practices whereby every so often somebody would run off and do something and the whole thing would come crashing down and nobody would know who had done what. (Manager C)

We had these feral groups doing their own thing, and we had ourselves doing our own thing, and we had IT operations. We didn't have anything related to really best practices. There were good people and I think people were doing best practices as they knew, but in terms of process, no. There was no formal process in place. (Manager D)

Standardization makes us more efficient and using common language, you get benefits out of using the same tools ... Our ways of dealing with issues and our ways of responding to critical and non-critical things is the same all across the university - a standard process for service. (Manager E)

The director of service delivery ultimately made the decision 'we're going to use ITIL because it's an industry standard'. (Manager F)

A future research area identified by de Vries is the role of company standards in cases of out-

sourcing IT activities (2006, p. 80). Two managers interviewed mentioned contrasting views in relation to outsourcing, firstly that outsourcing could be facilitated by adoption of standards:

There's a big push for outsourcing that sort of stuff, and it was recognised that we really couldn't outsource because we didn't really know what everybody did. Well, you could get someone else to do it but you'd be charged an arm and a leg for it because you'd have to go out and say well, look after our computing, and you'd get charged like a wounded bull. So what they needed to do actually in fact was streamline some services, and supply quality services before you could even think about doing that. So they needed to get quality in there. (Manager C)

In the old days where business units were told 'you will go to Group IT for your IT needs', we could see a time coming where they wouldn't have to do that. It hadn't actually happened, but we could see that time coming, so the Director of Service Delivery at the time said 'well what we need to do is get ourselves in a position where we are truly competitive so that ideally they won't even go looking because they'll know we're the best', and to him the way of doing that was that we have to improve. We have to show we're improving, but getting an industry recognised qualification would be a really good way of doing that and that's what kicked off our BS 15000 challenge ... To become the supplier of choice for internal customers. Rather than they having to come to us because that's the way it's done, we want them to choose to come to us. (Manager F)

From our interviews, it is clear that many organisations followed the standardization sequence described by de Vries and reproduced here as figure 1 (2003). All organisations relied heavily on the ITIL books and tailored the processes to suit their unique environments. In all cases managers required senior management commitment and

Figure 1. Processes in company standardization (de Vries, 2003, p. 28)

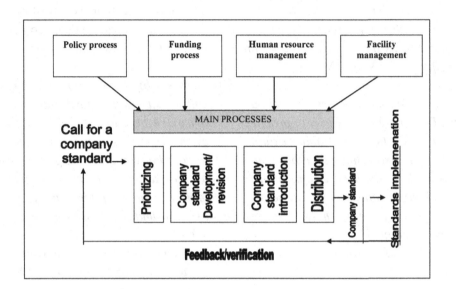

support to change policies and to secure funding for training and tools. Effort was required to manage workloads of staff involved and to procure and implement new facilities (hardware and software) to log calls and record assets and configurations.

ITIL Certification Education

Training is available from many accredited training providers such as Hewlett Packard, Pink Elephant, Lucid, TOAS, Mercury, and BMC Software. Professional qualifications based on the philosophy and content of ITIL are currently offered by six international examinations' institutes licensed by APMG to conduct certification examinations (APM Group, 2007):

- APMG specialise in the accreditation and certification of organisations, processes and people. APMG are an ITIL Examination Institute, who offer global accreditation and examination services for training providers.
- The Information Systems Examination Board (BCS-ISEB) is a wholly owned

subsidiary of the British Computer Society.
- With more than 6,000 members DANSK IT is a leading interest organization for IT-professionals in Denmark.
- DF Certifiering AB (DFC), is a wholly owned subsidiary to Dataföreningen i Sverige, the Swedish Computer Society with 26 000 IT-professionals as members in Sweden. DFC's role is to give accreditation to training providers and certify IT.
- The Examination Institute for Information Science in the Netherlands (EXIN) is a global, independent IT examination provider. EXIN establishes educational requirements and develops and organises examinations and learning tracks in the field of IT.
- Loyalist Certification Services (LCS) is a premier deliverer of ITIL certification exams in North America.

Since the release of version 3, the structure and content of the ITIL training courses have been revised. As illustrated in Table 2, there are three levels of professional qualifications available in

Table 2. ITIL Version 3 certification course structure (APMG-UK)

ITIL Advanced Qualification	
ITIL Expert Certification	
Managing across the Lifecycle	
Capability Stream (4 credits each) Planning, protection & optimisation Service offerings & agreements Release, control & validation Operational support & analysis	Lifecycle Stream (3 credits each) Service strategy Service design Service transition Service operations Continual service improvement
V3 Foundation (or upgrade from V2)	

ITIL-based IT service management with a fourth level proposed.

These qualifications enable organisations to identify the competence of individuals:

- The ITIL Foundation certificate is an entry-level qualification gained by successfully completing a one-hour multiple-choice exam. The exam focuses on foundation knowledge with regard to the ITIL terminology, structure and basic concepts and has comprehended the core principles of ITIL practices for Service Management.
- The ITIL Intermediate certificate refers to the courses on service lifecycle, service capability and managing across the lifecycle.
- The ITIL Expert certificate can be awarded to a candidate who has accumulated at least 22 credits.
- In the future, the ITIL Master certificate will be awarded to candidates who satisfy the advanced level requirements (details have not yet been announced).

In addition to the ITIL version 3 certificates, some of the Examination Institutes offer examinations for individuals based on ISO/IEC 20000 – the IT Service Management international standard.

Adoption of ITIL Certification

In 2005, it was claimed that EXIN International, the leading examination institute for ITIL training, had administered approximately 170,000 certificates to individuals (Computer Economics, 2005). Furthermore, in "the US alone, there are more than 200,000 IT staff who have gained ITIL certification, with the number doubling each year" (Evergreen, 2006).

To examine the demand for ITIL certification from employers, in January 2009, the authors queried the 9,983 IT&T jobs on Seek 'Australia's #1 Job Site' and found 413 Australian jobs requesting ITIL skills posted within the last 30 days. These positions were in the areas of Help Desk/Support, project management, business analysis, software engineering, networking, and training (Seek Ltd, 2009). This is a marked increase since May 2004 when Seek listed only 25 jobs asking for ITIL skills (Wilson, 2004). Although the number of IT&T jobs on the Australian Seek site has halved since June 2008, the proportion of advertisements mentioning ITIL has doubled. These statistics confirm reports in industry press that certification has become a 'recruiting filter' in Australia as well as in Europe (Schuller & Wheeler, 2006; Wilson, 2004).

One manager interviewed reported that ITIL skills have been included in the position descriptions (PDs) and are required of IT contractors:

I guess because we were redefining the PDs on an ongoing basis back in 2002 anyway as we were bringing staff on, and we were including ITIL as part of that. Almost all the PDs, certainly in my group all PDs go out with ITIL in them. When I go out for contractors they have to understand that these are processes we use and they have to have ITIL in them as part of the requirement. (Manager D)

But the manager at Organisation F did not agree with this approach, stating he is prepared to fund ITIL Foundations training for new recruits:

No, what we do is we put [ITIL Foundations] on as part of the induction. When you have new people come in, part of their standard training service to staff will be a one day ITIL overview. We encourage people to do the Foundation certificate but don't insist on it. (Manager F)

Therefore, based on reports in industry press and comments from the managers interviewed, it appears in answer to research question one (RQ1) that there is growing demand for education in IT service management.

IT SERVICE MANAGEMENT INTERNATIONAL STANDARD

In the 1990s, ITIL gained the support of the British Standards Institute and was extended and adopted as BS 15000 (Code of Practice for IT Service Management) in 1995. The 2nd edition of BS 15000, incorporating certification, was launched in June 2003. Australia followed this lead in July 2004 releasing AS 8018 ICT service management, based on BS 15000. The development of an international standard based on BS 15000 was fast tracked by the ISO/IEC joint technical committee one (JTC1) sub-committee seven (SC7). JTC1/SC7 is responsible for the elaboration of Information Technology standards. In December 2005, ISO member countries agreed to adopt ISO/IEC 20000 based on BS 15000.

The IT Service Management standard comprises two parts:

- part 1: specification. Promotes the adoption of an integrated process approach to effectively deliver managed services to meet the business and customer requirements (ISO/IEC, 2005a);
- part 2: code of practice. Provides guidance and recommendations based on industry consensus to service providers planning service improvements and/or seeking to be audited against ISO/IEC 20000-1:2005, and to auditors (ISO/IEC, 2005b).

ISO/IEC 20000 integrates the process-based approach of ISO's quality management system (ISO 9001:2000) by including the plan, do, check, act (PDCA) cycle and requirement for continual improvement. Part 1 of the standard contains ten sections: 1 scope; 2 terms and definitions; 3 requirements for a management system; 4 planning and implementing service management; 5 planning and implementing new or changed services; 6 service delivery process; 7 relationship processes; 8 resolution processes; 9 control processes, and 10 release process. Figure 2 shows the main components as described in sections 6 to 10.

Part 2 of the standard provides guidance to auditors and offers assistance to organizations that are to be audited against ISO/IEC 20000 or are planning service improvements (ISO/IEC, 2005b).

The Process of Achieving Certification to ISO/IEC 20000

To achieve ISO/IEC 20000 certification, companies must successfully undergo a third-party audit by an accredited conformity assessment body (CAB). The terms accreditation and certification have specific meanings in relation to international

Figure 2. Components of ISO/IEC 20000 (ISO/IEC, 2005a, p. 1)

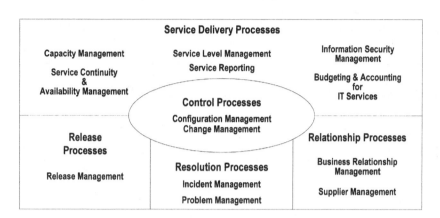

standards, and are in fact defined in EN ISO/IEC 17000 (Conformity assessment - Vocabulary and general principles). Accreditation: third-party attestation related to a conformity assessment body conveying formal demonstration of its competence to carry out specific conformity assessment tasks. Certification: third-party attestation related to products, processes, systems or persons (ISO/IEC, 2004).

A successful compliance audit is the culmination of months of planning, training, documentation and review. The qualified auditor seeks objective evidence (records, documents, etc.) to confirm that the activities of the organisation are in accordance with the documentation and the requirements of the relevant standard. The process to attain ISO/IEC 20000 certification varies depending on the size of the organisation, the breadth of its operation and the prior/existing level of standardization and documentation.

For example, Organisation F was able to gain ISO/IEC 20000 in a very short time frame on account of recently achieving BS 15000:

First of all I had to tell the auditor what you need to audit because he was new to it. I bought a book that told us what we had to prepare, and I went through it, and the auditor's list was different to mine. So we had to do it again, and my list was longer. There are 16 things that are different. They say there are 430 but most of them are wording changes – there are 16 fundamental changes you have to make where a process is changed to a procedure, or a procedure is changed to process, or some reports that you now must produce, whereas previously it said 'typically you will produce these'. I had a folder for 16 things (the evidence), so it's nowhere near as difficult to go from BS 15000 to ISO 20000 as it was to get BS 15000 in the first place, but you still have to be on your toes and make sure you have all the evidence. (Manager F)

An organisation seeking certification needs to select a conformity assessment body (CAB) to perform the audits. CABs in Australia and New Zealand are registered by JAS-ANZ (Joint Accreditation Scheme - Australia and New Zealand) to perform audits and grant certificates. On its web site, JAS-ANZ provides a list of all CABs it has accredited, and also a list of organisations certified to various standards by these CABs.

Other countries have similar bodies to JAS-ANZ, for example the United Kingdom Accreditation Service (UKAS). In the US, accreditation programs for management systems certification bodies are operated by the ANSI-ASQ National Accreditation Board; auditor certification and

Table 3. Summary comparison of ITIL and ISO/IEC 20000

	ITIL	ISO/IEC 20000
Origin	Late 1980s by Central Computer and Telecommunications Agency (CCTA)	Fast-tracked from BS 15000 2004, adopted Dec 2005
Evolution	ITIL V2 2001 ITIL V3 2007	BS 15000 was based on ITIL v2. Continuing by JTC1/SC7
Owner	OGC	ISO/IEC
Structure	5 core books: Service Strategy; Service Design; Service Transition; Service Operations; and Continual Service Improvement.	Part 1.Specification Part 2.Code of Practice
Certification	Individual, exams by examination institutes as approved by APMG	Organisations can be certified by a conformity assessment body

auditor training provider programs are operated by RABQSA International.

It is clear from the discussion above as summarised in Table 3 that there is a critical difference between ITIL certification and certification to ISO/IEC 20000: ITIL certification is awarded to individuals after successfully completing assessment from an examination institute, whereas ISO/IEC 20000 certification results from an audit of an organisational unit.

Although it is not known how many organisations have adopted ITIL, it is possible to analyse adoption of ISO/IEC 20000. As shown in Table 4, in January 2009, Japan with 48 organisations currently led the world in terms certification to ISO/IEC 20000 or BS 15000, closely followed by the UK (46) and India (38), then South Korea (35), and China (31) (itSMF, 2008). Germany (17), Taiwan (14), Switzerland and USA (both 12) also show high levels of adoption. There are a further 30 countries each with less than 10 certified organisations (itSMF, 2008).

To provide a graphic representation of the global adoption of ISO/IEC 20000, Figure 3 is provided.

Due to the conformance between ITIL and ISO/IEC 20000, ITIL certification will continue to be popular as an industry qualification for IT service management staff.

ROLE OF UNIVERSITIES

IT Service Management Education

The competition between traditional education providers and the increasing number of private sector companies which provide education and training, assessment of competencies and provision of credentials has received attention of community colleges in the US recently (Flynn, 2001). Stein et al. (2005) raise the concern that industry certification programs are perceived as *training* and are therefore not *educative*. Kurtus (1999) discriminates between the two based on the location of the training: "*Education* concerns remembering facts and understanding concepts. It is usually taught in school, although self-study is possible. *Training* concerns gaining skills and is taught either in trade schools or business training sessions". Further clarification from Tovey and Lawlor (2004) focus on the timing of the training: "Training is concerned with the development of knowledge and skills to be used immediately, or in the very near future, and deals with developing people who already have, or who are just about to enter, a job" (p. 24).

The distinction is further blurred by the practice of many professional bodies accrediting University programs to ensure graduates have the required skills to be admitted as members of a professional society. For example, the Austra-

Table 4. List of countries and number of organisations certified to ISO/IEC 20000 or BS 15000 (itSMF, 2008)

Country	Number of Certified Organisations
'Undisclosed'	2
Australia	3
Austria	5
Botswana	1
Brazil	2
China	31
Colombia	1
Czech Republic	6
Denmark	2
Finland	1
France	3
Germany	17
Hong Kong	7
India	38
Ireland	2
Italy	1
Japan	48
Kuwait	1
Latvia	1
Liechtenstein	1
Malaysia	2
Netherlands	3
Philippines	2
Poland	4
Qatar	1
Russia	1
Saudi Arabia	2
Singapore	1
Slovakia	1
South Korea	35
Spain	3
Sri Lanka	1
Switzerland	12
Taiwan	14
Thailand	3
Turkey	1
UK	46
United Arab Emirates	1
USA	12
TOTAL	318

Figure 3. ISO/IEC 20000 and BS15000 Certificates by Country

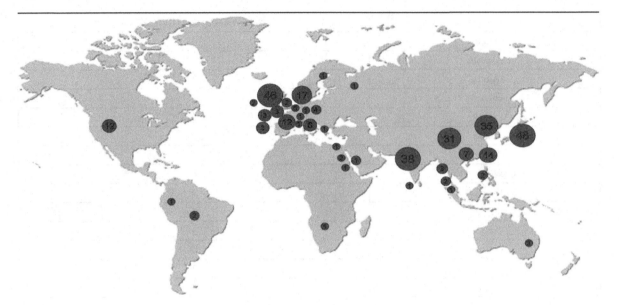

lian Computer Society considers the course and curriculum content, academic leadership and staff qualifications, and resources provided for students when accrediting courses as prerequisites for membership for graduates.

Although there are myriad accredited commercial providers offering ITIL training courses, after consulting colleagues and searching the internet, the authors found few universities are teaching ITIL, the exceptions include University of Southern Queensland (Rossi, 2006), Charles Sturt University (Rossi, 2008), University of Dallas Graduate School of Management (Thibodeau, 2007), Florida Atlantic University, Appalachian State University, University of Bergen in Norway (Iden, 2006), Tecnológico de Monterrey in Mexico, Victoria University in Australia (Jovanovic, Bentley, Stein, & Nikakis, 2006). In 2008, seven students at the University of Southern Queensland achieved the IT Service Management Foundation Certificate based on ISO/IEC 20000.

The analysis of a survey conducted in conjunction with itSMF USA revealed there is demand for graduates of IT programs who are knowledgeable about IT service management practices with at least 15,000 jobs per year in the U.S. (Conger, Venkataraman, Hernandez, & Probst, 2009). For any university prepared to provide ITIL Foundation training, there are many benefits possible. As well as the promise of an increase in the number of student enrolments and subsequent income, the reputation of the university could be enhanced as it would be seen as providing internationally recognised qualifications in response to demands from the business community. To ease the education path of students, the possibility would exist for recognition of prior learning by offering course credit to students who have achieved the ITIL Foundation certificate. Furthermore, as demonstrated by the research partnership between the University of Southern Queensland and itSMF Australia, opportunities for research would be encouraged and enhanced between the university and local business community (Rossi, 2006). These benefits support a positive response to the second research question (RQ2) posed in this paper: universities should provide education in relation to IT service management.

However, there are challenges to universities that consider including education on IT service management in their academic curricula:

- the authors have not been able to identify a suitable text book and teaching materials for a IT service management course.
- currently, there are few information systems (IS) academics with expertise in IT service management. IS academics would need funding to attend training courses.
- as discussed earlier, the continual upgrading of standards such as ITIL and ISO/IEC 20000 make it difficult to keep the course materials and academic skills up to date. The "cumbersome course curriculum approval systems" mentioned by Flynn (2001, p. 5) in relation to community colleges are also problematic for universities.
- the cost of the ITIL Foundation exam (currently US$150) would probably not be borne by the university and may be prohibitive for students, however it would be an career advantage for graduates to have covered the concepts.

Although this might appear to be a daunting list of challenges, some academic IS departments have overcome similar obstacles in providing courses related to other standards such as ISO/IEC 17799 (IT Security techniques - Code of practice for information security management) and facilitate certification to SAP and Microsoft qualifications. Many universities teach the Project Management Body of Knowledge (PMBOK) in IT Project Management courses. In this case students are given the option of taking the Project Management Institute exam for the certified Project Manager Professional (PMP) qualification.

Role of Universities in Standardization Education

With the increasing emphasis on governance and compliance since the Enron and other corporate scandals, many organisations are adopting industry-based standards. For example, in Australia, financial institutions must comply with many regulations (UCCC, FSRA, APRA); and hospitals apply for accreditation from the Australian Council on Healthcare Standards. Any company listed on the New York Stock Exchange must comply with the requirements of US Sarbannes-Oxley legislation. To improve their IT governance, many IT departments are adopting CobiT (Control objectives for information and related Technologies). However, regardless of whether the standard is focussed on the entire organisation or the IT department, all efforts to comply with standards involve IT staff, since records need to be kept and business processes changed for compliance.

The itSMF survey recently conducted by Cater-Steel et al. (2006) found that many firms are adopting multiple standards such as ITIL, CobiT, ISO 9000 and CMMI. The complexity associated with standards adoption raises the question: where do managers learn how to implement standards? Although aspects of human resource management, organisational behaviour and project management are included in both undergraduate and postgraduate offerings, there is an obvious need for universities to provide education in standardization, as well as in specific standards.

The need for education in the standardization process is recognised in the ITIL Service Manager course which prepares managers to plan and manage the introduction of the ITIL standard by addressing vital aspects such as communication, awareness, budget, executive commitment and involvement as well as process design, deployment and tool alignment.

CONCLUSION

In summary, the ITIL phenomenon has radically changed the discipline of IT service management. There is growing demand for IT staff to understand ITIL concepts and processes. With recognition of ITIL as the basis for the international standard for IT service management, it is important for universities to include ITIL concepts in programs to ensure graduates are prepared for the workplace. Furthermore, universities are urged to provide courses generally related to the development and implementation of standards in organisations.

This research has provided a comprehensive account of the content and evolution of ITIL from company framework to international standard. The structure of ITIL certification education is described, with accounts of increasing demand for ITIL certified staff confirmed by industry research.

Currently, it is impossible to determine how many organisations have adopted ITIL: the training certificates issued are the only measure of adoption at this time. On the other hand, all ISO/IEC 20000 certifications are recorded on a national basis. Future research will continue to analyse certification records to perform an international comparison of the up-take rate of the new standard.

Another area of research currently being undertaken by the authors concerns the need to provide validated evidence of the return on investment from adoption of ITIL. The relationship between best practice and cost reduction has been identified by de Vries as worthy of further research effort (2006, p. 79).

REFERENCES

APM Group. (2007). ITIL: Examination Institutes. Retrieved October 24, 2008, from http://www.itil-officialsite.com/ExaminationInstitutes/ExamInstitutes.asp

APMG-UK. APMG-UK's ITIL V3 Qualifications. Retrieved January 14, 2009, from http://www.apmgroup.co.uk/ITIL/ITILV3Qualifications.asp

Axios Systems. (2008). ITIL adoption surges despite confusion, says Axios survey. Retrieved January 14, 2009, from http://www.axiossystems.com/six/en/corporate/news/detail.php/211

Barton, N. (2004, July 8). This year's model: performance improvement complements IT best practices frameworks. *CIO, 2005*.

BSI Education. (2006). Standards and Education: Foundations for the Future. Retrieved September 6, 2006, from http://www.bsieducation.org/Education/HE/default.shtml

Casson, D. (2005). North American ITIL Assessment: an in-depth analysis of the current state and readiness of IT organisations to adopt ITIL-based processes [Electronic Version]. Retrieved August, from http://www.evergreensys.com/news_events/itilsurvey/PDF/2005NorthAmericanITILAssessment.pdf

Cater-Steel, A. P. (2009). IT Service Departments Struggle to Adopt a Service-Oriented Philosophy . *International Journal of Information Systems in the Service Sector, 1*(2).

Cater-Steel, A. P., & McBride, N. (2007). *IT Service Management Improvement – an Actor Network Perspective*. Paper presented at the European Conference on Information Systems.

Cater-Steel, A. P., & Pollard, C. (2008). *Conflicting views on ITIL implementation: managed as a project – or business as usual?* Paper presented at the International Conference on Information Resources Management (Conf-IRM).

Cater-Steel, A. P., & Tan, W.-G. (2005). *Implementation of IT Infrastructure Library (ITIL) in Australia: Progress and Success Factors*. Paper presented at the IT Governance International Conference.

Cater-Steel, A. P., Tan, W.-G., & Toleman, M. A. (2006). *Challenge of adopting multiple process improvement frameworks.* Paper presented at the European Conference on Information Systems, Goteborg, Sweden.

Cater-Steel, A. P., & Toleman, M. (2007a). Education for IT Service Management. *International Journal of IT Standards and Standardization Research, 5*(2), 27–42.

Cater-Steel, A. P., & Toleman, M. (2007b, 3-6 July). *The role of Universities in IT service management education.* Paper presented at the 11th Pacific Asia Conference on Information Systems, Auckland.

Cater-Steel, A. P., & Toleman, M. (2009). Education for IT Service Management Standards. In G. Kelley (Ed.), *Selected readings in information technology management: contemporary issues.* Hershey, PA: IGI Global.

Cater-Steel, A. P., Toleman, M., & Tan, W. (2006). *Transforming IT service management - the ITIL impact.* Paper presented at the 17th Australasian Conference on Information Systems.

Conger, S., Venkataraman, N., Hernandez, A., & Probst, J. (2009). (forthcoming). Market Potential for ITSM Graduates: A Survey. *ISM.*

de Vries, H. (2003). Learning by example- a possible curriculum model for standardization education. *ISO Bulletin, July,* 25-29.

de Vries, H. (2006). Best Practice in Company Standardization. *Journal of IT Standards & Standardization Research, 4*(1), 62–85.

Evergreen. (2006). Developing the Business Case for ITIL. Retrieved 16 Sept, 2006, from http://www.evergreensys.com/whitepapers_tools/whitepapers/BusinessValueITIL.pdf

Flynn, W. J. (2001). More than a matter of degree – credentialing, certification and community colleges [Electronic Version], 16, from http://www.nccet.org/associations/2158/NCCETcertification.pdf

Groves, L., Nickson, R., Reeve, G., Reeves, S., & Utting, M. (2000). A survey of software development practices in the New Zealand software industry. In *Proceedings of Australian Software Engineering Conference* (pp. 189-201). Canberra.

Hochstein, A., Tamm, G., & Brenner, W. (2005). *Service-Oriented IT Management: Benefit, Cost and Success Factors.* Paper presented at the 15th European Conference on Information Systems.

Iden, J. (2006). INFO317: IT Service Management. Retrieved September 25, 2006, from http://ugle.svf.uib.no/ifim/?kategori=716&strid=4539

Iden, J. (2009). Implementing IT Service Management: Lessons Learned from a University IT Department. In A. Cater-Steel (Ed.), *Information Technology Governance and Service Management: Frameworks and Adaptations* (pp. 333-349). Hershey, PA: Information Science Reference.

ISO/IEC. (2004). ISO/IEC 17000:2004 Conformity assessment - Vocabulary and general principles [Electronic Version].

ISO/IEC. (2005a). ISO/IEC 20000:2005 Information technology - Service management - Part 1: Specification [Electronic Version].

ISO/IEC. (2005b). ISO/IEC 20000:2005 Information technology - Service management - Part 2: Code of practice [Electronic Version].

ITIL Australia. *ITIL survival.* Retrieved 05 June 2006, 2006, from http://www.itilsurvival.com/ITILAustralia.html

itSMF. (2007). An Introductory Overview of ITIL V3 [Electronic Version]., itSMF. (2008). Certified Organisations. Retrieved 14 January, 2009, from http://www.isoiec20000certification.com/lookuplist.asp?Type=9

Jovanovic, R., Bentley, J., Stein, A., & Nikakis, C. (2006). Implementing Industry Certification in an IS curriculum: An Australian Experience. *Information Systems Education Journal, 4*(59), 3–8.

Kruithof, J., & Ryall, J. (1994). *The Quality Standards Handbook*. Melbourne: Information Australia.

Kurtus, R. (1999). The difference between education and training [Electronic Version]. Retrieved September 25 2006, from http://www.school-for-champions.com/training/difference.htm

Nerney, C. (2003). Survey: ITSM Needs to Pick Up Mindshare. Retrieved July 25 2005, from http://www.itmanagement.earthweb.com/service/print.php/3078431

Niessink, F., & van Vliet, H. (1998). Towards Mature IT Services. *Software Process Improvement and Practice, 4*(2), 55–71. doi:10.1002/(SICI)1099-1670(199806)4:2<55::AID-SPIP97>3.0.CO;2-T

OGC. (2006, 5 June 2006). Office of Government Commerce. ITIL IT Service Management: Glossary of Terms, Definitions and Acronyms. Retrieved from http://www.get-best-practice.biz/glossary.aspx?product=glossariesacronyms

Potgieter, B. C., Botha, J. H., & Lew, C. (2005, 10-13 July). *Evidence that use of the ITIL framework is effective.* Paper presented at the 18th Annual Conference of the National Advisory Committee on Computing Qualifications, Tauranga, NZ.

Praeg, C.-P., & Schnabel, U. (2006, 4-7 Jan). *IT-Service Cachet - managing IT-service performance and IT-service quality.* Paper presented at the 39th Annual Hawaii International Conference on System Sciences (HICSS'06), Kauai.

Praeg, C.-P., & Spath, D. (2009). Perspectives of IT-Service Quality Management: a Concept of Life-Cycle Based Quality Management of IT Services. In A. Cater-Steel (Ed.), *Information Technology Governance and Service Management: Frameworks and Adaptations* (pp. 381-407). Hershey, PA: Information Science Reference.

Purcell, D. E. (2006). Report on formation of the International Committee for Education on Standardization [Electronic Version].

Rossi, S. (2006, 12 July). University begins local ITIL adoption research. *Computerworld.*

Rossi, S. (2008, 28 March). Charles Sturt Uni leads ITIL accreditation. *Computerworld.*

Sallé, M. (2004). IT Service Management and IT Governance: review, comparative analysis and their impact on utility computing [Electronic Version], 25. Retrieved June 2, Schuller, H., & Wheeler, G. (2006, 31 May). An ITIL bit of knowledge. *Computerworld.*

Seek Ltd. (2009). Seek I.T.: Australia's #1 Job Site. Retrieved January 12, 2009, from http://it.seek.com.au

Stein, A., Nikakis, C., Bentley, J., & Jovanovic, R. (2005). The industry and education nexus: how one school tackled certification. In T. van Weert & A. Tatnall (Eds.), *Information and communication technologies and real-life learning - new education for the knowledge society* (pp. 255-261). MA: Springer/IFIP.

Tan, W., Cater-Steel, A., Toleman, M., & Seaniger, R. (2007). *Implementing centralised IT Service Management: Drawing Lessons from the Public Sector.* Paper presented at the Australasian Conference on Information Systems, Toowoomba.

Thibodeau, P. (2007, 19 September). Increasing Adoption of ITIL is Making Resistance Futile. *Computerworld.*

Tovey, M., & Lawlor, D. (2004). *Training in Australia: Design, Delivery, Evaluation, Management* (2nd ed.). Sydney NSW: Pearson Education.

Venkataraman, R., & Conger, S. (2006). Open Invitation to itSMF Academic Forum. In AISWORLD Information Systems World Network (Ed.).

Violino, R. (2005, July 25). Best-Practice Library Gains Fans. *Information Week* Retrieved November 10, 2005, from http://www.informationweek.com/story/showArticle.jhtml?articleID=166401916&tid=13690

Wilson, E. (2004, 11 May). Opening the book on ITIL. *Sydney Morning Herald.* Retrieved from http://www.smh.com.au/articles/2004/05/10/1084041321436.html

Wonacott, M. E. (2003). In Brief: Fast Facts for Policy and Practice No. 23: Industry-Sponsored Credentials [Electronic Version]. Retrieved from http://www.nccte.org/publications/infosynthesis/in-brief/in-brief23/inbrief23-indspon.pdf

Chapter 13

Factors Influencing the Lifetime of Telecommunication and Information Technology Standards

Knut Blind
Berlin University of Technology, Germany

INTRODUCTION

The dynamic technological changes in information and communication technology (ICT) influence the lifetimes of standards, an important dimension of the dynamics of standards. The need to change or adjust standards according to new trends in ICT has definitely increased in the last decade. Furthermore, some standards became obsolete, because new technologies led to completely new generations of standards. Consequently, standards have a life cycle defined by their publication and withdrawal dates, which represents a core element of the dynamics of standards.

Despite the high dynamics in ICT and the high relevance of standards for the development of ICT

and the related sectors (Blind, Jungmittag 2008), there is no systematic quantitative analysis which tries to investigate the life times as one important dimension or indicator of the dynamics of ICT standards and their driving factors. An exception is the contribution by Egyedi and Heijnen (2005), who focus on the internal revision processes of ISO (International Organization for Standardization). This paper presents results comparing different subcategories of ICT also taking country characteristics into account based on the data of the PERINORM database published by the national standard development organisations (SDOs) BSI (British Standards Institute), DIN (Deutsches Institut fuer Normung) and AFNOR (Association Française de Normalisation).

In contrast to the rather few quantitative studies, we can rely on a long tradition of conceptual

DOI: 10.4018/978-1-60566-946-5.ch013

analyses done by economists starting in the 1980s by the work of Arthur (Arthur 1989) applied in David´s study of the typewriter keyboard standard QWERTY (David 1985) and Farrell and Saloner´s game theory approach (Farrell, Saloner 1985; 1986). Based on network externalities, increasing returns but also information asymmetries these authors mainly explain the lock in effects of standardisation and the missing or insufficient dynamics of standards. Another kind of evolution of standards is discussed and illustrated by Swann (2000), who analyses the interplay between innovation and standardisation. Starting with a basic standard, which defines the specifications of some platform technology, the field for further innovation is set in using this basic technology for various applications.

Besides these very conceptual or theoretical approaches to deal with standards dynamics, several case study analyses exist, which focus on the standard maintenance and succession (Egyedi, Loeffen 2002) in order to answer the question how to deal with heritage relations between standards and on standard integrity (Egyedi, Hudson 2005) and in order to discuss control mechanisms that safeguard the integrity of (de facto) standards. This paper adds an additional methodological dimension to the analysis of the dynamics of standards by a strong focus on the life times of standards. The contribution of this paper to the emerging research on the dynamics of standards is twofold. First, the descriptive presentation of life times of standards focusing both on average publication years and survival times reflects on the one hand the historical development of ICT over time and on the other hand its dynamics in the various subfields. So far other indicators like scientific publications or patent applications are used to describe the development especially of new technologies, e. g. biotechnology or nanotechnology. The analysis of publications of standard documents extends the former exercises by a new more market and diffusion related dimension. Second, the characteristics of standard documents are used

to explain their life times. Here we borrow for the first time general approaches from bibliometrics and patent analysis in order to explain life times of standards as indicator for their value by documents' characteristics.

The remainder of the paper is structured as follows. First, we analyse the average lifetimes of standards in a quantitative manner, taking into account differences between countries. Since the simple approach of calculating the average lifetimes of historical standards does not allow us to include standards which are still alive, we have to apply a more sophisticated methodology, the so-called survival analysis, which was initially mainly applied in medical science. The application of this statistical approach produces average lifetimes of standards, taking into account the expected lifetime of standards which are still valid. This approach is crucial, especially for the analysis of ICT standards, because the number of valid standards relative to historical standards is rather high. Due to the very high relevance of international standards in the ICT sector and the high quality of this subsample, we concentrate the survival analysis especialy on the international standards including the standards released by the European standardisation bodies. The results of this analysis provide us with new insights about the expected lifetimes of standards differentiated by technology in the ICT area. The final step of our analysis tries to answer the question which causal factors influence the lifetimes of standards in the ICT sector. We present first insights by applying the so-called Cox regression, which allows us to identify whether some selected characteristics of a standard, like cross references or references to international standards, have a significant impact on its actual or expected lifetime. The approach to assess the importance of a technical document by analysing its references to other documents or being referenced in other documents has a long tradition in evaluating the value of patents by counting and analysing their citations.[1] The paper concludes with a brief summary of the main results, but also with some general recommendations regarding standardisation processes and the maintenance of standards derived from the new insights.

METHODOLOGICAL ISSUES

We will apply different methodological approaches to tackle the two major dimensions of our contribution. First, we will perform simple descriptive statistics of average publication and withdrawal years, then continue with survival time analyses, which allow us to take into account the numerous still valid documents, and finally conduct Cox regression analyses in order to identify significant factors influencing the lifetimes of standards, at least in the fields with sufficient information and observations.

For our analysis we use the PERINORM database edited by the three major national standardisation bodies in Europe, BSI in the United Kingdom, DIN in Germany, and AFNOR in France. The main characteristics of PERINORM edition 2004 relevant for our analysis are the following. Since we concentrate on the ICT sector, we select only the documents in the field of telecommunication and information technology, including office machines, by relying on the international classification of standards (ICS). Telecommunication is identified by the ICS code 33, information technology by the ICS code 35. The next level of subdivision of the two ICT-related fields will be illustrated in the tables used. In total, we rely on more than 78,000 documents in the field telecommunication and more than 31,000 documents in the field information technology and office machines. The majority of the documents have been published since the beginning of the 1990s.

In our analysis, we cover the following European countries: Austria (AT); Belgium (BE), Czech Republic (CZ), Switzerland (CH), Germany

(DE), Denmark (DK), Spain (ES); France (FR); Great Britain (GB), Italy (IT); Netherlands (NL); Norway (NO), Poland (PL); Russia (RU); Sweden (SE); Slovakia (SK); Turkey (TR). In addition, the set of international and European standards are included (IX).

The data quality is rather heterogeneous, since the databases of the founding countries France, Germany and Great Britain are of higher quality than those of most other countries. The data about the standards released by the international bodies is also of good quality. It has to be noted that the European and the international standards have to be included in the set of national standards, because of the requirement of CEN and ISO members to integrate and implement the European, respectively the international standards.

Although each document is described by almost 50 characteristics, we rely in our analysis mainly on the following search fields: Classification, Cross references, Expiry date, International relationship, Issuing body, Origin code, Publication date, Replaced by, Replaces, Status, Withdrawal date.

In the more sophisticated analyses, we have to restrict ourselves to those countries which provide high quality data for most of the relevant classification fields. Due to the differences between telecommunication and information technology and due to very large number of documents and descriptors, we have set up two separate databases.

DESCRIPTIVE RESULTS

In a first step, we analysed the average publication and withdrawal dates, differentiated both by technological area and by country. We concentrate on all standards documents, i.e. including drafts and pre-standards, by calculating the average of their publication date. In calculating withdrawal dates, we are able to consider just those documents which are already withdrawn. The difference between the

Table 1. Average publication and withdrawal dates in telecommunication differentiated by area of standardisation

Categories	Publication Date	Withdrawal Date
Telecommunications in general including infrastructure	1996.59	1998.13
Telecommunication services	1998.34	2000.56
Telecommunication systems including network (system) aspects	1996.25	1998.14
Telecommunication terminal equipment	1995.25	1999.18
Radio communications	1996.61	1998.06
Mobile services	1998.08	1998.11
Integrated Services Digital Network (ISDN)	1997.27	1998.27
Electromagnetic compatibility (EMC) including radio interference	1998.19	1999.63
Components and accessories for telecommunications equipment	1994.59	1998.73
Special measuring equipment for use in telecommunications	1993.28	1997.88
Audio, video and audiovisual engineering	1995.57	1997.66
Television and radio broadcasting	1996.76	1998.32
Fibre optic communications	1999.03	1999.43
Telecontrol telemetering includng supervising, cotrol and data acquisition	1997.11	1997.94

average publication and the average withdrawal dates gives a first indication of the dynamics of standards in the different subfields.

In Table 1, we present the average publication and withdrawal dates by technological area in telecommunication technology. The average publication dates vary between 1993 and 1998. The oldest documents can be found in the area of measuring equipment for use in telecommunication with an average publication date as far back as 1993. Standards on components and accessories for telecommunication equipment were published on average in 1994, those on telecommunication terminal equipment in 1995. In contrast, if we look at the standardisation fields with more recent average publication dates, we find standards for fibre optic communications with an average publication year of 1999. Standards for telecommunication services and mobile services are on average published in 1998. This first picture is in line with the technological and market development in telecommunication. First, standards are

needed to solve the general measurement and testing problems, then to secure the compatibility between components of the equipment and the terminal equipment itself. With the maturing of the technology and the market itself, we observe a shift in the focus from fixed to mobile telephony. This is also reflected by the delayed publication of standards for mobile services. Furthermore, the telecommunication industry experiences a further shift to service-related applications, i. e. at a later stage we observe the publications of standards structuring telecommunication services. In summary, the ranking of the average publication dates presents the historical development of the telecommunication technology, which means that the development of standards follows the technology life cycle in telecommunication.

Although Egyedi and Heijnen (2005) indicate that the average withdrawal dates are not good indicators for the expected lifetime of standards, we report in this section also the average withdrawal dates. However, we perform a more so-

Table 2. Average publication and withdrawal dates in Telecommunications for various countries

Country	Number of Standards	Publication Date	Withdrawal Date
International standards	18154	1995.26	1997.46
Austria	8377	1998.31	1999.27
Belgium	4679	1999.76	2001.64
Switzerland	1663	1995.18	1998.23
Czech Republic	3374	1998.25	2002.48
Germany	6983	1994.64	1997.30
Denmark	5355	1999.02	2000.21
Spain	1792	1996.13	1999.69
France	2927	1996.90	1999.17
United Kingdom	2029	1997.26	1999.77
Italy	19	1994.89	2002.33
Netherlands	5785	1997.44	1999.53
Norway	2467	1998.00	1998.44
Poland	1122	2000.02	2003.00
Russia	446	1988.95	1999.70
Sweden	4405	1997.46	1998.33
Slovakia	4654	1999.71	2000.69
Turkey	1422	1998.16	2002.00

phisticated analysis which allows us to calculate the expected lifetimes of standards in the next section. In general, we observe a rough correlation between average publication and withdrawal dates. However, the fields of standardisation which started relatively early are characterised by larger differences between withdrawal and publication dates. In the emerging fields of telecommunication standardisation, the differences between average withdrawal and publication date are smaller, which is caused by the fact that the majority of the standards in these areas are still alive. An exception is the area of telecommunication services, where a significant share of standards has obviously already been withdrawn

In Table 2, we present the average publication and withdrawal dates differentiated by country. The overview confirms that the country-specific databases differ significantly. On the one hand, we observe only small differences between aver-

ages of the large central European countries. On the other hand, the data of the eastern European countries indicate for Russia relatively old standards documents based on an average publication date before 1990, but for the Czech Republic, Slovakia, Poland and Turkey a rather young set of standards with an average publication year close to 2000. Whereas the Russian case is certainly influenced by a rather old and small national stock of standards, which has only recently been linked to the international standardisation activities. The other four countries are meanwhile linked to CEN or in case of telecommunication to ETSI, which means that they implement the stock of European standards in their national standardisation system. Since they possessed only a small stock of domestic standards, the implementation of the European stock of telecommunication standards rejuvenated the national stock of standards drastically. The European effect can also be observed in Belgium, which has no significant own standardisation activities.

In the next step, we look at the dynamics of standards in the field of information technology. In Table 3 we are again able to detect the life cycle of information technology in the averages of the publication dates. Standardisation started obviously in the field of office machines in general with an average publication date in 1986. In a next step, standards for data storage devices were published with an average publication date of just after 1990. A further standardisation step, microprocessor systems, underwent a standardisation phase with an average publication date of 1992. The remaining average publication dates do not differ significantly, because they are all within the interval between 1994 and 1996. The only exception is standards for the application of information technology, which were published on average in the year 1997.

The average withdrawal dates correlate rather closely with the average publication dates. Obviously, the historical standards for office machines are characterised by the largest difference between average publication and withdrawal date. Historically software standards have much shorter lifetimes.

The differentiation of information technology standards by country in Table 4 reveals a much more heterogeneous picture than in the field of telecommunication. The average publication year varies from 1992 to later than 1998.

For the eastern European countries, we find the pattern similar to the field of telecommunication of rather late publication and withdrawal dates. Russia is again characterised by a rather early average publication year of its standards. For the Netherlands, we even observe that the average publication year is later than the average withdrawal year, which is caused by the fact that only a few documents were withdrawn during the 1990s, but the majority of the documents were published since the end of the 1990s.[1] However, the homogeneous picture among the central European countries observed in the telecommunication sector cannot be detected in the information technology sector. Consequently, country-specific analyses are required in the following analytical steps.

Table 3. Average publication and withdrawal dates in information technology differentiated by area of standardisation

Categories	Publication Date	Withdrawal Date
Information technology (IT) in general	1995.33	1995.16
Character sets and information coding	1996.19	1997.69
Languages used in information technology	1996.01	1998.22
Software including software development, documentation, internet applications and use	1995.12	1996.08
Open systems interconnection (OSI)	1995.75	1998.11
Networking including LAN, MAN, WAN	1995.80	1998.11
Computer graphics	1994.53	1998.20
Microprocessor systems including PCs, calculators, etc.	1992.44	1997.19
IT terminal and other peripheral equipment including modems	1994.75	1996.77
Interface and interconnection equipment	1993.98	1995.26
Data storage devices	1990.49	1994.70
Applications of information technology	1996.88	1998.39
Office machines	1986.26	1993.52

RESULTS OF THE SURVIVAL ANALYSIS

As already indicated in the previous section, the approach to compare average withdrawal and publication dates is not robust and reliable enough to give indications about the average lifetimes of standards. In addition, the survival times indicate the dynamics within a field of standardisation, i.e. the shorter the higher the dynamics, whereas the average publication dates of standards may provide information about the development of a technology, which starts out with standards for hardware components and moves later to applications and services. Therefore, we apply the so-called Kaplan-Meier survival analysis (for technical details, see Norusis 1996). Survival analyses have their application origin in testing the effectiveness of medical treatments, espe-

cially on the survival times of patients. However, meanwhile the application of the methodology has been extended to analyses of the duration of unemployment and other economic phenomena, e.g. lifetime of companies (Cantner et al. 2004).

In the following, we present the results of survival analyses only applied to the final standard documents differentiated by country and technological area. In an explorative analytical step we compared the expected survival times of draft or pre-standards with those of standards themselves. We found very short survival times for all the draft and preliminary documents, irrespective of country and technological field. Because of this articifical phenomenon, we restrict our analysis to the sub-sample of final standard documents in contrast to the approach presented in the previous section. Since we differentiate in this analysis by country and field of technology, the number of

Table 4. Average publication and withdrawal dates in information technology differentiated by country

Country	Number of Standards	Publication Date	Withdrawal Date
International standards	9429	1995.44	1997.14
Austria	1552	1995.97	1997.65
Belgium	740	1996.07	2002.11
Switzerland	860	1993.14	1996.54
Czech Republic	1412	1998.22	2002.64
Germany	3396	1992.88	1995.41
Denmark	2384	1997.81	2000.10
Spain	642	1997.32	2001.72
France	1508	1993.57	1998.95
United Kingdom	2510	1996.67	1999.48
Italy	721	1995.02	2002.27
Netherlands	2086	1997.55	1993.58
Norway	484	1993.97	2000.45
Poland	493	1998.24	2003.00
Russia	519	1992.25	1999.76
Sweden	1561	1992.55	1997.04
Slovakia	814	1996.96	1999.39
Turkey	663	1996.93	n.a.

observations is sometimes reduced to a level which does not allow the application of the survival analysis. As we already observed significant differences between the considered countries in the average publication and withdrawal dates, consequently the expected survival times differ significantly between countries. In Figure 1, we present the expected survival times of telecommunications and information technology standards differentiated by country. The average international standard is alive 22.5 years in telecommunication and 16.5 years in the field of information technology.[2] The eastern European countries Poland, Russia and Slovakia are characterised by expected survival times of over 30 years; the same is true for Belgium with an expected survival time of over 40 years. In the database of these countries, there is a dominance of rather old standards, which are still alive. However, these results can also be generated by a very few standards published early, which are still alive, and a majority of rather new and probably international and European standards, which are also not yet withdrawn. Whereas the results of these countries are rather biased by some special effects, the calculations for the other European countries are more reliable. For these, we observe three clusters of countries. The survival times of standards in France and Great Britain are longer than the European standards. The Nordic and the central European countries, including the Czech Republic, have lower survival times. Whereas France and Great Britain still have a significant and slightly older stock of national standards, the other countries are obviously more heavily influenced by the standardisation activities at the European and international level, which requires the withdrawal of respective existing national standards. Here we also observe a difference between Germany, on the one hand, and France together with Great Britain on the other hand; Germany is obviously under a stronger international and European influence in the area of telecommunication standards. In general, the survival analysis confirms the country-specific heterogeneity of the standards life cycle

data already observed by analysing the average publication and withdrawal dates.

The variation of the survival times between countries can also be observed among the information technology standards. For most of the countries, we observe partly similar patterns as in the telecommunication area. On the one hand, Belgium and the eastern countries Poland and Russia are again characterised by very high expected survival times. On the other hand, in most central European countries, like e.g. Germany, the survival times of information technology standards are not very different from the set of international and European standards. Again, Austria represents an exception by having very low survival times of less than ten years. In contrast to the general pattern of shorter survival times of information technology standards in comparison to the telecommunication standards, the Dutch information technology standards last on average more than seven years longer than the Dutch telecommunication standards. The same is true for Norwegian, and to a limited extent, for Swedish standards.

The comparison of the survival times of telecommunication and information technology standards reveals the country-specific influence by the high correlation of the survival times in both technological fields. The major conclusion from the results of this working step is the requirement to calculate the data in a country-specific way. In the next step, we check whether – as expected and already indicated by the average publication and withdrawal dates – we find also technology-specific differences in the survival times.

In our presentation of the survival times differentiated by field of standardisation, we concentrate on the European and international standards, because the relevance of European and international standards for telecommunication and information technology is of much more relevance than national standardisation activities. Furthermore, the database of the European and international standards is much larger and more complete than the databases of the national stan-

Figure 1. Survival times of telecommunication and information technology standards in years by country

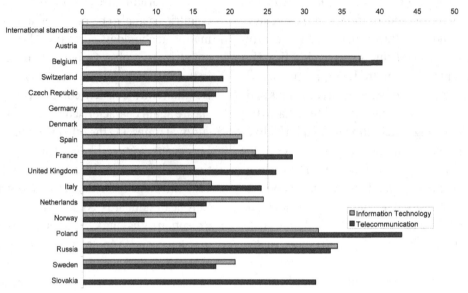

dards, which allows much more differentiated analyses. Bearing in mind the average survival time of 22.5 years of telecommunication standards in general, we concentrate just on the largest deviations from this mean value. The expected survival times for telecommunication terminal equipment standards are ten years longer than the average. This shows, on the one hand, that standardisation started in this area earlier than in the other sub-areas. Furthermore, the average lifetimes of historical documents, which are already withdrawn, has to be sufficiently long. Both explanations are consistent with reality. Since there is no other sub-area with significantly longer survival times than the average, we concentrate now on the sub-areas with rather short survival times. At first, we observe the rather short survival times of standards for mobile services, which are even lower also the very recent ETSI standards are taken into account. This phenomenon conforms to the explanation already made in the context of the average publication and withdrawal dates. The development of mobile services started

rather late in comparison to telecommunication standardisation in general, and consequently the expected survival times are rather short. Whereas the development of services always occurs in a rather late stage of the development of a technology and an industry, in telecommunication we observe the emergence of fibre optic communication since the late 1990s. Consequently, standardisation activities started later than in telecommunication in general. The standardisation activities to ensure electromagnetic compatibility (EMC) also started rather late, as seen above in the presentation of the average publication dates. Therefore, the expected survival times of these standards are around ten years and much shorter than those of telecommunication standards in general. Finally, the rather short survival times of standards related to Integrated Services Digital Network (ISDN) must be discussed. Although standardisation started rather early in this field, the expected lifetimes are shorter than comparative sub-areas (see Table 1 with the publication dates). Obviously, there have been more revisions of standards leading to withdrawals of existing standards and to a shortening of lifetimes.

Summarising the results of the survival analysis of international telecommunication standards, three main results have to be noted. First, the average survival times depend very much on the starting of respective standardisation activities, i.e. since standardisation for telecommunication hardware already took place before the 1990s, the expected survival times of these standards is much higher than those related to standards for mobile services, which were mostly released after the mid 1990s. This result confirms also that telecommunication standards were published rather early and turned out to be rather stable. Second, the survival times of standards in telecommunication reflect – in the same way as the average publication years – the life cycle of telecommunication technology areas, which started out with traditional hardware and equipment, then followed by application and services. Since fibre optic communication technology emerged only recently, the respective standards appeared in recent years, causing rather short survival times. Third, we detect some

technology-specific dynamics in the survival times, i.e. there are sub-areas in which standards are more frequently revised and withdrawn than in other areas. One example for such a sub-area are the international ISDN standards, which have consequently much shorter survival times than standards in other fields, which were published on average at the same time.

After the presentation and the analysis of the survival times of the international telecommunication standards, in the previous section of this section we will have a look at the survival times of the international information technology standards (Figure 3). On average, the survival time of an international information technology standard is 16.5 years and therefore five years less than the average telecommunication standard. This difference underlines that there is much more dynamics in the information technology standardisation compared to the telecommunication technology standardisation.

In contrast to the average survival times, we find an expected survival time of more than 20 years for standards for data storage devices. This

Figure 2. Survival times of international telecommunication standards in years by area of standardisation

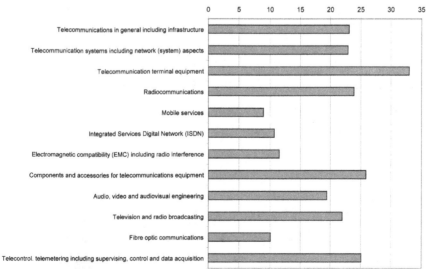

result is caused by the fact that standardisation in this area started rather early, already in the 1980s. Standards for software development and system documentation also have a survival time of 20 years, but the standardisation activities in this area were initiated on average five years later than for data storage devices. From this difference, we are able conclude that in the latter field standards are more frequently revised, adjusted to new generations of storage devices or even storage technologies than the more basic standards for software development, which focus more on general principles and terminologies. These obviously need less revisions and withdrawals over time.

If we focus on standardisation sub-areas with relatively short survival times, we identify open systems interconnection (OSI), networking and computer graphics. The latter field is obviously characterised by relatively high dynamics especially triggered by a rapid technical change, since standardisation activities started already relatively early. The OSI related standards have also a rather limited lifetime. In addition, if we

use the additional information on the average withdrawal dates, we find an early withdrawal year relative to the publication year. If we compare the OSI standards with the networking standards, we observe, on the one hand, a similar survival time, but a much later average withdrawal date, which allows us to conclude that in this sub-area a larger number of standards has already been withdrawn.

If we summarise the results of the survival analysis of international telecommunication and information standards together, we find the following main new insights. The survival times of telecommunication standards are much longer than for information technology standards, although the average publication dates do not differ significantly. Consequently, the dynamics within standards of information technology is much higher than those in telecommunication technology. In the latter field, the heterogeneity of the survival times is much higher, with rather low survival times of standards for mobile services and high survival times for telecommunication terminal equipment. In information technology, we just

Figure 3. Survival times of international information technology standards in years by area of standardisation

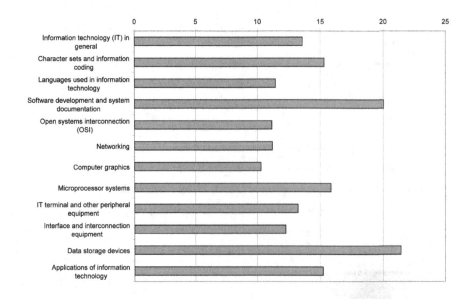

observe that standards for data storage devices and for software development and system documentation have a much higher survival time than the average for information technology standards. In the next section, we will try to identify factors influencing the lifetimes of standards.

FACTORS INFLUENCING THE SURVIVAL TIMES OF STANDARDS: RESULTS OF THE COX REGRESSION ANALYSIS

In the previous section, we calculated and interpreted the survival times of telecommunication and information technology standards. Despite the fact that country differences exist, in some cases caused by country-specific data quality, the analysis of the European and international standards showed that technology-specific reasons influence the survival times. In this final section, by applying the Cox regression methodology for a small selection of countries, we analyze which influences standard-specific characteristics have on the survival times of standards.

Based on the data which is available for each standard document, we developed the following specific hypotheses:

- If a standard amends another standard, then the expected lifetime is increased, because it has the character of a more basic and therefore longer lasting standard.
- If a standard is amended by another standard, then the expected lifetime is decreased, because the likelihood of a full substitution by another standard is higher.
- If a standard replaces another standard, its expected lifetime is higher, because the weaknesses of the predecessor standards have been solved.
- If a standard is replaced by another standard, its expected lifetime is lower, because of the replacement.

- If a standard has a cross reference to another standard, its expected lifetime is higher, because it is embedded in a whole network of standards, which is more stable than single and isolated standards.
- If a standard has a cross reference to another standard, its expected lifetime is lower, because it is embedded in a whole network of standards, which is more likely to be affected by external influences.
- If a standard has a reference to an international standard, its expected lifetime is lower, because the international standard is likely to change faster.
- If a standard has a reference to an international standard, its expected lifetime is higher, because the change of an international standard is likely to take more time.
- If a standard has a reference to regulation, its expected lifetime is higher, because changes in legislation take longer and its relevance is higher.
- If a standard contains more pages, its expected lifetime is higher, because the volume of codified knowledge is higher, which may cause further inertia (it may even represent the merger of various standards).

Since some data fields are not filled out for the selected countries, we had to restrict ourselves to testing some hypotheses only for a few or even a single country. Furthermore, we differentiate in general not by the sub-areas, because the number of observations is then too low to generate significant results.

In order to test the above hypotheses, we apply the so-called Cox regression model (for technical details, see Norusis 1996). This approach allows us to investigate whether and in what direction exogenous variables influence the survival probability of the standards documents. The methodology is a multiple regression or logistic regression analysis, which allows the inclusion of the still valid documents, like the Kaplan-Meier survival analysis.

Table 5. Meanings and names of exogenous variables

Meaning	Name of variable
Standard amends another standard	B_1: Amends
Standard is amended by another standard	B_2: Amended by
Standard replaces another standard	B_3: Replaces; B_{3a}: Number of replacements
Standard is replaced by another standard	B_4: Replaced by
Standard has a cross reference to another standard	B_5: Cross reference; B_{5a}: Number of cross references
Standard has a cross reference to an international standard	B_6: International reference; B_{6a}: Number of international references
Standard has a reference to legislation	B_7: Legislation
Number of pages	B_8: Pages

The cumulative survival function S(t), i. e. the proportion of the surviving cases at a particular point of time t, is the dependent variable. In a further step, the cumulative survival function at point t is calculated under the influence of the exogenous variables x_1 to x_n, which relate to the hypotheses above,as:

$$S(t) = [S_0(t)]^p, \qquad (1)$$

with $S_0 = S_0(t)$ as baseline survival function at time t, the exponent p is determined by

$$p = e^{(Bixi)} \text{ with } i = 1 \text{ to } n \text{ explaining variables.} \qquad (2)$$

The estimation of the coefficients B_1 to B_n will be solved by the Cox regression analysis. If all coefficients B_1 to B_n were equal to zero, then p would have the value of one and the baseline survival function would not be influenced by the exogenous variables (covariates). Positive coefficients B_i reduce the survival probability, negative ones increase the survival probability.

In the following Table 5, the exogenous variables for explaining the survival times of standards documents are summarised:

At first, we calculate separate regression models for each variable. In the Tables 6 and 7, the results for the telecommunication and information technology standards are summarised. We concentrate our analysis on the data of international, Austrian, Swiss, German, French, British and Dutch standards, but have to restrict ourselves to a sub-set of these countries for the variables "Amended", "Amended by" and "Legislation".

The results for the variables "Amended" and "Amended by" confirm for the selected countries that both documents which amended and were amended by another document have a significantly higher survival time than documents without this kind of cross references. Therefore, the first hypotheses, that if a standard amends another standard, then the expected lifetime is increased, is confirmed. Obviously amended standards have the character of a more basic and therefore longer lasting standard. However, if a standard is amended by another standard, then the expected lifetime is increased and not decreased. The explanation for this result to be observed in some countries may be that amendments obviously stabilise a standard in general and reduce the likelihood of a general withdrawal.

For the second couple of hypotheses focusing on replacements, we find a consistent picture for the evident hypothesis that if a standard is replaced by another standard, its expected lifetime is lower. However, the hypothesis that if a standard replaces another standard, its expected lifetime should higher, because the weaknesses

Table 6. Results of cox regression analysis for telecommunication standards

Variable	International standards		Austria		Switzerland		Germany		France		United Kingdom		Netherlands	
	B	Sig	B	Sig	B	ig	B	ig	B	ig	B	ig	B	Sig
B_1: Amends	-0.136	0.006	n.a	n.a.	n.a	n.a.	n.a	n.a.	n.a	n.a.	n.a.	n.a.	-3.622	0.000
B_2: Amended by	-0.558	0.000	n.a	n.a.	n.a	n.a.	n.a	n.a.	n.a	n.a.	0.238	0.124	-3.612	0000
B_3: Replaces	-0.432	0.000	-0.671	0.000	0.358	0.324	-0.473	0.000	0.379	0.250	0.375	0.009	0.547	0.000
B_{3a}: Number of replaces	-2.341	0.000	-0.403	0.000	0.146	0.529	-0.253	0.000	0.171	0.088	0.158	0.108	0.290	0000
B_4: Replaced by	3.600	0.000	5.139	0.000	3.075	0.000	2.538	0.000	4.402	0.000	2.829	0.000	6.143	0.000
B_5: Cross reference	0.142	0.000	-1.053	0.000	-0.350	0.014	0.183	0.000	-0.458	0.001	0.467	0.025	-4.682	0.000
B5a: Number of cross references	0.003	0.000	-0.025	0.000	-.026	0.002	0.005	0.000	-0.002	0.685	0.020	0.000	-1.334	0.000
B_6: International reference	0.047	0.039	0.600	0.000	1.064	0.142	0.779	0.000	0.241	0.160	-0.356	0.027	-0.214	0.523
B_{6a}: Number of international references	-0.096	0.000	0.303	0.000	0.084	0.219	0.102	0.000	0.067	0.295	-0.130	0.145	-0.604	0.000
B_7: Legislation	n.a	n.a.	n.a	n.a.	n.a	n.a.	0.338	0.000	n.a	n.a.	n.a	n.a.	n.a	n.a.
B_8: Pages	0.001	0.000	-0.002	0.000	0.02	0.170	0.003	0.000	0.002	0.264	0.005	0.001	0.000	0.000

of the predecessor standards have been solved, can only be confirmed for half of the countries considered. In the Netherlands, we even find a confirmation for information technology and a rejection for telecommunication standards. In telecommunication technology, the hypothesis is rejected only in Great Britain, in information technology also in France and Switzerland.

The testing of the hypotheses focusing on cross and international references reveal rather ambivalent results. For the standards in telecommunication technology, the hypothesis that if a standard has a cross reference to another standard, its expected lifetime is lower, because it is embedded in a whole network of standards, which is more likely to be affected by external influences, is confirmed by international, German and British standards. The analysis including in-stead the continuous variable of number of cross references confirms this result. However, the data from Austria, Switzerland, France and the Netherlands confirm the counter hypothesis. For the standards in information technology, the latter hypothesis is confirmed for all countries except for Germany and France. If we use the number of cross references, the data for Great Britain also confirm the hypothesis that the expected survival time of a standard will decrease with an increasing number of cross references.

The reference to an international standard decreases the expected lifetime of a telecommunication standard for the international, the Austrian and the German sample, whereas the longevity of standards in the British database increases. In information technology international references lead to a reduction of the lifetime, with the excep-

Table 7. Results of cox regression analysis for information technology standards

Variable	International standards		Austria		Switzerland		Germany		France		United Kingdom		Netherlands	
	B	Sig	B	Sig	B	ig	B	ig	B	ig	B	ig	B	Sig
B1: Amends	-0.267	0.000	n.a	n.a.	n.a	n.a.	n.a	n.a.	0.276	0.181	n.a.	n.a.	-3.085	0.002
B2: Amended by	-0.615	0.000	n.a	n.a.	n.a	n.a.	n.a	n.a.	-0.167	0.512	-0.291	0.004	-3.065	0002
B3: Replaces	-0.710	0.000	-0.630	0.000	0.382	0.027	-0.498	0.000	0.586	0.000	0.266	0.005	-0.449	0.000
B3a: Number of replacements	-0.372	0.000	-0.427	0.000	0.075	0.561	-0.248	0.000	0.294	0.000	0.143	0.001	-0.257	0010
B4: Replaced by	2.862	0.000	2.421	0.000	1.741	0.000	2.103	0.000	2.393	0.000	2.142	0.000	7.508	0.000
B5: Cross reference	-0.086	0.008	-1.091	0.000	-0.372	0.004	0.234	0.001	0.538	0.000	-0.354	0.001	-4.709	0.000
B5a: Number of cross references	-0.008	0.000	-0.053	0.000	0001	0.949	0.006	0.001	0.015	0.000	0.010	0.000	-1.095	0.000
B6: International reference	-0.218	0.000	0.400	0.030	1.072	0.011	0.215	0.000	0.449	0.001	0.131	0.265	-0.813	0.008
B6a: Number of international references	-0.046	0.000	0.013	0.733	-0.064	0.048	0.043	0.004	0.137	0.000	-0.018	0.764	0.067	0.433
B7: Legislation	n.a	n.a.	n.a	n.a.	n.a	n.a.	-0.238	0.175	n.a	n.a.	n.a	n.a.	n.a	n.a.
B8: Pages	0.001	0.000	-0.001	0.041	0.02	0.001	0.000	0.275	0.001	0.059	0.001	0.062	0.001	0.043

tion of the international[3] and the Dutch database. If we use the counts of international references, only the expected lifetime of standards of the Swiss and international databases increases with the number of international references.

Due to data restriction, we are only able to test the hypotheses for Germany that, if a standard has a reference to regulation, its expected lifetime is higher, because changes in legislation take longer and its relevance is higher. We find a rejection of this hypothesis in the telecommunication area and no significant relationship for information technology. One explanation for the rejection in the telecommunication area may be the liberalisation and deregulation of the telecommunication sector causing a rather frequent change of regulations, which also causes the pressure to adapt the referred standards more often.

Finally, we wanted to test whether the quantity of content in a standard measured by the number of pages has an impact on their survival times. In contrast to our hypothesis, that the more pages a standard contains, the higher its expected lifetime, the counter hypothesis is confirmed for most of the regressions. Only in Austria did larger standard documents have a longer expected life. The reason for this counterintuitive result is the recent trend to produce larger standards documents.

Since we observe rather heterogeneous results between the few countries considered, we had a more in-depth look at the sub-areas of the international standards.[4] For the following hypotheses out of the whole set of hypotheses, we find rather strong empirical evidence. Whereas there is no empirical support for the hypothesis that standards which amend other documents have a longer expected survival time, standards which are amended by other documents have a longer life expectancy in the majority of the subclasses. This contrasts our hypothesis, that a standard amended by another standard has a reduced expected lifetime, because the likelihood of a general substitution might be higher. In line with our hypothesis, there is strong empirical support for the fact that standard documents which replace previous documents have a longer life expectancy. Consequently, the number of documents being replaced increases the survival time of the respective standards. In addition, the ambivalent role of the existence of cross references or international cross references supports the two contradicting aspects of cross references. On the one hand, a standard with cross references to other standards is embedded in a whole network of standards, which should be more stable than single and isolated standards. On the other hand, a standard has cross references to other standards may be also influenced by changes in the area of the referenced standards. The link to a to a regulation is negative for German telecommunication standards, but slightly positive for German information technology standards. This means only for the later area, our hypothesis, that the expected lifetime is higher with a link to regulation, because changes in legislation take longer and its relevance is higher, is not confirmed. Finally, the survival time in the two areas in most countries decreases with an increasing number of page representing a larger volume of codified knowledge even the merger of various standards.

Summarising the results of the Cox regression, the following general new insights have to be reported. First, the document-specific information on predecessor and successor documents confirm, on the one hand, for the majority of countries and technological sub-areas that standards which replace a preceding document have a longer survival time compared to documents without a predecessor. Second, standards with a successor document have as expected a shorter expected lifetime. Third, the existence and the number of cross references have a heterogeneous influence on the lifetimes of standards, depending on the country and technological area considered. References to international information technology standards reduce the lifetime of standards at least for the majority of country-specific documents. Finally, the length of standard document measured by pages correlates negatively with its survival time, which is at first glance counter-intuitive. However, this result can be explained by the fact that standard documents published earlier are much shorter than recently published documents.

CONCLUSION

An analysis of the telecommunication and information technology standards published by formal international, European and national standardisation bodies was performed in order to identify patterns of the dynamics of standards and factors influencing the dynamics of standard. We were able to detect the patterns of dynamics both based on quantitative statistics of average publication and withdrawal years and expected survival times, which are consistent with well-known technology and market-related characteristics. However, we also find country-specific patterns which are caused either by institutional reasons, like the participation in the European standardisation activities, or by the quality of the database.

The analysis of factors influencing the dynamics of standards is restricted by two dimensions. First, we have to rely in general on the additional information which the database provides. Consequently, only a limited number of hypotheses can be tested. Second, the quality of the document-specific information is rather heterogeneous. Consequently, we had to restrict our analysis to a few selected countries and to the international and European standards. Nevertheless, the results of the analysis confirmed some of our hypotheses, but revealed also new insights. In general, the dynamics of standards depend both on country, but also technology-specific characteristics.

Since both the institutional framework, i. e. the processes in the national standardisation bodies, and the characteristics of technology, e. g. platform technology or application, are responsible for the lifetime of standards, further analyses have to take into account these two dimensions. Furthermore, approaches have to be developed which will allow us to match systematically additional information to each standard document, because this facilitates the testing of further more sophisticated hypotheses about the causes influencing the dynamics of standards.

Besides the further development of the conceptual and methodological analyses of the life times of standards, it has to be pointed out that new insights can be used for the improvement of standardisation processes. The observations that the lifetimes of standards are influenced both by related technology and the institutional framework should be considered by the standardisation bodies. First, different technologies require obviously specific adjustment or withdrawal strategies in standardisation. Consequently, standardisation bodies should be more aware of this heterogeneity and adapt their processes accordingly, always taking into account the continuous change in science, technologies and markets. The differences between countries call for two strategies. First, benchmarking exercises may help to identify best practices in the adaptation of processes to adjust, modify or even withdraw existing standards. Second, and even more important, is the necessity to homogenise the maintenance processes among countries in order to avoid inconsistencies causing risks for the development of technologies, but also common markets. This includes also a more homogeneous implementation or transfer of international and European standards into the body of national standards..

ACKNOLWEDGMENT

The author thanks for the financial contribution for the NO-REST project (507626) by the European Commission within the 6th Framework Programme. The paper was developed within the workpackage on the dynamics of standards of the NO-REST project. A previous version of the paper was published in the proceedings of the IEEE SIIT 2005 conference in Geneva and in the Journal of IT Standardisation Research.. Valuable comments by the coeditor of this special issue of this journal Mostafa Hashem Sherif significantly and the coeditor of this book Tineke Egyedi increased the quality of the paper. Remaining shortcomings are in the sole responsibility of the author.

REFERENCES

Arthur, W. B. (1989). Competing Technologies, Increasing Returns, and Lock-in by Historical Events. *The Economic Journal*, *99*, 116–131. doi:10.2307/2234208

Blind, K., & Jungmittag, A. (2008). The Impact of Patents and Standards on Macroeconomic Growth: A Panel Approach Covering Four Countries and 12 Sectors - The Empirical Economics of Standards. *Journal of Productivity Analysis*, *1*, 51–60. doi:10.1007/s11123-007-0060-8

Cantner, U., Dressler, K., & Krüger, J. (2004). Verweildaueranalysen in der empirischen Wirtschaftsforschung. *Das Wirtschaftsstudium*, *10*, 1287–1293.

David, P. A. (1985). Clio and the economics of QWERTY. *The American Economic Review*, *75*, 332–336.

Egyedi, T., & Heijnen, P. (2005). Scale of Standards Dynamics: Change in formal, international IT standards. In S. Bolin (Ed.), *The Standards Edge: Future Generation*. Bolin Communications.

Egyedi, T. M., & Hudson, J. (2005). A standard's integrity: can it be safeguarded? *IEEE Communications Magazine, 43*(2), 151–155. doi:10.1109/MCOM.2005.1391516

Egyedi, T. M., & Loeffen, A. G. A. J. (2002). Succession in standardization: grafting XML onto SGML. *Computer Standards & Interfaces, 24*(4).

Farrell, J., & Saloner, G. (1985). Standardisation, Compatibility and Innovation. *The Rand Journal of Economics, 16*(1), 70–83. doi:10.2307/2555589

Farrell, J., & Saloner, G. (1986). Installed Base and Compatibility: Innovation, Product Preannouncements, and Predation. *The American Economic Review, 76*, 943–954.

Hall, B., Jaffe, A., & Traijtenberg, M. (2001). *Market Value and Patent Citations: A First Look.* University of California, Berkeley: Institute of Business and Economic Research.

Norusis, M. (1996). *SPSS Advanced Statistics 6.1.* Chicago: SPSS Inc.

Swann, G. M. P. (2000). T*he Economics of Standardization, Final Report for Standards and Technical Regulations.* Directorate Department of Trade and Industry, Manchester: Univ. of Manchester.

ENDNOTES

[1] The standard data of Turkey do not provide even one document with a withdrawal date, which questions the quality of the Turkish data.

[2] The higher values in telecommunication technology are caused by the fact that the ETSI standards issued since 1998 are not included in the categoy of international standards.

[3] For the subset of international standards, an international reference is equal to a simple cross reference.

[4] The tables with the results are available from the author.

Chapter 14
IPR Policy of the DVB Project:
Negative Disclosure, FR&ND Arbitration Unless Pool Rules OK Part 1

Carter Eltzroth
DVB Project, Switzerland[1]

ABSTRACT

The DVB Project is a European-based standards forum that for close to 15 years has been developing specifications for digital video broadcasting, many now implemented worldwide. Its IPR policy has several novel elements. These include "negative disclosure," the obligation of each member to license IPRs essential to DVB specifications unless it gives notice of the unavailability of the IPR. This approach contrasts with the more common rule (e.g., within ANSI accredited bodies) calling for IPR disclosure and confirmation of availability on FR&ND terms. Other notable features of the IPR policy of DVB are arbitration and fostering of patent pooling. This article provides a commentary on the DVB's IPR policy and on its application. It also describes the work of the DVB in resolving IPR "gateway" issues when the perceived dominance of technology contributors, notably through control over IPRs, risked, in the view of some members, distorting new digital markets. In two cases, DVB has created a licensing mechanism to dispel these concerns. In addition to the quality of its technical work, DVB's success lies in its novel IPR policy and its ability to achieve consensus to resolve gateway issues.

INTRODUCTION

The DVB Project is a standards forum that has successfully developed a number of technical specifications for digital video broadcasting.[2]

Many of these have been adopted throughout the world. In Europe, the standards are at the core of digital television, and many have been mandated by the European Union.[3] Within the United States, DVB's specifications are used by satellite broadcasters and the U.S. cable industry and for mobile broadcasting. One of the reasons for the success of DVB has been a policy governing the intellectual property rights (IPRs) essential to its specifications. It contains a number of elements that were novel at the time of DVB's formation. The most notable is the commitment by all members to grant licences to IPRs on terms fair, reasonable, and nondiscriminatory (FR&ND) *unless* the holder gives notice of its unavailability. This rule on "negative disclosure" turns on its head the duty found in most standards bodies: affirmative disclosure of IPRs essential to a specification *together with* confirmation of a willingness to license on FR&ND terms.[4] Other unusual terms in DVB's policy included arbitration to settle IPR disputes and encouragement of patent pooling. This article examines the terms at length in the next section.

DVB's experience with "negative disclosure," the fostering of patent pools, and the other features of its IPR policy have served as a significant distinguishing factor of DVB specifications and have contributed to the widespread implementation of its technology. DVB's successful IPR policy is an important complement to the strength of the technology captured in its specifications. It is a central argument of this article that when making a choice among competing technologies, implementers have generally greater certainty of the extent of their exposure to costs—no more than FR&ND, even in the absence of disclosure—to be imposed by participating rights holders relevant to DVB specifications. This article argues that other standards bodies do not provide the same measure of certainty for implementers.

At the same time, DVB's policy has been subject to reassessment in light of the success or difficulties of practical application of its IPR rules. These difficulties have included problems associated with two licensing programs covering DVB standards; they have prompted the European Commission during 2007 to express its concerns directly to the DVB Project.[5] The IPR policy is also

assessed in an environment colored by concerns over "submarine patents," "patent ambushes," and doubts about the level of duty of care expected of participants in the standards process and where the policy framework is evolving to accommodate changes in regulation, judicial decisions, academic and scholarly literature, and other sources. This article discusses elsewhere the impact of developments such as the work of U.S. government agencies and the European Commission on the relationship between laws governing IPR and competition rules, the *Rambus* litigation, cases before DG Competition of the European Commission, and the work within ETSI in improving its own IPR policy.[6]

These changes have an impact throughout the standards process and the introduction of new technologies, and there is an abundant and growing literature on standards, IPR, and competition rules. A selection, undoubtedly unrepresentative, includes articles on the relationship between standard-setting and antitrust (Dolmans, 2002; Morse, 2003), the value *vel non* of a regime encouraging *ex ante* disclosure of essential IPR and licensing terms (Geradin et al., 2007; Ohana et al., 2003; Skitol, 2005; Updegrove, 2006), the analysis to be applied to patent pools (Raymond, 2002), the methodology for determining FR&ND (Einhorn, 2007; Layne-Farrar, 2006; Stoner, 2006; Swanson et al., 2005).

This article recounts the novelty and success of DVB's approach to IPR licensing. It seeks to demonstrate the following:

- DVB's policy of "negative disclosure," coupled with its fostering of patent pools, often provides to implementers of its specifications greater commercial certainty than other policies.
- This policy, in contrast with the more commonplace regime of affirmative disclosure, has been shown, perhaps paradoxically, to offer a greater level of accurate disclosure of IPRs essential to specifications.

- The IPRM Module, as a permanent body within DVB's structure, capably informs other DVB bodies of DVB's IPR policy and its regulatory context and provides a useful forum for exchange of views on licensing terms offered by rights holders.
- The DVB has thrived also from a "community-minded," or good faith, approach to its development of specifications; this has been complemented by a disclosure regime that does not require constant reference to lawyers and patent specialists on whether essential IPR has been validly disclosed and whether the owner offers terms falling within FR&ND.
- The IPR policy of the DVB Project has been operating for well over a decade; its flexibility has been demonstrated by its continuing usefulness despite the influx of new members from various industries and geographies; it remains a suitable framework for further innovations.

The balance of this section provides a background to the DVB Project and close to 15 years of developing technical specifications for digital video broadcasting. It also sets out the recent approaches adopted by competition authorities on the involvement of standards bodies in licensing arrangements for their standards and discusses developments on IPR policy within ETSI, a standards body central to DVB's work. The subsequent section presents a commentary on the DVB's policy on IPRs, as set out in Article 14 of its Memorandum of Understanding. DVB's arrangements for fostering the formation of voluntary licensing programs covering IPRs essential to its specifications and the tools DVB has adopted in that fostering process are set out in Part 2 of this article. DVB is at times more assertive in establishing licensing programs, notably when addressing perceived gateway or bottleneck issues; for example, in conditional access and in dominance of a technology supplier;

DVB's experiences in this area are also set out in Part 2, together with some conclusions pointing out the merits and failings of the DVB's policy on IPRs.

Background to DVB

The DVB Project is an association of more than 250 members working to develop specifications for digital video broadcasting.[7] Formed in September 1993, its activities are governed by a Memorandum of Understanding, which includes in its present form a separate article on the licensing of IPRs essential to its specifications.[8] The members are drawn from four sectors—consumer electronics, infrastructure provision, broadcasters and content providers, and regulators—and each of the four is entitled to a set number of seats on the Steering Board, DVB's governing body. Membership is worldwide.[9] A work item leading to a specification is launched within DVB by the preparation of commercial requirements in the Commercial Module. The commercial requirements determine the functionalities or performance characteristics to be achieved through the technical specification.[10] Based on these commercial requirements, the Technical Module develops the specification. The Steering Board thereafter adopts the specification, and it is delivered to a recognized standards body such as ETSI for completion of standardization.[11] Within the Steering Board (and in the modules and subgroups), decisions are generally made by consensus. The Steering Board has a mechanism to break deadlocks, but it has never been exercised.

The DVB offers a "bottom-up" approach to technological development. Within Europe, its structure, working method, and novel ties to regulators represented a departure from the view prevailing in the 1990s that the state (and European institutions) should take a leading role in industrial policy.[12] In broadcasting technology, this interventionist approach found its apogee in the work of the European Commission promoting

HD-MAC, an analog high-definition standard targeted at satellite broadcasters. As a result, a "triptych" of measures was adopted, compelling use of the HD-MAC standard, offering subsidies for programming and encouraging industry to coordinate market roll-out.[13] The "top-down" approach failed because of the reticence of broadcasters and its reliance on analog solutions at a time when digital technologies already looked more promising.[14]

As a result, DVB offered a number of innovations in its structure and work practices. Among these were the consensus-based decision process, inclusiveness across industrial sectors with a voice guaranteed to each sector in the Steering Board, participation by regulators from member states as a "college" within the membership, the focus on market requirements (as formulated by a Commercial Module), recognition that specification writing should meet a time-to-market test, and greater clarity on IPR licensing. Although operating under Swiss law as a not-for-profit association, DVB formed ties to formal institutions through agreements with ETSI and CENELEC, two standards bodies recognized under European law for standardization, and by the recognition by the European Commission and other EU institutions of DVB as their reference point for broadcasting technologies.

During its close to 15 years of existence, the DVB has developed more than 100 specifications. Among the most successful are its standards for terrestrial, satellite, and cable transmissions. For example, services based on its terrestrial standard, DVB-T, have been launched or are imminent in 27 countries; a further 24 have formally adopted the standard. Among other noteworthy specifications are those more recently adopted for a consumer product offering both reception of broadcasting and interactivity (the Multimedia Home Platform) and a specification based on DVB-T for delivery of broadcast transmission to smaller mobile devices such as cell phones (DVB-H).[15] DVB technologies

in broadcasting have been as successful as GSM in mobile telephony.

The United States has followed a different path in its development of digital television. Its standard setting, led by the efforts of the Advanced Television Standards Committee (ATSC), has been limited generally to a competing terrestrial specification that is now being rolled out by over-the-air broadcasters. ATSC's work was centered on a specification that could offer high-definition television (HDTV) so the purchaser could more easily appreciate the difference in technology.[16] Within the United States, other broadcaster services have taken up specifications from DVB's "toolbox." For example, both Echostar and DirecTV use the DVB-S specification for their satellite services, and market participants have not followed ATSC for introducing mobile broadcasting. Japan has created its own terrestrial specification, ISDB. ATSC has been taken up by Mexico and Canada and certain other territories; Japan's ISDB is the leading contender for terrestrial transmissions in Brazil.

This article generally presents the IPR policy of the DVB Project. It is based not only on published materials cited in the notes, but also on information drawn from the files of the DVB Project, including reports of the meetings of its Steering Board and the IPR Module.

Recent Regulatory Developments

This assessment of the IPR policy of the DVB Project is undertaken at a time of a shifting regulatory landscape. Authorities long appeared to disfavor meddling by standards bodies in licensing issues. Now competition authorities are openly signaling that there is little risk of a per se condemnation of ex ante royalty discussions within standards bodies. In addition, standards bodies are reviewing their IPR policies and practices in light of the series of decisions from the U.S. Federal Trade Commission and U.S. courts on the conduct of Rambus, a holder of essential IPR in a standard issued as a result of a process in which Rambus participated.[17]

A discussion of the IPR policy of a standards body can be undertaken only within the regulatory framework in which it operates. As a collective activity frequently comprised of competing commercial players, a standards body and its members must be wary of practices that violate competition rules. This is notably the case for the policy adopted and implemented by a body in respect to the licensing of IPRs essential for its standards. For example, the rejection of a candidate technology to be included in a specification on the basis that the owner's terms for licensing are not acceptable could be viewed as an impermissible collective boycott. As a result, the view long prevailing among standards bodies has been that any licensing, discussion of terms, or patent pooling effort should occur well outside a body's activities. In other words, a standards body should focus on the best technical solution to a technology challenge; licensing should be addressed after the solution is found and outside of the standards context. ETSI's attitude is representative. Its Guide on Intellectual Property Rights states:

Specific licensing terms and negotiations are commercial issues between the companies and shall not be addressed within ETSI. Technical Bodies are not the appropriate place to discuss IPR Issues. Technical Bodies do not have the competence to deal with commercial issues. Members attending ETSI Technical Bodies are often technical experts who do not have legal or business responsibilities with regard to licensing issues. Discussion on licensing issues among competitors in a standards making process can significantly complicate, delay or derail this process.[18]

DVB has generally followed this approach, and while its policy is innovative, it has adhered to the accepted position that a standards body should be reticent to set terms for licensing. This approach appeared to be supported by regulatory authorities.

Recent regulatory pronouncements indicate an evolution in the attitude of both the U.S. authorities and the European Commission. For example, in its 2004 guidelines on competition policy and technology transfer agreements, the European Commission indicated that it was prepared to accept that terms for licensing a contribution could be discussed before standard is adopted. It wrote:

In certain circumstances it may be more efficient if the royalties are agreed before the standard is chosen and not after the standard is decided upon, to avoid that the choice of the standard confers a significant degree of market power on one or more essential technologies.[19]

During 2005, the leading officials of the two agencies responsible for U.S. federal enforcement of antitrust laws adopted a similar position (Pate, 2005; Platt Majoras, 2005). These pronouncements on the shift in regulatory principles have now, in the United States, been applied in practice with the confirmation by the U.S. Department of Justice in business review letters that it would not take antitrust enforcement action against standards bodies whose policies require, in one case, working group members to disclose patents and patent applications, to commit to FR&ND licensing terms, to declare most restrictive licensing terms, and to submit to arbitration; and, in the other case, provide for a facility for disclosure of patents and letters of assurance for licensing terms.[20]

These agencies, together with the European Commission, have already, for a time, treated, as comporting with antitrust laws, patent pooling efforts when meeting certain procompetitive requirements as to essentiality of included IPRs, process of evaluation, and other matters.[21] As part of their more general review of the relationship between IPRs, standard-setting, and antitrust policy, the U.S. agencies have recently considered the place of patent pooling as a mechanism to achieve licensing efficiencies for bringing to market standardized technologies.[22]

Impact of Rambus Cases

In parallel with the hearings, public statements, and other regulatory action of the European Commission and U.S. agencies, the terms of an IPR policy in a standards body and the duties of a participant in that body have been the subject of extensive litigation. Briefly, Rambus, a technology provider, participated in the work of JEDEC, a standards body, which resulted in a new standard. At the time, Rambus had IPR relevant to that standard or to other work items within JEDEC. Rambus did not disclose this IPR but sued for infringement implementers of JEDEC standards.[23]

The precise elements of the claims and defenses are beyond the scope of this article. Rather, the continuing *Rambus* litigation is noteworthy for the tone it has set for the attitude of standards bodies to their IPR policies. Two conclusions have been drawn:

First, standards bodies have been brought to examine their policies in order to determine whether they are sufficiently precise to alert participants of their obligations of disclosure, licensing, etc of essential IPR. Here the policies of these bodies are measured against the detailed finding of the failings of JEDEC.[24] If a standards body finds that its policy falls short, it may well take steps to provide greater certainty to its members and to implementers by clarifying or where needed recasting its IPR rules.

Second, these bodies and their members are reviewing the duties which a standards participant owes to a body and its fellow participants. In other words, can the participant be held to a duty of care beyond that expected in normal commercial dealings, for example to a duty of good faith?[25]

ETSI and Disclosure

The shift in position by competition authorities suggests greater scope for action by standards bodies and their members when addressing the licensing of IPRs essential to their standards. At the same time, ETSI has been considering reforms of its IPR policy. ETSI's activities in this area are important because the majority of DVB's specifications are delivered to that body for formal standardization. Because of these close ties, there has been at times a tension between the DVB's policy of "negative disclosure" and ETSI's more familiar approach of affirmative disclosure and confirmation of licensing terms.[26]

This is not the first time ETSI's policy has been an important factor for DVB's. Shortly after its formation in 1988, ETSI adopted an interim policy that would have obliged members to license on FR&ND terms (unless essential IPR was withdrawn) and encouraged early disclosure of licensing terms, including a maximum royalty. This initial approach was abandoned in favor of a policy following the prevailing ISO model.[27]

More recently, ETSI has once again been engaged in a review of its IPR policy. The present review was prompted by a complaint brought by MicroElectronica to the European Commission that a declaration of a patent essential to an ETSI standard had been made by Sun Microsystems, Inc. (Sun) after the adoption of the standard. MicroElectronica asserted several claims, including that the declaration was impermissibly late; the declaration was in respect of a nonessential patent (i.e., MicroElectronica claimed it could make a noninfringing implementation of the standard); and Sun failed to satisfy the ETSI rule that it grant licences on FR&ND terms. The claim was brought to DG Competition on the basis of Microelectronica's assertion that the conduct of Sun, ETSI, and other ETSI members violated Article 81 of the EU Treaty. In respect of the Microelectronica claim, ETSI took corrective action to satisfy the

European Commission[28] and then took steps to reform its IPR policy.

The first tangible step was a rewording of the core disclosure obligation of ETSI members. The text in its present form reads (changes to the text are not in italic):

[E]ach Member shall use its reasonable endeavours, in particular during the development of a Standard or Technical Specification where it participates, *to inform ETSI of Essential IPRs* in a timely fashion. *In particular, a Member submitting a technical proposal for a Standard or Technical Specification shall, on a bona fide basis, draw the attention of ETSI to any of that Member's IPR which might be Essential if that proposal is adopted.* (ETSI, 2006)

After this perhaps modest amendment to the text of its policy, ETSI launched a more sweeping assessment. A number of options have been presented by ETSI members, including the value of making a general declaration of willingness to license early in standards work, a level of disclosure that matches specific claims in patents with standards, an ETSI framework for licensing agreements, patent "landscaping," a definition of FR&ND to include a royalty cap, enhancement to ETSI databases of submitted declarations, and so forth. The outcome of this review led to an ETSI process to facilitate ex ante terms and conditions.[29] It is important to note the impact of the ETSI process on DVB: the turbulence in the normally placid waters of ETSI's IPR policy could well spill over to DVB.

IPR POLICY OF THE DVB PROJECT

This section presents generally the policy adopted by DVB governing intellectual property rights essential to its specifications. It first describes DVB's work in formulating a policy and places that

activity in the context of regulatory and standards developments in the early and mid-1990s, notably the discussion within ETSI of its own policy. Subsequently, a detailed overview is offered, in the form of a commentary, of the text of Article 14 of the MoU, the basis for DVB's policy. DVB's copyright policy is then presented. The MoU includes a further key innovation: the fostering of voluntary licensing programs covering DVB specifications. This merits a fuller discussion.

DVB's Adoption of an IPR Policy

Issues relating to intellectual property rights were raised during the formation of DVB when it was operating informally as the European Launching Group—Digital Video Broadcasting. The ELG-DVB held several plenary meetings of potential members to discuss the text of a document, the Memorandum of Understanding, which would serve as its constituting text. At one of these meetings, a single paragraph was proposed as an IPR policy to the effect that members agreed to grant licences to their essential IPRs on FR&ND terms. The text was withdrawn, in part because it was a late addition when the MoU was close to signature, and because some colleagues believed that the IPR policy for DVB could be more ambitious. Once DVB was formed, the Steering Board, DVB's senior governing body, returned to the IPR issue and named two ad-hoc groups to develop a policy. This work produced a text that was adopted as an amendment to the DVB's MoU. The text of that "IPR Amendment" is in large measure identical to DVB's IPR policy today.

Regulatory and Industrial Context: ETSI, MPEG2, "MPEG 1½"

The formulation of DVB's IPR policy took place in the context of other regulatory and industrial developments. These included most notably the attempt by ETSI to complete its own policy on essential IPRs. In addition, DVB members were participants in (or actively followed) the work on the MPEG2 standard and the fringe effort to establish a pool covering MPEG2 patents. Finally, DVB early on had to confront a direct challenge to its activities: the risk that it would produce no more than "paper," unimplementable specifications that would lose out to proprietary technology.

ETSI's IPR Policy

DVB's work on its IPR policy was influenced by the parallel activity undertaken within ETSI. ETSI had been formed recently and was striving to develop rules to counter the risk that an ETSI member holding IPRs essentially could impose onerous terms on, or indeed block, implementation of a standard.

ETSI attempted to go beyond the IPR policy commonly used in the International Organization for Standardization (ISO) and its affiliates. The ISO policy contemplated that a standard could be withdrawn if blocking IPR prevented its use. The standards body could specify a new standard working around; in other words, avoiding the infringement of the blocking IPR. This model was suitable for freestanding products. But in the context of standards for essential interfaces for communications—the focus of ETSI's activities—there was often no alternative noninfringing solution. Moreover, once a standard is adopted within the telecommunications field, the whole industrial value chain is often committed. In the view of some during this initial period within ETSI, this gave disproportionate power to the holder of IPRs.

ETSIs attempted to solve this issue by a series of IPR measures, including imposing on members an *a priori* commitment to license (except in respect of identified IPRs withdrawn within six months of the launch of a work item) and binding arbitration. It also sought to require that members would license only for monetary consideration, notify ETSI of the maximum royalty, and apply these terms on a worldwide basis as the standards achieved broad acceptance. Several members,

however, complained to the European Commission, asserting that it amounted to a compulsory licence,[30] and ETSI was obliged to conform its policy to ISO's. The views of some leading members of DVB[31] were shaped by this experience, and they determined to use some of the same provisions in an IPR policy as DVB was launching its activities. Indeed, the constraints imposed on ETSI, a standards body formally recognized by EU institutions, were not present for DVB, a voluntary standards consortium.

MPEG2 Pooling Effort

Concurrently with DVB's steps to formulate its IPR policy, an intense effort was underway to complete a pool covering the patents essential to the MPEG2 specification. MPEG2 is a specification covering compression and other technologies; it is a necessary underpinning of DVB's work on digital broadcasting. The standards work was undertaken within the Moving Pictures Experts Group (MPEG) within ISO. The pooling activity, led by the U.S. entity CableLabs, was not formally part of ISO. Instead, consistent with the notion then prevailing under antitrust law calling for separation of standards work and licensing, the pooling activity was on the fringes of MPEG2. This effort would prove to be typical of such efforts: a jointly administered licensing program, making available under a single licence multiple patents, held by two or more entities, usually all relevant to a single standard or product. The patent holders participating in a pool may choose one of their number to act as administrator; in the case of the MPEG2 pool, the participants selected a third party for administration and pool promotion.[32] The effort ultimately resulted in the formation of a commercial licensing administrator, MPEG LA, and the completion of a licensing regime covering MPEG2 patents.[33]

The highly visible campaigning for an MPEG2 pool and the substantial resources devoted to the related patent search and formation of a licensing administrator were significant elements in the background to DVB's work on its IPR policy. It suggested that a formalized process for pooling could become commonplace in standards work, notably for broadcast technologies. This influenced the views of several participants in DVB's work, notably leading rights holders, and made more palatable the inclusion of a pooling option within an IPR text.

Challenge from "MPEG 1½"

One of the first work items of DVB was a specification for digital broadcast transmissions by satellite. Three leading European satellite broadcasters had confirmed that they would each delay introduction of digital services until completion of the DVB-S specification.[34] But shortly after DVB began developing its specification, there were press reports suggesting that a broadcaster wishing to implement DVB-S could well be blocked by the holders of patents essential to DVB-S demanding an onerous royalty or otherwise impeding use of its patent. The press reports indicated that an implementer would do better to buy a package of already existing, proprietary technology dubbed MPEG 1½, where the implementer would have certainty of the extent of its exposure to royalties. DVB's work then would be unavailing because the identity of the rights holders in DVB-S and their terms would be unknown. This would present to broadcasters and other implementers an unacceptable commercial risk of patent ambush and other practices. For this reason, DVB might produce merely a "paper standard" never to be implemented.

These reports spurred the DVB to address the need for an IPR policy. DVB members had already devoted significant resources in forming DVB. It enjoyed the support of the European Commission and Member State ministries. There was little desire to have this important initiative strangled at its inception by blocking patents. Shortly after the press reports, the DVB created the ad hoc groups on IPR, which led to the drafting of its licensing policy.[35]

DVB's Formulation of its IPR Policy

Based on that context—lessons learned from the debate over ETSI's policy and the other circumstances outlined previously— DVB set about formulating a policy covering DVB's specifications. As noted, shortly after formation, DVB created two ad hoc groups on IPR. Leadership of these groups was balanced: One group was chaired by a representative drawn from the equipment manufacturers' constituency and the second by a representative from pay television broadcasters. As work progressed, these groups often met together and were ultimately merged. The groups enjoyed a broad membership from throughout the DVB membership, and the text adopted represents, in addition to the experience of the ETSI debate and the other circumstances noted previously, a series of compromises across constituencies.

Among these compromises was a firm obligation imposed on DVB members to grant FR&ND licences to essential IPRs, coupled with a liberal but time-constrained right to withdraw IPR. This resulted in two windows for giving notice of unavailability: the first promptly after adoption of a specification; and the second, with stricter conditions, up to final standardization.[36] This compromise removed the need for affirmative disclosure of essential IPR. A second compromise was the grant of a right to arbitration to settle disputes about licensing terms for IPRs essential to a specification, coupled with the expiry of such right at the time of completion of a licensing program comprising patents essential to the specification.[37] Patent holders could have perceived that forming pools would be a relatively easy exercise, perhaps in light of the new formalized pooling mechanisms such as MPEG LA. As a result, in their view, the prospect of being taken to arbitration was remote.

The result of this activity within DVB was an amendment to its Memorandum of Understanding, adopted by the DVB's membership in October 1996. The operative language of the IPR Amendment through two successive restatements of the MoU has remained in large measure the same (and is discussed in detail next). The text has been changed to keep pace with the widening scope of DVB's activities[38] and to ensure that the policy is retroactive, covering all DVB specifications, including those released before adoption of the IPR policy.[39] In addition, the first version of the provision on forming patent pools, Article 14.9, set a hard date for completing the pooling arrangements. The original text of Article 14.9 called for pools to be completed by the second anniversary of the October 1996 adoption of the amendment. In its original form, the IPR Amendment was prepared under the assumption that DVB's work, with the completion of the basic transmission specifications, was virtually complete, and it would not undertake further work items. That expectation has, of course, proved to be widely off the mark, and the present Article 14.9 now sets the general rule that pools should be completed within two years from adoption of the underlying specification.

Text and Commentary of DVB's IPR Policy

The important elements of Article 14 MoU are considered next. Article 14.2, the general duty to offer FR&ND licences for essential IPRs, is presented first, together with its reach (members and their affiliates, Art. 14.4) and the technologies covered (Art. 14.5). The time limitations for negative disclosure, Articles 14.1 and 14.3, are then set out, together with the effect of notice on other members (Art 14.6). Article 14 also provides for enforcement of these IPR rules (arbitration, Art. 14.7); there are other remedies elsewhere in the MoU (e.g., Art 2.1, commitment "to purposes of DVB"). Other legal issues are considered, including retroactivity of the provisions (Art. 14.8), the effect of withdrawal from DVB (Art 15), and the relationship of DVB's rules with those of other standards bodies. Finally, the IPR Module, DVB's separate body to review IPR issues, is presented

(Art 9). The next section covers DVB's policy on copyright. (The provision forming the basis of DVB's fostering of patent pools, Article 14.9, merits a lengthier discussion; it is treated in Part 2 of this article.)

Obligation to License on FR&ND Terms

Article 14.2 MoU sets out the core obligation of DVB members in respect to licensing their IPRs essential to DVB specification. That section provides:

14.2 With respect to any IPRs, owned or controlled by the Member or any of its affiliated companies, under which it or any such affiliated company has the free right to grant or to cause the grant of licences and to the extent that such IPRs will be necessarily infringed when implementing any specification approved by the Technical Module, other than those that are notified under clause 14.1 hereof, each Member hereby undertakes, on its behalf and on behalf of its affiliated companies, that it is willing to grant or to cause the grant of non-exclusive, non-transferable, world-wide licences on fair, reasonable and non-discriminatory terms and conditions under any of such IPRs for use in or of equipment fully complying with such specification to any third party which has or will submit an equivalent undertaking with respect to any relevant IPRs it may have or obtain with respect to such specification.

Article 14.2 sets out the leading principal of the IPR policy. It provides that a member shall grant licences on terms FR&ND to IPRs that are necessarily infringed when implementing a DVB specification. "Intellectual property rights" is a broad term. In practice, the DVB's policy is focused on patents held by members; these are the subject, for example, of the pooling efforts (described further in this article). The status of patent applications and copyright are discussed elsewhere.[40]

The notion of "fair, reasonable, and nondiscriminatory" is not free from controversy. Indeed, it is sometimes contended that the expression is meaningless.[41] DVB has not attempted to offer a definition, in part because the discovery of price and other terms is generally left to the agreement of commercial actors and normally outside DVB's activities. However, DVB has provided a forum for discussion among DVB members of the licensing terms proposed by one or more rights holders and has developed other mechanisms (e.g., arbitration, fostering the pooling process) that may have an impact on terms.[42]

Terms based on FR&ND are to be available not just to other DVB members but also to "any third party" that wants to use DVB technology. There are some limitations on this duty. First, the IPR must be essential; that is, "necessarily infringed when implementing [the] specification." There is no duty if there are alternative technical means available to implement a DVB specification. The availability of an alternative has been understood to mean "from a technical point of view." The test is not based on the economic feasibility for the licensee to take up the alternative.[43] Second, the licensee must use the IPRs for "equipment fully complying with [the] specification." Finally, the licensing arrangement must be symmetrical: the licensee must make an "equivalent undertaking"; this is, agree to grant a license to the licensing member on FR&ND terms. This is a safeguard protecting the licensing member who deals with a licensee that is not a DVB member (and thus, otherwise not under the same duty as the licensor).

The rule on offering FR&ND terms is binding on DVB and its affiliated companies. Article 14.4 gives the definition of "affiliated companies":

14.4 As used in this Article 14, "affiliated company" shall mean, in respect of a Member,

any legal entity which directly or indirectly controls, is controlled by, or is under common control with the Member, but only as long as such control exists, where the term "control" means the ownership, directly or indirectly, of more than 50 % of the interest representing the right to vote or to manage the affairs of an entity.

The definition includes, for a DVB member, a company that becomes "affiliated" after the date of DVB membership; the acquired company's portfolio becomes subject to the FR&ND regime. Also in some cases, two or more DVB members can jointly own an entity that may, under the control arrangements among the owners, be treated as an affiliate of one or both members for the purposes of the IPR rules.

The rules offer a list of the technologies covered by the IPR policy. Article 14.5 provides:

14.5 This Article covers digital video broadcasting via satellite, cable, terrestrial and broadband wireless (MMDS, LMDS, etc) means and incorporating the global MPEG2 standard for source coding and multiplex to the extent possible, together with the relevant aspects of the related receiving equipment (including in each case scrambling) and does not cover associated matters such as conditional access. For the avoidance of doubt Article 14 does not cover the IPR arising from the MPEG2 standard itself.

The first sentence is intended to encompass the sweep of DVB specifications. All the specifications adopted by DVB fall under Article 14 (and are the subject of the "90-day notices" discussed later). The text conforms to the purpose clause of DVB at Article 1.3. It was designed to make clear, at an early stage in DVB's development, that certain technologies, while not fitting into a traditional definition of "broadcasting" such as multichannel multipoint distribution channel (wireless cable or MMDS), would nonetheless be subject to DVB's IPR rules. Today, if a list were still suitable, it would include, for example, DVB's specifications for television services received over the Internet (IPTV). If the text is changed in an amendment to the MoU, it is likely to list only the exclusions.

The section makes clear that the rules do not cover "associated matters such as conditional access" or the IPR arising from the MPEG2 standard. The exclusion of conditional access is part of the legacy of the "Conditional Access Package" under which certain DVB members promised to make available scrambling technology but reserved conditional access, treating it outside of DVB's technical work and its legal framework. The objective of the suppliers was to avoid an argument that the DVB's IPR terms required them to license their proprietary conditional access technology. Rather, these terms would come under the Conditional Access Package and ultimately the TV Standards Directive. The concern about "licensing creep" prompted the exclusion from the IPR rule of other "associated matters."

The section also excludes "IPR arising from the MPEG2 standard itself." The MPEG2 standard specified compression and other technologies related to digital television and other services. The work of MPEG2, an ISO body independent of DVB, was virtually complete when DVB launched its work on transmission standards. At the time of drafting the text that would become Article 14, the IPRs covering MPEG2 were the subject of a pooling campaign. For this reason, MPEG2 was excluded from Article 14.

"Negative Disclosure": Inability to License for FR&ND

As noted previously, DVB's policy reverses the normal mechanism of the IPR rules of a standards body. The common approach for standards bodies is to encourage disclosure and then to ask the rights holder to confirm it is willing to license on FR&ND terms. In DVB, disclosure is not required *unless* the holder cannot grant such licences. There are two windows for this "negative disclosure." The first occurs shortly after the specification is adopted by DVB. Section 14.1 provides:

14.1 Within 90 days from notification of approval of a specification by the Technical Module, each Member shall, on behalf of itself and its affiliated companies, submit to the chairman of the Steering Board a list of all the IPRs owned or controlled by the Member or any of its affiliated companies, to the extent that the Member knows that such IPRs will be necessarily infringed when implementing such specification and for which it will not or has no free right to make licences available.

The first window for disclosure opens when the DVB issues its "90-day letter" shortly after the Technical Module adopts a specification.[44] Often several specifications are listed in the letter. The member that cannot grant licences on FR&ND terms in respect to its IPRs essential to the specification submits within 90 days a list of its unavailable IPRs. There are two circumstances contemplated as the grounds for unavailability. First, the member is entitled to announce it "will not … make licences available" presumably in the exercise of its commercial judgment. In addition, it could give notice that it "has no free right to make licences available" if, for example, it has previously granted an exclusive right to a third party. To date, no list of unavailable IPRs has been submitted.

This provision is arguably generous to the rights holder; it allows the rights holder to signal, when the specification is virtually complete, that it is unwilling to grant a licence to essential IPR. This timing is consistent with the view widely shared among some DVB members that an obligation to make an earlier notice would not be productive because the specification would still be fluid. Until adoption by DVB's Technical Module, the final shape of the specification and its incorporated technologies are not certain. It is only at that point that a DVB member has all the information needed for a notice.[45] In addition, this first 90-day window offers a reasonable time for a DVB member to review its portfolio to determine if it has no free right to license a patent for an identified specification for FR&ND licensing. The task is easier in most cases because the internal review would not cover all relevant patents but only that smaller number of patents where, because of pre-existing licences or other contractual arrangements, there is a question of availability.[46]

The second window for negative disclosure closes when the DVB specification completes the standardization process within ETSI or another appropriate standards body. Article 14.3 states:

14.3 A Member shall have the right up until the time of final adoption as a standard by a recognised standards body of a specification approved by the Steering Board to declare to the DVB Steering Board that it will not make available licences under an IPR that was subject to the undertaking for licensing pursuant to article 14.2 above, only in the exceptional circumstances that the Member can demonstrate that a major business interest will be seriously jeopardised.

Here the DVB member makes a declaration that its essential IPR is unavailable because if it is compelled to grant a licence on FR&ND terms, "a major business interest would be seriously jeopardised." In the case of this section as well, no declaration of unavailability has ever been made, so it is difficult to identify the range of situations that would constitute a "major business interest" and serious jeopardy.[47] At one extreme, a member could arguably demonstrate serious jeopardy to a major business interest if application of DVB rules would trigger its bankruptcy.

The test of unavailability is different between Section 14.1 and Section 14.3. Section 14.1 is arguably more straightforward than Article 14.3. The member invoking Section 14.1 simply asserts the right to withdraw its IPR or claims it has no free right by operation of law or pre-existing contract in order to make its IPR available. Section 14.3 sets a higher threshold for unavailability because the member must demonstrate "jeopardy" to its "business interest." The circumstances leading a member to make a declaration under Section 14.3 are not based on its purely subjective assessment because the declaring member has to make a "demonstration" to the Steering Board. The Steering Board may offer its own views as to whether the member has satisfied the test of Article 14.3.[48]

While the text varies on the process to be followed for submitting a list of unavailable IPRs under Section 14.1 and making a declaration under Section 14.3, in both cases, the member should make its submission to the Chairman DVB.[49] The content is likely to be the same: a list of unavailable IPRs. The place of patent applications in such a list is not clearcut. In the case of a patent application, both windows may have closed before the patent issues. In such case, where the member would, with the issuance of the patent, have essential IPR *and* such IPR would be unavailable, it should, even while its application is pending, take one of the actions under Article 14.1 and Article 14.3.

The IPR rules apply equally to all members and all their IPRs essential to any DVB specification, whether they joined at DVB's inception or more recently. A prospective member could be concerned that at the time of joining, both windows for a specification could long have closed and it would not have an opportunity to give the notice of unavailability of its own IPR. Under these circumstances, DVB has, in response to a request, allowed a new member a further 90-day period so it could review its IPR portfolio.[50]

The MoU also addresses the concern that a member, submitting a list under Section 14.1

or declaring under Section 14.3, could take the position that it has put other members on notice of their infringement of essential IPR. Under U.S. legislation, a willful infringement could arguably subject the infringer to multiple actual damages.[51] DVB members have agreed, however, that neither action under Article 14 will have this effect. Article 14.6 provides:

14.6 Any notifications made by Members in connection with this Article 14 shall not constitute notice from any Member to any other Member (or any Observer) or constitute a charge or basis for a charge, of infringement of any IPR or related damages claim of any kind, for any purpose, under any applicable law.

Enforcement of Licensing Terms

The MoU expressly provides for arbitration as a remedy for violation of the IPR rules. Article 14.7 states:

14.7 Each Member hereby agrees, on its behalf and on behalf of its affiliated companies, that, subject to clause 14.9 of this Article 14, all disputes with any other Member of these statutes (MoU) regarding solely the terms and conditions of licences arising in connection with the undertaking in this Article 14 shall be finally settled under the Rules of Conciliation and Arbitration of the International Chamber of Commerce by three arbitrators appointed in accordance with such Rules. Arbitration shall take place in Frankfurt, Germany. German substantive law shall apply. The language of the arbitral proceedings shall be the English language unless agreed otherwise between the Members.

The scope of the arbitration provision is limited to "the terms and conditions of licences arising in connection with the undertaking in this Article 14." The general case contemplated would be a dispute between a member and a prospective licensee as to whether the terms offered satisfied FR&ND. Presumably, arbitration would also cover a member's refusal to license, whether in the context of a licensing dispute the member had made a satisfactory notice under Article 14.1 or Article 14.3 of the unavailability of its IPR, and other questions relating to provisions of Article 14. [52] The right to arbitration does not apply to specifications for which a licensing program has been established in conformity with Article 14.9.[53]

Arbitration can be invoked only by DVB members. This could be considered anomalous because the duty to license on FR&ND terms benefits "any third party" according to Article 14.2. A reason for this limitation in Article 14.7 is due to the novelty of including arbitration in the IPR rules of a standards body; in preparing the IPR rules, the drafter could well have intended to limit the universe of potential claimants.[54] At the same time, such a provision would make membership more attractive to the implementing community.

The arbitration provision specifies the applicable procedural and substantive law. The selection of rules of the International Chamber of Commerce is unexceptional and makes available a widely known body of arbitration procedures. The application of German substantive law and the choice of Frankfurt as the venue for the proceedings can be explained by the relative importance of Germany during the early days of DVB, based on such factors as the number of meetings of its governing bodies in Germany and the composition at the time of its senior management. It is DVB's expectation that the notion of "fair, reasonable and non-discriminatory" is well settled and that an outcome under Germany's substantive law would be no different than what could be expected from other jurisdictions.[55] Article 14.9 states that "all disputes ... *shall* be finally settled," indicating that arbitration is the exclusive means to resolves such disputes, precluding recourse to judicial proceedings.

Arbitration has its inconveniences; it can be expensive and unwieldy. The ICC court of arbitration can be a costly forum, especially when three arbitrators are required. At the same time, the MoU does not exclude other nonbinding forms of dispute resolution such as mediation and use of experts. Moreover, the approach adopted to complete the arrangements for licensing the Java components of MHP—review of terms by competition counsel and resolution of open points by mediation before his or her favorable opinion was delivered—could also be characterized as a form of mediation.[56]

The right to arbitration is an innovative development in DVB's rules.[57] It provides a mechanism for a relatively speedy resolution of a licensing dispute. It settles applicable law, procedure, and venue, reducing for the claimant the complexities of litigation and the exposure to dilatory pretrial practices. For the licensing member, it defines the class of potential claimants (members only) and confines the dispute to matters arising out of Article 14, arguably excluding ancillary claims often joined in a civil case. Overall, it was part of a calculus of avoiding ex ante disclosure of rights and licensing terms. The right was a development significantly beyond other IPR models. It was also one of the elements of IPR policy that had been proposed for ETSI but ultimately found to be more acceptable in a private law body such as DVB.

A further innovative feature of the arbitration provision is the explicit link to Article 14.9 and patent pooling. The assumption was that an acceptable range of royalties and other terms falling within an FR&ND framework, if not offered by the rights holder, could be determined through arbitration or through the pooling process. As noted, arbitration does not apply to specifications for which a licensing program has been completed. The prospect of the lapse of the arbitration provision is meant to serve as a spur for the completion

of patent pools.[58] Over time, this "spur" appears to be the most useful benefit because arbitration under Article 14.7 has indeed never been invoked. This is perhaps due to the costs involved. Or it is the result of the actions of rights holders to complete pools to avoid this remedy or by their offer of licensing terms, which, in the eyes of the implementers, are sufficiently FR&ND.

Arbitration is a right to be exercised by DVB members. DVB as an entity does not have a process set out in its MoU to penalize recalcitrant members, such as those refusing to offer their essential IPRs on FR&ND terms. At times there has been reference to the perceived failure of members to satisfy the duty under Article 2.1 to "commit themselves to the purposes" of the MoU; for example, if they notoriously promote a technology competing with DVB's or disparage a DVB specification. But this has not yet served as the basis for imposing a penalty such as expulsion on the offending members.[59]

Other Legal Issues

Several other provisions are relevant to the IPR rules of the DVB Project. These confirm that:

- The IPR rules set out in the MoU, even if adopted after the initial formation of the DVB, apply to all its specifications.
- A member's duty to offer FR&ND terms continues even if it chooses to withdraw from DVB.
- DVB's rules are not intended to displace the IPR policy of recognized standards bodies responsible for standardizing DVB specifications.

Date of Effectiveness of IPR Policy

As already indicated in section II.A, the IPR amendment to the Memorandum of Understanding was adopted some months after the formal inception of the DVB. One issue at the time was whether the members' licensing duty under the amendment would be retroactive to the date of DVB's formation. The amendment confirmed that the duty was retroactive; Article 14.8 in the present text reconfirms that position:[60]

14.8 Clauses 14.1 through 14.6 of this Article 14 to these Statutes (MoU) sustains in force the provisions of Article 19 of the previous version of the statutes (MoU) adopted by the General Assembly in accordance with the voting procedure pursuant Article 15 of that version and those provisions applied retrospectively.

Effect of Withdrawal from Membership

A member's duties under the MoU do not lapse at the time of its withdrawal. Article 15 provides a mechanism for withdrawal but states, "Such withdrawal shall not affect the existing obligations on the Member in its individual capacity." These obligations include the continuing duty to offer FR&ND terms in respect to its IPRs essential to specifications adopted before its withdrawal. This applies as well to those specifications that, when the member withdraws, are within the time periods for notice of unavailability. Other specifications will have been still in development at the time of the member's withdrawal. When these specifications are completed, DVB delivers to the former member (as it does to all current members) the "90-day notice," opening the window for submission of lists of unavailable IPRs.

Place of IPR Rules of Formal Standards Bodies

DVB develops specifications and looks to recognize standards bodies such as ETSI or CENELEC to adopt standards incorporating these specifications. These bodies have their own IPR policies

that follow the more common model requiring disclosure of essential IPR (positive disclosure) and confirmation that the IPR will be available on FR&ND terms. This model does not contradict DVB's approach but does present differences. In its MoU, DVB makes clear that its policy is not intended to displace those other policies. The chapeau to Article 14 states:

Recognising that the DVB Project is not a standards body, the DVB Project takes the basic position that if specifications made by the DVB group are being adopted as standard by a recognised standards body the IPR policy of that standards body should apply to such standards.

In practice, the two regimes are complementary:[61] the DVB policy compels FR&ND, subject to negative disclosure, and the standards body calls for positive disclosure and confirmation of licensing terms. (See further for a discussion of the merits *vel non* of a disclosure-based regime.) While expecting compliance with its own IPR policy, DVB also alerts its members to the need to adhere to the rules of the standards body to which its specification is delivered. For example, in the form of circular letter giving notice of the start of the 90-day period under Article 14.1 after adoption of a DVB specification, the DVB writes:

If you are a member of the standards body applicable to this specification, we expect you to comply with the IPR rules of that body. If you are not a member it is nonetheless good practice for you to comply with its IPR rules.[62]

Thus, in the case of a DVB member that is also a member of ETSI, it can remain silent during the 90-day window, as a result signifying that if it has essential IPRs, they are available for license on FR&ND terms. But once the specification has been submitted to ETSI, it must observe that body's disclosure rules.

DVB's IPR Module

The MoU also provides for a separate body within DVB, the Intellectual Property Rights Module, to treat IPR issues. The IPR Module is described as follows:

[A] forum for members to seek out solutions to any intellectual property issue that arise in relation to DVB specifications, within the framework of Article 14.

Article 9 MoU, as noted above, the European Launching Group—Digital Video Broadcasting—discussed the suitability of an IPR policy, and soon after formation, the DVB created two IPR ad hoc groups. These were merged into a single ad hoc group. After adoption of the first restated MoU in 1996, the work was formalized into the DVB's organizational structure as the IPR Module, equivalent to the other modules covering technical, commercial, and promotional matters.

One central function of the IPR Module is to provide a forum for exchange of views among members on the terms offered for licensing essential IPRs. It has served in this role notably for the terms offered by pools covering specifications for digital terrestrial broadcasting, Java, other technologies incorporated in the Multimedia Home Platform, and advanced video coding.[63] The IPR Module's function as forum is further discussed as one of the tools of DVB's fostering of patent pools. The IPR Module also has advised the Steering Board in IPR matters, developed a copyright policy, and reviewed the IPR policies of sister standards fora when the DVB is considering whether to enter into liaison arrangements.[64] In these matters, it reports to the Steering Board, which has sole power to "provide guidance on any questions of interpretation of the [Memorandum of Understanding],"[65] including in respect to Article 14 MoU.

The IPR Module is largely comprised of lawyers and patent specialists. Its membership is drawn from across DVB, reflecting its diverse industries and geographies. Like the other modules within DVB, the IPR Module has benefited from stable leadership; since inception, the IPR Module has had only three chairmen.[66] This has helped to ensure a strong institutional memory.

DVB's Copyright Policy

The term "intellectual property rights" as used in Article 14 MoU is generally limited to patents.[67] With the experience examining the licensing policies of Sun Microsystems, Inc. and with a new sensitivity to the issues arising out of the practice of normative referencing, DVB decided to formalize its policy on copyright. The DVB called upon its IPR Module to set out the policy; it was adopted (as a confirmation of DVB's practice) by the Steering Board in 2003.[68]

The text of DVB's copyright policy is unexceptional. Its operative language divides the rules for the use of contributed materials into provisions to accommodate DVB's drafting of specifications and those to allow implementation of the completed specification. For creating and drafting specifications and other DVB materials, the policy calls for contributors to grant to the DVB Project a licence to use, copy, and distribute, and to make derivative works of any contribution. Once the specification has been approved, the contributor grants to DVB a sublicensable licence (a) to use, copy, distribute, and make derivative works of its contribution to the specification, and to implement the specification, and (b) to use, make, reproduce, sell, and so forth, implementations. The policy further provides that ownership of specification and other DVB materials remains vested in DVB, with the right conferred on DVB members to make copies for their own use. Third parties may obtain rights to DVB materials by decision of the Steering Board.

DVB's copyright policy also contains a provision on referenced materials. As a result of convergence across industry sectors, DVB increasingly relies on and refers to the work of other fora in its specifications.[69] The policy requires that normatively referenced materials must be publicly available for evaluation without contractual restrictions (other than those reasonably intended to limit duplication and redistribution). For implementation of the normatively referenced materials, copyright licence must be available on FR&ND terms.

ENDNOTES

[1] I am grateful for the comments to earlier versions of this article offered by Anthony Dixon, Maurits Dolmans, Ruud Peters, Douglas Rosenthal, Stephen Temple, and Adam Watson Brown, by the anonymous reviewers of the *International Journal of IT Standards and Standardization Research*, and by colleagues within DVB, notably the members of the IPR Module; the remaining errors are my own. The views expressed in this article are my own and are not necessarily those of the DVB Project or any of its members. References are found at the end of Part 2 of this article.

[2] Information on the DVB Project can be found at www.dvb.org and further in this article.

[3] Directive 95/47/EC ... of 24 October 1995 on the use of standards for the transmission of television signals, OJ L 281/51 (23 November 1995) ("TV Standards Directive").

[4] The common practice of affirmative disclosure is found for example in the IPR polices of the American National Standards Institute (ANSI) and the International Organization for Standardization (ISO). ANSI is the umbrella organization for U.S. standard setting: it facilitates the development of standards through the accreditation of procedures used by standards developers and the approval of standards as American National Standards. ANSI's Patent Policy reads in part, "If an

ANSI-Accredited Standards Developer (ASD) receives a notice that a proposed [American National Standard ("ANS")] or an approved ANS may require the use of such a patent claim, the procedures in this clause shall be followed:

3.1.1 Statement from patent holder

The ASD shall receive from the identified party or patent holder either:

(a) assurance in the form of a general disclaimer to the effect that such party does not hold and does not currently intend holding any essential patent claim(s); or

(b) assurance that a license to such essential patent claim(s) will be made available to applicants desiring to utilize the license for the purpose of implementing the standard either:

   (i) under reasonable terms and conditions that are demonstrably free of any unfair discrimination; or

   (ii) without compensation and under reasonable terms and conditions that are demonstrably free of any unfair discrimination.

ANSI Essential Requirements s 3.1 available at www.ansi.org. (The text above takes effect in 2008; the prior text was substantial similar). ISO also follows the same practice of affirmative disclosure: ISO/IEC Directives Part 1 s 2.14, available at www.iso.org (when the originator of a proposal, or any other party involved in preparing a document, becomes aware of a patent covering the proposal, then it shall ask the holder to confirm it is willing to grant licenses on reasonable and nondiscriminatory terms). Thereafter, the declaration of the rights holder is generally made publicly available; if the holder refuses to confirm it is willing to grant licenses on FR&ND terms, then the situation is referred back to the drafting committee, presumably to reopen the standard and to specify an alternative that does not infringe on the patent. The comparable provisions of the European Telecommunications Standards Institute are discussed later in the text. (Note that the obligation of a rights holder participating in standard setting to give notice is unclear. Also the participant's duty to grant FR&ND licences is not unambiguous.)

5   Letter dated 4 May 2007 of Fabio Colasanti, European Commission, DG Infos, addressed to Dr. Theo Peek, Chairman DVB.

6   *Rambus,* changes to the IPR policy within ETSI and other developments are discussed further in this article.

7   Information on the DVB Project can be found at www.dvb.org. A summary of the technical work of the DVB Project is set out by the chairman of its Technical Module in Reimers (2004). A broader history of digital television in Europe is available (Bell, 2007).

8   The Memorandum of Understanding further amended and restated (on 13 December 2000) for the development of harmonized Digital Video Broadcasting (DVB) services based on European specifications (MoU). Article 14 MoU sets out the IPR policy of the DVB Project.

9   Membership includes, in addition to long-established commercial companies, entities from the open-source community and cleanroom implementers.

10 Within DVB, "commercial requirements" do not include, for example, price points for consumer equipment or other implementations of DVB specifications. Recently, commercial requirements have begun to describe acceptable terms for licensing of IPRs essential to implementing the resulting specification.

11 In addition to the Commercial Module and the Technical Module, the MoU establishes the Intellectual Property Rights Module (IPR Module) and the Promotion and Communications Module responsible for DVB's presence at trade shows and for promoting DVB standards in non-European territories. Ad hoc groups also report to the Steering Board, covering such matters as budget, membership, and contacts with regulatory bodies.

12 See from the abundant literature at the time on "Rhenan capitalism" (contrasting with the Anglo-American model) (Delmas, 1991).

13 See, among others, Council Directive of 3 November 1986 on the adoption of common technical specifications of the MAC/packet family of standards for direct satellite broadcasting, OJ L 311/28 (6 November 1986); Council Directive 92/338 of 11 May 1992 on the adoption of standards for satellite broadcasting of television signals, OJ L 137/17 (20 May 1992). Some elements of the triptych were salvaged in later EU legislation; for example, the TV Standards Directive, *supra* n. 3.

14 The technical aspects of the evolution in television technology are set out in Wu, et al. (2006).

15 The MHP specification has been adapted for other broadcasting environments such as OpenCable Application Platform (OCAP) by the U.S. cable industry for bidirectional household equipment, the U.S. Federal Communications Commission, In the Matter of Implementation of Section 304 of the Telecommunications Act of 1996, Commercial Availability of Navigation Devices, Compatibility between Cable Systems and Consumer Electronics Equipment, CS Docket No 97-80; as B23 by ARIB, the Japanese broadcast standards body; and is a component in the Blue-ray disc specification. DVB-H, in spring 2007, underwent trials in a number of territories, including Europe and the United States.

16   There were different market considerations in the United States and Europe. In Europe, analog picture quality, based on the PAL and SECAM standards, was generally superior. The advantage presented by digital compression technologies to European viewers was the greater number of broadcasting services. In contrast, Americans already enjoyed a multitude of analog services through cable or satellite networks; HDTV through ATSC is a distinctive improvement over the NSTC analog standard. In any event, DVB's "toolkit" offers both HDTV and standard definition television.

17   In the matter of Rambus, Inc. (U.S. Federal Trade Commission, docket no 9302) Opinions of the Commission (31 July 2006) (as to liability) (5 February 2007) (as to remedy). The FTC's liability opinion also summarizes *Rambus, Inc. vs. Infineon Techs AG*, 313 F3d 1081 (Fed Cir 2003) and other non-FTC judicial developments. The FTC decisions are now (December 2007) the subject of appeals before the U.S. Court of Appeals (DC Cir, Nos 07-1086, 07-1124).

18   See, for example, ETSI (2007). To the same effect, International Telecommunications Union, ITU-T Patent Policy at preamble para 2.2, available at http://www.itu.int/ITU-T/dbase/patent/patent-policy.html ("negotiations ... are left to the parties concerned and are performed outside the ITU"). Alliance for Telecommunications Industry Solutions, Operating Procedures at para 10.4, available at http://www.atis.org/ATSIop.pdf ("[A]ll negotiations and discussions of license terms shall occur between the patent owner and the prospective licensees outside the deliberations of Forum or Committee [of ATIS]. No discussion or negotiation shall be permitted in any Forum or Committee"), and ISO/IEC Directives Part I (5th ed. 2004 Geneva) s 2.14 .2(b) ("Such negotiations [of licensing terms] are left to the parties concerned and

are performed outside ISO and/or IEC").

19   European Commission, Guidelines on the application of Article 81 of the EC Treaty to technology transfer agreements (2004/C 101/02) (27 April 2004) para 225.

20   VITA Business Review Letter (30 October 2006), available at www.usdoj.gov/atr/public/ busreview/219380.htm and IEEE Business Review Letter (30 April 2007), available at www.usdoj.gov/atr/ public/ busreview/222978.htm.

21   European Commission, *Commission approves a patent licensing programme to implement the MPEG-2 standard* (IP/98/1155) (18 December 1998), MPEG-2 Business Review Letter (26 June 1997), available at www.usdoj.gov/atr/public/busreview/1170.htm ("MPEG2 Business Review Letter"); DVD 3C Business Review Letter (16 December 1998), available at www.usdoj.gov/atr/public/busreview/2121.pdf; European Commission, *Commission approves a patent licensing programme to implement the DVD standard* (IP/00/1135) (9 October 2000), DVD 6C Business Review Letter (10 June 1999) available at http://www.usdoj.gov/atr/public/busreview/2485.pdf; DVB-T Notification, Case COMP/C-3-38143, OJ C 174/6 (19 June 2001); and European Commission, *Antitrust clearance for licensing of patents for third generation mobile services (IP/02/1651) (12 Nov 2002)*, 3GPP Patent Platform Partnership Business Review Letter (12 November 2002), available at www.usdoj.gov/atr/public/busreview/200455.pdf.

22   See US FTC (2003) (summarizing Carl Shapiro, Navigating the Patent Thicket, on pools "to facilitate orderly transfer of intellectual property at lower combined rates and higher combined profits," avoiding Cournot's complements problem); 42 (pools "have become critically important mechanisms for enabling widespread use of new technologies that require access

to a multitude of patents dispersed among a multitude of parties," quoting Stephen Fox, Hewlett Packard). See US DoJ & US FTC (2007) (discussing solutions to patent hold-up). The fostering of patent pools is an important feature of DVB's overall IPR policy.

23 *Rambus, supra* n 17.

24 *Rambus, Inc. vs. Infineon Techs.* AG, 318 F3d 1081 (Fed Cir 2003).

25 See, for example, Abbott and Gebhard (2006) ("[F]irms participating in SSOs should exercise good faith efforts to abide by any disclosure policy and otherwise conduct themselves in good faith through the process"); and *Broadcom vs. Qualcomm*, 501 F 3d 279 (3d Cir 2007) (finding assertion of broken FR&ND promise to standards body could be basis for antitrust claim). The *Rambus* litigation is not discussed further in this article. At the time of the decision in the U.S. Federal Circuit, *supra* n 17, DVB examined its Article 14 MoU and its practices, and concluded that these did not present the same issues as found in JEDEC: Article 14 MoU is an unambiguous rule for licensing on FR&ND terms unless an IPR has been notified as unavailable; the timing of the duty is clear: it attaches at the time of membership, subject to notices of unavailability submitted within strict time limits; the rules are confined to essential IPR; and the scope for "gaming" the rules by a DVB member is not likely in light of *Magill* ECJ (6 April 1995) and *IMS* ECJ (29 April 2004), to be tolerated in the European Union.

26 On elements of this tension, see discussion of the chapeau to Article 14.

27 The controversy surrounding the ETSI interim IPR policy and its rejection by the European Commission influenced the work within DVB on its own IPR policy.

28 The corrective action was removal of Sun's declaration. For an explanation of this action, together with a statement from Sun, see http://webapp.etsi.org/ipr/IPRList.asp?Project=&Countries=&y=6&OrderBy=DECLARATION_DATE&AppNumber=&ETSIDeliverable=TS 101 476&Notes=&Order=ASC&Country=&separator=%2C%2C %3B%2C -&Company=Sun Microsystems%2C Inc.&Title=&OpProjects=or&PatentNumber=&Operator=or&Year=&Day=&x=31&Month=
ETSI disclaims any review of declarations of essentiality. The Commission process that led to its decision is not pellucid. English courts examine the issue of "nonessentiality" of declarations submitted to ETSI. See *Nokia Corporation vs. InterDigital Technology* (2006) EWHC 802 (Pat).

29 ETSI GA ad hoc group on IPR Review, List of Topics, ETSI GA/IPRR06(06)02 (2 August 06). Other standards bodies have adopted novel approaches to IPR. For example, W3C allows only technology that is royalty free. http://www.w3.org/Consortium/Patent-Policy-20040205/#def-RF. MPEG has proposed the development of specifications using technology where the term of patent protection has expired. Members of the Blu-ray Disc association agree that the "aggregate of … all licences … shall not block, frustrate or harm acceptance of any Blu-ray Disc format as a worldwide standard or development of products complying with any … format or commercialization of the same." Blu-ray Disc charter clause 15(4). Holders of patents essential to W-CDMA agreed "to set a benchmark … to achieve fair and reasonable royalty rates … to be at a modest single digit level … targeted cumulative 5% level." www.3gpp.co.uk/PR/November 2002/4377.htm.

30 ETSI interim IPR policy, OJ C 076, 28 March 1996, pages 05-07. As a measure of

the evolution of the regulatory landscape, it is not certain that the European Commission would today take the same view of all the provisions it rejected in the mid-1990s. For the Commission's overall position at the time of DVB's formation, see European Commission, Intellectual property rights and standardization, COM 92 (445) final (27 October 1992).

[31] Stephen Temple, who was an initial member of DVB's Steering Board and also the Chairman of ETSI's Technical Assembly, has provided much of the background of this section.

[32] There is a rich literature on pooling, its advantages to licensors and licensees, and the arrangements acceptable to regulatory authorities. For business review letters issued by the U.S. Department of Justice and related decisions of the European Commission on licensing programs, see *supra* n 21.

[33] The arrangements for MPEG LA and the MPEG2 pool are set out in MPEG-2 Business Review Letter, *supra* n 21. There have been prior pools (e.g., in the optical storage field since 1983), but these were generally led by a rights holder and less visible than MPEG LA's well-funded effort.

[34] The announcement that the broadcasters were willing to postpone commercialization of satellite services until they could implement DVB-S was significant, because one had previously rejected a new, untested analog satellite standard promoted by European institutions in favor of an "off-the-shelf" technology.

[35] Perhaps ironically, during the later pooling process for DVB-S and other early specifications, no declared IPR was found to be essential for DVB-S.

[36] See discussion *infra* on Arts 14.2 (duty to grant FR&ND licences) and 14.1 and 14.3 (windows for "negative disclosure"). One participant in the formulation of the policy recalls more of a rudimentary calculus than

a "compromise": "it was generally accepted by members at the time" that a rights holder should either withdraw its essential IPRs or license on FR&ND terms.

[37] See discussion *infra* on Art 14.7 (arbitration) on patent pooling.

[38] See discussion *infra* on Art 14.5.

[39] See discussion *infra* on Art 14.8.

[40] On patent applications, see discussion on "negative disclosure"; DVB's copyright policy is also discussed.

[41] See Broadcom vs. Qualcomm, supra n. 25 and the articles cited in the text following n.6.

[42] See discussion *infra* on Art 14.7 (arbitration) on pooling.

[43] There are other tests for "essentiality," notably in the context of patent pooling. See, for example, Guidelines, *supra* n 19 at paras 215–222 (favoring pools comprised of essential technologies "if there are no substitutes for the technology inside or outside the pool and the technology … constitutes a necessary part of the package" to produce the product); and the different tests proposed in the business review letters relating to patent pools cited *supra* n 21 (ranging from "technically essential to compliance" to "literally essential" or "for which there is no "realistic" alternative [i.e., not] economically feasible").

[44] That is, before the DVB Project has completed its own process for adopting the specification. After approval by the Technical Module, the specification is reviewed and adopted by the Steering Board and thereafter delivered to the appropriate body, such as ETSI, for standardization.

[45] The notice could arguably be given for any commercial reason or for no reason. On the other hand, a bald notice of unwillingness to license may be viewed as abusive and in breach of a duty of good faith and "community-mindedness," which are pillars of DVB's activities.

46   At the same time, the review of relevant patents—the more comprehensive task—could put the member in a position to make a declaration for a pooling effort covering the specification, and to meet its obligations for positive disclosure in the standardizing body.

47   It is also difficult to anticipate precisely the response of DVB to a notice of unavailability. The MoU is silent on the point. It is likely that it would follow the model of other standards fora and strip out the technologies burdened by the unavailable IPR. Other approaches might be invoked, such as calling for the rights holder to offer better terms.

48   And the validity of the declaration could also be subject to review under arbitration contemplated by Article 14.7 discussed later.

49   Note that while the second window is fairly certain to close later, it is possible that the two windows will be open concurrently for a time.

50   The request was somewhat surprising because the prospective member, during the period when considering whether to join, was presumably weighing the impact of the IPR policy on its portfolio. In the event, the new member submitted no notice of unavailability during the supplemental 90-day "window pane."

51   35 U.S.C. s 284 (court may assess damages up to three times the reasonable royalty).

52   A properly framed demand for arbitration could presumably include claims based on competition law. See Dolmans and Grierson (2003).

53   On DVB's fostering of patent pools, see further in the article.

54   The text was drafted when DVB had less than 100 members. DVB has today more than 250 members, so the number of potential claimants has grown considerably. A nonmember implementer is a third-party beneficiary of the member's FR&ND licensing duties under the MoU and could seek a judicial remedy or propose ADR.

55   Art. 14.7 covers only "this Article 14." The MoU does not otherwise have a choice of law provision but is governed by Swiss law.

56   On technical aspects, the MHP process also created an explicit "feedback mechanism" providing for resolution of a conflict between the MHP specification and test application or a valid implementation. See DVB Project (2003).

57   At the same time as DVB's rules were being considered, the World Intellectual Property Organization was forming the WIPO Arbitration and Mediation Center. (See http:// arbiter.wipo.int.) On the attractiveness of arbitration to resolve IPR disputes in the standards environment, see Brenning (2002) (as a safeguard, "the SSO could build in an arbitration mechanism for breaches of its internal rules. This would solve the problem of the long lead time of the Commission's procedure" when it responds to a challenge, based on competition law, to licensing terms). Compare papers presented in the context of the FTC's review of intellectual property and standards (Balto & Prywes, 2002) ("Standard-setting groups should be encouraged to require alternative dispute resolution procedures for resolving disputes about licensing terms. For example, ADR would be useful to determine whether licensing terms offered to one firm are" RAND) (Holleman, 2002) (challenging among other points any role for a standards body in resolving disputes relating to patents or licensing terms). IPR matters now represent some 7% of the ICC caseload.

58   A licensing program covering a specification terminates the right to arbitration. Such a licensing program must, under the terms of Art 14.9, be notified within two years of the Art 14.1 notification. Art. 14.9 provides that the right to arbitration "shall come into force two years after the [Art. 14.1] notification"

unless the pool is formed. In other words, the right is suspended; if a pool is successfully formed, the right is terminated.

[59] DVB does have a mechanism for suspending and expelling members for failure to pay the annual membership fee.

[60] Similarly, a new member is held to the FR&ND standard in respect to all DVB specifications, including those adopted before its membership.

[61] As a practical matter, the match between DVB and ETSI rules does not appear to be perfect. Some DVB members argue that they are excused from ETSI disclosure duties because it is enough for ETSI to know that the DVB specification is covered by its FR&ND rules (absent a notice of withdrawal). This argument is generally not favored by DVB. Moreover, ETSI notes the disparity between disclosures on the ETSI IPR database for DVB specifications and the many thousands for telecoms specifications. See http://www.etsi.org/WebSite/AboutETSI/LegalAspects/iprdb.aspx. This may be at least partly attributed to the differences in competitive conditions between industrial sectors.

[62] The form of the circular letter is set out in an annex to Corrigenda and Addenda no 1 to DVB Blue Book A066 rev 1 (Geneva, September 2004) available at www.dvb.org/documents//sb1392%5B1%5D.iprm0430.MHP%20A066r1%20corrigenda%20and%20addenda.pdf.

[63] The patents essential for digital terrestrial broadcasting (DVB-T) are licensed through MPEG LA, www.mpegla.com; Sun's Java technologies in MHP through ETSI, www.etsi.org; other technologies in MHP through Via Licensing, www.vialicensing; advance video coding (MPEG 4(10)) through both MPEG LA and Via Licensing.

[64] Recently, DVB has entered into liaison arrangements with sister standards fora. Under these arrangements, DVB and the sister forum may agree to exchange documents, to make normative reference to specifications, or indeed to incorporate materials into each other's documents. Before entering into these liaisons, DVB reviews the IPR policy of its potential partner to determine if there is rough parity with its own. In some circumstances, there has been no difficulty finding equivalence; in others, the sister forum has changed its policy to align with DVB's; and in some cases, DVB has accepted that it cannot expect to bring a sister forum to renounce, for example, an ANSI-based "awareness" policy.

[65] Art 17 MoU.

[66] A chairman of one of the two early ad hoc groups became Chairman DVB; the other, who became the first chairman of the IPRM, now serves as Legal Director DVB.

[67] See discussion previously on Article 14.2 MoU

[68] The policy was adopted by the Steering Board in its document SB 41 (03) 27. It is available at www.dvb.org/membership/ipr_policy/copyright_policy. The discussion of the policy in this article is a summary; reference should also be made to the text of the policy itself.

[69] For example, DVB's MHP specification includes some 70 normative references. Indeed, at its inception, DVB made clear that it expected to build on the standards work of MPEG within ISO; it did not intend to recreate the work completed by another standards body.

This work was previously published in the International Journal of IT Standards and Standardization Research, Vol. 6, Issue 2, edited by K. Jakobs, pp. 21-47, copyright 2008 by IGI Publishing (an imprint of IGI Global).

Chapter 15
Structural Effects of Platform Certification on a Complementary Product Market:
The Case of Mobile Applications

Ankur Tarnacha
Pennsylvania State University, USA

Carleen Maitland
Pennsylvania State University, USA

ABSTRACT

This article examines the structural effects of platform certification on the supply of complementary products. Drawing on the exploratory case of mobile application markets, the article highlights the broader market effects of competing platforms and their certifications on a platform-based complementary product market. The case suggests that platform certifications influence market intermediation, entry barriers, and deployment fragmentation. We present these market effects in a conceptual model that can be applied to understand similar complementary product markets. As such, the article contributes to the literature on compatibility standards by emphasizing some of the complementary product market effects of employing certification in enhancing compatibility.

INTRODUCTION

One of the challenges resulting from complex, specialized information technology systems has been maintaining vertical compatibility, typically through compliance to a standard, while ensuring the development of a vibrant market of complementary goods. One tool used to foster compatibility is that of platforms, which are technology architectures composed of subsystems and interfaces between those subsystems and the external environment (Greenstein, 1998; Meyer

& Seliger, 1998; West & Dedrick, 2000). The interfaces provide access to platform subsystem functionality that can be used to design complementary products. Standardized platform interfaces in that sense facilitate vertical compatibility between the product implementing the platform and the complementary product (Schmidt & Werle, 1998). However, without consistent interface implementation, compatibility can suffer (Egyedi & Dahanayake, 2003; Egyedi & Hudson, 2005). As vertical incompatibilities reduce complementary network externalities for the platform (Gandal, 1995; West & Dedrick, 2000), it is in the best interest of platform promulgators (firms or industry alliances that develop, promote, or support a particular platform) to ensure its "correct" implementation and use.

Extant literature has discussed various strategies to ensure compatibility, including standards certification, wherein products are assessed for conformance to a developed standard (see, for instance, Egyedi and van Wendel de Joode, 2003). Research has primarily investigated the strategic implications of compatibility certification for the standard promulgators and organizations directly involved in the implementation (Egyedi, 2001b; Rada, 1996), with little emphasis on how certification influences the market of *complementary products*. As complementary products contribute to the value of the platform and are often more closely aligned with end users, understanding these effects will have broad implications not only for suppliers of technology but for end users as well.

In this article, we explore the structural effects of platform certification (the conformance of a platform's complementary product to the platform-sponsor-defined best practices in platform interface usage). In particular, we seek to answer the question: What are the structural effects of platform certification on a platform's complementary product market? We examine these market effects using an exploratory case (Yin, 1994) of the mobile applications market,

where multiple mobile computing platforms competing for dominance offer mobile application certification programs. The data for the case were gathered from 18 open-ended interviews with the top-management of mobile application vendors in the United States in the fall of 2005. These data were supplemented by several on-site interviews with the top-management team and certification program managers at a leading global certification intermediary in the summer of 2006. Further, the case is supported by secondary sources such as trade press articles and news released by various platform promulgators. Our analysis is exploratory in nature, and as such, the goal is to identify relationships in the case of mobile applications market, which can be more systematically investigated in the future.

The article is structured as follows. We first review the extant literature on compatibility standards, platforms, and certification. Subsequently, we present the case of mobile applications markets, wherein we first provide an overview of the market highlighting the prevalence of computing platforms, their implementations, and certifications. We then present some of the observed market effects of platform certification on the mobile applications market. The case is followed by the discussion of these effects, grounding them in the standards and information technology literature. Finally, we conclude with recommendations for future research.

LITERATURE REVIEW

Compatibility Standards and Platforms

While standards exist in various forms (David & Greenstein, 1990; David & Steinmueller, 1994; Tassey, 2000), one of the more common classification schemes distinguishes reference, minimum quality, and "interface" or compatibility standards (David & Greenstein, 1990).

Reference and minimum quality standards provide benchmark characteristics that define the quality, performance, or other desirable attributes of the standardized product. Compatibility standards, on the other hand, are identified as a set of technical specifications that provide an interface to develop compatible complementary products. Compatibility standards in that sense provide "vertical compatibility" across two complementary components such as a printer and cartridge or a computer hardware and software (Schmidt & Werle, 1998). Compatibility standards assure that a complementary product can be successfully integrated into a larger system built from subsystems conforming to the same compatibility standard and serve as a functional subsystem.

From an economic perspective, compatibility decisions in networked industries are influenced by network externalities, which can be direct or indirect (Katz & Shapiro, 1985, 1986). While direct network externalities result from the increased utility a consumer derives from a product with increased users (e.g., a telephone network), indirect network externalities result from the increased availability of complementary products (e.g., a telephone). Research on network externalities has been elucidated by the "complementary product" or "hardware/software" paradigm (Church & Gandal, 1992; Katz & Shapiro, 1994), which emphasized the importance of indirect or complementary network externalities in influencing technology adoption (Church & Gandal, 1993), market structure (Economides & Salop, 1992), and strategic behaviors of firms in vertically networked industries (Church & Gandal, 1992; Matutes & Regibeau, 1987). Further, various empirical studies have documented the influence of complementary network externalities on the economics (Brynjolfsson & Kemerer, 1996; Gandal, 1995) and structural evolution of ICT industries (Bresnahan & Greenstein, 1999; Gallagher & Park, 2002; West & Dedrick, 2000).

The complementary product paradigm has also been explored in the compatibility literature

under the term "platform," which is technology architectures that provide a framework for developing complementary products (Bresnahan & Greenstein, 1999; West & Dedrick, 2000). Computing platforms have been viewed as a cluster of technically standardized components called Application Programming Interfaces (APIs) that define the interaction of complementary applications designed for the platform (Greenstein, 1998). These APIs provide the necessary information for developers to design applications compatible with the given platform. Hence, API clusters or computing platforms mediate software compatibility (West & Dedrick, 2000) and in that sense can be referred to as a "compatibility standard" (David & Greenstein, 1990).

Platforms, as compatibility standards, have had significant effects on the evolution of the computing industry in general (see Greenstein, 1998; Bresnahan & Greenstein, 1999), as well as in various ICT industry segments in particular (Gandal, Greenstein & Salant, 1999; Iversen & Tee, 2006; Karvonen & Warsta, 2004; Tilson & Lyytinen, 2006; West & Dedrick, 2000). For instance, in the mobile computing industry segment, Karvonen and Warsta (2004) highlight the importance of development platforms in providing access to various technological layers of mobile computing. Iversen and Tee (2006) further document the case of the Symbian platform in shaping the evolving industry structure in the mobile telecom sector. Studies have also documented the strategic implications of developing and managing platforms (Garud & Kumaraswamy, 1993; Methlie & Gressgård, 2006; Windrum, 2004) as well as their adoption by organizations (West & Dedrick, 2006).

Platforms, Compatibility, and Certification

Development and specification of compatibility standards is an important facet of ensuring compatibility. However, without consistent implementation, compatibility can suffer (Egyedi & Dahanayake, 2003; Egyedi & Hudson, 2005). This is particularly true for platforms, as they are complex technological systems that encapsulate multiple component interfaces and their relationships. Although the specifications for component interfaces are documented to explicitly provide information about their usage, their complexity can leave room for interpretation and, hence, inconsistent implementations (Egyedi & Dahanayake, 2003). Varying implementations are a central issue for compatibility standards, particularly complex computing platforms, as inconsistent implementations can create incompatible products and reduce complementary network externalities, thereby defeating the very purpose of a platform. Hence, in many cases, it is in the best interest of platform promulgators (i.e., firms or industry alliances that develop, promote, or support a particular platform) to ensure "correct" implementation and use.

Various studies have examined the issue of managing compatibility and implementations. Egyedi and van Wendel de Joode (2004), for instance, identify coordination mechanisms that can be used to manage compatibility in open source software. These coordination mechanisms include the use of regulation (through contracts, licenses, and member agreements), operations (through reference implementations, tools, and training), and authority (through gatekeepers and hierarchies) that can converge the strategic behavior of various stakeholders toward compatibility (Egyedi & van Wendel de Joode, 2004). Further, Egyedi (2001), discusses various strategies employed by Sun Microsystems to foster compatibility of the Java technology. She highlights compatibility fostering "input controls" such as providing training and software development kits (SDKs) during the early stages of specification development, as well as "output controls" such as providing reference implementation and compatibility certification and logos during the later stages of specification

implementation (Egyedi, 2001a, 2001b). Output controls are particularly relevant for platform standards, as they can be employed to control implementation variations of proprietary as well as open platforms (Egyedi, 2001a). Compatibility certifications wherein products are assessed for conformance to a developed standard is one such output control, which can be employed by platform promulgators to ensure vertical compatibility.

Despite the use of compatibility certification by industry consortia such as CTIA[1] and firms such as Sun and Microsoft[2], not to mention the long history of reference and minimum quality certification employed by various governmental agencies (e.g., in the United States, FCC-EA[3] and in the EU, CE markings[4]) as well as international quasigovernmental standards development and compliance organizations such as IEC[5] and UL[6], there has been little academic research on the topic of certification (studies on Java and other open source software compatibility strategies by Egyedi are notable exceptions).

While fostering compatibility is an important goal, the mechanisms used to drive compatibility can have implications for the suppliers of complementary goods that in turn add value to the standardized technology. Although research on compatibility recognizes certification as a mechanism to foster compatibility, it does not directly address the resulting competitive landscape of the complementary product market. Thus, research on the effects of compatibility certifications for the complementary product market is needed and, to the best of our knowledge, has not been performed.

In this article, we address this gap by reporting on our exploration of the market effects of multiple compatibility standards certifications in the emerging mobile computing industry, where complementary mobile applications are certified for compatibility on various evolving computing platforms.

THE CASE OF MOBILE APPLICATIONS MARKET

The mobile industry is comprised of multiple interrelated segments, while a complete depiction of the mobile industry might best be achieved using a so-called value network or ecosystem model; here, for the sake of simplicity, we employ a value chain metaphor (Porter, 1985). Examining the value chain from the mobile application perspective, researchers have identified five core segments in the mobile industry (Barnes, 2002; Karvonen & Warsta, 2004). These segments include (1) the mobile content providers that create, aggregate, and distribute mobile content; (2) mobile application developers/vendors that develop and distribute software providing computational functions such as e-mail/chat clients, word/spreadsheet processing, and mobile games on mobile devices; (3) mobile platform providers that provide the necessary implementation tools for deploying mobile applications; (4) mobile device manufacturers that provide information processing capable mobile devices; and (5) mobile network operators that deploy and manage mobile network infrastructure to provide mobile access to end users.

In this article, we are primarily interested in mobile application developers as they develop complementary applications for mobile computing platforms. These application developers are essentially software development agencies that specialize in developing applications for mobile devices. They are the core technical facilitators of the emerging medium, with a high degree of interdependence with the various segments of the mobile value chain.

Computing Platforms and Certification

As mobile applications execute on mobile devices, they typically interact with various technologi-cal layers such as the mobile operating system, device hardware, and the network infrastructure (Karvonen & Warsta, 2004). Depending on its functionality, an application might interact with many interfaces across these layers. This interaction is achieved by APIs, which provide access to the layer-specific features required by the application. For instance, a location-based multimedia application might require and use the mobile network's location APIs for mapping; the mobile device's camera-controlling APIs for collecting visual imagery, and the operating system's file-system APIs for data storage. While APIs enhance interoperability, they also limit applications to devices and networks that have those specific APIs.

In order to circumvent the complex dependency of mobile applications across multiple layers, various computing platforms have been developed. These platforms essentially package available APIs at various layers and provide a standardized mechanism to access various layer-specific features. In the mobile environment, operating systems such as Symbian-OS, Palm-OS, and Windows Mobile have been extended to provide access to layer-specific features. Additionally, middleware platforms such as Sun's Java ME and Qualcomm's BREW provide APIs that indirectly provide access to various layer-specific features. While these middleware platforms have the same basic aims, they differ in their development and management. Java ME, for instance, is a semi-open standardization initiative that has evolved from its success in the desktop and server markets[7]. Similar to Java, it is a platform that runs on top of a mobile operating system, allowing Java ME applications to execute on Java ME-implementing devices. BREW, on the other hand, is a proprietary standard developed by Qualcomm that is specifically designed for network operators. Similar to Java ME, it is a development platform that runs on top of a mobile operating system, allowing BREW applications to execute on various BREW-implementing mobile devices[8].

While the purpose of a platform is to provide integrated access to various components through APIs, due to rapid device and network innovations, both operating systems and middleware platforms are often not able to provide full device- and network-specific functionalities. Device manufacturers, realizing this dependency, provide their own flavors of integrated device-specific platforms. Nokia, for instance, provides platforms such as Nokia Series 60 and 80 that are based on the integration of Symbian and Nokia device APIs. RIM's Blackberry is another example, where additional Blackberry-specific APIs are integrated with the Java ME platform. As the complex integration of multiple APIs takes on various forms, we use the term "computing platform" to refer to the mobile operating systems (e.g., Symbian-OS, Palm-OS, and Windows Mobile), middleware platforms (e.g., Java ME and BREW), as well as device-specific platforms (e.g., Nokia Series 60 and 80, and Blackberry Java).

Contributing to the complexity of various computing platforms are the certification programs sponsored by operating system and middleware platform promulgators such as Symbian, Microsoft, Sun, and Qualcomm. Further, various device manufacturers sponsor certification programs that partially or completely adopt certification criteria from platform promulgators. Motorola, for instance, sponsors separate certification programs for testing Java ME applications and Windows Mobile applications (Mahmoud, 2002; Motorola, 2006)[9]. Furthermore, various network operators also sponsor customized certification programs to ensure proper application behavior on their networks[10].

These certification programs are essentially designed to test and verify the adherence of mobile applications to a platform sponsor's defined best practices in platform usage to allow appropriate application execution. The certified applications are digitally signed and can use proprietary logos for deployment on various mobile operator networks for eventual end-user consumption.

From the application developer's perspective, these certification programs are critical, as most network operators mandate that applications be certified prior to deployment[11]. The prevalence of computing platforms and their certification programs provides an opportunity to explore the effects of certification on a complementary product market. In the following section, we examine these effects in the mobile applications market.

Market Effects of Platform Certification

Clearly, the attempt to mitigate the complex nature of mobile technologies through the creation of application development platforms has, at least temporarily, been thwarted by the emergence of multiple competing platforms that enjoy a varying degree of support from actors across the mobile value chain. While the competitive dynamics surrounding the emergence, adoption, and support of various platforms in the mobile value chain is bound to influence the structural landscape of the entire value chain, in this article we focus on some of the core issues raised by the prevalence of platforms and their certification programs upstream in the value chain.

It was expected that the multiplicity of platforms coupled with high prevalence of certification would have structural and strategic implications for the complementary mobile applications market. In order to investigate these possible effects, we conducted 18 open-ended interviews of the top management of mobile application vendors that develop and distribute mobile applications across multiple platforms, during the fall of 2005 in the United States. In addition, several on-site discussions and interviews with the top management team and certification program managers at National Software Testing Labs (NSTL), a leading global certification intermediary providing certification for multiple certification programs, were also conducted in the summer of 2006[12]. Based on these interviews and secondary sources such as trade press articles and publicly available documentation of certification programs, we outline some of the compatibility-driving service niches and their consequent effects on the mobile applications market.

Compatibility Services and Certification Intermediation

The existence of multiple platforms creates vertical application compatibility issues, wherein the applications based on one platform standard are not able to execute on devices and networks supporting another. Given this situation, we sought to find how developers deal with this issue. Accordingly, they reported that the vertical incompatibilities have given rise to various types of services that assist application developers in reaching consumers using mobile devices implementing various platforms.

An important category of such services is *compatibility and interoperability testing.* Such testing services test applications for compatibility with various mobile devices implementing the platform on which the application was developed. The service provides compatibility test reports based on test plans, which are either designed by the compatibility service providers or negotiated between the compatibility service provider and the developer. In addition to testing services, application migration services known as *cross-platform application porting* are also abundant, wherein applications are reprogrammed and migrated to execute on a competing platform. Although various technological tools are available to developers that assist in developing applications for multiple platforms simultaneously,[13] such tools often do not achieve complete compatibility. All the developers interviewed reported that such cross-platform application porting services are quite commonly used to systematically redesign and reprogram an application to execute on competing platforms.

Although such services are common in markets where multiple standards compete for dominance,

the mobile applications market diverges from other markets with multiple competing standards due to the prevalence of platform certification. In addition to various compatibility, interoperability, and cross-platform porting services, the use of *certification services* has become a necessity in the business of mobile application development and distribution. In addition to application testing on various certification test criteria, certification services also manage the applications through various certification processes of application submission, testing, and signing. All the application developers we interviewed underscored the importance of certification services in the mobile applications market.

Existence of these service niches (i.e., compatibility testing, application porting, and certification services) has had some key structural effects on the mobile applications market. One such effect comes in the form of certification intermediation. Platform certification sponsors typically outsource certification testing to specialists often referred to as Authorized Testing Labs (ATLs). Some of the major application platform certification programs and their authorized certification labs are shown in Table 1. Although the ATLs are agents of certification sponsors in certifying applications, they are in a unique position to serve multiple certification programs simultaneously and address the certification service niche comprehensively. In that sense, they act as intermediaries in the market by serving both the platform certification sponsors and the mobile application developers. We refer to this phenomenon as *certification intermediation.*

In the mobile applications market, certification intermediaries aggregate technical resources, such as an inventory of various mobile devices supporting various platforms, to perform certification testing. Certification intermediaries procure most, if not all, devices available in the market. The procurement sometimes also involves obtaining precommercial mobile devices, which are typically supplied by certification sponsors.

Table 1. Key mobile platform certification programs, sponsors, and authorized certification labs

Platform	Certification Program	Certification Sponsor	Authorized Certification Labs*
BREW	True BREW[14]	Qualcomm	NSTL
Java ME	Java Verified[15]	Sun Microsystems	Babel Media, Capgemini, NSTL, and RelQ
Symbian-OS	Symbian Signed[16]	Symbian	Capgemini, Mphasis, and NSTL
Windows Mobile	Designed for Windows Mobile with Mobile-2Market[17]	Microsoft	QualityLogic, NSTL, and Veritest

*Source: Certification program Web sites, accessed May 2007

Additionally, these intermediaries also buy access to multiple network operator voice and data service plans to test applications on live networks.

In addition to aggregating technical resources, certification intermediaries face risks typically related to certification programs. The ability to achieve and maintain the designation of an authorized test lab for a certification program by generating and managing a steady volume of application certifications is one such risk. In the longer term, certification intermediaries face risks from the possible dissolution of the certification program altogether[18]. Competition also exists with other application testing labs, although the number is fairly limited (approximately 10 worldwide).

As aggregators of various technical resources facing risks associated with the certification programs, certification intermediaries have incentives to diversify across service niches such as compatibility testing, porting, and other quality assurance services such as functionality, usability, and performance testing. Certification intermediaries are able to leverage their technical expertise and access to resources (often exclusive such as access to precommercial mobile devices and platform upgrades) to provide such additional services. By positioning themselves as a one-stop-shop for getting applications to the market, most certification intermediaries have

evolved as a critical resource for mobile application developers.

In their activities, certification intermediaries support both the platform certification sponsors and the application developers. As a technical enterprise requiring both technical competency and detailed information about evolving platforms, certification intermediaries are critically positioned to influence the emerging mobile applications market. In the following section, we present some of the implications of certification intermediation on the supply of mobile applications.

Supply-Side Market Effects

As the core technical facilitators of mobile content in the mobile value chain, application developers essentially represent the supply side that delivers mobile applications and services to consumers. Our interviews with the application developers pointed to two essential supply-side effects of prevalent platforms and their certification programs on the mobile applications market; namely, the degree of *deployment fragmentation* and extent of *market entry barriers*. We describe each in turn.

Application developers attempt to address various specialized niches, which are characterized by specific mobile application functionalities such as navigation, monitoring and tracking applications for fleet management, games, ringtones, and screen-saver applications for entertainment. Irrespective of the addressed niche, the interviewed application developers indicated that all developers must first contend with multiple platforms and their varying implementations on various mobile devices. It essentially necessitates the development of multiple application versions to target a particular customer segment. For instance, in order to develop a specialized application for a segment of customers (e.g., truck drivers or Hispanic immigrants), the application developer has to provide multiple versions of the same functional application so it can execute on various platforms and their implementations on mobile devices used by the intended customer segment. From the developer's perspective, this fragments the market along multiple operating systems and middleware platforms, as well as along their various implementations on a plethora of mobile device models. We refer to this fragmentation as *deployment fragmentation*, which restricts application deployment across multiple platforms ("between-platform" deployment fragmentation) as well as their varied implementations on mobile devices ("within-platform" deployment fragmentation).

Although certification does not directly influence the between-platform deployment fragmentation, it was expected that certification can, at least partially, address the within-platform deployment fragmentation. However, the developers we interviewed noted that the certification testing criteria are typically very basic, and applications are only tested on limited mobile devices. Additional testing on mobile devices implementing the same platform requires additional certification fees. Further, the developers also experienced different levels of within-platform deployment fragmentation across platform standardization approaches. Open platforms such as Java ME, in spite of platform certification, seem to exhibit greater within-platform deployment fragmenta-

tion compared to proprietary platforms such as BREW[19]. Platform certification in that sense does not comprehensively address the within-platform deployment fragmentation, even though it provides a framework to manage variability in platform implementations.

Another market effect of multiple platforms, their implementations, and platform certification is an increase in entry barriers for application developers. As discussed earlier, multiple platforms and their implementations necessitate creation of multiple versions of an application in order to sell it to its intended customer segment. This creates additional costs for developing an application, reducing the return on investment in developing new applications and thereby reducing the incentive to enter a new market segment. For established application developers, such costs can be spread over multiple applications they develop and sell. However, for new market entrants, such costs act as entry barriers. The interviewed developers suggested various reasons for the same. First, mobile operators typically do not deploy uncertified applications on their networks for eventual sale to their subscribers. A developer entering the market has to certify the application to make a sale, thereby increasing application development and deployment costs relative to an environment without certification. Second, ATLs are given the flexibility by the certification sponsors to provide volume discounts for certification. Volume discounting assists incumbent application developers that develop and certify multiple applications. However, it provides a competitive disincentive to market entrants who compete with incumbents for new applications, as market entrants typically cannot offer multiple application volume. Finally, the certification costs are based on testing an application on one handset model. As the number of targeted handsets to reach the intended consumer segment increases, the certification costs skyrocket, increasing the upfront application deployment costs. To understand the magnitude of such upfront costs, the range and average pricing for

Table 2. Platform certification program pricing

Platform Certification Program	Application Certification Price *per application per handset*	
	Range	Average Price
True BREW	€ 700	€ 700
Java Verified	€ 150 - € 500	€ 240
Symbian Signed	€ 185 - € 560	€ 332
Designed for Windows Mobile with Mobile2Market	€ 196 - € 314	€ 275

Source: Program sponsor websites and own calculations, accessed May 2007

the major platform certification *per handset* are presented in Table 2. According to the interviewed developers, the number of targeted handset models typically range from tens to hundreds, creating sunken certification investments of thousands of Euros, which are often higher compared to the application development cost itself. In that sense, certification raises the entry barriers for the supply of mobile applications and potentially hampers innovation as well[20].

Certification intermediation, together with mobile application deployment fragmentation and entry barriers, constitute the market effects of multiple platforms, their implementations, and the prevalence of platform certification on the supply of mobile applications. In the following section, we discuss the implications of these findings for similar complementary product markets that are characterized by compatibility standards or platform certification.

DISCUSSION

The case of platform certifications in the mobile application market provides the basis for investigating the overarching research question: What are the structural effects of platform certification on a platform's complementary product market? In this section, we analyze this question, drawing

on the literature on compatibility standards and industrial organization. We conceptualize how platform certification can alter the market effects of competing platforms. For analytical clarity, we first discuss the issue of vertical compatibility and identify the market mechanisms that can potentially address it, and then discuss the implications of these mechanisms on the complementary product market.

As has been observed, vertical compatibility cannot be ensured by standardization and documentation of platform specifications because incompatibilities can result from inconsistent or selective implementation and use of a standardized platform (Egyedi & Dahanayake, 2003; Egyedi & Hudson, 2005). However, in some cases, these incompatibilities can be resolved by the market ex-post through provision of various tools such as cross-standard product converters, adapters, and gateways (Farrell & Saloner, 1992). On the other hand, in cases of rapid technological change and where multiple platforms and their varied implementations exist, such incompatibility-resolving-tools can become technically and economically unfeasible. In such a situation, the service niche of compatibility and interoperability testing assume greater significance. Further, demand for "ancillary services" such as cross-platform product migration and quality assurance services such as performance, functionality, and usability testing,

Figure 1. Market effects of platform certification on complementary product market

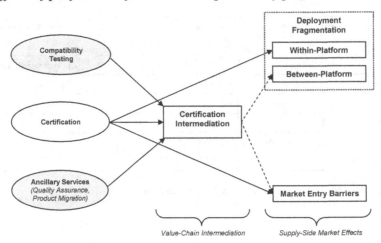

can also be enhanced. Although such ancillary services do not resolve vertical incompatibilities, their demand increases as the functioning of the complementary product becomes intricately coupled with the implementation of the underlying platform.

Platform promulgators can also proactively address vertical incompatibilities through certification of complementary products and use of proprietary compatibility logos (Egyedi & van Wendel de Joode, 2003). Platform certification in the mobile applications market can be viewed as such a mechanism, where platform promulgators exercise authority and act as "gatekeepers" (Egyedi & van Wendel de Joode, 2004) over platform implementations and use by authorizing certification labs. In that sense, the authoritative mechanism of platform certification attempts to reduce implementation variation and increase complementary product compatibility through validation by experts (platform promulgators and authorized testing labs).

This raises two questions: Do these authoritative mechanisms achieve their goals, and what other effects do they generate? Based on the findings from the mobile applications market, we outline the structural implications of these mechanisms on the complementary product market as

depicted in Figure 1. Starting on the lefthand side, the model presents the *primary market effects* (bold lines) of certification, compatibility testing, and ancillary services on three outcomes; namely, value chain intermediation, the level of deployment fragmentation, and the extent of entry barriers in the complementary product market. In turn, value chain intermediation, in the form of certification intermediation, produces *secondary market effects* (dotted lines) by further influencing market fragmentation and entry barriers of the complementary product market. We consider each in turn.

One of the primary effects of platform certification is on the degree of fragmentation in the complementary product market. In general, certification aims to ensure consistent use of the platform in designing complementary products, thereby addressing within-standard vertical incompatibilities of complementary products. In theory, the initially disjointed submarkets of various product versions for varying platform implementations are merged by certification, thereby reducing within-platform deployment fragmentation of the complementary product market. However, the case of mobile applications market suggests that this effect depends on the certification test criteria and the standardization approaches of the platform.

In addition, platform certification can also influence the entry barriers for the complementary product market. In particular, the cost of certification is incurred by complementary product developers. These costs can be especially daunting for market entrants, which typically do not offer multiple products during the startup phase and therefore are unable to take advantage of potential volume certification discounts. Hence, compared to a market without certification, *ceteris paribus*, a market with certification increases market entry barriers in the complementary product market.

Furthermore, certification also creates an opportunity for intermediation. Of course, the existence of certification intermediation largely depends on the platform promulgator outsourcing certification testing. However, the decision to outsource certification testing can be motivated by the need to obtain third-party objectivity as well as the availability of expertise in performing related services (Biglaiser, 1993; Choi, 1998). As discussed earlier, in markets with multiple platforms and their varied implementations, compatibility testing and related ancillary services are in greater demand. Therefore, both third-party objectivity and expertise can be acquired through outsourcing certification testing to firms providing such related services. Hence, it follows that the structural outcome of certification intermediation is more likely in markets where compatibility testing and related ancillary services are in greater demand.

The existence of certification intermediation can, in turn, have secondary market effects on the complementary product market. Given that multiple platforms compete in the market, certification intermediaries can potentially build on the expertise gained through services such as compatibility testing to diversify across multiple platforms. Certification intermediaries can increase both economies of scope and scale by aggregating multiple certifications and related services. Such aggregations are especially common in digital industries (Resnick, Zeckhauser & Avery, 1994; Sarkar, Butler & Steinfield, 1995; Whinston, Stahl & Choi, 1997).

Such economies (given competing intermediaries) may be passed on to the complementary product developers, thereby potentially reducing entry costs and barriers as compared to the case with certification alone. Additionally, certification intermediaries, with their increased expertise on certifying multiple platforms, can provide aggregate economies of scale across all platforms, thereby reducing complementary product development costs across multiple platforms. In that sense, they can reduce the impact of between-platform deployment fragmentation in the complementary product market.

CONCLUSION

In the rapid evolution of information technologies, platform certification represents an important mechanism for facilitating vertical compatibility. However, in markets with competing platforms and their varied implementations, the requirement to certify across a variety of platforms may stifle the development of a rich variety of complementary products. To date, there has been little research on the complementary product market effects of platform certification. Drawing on evidence from a case study of the mobile application market, the research presented here provides insights into the effects of platform certification for a complementary product market.

Our exploratory research finds that in the mobile industry, platform certification has three effects; namely, intermediation within and between platform deployment fragmentation and entry barriers. If one assumes, however, that platform certification and competition are inevitable, attention should focus on the effects of intermediation. As compared to an unintermediated market, our research suggests that certification intermediaries may potentially mitigate some of the negative effects of a platform competition through their beneficial impact on between-platform deployment fragmentation and a potential reduction in entry barriers. Interestingly, in the case that an intermediary is able to certify for more than one program, it is likely to possess valuable information about the supply of complementary products to the various platforms and to some extent the true state of the platform competition. Clearly, the value of this information is dependent on the structure of the intermediation market, with a monopoly certification provider holding fairly complete information as compared to intermediaries in a competitive market.

Thus, through identification of the market effects of platform certification as a means for managing compatibility, this work contributes to both the broader literature on compatibility standards as well as standards competition. However, our analysis is exploratory in nature, and hence, the conceptual model requires more systematic validation before its generalizability to other similar product markets can be assessed. Particular characteristics of the mobile industry that may have influenced our findings include that the suppliers of the complementary goods (mobile applications) are numerous, generally small, and often require only relatively low levels of investment, which encourages entry. This, in addition to the global nature of application supply, may have influenced the certification outsourcing decision, which in turn generated certification intermediation. Assessing the extent to which our findings are valid in, for example, more concentrated complementary product markets requires further research. Future research might also evaluate the effects of certification intermediation on extending indirect platform network externalities. Models might also be developed to improve understanding of the role of certification intermediaries across a range of software development activities to assess the generalizability of their benefits. In addition to systematic assessment of the model presented

here in both similar and dissimilar contexts, future research might attempt to model the influence of compatibility certification on the standards competition to assess whether certification serves to extend or shorten the life of such competitions.

REFERENCES

Barnes, S.J. (2002). The mobile commerce value chain: Analysis and future developments. *International Journal of Information Management, 22*(2), 91–108.

Biglaiser, G. (1993). Middlemen as experts. *RAND Journal of Economics, 24*(2), 212–223.

Bresnahan, T.F., & Greenstein, S. (1999). Technological competition and the structure of the computer industry. *The Journal of Industrial Economics, 47*(1), 1–40.

Brynjolfsson, E., & Kemerer, C.F. (1996). Network externalities in microcomputer software: An econometric analysis of the spreadsheet market. *Management Science, 42*(12), 1627–1647.

Choi, S. (1998). Market lessons for gatekeepers. *Northwestern University Law Review, 92*(3), 916–966.

Church, J., & Gandal, N. (1992). Network effects, software provision, and standardization. *The Journal of Industrial Economics, 40*(1), 85–103.

Church, J., & Gandal, N. (1993). Complementary network externalities and technological adoption. *International Journal of Industrial Organization, 11*(2), 239–260.

David, P.A., & Greenstein, S. (1990). The economics of compatibility standards: An introduction to recent research. *Economics of Innovation and New Technology, 1*, 3–41.

David, P.A., & Steinmueller, W.E. (1994). Economics of compatibility standards and competition in telecommunication networks. *Information Economics and Policy, 6,* 217–241.

Economides, N., & Salop, S.C. (1992). Competition and integration among complements, and network market structure. *The Journal of Industrial Economics, 40*(1), 105–123.

Egyedi, T.M. (2001a). Strategies for de facto compatibility: Standardization, proprietary and open source approaches to Java. *Knowledge, Technology, and Policy, 14*(2), 113–128.

Egyedi, T.M. (2001b). Why JavaTM was -not standardized twice. *Computer Standards & Interfaces, 23*(4), 253–265.

Egyedi, T.M., & Dahanayake, A. (2003). *Difficulties implementing standards.* Proceedings of the 3rd IEEE Conference on Standardization and Innovation in Information Technology, Delft, The Netherlands.

Egyedi, T.M., & Hudson, J. (2005). A standard's integrity: Can it be safeguarded. *IEEE Communications Magazine, 43,* 151–155.

Egyedi, T.M., & van Wendel de Joode, R. (2003). *Standards and coordination in open source software.* Proceedings of the Standardization and Innovation in Information Technology (SIIT 2003), Delft, The Netherlands.

Egyedi, T.M., & van Wendel de Joode, R. (2004). Standardization and other coordination mechanisms in open source software. *International Journal of IT Standards & Standardization Research, 2*(2), 1–17.

Farrell, J., & Saloner, G. (1992). Converters, compatibility, and the control of interfaces. *The Journal of Industrial Economics, 40*(1), 9–35.

Gallagher, S., & Park, S.H. (2002). Innovation and competition in standard-based industries: A historical analysis of the U.S. home video game market. *IEEE Transactions on Engineering Management, 49*(1), 67–82.

Gandal, N. (1995). Competing compatibility standards and network externalities in the PC software market. *The Review of Economics and Statistics, 77*(4), 599–608.

Gandal, N., Greenstein, S., & Salant, D. (1999). Adoptions and orphans in the early microcomputer market. *The Journal of Industrial Economics, 47*(1), 87–105.

Garud, R., & Kumaraswamy, A. (1993). Changing competitive dynamics in network industries: An exploration of Sun Microsystems' open systems strategy. *Strategic Management Journal, 14*(5), 351–369.

Greenstein, S. (1998). Industrial economics and strategy: Computing platforms. *IEEE Micro, 18*(3), 43–53.

Iversen, E.J., & Tee, R. (2006). Standards dynamics and industrial organization in the mobile telecom sector. *Info: The Journal of Policy, Regulation and Strategy for Telecommunications, Information and Media, 8*(4), 33–48.

Karvonen, J., & Warsta, J. (2004). *Mobile multimedia services development: Value chain perspective.* Proceedings of the 3rd International Conference on Mobile and Ubiquitous Multimedia MUM '04, College Park, Maryland.

Katz, M.L., & Shapiro, C. (1985). Network externalities, competition, and compatibility. *The American Economic Review, 75*(3), 424–440.

Katz, M.L., & Shapiro, C. (1986). Technology adoption in the presence of network externalities. *The Journal of Political Economy, 94*(4), 822–841.

Katz, M.L., & Shapiro, C. (1994). Systems competition and network effects. *The Journal of Economic Perspectives, 8*(2), 93–115.

Mahmoud, Q.H. (2002). *Testing wireless Java applications.* Retrieved August 1, 2007, from http://developers.sun.com/techtopics/mobility/midp/articles/test/

Matutes, C., & Regibeau, P. (1987). Standardization in multi-component industries. In H.L. Gabel (Ed.), *Product standardization and competitive strategy*. Amsterdam, The Netherlands: Elsevier Science.

Methlie, L.B., & Gressgård, L.J. (2006). Exploring the relationships between structural market conditions and business conduct in mobile data services markets. *Journal of Electronic Commerce Research, 7*(1), 14.

Meyer, M.H., & Seliger, R. (1998). Product platforms in software development. *Sloan Management Review, 40*(1), 61.

Motorola. (2006). *Motorola Q Developer Guide*. Retrieved August 1, 2007, from http://developer.motorola.com/docstools/developerguides/

Porter, M.E. (1985). *Competitive advantage: Creating and sustaining superior performance*. New York: The Free Press.

Rada, R. (1996). Who will test conformance? *Communications of the ACM, 39*(1), 19–22.

Resnick, P., Zeckhauser, R., & Avery, C. (1994). *Roles for electronic brokers*. Proceedings of the Telecommunications Policy Research Conference, Arlington, Virginia.

Sarkar, M.B., Butler, B., & Steinfield, C. (1995). Intermediaries and cybermediaries: A continuing role for mediating players in the electronic marketplace. *Journal of Computer Mediated Communication, 1*(3).

Schmidt, S.K., & Werle, R. (1998). *Co-ordinating technology: Studies in the international standardization of telecommunications*. Cambridge, MA: MIT Press.

Tarnacha, A., & Maitland, C.F. (2006). *Entrepreneurship in mobile application development*. Proceedings of the Eighth International Conference on Electronic Commerce, Fredericton, New Brunswick, Canada.

Tarnacha, A., & Maitland, C.F. (Forthcoming). The effects of standards competition on market entry: The case of the mobile application markets. In *The standards edge: Unifier or divider?* The Bolin Group.

Tassey, G. (2000). Standardization in technology-based markets. *Research Policy, 29*(4-5), 587–602.

Tilson, D., & Lyytinen, K. (2006). The 3G transition: Changes in the US wireless industry. *Telecommunications Policy, 30*(10/11), 569–586.

West, J., & Dedrick, J. (2000). Innovation and control in standards architectures: The rise and fall of Japan's PC-98. *Information Systems Research, 11*(2), 197–216.

West, J., & Dedrick, J. (2006). Scope and timing of deployment: Moderators of organizational adoption of the Linux server platform. *International Journal of IT Standards & Standardization Research, 4*(2), 1–23.

Whinston, A.B., Stahl, D.O., & Choi, S.-Y. (1997). *The economics of electronic commerce*. Indianapolis, IN: MacMillan Publishing Company.

Windrum, P. (2004). Leveraging technological externalities in complex technologies: Microsoft's exploitation of standards in the browser wars. *Research Policy, 33*(3), 385–394.

Yin, R.K. (1994). *Case study research: Design and methods* (2nd ed.). Thousand Oaks, CA: Sage Publications Inc.

ENDNOTES

[1] Various CTIA-sponsored certifications can be found at http://www.ctia.org/business_resources/certification/

[2] See, for instance, the Windows Logo Program available at http://www.microsoft.com/whdc/winlogo/default.mspx

[3] See, for instance, the Equipment Authorization (EA) certification available at http://www.fcc.gov/oet/ea/

[4] The CE health and safety certification details can be found at http://www.cemarking.net/

[5] Various IEC-sponsored certifications can be found at http://www.iec.ch/helpline/sitetree/conformity/

[6] Various UL conformity assessment marks can be found at http://www.ul.com/

[7] The Java ME standard was established and is managed by an expert group of leading mobile device manufacturers, wireless carriers, and software vendors using the traditional Java Community Process (JCP) of developing publicly available specifications.

[8] In addition to being an application platform, BREW also incorporates an application distribution system that allows end users to shop, purchase, download, and install software over the operator's network. This combination provides network operators with a vertically integrated distribution control system that streamlines the development, deployment, and billing of applications for both developers and the network operator. For details, see BREW Developer home hosted at http://brew.qualcomm.com/brew/en/developer/overview.html

[9] Nokia as a device platform promulgator also used to provide a certification program called NokiaOK, which they later merged with Symbian. See Nokia OK press release at http://press.nokia.com/PR/200203/853384_5.html

[10] Examples of such programs include Cingular Certified Solution (http://developer.cingular.com/developer/testing/index.jsp?itemId=400025), Sprint Application Testing (http://developer.sprint.com/site/global/develop/p_testing/p_virtual_dev_lab/p_virtual_dev_lab1.jsp), and Virgin Mobile Certification (www.nstl.com/about_nstl/press_docs/virginmobile.pdf), to name a few.

[11] As examples, see VerizonWireless' requirement for True BREW Certification at http://www.vzwdevelopers.com/aims/public/BrewLanding.jsp, and Orange requirements for Industry Standard Testing at http://www.orangepartner.com/site/enuk/develop/v_devcentre/tools/p_compatibility_test.jsp#5

[12] As NSTL has provided certification services for various PC and mobile technologies for over a decade, they are in a unique position to provide insights into this somewhat ignored service niche of certification.

[13] For example, software tools like AppForge Crossfire and Tira Jump Product Suite enable developers to create different platform versions of an application.

[14] The program details can be accessed from http://brew.qualcomm.com/brew/en/developer/overview.html

[15] The program details can be accessed from http://javaverified.com/

[16] The program details can be accessed from https://www.symbiansigned.com/

[17] The program details can be accessed from http://msdn2.microsoft.com/en-us/windowsmobile/bb250547.aspx

[18] The dissolution of NokiaOK certification and its merger with the Symbian Signed is an example of such a risk.

[19] For a detailed comparison of the effects of open and proprietary standards on market fragmentation in the mobile applications market, see Tarnacha and Maitland (Forthcoming).

[20] For a discussion on the effects of standards on entry barriers and entrepreneurial innovation in the mobile applications market, see Tarnacha and Maitland, 2006).

This work was previously published in the International Journal of IT Standards and Standardization Research, Vol. 6, Issue 2, edited by K. Jakobs, pp. 48-65, copyright 2008 by IGI Publishing (an imprint of IGI Global).

Compilation of References

Abbate, J. (1999). *Inventing the Internet*. Cambridge, MA: MIT Press.

Acyl, A., & Borde, J. M. (2003). *Training and education for standardization in Europe – Volume 1 – Survey report*. Paris: Akela Business Engineering.

Administrative Complaint (2002), Docket No 9302, 18 June 2002.

Adner, R., & Levinthal, D. A. (2004). What is not a real option: Considering boundaries for the application of real options to business strategy. *Academy of Management. The Academy of Management Review, 29*(1), 74.

Ahuja, G., & Katila, R. (2001). Technological acquisitions and the innovation performance of acquiring firms: A longitudinal study. *Strategic Management Journal, 22*, 197-220.

Akrich, M. (1992). The description of technical objects. In J. Law, & W. E. Bijker (Eds.), *Shaping technology/ building society: Studies in socio-technical change*. Cambridge, MA: MIT Press.

Albrecht, C.C., Dean, L.D., & Hansen, J.V. (2003).Market place and technology standards for B2B ecommerce: Progress and challenges. In J.L. King & K. Lyytinen (Eds.), *Proceedings of MISQ Special Issue Workshop on Standard Making: A Critical Frontier for Information Systems*. Minneapolis: MIS Quarterly (pp. 108-209).

AL-Gahtani, S.S., & King, M. (1999). Attitudes, satisfaction and usage: Factors contributing to each in the acceptance of information technology. *Behaviour & Information Technology, 18*(4), 277-297.

Ali, A., Krapfel, R., Jr., & LaBahn, D. (1995). Product innovativeness and entry strategy: Impact on cycle time and break-even time. *Journal of Product Innovation Management, 1995*(12), 54-69.

Alkio, M. (2003, March 9). Kovaa peliä patenteilla. *Helsingin Sanomat*, p. E3.

Allen, J. P. (2004) Redefining the network: Enrollment strategies in the PDA industry, *Information Technology & People 17*(2), 171-185.

American National Standards Institute (ANSI) (2005a). *United States Standards Strategy*.

Amorim, C. S. (2008) Global perspectives and Strategies for Education about Standardization. Presentation at 3rd ICES Workshop, Gaithersburg, 2008-02-21—22, http://www.standards-education.org (last accessed 2008-11-09).

Amram, M., & Kulatilaka, N. (1999). *Real options*. Boston: Harvard Business Press.

Anderson, P., & Tushman, M. L. (1990). Technological discontinuities and dominant designs: A cyclical model of technological change. *Administrative Science Quarterly, 35*(4 Dec), 604-633.

Anh, V.T. (2006). An introduction—The history of standardisation. In W. Hesser, A. Feilzer, & H. de Vries (Eds.), *Standarisation in companies and markets*.

ANSI. (2003). *Guidelines for implementation of the ANSI Patent Policy*.

ANSI. (2003). *Patent policy*.

ANSI. (2005). *Overview of the U.S. Standardization System.*

APM Group. (2007). ITIL: Examination Institutes. Retrieved October 24, 2008, from http://www.itil-official-site.com/ExaminationInstitutes/ExamInstitutes.asp

APM. (2005). Association for project management overview. Retrieved August 24, 2005 from, http://www.apm.org.uk/page.asp?categoryID=3&subCategoryID=21&pageID=0

APM. (2006). *Body of knowledge: Version 5.* High Wycombe, UK: Association of Project Managers.

APMG-UK. APMG-UK's ITIL V3 Qualifications. Retrieved January 14, 2009, from http://www.apmgroup.co.uk/ITIL/ITILV3Qualifications.asp

Archibugi, D., & Pianta, M. (1996). Measuring technological change through patents and innovation surveys. *Technovation, 16*(9), 451-468.

Arellano, M. (1999). Fast company: Nortel's long involvement with OC-192 research is helping it dominate the market. *Tele.com, 4*(17), 42.

Arthur, W. B. (1988). Self-Reinforcing Mechanisms in Economics. *The Economy as an Evolving Complex System* (pp. 9-31). SFI Studies in the Sciences of Complexity, Addison-Wesley Publishing Co.

Arthur, W. B. (1989). Competing technologies, increasing returns, and lock-in by historical events. *The Economic Journal, 99,* 116–131. doi:10.2307/2234208

Arthur, W. B. (1996). Increasing returns and the new world of business. *Harvard Business Review*(July-August), 100-109.

Artych, R. (2003). *Methodology for the Design of Useful Implementations of Communications Protocols.* Unpublished doctoral dissertation, Warsaw University of Technology. (In Polish)

Artych, R., & Brzeziński, K. M. (1999). External Conformance Requirements: Concepts, Methods and Tools. In *Proceedings of the 12th International Workshop on Testing of Communicating Systems (IWTCS '99)* (pp. 363–378). Budapest: Kluwer.

Asaravala, A. (2004, April 24). Forgent sues over JPEG patent. *Wired News.* Retrieved August 29, 2006, from http://www.wired.com/news/business/0,1367,63200,00.html

ASTM Standardization News. (2003). Standards education in the United States: A Roundtable. *ASTM Standardization News, 31*(6), 41–47.

Autio, E. (1997). New, technology-based firms in innovation networks: Symplectic and generative impacts. *Research Policy, 26*(3), 263-281.

Axelrod, R. (1984). *The evolution of cooperation.* New York: Basic Books.

Axelrod, R., et al. (1995). Coalition formation in standard-setting alliances. *Management Science, 41*(9), 1493-1508.

Axios Systems. (2008). ITIL adoption surges despite confusion, says Axios survey. Retrieved January 14, 2009, from http://www.axiossystems.com/six/en/corporate/news/detail.php/211

Bacharach, S. (1989). Organizational theories: Some criteria for evaluation. *Academy of Management Review, 14*(4), 496-515

Baldwin, C. Y., & Clark, K. B. (2000). *Design rules.* Cambridge, MA: The MIT Press.

Baldwin, C. Y., & Clark, K.B. (2005). Designs and design architecture: The missing link between "knowledge" and the "economy." Advancing Knowledge and the Knowledge Economy. Washington, DC.

Balto, D.A., & Wolman, A.M. (2003). Intellectual property and antitrust: General principles. *IDEA The Journal of Law and Technology, 43*(3), 396-474.

Barnes, S.J. (2002). The mobile commerce value chain: Analysis and future developments. *International Journal of Information Management, 22*(2), 91–108.

Barnett, M. L. (2003). Falling off the fence? A realistic appraisal of a real options approach to corporate strategy. *Journal of Management Inquiry, 12*(2), 185.

Barney, J. (1991). Firm resources and sustained competitive advantage. *Journal of Management, 17*(1), 99-120.

Barton, N. (2004, July 8). This year's model: performance improvement complements IT best practices frameworks. *CIO, 2005.*

Baskin, E., Krechmer, K., & Sherif, M. (1998). The six dimensions of standards: Contribution towards a theory of standardization. In L. A Lefebvre, R. M. Mason, & T. Khalil (Eds.), *Management of Technology, Sustainable Development and Eco-Efficiency* (pp. 53-62). Amsterdam et al: Elsevier.

Bekkers, R., Duysters, G., & Verspagen, B. (2002). Intellectual property rights, strategic technology agreements and market structure. The case of GSM. *Research Policy, 31,* 1141-1161.

Bekkers, R., Verspagen, B., & Smits, J. (2002). Intellectual property rights and standardization: The case of GSM. *Telecommunications Policy, 26*(3-4), 171-188.

Belleflamme, P. (1999). Assessing the diffusion of EDI standards across business communities. *EURAS Yearbook of Standardization, 2,* 301-324.

Benham, L. (1980). The demand for occupational licensure. In S. Rottenberg (Ed.), *Occupational licensure and regulation.* US: American Enterprise Institute for Public and Policy Research, pp. 13-25.

Benkler, Y. (2001). Coase's penguin, or, Linux and the nature of the firm. *Yale Law Journal, 112*(3), 367-445.

Benoliel, D. (2003). Cyberspace Technological Standardization: An Institutional Theory Retrospective, 18 Berkeley Tech. L.J. 1259 (2003).

Berlind, D. (2002a, April 16). IBM drops Internet patent bombshell. *Tech Update.*

Berlind, D. (2002b, April 25). The hidden toll of patents on standards. *Tech News on ZDNet.* Retrieved August 29, 2006, from http://news.zdnet.com/2100-9595_22-891852.html

Berman, V. (2005, January-February). Is it time to reexamine patent policy for standards? *IEEE Design & Test of Computers,* 71-73.

Berner-Lee, T. (1999). *Weaving the Web: The original design and ultimate destiny of the World Wide Web.* San Francisco: Harper.

Bessen, J. (2003). *Strategic patenting of complex technologies* (Working Paper). Research on Innovation.

Biglaiser, G. (1993). Middlemen as experts. *RAND Journal of Economics, 24*(2), 212–223.

Bijker, W. E. (1995). *Of bicycle, bakelites, and bulbs: Toward a theory of sociotechnical change.* Cambridge: The MIT Press.

Bijker, W.E. (1987). The social construction of Bakelite: Toward a theory of invention. In W.E. Bijker, T. P. Hughes, & T. Pinch (Eds.), *The social construction of technological systems.* Cambridge: MIT Press.

Bix, B. H., & Winn, J. K. (2006). Diverging Perspectives on Electronic Contracting in the US and EU. *Cleveland Marshall Law Review.*

Blind, K. (2004). *The Economics of Standards – Theory, Evidence, Policy.* Cheltenham, UK / Northampton, MA, USA: Edward Elgar.

Blind, K. (2006). Explanatory factors for participation in formal standardisation processes: Empirical evidence at firm level. *Economics of Innovation and New Technology, 15*(2), 157-170.

Blind, K., & Jungmittag, A. (2008). The Impact of Patents and Standards on Macroeconomic Growth: A Panel Approach Covering Four Countries and 12 Sectors - The Empirical Economics of Standards. *Journal of Productivity Analysis, 1,* 51–60. doi:10.1007/s11123-007-0060-8

Blind, K., & Thumm, N. (2004). Intellectual property protection and standardization. *International Journal of IT Standards & Standardization Research, 2*(2), 61-75.

Blind, K., Bierhals, R., Thumm, N., Hossain, K., Sillwood, J., Iverser, E., et al. (2002). *Study on the interaction between standardisation and intellectual property rights* (EC Contract No G6MA-CT-2000-02001, 2002).

Blind, K., Edler, J., Nack, R., & Strauß, J. (2001). *Micro- and macroeconomic implications of the patentability of software innovations. Intellectual property rights in information technologies between competition and innovation* (Study on Behalf of German Federal Ministry of Economics and Technology).

Bloomfield, R.S. (1999). A perspective on advancing standards research and education—Building in the telecommunications scene. *ISO Bulletin, 29*(6).

Blum, D., Gebel, G., & Moench, D. (2004). *Burton Group Report on the Federal E-Authentication Initiative* (August 30, 2004). Retrieved from http://www.cio.gov/eauthentication/documents/BurtonGroupEAreport.pdf.

Blum, U. (2005). Lessons from the past: Public standardization in the spotlight. *International Journal of IT Standards & Standardization Research, 3*(1), 1-20.

Boland, R. J. J., & Tenkasi, R. V. (1995). Perspective making and perspective taking in communities of knowing. *Organization Science, 6*(4), 350-372.

Borde, J.-M. (2004). *Training and education for standardization in Europe – Survey report.* In F., Bousquet et al. (Eds), *EURAS Proceedings 2004* (pp. 157-170). Aachener Beiträge zur Informatik Vol. 36. Aachen, Germany: Wissenschaftsverlag Mainz in Aachen.

Bowker, G., & Star, S. (1999). *Sorting things out: Classification and its consequences.* London: MIT Press.

Bowman, E. H., & Hurry, D. (1993). Strategy through the options lens: An integrated view of resource investments and the incremental-choice process. *Academy of Management Review, 18*(4), 760-782.

Boyatzis, R.E. (1982). *The competent manager: A model for effective performance.* New York: Wiley.

Bredillet, C. (2003). Genesis and role of standards: Theoretical foundations and socio-economical model for the construction and use of standards. *International journal of Project Management, 21*(6), 463-470.

Bresnahan, T.F., & Greenstein, S. (1999). Technological competition and the structure of the computer industry. *The Journal of Industrial Economics, 47*(1), 1–40.

Brown, D. (2005). Raise HR's stature by raising the bar for qualification. *Canadian HR Reporter, 18*(6), 5-8.

Brunnermeier, S.B., & Martin, S.A. (1999). *Interoperability cost analysis of the U.S. automotive supply chain.* Project Number 7007-03, Research Triangle Park. North Carolina: Research Triangle Institute.

Brynjolfsson, E., & Kemerer, C.F. (1996). Network externalities in microcomputer software: An econometric analysis of the spreadsheet market. *Management Science, 42*(12), 1627–1647.

Brzeziński, K. M. (1998). Towards Formality of Technical Requirements for Protocols. In *Proceedings of the 9th European Workshop on Dependable Computing (EWDC'98)* (pp. 71–74). Gdańsk.

Brzeziński, K. M. (2005). Embedded Capability Relations to Aid the Industrial Usability of Telecommunications Standards. In *Proceedings of the 4th International Conference on Standardization and Innovation in Information Technology (SIIT 2005)* (pp. 55–63). Geneva.

Brzeziński, K. M. (2005). Formalizing Operator Requirements for the Development of Telecommunications Networks and Services. In *Proceedings of the 8th International Conference on Telecommunications (ConTEL 2005)* (pp. 611–618). Zagreb.

Brzeziński, K. M. (2007). Network Operators' Requirements and the Structure of Telecommunications Standards. [JITSR]. *International Journal of IT Standards and Standardization Research, 5*(1), 103–117.

Brzeziński, K. M., Gajowniczek, P., Grzegorzewski, M., Karwowski, K., Kukliński, S., Średniawa, M., et al. (2008, December). *Converged services in a heterogeneous NGN / CSN environment. Volume 1–3.* (Research Project no. 501E/1036/4470). Warsaw: Warsaw University of Technology, on contract from CBR TP (Telekomunikacja Polska, R&D Department). (In Polish; not publicly available)

BSI (Eds). (2006). *BS 8900:2006 guidance for managing sustainable development.* BSI British Standards.

BSI Education. (2006). Standards and Education: Foundations for the Future. Retrieved September 6, 2006, from http://www.bsieducation.org/Education/HE/default.shtml

Byrne, B.M., & Golder, P.A. (2002). The diffusion of anticipatory standards with particular reference to the ISO/IEC information resource dictionary system framework standard. *Computer Standards & Interfaces, 24*(5), 369-379.

Calderone, L.L., & Custer, T.L. (2005, November). *Prosecution laches as a defense in patent cases.* Flaster Greenberg Attorneys at Law. Retrieved August 29, 2006, from http://www.flastergreenberg.com/pdf/PatentArtic_prf3.pdf

Callon, M. (1986). Some elements of a sociology of translation: Domestication of the scallops and the fishermen of St Brieuc Bay. In J. Law (Ed.), *Power, action and belief: A new sociology of knowledge?* London: Routledge & Kegan Paul.

Callon, M. (1992). Techno-economic networks and irreversibility. In J. Law (Ed.), *A sociology of monsters: Essays on power, technology and domination.* London: Routledge.

Callon, M., & Law, J. (1989). On the construction of sociotechnical networks: content and context revisited. *Knowledge and Society, 8*, 57-83.

Calzadilla-Sarmiento, B. (2005). Training services Supporting International Standards development. *ISO Focus, 2*(3), 16–19.

Cameron, K. (2005). *The Laws of Identity.* Retrieved from http://www.identityblog.com.

Cantner, U., Dressler, K., & Krüger, J. (2004). Verweildaueranalysen in der empirischen Wirtschaftsforschung. *Das Wirtschaftsstudium, 10*, 1287–1293.

Caplan, P. (2003). *Patents and open standards* (White paper prepared for the National Information Standards Organization).

Carey, J. (1953). Uniform standards for professional qualifications. *Journal of Accountancy, 95*, 36-37.

Cargill, C. F. (1989). *Information technology standardization: Theory, process, and organizations.* Redford, MA: Digital Press.

Carley, K. (2006). Dynamic network anlysis: Summary of the NRC workshop on social network modeling and analysis. In R. Breiger, & K. Carey (Eds.), National Research Council, Washington D.C.

Casson, D. (2005). North American ITIL Assessment: an in-depth analysis of the current state and readiness of IT organisations to adopt ITIL-based processes [Electronic Version]. Retrieved August, from http://www.evergreen-sys.com/news_events/itilsurvey/PDF/2005NorthAmericanITILAssessment.pdf

Cater-Steel, A. P. (2009). IT Service Departments Struggle to Adopt a Service-Oriented Philosophy . *International Journal of Information Systems in the Service Sector, 1*(2).

Cater-Steel, A. P., & McBride, N. (2007). *IT Service Management Improvement – an Actor Network Perspective.* Paper presented at the European Conference on Information Systems.

Cater-Steel, A. P., & Pollard, C. (2008). *Conflicting views on ITIL implementation: managed as a project – or business as usual?* Paper presented at the International Conference on Information Resources Management (Conf-IRM).

Cater-Steel, A. P., & Tan, W.-G. (2005). *Implementation of IT Infrastructure Library (ITIL) in Australia: Progress and Success Factors.* Paper presented at the IT Governance International Conference.

Cater-Steel, A. P., & Toleman, M. (2007). Education for IT Service Management. *International Journal of IT Standards and Standardization Research, 5*(2), 27–42.

Cater-Steel, A. P., & Toleman, M. (2007, 3-6 July). *The role of Universities in IT service management education.* Paper presented at the 11th Pacific Asia Conference on Information Systems, Auckland.

Cater-Steel, A. P., & Toleman, M. (2009). Education for IT Service Management Standards. In G. Kelley (Ed.), *Selected readings in information technology management: contemporary issues.* Hershey, PA: IGI Global.

Cater-Steel, A. P., Tan, W.-G., & Toleman, M. A. (2006). *Challenge of adopting multiple process improvement frameworks.* Paper presented at the European Conference on Information Systems, Goteborg, Sweden.

Cater-Steel, A. P., Toleman, M., & Tan, W. (2006). *Transforming IT service management - the ITIL impact.* Paper presented at the 17th Australasian Conference on Information Systems.

Cegielski, C. (2004). Who values technology certification? *Communications of the ACM, 47*(10), 103-105.

Cegielski, C., Rebman, C., & Reithel, B. (2003). The value of certification: An empirical assessment of the perceptions of end-users of local area networks. *Information Systems Journal, 13*, 97-107.

Center for Global Standards Analysis. (2004). *Report on a Survey of Schools of Engineering in the United States concerning Standards Education.* Washington, DC: The Catholic University of America.

Chamberlin, E.H. (1953). The product as an economic variable. *Quarterly Journal of Economics, Vol. 67*(1).

Chaudhuri, S., & Tabrizi, B. (1999). Capturing the real value in high-tech acquisitions. *Harvard Business Review, 77*(5), 123-130.

Chesbrough, H. (2003). *Open innovation.* Harvard Business School Press.

Chiao, B., Lerner, J., & Tirole, J. (2005). *The rules of standard-setting organizations: An empirical analysis.* Unpublished Manuscript, Harvard Business School.

Chiesa, V., Manzini, R., & Toletti, G. (2002). Standard-setting processes: Evidence from two case studies. *R & D Management, 32(*5), 431.

Choi, D. & de Vries, H.J. (2010). Standardization as Emerging Content in Technology Education at all Levels of Education. *International Journal of Technology and Design Education, 20*(?) *(forthcoming).*

Choi, D. (2008, Ed.). *APEC SCSC Education Guideline 1: Case Studies of How to Plan and Implement Standards Education Programs.* Singapore: APEC.

Choi, D., de Vries, H. J., & Kim, D. (2009). Standards Education Policy Development: Observations based on APEC Research. *International Journal of IT Standards and Standardization Research, 7*(2), 43–63.

Choi, S. (1998). Market lessons for gatekeepers. *Northwestern University Law Review, 92*(3), 916–966.

Christensen, C. M., Suarez, F. F., & Utterback, J. M. (1998). Strategies for survival in fast-changing industries. *Management Science, 44*(12), S207-S220.

Church, J., & Gandal, N. (1992). Network effects, software provision, and standardization. *The Journal of Industrial Economics, 40*(1), 85–103.

Church, J., & Gandal, N. (1993). Complementary network externalities and technological adoption. *International Journal of Industrial Organization, 11*(2), 239–260.

Clark, D. (2002, October). Do Web standards and patents mix? *Computer,* pp. 19-22.

Clark, R. (2002, July 19). *Concerning recent patent claims.* Retrieved August 29, 2006, from http://www.jpeg.org/newsrel1.html

Clarkson, K., & Muris, T. (1980). The federal trade commission and occupational regulation. In S. Rottenberg (Ed.), *Occupational licensure and regulation. .* US: American Enterprise Institute for Public and Policy Research, pp. 107-141.

Cohen, W. M., & Levinthal, D. A. (1990). Absorptive capacity: A new perspective on learning and innovation. *Administrative Science Quarterly, 35*, 128-152.

Cohen, W.M., Nelson, R.R., & Walsh, J.P. (2000, February). *Protecting their intellectual assets: Appropriability conditions and why U.S. manufacturing firms patent (or not)* (NBER Working Paper Series).

Commission, E. U. (1999). eEurope: An Information Society for All. Communication on a Commission Initiative for the Special European Council of Lisbon, 23 and 24 March 2000. Retrieved from http://europa.eu.int/eur-lex/en/com/cnc/2001/com2001_0428en01.pdf

Commission, E. U. (2006). Report on the operation of Directive 1999/93/EC on a Community framework for electronic signatures. Brussels 15.3.2006 COM(2006) 120 Final.

Conger, S., Venkataraman, N., Hernandez, A., & Probst, J. (2009). (forthcoming). Market Potential for ITSM Graduates: A Survey. *ISM*.

Congress of the United States. (1990). Office of Technology Assessment, Critical Connections, US Government Printing Office. Darwin, C. (1895). *The Origin of the Species by means of natural selection*. D. Appleton and Co.

Coombs, C.R., Doherty, N.F., & Loan-Clarke, J. (2001). The importance of user ownership and positive user attitudes in the successful adoption of community information systems. *Journal of End User Computing, 13*(4), 5.

Cover, R. (2005). The Cover Pages: Security Assertion Markup Language (SAML). Retrieved from http://xml.coverpages.org/saml.html

Crawford, L. (2004). Global body of project management knowledge and standards. J. Pinto, & G. Morris (Eds.), *The wiley guide to managing projects*. New York: Wiley, 1150-1196.

Crawford, L. (2004). Professional associations and global initiatives. J. Pinto, & G. Morris (Eds.), *The wiley guide to managing projects*. New York: Wiley, 1389-1402.

Critical Issues in ICT Standardization. (2005, April). ICT Focus Group report. ICT Standards Board. Available from http://www.ict.etsi.org/publications.htm

Croley, S. P. (1998). Theories of regulation: Incorporating the administrative process. *Columbia Law Review, 98*(1), 1-168.

Cunningham, A. (2005). Telecommunications, intellectual property, and standards. In I. Walden, & J. Angel (Eds.), *Telecommunications law and regulation*. Oxford.

Damsgaard, J., & Lyytinen, K. (2001). The role of intermediating institutions in the diffusion of electronic data interchange (EDI): How industry associations intervened in Denmark, Finland, and Hong Kong. *The Information Society, 17*(3), 197-210.

David, P. A. (1985). Clio and the economics of QWERTY. *The American Economic Review, 72*(2), 332-337.

David, P. A. (1995). Standardization policies for network technologies: The flux between freedom and order revisited. In R. W. Hawkins, R. Mansell, & J. Skea (Eds.), *Standards, innovation and competitiveness: The politics and economics of standards in natural and technical environments.* Aldershot, UK: Edward Elgar.

David, P. A., & Greenstein, S.M. (1990). The economics of compatibility standards: An introduction to recent research. *The Economics of Innovations and New Technology, 1*(1/2), 3-41.

David, P. A., & Steinmueller, W.E. (1994). Economics of compatibility standards and competition in telecommunication networks. *Information Economics and Policy, 6*(3,4), 217-241.

Davidson, E. (2002). Technology frames and framing: Socio-cognitive investigation of requirements determination. *MIS Quarterly, 26*(4), 329-358.

Davis, F.D. (1993). User acceptance of information technology: System sharacteristics, user perceptions and behavioural impacts. *International Journal of Man-Machine Studies, 38*(3), 475-487.

de Vries, H. (2003). Learning by example- a possible curriculum model for standardization education. *ISO Bulletin, July,* 25-29.

de Vries, H. J. (1999). *Standardization – A Business Approach to the Role of National Standardization Organizations.* Boston / Dordrecht / London: Kluwer Academic Publishers.

de Vries, H. J. (2001). IT Standards Typology. In K. Jakobs (Ed.), *Advanced Topics in Information Technology Standards and Standardization Research* (Vol. 1, pp. 1–26). IGI Publishing.

de Vries, H. J. (2001). Standardization - a New Discipline? In *Proceedings of the 2nd IEEE Conference on Stan-*

dardization and Innovation in Information Technology (SIIT 2001) *(pp. 91–105).*

de Vries, H. J. (2002. Standardization – Mapping a Field of Research. In S. Bolin (Ed.), *The Standards Edge* (pp. 99-121). Ann Arbor, MI: Bollin Communications.

de Vries, H. J. (2005). *Standardization Education.* In M.J. Holler (Ed.), *EURAS Yearbook of Standardization, Vol. 5, Homo Oecomomicus, XXII* (1) (pp. 78-80). Munich: Accedo Verlagsgesellschaft.

de Vries, H. J. (2006). Competing E-Purse Systems: A Standards Battle. *Journal of Cases on Information Technology, 8*(1), 1–15.

de Vries, H. J., & Egyedi, T. M. (2007). Education about Standardization – Recent Findings. *International Journal of IT Standards and Standardization Research, 5*(2), 1–16.

de Vries, H. J., & Slob, F. J. C. (2006). Best Practice in Company Standardization. *International Journal of IT Standards and Standardization Research, 4*(1), 62-85.

Dean, P.J. (1997). Examining the profession and the practice of business ethics. . *Journal of Business Ethics, 16*, 1637-1649.

DeCarolis, D. M., & Deeds, D. L. (1999). The impact of stocks and flows of organizational knowledge on firm performance: An empirical investigation of the biotechnology industry. *Strategic Management Journal, 20*(10), 953-968.

Dedrick, J., & West, J. (2003). Why firms adopt open source platforms: A grounded theory of innovation and standards adoption. In J.L. King & K. Lyytinen (Eds.), *Proceedings of MISQ Special Issue Workshop on Standard Making: A Critical Frontier for Information Systems.* Minneapolis: MIS Quarterly, (pp. 236-257).

Delio, M. (2004). Solving the Identity Crisis. *InfoWorld, 36*, 34.

Dickerson, K. (2005). *The Paramount Importance of Standards to Operators, Vendors and Users.* Keynote speech at the 4th International Conference on Stan-

dardization and Innovation in Information Technology (SIIT 2005).

Dickerson, K. (2007). *BT's use of Open Standards and Open Source.* Invited speech at the 5th International Conference on Standardization and Innovation in Information Technology (SIIT 2007).

Dierickx, I., & Cool, K. (1989). Asset stock accumulation and sustainability of competitive advantage. *Management Science, 35*(11), 1504-1513.

Dixit, A. K., & Pindyck, R. S. (1994). *Investment under uncertainty.* Princeton, NJ: Princeton University Press.

DLA. (2004). *European intellectual property survey.*

Dobson, B. (2005). Greater efficiency, reduced cost. *Defence Management Journal, 28*, 25-26.

Dreverman, M. (2005). *Adoption of product model data standards in the process industry.* Eindhoven University of Technology, Eindhoven, Netherlands.

Dumortier, J. (2004). Legal Status of Qualified Electronic signatures in Europe. In S. Paulus, N. Pohlmann, & H. Reimer (Eds.), *ISEEE 2004—Securing Electronic Business Processes.* Vieweg.

Dumortier, J., Kelm, S., Nilsson, H., Skouma, G., & Van Eecke, P. (2003). Legal and market aspects of the application of Directive 1999/93/EC and practical applications of electronic signatures in the Member States, the EEA, the Candidate and Accession countries, 20 October 2003.

Duncan, W.R. (1998). Presentation to council of chapter presidents. *PMI Annual Symposium.* October 10, Long Beach, CA, USA.

ECITB. (2002). *National occupational standards for project management: Pre-launch version.* Kings Langley: Engineering Construction Industry Training Board.

Economides, N., & Salop, S.C. (1992). Competition and integration among complements, and network market structure. *The Journal of Industrial Economics, 40*(1), 105–123.

Egan, M. (2002). Setting Standards: Strategic Advantage in International Trade. *Business Strategy Review, 13*(1), 51–64. doi:10.1111/1467-8616.00202

Egyedi, T. (2005). *Consortium problem redefined: Negotiating 'democracy' in the actor network standardization.* Unpublished working paper, Department of Information and communication Technology, Faculty of technology, Policy and Management, Delft University of Technology.

Egyedi, T. M. (2000). Institutional dilemma in ICT standardization: Coordinating the diffusion of technology? In K. Jacobs (Ed.), *Information technology standards and standardization: A global perspective*, 48-62. Hershey, London: Idea Group Publishing.

Egyedi, T. M. (2001). *Beyond Consortia, Beyond Standardisation? New Case Material and Policy Threads.* Final Report for the European Commission.

Egyedi, T. M. (2002). Standards Enhance System Flexibility? Mapping Compatibility Strategies onto Flexibility Objectives. In *Proceedings of the EASST 2002 conference.*

Egyedi, T. M. (2007). *IEC Lecture Series: The importance of Standards.* Geneva: IEC (CD).

Egyedi, T. M., & Hudson, J. (2005). A standard's integrity: can it be safeguarded? *IEEE Communications Magazine, 43*(2), 151–155. doi:10.1109/MCOM.2005.1391516

Egyedi, T. M., & Loeffen, A. G. A. J. (2002). Succession in standardization: grafting XML onto SGML. *Computer Standards & Interfaces, 24*(4).

Egyedi, T., & Heijnen, P. (2005). Scale of Standards Dynamics: Change in formal, international IT standards. In S. Bolin (Ed.), *The Standards Edge: Future Generation.* Bolin Communications.

Egyedi, T.M. (2001). Strategies for de facto compatibility: Standardization, proprietary and open source approaches to Java. *Knowledge, Technology, and Policy, 14*(2), 113–128.

Egyedi, T.M. (2001). Why JavaTM was -not standardized twice. *Computer Standards & Interfaces, 23*(4), 253–265.

Egyedi, T.M., & Dahanayake, A. (2003). *Difficulties implementing standards.* Proceedings of the 3rd IEEE Conference on Standardization and Innovation in Information Technology, Delft, The Netherlands.

Egyedi, T.M., & van Wendel de Joode, R. (2003). *Standards and coordination in open source software.* Proceedings of the Standardization and Innovation in Information Technology (SIIT 2003), Delft, The Netherlands.

Egyedi, T.M., & van Wendel de Joode, R. (2004). Standardization and other coordination mechanisms in open source software. *International Journal of IT Standards & Standardization Research, 2*(2), 1–17.

Eisenhardt, K. M., & Martin, J. A. (2000). Dynamic capabilities: What are they? *Strategic Management Journal, 21*, 1105-1121.

Ellison, C. M., & Schneier, B. (2000). Ten Risks of PKI: What You're Not Being Told about Public key infrastructure. *Computer Security Journal, 16*(1), 1–7.

ENAA. (2002). *P2M: A guidebook of project & program management for enterprise innovation: Summary translation. Revision 1.* Tokyo, Japan: Project Management Professionals Certification Center (PMCC).

Eolas Technologies Incorporated and the Regents of the University of California v. Microsoft Corporation, Case Nr. 04-1234, Federal Circuit, 2 March 2005.

ETSI EG 201 058. (2003). *Implementation Conformance Statement (ICS) proforma style guide* (V1.2.4).

ETSI EG 202 237. (2007). *MTS; Internet Protocol Testing (IPT); Generic approach to interoperability testing.* (V1.1.2).

ETSI EG 202 568. (2007). *MTS; Internet Protocol Testing (IOT); Testing: Methodology and Framework* (V1.1.3).

ETSI ES 201 873. (2008). *MTS; The Testing and Test Control Notation version 3.*

ETSI ES 202 553. (2008). *MTS; TPLan: A notation for expressing Test Purposes* (V1.1.1).

ETSI ETS 300 406. (1995). *MTS; Protocol and profile conformance testing specifications; Standardization methodology.*

ETSI MBS. (n.d.). *Making Better Standards.* Electronic publication. Available from http://portal.etsi.org/mbs (accessed 15 Jan. 2009)

ETSI SR 001 262. (2004). *ETSI drafting rules.*

ETSI. (2005). *IPR policy.*

EU Commission (2007). Communication from the Commission to the European Parliament, the Council, the European Economic and Social Committee and the Committee of the Regions. Radio Frequency Identification (RFID) in Europe: Steps Toward a Policy Framework, COM (2007) 96 final.

EU Commission (2008, February 8). *European ICT Standardisation Policy at a Crossroads: A New Direction for Global Success.*

EU Commission (2009, January 28). VAT: Commission proposes a review of the VAT rules on invoicing with a view to reduce burdens on business and to help Member States tackle fraud. IP/09/132.

European Commission. (2006). *Website, Enterprise and Industry, Standardization.* Retrieved from http://ec.europa.eu/enterprise/standards_policy/academic_network/catalogue.htm#Universities #Universities

European Data Protection Supervisor (2008). Opinion of the European Data Protection Supervisor on the Communication from the Commission on RFID in Europe, 2008 O.J. (C 101) 1.

Evergreen. (2006). Developing the Business Case for ITIL. Retrieved 16 Sept, 2006, from http://www.evergreensys.com/whitepapers_tools/whitepapers/BusinessValueITIL.pdf

Evolution of Global Networks. (2001). In *Global Networks and Local Values: A Comparative Look at Germany and the United States* (pp. 23–45). National Academy Press.

Faraj, S., Kwon, D., & Watts, S. (2004). Contested artifact: Technology sensemaking, actor networks, and the shaping of the Web browser. *Information Technology & People 17*(2), 186-209.

Farrell, J. (1996). *Choosing the rules for formal standardization.* UC Berkeley.

Farrell, J., & Saloner, G. (1985). Standardisation, compatibility and innovation. *The Rand Journal of Economics, 16*(1), 70–83. doi:10.2307/2555589

Farrell, J., & Saloner, G. (1986). Installed base and compatibility: Innovation, product preannouncements, and predation. *The American Economic Review, 76*(5), 940-955.

Farrell, J., & Saloner, G. (1992). Converters, compatibility, and the control of interfaces. *The Journal of Industrial Economics, 40*(1), 9–35.

Farrell, J., & Saloner, G. (1988). Coordination through committees and markets *The RAND Journal of Economics, 19*(2), 235-252.

Farrell, J., Saloner, G. (1988). Dynamic competition with switching costs. *The Rand Journal of Economics, 19*(1), 123-137.

Federal Trade Commission v. Dell Computer Corp., FTC File No. 931 0097, 2 November 1995.

Feldman, R.P., & Rees, M.R. (2000, July). The effect of industry standard setting on patent licensing and enforcement. *IEEE Communications Magazine*, pp. 112-116.

Ferguson, K. (1999). 20/20 foresight. Retrieved August 29, 2006, from http://www.forbes.com/1999/04/19/feat.html

Fichman, R. G., & Kemerer, C. F. (1993). Toward a theory of the adoption and diffusion of software process innovations. *IFIP Transactions A-Computer Science and Technology*, A-45, 23-30.

Fichman, R.G. (1992). Information technology diffusion: A review of empirical research. In J.I. Degross, J.D. Becker & J.J. Elam, (Eds.). *Proceedings of the Thirteenth international Conference on information Systems*, (pp. 195-206).

Fichman, R.G., & Kemerer, C.F. (1993b). Adoption of software engineering process innovations: The case of object orientation. *MIT Sloan Management Review, 34*(2), 7-22.

Flynn, W. J. (2001). More than a matter of degree – credentialing, certification and community colleges [Electronic Version], 16, from http://www.nccet.org/associations/2158/NCCETcertification.pdf

Folta, T. B., & O'Brien, J. P. (2004). Entry in the presence of dueling options. *Strategic Management Journal, 25*, 121-138.

Forgent Networks. (2006). *Intellectual property, '672 patent cases*. Retrieved August 29, 2006, from http://www.forgent.com/ip/672cases.shtml

Frank, S.J. (2002, March). Can you patent an industry standard? *IEEE Spectrum*.

Friedman, M. (1962). Capitalism & freedom. Chicago: University of Chicago Press.

FTC. (2003). *To promote innovation: The proper balance of competition and patent law and policy*.

Funk, J. L. (2002). *Global competition between and within standards: The case of mobile phones*. New York: Palgrave.

Furman, J., & Stern, S. (2004). *Climbing atop the shoulders of giants: The impact of institutions on cumulative research*. Unpublished Manuscript, Northwestern University.

Gabel, H. L. (1991). *Competitive strategies for product standards: The strategic use of compatibility standards for competitive advantage*. London: McGraw-Hill Book Company.

Gadamer, H.-G. (1975). *Truth and method* (G. Barden & J. Cumming, Trans.). New York: Seabury Press.

Gallagher, S., & Park, S.H. (2002). Innovation and competition in standard-based industries: A historical analysis of the U.S. home video game market. *IEEE Transactions on Engineering Management, 49*(1), 67–82.

Gallivan, M.J. (2001). Organizational adoption and assimilation of complex technological innovations: Development and application of a new framework. *SIGMIS Database, 32*(3), 51-85.

Gandal, N. (1995). Competing compatibility standards and network externalities in the PC software market. *The Review of Economics and Statistics, 77*(4), 599–608.

Gandal, N., Gantman, N., & Genesove, D. (2007). Intellectual property and standardization committee participation in the US modem industry. In S. Greenstein, & V. Stango (Eds.), *Standards and public policy*. Cambridge University Press.

Gandal, N., Greenstein, S., & Salant, D. (1999). Adoptions and orphans in the early microcomputer market. *The Journal of Industrial Economics, 47*(1), 87–105.

Garfinkel, S. (2005). Design Principles and Patterns for Computer Systems That Are Simultaneously Secure and Usable, MIT Ph.D. dissertation. Retrieved from http://www.simson.net/thesis/

Garud, R., & Kumaraswamy, A. (1993). Changing competitive dynamics in network industries: An exploration of Sun Microsystems' open systems strategy. *Strategic Management Journal, 14*(5), 351–369.

Garud, R., Jain, S., & Kumaraswamy, A. (2002). Institutional entrepreneurship in the sponsoring of common technological standards: The case of Sun Microsystems and Java. *Academy of Management Journal, 45*(1), 196-214.

Gaynor, M., & Bradner, S. (2001). *The real options approach to standardization*. Paper presented at the Hawaii International Conference on Systems Sciences, Honolulu, HI.

George, T. (2002). Employees raise the bar on certification. *Information Week, 896*, 76-77.

Gerundino, D. (2005). Learning-by-doing: the ISO e-learning programme. *ISO Focus, 2*(3), 12–14.

Gerundino, D. (2007). ISO e-learning completed! – A convenient, practical and fun way to become a standardization expert. *ISO Focus, 4*(11), 39–43.

Gessa, N. (2007). *An Ontology-based Approach to Define and Manage B2B Interoperability*. Unpublished doctoral dissertation, University of Bologna.

Gherardi, S., &Nicolini, D. (2000). To transfer is to transform: The circulation of safety knowledge. *Organization, 7*(2), 329-348.

Gibb, B., & Damodaran, S. (2003). *ebXML: Concepts and Application*. Indianapolis: Wiley Publishing.

Glassie, J. (2003). Certification programs as a reflection of competency. *Association Management, 55*(6), 17-18.

Glenny, M. (2001, February). How Europe Can Stop Worrying and Learn to Love the Future.*Wired.com, 9.02*. Retrieved from http://www.wired.com/wired/archive/9.02/misha.html

Global RFID Interoperability Forum for Standards (GRIFS) (2008). D1.3 RFID Standardisation State of the Art Report Version 1.

Gohring, N. (2005). Qualcomm files a second suit against Broadcom. *InfoWorld*. Retrieved August 29, 2006, from http://www.infoworld.com/article/05/10/21/HNqualcommsecondsuit_1.html

Gohring, N. (2005). Qualcomm files patent infringement suit against Nokia. *InfoWorld*. Retrieved August 29, 2006, from http://www.infoworld.com/article/05/11/07/hnqualcommsuit_1.html

Gonczi, A., Hager, P., & Athanasou, J. (1993). *The development of competency-based assessment strategies for the professions*. Canberra, Australia: Australian Government Publishing Service.

GovTrack.us. 109th Congress, H.R. 2795: Patent Act of 2005. Retrieved August 29, 2006, from http://www.govtrack.us/congress/bill.xpd?bill=h109-2795

Graham, J. D. (2002). *Office of Management & Budget: An Overview of the U.S. Regulatory System*. Retrieved from http://www.whitehouse.gov/omb/inforeg/pres_mgmt_regulatory_state.html

Graham, S.J.H., & Mowery, D.C. (2002, June 6-8). *Submarines in software? Continuations in U.S. software patenting in the 1980s and 1990s*. Paper presented at the DRUID Summer Conference on Industrial Dynamics of the New and Old Economy—Who is Embracing Whom?, Copenhagen/Elsinore.

Granstrand, O. (1999). *The economics and management of intellectual property*. Edward Elgar Publishing.

Grant, R. M., & Baden-Fuller, C. (2004). A knowledge accessing theory of strategic alliances. *Journal of Management Studies, 4*, 61-84.

Greenstein, S. (1998). Industrial economics and strategy: Computing platforms. *IEEE Micro, 18*(3), 43–53.

Greenstein, S., & Stango, V. (Eds.). (2005). *Standards and public policy*. Cambridge: Cambridge Press.

Grindley, P. (2002). *Standards, strategy and policy*. Oxford.

Groves, L., Nickson, R., Reeve, G., Reeves, S., & Utting, M. (2000). A survey of software development practices in the New Zealand software industry. In *Proceedings of Australian Software Engineering Conference* (pp. 189-201). Canberra.

Gulati, R. (1995). Does familiarity breed trust? The implications of repeated ties for contractual choice in alliances. *Academy of Management Journal, 38*, 85-112.

Hahn, R.W. (2001, March). Competition policy and the new economy. *Milken Institute Review*, 34-41.

Haleblian, J., & Finkelstein, S. (1999). The influence of organizational acquisition experience on acquisition performance: A behavioral learning perspective.*Administrative Science Quarterly, 44*(1), 29-56.

Hall, B., Jaffe, A., & Traijtenberg, M. (2001). *Market Value and Patent Citations: A First Look*. University of California, Berkeley: Institute of Business and Economic Research.

Hall, B., Jaffe, A., & Trajtenberg, M. (2002). The NBER patent citations data file: Lessons, insights, and methodological tools. In A. Jaffe, & M. Trajtenberg (Eds.), *Patents, citations and innovations: A window on the knowledge economy*. Cambridge: MIT Press.

Hall, B., Jaffe, A., & Trajtenberg, M. (2005). Market value and patent citations. *RAND Journal of Economics, 36*(1), 26-38.

Hall, B., Mairesse, J., & Turner, L. (2005). *Identifying age, cohort and period effects in scientific research productivity.* Unpublished Manuscript, University of California at Berkeley.

Hanseth, O., et al. (2006). Reflexive standardization: Side-effects and complexity in standard-making. *MIS Quarterly,* forthcoming.

Hanseth, O., Monteiro E., & Halting, M. (1996). Developing information infrastructure: The tension between standardisation and flexibility. *Science, Technologies, and Human Values, 21*(4), 407-426.

Hanson, D. (2005). *CE Marking, Product Standards and World Trade.* Cheltenham, UK / Northampton, MA, USA: Edward Elgar.

Haug, T. (2002). A commentary on standardization practices: Lessons from the NMT and GSM mobile telephone standards histories. *Telecommunications Policy, 26*(3-4), 101-107.

Hawkins, R. W. (1995). Introduction: Addressing the p*roblématique* of standards and standardization. In R. W. Hawkins, R. Mansell, & J. Skea (Eds.), *Standards, innovation and competitiveness: The politics and economics of standards in natural and technical environments.* Aldershot, UK: Edward Elgar.

Hayek, F. A. (1973). *Law, Legislation and Liberty, Volume 1: Rules and Order.* London: Routledge & Kegan Paul.

Hayward, M. L. A. (2002). When do firms learn from their acquisition experience? Evidence from 1990-1995. *Strategic Management Journal, 23*(Jan), 21-39.

Heinze, W.F. (2002, May). Dead patents walking. *IEEE Spectrum,* 52-54.

Heisenberg, D. (2005). *Negotiating privacy: the European Union, the United States, and personal data protection.*

Heitmeyer, C. L. (1998). On the Need for Practical Formal Methods. In *Proceedings of the 5th International Symposium on Formal Techniques in Real-Time Fault Tolerant Systems (FTRTFT)* (p. 18-26). (Invited paper)

Hemphill, T.A. (2005, January). Technology standards development, patent ambush, and US antitrust policy. *Technology in Society, 27*(1), 55-67.

Hesser, W., & Czaya, A. (1999). Standardization as a subject of study in higher education – A vision. *ISO Bulletin, 30*(6), 6–12.

Hesser, W., & Inklaar, A. (1998). *An Introduction to Standards and Standardization,* DIN Normungskunde Band 36 (p. 35). Berlin: Beuth Verlag GmbH.

Hesser, W., & Siedersleben, W. (2008). Standardization goes East – The European-Asian academic network – International and multimedia-based. *ISO Focus, 4*(11), 21–24.

Hesser, W., Feilzer, A. J., & de Vries, H. J. (Eds.). (2007). *Standardisation in Companies and Markets* (2nd ed.) Hamburg: Helmut Schmidt University.

Heywood, L., Gonczi, A., & Hager, P. (1992). *A guide to development of competency standards for professions.* Canberra, Australia: Australian Government Publishing Service.

Heywood, P., Jander, M., Roberts, E., & Saunders, S. (1997). Standards: The inside story. *Data Communications*(March), 59-72.

Higuchi, T. (1996). *Dig shi Huang-ti* (Shikotei wo Horu in Japanese), Gakuseisha.

Hjelm, B. (2000). Standards and intellectual property rights in the age of global communication: A review of the international standardization of third-generation mobile system.

Hochstein, A., Tamm, G., & Brenner, W. (2005). *Service-Oriented IT Management: Benefit, Cost and Success Factors.* Paper presented at the 15th European Conference on Information Systems.

Hodges, C. (2005). European Regulation of Consumer Product Safety. Oxford University Press.

Hosein, I., Tsiavos, P., & Whitley, E.A. (2003). Regulating architecture and architectures of regulation: Contributions from information systems. *International Review of Law Computers & Technology, 17*(1), 85-97.

Howcroft, D., Mitev, N., & Wilson, M. (2004). What we may learn from social shaping of technology approach. In J. Mingers, & L. Willcocks (Eds.), *Social theory and philosophy for information systems.* Chichester: John Wiley, pp. 329-371.

Hughes, T. (1987). The evolution of large technological systems. In W. Bijker, T. Hughes, & T. Pinch (Eds.), *The sociological construction of technological systems.* Cambridge, MA: The MIT Press.

Için, O. (1994). *Standardizasyon ve Kalite.* Istanbul: Türk Standardlari Enstitüsü.

Iden, J. (2006). INFO317: IT Service Management. Retrieved September 25, 2006, from http://ugle.svf.uib. no/ifim/?kategori=716&strid=4539

Iden, J. (2009). Implementing IT Service Management: Lessons Learned from a University IT Department. In A. Cater-Steel (Ed.), *Information Technology Governance and Service Management: Frameworks and Adaptations* (pp. 333-349). Hershey, PA: Information Science Reference.

IETF RFC 2119. (1997). *Key words for use in RFCs to indicate requirements levels* (S. Bradner, Ed.).

IETF. (2005). Intellectual property rights in IETF technology.

Informamedia.com. (2006, March 1). ETSI acts on unfair, unreasonable and discriminatory IPRs. *Informamedia. com.*

Inkpen, A. C., Sundarum, A. K., & Rockwood, K. (2000). Cross-border acquisitions of US

Intel. (2005). *Intel Capital Portfolio*, Vol. 2005.

IPMA. (1999). G. Caupin, H. Knopfel, P. Morris, E. Motzel, & O. Pannenbacker (Eds.). *ICB: IPMA competence baseline, Version 2.* Germany: International Project Management Association.

IPMA. (2003). *Research and development.* www.ipma. ch/

IPO. (n.d.). *21ˢᵗ Century Patent Coalition: "Submarine patents" ARE a significant problem.* Retrieved August 29, 2006, from http://www.ipo.org/contentmanagement/ contentdisplay.cfm?contentid=7334

ISO Focus (2007). Education for all. Special issue. *ISO Focus, 4*(11).

ISO Focus (2010). Special issue on education. *ISO Focus, 7*(1).

ISO. (1997). *ISO 10006: 1997: Quality management: Guidelines to quality in project management.* Geneva: International Organization for Standardization.

ISO. (2006). ISO Web site. Retrieved February 22, 2006, from http://www.iso.org/iso/en/isoonline.frontpage

ISO/IEC 9646. (n.d.). *Conformance testing methodology and framework.*

ISO/IEC. (2004). ISO/IEC 17000:2004 Conformity assessment - Vocabulary and general principles [Electronic Version].

ISO/IEC. (2004). *ISO/IEC Directives, Part 2. Rules for the structure and drafting of International Standards* (5th ed.).

ISO/IEC. (2005). ISO/IEC 20000:2005 Information technology - Service management - Part 1: Specification [Electronic Version].

ISO/IEC. (2005). ISO/IEC 20000:2005 Information technology - Service management - Part 2: Code of practice [Electronic Version].

ITIL Australia. *ITIL survival.* Retrieved 05 June 2006, 2006, from http://www.itilsurvival.com/ITILAustralia. html

itSMF. (2007). An Introductory Overview of ITIL V3 [Electronic Version]., itSMF. (2008). Certified Organisations. Retrieved 14 January, 2009, from http://www. isoiec20000certification.com/lookuplist.asp?Type=9

ITU-T (2005). *Patent policy implementation guidelines.*

ITU-T Z.150. (2003). *User Requirements Notation (URN) – Language requirements and framework.*

ITU-T Z.450. (2003). *Quality aspects of protocol-related Recommendations.*

Iversen, E.J., & Tee, R. (2006). Standards dynamics and industrial organization in the mobile telecom sector. *Info: The Journal of Policy, Regulation and Strategy for Telecommunications, Information and Media, 8*(4), 33–48.

Jacobs, P. (2005, December). Qualcomm defends patent licensing programme. *wirelessweb.* Retrieved August 29, 2006, from http://wireless.iop.org/articles/news/6/12/6/1

Jaffe, A., & Trajtenberg, M. (2002). *Patents, citations and innovations: A window on the knowledge economy.* Cambridge: MIT Press.

Jakobs, K. (2001, Ed.). *IT Standards and Standardization: A Global Perspective.* Hershey, PA: Idea Group Publishing.

Jakobs, K. (2003). *Information Technology Standards, Standards Setting and Standards Research.* Presented at Stanhope Center's Roundtable.

Jakobs, K. (2006). Shaping user-side innovation through standardisation: The example of ICT. *Technological Forecasting & Social Change, 73*(1), 27-40.

Jakobs, K. (2006, Ed.). *Advanced Topics in Information Technology Standards and Standardization Research, Vol. 1.* Hershey, PA: Idea Group Publishing.

Janney, J. J., & Folta, T. B. (2003). Signaling through private equity placements and its impact on the valuation of biotechnology firms. *Journal of Business Venturing, 18*(3), 361-380.

Jarvenpaa, S., Tiller, L.E.H., &Simons, R. (2003). Regulation and the Internet: Public choice insights for business organizations *California Management Review, 46*(1), 72-85.

JEDEC. (2004). White paper: The vital role of standard-setting organizations and the necessity of good faith and fair play among participants. *JEDEC 2004 Symposium: The Future of Standards Setting, Legal, Marketplace and Consumer Implications.* Available at: http://www.standardsconference.org/docs/WhitePaper_1-14-05.pdf

Jørgensen, U., & Sørensen, O. (1999). Arenas of development: A space polulated by actor-worlds, artefacts, and surprises. *Technology Analysis and Strategic Management, 11*(3), 409-429.

Jovanovic, R., Bentley, J., Stein, A., & Nikakis, C. (2006). Implementing Industry Certification in an IS curriculum: An Australian Experience. *Information Systems Education Journal, 4*(59), 3–8.

Karim, S., & Mitchell, W. (2000). Path-dependent and path-breaking change: Reconfiguring business resources following acquisitions in the U.S. medical sector, 1978-95. *Strategic Management Journal, 21*, 1061-1081.

Karnoe, P., &Garud, R. (2005). Path creation and dependence in the Danish wind turbine field. In J. Porac, & M. Ventresca (Eds.), *Constructing industries and markets.* New York: Elsevier.

Karvonen, J., & Warsta, J. (2004). *Mobile multimedia services development: Value chain perspective.* Proceedings of the 3rd International Conference on Mobile and Ubiquitous Multimedia MUM '04, College Park, Maryland.

Katz, M. L., & Shapiro, C. (1986). Technology adoption in the presence of network externalities. *Journal of Political Economy, 94*(4), 822-841.

Katz, M.L., & Shapiro, C. (1985). Network externalities, competition, and compatibility. *The American Economic Review, 75*(3), 424–440.

Katz, M.L., & Shapiro, C. (1994). Systems competition and network effects. *The Journal of Economic Perspectives, 8*(2), 93–115.

Kauhaniemi, M. (2003). *How STEP and related B2B standards support integrated product data exchange in the Web environment.* T-86.161 Special Topics in Information Technology for Production II. Helsinki: Helsinki University of Technology.

Keil, T. (2002). De-facto standardization through alliances–Lessons from Bluetooth. *Telecommunications Policy, 26*(3-4), 205-213.

Kemmerer, S. (Ed.). (1999). *STEP: The grand experience.* Gaithersburg, MD: National Institute of Standards and Technology.

Kim, D. (2006). Private email to the author from D. Kim, researcher at KSA (Korean Standards Association) directly responsible for the "university standardization course," November 16, 2006.

Kim, D. (2006). *Standards Education in Korea–University Education Program.* Presentation at The Future of Global Education in Standards conference in Tokyo, Japan, February 6, 2006.

Kim, L. (1997). The dynamics of Samsung's technological learning in semiconductors. *California Management Review, 39*(3), 86-100.

King, J. L., &West, J. (2002). Ma bell's orphan: US cellular telephony, 1974-1996. *Telecommunications Policy, 26*(3-4), 189-204.

King, J. L., et al. (1994). Institutional factors in information technology innovation. *Information Systems Research, 5*(2),139-169.

Kipnis, J. (2000, July). Beating the system: Abuses of the standards adoption process. *IEEE Communications Magazine,* pp. 102-105.

Kirsch, E.D. (2000). International standards participation: Lessons from Townshend & Dell. *International Lawyers Network. The bullet"iln", 1*(2). Retrieved August 29, 2006, from http://www.ag-internet.com/push_news_one_two/internationalstandards.htm

Kirton, J.J., & Trebilcock, M.J. (2004). *Hard choices, soft law: Voluntary standards in global trade, environment, and social governance.* Ashgate.

Knight, H.J. (2001). *Patent strategy for researchers and research managers.* John Wiley & Sons.

Kogut, B., & Kulatilaka, N. (1994). Operating flexibility, global manufacturing, and the option value of a multinational network. *Management Science, 40*(1), 123.

Kotter, J.P., Collins, J., Pascale, R., Duck, J.D., Porras, J., & Athos, A. (1998). *Harvard business review on change.* Boston, MA.: Harvard Business School

Kratzman, V.A. (2005). *Technology transfer mid-term report next step recommendations.* FINPRO.

Krechmer, K. (1996). Technical standards: Foundations of the future. *Standardview, 4*(1), 4-8.

Krechmer, K. (2000). *Standards Mark the Course of Economic Progress.* A revised version of a paper presented at the International J.A. Schumpeter Society Economics Conference, Manchester, England.

Krechmer, K. (2002). Cathedrals, Libraries and Bazaars. In *Proceedings of the 2002 ACM symposium on Applied computing* (p. 1053-1057).

Krechmer, K. (2004). Standardization and innovation policies in the information age. *International Journal of IT Standards & Standardization Research, 2*(2), 49-60.

Krechmer, K. (2005). *The mathematical basis of standards.* Proceedings of the 4th International Conference on Standardisation and Innovation in Information Technology (SIIT).

Krechmer, K. (2005, January). *Communications standards and patent rights: Conflict or coordination?* Paper presented at the Economics of the Software and Internet Industries Conference, Tolouse, France.

Krechmer, K. (2007). Teaching Standards to Engineers. *International Journal of IT Standards and Standardization Research, 5*(2), 17–26.

Kruithof, J., & Ryall, J. (1994). *The Quality Standards Handbook.* Melbourne: Information Australia.

KSA. (2003). *International Workshop to develop a Standardization Education Model.* Seoul: KSA.

KSA. (2007). *Future Society and Standards.* Seoul: KSA (in Korean).

Kuner, C. (1997). *Final Version of the Digital Signature Law with Commentary.* Retrieved from http://www.kuner.com/data/sig/digsig4.htm

Kuner, C. (1998). *German Consumer Association Denounces EU Draft Digital Signature Directive.* Retrieved from http://www.kuner.com/data/sig/verbrauc.htm

Kuner, C. (1998). *Remarks of the German Government on the EU Draft Directive concerning Electronic and Digital Signatures.* Retrieved from http://www.kuner.com/data/sig/gov_ger_eu-draft.htm

Kurihara, S. (2008). Compatibility of free trade with health, safety, and environment. In S. Bolin (Ed.), *The standards edge: Unifer or divider?* Bolin Communications.

Kurokawa, T. (2005). Developing Human Resources for International Standards, Science and Technology Trends . *The Quarterly Review, 17,* 34–47.

Kurokawa, T. (2005). Developing Human Resources for International Standards. *The Quarterly Review, 5*(17), 34–47.

Kurtus, R. (1999). The difference between education and training [Electronic Version]. Retrieved September 25 2006, from http://www.school-for-champions.com/training/difference.htm

LaBarba, L. (1999). Nortel tunes into lasers: New units push envelope toward sparing concept. *Telephony, 236*(9), 22.

Labsystems Oy v. Biohit Oy. HO S 94/1922. Finnish Court of Appeal.

Lamberti, H.-J. (2005). Securing Electronic Transactions, 9:9 Electronic Banking Law and Commerce Report 5.

Langley, A. (1999). Strategies for theorizing from process data. *Academy of Management Review, 24*(4), 691-710.

Latour, B. (1987). *Science in action: How to follow scientists and engineers through society* (1st ed.). Milton Keynes: Open University Press.

Latour, B. (1992). Where are the missing masses? The sociology of a few mundane artifacts. In W. E. Bijker, & J. Law (Eds.), *Shaping technology/building society: studies in sociotechnical change.*Cambridge, MA: MIT Press.

Latour, B. (1995). *Social theory and the study of computerized work wites.* Paper presented at the IFIP WG8.2, Cambridge, UK.

Latour, B. (1997). *On actor-network theory: A few clarifications.* ANT Resource, Centre for Social Theory and Technology, Keele University.

Latour, B. (1999). *Pandora's hope: Essays on the reality of science studies.* Cambridge, MA: Harvard University Press.

Law, J. (1992). Notes on the theory of the actor-network: Ordering, strategy, and heterogeneity *System Practice, 5*(4), 379-393.

Lawless, M. W., & Anderson, P. C. (1996). Generational technological change: Effects of innovation and local rivalry on performance. *Academy of Management Journal, 39*(5), 1185-1217.

Leduc, G. (1992). A Framework Based on Implementation Relations for Implementing LOTOS Specifications. *Computer Networks and ISDN Systems, 25,* 23–41. doi:10.1016/0169-7552(92)90122-7

Leeds, D. D. (1997). Raising the Standard: Antitrust Scrutiny of Standard-Setting Consortia in High Technology Industries, 7 Fordham Intell. Prop. Media & Ent. L.J. 641 (1997).

Leffler, K. (1980). Commentary. In S. Rottenberg (Ed.), *Occupational licensure and regulation.* USA: American Enterprise Institute for Public and Policy Research, 287-295.

Leiblein, M. J. (2003). The choice of organizational governance form and performance: Predictions from transaction cost, resource-based and real options theories. *Journal of Management, 29*(6), 937-961.

Leland, H. (1979). Quacks, lemons, and licensing: A theory of minimum quality standards. *Journal of Political Economy, 87*(6), 1328-1346.

Leland, H. (1980). Minimum-quality standards and licensing in markets with asymetric information. In S. Rottenberg (Ed.), *Occupational licensure and regulation.* USA: American Enterprise Institute for Public and Policy Research, 265-284.

Lemelson Foundation. (n.d.). Jerome H. Lemelson. Retrieved August 29, 2006, from http://www.lemelson.org/about/bio_jerry.php

Lemley, M. (2002). Intellectual property rights and standard setting organizations. *California Law Review, 90*, 1889 -1981.

Lemos, R. (2002, July 23). Finding patent truth in JPEG claims. *CNET News.com*. Retrieved August 29, 2006, from http://news.com.com/Finding+patent+truth+in+JPEG+claim/2100-1001_3-945686.html

Lenn, M.P. (1997). Introduction. In M.P. Lenn, & L. Campos (Eds.), *Globalization of the professions and the quality imperative: Professional accreditation, certification and licensure*. Madison WI: Magna Publications, Inc.

Leonard-Barton, D. (1992). Core capabilities and core rigidities: A paradox in managing new product development. *Strategic Management Journal, 13*, 111-125.

Lessig, L. (1999). *Code and other laws of cyberspace*. New York: Basic Books.

Lessig, L. (1999). The law of the horse: What cyberlaw might teach. *Harvard Law Review, 113*(2), 501-549.

Lo, A.M. (Jupiter Networks, Inc). (2002). *A need for intervention: Keeping competition alive in the networking industry in the face of increasing patent assertions against standards*. FTC/DOJ Hearings on Competition and Intellectual Property Law and Policy In the Knowledge-Based Economy—Standard Setting and Intellectual Property, 18 April 2002.

Loffredo, D. (1998). *Efficient database implementation of EXPRESS information models*. Rensselaer Polytechnic Institute.

London School of Economics (2005). *The Identity Project: An assessment of the UK Identity Cards Bill and its implications*.

LSC Group. (2002). RAMP *white paper-Driving down the cost of spares provisioning* (Issue 2). Bath: Warship Support Agency.

Lucky, R.W. (2006, September). Unsystematic Engineering. *IEEE Spectrum*.

Lyytinen, K., & Fomin, V.V. (2002). Achieving high momentum in the evolution of wireless infrastructures: The battle over the 1G solutions. *Telecommunications Policy, 26*(3-4), 149-170.

M&E Consultants. (2001). *Report on a survey of other NSBs Educational Activities*. East Barnet, Herfordshire, UK: M&E consultants.

Madden, G., Rao, P. M., & Galvin, P. (2002). *Technological competency of leading ICT firms: US patent data evidence*. Paper presented at the International Telecommunications Society, Seoul, South Korea.

Mahmoud, Q.H. (2002). *Testing wireless Java applications*. Retrieved August 1, 2007, from http://developers.sun.com/techtopics/mobility/midp/articles/test/

Mähring, M. et al. (2004). Trojan actor-networks and swift translations: Bringing actor-network-theory to IT project escalation studies. *Information Technology & People, 17*(2), 210-238.

Malone, S. (2005, November 1). *Microsoft loses Eolas Supreme Court appeal*. PC Pro. Retrieved August 29, 2006, from http://www.pcpro.co.uk/news/news/79431

Mangematin, V., & M. Callon. (1995). Technological competition, strategies of the firms and the choice of the first users: The case of road guidance technologies. *Research Policy, 24*(3), 441-458.

Manninen, A. T. (2002). *Elaboration of NMT and GSM standards: From idea to market*. Unpublished PhD Thesis, University of Jyvaskyla.

Männistö, T., Peltonen, H., Martio, A., & Sulonen, R. (1998). Modelling generic product structures in STEP. *Computer-Aided Design, 30*(14), 1111-1118.

Mansell, R., & Silverstone, R. (1996). *Communication by design: The politics of information and communication technologies. Oxford:* Oxford University Press.

Marasco, A. (ANSI). (2003, October 30). *IPR and standards*. Presentation at AIPLA.

March, J. G. (1991). Exploration and exploitation in organizational learning. *Organization Science, 2*(1), 71-78.

Marin, L. J. A. (2008) Global perspectives and Strategies for Education in Standardization. Paper presented at 3rd ICES Workshop, Gaithersburg, 2008-02-21—22, http://www.standards-education.org (last accessed 2008-11-09).

Markiewicz, K. (2004). *University patenting and the rate of knowledge exploitation.* Unpublished Manuscript, University of California at Berkeley.

Markoff, J. (2002, July 29). Patent claim strikes an electronics nerve. *The New York Times.*

Markus, L., et al. (2006). Industry-wide IS standardization as collective action: The case of the US residential mortgage industry. *MIS Quarterly,* forthcoming.

Markus, M. L., & Robey, D. (1988). Information technology and organizational change: Casual structure in theory and research. *Management Science, 34*(5), 583-598.

Mason, H. (2002). ISO 10303–STEP: A key standard for the global market. *ISO Bulletin,* April (1), 9-13.

Matsumoto, C. (2001). Rivals vie to reshape net topology. *Electronic Engineering Times*(1183), 1,16.

Matutes, C., & Regibeau, P. (1987). Standardization in multi-component industries. In H.L. Gabel (Ed.), *Product standardization and competitive strategy.* Amsterdam, The Netherlands: Elsevier Science.

Mayer, D., & Kenney, M. (2004). Economic action does not take place in a vacuum: Understanding Cisco's acquisition and development strategy. *Industry and Innovation, 11*(4), 299.

McEuen, D. (2000). DWDM: Increasing the capacity of optical networks. *ElectronicNews, 46*(27), 16.

McGarity, T. O. (1996). The Expanded Debate over the Future of the Regulatory State, 63 U. Chicago Law Rev. 1463.

McGrath, R. G. (1997). A real options logic for initiating technology positioning investments. *Academy of Management: The Academy of Management Review, 22*(4), 974-996.

McGrath, R. G., Ferrier, W. J., & Mendelow, A. L. (2004). Real options as engines of choice and heterogeneity.

Academy of Management: The Academy of Management Review, 29(1), 86-101.

Megantz, R.C. (2002). *Technology management. Developing and implementing effective licensing programs.* John Wiley & Sons.

Mehta, A., Rysman, M., & Simcoe, T. (2005). *Identifying age profiles of patent citations.* Unpublished Manuscript, Boston University.

Meister, D. (2004). *STEP through 20 years: Lessons and theoretical implications.* Working paper edn. Faculty of Information Systems, Richard Ivey School of Business, The University of Western Ontario, Canada.

Messerschmitt, D.G., & Szyperski, C. (2003). *Software ecosystem.* The MIT Press.

Methlie, L.B., & Gressgård, L.J. (2006). Exploring the relationships between structural market conditions and business conduct in mobile data services markets. *Journal of Electronic Commerce Research, 7*(1), 14.

Meyer, M.H., & Seliger, R. (1998). Product platforms in software development. *Sloan Management Review, 40*(1), 61.

Miele, A.L. (2000). *Patent strategy: The manger's guide to profiting from patent portfolios.* John Wiley & Sons.

Miller, A. S. (1995). Environmental Regulation, Technological Innovation and Technology-Forcing, Natural Resources & Environment, Fall 1995 at 64.

Miller, K. D., & Folta, T. B. (2002). Option value and entry timing. *Strategic Management Journal, 23*, 655-665.

Mitchell, W. (1989). Whether or when? Probability and timing of incumbent's entrance into emerging industrial subfields. *Administrative Science Quarterly, 34*(2), 208-230.

Mitra, P., Purao, S., Bagby, J.W., Umapathy, K., & Sharoda, P. (2005). *An empirical analysis of development processes for anticipatory standards.* NET Institute Working Paper No. 05-18 http://ssrn.com/abstract=850524

MoD CDMA. (2004). *Ministry of defence policy on the use of XML.* Retrieved June 24, 2005, from http://www.cdma.mod.uk/suppinfo/xmlpolicy-v1_0.doc

MoD SSE. (2005). *Support solutions envelope–Data standards*. Retrieved March 16, 2005, from http://www.ams.mod.uk/ams/content/docs/sse/v3_3_archive/ikm%20&%20c4i/gp_3_ed1.htm

MoD SSE. (2005). *Support solutions envelope—Engineering & asset management*. Retrieved March 16, 2005, from http://www.ams.mod.uk/ams/content/docs/sse/v3_3_archive/eam.htm

MOD. (2005). *Recent trends in service and civilian personnel numbers, at 1 April each year*. Retrieved November 10, 2005, from http://www.dasa.mod.uk/natstats/ukds/2005/c2/table21.html

Mohr, L. B. (1982). *Explaining organizational behavior*. San Francisco: Jossey-Bass.

Morgan, R. L., et al. (2004). Federated Security: The Shibboleth Approach. *Educause Quarterly, 27*(4). Retrieved from http://www.educause.edu/apps/eq/eqm04/eqm0442.asp

Morris, P.W.G. (1994). *The management of projects*. London: Thomas Telford.

Moseley, S., Randall, S., & Wiles, A. (2004). In Pursuit of Interoperability. *International Journal (Toronto, Ont.), 2*(2), 34–48.

Motorola. (2006). *Motorola Q Developer Guide*. Retrieved August 1, 2007, from http://developer.motorola.com/docstools/developerguides/

Mouly, M., & Pautet, M. –B. (1992). *The GSM system for mobile communications*. Palaiseau, France: Michael Mouly and Marie-Bernadette Pautet.

Mowery, D.C., & Simcoe, T. (2002). Is the Internet a US invention? An economic and technological history of computer networking. *Research Policy, 31*(8-9), 1369-1387.

Mueller, J.M. (2001). Patenting industry standards. *John Marshall Law Review, 34*(897).

Munir, K. A. (2003). Competitive dynamics in face of technological discontinuity: A framework for action. *Journal of High Technology Management Research, 14*(1), 93.

Muriithi, N., & Crawford, L. (2003). Approaches to project management in Africa: Implications for international development projects. *International Journal of Project Management, 21*, 309-319.

Mustonen-Ollila, E., & Lyytinen, K. (2003). Why organizations adopt information system process innovations: A longitudinal study using diffusion of innovation theory. *Information Systems Journal, 13*(3), 275-297.

Naraine, R. (2002, May 10). Qualcomm rejects Nokia patent cap proposal. *internetnews.com*. Retrieved August 29, 2006, from http://www.interetnews.com/wireless/article.php/1116381

Naraine, R. (2002, May 8). Nokia calls for 5% cap on 3G patent royalties. *internetnews.com*. Retrieved August 29, 2006, from http://internetnews.com/wireless/article.php/1041561

National Commission on Excellence in Education. (1983). A nation at risk: The imperative for educational reform. Washington, US: Government Printing Office (Accessed online at: http://www.ed.gov/pubs/NatAtRisk/findings.html).

Nelson, M. L., Shaw, M. J., & Qualls, W. (2005). Inter-organizational system standards development in vertical industries. *Electronic Markets, 15*(4), 378-392

Nerney, C. (2003). Survey: ITSM Needs to Pick Up Mindshare. Retrieved July 25 2005, from http://www.it-management.earthweb.com/service/print.php/3078431

Newman, M., & Robey, D. (1992). A social process model of user-analyst relationships. *MIS Quarterly, 16*(2), 249-266.

Nickerson, J. V., & zur Muehlen, M. (2006). The social ecology of standards processes: Insights from Internet standard making. *MIS Quarterly*, forthcoming.

Niessink, F., & van Vliet, H. (1998). Towards Mature IT Services. *Software Process Improvement and Practice, 4*(2), 55–71. doi:10.1002/(SICI)1099-1670(199806)4:2<55::AID-SPIP97>3.0.CO;2-T

Nilakanta, S., & Scamell, R.W. (1990). The effect of information sources and communication channels on the eiffusion of innovation in a data base development environment. *Management Science, 36*(1), 24-40.

Nokia. (2005, November 7). *Nokia responds to reports of Qualcomm GSM patent infringement suit.* Retrieved August 29, 2006, from http://press.nokia.com/PR/200511/1019958_5.html

Nokia. (2005, October 28). *Leading mobile wireless technology companies call on European Commission to investigate Qualcomm's anti-competitive conduct.* Retrieved August 29, 2006, from http://press.nokia.com/PR/200510/1018639_5.html

Norusis, M. (1996). *SPSS Advanced Statistics 6.1.* Chicago: SPSS Inc.

O'Reilly, C. (1998). Cisco Systems: The acquisition of technology is the acquisition of people. In S. G. S. o. Business (Ed.). Palo Alto, CA: Stanford University.

Oakes, C. (1998). ADSL Standard: Divided Tech, United Companies: Wired News.

OASIS. (2005). *IPR policy.*

OECD. (2004). *Patents and innovation: Trends and policy challenges.* Retrieved August 29, 2006, from http://www.oecd.org/dataoecd/48/12/24508541.pdf

OECD. (2005). *Compendium of patent statistics.* Retrieved August 29, 2006, from http://www.oecd.org/dataoecd/60/24/8208325.pdf

OGC. (2006, 5 June 2006). Office of Government Commerce. ITIL IT Service Management: Glossary of Terms, Definitions and Acronyms. Retrieved from http://www.get-best-practice.biz/glossary.aspx?product=glossariesacronyms

Ohana, G. (Cisco Systems, Inc). (2005. October 6). Intellectual property rights: Policies in standard-setting: Areas of debate. In *Proceedings of From A to Veeck: Standardization and the Law, 2005 ANSI Annual Conference.* Retrieved August 29, 2006, from http://public.ansi.org/ansionline/Documents/Meetings%20and%20Events/2005%20Annual%20Conference/Legal%20Conference/Ohana-Panel%20I.pdf

Orlikowski, W., & Gash, D. (1994). Technology frames: Making sense of information technology in organizations. *ACM Transactions on Information Systems, 12*(2), 147-207.

Out-law.com. (2005, November 31). Mobile-makers say 3G patent licensing breaks antitrust laws. Retrieved August 29, 2006, from http://www.out-law.com/page-6280

Oxley, J. E. (1999). Institutional environment and the mechanisms of governance: The impact of intellectual property protection on the structure of inter-firm alliances. *Journal of Economic Behavior & Organization, 38*(3), 283-309.

Pakes, A. (1986). Patents as option: Some estimates of the value of holding European patent stocks. *Econometrica, 54*(4), 755-784.

Patterson, M. R. (2002). Inventions, industry standards, and intellectual property. *Berkeley Technology Law Review, 17*(3), 1-42.

Pelkmans, J. (1987). The New Approach to Technical Harmonization and Standardization. *Journal of Common Market Studies, 25*(3), 249. doi:10.1111/j.1468-5965.1987.tb00294.x

Pelkmans, J. (2001). The GSM standard: explaining a success story. *Journal of European Public Policy, 8*(3), 432–453. doi:10.1080/13501760110056059

Pells, D.L. (1996). Introduction. In J.S. Pennypacker (Ed.), *The global status of the project management profession.* Sylva, NC: PMI Communications, , ix–xii.

Pentland, B. T. (1999). Building process theory with narrative: From description to explanation. *Academy of Management Review, 24*(4), 711-724.

Perens, B. (n.d.). *The problem of software patents in standards.* Retrieved August 29, 2006, from http://perens.com/Articles/PatentFarming.html

Peteraf, M. A. (1993). The cornerstones of competitive advantage: A resource-based view. *Strategic Management Journal, 14*, 179-191.

Peterson, S.K. (Hewlett-Packard Company). (2002). *Consideration of patents during the setting of standards.* For FTC and DOJ Roundtable, Standard Setting Organizations: Evaluating the Anticompetitive Risks of Negotiating IP Licensing Terms and Conditions Before A Standard Is Set, 6 November 2002.

Peterson, S.K. (Hewlett-Packard Company). (2002). *Patents and standard-setting processes.* FTC/DOJ Hearings on Competition and Intellectual Property Law and Policy in the Knowledge-Based Economy, 18 April 2002.

Pettigrew, A. M. (1997). What is a processual analysis? *Scandinavian Journal of Management, 13*(4), 337-348.

Pinch, T. J., & Bijker, W.E. (1987). The social construction of facts and artifacts: Or how the sociology of science and the sociology of technology might benefit each other. In W. E. Bijker, T. P. Hughes, & T. J. Pinch (Eds.), *The social construction of technological systems: New directions in the sociology and history of technology.* Cambridge: MIT Press.

PMI. (2003). *PMI chapters outside the United States.* Retrieved June 26, 2003 from, www.pmi.org/info/GMC ChapterListingOutsideUS.asp#P128 1923

PMI. (2003). PMI Sydney chapter. Retrieved June 26, 2003 from, http://sydney.pmichapters-australia.org.au/

PMI. (2004). A guide to the project management body of knowledge. PA, US: Project Management Institute.

PMI. (2005). *PMI chapters.* Retrieved August 24, 2005 from, http://www.pmi.org/prod/groups/public/documents/info/gmc_chaptersoverview.asp

PMI. (2005). *PMI project management standards program.* Retrieved August 24, 2005 from, http://www.pmi.org/prod/groups/public/documents/info/pp_pm-standardsprogram.asp

PMI. (2006). Project management institute fact sheet. Retrieved March 9, 2006 from, http://www.pmi.org/info/GMC_MemberFACTSheetJan06.pdf

Poltorak, A.I., & Lerner, P.J. (2004). *Essentials of licensing intellectual property.* John Wiley & Sons.

Porter, M.E. (1985). *Competitive advantage: Creating and sustaining superior performance.* New York: The Free Press.

Potgieter, B. C., Botha, J. H., & Lew, C. (2005, 10-13 July). *Evidence that use of the ITIL framework is effective.* Paper presented at the 18th Annual Conference of the National Advisory Committee on Computing Qualifications, Tauranga, NZ.

Praeg, C.-P., & Schnabel, U. (2006, 4-7 Jan). *IT-Service Cachet - managing IT-service performance and IT-service quality.* Paper presented at the 39th Annual Hawaii International Conference on System Sciences (HICSS'06), Kauai.

Praeg, C.-P., & Spath, D. (2009). Perspectives of IT-Service Quality Management: a Concept of Life-Cycle Based Quality Management of IT Services. In A. Cater-Steel (Ed.), *Information Technology Governance and Service Management: Frameworks and Adaptations* (pp. 381-407). Hershey, PA: Information Science Reference.

Prescott, M.B., & Conger, S.A. (1995). Information technology innovations: A classification by IT locus of impact and research approach. *SIGMIS Database, 26*(2-3), 20-41.

Priem, R. L., & Butler, J. E. (2001). Tautology in the resource-based view and the implications of externally determined resource value: Further comments. *Academy of Management Review, 26*(1), 57-66.

PROSTEP, (2004). *Organization/history (ISO).* Retrieved July 15, 2004, from http://www.prostep.org/en/services/was/orga/

Purcell D. E. & Kelly, W. E. (2003). Adding value to a standards education: lessons learned from a Strategic Standardization course. *ISO Bulletin,* 34-34. .

Purcell, D. E. (2005). *IEC Lecture Series: International Standardization in Business, Industry, Society and Technology.* Geneva: IEC (CD).

Purcell, D. E. (2006). Report on formation of the International Committee for Education on Standardization [Electronic Version].

Purcell, D. E. (2006). *Strategic Standardization Syllabus.* Washington, DC: Catholic University of America, School of Engineering.

Purcell, D.E. (2005). Report to the center for global standards analysis on Beijing information technology standard international forum. Retrieved from http://www.ieee.org/potal/cms_docs/erudation/setf/newsitems/beijingreport.doc

PwC Advisory. (2006). *2006 patent and trademark damages study.*

Rada, R. (1996). Who will test conformance? *Communications of the ACM, 39*(1), 19–22.

Rada, R., & Berg, J. (1995). Standards: Free or sold? *Communications of the ACM, 38*(2), 23-27.

Rahnasto, I. (2003). *Intellectual property rights, external effects, and anti-trust law.* Oxford University Press.

Rambus, Inc v. Infineon Technologies AG. No. 01-1449. Federal Circuit, 29 January 2003.

Ramiller, N. C. (2005). Applying the sociology of translation to a system project in a lagging enterprise. *Journal of Information Technology Theory and Application, 7*(1), 51-76.

Rao, P. M., Vemuri, V., K. , & Galvin, P. (2004). The changing technological profile of the leading ICT firms: Evidence from U.S. patent data, 1981-2000. *Industry and Innovation, 11*(4), 353-372.

Red Herring. (2006, February 3). JPEG patent reexamined. Retrieved August 29, 2006, from http://www.redherring.com/Article.aspx?a=15582&hed=JPEG+Patent+Reexamined&sector=Industries&subsector=Computing

Regan, K. (2005, July 5). Broadcom suit accuses Qualcomm of antitrust tactics. *E-Commerce Times.* Retrieved August 29, 2006, from http://www.ecommercetimes.com/story/44395.html

Reihlen, H. (1999). Is standardization a standard career? *ISO Bulletin, 30*(6), 2.

Reingold, J. (2006, January). *Patently aggressive.* 102. Retrieved August 29, 2006, from http://www.fastcompany.com/magazine/102/patents.html

Resnick, P., Zeckhauser, R., & Avery, C. (1994). *Roles for electronic brokers.* Proceedings of the Telecommunications Policy Research Conference, Arlington, Virginia.

Revesz, R. (2001). Federalism and Regulation: Some Generalizations. In D. C. Esty & D. Géradin (Eds.), *Regulatory competition and Economic Integration: Comparative Perspectives* (pp. 3-29). New York: Oxford University Press.

Rivette, K., & Kline, D. (2000). *Rembrandts in the attic.* Harvard Business School Press.

Robey, D., & Newman, M. (1996). Sequential patterns in information systems development: An application of a social process model. *ACM Transactions on Information Systems, 14*(1), 30-63.

Robinson, G. (1999). There are no Standards for Making Standards. In *Proceedings of the 1st IEEE Conference on Standardization and Innovation in Information Technology (SIIT 1999).* (Invited paper)

Rogers, E.M. (2003). *Diffusion of innovations* (5th ed). New York: Simon & Schuster International.

Rogoski, R. (1997). *In the past, the future: Cisco System's RTP chief says partnering key to firm's success.* Bizjournals.com (Feb 10).

Rosenkopf, L., & Tushman, M. L. (1998). The co-evolution of technology and organization. *Industrial and Corporate Change, 7,* 311-346.

Rossi, S. (2006, 12 July). University begins local ITIL adoption research. *Computerworld.*

Rossi, S. (2008, 28 March). Charles Sturt Uni leads ITIL accreditation. *Computerworld.*

Rushby, J. (2000). Disappearing Formal Methods. In *5th Int. Symposium on High Assurance Systems Engineering (HASE)* (pp. 95–96). Albuquerque. (Invited paper)

Rycroft, S., & Tully, M. (2007). Building an Information Security Meta Standard. *BT Technology Journal*, *25*(1), 37–40. doi:10.1007/s10550-007-0006-8

Rysman, M., & Simcoe, T. (2006). *Patents and the performance of voluntary standard setting organizations.* Unpublished Manuscript, Boston University.

Sahay, S., & Robey, D. (1996). Organizational context, social interpretation and the implementation and consequences of geographical information systems. *Accounting, Management and Information Technologies*, *6*(4), 255-282.

Sallé, M. (2004). IT Service Management and IT Governance: review, comparative analysis and their impact on utility computing [Electronic Version], 25. Retrieved June 2, Schuller, H., & Wheeler, G. (2006, 31 May). An ITIL bit of knowledge. *Computerworld.*

Sarkar, M.B., Butler, B., & Steinfield, C. (1995). Intermediaries and cybermediaries: A continuing role for mediating players in the electronic marketplace. *Journal of Computer Mediated Communication, 1*(3).

Sarvas, R., & Soininen, A. (2002, October). *Differences in European and U.S. patent regulation affecting wireless standardization.* Paper presented at the International Workshop on Wireless Strategy in the Enterprise, Berkeley, California.

Schepel, H. (2005). The constitution of private governance: product standards in the regulation of integrating markets.

Schmidt, S.K., & Werle, R. (1998). *Co-ordinating technology: Studies in the international standardization of telecommunications.* Cambridge, MA: MIT Press.

Schoechle, T. (2003). Digital Enclosure: The Privatization of Standards and Standardization. In *Proceedings of the 3rd IEEE Conference on Standardization and Innovation in Information Technology* (SIIT 2003) *(pp. 229–240).*

Schrage, M. (2004). Hiding behind certification: An over-reliance on IT sheepskins is a recipe for disaster. *CIO, 17*(17), 1.

Seek Ltd. (2009). Seek I.T.: Australia's #1 Job Site. Retrieved January 12, 2009, from http://it.seek.com.au

Shadish, W. R., Cook, T.D., & Campbell, D.T. (2002). *Experimental and quasi-experimental designs for generalized causal inference* (2ⁿᵈ ed.). Houghton Mifflin.

Shaffer, G. (2002). Reconciling Trade and Regulatory Goals: The Prospects and Limits of New Approaches to Transatlantic Governance Through Mutual Recognition and Safe Harbor Agreements. *Columbia Journal of European Law*, *9*, 29–77.

Shapiro, C. (2001). *Navigating the patent thicket: Cross licenses, patent pools and standard setting.*

Shapiro, C., & Varian, H. (1998). *Information rules: A strategic guide to the network economy.* Cambridge, MA: Harvard Business School Press.

Shapiro, S., Richards, B., Rinow, M., & Schoechle, T. (2001). Hybrid Standards Setting Solutions for Today's Convergent Telecommunications Market. In *Proceedings of the 2nd IEEE Conference on Standardization and Innovation in Information Technology (SIIT 2001)* (pp. 348–351).

Sheremata, W. A. (1998). New issues in competition policy raised by information technology industries. *The Antitrust Bulletin*, *43*(3/4), 547-582.

Sherif, M. H. (2001, April). A Framework for Standardization in Telecommunications and Information Technology. *IEEE Communications Magazine*, *39*(4), 94–100. doi:10.1109/35.917510

Sherif, M. H. (2003). When is Standardization Slow? [JITSR]. *International Journal of IT Standards and Standardization Research*, *1*(1), 19–32.

Shurmer, M., & Lea, G. (1995, June). Telecommunications standardization and intellectual property rights: A fundamental dilemma? *Standardview, 3*(2).

Simcoe, T. (2004). *Design by committee? The organization of technical standards development.* Dissertation, University of California at Berkeley.

Simon, H. A. (1977). *The new science of management decision* (rev. ed.). Englewood Cliffs: Prentice-Hall.

Simons, C. A. J. (1999). Education in standardization – Getting structured common sense into our society – The personal opinion of a standards-educator. *ISO Bulletin, 30*(6), 13–16.

Sobel, J. (2001). On the dynamics of standards. *RAND Journal of Economics, 32*(4), 606-623.

Soh, P.-H., & Roberts, E. B. (2003). Networks of innovators: A longitudinal perspective. *Research Policy, 32*(9), 1569.

Soininen, A. H. (2005).Open Standards and the Problem with Submarine Patents. Proceedings SIIT 2005 pp. 231-244 4th International conference on standardization and innovation in information technology.

Sørensen, K. H., & Williams, R.(2002). *Shaping technology, guiding policy: Concepts, spaces and tools.* Cheltenham: Edward Elgar.

Spivak, S. M., & Brenner, F. C. (2001). *Standardization Essentials – Principles and Practice.* New York / Basel: Marcel Dekker Inc.

Spivak, S. M., & Kelly, W. E. (2003). Introduce strategic standardization concepts during higher education studies… and reap the benefits! *ISO Bulletin, 34*(7), 22–24.

Spivak, S. M., &Brenner, F.C. (2001). *Standardization essentials: Principles and practice.* New York: Marcel Dekker, Inc.

Steele, R. (2004). Standards as an indicator of maturity? … and an opportunity for customer and industry advantage? *International Journal of IT Standards & Standardization Research, 2*(1), 42-45.

Steensma, H. K., & Fairbank, J. F. (1999). Internalizing external technology: A model of governance mode choice and an empirical assessment. *The Journal of High Technology Management Research, 10*(1), 1-35.

Stein, A., Nikakis, C., Bentley, J., & Jovanovic, R. (2005). The industry and education nexus: how one school tackled certification. In T. van Weert & A. Tatnall (Eds.), *Information and communication technologies and real-life learning - new education for the knowledge society* (pp. 255-261). MA: Springer/IFIP.

Steinmueller, E. (2005). *Technical compatibility standards and the co-ordination of the industrial and international division of labor.* Paper presented at NSF Academics conference on Advancing Knowledge and the Knowledge economy.

Stern, J. (2003). Train the standardizers, or how to become step-by-step an expert in standardization. *ISO Bulletin, 34*(7), 20–21.

Stern, R. (2001). More standardization skullduggery. *IEEE Micro, 21*(4), 12-15,69.

Stewart, J., &Williams, R. (2005). The wrong trousers? Beyond the design fallacy: Social learning and the user. In H. Rohracher (Ed.), *User involvement in innovation processes: strategies and limitations from a socio-technical perspective.* Munich: Profil-Verlag.

Stretton, A. (1994). A short history of project management: Part one: the 1950s and 60s. *Australian Project Manager, 14*(1), 36-7.

Stroyd, A.H. (2000). *Lemelson bar coding patents: Attempting to sink the submariner.* Retrieved August 29, 2006, from http://www.mhia.org/PSC/pdf/Lemelson.PDF

Suchman, L. (2000). Organizing alignment: A case of bridge-building. *Organization, 7*(2), 311-327.

Surowiecki, J. (2006, December 26/January 2). Blackberry picking. *The New Yorker*, Financial Page.

Swann, P. (2000). *The economics of standardization.* Retrieved January 24, 2004, from http://www.dti.gov.uk/strd/fundingo.htm#swannrep

Symbol Technologies Inc. v. Lemelson Medical, Education & Research Foundation. 277 F.3d 1361, 1363. Federal Circuit, 2002.

Symbol Technologies, Inc et al. v. Lemelson Medical, Education & Research Foundation. LP et al., 422 F.3d 1378. Federal Circuit, 2005.

Tan, W., Cater-Steel, A., Toleman, M., & Seaniger, R. (2007). *Implementing centralised IT Service Management: Drawing Lessons from the Public Sector.* Paper presented at the Australasian Conference on Information Systems, Toowoomba.

Tapscott, D., & Williams, A.D. (2006). *Wikinomics*, Portfolio.

Tarnacha, A., & Maitland, C.F. (2006). *Entrepreneurship in mobile application development*. Proceedings of the Eighth International Conference on Electronic Commerce, Fredericton, New Brunswick, Canada.

Tarnacha, A., & Maitland, C.F. (Forthcoming). The effects of standards competition on market entry: The case of the mobile application markets. In *The standards edge: Unifier or divider?* The Bolin Group.

Tassey, G. (2000). Standardization in technology-based markets. *Research Policy, 29*(4-5), 587–602.

Teece, D. J., & Sherry, E. F. (2003). Standards setting and antitrust. *Minnesota Law Review, 87*(6), 1913-1994.

Teece, D. J., Pisano, G., & Shuen, A. (1997). Dynamic capabilities and strategic management. *Strategic Management Journal, 18*(7), 509-533.

Teece, D.J. (2000). *Managing intellectual capital.* Oxford University Press.

Thibodeau, P. (2007, 19 September). Increasing Adoption of ITIL is Making Resistance Futile. *Computerworld.*

Tiebout, C. (1956). A Pure Theory of Local Expenditures. *The Journal of Political Economy, 64,* 416–424. doi:10.1086/257839

Tilson, D., & Lyytinen, K. (2006). The 3G transition: Changes in the US wireless industry. *Telecommunications Policy, 30*(10/11), 569–586.

Toivanen, O. (2005). *Choosing standards.* Unpublished Manuscript, University of Helsinki.

Tovey, M., & Lawlor, D. (2004). *Training in Australia: Design, Delivery, Evaluation, Management* (2nd ed.). Sydney NSW: Pearson Education.

Townshend v. Rockwell International Corp. and Conexant Systems, Inc., 55 U.S.P.Q.2d 1011. Northern District of California, 2000.

Tushman, M. L., & Rosenkopf, L. (1992). Organizational determinants of technological change: Towards a sociology of technological evolution. *Research in Organizational Behavior, 14,* 311-347.

Tyler, T. (1990). *Why People Obey the Law.* New Haven: Yale University Press.

Van de Ven, A. H., & Poole, M.S. (1995). Explaining development and change in organizations. *Academy of Management Review 20*(3), 510-540.

Van de Ven, A. H., & Huber, G. (1990). Longitudinal field research methods for studying processes of organizational change. *Organization Science, 1*(2), 213-219.

Van de Ven, A. H., et al. (1999). *The innovation journey.* New York: Oxford University Press.

van Wegberg, M. (2004). Standardization and competing consortia: The trade-off between speed and compatibility. *International Journal of IT Standards & Standardization Research, 2*(2), 18-33.

Varchaver, N. (2001, May 3). *Jerome Lemelson the patent king.* Retrieved August 29, 2006, from http://www.engin.brown.edu/courses/en90/fall/2003/Lemelson%20Fortune%20may%2014%202001%20article.pdf

Venkataraman, R., & Conger, S. (2006). Open Invitation to itSMF Academic Forum. In AISWORLD Information Systems World Network (Ed.).

Venkatesh, V., Morris, M., Davis, G., & Davis, F. (2003). User acceptance of information technology: Toward a unified view. *MIS Quarterly, 27*(3), 425-478.

Verman, L. C. (1973). *Standardization – A New Discipline.* Hamden, CT: Archon Books.

Vermeulen, F., & Barkema, H. (2001). Learning through acquisitions. *Academy of Management Journal, 44*(3), 457-476.

Vermont, S. (2002). The economics of patent litigation. In B. Berman (Ed.), *From ideas to assets. Investing wisely in intellectual property.* John Wiley & Sons.

Violino, R. (2005, July 25). Best-Practice Library Gains Fans. *Information Week* Retrieved November 10, 2005, from http://www.informationweek.com/story/showArticle.jhtml?articleID=166401916&tid=13690

Virilli, F. (2003). Design, sense-making and negotiation activities in the Web services standardization process. In J. King, & K. Lyytinen (Eds), Standard making: A critical research frontier for information systems. Proceedings of a Pre-conference Workshop at ICIS, December 12-14, Seattle, 2003, Washington, available at http://www.si.umich.edu/misq-stds/proceedings/index.html

Von Weizsacker, C.C. (1984). The costs of substitution. *Econometrica, 52*(5), 1085-1116.

Vu, T. A. (2006). *An Introduction – The History of Standardization.* In W. Hesser, et al. *Standardization in Companies and Markets* (pp. 35-60). Hamburg: Helmut Schmidt University Hamburg.

W3C (2004). *Patent policy.*

W3C. (2004). *QA Framework: Test Guidelines (Working Draft, 25 Feb. 2004).*

Walsham, G. (1997). Actor-network theory and IS research: Current status and future prospects. In A. Lee, J. Liebenau, & J. DeGross (Eds.), Information systems and qualitative research. London: Chapman and Hall, pp. 466-480

Walsham, G., & Sahay, S. (1999). GIS for district level administration in India: Problems and opportunities. *MIS Quarterly, 23*(1), 39-66

Warken, M. (2006). *From Testing to Anti-product Development.* Presented at the TTCN-3 User Conference (T3UC), Berlin.

Warner, A.G. (2003). Block alliances in formal standard setting environments. *International Journal of IT Standards and Standardization Research, 1*(1), 1-18.

Watabiki, H. (1994). World history talked by goods (Mono ga Kataru Sekaishi in Japanese), Seibunsha.

Watts, J.J.S., & Baigent, D.R. (2002). Intellectual property, standards and competition law: Navigating a minefield. *IEEE*, 837-842.

Weick, K. E. (1989). Theory construction as disciplined imagination. *Academy of Management Review, 14*(4), 516-531.

Weick, K. E. (1993). The collapse of sensemaking in organizations: The Mann Gulch disaster. *Administrative Science Quarterly, 38*(4), 628-652.

Weick, K. E. (1995). *Sensemaking in organizations.* London: Sage Publications.

Weiser, P. J. (2003). The Internet, innovation, and intellectual property policy. *Columbia Law Review, 103*(3), 534-613.

Weitzel, T., Beimborn, D., & König, W. (2006). A unified economic model of standard diffusion: The impact of standardization cost, network effects and network topology. *MIS Quarterly,* forthcoming.

Werle, R. (2000). *Institutional aspects of standardization: Jurisdictional conflicts and the choice of standardization organizations.* Koeln: Max-Planck Institute for Social Science Research.

Wernerfelt, B. (1984). A resource-based view of the firm. *Strategic Management Journal, 5*, 171-180.

Wernerfelt, B., & Karnani, A. 1987. Competitive strategy under uncertainty. *Strategic Management Journal, 8,* 187-194.

West, J. (1999). Organizational decisions for I.T. standards adoption: Antecedents and consequences. In *Proceedings of the 1st IEEE Conference on Standardisation and Innovation in Information Technology,* (pp. 13-18).

West, J. (2003). The role of standards in the creation and use of information systems. In J.L. King & K. Lyytinen (Eds.), *Proceedings of MISQ Special Issue Workshop on Standard Making: A Critical Frontier for Information Systems,* (pp. 314-325).

West, J., & Dedrick, J. (2000). Innovation and control in standards architectures: The rise and fall of Japan's PC-98. *Information Systems Research, 11*(2), 197–216.

West, J., & Dedrick, J. (2006). Scope and timing of deployment: Moderators of organizational adoption of the Linux server platform. *International Journal of IT Standards & Standardization Research, 4*(2), 1–23.

Westman, R. (1999, October). The battle of standards—And the road to peace. *On—The New World of Communication*, pp. 26-30.

Wheelwright, S. C., Holloway, C. A., Kasper, C. G., & Tempest, N. (1999). *Cisco Systems, Inc: Acquisition integration for manufacturing.* Cambridge, MA: Harvard Business School.

Whinston, A.B., Stahl, D.O., & Choi, S.-Y. (1997). *The economics of electronic commerce.* Indianapolis, IN: MacMillan Publishing Company.

Wikipedia. (2005). Retrieved September 9, 2005 from, http://www.wikipedia.org/

Williams, R., & Edge, D. (1996). The social shaping of technology. *Research Policy, 25*, 865-899.

Willis, J.L. (2004). What Impact Will E-Commerce Have on the U.S. Economy? *Federal Reserve Bank of Kansas City Economic Review*, 2nd Quarter.

Wilsher, R., & Hill, J. (2003, October 12). A report prepared on behalf of the Department of Trade and Industry into the impact in the United Kingdom of the EC Electronic signatures Framework Directive. DTI TFBJ/C/003/006 IX.

Wilson, E. (2004, 11 May). Opening the book on ITIL. *Sydney Morning Herald.* Retrieved from http://www.smh.com.au/articles/2004/05/10/1084041321436.html

Windrum, P. (2004). Leveraging technological externalities in complex technologies: Microsoft's exploitation of standards in the browser wars. *Research Policy, 33*(3), 385–394.

Winn, J. K. (2001). The Emperor's New Clothes: The Shocking Truth about Digital Signatures and Internet commerce. *Idaho Law Review, 37*, 353.

Wireless Watch. (2005, November 15). *The Register.* Qualcomm IP battle hots up. Retrieved August 29, 2006, from http://www.theregister.co.uk/2005/11/15/qualcomm_ip_battle/

Wireless Watch. (2005, November 29). Mobile patents war shifts to email. *The Register.* Retrieved August 29, 2006, from http://www.theregister.co.uk/2005/11/29/mobile_email_patents_war/

Woiceshyn, J. (1997). Literary analysis as a metaphor in processual research: A story of technological change. *Scandinavian Journal of Management, 13*(4), 457-471.

Wolfson, A., Trebilcock, M., & Tuohy, C. (1980). Regulating the professions: A theoretical framework. In S. Rottenberg (Ed.), *Occupational licensure and regulation. US: American Enterprise Institute for Public and Policy Research*, pp. 180-214.

Wonacott, M. E. (2003). In Brief: Fast Facts for Policy and Practice No. 23: Industry-Sponsored Credentials [Electronic Version]. Retrieved from http://www.nccte.org/publications/infosynthesis/in-brief/in-brief23/inbrief23-indspon.pdf

Wong, W. (2002, April 18). IBM ebMXL patent plan royalty-free. *Tech Update.*

WTO Committee on Principles for the Development of International Standards. (2000). Decisions and Recommendations adopted by the Committee since 1 January 1995, G/TBT/1/Rev.8, 23 May 2002, Section IX.

Xia, M., Zhao, K., & Shaw, M.J. (2003). Open E-business standard development and adoption: An integrated perspective. In J.L. King & K. Lyytinen (Eds.), *Proceedings of MISQ Special Issue Workshop on Standard Making: A Critical Frontier for Information Systems*, Minneapolis: MIS Quarterly, (pp. 222-235).

Yin, R.K. (1994). *Case study research: Design and methods* (2nd ed.). Thousand Oaks, CA: Sage Publications Inc.

Zachariades, A. (n.d.). *Protypation Digest – Contents' plan.* Thessaloniki, Greece: Union of Hellenic Scientists for Protypation and Standardization.

Zahra, S. A., & George, G. (2002). Absorptive capacity: A review, reconceptualization, and extension. *Academy of Management Review, 27*(2), 185-203.

Zander, U., & Kogut, B. (1995). Knowledge and the speed of the transfer and imitation of organizational capabilities: An empirical test. *Organization Science, 6*(1), 76-92.

Zhang, J., & Warren, T.L. (2003). *SMEs and STEP.* Contract Number F34601-95-D-00376. Oklahoma State University School of Industrial Engineering and Management: Computer Assisted Technology Transfer (CATT) Research Program.

Zmud, R.W. (1983). The effectiveness of external information channels in facilitating innovation within software development groups. *MIS Quarterly, 7*(2), 43-58.

Zollo, M., & Singh, H. (2004). Deliberate learning in corporate acquisitions: Post-acquisition strategies and integration capability in U.S. bank mergers. *Strategic Management Journal, 25,* 1233-1256.

Zollo, M., & Winter, S. G. (2002). Deliberate learning and the evolution of dynamic capabilities. *Organization Science, 13*(3), 339.

Zollo, M., Reuer, J. J., & Singh, H. (2002). Interorganizational routines and performance in strategic alliances. *Organization Science, 13,* 701-713.

About the Contributors

Kai Jakobs joined Aachen University's (RWTH) Computer Science Department as a member of the technical staff in 1985. Over the years, his research interests moved away from the technical nuts and bolts of communication systems to socio-economic aspects with a focus on IT standardization. He is the co-author of a text book on data communications and more recently, five books on standards and standardization in IT. He has been on the program committees of numerous international conferences, and has also served as an external expert on evaluation panels of various European R&D programs, on both technical and socio-econimic issues. He holds a PhD in computer science from the University of Edinburgh.

* * *

Knut Blind is professor for innovation economics, Faculty for Economics and Management, at Berlin University of Technology. He is also head of the Department of Regulation and New Markets'at the Fraunhofer Institute for Systems and Innovation Research, headquartered in Karlsruhe, Germany. For 10 years he has been active in innovation and standardisation research leading to numerous publications. In the last few years, he extended his research focus to also cover the analysis of the relation between innovation and regulation.

Krzysztof M. Brzezinski is an Assistant Professor at the Institute of Telecommunications, Warsaw University of Technology, Poland. He obtained his M.Sc. in 1984 (for work on switching system management) and Ph.D. in 1995 (for work on broadcast concepts in design) from the same University. His interest in standards is rooted in a more general context of formalized system development. He specializes in formal verification/validation by active and passive testing. For many years dr Brzezinski has consulted the TP – Telekomunikacja Polska, the leading Polish network operator, on the issues of service and infrastructure development and testing. He was the project or task leader in numerous projects run by the R&D department of this Operator, including those that led to the development of the TP's ISDN and IN networks (he is the author of TP's Technical Requirements for DSS1, ISUP, INAP and other protocols / platform elements) and to the adoption of the formalized testing methodology. Dr Brzezinski is the author of two books, several book chapters, more than 40 published papers, and numerous technical reports.

Aileen Cater-Steel is a senior lecturer of information systems at the University of Southern Queensland, Australia. Her current research interests are IT service management and software process improvement. She has also published research related to IT governance, software development standards, organizational and national culture, and electronic commerce. Prior to her university appointment, Aileen worked in private and government organizations where her career progressed from programmer to systems analyst, project manager, and then to IT manager.

Lynn Crawford is a world leader in the field of project management competency. Her research into the assessment of competence for project managers has lead to the development of international teams of researchers and practitioners in developing global competency standards and global bodies of knowledge. Her research strengths address the areas or Hard & Soft systems, Project Governance, Program management, Project categorisation and corporate project management capability. She is currently the director of the Project Management Research Unit at the University of Technology Sydney and a Professor in Project Management at ESC Lille, France.

Ray Dawson obtained BSc and masters degrees from Nottingham University before entering industry with Plessey Telecommunications in 1977. While working as a software developer and configuration manager at the company he developed an interest in 'best practice' working methods. This became a research interest when he joined Loughborough University as a lecturer in 1987. He then combined this interest with knowledge management and is now leader of the multi-disciplinary Knowledge Management Research Group at Loughborough University. This group works with organisations to provide Knowledge Management problem solutions, which are both practical and cost-effective. Ray Dawson is a Fellow of the British Computer Society, a Chartered Engineer and a Chartered IT Professional.

Henk J. de Vries is an associate professor of Standardization at Rotterdam School of Management, Erasmus University in Rotterdam, The Netherlands, department of Management of Technology and Innovation. His education and research concern standardization from a business point of view. From 1994 until 2003, de Vries worked with NEN, Netherlands Standardization Institute, in several jobs, being responsible for R&D during the last period. Since 1994, he has an appointment at the Erasmus University's School of Management and since 2004, he has been working full-time at this university. De Vries is the author of 250 publications, including several books, on standardization.

Tineke Egyedi (PhD) is a senior researcher Standardization at the Delft University of Technology. Earlier she worked for KPN Research, the Royal Institute of Technology in Sweden, and the University of Maastricht. Her research is funded by the Dutch science foundation, the NGI foundation, industry, and government. She has participated in several European projects, chaired IEEE standardization conferences/ program committees, and is (associate) editor of two international journals on standardization. She has published widely. She is president of the European Academy for Standardization (EURAS) and vice-chair of the International Cooperation for Education about Standardization (ICES).

Carter Eltzroth is Legal Director of the DVB Project, Geneva. He assists in other activities relating to patent licensing, formation of licensing programmes, and other IPR issues linked to standards. He is also involved, on behalf of broadcasters, the World Bank and other multilateral institutions, in regulatory and public policy issues impacting broadcasting in Europe and in developing countries. He is former Secretary General of the Association Européenne pour la Protection des Œuvres et services Cryptés (AEPOC). Carter Eltzroth obtained an MA (Oxford) in literae humaniores and a JD (Columbia).

A dual Belgian/US national, he is a member of the New York bar. He can be reached at celtzroth@ helikon.net.

James F. Fairbank is an Associate Professor of Management at Pennsylvania State University. His research and teaching interests include strategic management and entrepreneurial venturing. His research interests include the strategic use of information technology, performance implications of benchmarking other organizations, and now to enhance organizational innovation. Dr. Fairbank was an officer in the U.S. Navy and has industry experience as a manger in large and small companies.

Vladislav V. Fomin is an associate professor at the department of Information Systems and Decision Sciences at the GSCM-Montpellier Business School in France. His prior positions included a research scientist at the Faculty of Policy, Technology and Management, Delft University of Technology (2006), an assistant professor at the department of Informatics, Copenhagen Business School (2004-6), and visiting assistant professor at the School of Information at the University of Michigan (2001-3). Current research interests include standard making processes in the field of information and communication technologies (ICT) and studies of ICT infrastructure development and design.

Thomas Keil is professor of strategic management at Helsinki University of Technology (TKK) and serves as the Academic and Managing Director of the TKK Executive School of Business Oy. Thomas holds DSc (Tech) and Lic. Tech degrees from Helsinki University of Technology and a MSc degree (Dipl. Wirsch.-Ing.) from Darmstadt University of Technology. Thomas' research focuses on standardization, corporate entrepreneurship, mergers and acquisitions, strategic alliances, and strategic management in high-tech industries. Thomas' work has been published in leading European and North-American journals including Harvard Business Review, Sloan Management Review, Entrepreneurship Theory & Practice, Journal of Management, Journal of Management Studies, and has won several international awards.

Timothy King graduated in 1990 and obtained his PhD in 1994. Both degrees are in Mechanical Engineering from Imperial College, London. Since 1986, he has been interested in the exploitation of computer technology to support the engineering process. He worked in research and academia in Japan from 1994 to 1998. Since 1998, he has worked as a consultant for LSC Group in the UK, specializing in enterprise integration and information and knowledge management. He is active in the development of International Standards. He is Head of the UK delegation to ISO/TC184/SC4 (Industrial Data) and Convener of ISO/TC184/SC4/WG13 (Industrial Data Quality). Dr. King is a Chartered Engineer (Institution of Mechanical Engineers) and Chartered Information Technology Professional (British Computer Society).

Ken Krechmer (krechmer@csrstds.com) has participated in communications standards development from the mid 1970's to 2000. He actively participated in the development of the International Telecommunications Union Recommendations T.30, V.8, V.8bis, V.32, V.32bis, V.34, V.90, and G.994.1. He was the technical editor of Communications Standards Review and Communications Standards Summary 1990 -2002. In 1995 and 2000 he won first prize at the World Standards Day paper competition. He was Program Chair of the Standards and Innovation in Information Technology (SIIT) conference in 2001 (Boulder, CO), 2003 (Delft, Netherlands) and 2005 (Calgary, Canada). In December, 2006 he received the joint second prize in the IEC Centenary Challenge. He is a lecturer at the University of

Colorado, Boulder, CO, USA and a Senior Member of the IEEE. His current activities are focused on research and teaching about standards.

Shiro Kurihara graduated from the department of electrical engineering, the University of Tokyo in 1971 and entered into the Ministry of International Trade and Industry. He obtained Ph.D. in economics from the Johns Hopkins University in 1980. He was research fellow in the foreign policy studies in the Brookings Institution and has held various posts in the Ministry, namely, director for international standardization, director for superconductivity and so on. He also served as director for research grants in the International Human Frontier Science Program Organization in Strasbourg, France. He was appointed as professor in the faculty of commerce, Hitotsubashi University in 1994. He chaired the first International Committee for Education on Standardization held in Tokyo in February 2006.

Kalle Lyytinen is Iris S. Wolstein professor Case Western Reserve University, USA, adjunct professor at University of Jyvaskyla, Finland, and visiting professor at University of Loughborough U.K. He serves currently on the editorial boards of several leading IS journals including Journal of AIS (Editor-in-Chief), Journal of Strategic Information Systems, Information&Organization, Requirements Engineering Journal, Information Systems Journal, Scandinavian Journal of Information Systems, and Information Technology and People, among others. He is AIS fellow (2004).. He has published over 180 scientific articles and conference papers and edited or written eleven books on topics related to nature of IS discipline, system design, method engineering, organizational implementation, risk assessment, computer supported cooperative work, standardization, and ubiquitous computing among others. He is currently involved in research projects that looks at the IT induced radical innovation in software development, IT innovation in architecture, engineering and construction industry, design and use of ubiquitous applications, and the adoption of broadband wireless services in the U.K., South Korea and the U.S.

Carleen Maitland is an assistant professor in the College of Information Sciences and Technology at Penn State University, USA. She received a Ph.D. in the Economics of Infrastructure from Delft University of Technology, the Netherlands, in 2001 as well as undergraduate and graduate degrees in engineering from Worcester Polytechnic Institute and Stanford University. With over 10 years of experience, Dr. Maitland's research has focused on the international and inter-organizational context of ICT deployments, particularly in the wake of technological change, and the ways in which national and regional policies influence market development. Her work has been funded by the European Commission, the U.S. Department of Commerce, the U.S. National Science Foundation, and IBM, among others, and has resulted in over 30 journal articles, book chapters and referred conference proceedings.

Julien Pollack is a researcher currently engaged at the University of Technology, Sydney. His main areas of research include systems thinking, complexity theory, project management, and strategic planning. He has a background in information systems development. His previous experience also includes public sector strategy development and delivery, and theatrical projects.

Steve Probets has been a lecturer in the Information Science Department at Loughborough University for five years. Prior to that he worked in the Electronic Publishing Group at Nottingham University. His research interests lie in the Knowledge Management and Electronic Publishing domains. Steve has been involved in a range of research projects ranging from investigations into the development of the scholarly publishing industry to projects, which have developed XML schemes for adding semantics to data. Adoption issues for new technologies and business models are of interest

Marc Rysman is an Associate Professor in the Economics Department at Boston University. He received a BA from Columbia University in 1992 and a Ph.D. in Economics from the University of Wisconsin in 1999. He specializes in industrial organization and emphasizes empirical estimation of industrial phenomena. Rysman's research focuses on issues of network effects, standardization and two-sided markets. He also teaches on antitrust and regulation.

Tim Simcoe is Assistant Professor of Strategic Management at the Joseph L. Rotman School of Management, University of Toronto. His current research focuses on the political economy of compatibility standards as well as their impact on economic and technological change. Tim earned his M.A. in Economics and his Ph.D. in Business Administration from the University of California, Berkeley in 2005. Prior to that, he worked as a consultant in the economic and information technology practices of Ernst & Young LLP, and as a research assistant for the U.S. Council of Economic Advisers.

Aura Soininen, LL.M., is currently in the process of completing her PhD (Econ.) on patents in the ICT Sector at the Lappeenranta University of Technology, Department of Business Administration. Furthermore, she works as an associate lawyer in Attorneys at Law Borenius & Kemppinen, Ltd with a specific focus on patent law, IPR strategies and questions related to the pharmaceutical industry and biotechnology. Aura received her Master of Laws degree in 2002 (University of Helsinki), and has also studied biochemistry. After graduation she worked several years as a Researcher at the Helsinki Institute for Information Technology (HIIT). During her employment at HIIT she spent a year and a half at the UC Berkeley, US, where she was a visiting scholar at the School of Information Management and Systems. She has also taught Information Technology Law at the Helsinki University of Technology and worked as a trainee in Labour Court.

Ankur Tarnacha is a Ph.D. candidate at the College of Information Sciences and Technology, The Pennsylvania State University. He holds a Masters degree in Electrical Engineering from The Pennsylvania State University with a concentration in wireless networks. Prior to his graduate work he worked software architect in the Indian telecom sector. His research interests include competitive and collaborative dynamics in wireless markets, standards competition, mobile commerce, and evolution of the telecommunications industry.

Josephine Thomas obtained a BEng and masters degree before completing her PhD in Information Science at Loughborough University in 2006. Her research focused on the critical issues surrounding the adoption and diffusion of data-exchange standards. Since November 2006, she has been working in the Information Engineering team in the Strategic Research Centre at Rolls-Royce. Her main role is to facilitate the adoption of a rich set of tools and techniques for the representation, acquisition and exploitation of knowledge within Rolls-Royce. These tools and techniques draw from a wide variety of disciplines and technologies, including Artificial Intelligence, Intelligent Agents, Cognitive Science, Neurobiology, Statistics, Probability Theory, Signal Processing and Control Theory. Josephine Thomas is also a Director and the Company Secretary of the Natural Computing Applications Forum.

Mark Toleman is a professor of information systems at the University of Southern Queensland. His research interests are wide and include IT service management, IT governance, systems development methodologies, research-practitioner nexus, novice developers, and information systems education. He has published over 100 articles in books, refereed journals, and refereed conference proceedings.

Alfred G. Warner is an Assistant Professor in Management at Pennsylvania State University. His research interests include response of firms and industries to innovation, the emergence of standards and their interaction with increasing returns to adoption markets. His teaching interests are in strategy and innovation management. Dr. Warner has prior experience with Butler Manufacturing, Devine Lighting, and Holophane Lighting, and consulting experience with an e-business startup.

Jane K. Winn is the Charles I. Stone Professor at University of Washington School of Law, and a director of the UW Law School Division of Law, Technology & the Arts. A graduate of Queen Mary College, University of London and Harvard Law School, Professor Winn teaches commercial law, including the law of electronic commerce, and comparative law. She is the coauthor of the treatise Law of Electronic Commerce (4th edition 2009, semi-annual updates) as well as numerous articles on commercial, comparative and technology law topics. Copies of those articles are available on her website at http://www.law.washington.edu/faculty/winn/. Winn practiced with Shearman & Sterling in New York City, taught at Southern Methodist University in Dallas, and visited at University of California-Berkeley before joining UW Law School in 2002. She is a member of the American Law Institute and an advisor to its Principles of Software Contracts project, and has been a Senior Fellow of the University of Melbourne School of Law since 2001. Her current research interests include electronic commerce law developments in the US, EU and Greater China, including information security, electronic contracting and the role of standards in the globalization of markets.

Index